The Education of Jane Addams

POLITICS AND CULTURE IN MODERN AMERICA

Michael Kazin, Glenda Gilmore, and Thomas J. Sugrue, Series Editors

Books in the series narrate and analyze political and social change in the broadest dimensions from 1865 to the present, including ideas about the ways people have sought and wielded power in the public sphere and the language and institutions of politics at all levels—national, regional, and local. The series is motivated by a desire to reverse the fragmentation of modern U.S. history and to encourage synthetic perspectives on social movements and the state, on gender, race, and labor, on consumption, and on intellectual history and popular culture.

The Education of
Jane Addams

Victoria Bissell Brown

PENN

University of Pennsylvania Press
Philadelphia

10   9   8   7   6   5   4   3   2   1

Published by
University of Pennsylvania Press
Philadelphia, Pennsylvania 19104-4011

Library of Congress Cataloging-in-Publication Data

Brown, Victoria (Victoria Bissell)
    The education of Jane Addams / Victoria Bissell Brown.
       p.   cm.—(Politics and culture in modern America)
    Includes bibliographical references (p.   ) and index.
    ISBN: 0-8122-3747-1 (cloth : alk paper)
    1. Addams, Jane, 1860–1935. 2. Women social reformers—United States—
Biography. 3. Women social workers—United States—Biography. I. Title. II. Series.
HV28.A35B76   2003
361.92 B 21

                                            2003053337

To Jimbrown

Contents

Introduction

On a spring evening in 1895, Jane Addams stood before an over-flow crowd in the meeting room of New York City's United Charities Building and announced that "there is nothing so dangerous as being good to people." She had traveled to New York from her home in Chicago to share her reflections on the similarities between King Lear and George Pullman. Pullman was the railway car magnate whose much touted benevolence to his workers had been answered with a walkout at his Chicago plant and a nationwide railway sympathy strike that drew capital, labor, and the state into a violent, costly showdown. The lesson Addams drew from that brief conflagration the previous spring was that Pullman, like Lear, had contradicted the terms of generosity; both men had used kindness to acquire power, not to redistribute it, and had thereby revealed the selfish nature of benevolence. The key to genuine service, Addams told this crowd of charity workers, was not to be "good to people" but to be "good with people." The secret of success in all social action could, she said, be summed up in one word: "cooperation."[1]

Addams did not deliver this message in a fevered tone or punctuate it with fists in the air. Whether on a public platform or in the drawing room of her Hull-House settlement, she adopted a sedate, sturdy posture and spoke in calm, measured cadences, projecting her cultured voice with confidence and clarity. There was nothing in her speaking manner to contradict her appearance as a small and unadorned woman of thirty-four years. Listeners found her style "perfectly easy," "unstudied," "modest and sensible," "unemphatic but convincing." Some observers thought her "dainty," others found her "dignified." A chorus of commentators noted that her soft face was dominated by "luminous" eyes whose depth seemed to suggest the measure of Addams's soul.[2]

By the spring of 1895, it was not unusual for crowds to turn out to hear Addams speak anywhere from San Francisco to Boston. She had, by then, been in public life for more than five years, becoming well known in reform circles as the "guiding spirit" of Hull-House, the settlement house she had established on Chicago's Halsted Street.[3] Opened in the fall of 1889 in a dirty, crowded, neglected quarter just southwest of the prosperous downtown, Hull-House

1. Jane Addams at age thirty-five, in 1895. (University of Illinois at Chicago, University Library, Jane Addams Memorial Collection, neg. no. 1437)

was one of the first settlements in the United States. It quickly became the most successful effort by privileged, white Northerners to take up residence among a city's working poor and offer their tastes, training, and talents to their neighbors.

Addams was regarded as one who could speak with authority on the distinction between being good "to" people and being good "with" them because she had demonstrated her capacity for cross-class cooperation in her daily conduct among her immigrant neighbors. Every week, a thousand of those neighbors visited Hull-House for one activity or another, and that level of voluntary participation in clubs, classes, and social events convinced sympathetic observers in the press and public that "the gentle, the earnest, the noble woman" who presided over Hull-House "must be doing great and beautiful work."[4]

Jane Addams appeared on the Chicago scene in 1889, at the end of a decade in the city's history marked by labor protest against employers' exploitation and working-class hostility to patronizing Protestant philanthropy. Addams introduced the British settlement scheme to Chicago labor activists, women reformers, and liberal clergy, who were hungry for practical, productive alternatives to the class alienation borne of laissez-faire capitalism and condescending charity. Those who became Addams's allies in Chicago represented that vanguard of urban Americans coming to the fore in every major city, ready to challenge the economic and political rules that had dominated the landscape since the triumph of northern industrial capitalism in the Civil War. Like Addams, many of her reform allies had grown up during the postwar decades of excess that Mark Twain titled "the Gilded Age" and had enjoyed wealth and comfort in those decades. Like her, they had embraced the credo of responsible stewardship that was supposed to vindicate the inequitable distribution of wealth in the democracy. But by the end of the 1880s, many of these children of the Gilded Age, including Jane Addams, feared the corruption of that stewardship when it came cloaked in the unforgiving name of social Darwinism.

Addams and her colleagues in Chicago and around the country launched in the 1890s what they themselves regarded as a "progressive" era. They felt moved by spiritual and democratic longings for a society in which stewardship was a responsibility shared by all and individual rights operated in harmony with community interests. Addams was present at the start of a twenty-year cavalcade of civic activism dedicated to the principle that, in order for a democracy to function, the entire community—from individuals to the national state—must take an affirmative role in securing the most basic conditions of health, education, and welfare so that every citizen could be optimally equipped to participate in the democracy. During her lifetime of advocacy for this position, Addams contributed to the redefinition of the role of the democratic state in regulating economic relations and redefined, in the process, women's role as participating citizens in that state. She was, throughout this period, regarded as one of the Progressive Era's most effective organizers and most articulate philosophers.

In the forty years that passed between her speech at New York's United Charities Building and her death from cancer in May 1935, Jane Addams managed the ever expanding, always esteemed program at Hull-House. By 1910, when she published her enormously successful autobiography, *Twenty Years at Hull-House*, the settlement comprised thirteen buildings encircling an entire square block at Halsted and Polk Streets and served several thousand visitors a week. Hull-House operated as a meeting ground for working-class neighbors, labor unionists, artists, ethnic club members, intellectuals, religious liberals, anarchists, socialists, businessmen, feminists, government investigators, foreign dignitaries, teenage athletes, and children in search of a music class, jungle gym, or free bath. It served, as well, as a catalyst for social legislation, political reform, social science theory, and labor organizing at the city, state, and national levels. Addams was the steady hand at the helm of Hull-House, attracting extraordinarily gifted, innovative women and men around her and adroitly leading them in the development of the social service programs and legislative agendas that came to typify the Progressive Era.

At the same time, Addams became a national figure by delivering thousands of speeches, writing more than a dozen books, and publishing more than five hundred articles in venues as diverse as the *Ladies' Home Journal, Annals of the American Academy of Political and Social Sciences*, and *Machinist's Monthly Journal*.[5] She had strong ties to the University of Chicago, becoming closely affiliated with that institution's leading lights, including John Dewey, and contributing to the "Chicago school's" creation of both sociology and social work as academic disciplines.[6] She was active in labor mediation and labor legislation, was a founding member of the NAACP, served on the Chicago School Board, was the paid garbage inspector for her ward (the only paid position she ever held), staged unsuccessful political campaigns against corrupt ward bosses, worked on state programs for the criminal and the insane, was president of the National Conference of Charities and Corrections, and, from 1911 to 1914, was a vice president of the National American Woman Suffrage Association.

In an uncharacteristic departure from her avowedly nonpartisan stance, Addams threw herself into Teddy Roosevelt's Progressive Party campaign of 1912, becoming the first American woman to give a nominating speech at a presidential convention and even endorsing the campaign's *Jane Addams's Song Book*. Typically, she preferred to serve as an honest broker between partisans. Over the course of her career, she mediated disputes between workers and employers, landlords and tenants, radicals and the police, citizens and politicians, judges and defendants, students and teachers, parents and children, husbands and wives. She traveled to several continents as a distinguished visitor, sat on countless boards and advisory committees, organized thousands of meetings and conferences, and counseled presidents, governors, mayors, senators, and congressional representatives.

At all times and in every possible way, Addams was a committed pacifist who viewed conflict and violence as the natural enemies of social progress. That conviction dictated that she operate as a moderate, mediating figure in American life for close to thirty years. Once the United States entered World War I in 1917, however, pacifism was anything but a moderate position and Addams joined the much reviled ranks of war resisters. Virtually overnight, her trusted image as a calm negotiator was recast in unpatriotic terms; war enthusiasts denounced her as a dangerous subversive for her uncompromising stance in the name of mediation. Undeterred, Addams founded the Women's International League for Peace and Freedom (WILPF) and pursued pro-peace activities for the remainder of her life. She survived the 1920s, determinedly shepherding both Hull-House and WILPF through an antiprogressive era, and was vindicated for her peace activism when she became, in 1931, the first American woman to win the Nobel Peace Prize. Despite age and declining health, she stayed fully engaged in public life into the 1930s. Just weeks before Addams's death in 1935, at a dinner honoring WILPF, Eleanor Roosevelt praised her predecessor in reform. "You were a pioneer," said the first lady, "and are still pioneering."[7]

In the spring of 1895, when she was addressing the gathering in the United Charities Building in New York, Jane Addams was just launching her reform career. Her first five years "in the fray," however, had sharpened her philosophy to the point she made that evening.[8] Her call for "cooperation" was no tepid request for polite handshakes all around; it was a rigorous challenge to her listeners to take seriously the motives and interests of others and to seek collective solutions that reflected the "widest vision" of the common good. In "A Modern Lear," the published version of Addams's analysis of George Pullman and the strike he refused to arbitrate, she tapped into her own and others' family experiences to explore the tragic consequences when parents—and employers—ignored the interests of those they presumed to govern, stubbornly insisting on outmoded deference from individuals who sought "frank equality."[9]

Convinced that her era was caught up in "the sweep of a world-wide moral impulse" demanding the dignity of every individual, Addams also insisted that her generation bore "the responsibility of tolerance." Class warfare would not bring economic justice any more than civil war had brought racial justice. The age required that every member of the society, across divisions of class, race, ethnicity, and sex, rise above selfishness and pursue "mutual interest in a common cause." Justice, said Addams—and she said it more than once—could come only through "affectionate interpretation" of others' needs and motives. In evoking the King Lear story to guide her audience through memories of autonomy sought and won, Addams called up the image of Lear's daughter Cordelia, who braved the consequences of standing up for independent principle. Addams could have been describing herself, standing before the crowd in New York City in May 1895, when she said that Cordelia was "transformed by a dignity which recast her speech and made it self-contained, as is becoming a citizen of the world."[10]

The Education of Jane Addams is about how a daughter of America's small-town prairie elite was transformed by the dignity of her own philosophy and arrived on that New York platform by her thirty-fifth year. The story told here traces Addams's evolution from an ambitious, arrogant youth caught up in heroic dreams of individual triumph to a young woman humbled by ill health, family duty, and spiritual doubt. It examines the process of emotional and philosophical growth that allowed the young Jane Addams to transcend the conceits of her youth, and then follows her path to Chicago, where she sought salvation in collective, cooperative action and enjoyed greater fame and success than she could have imagined in her schoolgirl fantasies. Her dreams of a life as a public figure carried her furthest, it turned out, when she folded ambition for herself into ambition for democracy.

Just as Addams charted Cordelia's development in "A Modern Lear," noting her "first dawn of character" and her ultimate devotion to a principle larger than self, so this work traces Addams's quest for a purpose beyond what she called "the great I," her search for a way to find herself by losing herself.[11] As in the Cordelia story, this narrative examines the difficult peace Addams negotiated with her family once she decided, in her late twenties, to define herself as more than a daughter and a sister. But this story extends beyond that declaratory moment of independence. It follows Addams into Hull-House to see how she applied the lessons she had learned along the way and shows how the first years of the settlement experience further educated her for a life in progressive social reform. She continued to learn, of course; she continued to see herself, in fact, as the reformer ever in need of reform. This account stops in 1895, however, in order to stay true to its focus on how it was that Jane Addams became Jane Addams.

I did not set out to write an entire book on this young woman. I began this project assuming, like everyone else who had written about Jane Addams, that the story of her youth was mere preface to the "real" story of her public career, which was the story I intended to reexamine. In retrospect, I can see that it was my struggle with Jane Addams's handwriting that explains how, and why, I came to write this coming-of-age story. The first time I tried to read Addams's adult scrawl, I tearfully despaired of ever deciphering, much less analyzing, her correspondence. The strategy I settled upon for handling this problem was to start back with Addams's childhood writings (and her childhood penmanship) and simply learn to read her hand by sequentially mastering each new idiosyncrasy she acquired over the course of her adolescence and young womanhood. The method worked; by the time I read Addams's hasty notes from Hull-House, I could decode what she was saying. But also by that time, two connected realities had sunk in: first, there was an enormous amount of wonderful material from her youth that had never been analyzed and, second, familiarity with this early material, like familiarity with her early handwriting, was requisite for understanding the public, adult Jane Addams. Grasp of her handwriting became a metaphor for comprehending her life.

The process I used to arrive at this realization would not have been possible without the microfilm edition of the Jane Addams Papers. Since the 1985 publication of the eighty-three reels of Addams's correspondence, clippings, writings, settlement records, and organizational records, scholars have been free to roam through the surviving documents from her life. Access to the thousands of letters and records that Mary Lynn Bryan and Nancy Slote amassed for the microfilm edition from some six hundred archives allowed me to immerse myself in the first thirty-four years of Addams's life. The microfilm afforded me the luxury of transcribing every letter, essay, and article without prejudging its significance. That method allowed unanticipated meanings and patterns to emerge gradually from the documents.

I did not, of course, begin my work innocent of assumptions about Jane Addams. The standard narrative on her early years was familiar ground: she was the youngest child in a wealthy Illinois family and when her mother died she poured her adoration into her powerful father, whose death left her so paralyzed by unresolved guilt and anger over her stifled ambitions that she spent seven years after graduation from college in ill health and idleness, aimlessly wandering through Europe until an epiphany at a Madrid bullfight convinced her to open a settlement house and live the admirable, if emotionally bloodless, life of a secular saint.[12] I was never particularly satisfied with this story but did not expect to spend fifteen summers of my life unpacking it.

The more time I spent with Addams's surviving papers, however, the more I was drawn into three aspects of her development that were inadequately etched in the existing image of the young Jane Addams. I became fascinated by the story of her political and spiritual conversion from an aspiring elite steward for whom Christian teachings were a tool, not a faith, to a practicing democratic pacifist for whom Christian teachings were a faith, not a religion. At the same time, I was intrigued by Addams's elusive personal style, her capacity for inspiring others' love and devotion while never quite revealing herself. Finally, I was struck over and over again by the contrasts between the young woman emerging from the surviving sources and the picture Jane Addams had created in her autobiography, a picture that obliquely conveyed her personal style. It was an irrepressible interest in these three facets of Jane Addams's journey to an adult career that persuaded me to write *The Education of Jane Addams*.

Over time, I have come to see how fitting it is, in the case of Addams, to focus so intently on the gradual steps she took in her emotional and philosophical development. Addams herself, as an adult philosopher, always insisted on attention to the evolutionary process by which an individual or a social condition came to be; she always wanted to know the particular roots of any human dilemma, and she always wanted to invent solutions that fit the lived experience of those affected. By tracing the evolution of Addams's own approach from arrogant heroics to democratic process, we can appreciate why her lived experience convinced her that we learn best about life from life itself. A developmental approach also protects us from the romantic tendency to write mythic tales in which the unknown Jane Addams was somehow destined to become the world-famous Jane Addams. She herself scoffed at such ahistorical renditions of real life, urging us to recognize "the essential provisionality of everything" and to replace heroic fairytales with the messy truth of multiple contingencies.[13]

Ironically, most of the myths that exist about Jane Addams can be traced back to her own autobiography, *Twenty Years at Hull-House*, which is a rich but slippery source of information on her life before settlement in Chicago. In 1909, when she wrote *Twenty Years*, Addams was the most famous and most influential woman in America; that year, *Current Literature* titled a feature about her "The Only Saint America Has Produced."[14] Writing from that lofty perch at the height of the Progressive Era, Addams aimed to advance her reform philosophy with the aid of an attractive, accessible life story; her purpose was not to engage in a public act of self-revelation. There are, for that reason, sizable gaps between the sleek and engaging tale she told in her autobiography and the more intricate and challenging story that emerges from her papers. This study examines those gaps, rather than relying on the autobiography itself, to gain access to her emotional life. Much in the way of biographical truth may be discerned in Addams's autobiographical fictions, so while events reported in the autobiography may be invented, the emotional messages embedded in those reports are quite genuine. As Jane Addams herself said, several years after writing *Twenty Years*, there is a "mysterious autobiographical impulse which makes it more difficult to conceal the truth than to avow it."[15] Even as she revised the narrative details of her life, Addams still conveyed much of her felt experience.

This study of Addams's development urges respect for the emotional authenticity of the autobiography while arguing for a careful reexamination of the evidence on her life. Given the continuing interest in Addams as a representative of America's first generation of college women and as the premier female reformer of the Progressive Era, it seems only prudent to pause and test the foundation of our understanding of Jane Addams. Wise historical practice counsels that we take some time to examine the surviving data from her youth and construct a narrative independent of the mythology, one that realistically embeds her in a particular time and place, in a particular family and school, in a particular set of class and gender constraints, and in a particular grouping of ideological and emotional dilemmas.

The stories Addams told in her autobiography, which have assumed mythic proportions in the frequent retelling, were sincerely meant to make the point that we learn from lived experiences. But the political lessons Addams sought to teach in *Twenty Years* required, in her mind, that she recast and rearrange many of her experiences for heuristic purposes. As a result, she condensed the course of her own development and skewed our understanding of the exact, halting steps she took toward shaping her adult personality and politics. The progress in our thinking about U.S. women's history and U.S. social history, as well as in our approach to biography and autobiography, has made this a propitious time to recover Jane Addams from the mists of myth and restore to her the craggy contingencies that make her life far more complex and interesting than any smooth myth can ever be.

The Education of Jane Addams portrays a young woman bent toward self-protective diplomacy by a tangled family dynamic in which the safest—not the most threatening—figure was her father, John Huy Addams, whose paternal example raised young Jane's expectations of generosity from powerful men and imbued her with confidence in her capacity to work with such men as a colleague.[16] John Addams's daughter does not appear here as a sickly girl yearning with compassion for the poor, but as an ambitious, intellectual adolescent whose dreams of heroic stewardship were thwarted by her struggles with Christianity and her father's sudden death when she was just twenty. Thrust into private confinement as family caretaker for the demanding, egocentric characters who survived her father's death, Jane Addams learned some important and humbling lessons and honed her talent for detached mediation by serving as the family peacemaker.

The young woman who emerges from these pages was not raised for female idleness but for community service; her nascent talent was less for friendship than for leadership and her first interest was less in the plight of the downtrodden than in the potential powers of the elite. Her journey from that youth to Hull-House involved less invalidism and more religious questioning than the standard story allows, and as much softening as toughening. At the heart of Jane Addams's education was her struggle with faith and religion, and the story here traces the momentum of that struggle as it carried her toward the philosophy of democratic pacifism articulated in "A Modern Lear." Given Addams's youthful ambition, the stakes in her religious struggle were high because no American woman in the 1880s could claim the voice of respectable, responsible stewardship without the justification of faith. Rejecting the shallow piety she encountered at Rockford Female Seminary, Jane Addams was compelled to dig deeper, and that excavation strengthened her soul, giving her the spiritual stamina for a lifetime of rough and dirty work.

Because the salvation Addams fashioned was secular, and because her autobiography has been read as dismissive of religion, it comes as something of a surprise to discover how much of her young womanhood was devoted to a quest for authentic spirituality. Once made, however, that discovery goes far to explain why her adult life was devoted to the politics of mediation, not the politics of partisanship. At the same time, the surviving epistolary record testifies that her mediator's inclination toward dispassion was not a quality she had to acquire but one she had to train. As Addams matured, she learned when and how to lower the emotional boundaries she had drawn around herself in youth. Once she fashioned a democratic, pacifist philosophy that suited her temperament, Addams's dispassion shifted from cool to warm, resting not at a safe distance from others but in confident devotion to them.

When James Weber Linn was writing the first biography of his beloved aunt, he shared with her his stylistic struggle to "properly set forth," "without exaggeration," her quality of impersonality. In response, his dispassionate Aunt Jane angrily denied that she was at all impersonal. From her point of view, such a characterization ignored the years she had spent as a young woman shedding her elitist detachment from others and embracing her committed place alongside her fellows. That deeply personal process had required her delicate extrication from an absorbing family and the wholly experimental transfer of her mediation skills to the public arena. In order to harness her bent for detachment to a heartfelt calling, Addams risked personal failure, rejection, and shame. The affection she "shone alike on the just and the unjust" represented, from her point of view, not an impersonal suspension of her truest sentiments but a hard-won expression of them.[17]

Jane Addams's penchant for "affectionate interpretation" of the human condition has invited an array of biographical analyses stretching from worshipful hagiography to profane pathography. While this work positions itself squarely against sentimental renderings that have etherealized Addams beyond recognition or destiny studies that have deprived her of the evolutionary process she held dear, it also situates itself apart from skeptical biographers who have distrusted Addams's politics or her psyche—or both. The strongest and most enduring portrait of Addams, drawn in the early 1970s when mediation seemed timid, criticized her "habit" of seeing both sides in a conflict, treating it as the result of her emotional need to be loved, not as a mature philosophical position. While this view had the virtue of treating Addams as a complex figure, it ultimately ignored the considerable anger which Addams withstood from partisans wishing her to enlist with them, and it dismissed her steadfast commitment to peaceful, democratic mediation as merely a psychological inability to ever become "the impassioned advocate of any cause." Thus, Addams's political and psychological strength came into question because she ostensibly failed to "follow the logic of her position" into the Socialist Party or into the war to save democracy.[18]

In an era influenced more by Freud than feminism, even Addams's choice of a career over marriage was, at one time, read as an unsettling sign of maladjustment requiring explanation. So strong was the cultural recoil from any hint of same-sex attachments that many of Addams's admiring biographers preferred to cast her as a woman bereft of any personal life who selflessly channeled her neurosis into good works rather than consider the abundant evidence of her complicated bond with Ellen Gates Starr and her rich and satisfying partnership with Mary Rozet Smith. For three decades historians of women have sought to rescue us from such dehumanizing distortions, though they persist.[19] At the same time, however, modern feminist analyses continue to be drawn to caricatures of Addams as a victim of a paternal repression that supposedly made her both an invalid and a rebel.[20] In these matters, as in so many others, Addams's experience defies our standard categories. If we fail to examine Addams as a daughter or as loving female partner, we deprive ourselves of a full understanding of exactly how and why she conducted herself as she did in her public life.

Sophisticated discussions of Jane Addams in recent years have greatly aided my own progress in analyzing her development. Among philosophers there is a new interest in her as a democratic pragmatist and ethicist; among historians there is a revised appreciation of her commitment to mediation and an interest in the political dilemmas implicit in such a commitment; among feminist scholars there is acceptance of her pacifist recoil from anger and a new attention to her grounding of women's power in female experience rather than female nature.[21] Among Americans weary of the politics of vitriol, there is an attraction to prodemocratic leaders who advocated compromise and civility and meant it. *The Education of Jane Addams* shares in this spirit of renewed interest in Addams by exploring the preparatory process by which she defined and then redefined herself as an unsanctified female steward in Gilded Age America.

When James Weber Linn was finishing his biography of his Aunt Jane, just at the time of her death in 1935, a Hull-House colleague exclaimed on what a "baffling job a biography of J. A. would be!" The chronicle would not be difficult, she thought, for it was "no doubt well documented and easy to develop." But how, she wondered, could a biographer "get across such a subtle and unique personality?"[22] My hope in writing this biography is that by tracing how Jane Addams became Jane Addams, her "subtle and unique" personality—and politics—will baffle us all a little less.

My guide in this effort has been the feminist philosopher Charlotte Perkins Gilman, who once said that Jane Addams's mind had "more 'floor space' in it than any other I have known. She could set a subject down, unprejudiced, and walk all around it, allowing fairly for every one's point of view."[23] That comment has stayed with me as not only the best description of Addams I have ever read but also the wisest advice to anyone writing about her. The task requires walking all the way around the record, taking in the emotional elusiveness and the warmth, the ambition and the self-doubt, the managerial control and the democratic spirit, trusting that her complexities do not make her a hypocrite, that denying them cannot make her a saint, and that an affectionate interpretation does not preclude candor.

Jane Addams had forty more years of active labor ahead of her in 1895; her education was by no means complete, but the fundamentals were in place and would not change. The mission that was impersonal for some was profoundly personal for her; it was, as she said in "A Modern Lear," the call "to touch to vibrating response the noble fibre in each man, to pull these many fibres, fragile, impalpable and constantly breaking, as they are, into one impulse" and to work together toward "the uncertain future which lies ahead of us."[24]

Chapter 1
Self-Made Man

Three weeks before Jane Addams celebrated her twenty-first birthday, her father's appendix burst and he died. Amid the bone-chilling grief she suffered in that August of 1881, Jane received a letter from her brother-in-law, the Reverend John Linn. In what remains as the single most explicit and sustained comment on this father-daughter bond, Linn observed that the "poignancy" of Jane's grief arose from "the fact that your heart and life were wrapped up with your Pa." Jane's dependence on her father's encouragement and support was profound, said Linn, because "your life aims were high enough and your plans broad enough so that he could take an interest in them and it was his great delight to prepare you for your mission."[1]

John Linn was not the sort of man to imagine, on his own, that women had high aims or a worldly mission. For him to write such words to his wife's youngest sister, he must have observed not only Jane Addams's youthful ambition but also her father's investment in that ambition. Neither Rev. Linn—nor Jane Addams—had any idea, in August 1881, just what her "mission" might be. In fact, the letter makes clear that Linn was not entirely approving of Jane's ambition; he cautioned her against the "danger" of being "governed" by a "desire of preeminence," and he encouraged her to seek refuge and guidance in Christ. But the whole premise of Linn's letter was that Jane Addams should draw strength from the memory of her father's pride and joy in her "life aims."[2]

When she was almost fifty years old and writing her autobiography, Jane Addams chose to dedicate it to "the memory of my father" and also chose to string her childhood memories on the "single cord" of her father's story. She told her readers that she settled upon this narrative line because it was "simpler."[3] It was certainly simpler than exploring her feelings about the diligent mother who died when Jane was only two years old, and most definitely simpler than describing the influence of the prideful stepmother who appeared when Jane was eight. Moreover, it was politically useful for Jane Addams, in 1910, to legitimize her female ambition with autobiographical tales of paternal encouragement. But Rev. Linn's letter from the summer of 1881 suggests that there was more than contrivance at work in Addams's decision to focus her childhood story on her father. Indeed, Linn's words, combined with all of the other surviving evidence, challenge the gothic speculation that Jane Addams created her career in defiance of a dead father who had denied her ambition. It appears far more likely that Jane Addams, like so many other nontraditional females of her era, benefited from the encouragement of an interested, interesting father.[4]

John Addams was the only man to whom Jane Addams was ever subordinate. As unequal relationships go, theirs appears to have been notably harmonious. Jane Addams seems to have been true to the spirit, if not all the details, of their life together when she wrote that her father "held fast my supreme affection" and "first drew me into the moral concerns of life."[5] John Addams lived in his daughter's memory as a warm, sturdy figure of authority, the sort of father who raises children with the capacity to believe in rational justice and disinterested morality. He stood in her mind as an exemplar of fair-minded, generous stewardship, a man whose public stature as a miller, a banker, and an Illinois state senator was consistent with the reserved but kindly father she knew at home. At the time of her father's death, Jane wrote: "My own vivid recollection of John H. Addams is the fact that he was a man of purest and sternest integrity and that bad men feared him. . . . He was the uncompromising enemy of wrong and of wrong doing. He was a leader as well as a safe and fearless advocate of right things in public life."[6]

That a grieving daughter would write such a civic-minded assessment of her father in a private notebook says much about the particular way in which the young Jane Addams made sense of her father's life and death. Thirty years later, she would recall that the "first comfort" she experienced in that bleak time of mourning came from a teacher who spoke not of resignation to God's will but of Plato and the "permanence of excellence." Near the end of her own life, Addams published a collection of eulogies titled *The Excellent Becomes Permanent*.[7] Labor and service were the only answers she could offer up to death. Senator Addams had not bequeathed to Jane any faith in a heavenly afterlife; that was for others to imagine. Instead, Jane Addams credited her father with teaching her that solid work in this life—and "fearless" advocacy of "right things"—were the one sure route to immortality.

If John Addams was important in encouraging Jane's ambition and teaching her the value of hard work, he was equally important in shaping her political ideology. John Addams's life was a testament to the Whig belief in a harmonious society, in the capacity for men of good will and reason to find mutual interests and to make rational compromises to advance those interests. Mediation in all things was to become Jane Addams's ideological lodestar, and the original dust for that star has to be traced back to her "Pa."*

---

* In the Addams family, the "a" in the terms "Pa" and "Ma" were pronounced as one would pronounce the "a" in "pap" or "map."

Jane grew up under her father's tutelage in a large gray brick house perched on a shaded mound close by Cedar Creek in northern Illinois. John Addams had moved his young family into this substantial new home in Cedarville in 1854, six years before Jane's birth. Across the road, John Addams's creek-fed grist mill kept up a steady clatter throughout Jane's childhood. The Addams house was then, and remains today, the largest house in Cedarville, a town of fewer than a thousand residents when Jane Addams was born there in 1860. Cedarville lies just about five miles north of Freeport, the leading community in Stephenson County. It was in Freeport, which had five times the population of Cedarville, that John Addams opened the Second National Bank in 1864, and, in 1867, the Protection Life Insurance Company and the Buckeye Mutual Fire Insurance Company.[8]

On those occasions when the young "Jennie" Addams walked with her Pa down the streets of Cedarville or Freeport, she would have seen that other men—men in overalls, men in cutaway coats—smiled upon seeing her father in his "high and shining silk hat," nodded and touched their own hats, approached him, conferred with him, appealed to him, respected him.[9] Farmers and grocers, laborers and blacksmiths, teachers and preachers, Americans and Germans all had dealings with John Addams, and an observant child would have seen that. As well, she would have seen that her Pa was no democrat. Not for him the back-slapping camaraderie of the saloon. He was a gracious, serious Whig of a man who willingly engaged in purposeful dealings with any citizen, rich or poor, and was comfortable with the delicate balance of power which settlers of unequal means had forged on the prairie of northern Illinois. As a young man, John Addams had sworn off "frivolous conversation," but as a mature man of substance, he enjoyed the respectful confidence of his neighbors.[10] Watching her Pa conduct business, Jane would have seen the decorum and deference common to nineteenth-century Americans who believed that merit was rewarded—with both responsibility and privilege.

In 1870, when Jane Addams was ten years old, her father told the census taker for Buckeye Township that he was worth $60,000 in real property and $20,000 in personal property. Since the median real wealth in the township that year was $2,700 and the median personal wealth was $600, John Addams occupied, objectively speaking, an elite position in his community.[11] When, in her autobiography, Jane Addams chose to describe her father as a "self-made man," she was stretching, not violating, the truth.[12] Senator Henry Clay coined the term to describe men dedicated to self-improvement and public improvement, and in that sense John Addams was a self-made man. He had been launched in Illinois with the help of some money, but his own labor had turned that start into a great deal more.

Born near Reading, Pennsylvania, in July 1822, John Addams spent the first twenty-two years of his life in the southeastern part of that state. The seventh of ten children born to Samuel Addams and Catherine Huy Addams, John was the third son in a family four generations removed from its English roots.[13] Samuel Addams fared well enough as a farmer to send John to boarding school

2. Portrait of Jane Addams's father, Senator John Huy Addams. (University of Illinois at Chicago, University Library, Jane Addams Memorial Collection, neg. no. 510)

at Washington Hall Collegiate Institute when he was sixteen and seventeen.[14] John Addams's later correspondence and personal library suggest the classical reading characteristic of ante-bellum Yankees devoted to self-improvement, but apart from a year's stint teaching school, his life was devoted to practical enterprise, not scholarship.

By the age of eighteen, Addams was apprenticed to Enos Reiff, a flour miller in Ambler, just north of Philadelphia. It was there that John met his future wife, Sarah Weber, the sister of Enos Reiff's wife, Elizabeth. Sarah was five years older than John and endowed with a boarding-school education and tall, angular good looks. She was, in addition, positioned to inherit a comfortable sum from the successful milling business that her father, Colonel George Weber, owned in Kreidersville, Pennsylvania. At age twenty-five, in 1842, Sarah Weber was still unmarried, perhaps by choice, perhaps because her father had deemed an earlier suitor unworthy. Whatever the cause, Sarah Weber's interest in matrimony coincided nicely with John Addams's interest in her and with Col. Weber's approval of the match.[15] Apparently, both Sarah and Col. Weber saw something of promise in the young man with jet black hair and silvery blue eyes.

The honeymoon in the summer of 1844 took them to Niagara Falls—a stop on the way between Pennsylvania and the couple's new home in Illinois. John Addams's diary from the trip recorded the "wonderful" beauty of the falls and the time-consuming "foolishness" of fancy hotel dining, as well as loving concern over his bride's seasickness on the voyage across Lake Michigan to Illinois. The diary also revealed a young man preoccupied with the opportunities and the risks ahead. His father had agreed to put up the money to buy a home and mill in Illinois, but that put a burden on John to find a suitable site.[16] Though he thought the prairie lands were "some of the prettiest a man could wish to see" and believed "there is no finer agricultural country known in the world," the young John Addams was still nervous about his prospects.[17]

The young couple's four-month search for a home and mill was fraught with anxiety. One day John Addams was "depressed," another day "quite elated"; maybe this was the right location, maybe that was the right price. Ninety years later, when Jane Addams finally read her father's 1844 diary, she was "amazed" to encounter this "qualmish" young man, so unlike the sturdy figure she had known.[18] But by the time Jane knew her father, he was a financial success. His disquiet in 1844 is a measure of his discomfort with being "loaded with debt." It was, he knew, "no trifling business to effect a purchase in which one is to make use of a kind father's money."[19] John and Sarah finally settled on the mill in Cedarville, chosen because it was beautiful, because their neighbors were friends and cousins from Pennsylvania, and because it lay in "a neighborhood where there will always be work plenty." John's father put up the substantial $4,600 needed to purchase the Cedar Creek mill and its surrounding 675 acres, and later advanced the additional $4,000 needed to renovate the mill, leaving John with the keenly felt need to be "very careful with the trust imposed upon me."[20] By the time the newlyweds settled in, Sarah was pregnant and John was determined to "ensure a good and honorable living to self and beloved" and to prove himself worthy of others' trust. Daily he prayed to "not disappoint my dear Parents."[21]

Sarah reported that John was so "busy in the mill" that they could not return visits paid by new neighbors. But despite working "day and night," John managed to make time for Stephenson County meetings to discuss the desperate need for a railroad.[22] Without cheap and easy access to eastern marketplaces, grain farmers—and millers—could not maximize their investment on the prairie. Back in the 1830s, Chicago businessmen had plotted out a rail line from their port on Lake Michigan to the port of Galena on the Mississippi, but the Panic of 1837 and the ensuing financial debacle in Illinois had scuttled those plans. By 1845, however, the state's population was booming, the economy was back on its feet, optimism about internal improvements had returned, and the locals were ready to invest in the Galena and Chicago Union Railroad.[23] John and Sarah could not possibly have started up their lives in Illinois at a more propitious moment.

It is this propitiousness—the way in which enterprise, opportunity, personal wealth, and community good all coincided during John Addams's early days in Illinois—that is central to understanding his influence on his daughter. He would grow very rich off the Galena and Chicago Union line but, because of unique circumstances, Addams's baptism as a businessman would be entirely harmonious, typified by what one local historian called "cooperation and unity of interest."[24]

Parochial fears of intercity competition scared off investors in Chicago, ninety miles southeast, and Galena, thirty-five miles southwest. The proposed railroad's directors then turned to farmers and villagers along the route, asking them to invest $100 apiece in railroad stock.[25] The Galena and Chicago Union Railroad became, of necessity, a "pay-as-you-go, farmer's railroad."[26] Between 1846 and 1853, as the line inched its way toward Freeport, local dollar by local dollar, John Addams canvassed among his ten thousand neighbors in Stephenson County, imploring them to invest in the railroad, promising them that the route would go through Freeport, and guaranteeing them a return on their investment. In the process, he raised $14,000 for the railroad and became "the best-known man in the district."[27]

The railroad that Addams convinced his neighbors to support became, during the 1850s, the most profitable line in the United States, averaging annual dividends of more than 16 percent.[28] The tonnage and value of grain shipped out of Freeport soared in these years, as did the amount and value of goods imported, the size of the local population, and the price of land. Little wonder that, years after his death, the people of Freeport still praised John Addams for bringing the railroad through their town.[29] And while we do not know how much Addams himself invested in the railroad, we do know that his total wealth in 1860 was almost $50,000 more than the $17,000 he listed back in 1850.[30] As a devoted Whig and an admirer of Henry Clay's "American System," the thirty-eight-year-old John Addams heartily embraced this lesson in mutuality between community leaders, private enterprise, and the people.[31]

By 1860, the year of Jane Addams's birth, her father's pioneer prayers for success had been amply rewarded. In 1858, he was able to spend $10,000 in building an entirely new grist mill near the one renovated for $4,000 back in 1844.[32] He and Sarah had long since moved beyond their first, little house on the prairie and were well settled into their gray stone manse and the prosperity it bespoke. Before giving birth to "Jennie," Sarah Addams had birthed seven babies and buried three of them. Her two older daughters, Mary, aged fifteen, and Martha, aged ten, were quiet, responsible girls; the sort who read books and wrote letters and helped their mother with household chores. By contrast, the two younger children—Weber, aged eight, and Alice, aged seven—were hellions; they risked life and limb by playing in the mill race or jumping on the back of the family's prize bull and bellowed and kicked against closed doors when banished for their (frequent) misbehavior.[33]

Sarah Addams presided over these children and her busy household with the matter-of-fact dignity often ascribed to her husband. She was a wealthy woman, but not a woman of leisure. For Sarah Addams, wealth meant responsibility more than luxury. There were mill hands to tend to, the two "hired girls" from the neighborhood to supervise, and community duties to shoulder. When the township held a Teachers' Institute, John and Sarah Addams hosted six participants; when the town needed a library, the Addams's living room housed the books; and when Stephenson County held its annual fair, Sarah and her husband served as judges for the flower contest.[34]

Through her ladies' sewing circle, Sarah Addams raised funds for Cedarville's first meeting house, but neither she nor her husband ever joined a church in town. Back in Pennsylvania, Sarah had professed her faith by joining the Reformed Church, but the man she married was not, and never became, a "saved" Christian. Together, however, they alternated Sundays between the Methodist and Presbyterian meetings, and John testified to his moral principles by belonging to the Stephenson County Bible Society and teaching in the local, non-denominational, "union" Sunday School, which brought together all of Cedarville's Protestant students.[35] John shepherded the Addams children out of the house every Sabbath morning for Sunday School, leaving Sarah free to dress for church. Her husband was no dandy, but when Sarah reached the pew of whichever church they were attending that week, John stood and bowed and allowed his wife to glide around him before resuming his seat. This bit of ceremony passed for gallantry in Cedarville, Illinois, in the 1850s, and underscored the Addamses' stature as the leading family in town.[36]

In 1854, six years before Jane Addams's birth and Abraham Lincoln's election to the presidency, John Addams was elected to the Illinois State Senate from Stephenson County. He ran on a fusion ticket, as a Whig and a Republican, signaling his Whig loyalty to the Missouri Compromise that Henry Clay fashioned in 1820 and to the Clay-sponsored Compromise of 1850. John Addams subscribed thoroughly to Senator Clay's philosophical commitment to the basic principle of compromise; it suited Addams's temperament, it suited his nonsectarian religiosity, and—until the Kansas-Nebraska Act of 1854—it suited the times.[37] But by the winter of 1855, when John Addams entered the Illinois Senate, Henry Clay was dead and so, apparently, was the Whig Party. The triple blow of the Fugitive Slave Act, the Kansas-Nebraska Act, and the Dred Scott decision had sent Whigs staggering in at least four directions, some into the arms of the proslavery Democrats, others into the ranks of the nativist Know-Nothings, a few into the abolitionist camp, and many into the emerging fold of the "free-soil" Republicans.

For John Addams, situated in a northern Illinois county known for its free-soil sympathies, this political crisis—like the Galena and Chicago Railroad investment—posed no conflict between conscience, self-interest, and community interest. All were consonant in John Addams's world. He quickly aligned with the majority of his neighbors in the new Republican Party believing that loyalty to Henry Clay's compromises required, finally, an uncompromising stand on union and on territorial limits to slavery.[38]

It is regrettable that Jane Addams, writing her autobiography in 1909, did not point to Henry Clay and the family legacy of stewardship, harmony, and principled compromise in describing her father's political orientation. If she had, the world might have gained a better understanding of Jane Addams's own political lineage. In 1909, however, the Civil War was still the nation's defining political moment and Jane Addams chose to identify her father not with Henry Clay, the great compromiser, but with Abraham Lincoln, the great emancipator.[39] That decision served two purposes: it usefully linked her own reform politics to America's victorious commander rather than to a defeated compromiser. At the same time, it accurately reflected the fact that, as important as Clay had been in shaping John Addams's fundamental views on civic life, Abraham Lincoln and his Republican Party were the key elements in John Addams's political career.[40]

Senator Addams's views on slavery were firm but decidedly moderate in regard to limiting slave expansion. He had opposed the annexation of Texas and what he called "the propagation" of slavery into new territories back in 1845, and he first ran for state senate against the Kansas-Nebraska Act.[41] The Democrats' *Freeport Bulletin* did its best to discredit the anti-Nebraska position, always referring to the Republicans as the "Black Republicans" or the "Abolitionist Republicans," but John Addams was not frightened off by such labels. As a Stephenson County delegate to the Republican Party's first statewide meeting in Springfield in 1854, and again at the Bloomington convention two years later, Addams saw firsthand that this was no radical band of abolitionists.[42]

The Republican Party platform in Illinois was focused narrowly on the matter of slave expansion, limiting itself to what Jane Addams later called "Mr. Lincoln's 'best possible.'"[43] It was this moderation that made the party a perfect fit for John Addams. Twenty years later he would tell an audience that "many of us did not relish" the Compromise of 1850, but "said if it would satisfy the South we would be content." It was only with the Kansas-Nebraska Act of 1854, when aggressive, uncompromising, proslavery forces "opened up the whole slavery question again," explained Addams, that Whigs like himself "nobly determined to take a firm stand for liberty . . . that slavery should spread no farther."[44]

The Civil War story that Jane Addams heard while growing up in the 1870s was not the abolitionist story of a crusade for universal human freedom; it was the Whig story of a breakdown in reason and civility. At every Republican rally and Fourth of July picnic, in every parlor conversation between her father, his neighbors, and his political colleagues, and certainly in every history class, she learned about an American civil war forced upon the sober, moral North by Southern men whose slaveowning had corrupted their hearts and minds. She learned about a campaign of Southern aggression with which John Addams and his new Republican Party simply could not compromise.

During the Great War that later shaped Jane Addams's life, she learned, like her father, that a belief in mediation occasionally necessitates intransigence. In Jane's case, the lesson reconfirmed her acquired commitment to pacifism. While that commitment certainly owed something to her father's Whiggish devotion to civility and compromise, it was not a direct legacy of her father's experience in the Civil War. The lessons John Addams drew for his daughter from the Civil War were not about peace but about victory. They were about the importance of a strong national government, an "American System" for the whole economy, and activist intervention by the citizenry working together through the state. So while Jane Addams did not inherit her pacifism from her father, she did carry into the Progressive Era a substantial legacy from his Republican ideology.[45]

It is a testament to the selectivity of memory that readers of Jane Addams's autobiography have long chosen to focus their attention on her fleeting references to her father's "Quaker tendencies" while overlooking the fact that her narrative is suffused with childhood memories of military regalia and the honor of war service.[46] As an adult, and in private, she explicitly denied any Quaker parentage, but Jane Addams never disavowed that erroneous reputation in public, perhaps because she sought to provide herself with a legitimate, religious source for her own pacifism. Whatever the motive in suggesting that her father was a Quaker, the effect was to divert attention from John Addams's role in aiding the war effort and his political identity as a fiercely loyal Union man.[47]

Senator Addams did not actually fight in the Civil War. He was a thirty-nine-year-old father of five and in his fourth two-year term as an Illinois state senator when the Confederates fired on Fort Sumter. He could have enlisted and obtained a commission as an officer; men in similar circumstances did. Instead, Senator Addams focused on serving his local district, adhering to a pattern that characterized his whole political career. When he was down in Springfield, he provided legislative support for Governor Richard Yates's Republican administration, and his eldest daughter, Mary, helped him oversee the progress of enlistments in Stephenson County.[48] When he was back home, he campaigned so effectively for enlistments that the *Illinois State Journal* singled out the exertions of the senator from "Little Stephenson County." In the aftermath of the 1861 disaster at Bull Run, Senator Addams so energetically roused his constituents that the district raised three full companies within a few days, and Company G of the 93rd Illinois Volunteer Infantry was called "The Addams Guards."[49] In fact, Stephenson County sent so many young men into service—voluntarily—that Addams successfully lobbied for his district's exemption from the 1864 draft.[50]

Jane Addams never reflected publicly on just how hugely fortunate it was that her father did not enlist in the Union Army. But that calculation is easy enough to make, for in January 1863, when little Jennie was just over two years old, her mother, Sarah, died. The cause of death appears to have been eclampsia, a toxemic state particular to pregnancy. Sarah was seven months pregnant that January, when she ventured out into a snowy night to aid the wife of a mill worker who was in labor. Upon returning home, she went into convulsions. These ceased when the doctor "removed" her lifeless female baby, but by then Sarah lay unconscious. Her brother, George Weber, had settled in the Cedarville area by 1863 and was in attendance during his sister's final days.

According to his letter to the family in Pennsylvania, "The first we noticed of any consciousness was [when] their little daughter, Jenny, cried out with a loud shriek. Sarah raised up in bed but oh the wild look she had. She soon sank back again."[51]

John Addams had rushed home from Springfield, where the senate was in session, and waited. Two days later, his "beloved" of twenty years—and the mother of their five children—was dead. George Weber reported to the folks back home that John took his wife's death "severely to heart" and that he was "much perplexed what to do in regard of his dear family."[52] Single fathers were not common in Stephenson County, Illinois, in 1863, but John Addams had become one. And Jennie Addams was about to start centering upon him "all that careful imitation which a little girl ordinarily gives to her mother's ways and habits."[53]

Chapter 2
The Predominant Elements of Her Character

Jennie Addams may have been motherless, but she was never un-mothered. Her eldest sister, Mary, was eighteen years old at the time of Sarah Addams's death and quickly moved into position as a surrogate mother to thirteen-year-old Martha, ten-year-old Weber, nine-year-old Alice, and two-year-old Jennie. Decades later, Jane Addams spoke about how "a household of children, whose mother is dead . . . perform unaccustomed offices for each other and awkwardly exchange consolations." Indeed, the adult Jane Addams believed that she owed Mary "everything." In 1890, when a niece was fearful that her own mother might die, Addams reached back twenty-five years to "my horrible dream every night" that Mary would die and there would be "no one to love me."[1]

There would, of course, have been others to love her: Polly Beer, the family housekeeper in these years; Sarah Addams's brother, George, and John Addams's brother, James, both of whom lived in the area; not to mention Cedarville's close community of some seven hundred neighbors. Motherless though she was, the toddler Jennie Addams was embedded in a safe and attentive circle of responsible, caring adults. None, however, not even Mary, occupied as central a place in that circle as her Pa. Like so many of her later female colleagues in social reform, Jane Addams looked to her father as a strong, steady source of comfort and security and was not disappointed.[2]

In the first year after Sarah's death, John was home a great deal, overseeing the mill and appearing only infrequently at the twenty-third session of the Illinois State Senate. The following year, he resumed his winter duties in Springfield but often took a train home for the weekend. The year after Sarah died, John Addams also opened the Second National Bank of Freeport. This meant a five-mile carriage ride into town every day, but a return to the family circle every evening. Mary Addams and Polly Beer undoubtedly gave young Jennie her baths and meals and little scoldings in the years immediately following her mother's death, but it was Pa who dominated her mental landscape and her field of memory. Whether at home or away, he became the object of Jennie's "adoring affection." All the children sent kisses to Pa in Springfield, but Jennie sent him "ten kisses." When he was home, she trotted beside him, "doglike" and eager for his company. When she dreamt her "horrible dream" about Mary dying, she found solace with her father. From him came "comfort," "relief," "the sense that the knowledge . . . was shared," "a new fellowship . . . because we had discussed [death] together."[3] It is not necessary to take literally every story Addams told about her father in her autobiography in order to draw meaning from her emotional memory of a caring and involved parent. What she wrote about her father is, in fact, consistent with the picture emerging from modern research on nineteenth-century Northern fathers and quite consistent with others' recollections of Stephenson County's senator.[4]

John Addams's grandson, Mary's eldest son, was nine years old when his grandfather died, old enough to have acquired a strong sense of the man. He later recalled Senator Addams as the "one figure who stands out in my childhood memories for he was so very big to me and grave and I was always wondering what his thoughts must be—and yet I was so absolutely certain of his love and knew that if I did dare to speak to him, a certain look would come into his eyes and I felt that he was never putting me off or only seeming to listen."[5] In an era when middle-class men could exhibit a greater range of playfulness, sentimentality, and attentiveness than historians have often recognized, John Addams appears to have been among the attentive ones, among those who believed that children needed to be listened to and taken seriously. Neither frolicsome nor mawkish by nature, Senator Addams adopted an avuncular, respectful stance toward children. When little boys visited the bank, he came from behind the counter to shake their hands and tousle their hair. Should he encounter a youngster walking on the road to Freeport, he would give him a buggy ride behind his "fine team of horses" and "quiz" him about his life and his thoughts. Decades after John Addams's death, men told Jane Addams that they had known her father "very well in the way a boy knows a man," or "as well as any growing lad could know an esteemed elder."[6] The fact that John Addams was a man of great public and private dignity, even reserve, did not prevent him from being accessible to children.

Neighbors regarded Addams as a "kind and indulgent father," and in the world he inhabited, this was a compliment.[7] He monitored his children's health and studies with care, doling out praise and encouragement with affection, writing news of his senate activities (even sending home a senate seating chart so the children could picture the scene), signing his letters "your friend" as easily as he signed "your father."[8] Should a paternal word of criticism be called for, it was offered with characteristic restraint. When Alice was habitually late to the breakfast table during a vacation at home from school, her father "did not say much." Later, however, he felt compelled to write of his displeasure at her "indifference to punctuality." He was, he explained, a businessman and knew "how annoying tardiness is in small things."[9] No threats or punishments were offered, but when Alice asked permission to take a special railway trip that spring, her father tweaked her by expressing doubt that she would ever catch such an early morning train.[10] In the end, Alice was allowed to go, as she was allowed to do most everything she wanted to do, but John Addams had made his point: he expected a daughter to be every bit as level-headed and responsible as a son.

Jane Addams never wrote about her mother in any surviving letter, speech, article, or book. Had she wished to create a maternal legacy for herself, she could have drawn on others' memories and her own considerable skills as a storyteller to connect herself to the industrious female stock that bore her. At the very least, she could have quoted from Sarah Addams's obituary describing her as "a woman who will be missed everywhere—at home, in society, in the church, in all places where good was to be done and suffering to be relieved. Possessed of means, and with a heart ever alive to the wants of the poor, she was always present when sympathy was needed or aid required. She lived a life of usefulness and has gone to her reward."[11] Jane Addams's readers would have loved such words and their intimations of the daughter's destiny, but the daughter never used them. When a publisher asked her, in 1914, for an article on Sarah, Addams wrote an uncharacteristically terse reply, explaining that it would be "quite impossible" for her to fulfill such a request because her mother "died when I was a baby." And when asked, on a 1925 "heredity" questionnaire, which parent had influenced her, Addams replied that "the predominant elements" of her character had come from her father.[12]

It was not that Jennie Addams was unaffected by her mother's death; her recollections of childhood are suffused with memories of death and abandonment. "One's throat goes dry over this old fear of death," she wrote at age fifty-five, "your heart contracts."[13] But the lesson Addams took from her mother's death, the lesson she chose to inject into these recollections, was that her father had been her greatest source of comfort, honesty, and wisdom. He was not only her guide in understanding her mother's death, but in understanding her sister Martha's death from typhoid fever four years later when Martha was just seventeen and Jennie was only six. Laced throughout these years of family tragedy there was also the national tragedy that Pa had to explain in terms Jennie could grasp: the community grief when neighbors' sons died in the distant Civil War, and the tears shed by everyone, even her father, when the president, Illinois's favorite son, was assassinated.[14]

Jane Addams later credited her father with providing the philosophical armor she needed to meet and make sense of "the prowling terror," "the formless peril," "the shadowy dangers," "the miserable dread," in short, all the images she associated with death.[15] Plenty of people around her could call up a child's fear of those forces. There were the neighbors who believed that the unsanctified would burn in hell and even Jane's uncle George Weber, Sarah's evangelical brother, could only "hope" that his wealthy sister had "died in peace."[16] In contrast to such judgmental voices, Jane described her father as "much too wise to grow dogmatic on the great theme of death."[17] Having foregone the faith of a "professing Christian," Senator Addams preached the value of honesty "with yourself inside" and "doing good among his fellow beings"; he resisted expressing certitude about the unknowable.[18] So while John Addams's pious daughter Mary consoled herself, in the months following her mother's death, with the thought that "our Father in heaven doth all things well," John Addams merely sighed over "how fleeting and uncertain life is."[19] Where Mary—and Uncle George—saw the workings of the divine in events, John sought the divine in humans' noble response to events. In this fundamental matter, Jane would fashion herself as her father's spiritual compatriot.[20]

Stories of Jennie Addams as a child sending kisses to her father seem to suggest a fragile, lonely little girl. She was, after all, the household's motherless baby; her surviving siblings—Mary, Weber, and Alice—were between seven and sixteen years older than she and could reminisce about a mother Jennie barely knew. In Alice's memory, complicated by the mix of admiration and resentment she later felt for her famous sister, Jennie was a "petted," "selfish," "willful" child whose family was so "quickly responsive to her moods and childish tempers" and so catered to her "delicate" health that she "came to feel her own way was without question the right one." Jane also recalled herself as "delicate" and as the special object of her father's leniency, but she focused on a child whose spine was made "crooked" by tubercular abscesses and whose loneliness was more notable than her willfulness.[21] Family letters temper these recollections, for they made frequent mention of other relatives' illnesses but said nothing of Jennie's ailing spine—or her willfulness. Indeed, the few mentions of Jennie in the first eight years of her life describe her as a charming and "lovable" child who amused Mary with inquiries about "when her little finger would grow as long as the others."[22]

At age eight, the ostensibly delicate Jennie Addams sustained yet another dramatic change in her life when Anna Haldeman, her new stepmother, joined the Cedarville household. All notions of Jennie Addams as a frail, lonely, self-absorbed little girl must be revised with the advent of Anna—and George, the seven-year-old stepbrother Jennie acquired in the bargain. The Freeport widow whom Senator Addams chose as his second wife was not inclined to let a female competitor for pity and attention grow up in any home of hers. To the extent that Jennie was ever pampered or indulged, it was not for long. When Anna took command of the Addams home in the fall of 1868 she had every reason to turn her youngest stepchild into a healthy, cheerful, obedient daughter. In so doing, she satisfied her own and the Senator's definition of a good mother, kept firm control of the family spotlight, and added immeasurably to the quality of Jane Addams's childhood and to the complexity of her character.

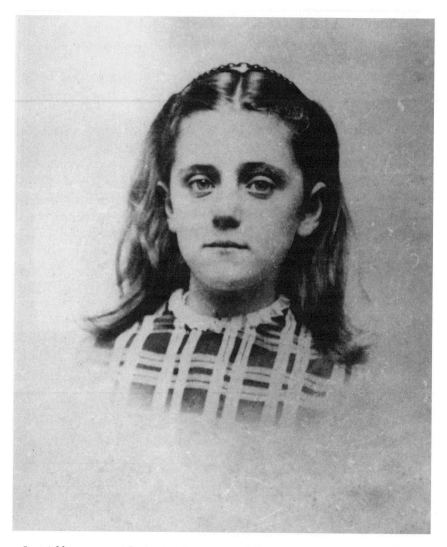

3. Jane Addams at age eight, in 1868. (University of Illinois at Chicago, University Library, Jane Addams Memorial Collection, neg. no. 2766)

Still, the upheaval in Jennie's life in the fall of 1868 was tremendous. That summer she had nestled comfortably in a home run by her Pa, her sisters Mary and Alice, and her brother Weber. In September, Alice departed for Rockford Female Seminary and Weber enrolled at the University of Michigan at Ann Arbor. Then, suddenly, in November, Pa brought home a new wife and brother. No sooner had Christmas passed than Pa went off to the senate in Springfield, leaving Jennie alone with a woman whom she was to call "Ma" and a stepbrother who wanted to play. The center of gravity in the household had shifted irrevocably and Jennie initially resisted. One family friend with distinct memories of Jennie "as a little girl tripping about your father's house" could recall, a quarter century later, "how much more acceptable to you was the service of love from your eldest sister than the word of authority from your step-mother."[23]

Sooner rather than later, Jennie settled in to her new family. She was not so spoiled or willful as to challenge the domestic arrangements of her elders, not when surrounded by multiple encouragements to adjust. Her beloved Pa obviously wanted her to accept her new Ma, and her older sisters welcomed Anna warmly, happy to have a maternal figure in the home who offered a respite from some of the household burdens they had been carrying.[24] Anna, meanwhile, conveyed her enjoyment of children. When she was not persuading Jennie of the legitimacy of her authority, she delighted in her stepdaughter's play with her son. The Senator, down in Springfield, begged for daily letters from his bride about "the doings" of his "now doubly dear home," and Anna wrote assuringly, "to be termed 'Mother' or 'Ma' by such warm-hearted, kind children, does not after all make the position as hard as I had supposed for me to fill." She noted in particular that "the two little ones," Jennie and George, kept her from having "the blues."[25] Although Anna complained from the start, as she would for the rest of her life, about cool treatment from John's neighbors in Cedarville, she did not complain about the children. In that area, in which Anna was most confident and John most solicitous, the newlyweds shared a sincere determination to succeed.[26]

If there was a campaign to win Jennie over to Anna, then the secret and most fortunate weapon was George Haldeman. His introduction into the big gray house in Cedarville meant that Jennie Addams was no longer the isolated, motherless baby among older, more knowing siblings. She was now the full and equal member of a brother-sister team on which both players had lost a parent in early childhood. The Addams household now revolved around Jennie and George while older brothers and sisters spun off into their own orbits. The two children shared everything, including Anna's love of spontaneous play—and her equally spontaneous fits of temper. For Jennie, Anna represented a wholly new emotional experience: fiery, impulsive, and dramatic. Her temperament was entirely different from Pa's emotional reserve, her methods of household management were far removed from the prairie practicality Mary had learned from Sarah, and her passionate style of motherhood, for good and ill, exposed young Jennie to a range of emotional expression uncommon in the village of Cedarville. Along with offering companionship, George Haldeman served Jennie as an experienced guide in dealing with his mother's moods. As childhood partners, "both children felt the storm as well as the sunshine of Anna's gracious but complicated character."[27]

Anna Hostetter Haldeman Addams was not an easy woman. On that point, everyone agreed. People either loved her "extravagantly" or disliked her "thoroughly." Her most adoring grandchild, Marcet, described her as a "beautiful, high-spirited" creature whose moods alternated between "sweeping tendernesses" and "explosions and irritations."[28] Her less adoring grandchild, James, called her "handsome in a terrifying sort of way," the sort of strong character around whom circulate legends of willfulness "and cruelty of purpose."[29] Even the staid authors of *The History of Stephenson County* departed from their dry writing style long enough to comment on the "often tempestuous though culturally stimulating home environment" created by the second Mrs. John Addams: "No one ever thought of her as belonging to Cedarville although she was of great interest to the little community. . . . She never became, or wanted to become, a real neighbor in the village except to the children. Part of the charm of this many-sided woman was her rapport with children. For years she gave her own birthday party, inviting a half-dozen or so children and giving them a glorious afternoon."[30]

Anna Hostetter was thirty-nine years old when she married John Addams. Born in Pennsylvania in 1829, Anna lost both her mother and a sister when she was quite young. She had moved to northern Illinois in 1845, at the age of sixteen, with her two older brothers, both physicians, who set up practice in Mt. Carroll, just thirty miles southwest of John Addams's mill. Still in her teens when she married William Haldeman, a grain miller from Freeport, she had given birth to four sons by the time she was thirty-two. Her firstborn, Henry—always called "Harry"—was already twenty years old and living away from home when Anna remarried. By that time, her two middle sons had died from separate childhood illnesses, leaving her youngest, George, to accompany her to Cedarville.[31] If Jennie Addams was John's indulged baby, George was Anna's. Her lifelong grief over the loss of her mother, her sister, her two sons, and her first husband caused Anna to pour all of her emotional energy into her two surviving boys. She believed that they were both meant for great missions in life, and she was determined to have them realize their destinies.[32]

The Haldeman family had lived comfortably in Freeport from 1847 to

1866. William had not fought in the Civil War; instead, he had competed vig-orously with John Addams in the grain business.[33] He had told the census taker that he owned $10,000 in real property in 1860—a fraction of the $46,000 John Addams owned—but plenty to provide Anna and the boys with a pleasant home, fashionable clothes and furniture, a piano, good riding horses, and the small luxuries necessary for gracious entertaining in a midwestern town at midcen-tury.[34] Still, Anna was prone to bouts of depression, and neighbors' "rebuffs"— real and imagined—left her feeling "so homeless, so friendless" when William was away that she became consumed with doubt about "every body and every thing."[35] Though she loved the outdoors and was blessed with a strong constitution, Anna saw herself as delicate and poetically sensitive. Her nerves, she thought, were poised to vibrate to the most subtle disturbances and "like the Aspen leaves rustle and shake even when there is seemingly no breeze to move them."[36]

William Haldeman's death in the spring of 1866 had left Anna and the boys with some inheritance—Harry and George were each worth $8,000 in 1870—but Anna was not equal to the task of managing the estate in a way that would permanently support her tastes or her ambitions for her sons.[37] Her brother had warned Anna against her inclination to feel bitter, and she cer-tainly endeavored to keep up appearances.[38] She held on to her house in Free-port, sent Harry to Leipzig, Germany to study music, and gave piano lessons to local children—including, before her untimely death, John Addams's second daughter, Martha. In good times and bad, Anna Haldeman was well dressed and well coiffed and could always command a room with a witty remark and the dramatic sweep of one beautiful hand.[39]

When John Addams first attempted courtship in the spring of 1868, the widow Haldeman declined his overtures, claiming that her "sympathies" did not accord with his. But her candor only heightened Addams's appreciation of the "nobleness" of Anna's character.[40] If the rebuff was a feminine ploy, it worked. Within weeks, the two single parents were openly courting. Anna, after all, had to be practical. Senator Addams was certainly practical. She was a widow with children (and a dwindling estate); he was a widower with children (and a growing estate). She was equipped to mother his children; he was in a position to provide her sons with the prestigious father Anna felt they deserved. John's first letters to Anna noted "the peculiar position we both occupy . . . both of us having families," but he was quick to comment as well on his great respect for Anna and his great pleasure in her company. He was clearly drawn to this lively, artistic woman who was tall and angular like Sarah, but different in every other regard. In June, John addressed Anna as "Dear Madam" and closed "Yours truly." By October, she was "my dear" and John was "truly and affectionately yours."[41] In mid-November, they wed.

If the marriage was a calculated one, Anna masked it well with playful references to herself as the "sometime disturber" of her new husband's rest and tender assurances that he had "about all" of her love "from the first of my being your wife." She surely agreed with her brother that the Senator deserved her "highest and best efforts to make him happy," and undoubtedly enjoyed the status and protection her new husband offered. It cannot have taken great effort for Anna, who "loved to attract and please" men, to turn her well-honed charms on the most respected man in the county.[42] She was aided in her effort by several significant compatibilities. They were both Republicans, of course, and both of their families were from Pennsylvania. These were not unusual commonalities in Stephenson County, Illinois, but not unimportant ones either. Much more notable was their religious compatibility. Unlike many women John Addams might have courted in Stephenson County, Anna Haldeman was not a sectarian or evangelical Protestant. As commonsensical in theology as her second husband, Anna believed that "to do good for our fellow beings . . . is all the religion worth one Christian thought."[43] Though this belief did not inspire in Anna the same enthusiasm for community stewardship that Sarah Addams had shared with John, it ensured that the Senator's new wife would not be importing dogmatic religiosity into his home; the religious views Jennie would hear from Anna were consistent with those she heard from her Pa.[44] In keeping with these liberal tendencies was Anna Haldeman's attitude toward child-rearing, another important area of agreement between the new heads of this blended family.

Like her second husband, Anna aligned herself with the increasingly popular view that "gentle measures" were more effective than harsh discipline in guiding children. Neither Anna nor John Addams subscribed to earlier beliefs in the necessity of "breaking" a child's "will"—guiding it, yes, channeling it in productive directions, yes, but never assaulting the child's God-given, individual self. Along with many other Northern, liberal, middle-class parents in these years, Anna and John sought to enlist their children in the willing service of domestic and social order through inspirational stories of heroism, not threatening tales of punishment. Both Anna and John Addams were more likely to play upon a child's sense of pride than sense of shame, more likely to bribe than punish, more likely to prick than pummel a young conscience.[45] As luck would have it, these were strategies best suited to rearing an industrious child like Jennie Addams.

Anna was not always able to enact her enlightened principles of child nurture. She lost her temper, she yelled, she probably turned red in the face and perhaps even cried with frustration, right in front of the children. These outbursts were expressions of Anna's temperament, however, not her philosophy of childrearing; she did not believe in terrorizing children as a policy, she simply could not discipline her passions to conform to her ideals. Her brother urged her to seek "calm deliberate concessions" if she wished to make herself, and others, happy, but while Anna aimed for happiness, calm deliberation was not always within her reach.[46] These traits of temperament bore benefits as well as costs in the Addams household. Thanks to her passionate nature, Anna probably brought more sentimentality, and perhaps more physicality, to her childrearing than John did, a difference that fit comfortably within the gender distinctions of the day. Anna's rages were probably less easy to accommodate. The record is silent on precisely what John Addams thought of his new wife's outbursts or how he handled them; one suspects he practiced forbearance, even withdrawal, at such times. One suspects Anna felt abandoned at such times. But these are merely suspicions. What seems quite clear is that when John and Anna Addams went into partnership to raise Jennie and George, they agreed on the fundamental principles of the enterprise.

In the years between Anna and George's arrival in Cedarville in 1868 and Jane Addams's departure for Rockford Female Seminary in 1877, Jane emerged from a pampered, frail childhood into a vigorous, more self-confident adolescence. Throughout those years, her daily life was thoroughly entwined with George Haldeman's. Anna did not countenance much mooning about the house, so Jennie and George were up and out, playing in the yard, playing in the barn, playing by the creek.[47] All the business of childhood—all the industrious play, all the invention and experimentation and exploration, all the mastery of

4. Jane Addams with Cedarville classmates in 1872. She is second from the left, in front standing row. George Haldeman is at the center of the row of seated boys. (Rockford College Archives)

academic and social skills, all the negotiating for approval and autonomy from parents—every bit of it occurred for Jane in tandem with George.

When she was fourteen and keeping a daily diary, Jane wrote newsy and unsentimental reports on her activities with George. They went sledding on the creek together, had snowball fights in which "George says he beat but he didn't," went to the traveling magic show and to singing class, "nearly killed ourselves playing hopscotch but had a good deal of fun," rode horseback, wrote and illustrated "romantic tales" side by side, played croquet, formed the Science Almanacs Association with only themselves as members, performed piano duets for company ("with *some* grumbling"), perfected their chess game, wrote poems using George's "original alphabet," and suffered through the mumps together at age sixteen.[48]

This matter-of-fact record of daily activities challenges the historical stereotype of the Victorian American home as a site of rigid gender segregation where girls were grounded in the parlor by stifling rules of decorum. It is, however, consistent with the testimonies of females in Jane Addams's cohort who recalled active play with boys who were relatives and neighbors; it is also consistent with studies of childhood play conducted in the late nineteenth century, and consistent with the advice literature and post–Civil War novels endorsing "tomboyism" as healthy preparation for the demanding life of a wife and mother. Northern middle-class parents needed no feminist impulses in order to want vigorous daughters who would be competent partners to their husbands and capable managers in widowhood—or spinsterhood. So while girls were typically excluded from boys' hiking, hunting, and fishing excursions, they were regular participants in horseback rides, sledding, ice skating, games, contests, musicales, dramas, reading and drawing clubs. Boys (and girls) may have valued distinctly masculine activities over more feminine ones, but that did not preclude regular, casual mixing in a common social space of childhood play where age and ability might influence the hierarchy as much as gender.[49]

If there was anything exceptional in the camaraderie Jennie and George enjoyed in Cedarville in the 1870s, it was not Jennie's access to play with George but George's dependence on play with Jennie. When, for example, George, at age ten, went away for a visit, all of his surviving letters home were addressed to Jennie. The following year, when Jennie went to visit Anna's family in Mt. Carroll, Anna reported that George was "very happy at home only he misses Jennie very much," adding that his refusal to accompany Jennie on this trip away from home was typical of George, "queer boy that he is."[50] It was blood, not gender, that dictated Anna's position in this scenario; her self-declared sensitivity was not a female trait she saw reflected in Jane but a special bond between herself and her baby boy.

As George and Jennie got older, Anna extended herself to provide a wholesome, lively social life for the two teenagers. Whatever her discomfort with her adult neighbors in Cedarville, Anna loved entertaining young people, so night after night the Addams's parlor was a site for card games, charades, blind man's bluff, singing, spelling contests, natural history games, taffy pulls, and oyster suppers. Typically, George was the only male participant in the parlor gatherings. Jennie regularly invited her girlfriends over to join in the play with Anna and George, but Anna's "queer boy" did not extend invitations to other boys in town, and Senator Addams absented himself unless there was a spelling contest (where he reigned as champion).[51]

In adolescence, Jane Addams "read and re-read" *Little Women* and admired Alcott's "ideal hero," Laurie.[52] Here was a sensitive fellow who enjoyed being the sole boy playing games contrived by girls, who thought girls just as smart as boys, and who liked Jo the best. Similar to Jo, Jennie seems to have been oblivious to any potential for romance with George, her "Laurie." Though Jane Addams would, as an adult, write with great sensitivity about the first stirrings of adolescent sexuality, she gave no voice to such stirrings in the notably unromantic letters and diary entries that have survived from her youth. At age fourteen, she pronounced other girls' sentimental displays over boys to be "disgusting"[53] and told a cousin that she thought "Platonic love, or rather pure sacred friendship" was "so much higher than what is generally implied in the word love." In that same letter, Jane critiqued Alcott's *Rose in Bloom*, where the tragic hero, Charlie, who was "something like Laurie," might have turned "out all right" if Alcott's heroine, Rose, "had sufficiently exerted herself." Unlike other, more voluble girls of her generation, Jane did not comment on whether she felt any duty to bring her shy step-brother "out all right."[54]

In the same years that Jane and George shared their social life, they also shared the academic life of Cedarville's small school. Their parents had the cultural inclination and the economic means to keep both children in the classroom throughout each school year until they graduated from their one-room high school on the second floor of Cedarville's brick schoolhouse. Since only 50 percent of schoolage children in Illinois were in regular attendance at even the elementary level, Jane and George's steady advancement through the grades reflects the relative privilege they enjoyed.[55] Still, theirs was a manifestly small-town education, with classes of perhaps a dozen to two dozen students representing a span of ages and levels of commitment to the academic enterprise. The curriculum was basic, advancing from reading, writing, spelling, and arithmetic to Latin, algebra, botany, and "natural philosophy." Thanks to Cedarville's rather pedestrian teachers, the instruction was generally rote.

In the diary she kept at age fourteen, Jane was most expressive when writing about school. She openly detested the "pokey," "humdrum" drudgery of the Cedarville schoolhouse and could get her "angry passions stirred up considerable against Mr. Moore" for being such a bad teacher.[56] It is not difficult to imagine her finding support for this sentiment from Anna, who often became passionate in her anger at "pokey" Cedarville. Nor is it difficult to imagine John Addams, distinguished member of the Cedarville School Board, raising an eyebrow at his daughter's complaints. In May of her sophomore year, Jane "felt ashamed" of herself for complaining so much about school, but admitted she was "sick and tired of it" and "crept like a snail unwillingly . . . through all of the exercises." She took small glee in Mr. Moore's inability to work a "simple" math problem and noted with disdain that this inadequate man was "ever lastingly picking his nose."[57]

The joy in Jane Addams's Cedarville school life derived from partnership with George and from opportunities to show off her academic talents. She could not be the center of family attention in Anna's household, but she could gain the spotlight in school. Though American society made little room for the educated female adult in the 1870's, America's common schools rewarded girls every day for their decorum and precise recitations. Indeed, American education was moving toward a time when girls' notable success in the classroom would evoke fears of the feminization of education.[58] In Cedarville in the 1870s, however, school achievement was not the exclusive province of either girls or boys. Jane and George moved in tandem toward the more advanced subjects, with Jane taking pride in their shared achievements. So linked was their academic progress that when Anna's sensitive son missed school because of "one of his old spells," Jennie did not recite her Latin. "I would have to wait on George anyway," she reasoned, "and we might just as well go together."[59] Against her other classmates, Jane was a scrappy competitor, but not against George. In her stepbrother's case, Jane presumed that academic honors would be shared, and she prized the place they occupied, as a team, at the head of the class.

The school's monthly recitation days were Jane's favorite school days. She delighted when as many as forty-two neighbors were in the audience alongside her Pa and Ma, but also declared it "a grand day for our exercises" when Pa and Ma were joined by just a few others.[60] The Senator and Mrs. Addams regularly came to hear Jane and George recite their Latin translations of Caesar's *Commentaries on the Gallic Wars*, work through math examples, or display their command of patriotic poetry like "Day Is Done," and they put as much stock in Jane's recitations as in George's.[61] In a letter to Alice when Jane was twelve, Anna commented with obvious pride that "Jennie and George did themselves . . . great credit" in their school exams.[62] Jane's reports, in her diary, about getting help with her math from Pa and George and even her brother Weber suggest that the men in the family did not think it was silly for a girl to seek mastery of the subject.[63] So, too, Jane's report to a cousin that she had made an "arrangement" with her father to read "a certain amount of history first" each day, before turning to her "more interesting" novels, indicates that Senator Addams regarded his daughter's education as a serious matter worthy of attention.[64]

Jane Addams's girlhood in the big gray house in Cedarville did not inspire in her a strong identification with the "cause" of womanhood. She expressed momentary irritation over male domination of the high school literary society, but was just as inclined to express irritation at girls for being "stupid" or sentimental and quite happily reported that she and a girlfriend had moved to the "boys' side" of the classroom where it was "ever so much plesanter" than on the "girls' side."[65] Rather than feeling estranged from men, Jane's youthful experiences led to her think that she could negotiate the world of men on her merits and easily surpass fools like Mr. Moore. Anna's pronounced femininity offered no model of partisan affiliation with female culture. Jane's stepmother was, instead, an admirer of men's world and channeled her ambition toward pleasing men and promoting their interests. The flaws in this stance might have been more obvious to Jane had her father and George evinced a more oppressive masculinity. But they did not. The two males to whom she was closest while growing up accepted Jane as an intellectual and social equal, leaving her—with all her love of industry, achievement, and attention—to assume that Anna's admiration for the world of men was perfectly sensible. Only much later would Jane Addams realign her loyalties and identify with an assertively female political culture.

Within the nuclear family that Anna and John created for Jane and George between 1868 and 1877, Jane emerged as the stronger, sturdier of the two children. This suited Anna's need to provide inspiration for her shy George and left the household's field of female "sensitivity" less crowded. It also suited John's respect—and his community's respect—for industrious, capable women, women who could serve as civic stewards in their own right. It occurred to no one at the time that they might be setting Jane on a trajectory that would take her out of their orbit. Nor did it occur to her that the competencies she was honing might collide with her family's or her society's gender assumptions. In the big house in Cedarville in the mid-1870s, the attention of the Addams family was not focused on Jennie. There were larger and more immediate dramas to attend to, both within the family and on the political scene. Amid those dramas, it was Jennie's role to be a reliable, cheerful, studious girl who could serve the distinctly different needs of both her parents. In that regard, she was indubitably being trained for womanhood.

5. The Addams home in Cedarville, Illinois. Anna Haldeman Addams is standing on the balcony. (University of Illinois at Chicago, University Library, Jane Addams Memorial Collection, neg. no. 1682)

Chapter 3

Sober, Serious, and Earnest

In July 1876, while attending the United States Centennial Exposition in Philadelphia, Jane Addams paid a visit to one of the nation's leading phrenologists, John L. Capen. Anna Addams had, apparently, already had her cranium analyzed at the Chicago Institute of Phrenology. Now it was Jane's turn. By submitting themselves to these quiet professional examinations, the Addams women were participating in a process that many scientific thinkers of the day accepted as perfectly valid. The study of the conformation of the skull was widely regarded as a reliable means for assessing mental faculties and individual character. Most practicing phrenologists were trained and loyal adherents to the principles of the field and believed that the judgments they made about a subject's character were based on objective skull measurements and manipulations. However, in order to be successful, which is to say, in order to produce reports that clients would regard as perceptive, phrenologists needed to be close observers of subtle behavior and needed to engage their clients in the sort of casual but informative conversation that would provide clues to the personality they thought they were discerning through examination of the bumps and curves of the head.[1] Capen must have been very good at his job. The descriptions he wrote of Anna and Jane square remarkably well with others' reports and serve to capture a notable contrast in the way each woman presented herself to the world.

Anna, at age forty-eight, conducted herself as a woman who was "vigorous," "sensitive," "intuitive," possessing a "great deal of energy, excitability," the "first to come to a quick conclusion," one whose "prejudices," "imagination," and "appetites" were "very strong," and one with "a good bit of girlishness left" in her.[2] Jane, on the eve of her sixteenth birthday, impressed Capen as "womanly and matronly," with an "intellect beyond average," an "evenness of temperament," an inclination to be "sober, serious, and earnest," as well as "skeptical," "prudent and careful." Though he detected "timidity" in the adolescent and "lack of confidence in herself," Capen also claimed to find evidence in her craniology that she would "do anything from principle, believe nothing without good reason," and concluded that there was "an element of toughness in her that will endure a good deal." She had, thought Capen, the makings of a "good chess player" or "financier."[3]

A year earlier, Jane had described a local lecture by a female phrenologist as a "string of gab," and Capen likely picked up that "skeptical" stance. Still, the Addams family library contained at least two serious books on phrenology, so it is also likely that these sessions with Capen were no mere lark.[4] Moreover, someone in the family saved the reports Capen wrote. Over the years, while letters were lost, records were discarded, and speeches disappeared, these phrenology reports survived as a quirky confirmation of the claims others would make about Anna's and Jane's personalities. The girlish mother and matronly daughter stand as the two feminine poles between which family dramas were

6. Jane Addams, Anna Haldeman Addams, and George Haldeman at the Centennial Exposition in Philadelphia, 1876. (University of Illinois at Chicago, University Library, Jane Addams Memorial Collection, neg. no. 502)

played out in the 1870s, Anna always near the center of those dramas, Jane usually in the wings. And the summer of 1876 capped a year of both small and large family dramas. Jane's eldest sister, Mary, had borne her second child that year, and both of her siblings, Weber and Alice, the hellions who had grown up "almost like twins," had married.[5] As the family's "sober" and "earnest" daughter, Jane Addams made accommodations around the edges of these events, pulling the attention in her direction only on recitation days at school.

Mary had departed the family's Cedarville house when she married the Reverend John M. Linn in 1871, three years after Anna relieved her of the responsibility of caring for John Addams's household. She first set up housekeeping in nearby Durand, where Rev. Linn was the Presbyterian minister. Jane and her father relished overnight visits from Mary and her first baby, John, whenever Rev. Linn had to travel for work.[6] By 1876, when Mary's second child, James, was born, the presbytery had moved the Linns farther away, to Winnebago, Illinois, and Mary was learning to cope on her own. Back in Cedarville, the family was attending to other matters.

Weber married Laura Shoemaker, a young woman from the neighboring village of Lena, in March 1876, when he was twenty-four years old. The marriage came at the end of eight rather bumpy years in Weber's life. He had entered the University of Michigan in the fall of 1868, just at the time his father married Anna Haldeman. Illness forced him back to Cedarville within a few months, creating an uncomfortable situation for all since Weber was far less accepting than his sisters of his father's new wife. In the apparent hope that physical labor (and time spent with his dead mother's family) would be restorative, Weber went off to work at his Uncle Enos Reiff's mill in Pennsylvania. Foreshadowing the advice that Jane would receive in the 1880s, Weber was discouraged from all studying while he recovered his health.[7]

Weber never did return to school—or to his father's home. With Mary acting as the honest broker between her solicitous father and quiet brother, an agreement was reached that he would return to Cedarville but live in his own house. His father gave him management responsibilities at the mill and 500 acres to farm (at a time when John Addams's own brother farmed only 170 acres in Stephenson County).[8] Thereafter, Weber stopped by the house on Cedar Creek often enough for dinner, occasionally engaging in the parlor amusements and just as occasionally taking Jennie with him to visit his sweetheart, Laura, in Lena. After Weber and Laura were married, they remained on the adjoining farm. But in years to come, as Weber's mental and physical health fluctuated, he would have a far more distant relationship with his stepmother than proximity might predict.[9]

Whatever the strains between Weber and Anna, it was probably not his courtship of Laura Shoemaker that occupied the Addams family's attention in the fall of 1875. The central drama of those months revolved around the announcement by Jane's sister Alice that she intended to marry Anna's eldest son, Harry Haldeman. That news occasioned a "war of some sort" in the Addams household.[10] Jane certainly had known about the romance; her diary mentioned that Alice showed her younger sister a "very sweet" love letter from Harry months earlier.[11] But nowhere in Jane's 1875 diary did she give voice to the opinions she conveyed, years later, to her nephew: that the courtship was "tempestuous," that the stepbrother and stepsister were "violently in love" and that "the parents of both" were "vigorously opposed" to their marriage.[12]

Alice had been packed off to Europe in the summer of 1875, but distance did no more to cool the couple's ardor than it did to soothe their parents' worry. The problem was not the propriety of a stepbrother marrying a stepsister; Harry and Alice had not grown up together, and there was nothing incestuous in the match. But Anna doubted that her middle stepdaughter was good enough for her prized eldest son; her criticisms of Alice pushed Harry to exclaim, "I think more of her than she does of me and always expect to."[13] Senator Addams would likely have agreed with Harry's suggestion that Alice was the more estimable of the two young lovers. When Alice was in Europe, her father praised her for being "sensible" enough not to "waive your temperance principles" at a banquet, a not-so-subtle reference to Harry's habitual intemperance and lack of good sense.[14] Harry's letters home over the previous five years had revealed a self-indulgent young man who was quick to blame others for his own problems and disdained many of the beliefs and traditions that undergirded John Addams's world. In his twenties, Harry Haldeman had all the makings of what he would ultimately become: a cynical, self-important, bitter alcoholic. When his "vices" forced him to leave medical school at the University of Michigan in 1870, Harry blamed "unfeeling relatives" and "the unwillingness of friends to lend a helping hand," railed against the unfair obstacles he faced as a "self-made man," and mocked churchgoers as "frigid souls" conned by wicked clergy into trying to "wheedle Jove." On those occasions when all of this self-pity shifted from vitriolic to sentimental, he confessed to homesickness and to feeling "as much of a baby now" as when he had gone to Leipzig at age twenty. But after bragging to his mother that "few have gone so low and reformed," Harry turned to courting his stepsister.[15]

Alice, at age twenty-three, was blind to Harry's weaknesses. She saw the charm and wit and musicality. She saw a (fairly) handsome, twenty-eight-year-old would-be physician who wrote plays and poetry and could quote philosophers.

It took John Addams's more practiced, paternal eye to detect the dangers that lay ahead. He saw how vanities and instabilities that could be tolerable in Anna would be disastrous in a providing husband.[16] But despite John and Anna's shared opposition to the marriage, they could not mount a unified campaign against it. Each spouse was in the awkward position of thinking the other's child an unworthy partner for his or her own offspring. Alice and Harry had their parents over a barrel, and the wedding went forward in October 1875, shortly after Jane's fifteenth birthday.

The marriage did prove stabilizing for Harry. With Alice's encouragement, he graduated from Chicago Medical School at Northwestern University in 1878 and set up practice in Mitchellville, Iowa, near a popular hot spring. Still, for all his efforts at respectability, Harry's addictions, and the bitter self-pity that induced them, would shadow the Addams family for years to come. James Weber Linn, the son Mary bore in the spring after Alice and Harry wed, later claimed that Harry "did not much affect Jane Addams's life," but that was not true.[17] The marriage of this misanthropic stepbrother to her sister created complex and enduring fissures in Jane Addams's family life. It also created new expectations in Anna's mind about Jane's relationship with her stepbrother, George, expectations that Jane would never be able to satisfy.

At sixteen, Jane was not particularly communicative about any of these developments in the family; reflective self-expression did not characterize her writing during these years in Cedarville. Her letters said more about Charles Dickens than about Weber, Alice, or Harry, and her diary entries recorded more parlor games, croquet matches, and school recitations than reflections on matters of the soul. There was the occasional mention of church sermons about "Christians and their duties" and Sunday School debates over whether Samson was a good man or a bad man (Jane's class "came to the conclusion that he was decidedly *not* a good man," but "Pa's class came to a somewhat different conclusion"). Jane, however, wrote no anguished entries over whether she was a good enough Christian—or a good enough daughter. There was certainly no expression of faith that would explain why Jane wore an ornate crucifix around her neck in 1876 photos, leaving open the possibility that the religious jewelry was a souvenir from Alice's European tour.[18]

Unlike other adolescent females of her generation, Jane did not retreat into journal writing as a way to independently explore her spiritual status or her place in family dynamics. When a relative of Anna's died suddenly, Jane admitted to her diary that she "didn't know how to feel, I don't believe I can feel." She, who had survived the deaths of a mother and a sister, did "wonder" how she "acted" in response to the news, for her strongest impulse was "not to

7. Alice Addams, in Europe in 1875, before her marriage to Harry Haldeman. (Swarthmore College Peace Collection)

8. Henry (Harry) Winfield Haldeman in 1874. (Swarthmore College Peace Collection)

give in to it." This precocious capacity for safe distancing from intense emotion came across to Capen, the phrenologist, as "true, steady and uniform, and self-sacrificing." He did not consider the element of self-protection.[19]

Capen predicted that if Jane found herself "imposed upon," she "would become indignant," but Jane never expressed indignation at her relatives in her diary.[20] Even when Anna's perpetual difficulties with household servants created extra household work for Jane, she adopted her father's inclination to "look on the charitable side" of Anna's vexations. Jane matter-of-factly prepared her father's meals when the family was between maids and calmly accepted Anna's negative judgment of her stepdaughter's cooking.[21] The fact that Anna never did "anything more useful with her hands than adjust the objects in the room, care for her flowers and strum a guitar" did not occasion any mention in a diary that was vulnerable to Anna's prying eyes.[22] The only complaints that made their way to the page were always directed at individuals outside the family. Within the family, Jane admitted only peace and harmony, and that served the family, and her father, quite well.

By the mid-1870s, when Jane was a teenager and John Addams was in his fifties, circumstances encouraged them both to take special pleasure, and comfort, in each other. The Senator was surrounded by weak, unpromising sons who showed no signs of ever exhibiting his drive and discipline, yet he enjoyed the daily company of an ambitious and attentive daughter. She, by the same note, faced an unimpressive roster of male models: fragile Weber was dependent on his father's largesse, bitter Harry was dependent on alcohol and Alice, sensitive George was dependent on Anna—and Jane. Even her schoolteacher, Mr. Moore, was a poor excuse for a scholar. Only Pa was fit to teach the qualities of leadership, decisiveness, and dependability that the era associated with independence and citizenship, all qualities that Jane was eager to acquire.

Rev. Linn caught the mutuality in their relationship when he reminded Jane of her unusual access to her Pa. "Not every daughter has such a father," he observed, adding, "you knew all that he suffered and you tried to comfort him. In this you were successful. No one could ever have been more so."[23] In her autobiography, Jane Addams chose to emphasize the traditionally masculine aspect of their bond by recalling her father's tutorials in ethics and politics and suggesting that her privileged place in her father's life, unoccupied by any worthy son, had allowed her to disassociate citizenship and stewardship from gender. But Rev. Linn noted the feminine "comfort" she provided to her Pa. In maturity, Jane Addams would bridge the duality, drawing on a whole spectrum of skills acquired in her Pa's study.

Jane comforted her father not by siding with him against the rest of the family but, rather, by keeping peace in the family, by serving the competing needs of the family, and by mediating between those needs. The evenings Jane spent playing in the parlor with Anna and George freed John Addams to read quietly in another room; her partnership with George in school relieved the family of worry about the boy's reclusive tendencies, and her curiosity about politics and religion gave her father opportunities for the intellectual companionship that his marriage could not provide. In all of these roles, Jane drew solace from the belief that none of the household tensions were about her; she was the oil, not the troubled water. At school, in public, she could draw attention to herself and enhance family pride; at home, she stood aside, occupying an emotionally safe perch from which to guide others away from conflict.

Well before Jane was a teenager, her Pa had retired from the political battlefield of Reconstruction politics. When she was ten, in 1870, Senator Addams voluntarily relinquished his seat in the Illinois State Senate. He had served for fifteen years; no one in the legislature had served longer. He resolved to "have no more of it" because he was bored and wanted "the pleasure of enjoying the society of my dear family." Family lore has held that Anna relished the social life available to her as a senator's wife in Springfield and had ambitions to go to Washington, D.C., so she argued against John's decision to retire from public office. But it must have been futile to argue with a husband who insisted that the whole process of legislating had become "quite disgusting" to him and he would rather be "alone in a room with one held most dear" than stuck in endless committee meetings.[24]

When John Addams talked with Jane about "the grave march of public affairs," he spoke as a man who had gone into politics for a unified cause, not a contentious career.[25] The free soil fever that had drawn Addams to Springfield was the political equivalent of a revival meeting. The birth of the Republican Party and Lincoln's victory in 1860 were John Addams's civic epiphany, his great awakening. Between 1854 and 1865, the cause was clear, the sides well marked, and John Addams's multiple interests were harmonious. Legislation that supported railroads as well as schools, banks as well as military pensions, insurance companies as well as poor relief, all served the Northern crusade for free labor and free men. These interests did not conflict, and a man like Addams, with deep roots in the Whig Party, did not doubt the need for government activism in all these directions. Nor did he pause in voting to end Illinois's racist "Black Laws," or in approving both the Thirteenth Amendment to the Constitution ending slavery and the Fourteenth Amendment making black men citizens with due rights.[26]

Illinois politics in the years following the Civil War were not nearly so uplifting. From lofty, wartime pronouncements against slaveocracy, Republican legislators descended into intra-party wrangles over kickbacks on the new state penitentiary.[27] John Addams was ill prepared for the corruption of legislative business that ensued in Springfield in the late 1860s. According to the harmonious ideology he had embraced in the start-up days of the Galena and Chicago Union Railroad, government support of business, through subsidies and bills of incorporation, was an enlightened strategy. An active government could rescue Illinois from the backward, antibusiness Democrats and deliver it unto prosperity. Confident that state, community, and business interests were mutual, Senator Addams routinely voted for special bills of incorporation, even when the legislators introducing those bills were among the local businessmen who stood to profit from them.

Addams himself sponsored two bills in 1867 that increased his personal wealth: he introduced an act enabling the formation of "rural mutual assessment insurance companies" and then promptly established the Buckeye Mutual Fire Insurance Company in Freeport with his brother, James, as the "traveling agent," and he introduced a bill to incorporate the Protection Life Insurance Company in Freeport and then became president of that company. These votes were not, in his eyes or anyone else's, tainted. He had, after all, introduced legislation in 1865 providing for state regulation of insurance companies, and had introduced a bill in 1867 to regulate corporations.[28] If asked, Addams would have argued that his sponsorship of such bills represented the sound business judgment of a public servant whose own interests coincided with the community's interest in having reliable insurance companies.

The "orgy of logrolling" and payoffs that tainted the Illinois legislative sessions in 1867 and 1869 made a mockery of John Addams's faith in the honor of the system. The corruption also sparked a voters' demand for a constitutional convention to overhaul the legislature and throw out the "bullies, strumpets, vagrants, and sneak thieves" running the state.[29] Freeport's Democratic press did not include Senator Addams in its attacks on the new breed of politicians who were getting rich off Springfield bribes instead of running legitimate businesses. No one placed Addams among those responsible for escalating the number of bills for incorporation and bowing to corporate interests that were distant from local communities. But while there is no sign anywhere that John Addams was involved in the corruption, there is evidence that he was affected by it. In 1869, as chairman of the Senate's Finance Committee, Addams suddenly began voting "no" on all special acts for bank incorporations. Sometimes, he voted entirely alone, sometimes he voted (no doubt uncomfortably) with a couple of antibank Democrats, and occasionally he was joined by a Republican or two.[30] Little wonder that John Addams wrote weary letters home while sitting in the senate's interminable meetings in the winter of 1869. Republican politics had lost its spiritual center; what had once been compelling now held "nothing of interest" for the man who still listed himself as a "miller"—not a banker—in the senate roll.[31]

By the time he retired from the state senate in 1870, John Addams was an anachronism in Illinois politics. The *Freeport Journal* might have been able to imagine its favorite son as a viable candidate for U.S. Congress in 1869 because his record was "as pure as crystal," because he had "not an enemy in the county," and because he had not been "engaged in the fierce political contests which we have witnessed during the last four or five years."[32] But the truth was that those very qualities made Addams a political nobody in postwar Illinois. Despite his unusual record of persistence in the senate, he was never mentioned in any political histories of the state or in any of his colleagues' memoirs. He appears on no one's list of "distinguished" Illinois men of the era and figures in none of the elaborate stories about Springfield wheeling and dealing.[33] When the Senator died, Jane wrote that "he was respected for his stern honesty and tricksters either in politics or in legislative halls were afraid of him."[34] However accurate her testament to his honesty, the record forces the conclusion that Jane Addams's father was a big man at home but not a major player in the smoke-filled rooms of Springfield. After fifteen sessions, he took his quaint notions of stewardship back to Stephenson County and tended to his family and his businesses.

Under her father's at-home tutelage, the adolescent Jane Addams was thoroughly steeped in her father's equation of party loyalty with patriotism and patriotism with a strong federal government. Any threat to the Union—or the Republican Party—was an invitation to the reimposition of a pro–states' rights, anti-Negro agenda.[35] As a girl of seventeen, Jane enjoyed politics "very much," followed the Hayes-Tilden election with great interest, and missed the "excitement" when it was over.[36] But John Addams's daughter was quite ready to criticize the Republican Hayes administration when it appeared to be selling out the Union cause. Echoing sentiments she undoubtedly heard in her father's study, young Jane Addams confidently asserted that the South should be "treated with justice, not mercy." She reasoned it was perfectly fair to favor Republicans for public jobs in the former Confederacy because "to the victor belong the spoils." For her, as for her father, any "meekness" toward the rebels was "weakness," and the removal of troops from the South constituted an abandonment. "If Congress," she wrote in 1877, "now yields one inch of the principle advanced [in our late war], it will make all that terrible loss of life mere butchery."[37]

Jane Addams would always be sensitive on this matter of "the terrible loss of life" and sensitive, as well, to the political lessons that her father taught her during their private moments of respite from the family's dramas. Though she later chose to draw her paternal political lineage through Abraham Lincoln and Joseph Mazzini, two democratic icons for her generation of Americans, the real connection between father and daughter had less to do with democracy and more to do with republicanism. Jane Addams imbibed two political principles in her father's house: a belief in the government's duty to foster a fair and honest climate for economic opportunity, and a belief that those who had already benefited from that opportunity were charged to act as community stewards for the rest. These filial lessons in the obligations of states and stewards skirted the egalitarian ethic that Jane Addams would later espouse (and later try to ascribe to her father), but were not incompatible with it. Indeed, her father's republican ideology would always inform her brand of democracy and shape the direction of her political evolution.

In writing her autobiography, Jane Addams sought to evoke the feel of that "score" of "early conversations" she had with her father about "impersonal and international relations."[38] For help, she turned to Elizabeth Barrett Browning's epic poem *Aurora Leigh*, in which the heroine praised the loving care her father bestowed after death took the four-year-old's mother. Addams identified with this story of an "austere" father who awkwardly conveyed his affection by sharing all he knew, which meant giving his daughter a son's education in classical literature. Indeed, Addams quoted Browning in order to say of her own father:

He wrapt his little daughter in his large
Man's doublet, careless did it fit or no.[39]

Addams left open the question of just how careless, that is to say, just how unconscious, either father or daughter were when engaged in their informal tutorials. John Linn observed that John Addams took "delight" in preparing Jane for her "mission," but conveyed no sense that the father and daughter ever jointly defined that mission.[40] The autobiographical tale Addams spun about childhood longings to build a "large house . . . right in the midst of horrid little houses" is contradicted by adolescent writings in which she recoiled from the charity work of pious missionaries.[41] Traces from the late 1870s do suggest, however, that Jane was beginning to hope that her scholastic achievements would take her away from the domestic routines Anna found so dull and to dream that all her pleasure in public recitations and "impersonal" relations might be part of a different sort of female life.

Neither Jane nor her father had the vision in 1876 to see beyond the era's gender boundaries and imagine young Jane Addams wielding independent public power. That did not mean, however, that either regarded paternal political tutelage as frivolous. Both knew that a certain class of American women were eligible for community stewardship and that John Addams's own achievements had earned a place for his daughter in that circle of female stewards. Though the Senator shared Anna's dislike of "strong-minded women" in public life and regarded Elizabeth Cady Stanton as "bordering on the egotistical," he still referred to woman suffrage as "our" side, and—like so many fathers of her generation's achieving women—he did encourage Jane in the subversive belief that her understanding of politics and her knowledge of history actually mattered.[42]

Anna was not irrelevant to Jane's early training as a community steward. Though the second Mrs. Addams never assumed the duties of female stewardship, she shared the style and carriage of that privileged class of American women, and she schooled Jane in its fundamentals. The household in which Anna raised Jane and George was materially different from the one which Mary had inherited from Sarah Addams. As mistress of the house, Anna installed a new bay window for the living room, a more formal set of china and linens for the dining room, and a $700 ebony piano in the parlor.[43] When Mary Addams ran her father's house, the girls in the family wore dresses Mary sewed for them.[44] After Anna took charge, Jane's clothes came from stores or dressmakers, and Anna made frequent trips to Freeport for new dresses, collars, handkerchiefs, or combs for herself and Jane.[45]

It is likely that Jane grew up hearing some debate in the household about unnecessary displays of wealth. In the first blush of marriage, John Addams had relished all the "fixing of ribbons" that accompanied his shared toilet with Anna.[46] But the Senator was, in the everyday, a sober steward to Yankee and German neighbors who were known as "masters of economic understatement," and he was anxious to distance himself from the corrupt ostentation in Springfield.[47] In 1871, when Jane was eleven years old, she wrote excitedly to Alice about getting a new "waterproof" coat, one that she thought "a great deal nicer than any other ever was."[48] Almost forty years later, in her autobiography, Addams recalled being "arrayed in a new cloak, gorgeous beyond anything I had ever worn before" and feeling "chagrined" by her father's suggestion that she, instead, wear her old cloak to Sunday School because it "would not make the other girls feel bad."[49]

Like many stories in Jane Addams's autobiography, this one feels like an apocryphal snapshot of a more panoramic theme in the Addams family. In this case, the theme revolves around whether and how to enjoy the luxuries that can come with wealth. The issue was never fully resolved at home, and Jane Addams would struggle with it her entire life. On the one hand, Jane shared her father's admiration for pioneer simplicity and humility (and his understanding of the political symbolism of cloth coats). On the other hand, Jane's father had provided her with wealth and with a stepmother who taught her how to spend it. Though never an extravagant person, Jane Addams always enjoyed beautiful, well-made things. Her later critique of industrial production, though ultimately fueled by concerns over economic democracy, was initially informed by her stepmother's genteel lessons in discriminating between the shoddy and the fine.

On the eve of her departure for Rockford Female Seminary in 1877, Jane Addams—still called Jennie at home—was a poised, self-contained adolescent. At five feet, three inches and weighing only ninety-five pounds, she stood thin and erect, with brown hair tucked in a bun on the back of her head (as it would be for the rest of her life), dark brown eyes set so deep that they always seemed a bit sad, and a nose dotted with eight freckles but, to her critical eye, "expressing no character whatsoever."[50] Her investment, or Anna's, in her appearance is evident in a surviving photo in which Jane is sporting not only the ornate crucifix necklace but earrings and faintly curly hair as well. If Jane ever was the frail, withdrawn little girl of autobiographical fame, she was definitely not such a pathetic figure in adolescence. Any childish tendencies she may have had toward stubbornness had been shined to a civilized gloss of teen pride in her emerging rectitude. As Jennie grew from childishness to pubescent poise, Anna's preening example pointed the way to a certain tilt of the chin, a certain cock of the eye. What might have been shyness, or even willfulness, became instead a fragile self-possession that made the teenage Jane Addams appear precociously dignified. She could walk down the streets of Cedarville or Freeport or even Chicago with as much refinement in her carriage as Anna and as much righteousness in her heart as John.

By the time she left home, Jane had practice in keeping her own counsel, mediating the tensions between strong individuals, and diverting her attention from personal worries by thinking about books, ideas, performance, and politics. Modeling her father's self-restraint and her stepmother's aristocratic airs, she found a way to rise above girlish manners, schoolroom crushes, and family squabbles. Over the "large man's doublet" her Pa wrapped her in, young Jane pulled on a second layer of protection: the cloak of equanimity. Anna's unseemly displays of self-indulgent temper would not become Jane's style. Jane would take pride in not being prideful. The "strong will" that the discerning phrenologist identified in 1876 did not lean in Anna's direction.[51] If it had, there might have been endless feminine tussles with Anna over dresses and boys and kitchen duties. But Jane Addams showed no interest in boys (except in her Platonic love for George), and she obediently deferred to Anna on matters of clothing and cooking. The strong will came out, instead, in ways that would not conflict with Anna and in ways that would please her father: in attention to her schoolwork, to the reading Pa assigned, and to smoothing

9. Jane Addams at age seventeen, before leaving home for Rockford Female Seminary. (Swarthmore College Peace Collection)

family tensions. The cost to the young Jane Addams of all this accommodation and self-containment would be deferred. In adolescence, in the big gray house by Cedar Creek, it served and served nicely.

John Addams sent his youngest daughter off to Rockford with a more urgent sense of the connection between books, ideas, and public life than he, or most fathers, gave to other daughters, and equipped her, as well, with diplomatic skills that would be useful at the seminary. Anna, meanwhile, sent her with a greater appreciation for art, music, literature, fashion, and the aesthetics of nature than Jane would ever have received at her father's hand or, likely, at her own mother's hand. And tucked between the folds of all the other lessons Anna taught Jane was a persistent, and quite useful, lesson in how to navigate around a charismatic, egocentric authority. Jane Addams's young, comfortable life in Cedarville had been sheltered, to be sure, but not simple. Against its complexities, she had woven a self-possessed resilience that would shape her success beyond the village and the big gray house on Cedar Creek.

Chapter 4
Bread Givers

Rockford Female Seminary was perched on a hill overlooking the Rock River, about thirty miles east of Freeport. In September 1877, the city of Rockford was larger and busier than Freeport, with more manufacturing and a more diverse population. It was also four times the size of the village of Cedarville and much noisier than John Addams's grist mill. But the urban surroundings did not affect Jane Addams, who had "but little" contact with the city during her four years at seminary. Like her one hundred schoolmates, Jane spent those years scurrying between the seminary's three "fine, well-proportioned, strongly built" brick buildings: the chapel, the dormitory, and the recitation hall. Despite her efforts to break down the barriers between town and gown, Jane's seminary years were largely spent isolated from the world around her.[1]

10. The campus of Rockford Female Seminary as it appeared when Jane Addams was a student. (Rockford College Archives)

Living accommodations at Rockford Female Seminary in 1877 were not nearly as comfortable as those John and Anna had provided back home in Cedarville. Two students shared a small, gaslit room equipped with two wooden chairs "painted drab," a woodbox and stove, a table and bed, a wash-bowl and pitcher, and a built-in credenza with three shelves above and three drawers below. At the time of Jane's arrival, the school boasted new bathrooms and a renovated gymnasium, but the dining room remained simple and aus-tere, and the smelly laundry room still abutted the classrooms.[2]

Jane Addams would soon impress her classmates as the most poised and mature among them, but on her first day, recalled one classmate, she "looked as I know I was feeling, very trembly inside . . . young and worried."[3] Six other equally young, equally worried girls entered that fall's first-year collegiate class alongside Jane. As a group, they joined the school's twenty-seven other colle-giate students, nine "partial collegiates," forty-one "Preparatory" students, and twenty-one "Normal School" and "Special" students. Over two-thirds of the Rockford student body was from Illinois, and almost one-third was from Rockford itself. The vast majority of the seminary's out-of-state students were from Iowa and Wisconsin. Together, the students comprised a close-knit and homogeneous community of white, middle-class midwestern daughters from the region's prosperous farming villages and towns.[4]

Reigning over this intense community of 105 students and twenty faculty members was Miss Anna Peck Sill, the founder and headmistress of Rockford Female Seminary.[5] Sill was sixty-one years old in the fall of 1877, when Jane Addams, who had just turned seventeen, enrolled at the seminary. As a living relic of the Second Great Awakening, Sill inspired equal measures of reverence, respect, and resentment in her young charges. Addams later captured the pres-sure Sill brought to bear upon the students when she wrote that they were "conscious of the heroic self-sacrifice made in their behalf, [and] felt that each minute of the time thus dearly bought must be conscientiously used."[6]

Rockford students knew what Miss Sill had accomplished in her life. They knew that she had moved to Illinois from the "burned-over district" of upstate New York in the late 1840s, bringing with her the revival movement's enthusi-astic acceptance of Jesus as a personal savior. They knew she had come to answer the call of the Congregationalists who wanted to create a "sister school" for Beloit College, the all-male academy in southern Wisconsin where George Haldeman was enrolled in the fall of 1877.

Rockford students knew, too, that Sill had built up the seminary from vir-tually nothing over the course of three decades, meeting at first with twenty local girls in a rent-free room in the courthouse building and then, brick by brick, erecting the respected campus they now inhabited. They certainly knew

11. Anna Peck Sill, headmistress of Rockford Female Seminary when Jane Addams was a student. (Rockford College Archives)

that Miss Sill could be autocratic and demanding with her board of trustees, her faculty, and the Rockford community. And it is probable that her students in the 1870s knew that Sill, nearing retirement, was determined to see Rockford fulfill its original charter by becoming a true college and granting bachelor of arts degrees. The more discerning students, including Jane Addams, undoubtedly saw the contrast between Sill's imperious conduct and her claim that the seminary's mission was to train females to do their humble, domestic, silent Christian duty. "What matter if [women's] power be behind the throne?" asked Sill, who had never relinquished her own throne. "The most potent forces," she loudly proclaimed, "are silent forces."[7]

Anna Sill provided Jane Addams with an impressive model of an unmarried career woman running an institution with more determination than funds, a woman who breathed tangible reality into her philosophical convictions. But because her religious convictions embraced the century's most conservative gender constructs, Sill was also a confusing, even maddening, female leader. On the one hand, Sill wanted Rockford graduates to be "Christian Mothers and Missionaries for the Evangelization of the World" and insisted that "the chief end of women's education" was to "elevate and purify and adorn the home." On the other hand, she offered no domestic science courses at Rockford and clearly favored those graduates who became missionaries, rather than housewives or even teachers. Sill's own theological tradition required that she deny her personal ambition, so she mourned for "those olden days" when women did not "clamor for *rights*" but embraced, instead, their "queenly" role as "mother and teacher." Disclaiming any sense of entitlement to her own celibate, nondomestic life, Sill insisted that the "primary motive which led me to acquire an education was that I might lay it at the Savior's feet, and thus be of some service to his cause."[8]

Just at that moment in Jane's adolescence when questions of autonomy and personal ideology were most precious, private, and vulnerable, she found herself under the watchful authority of a woman who actively urged a set of rigid, orthodox beliefs on her captive students. "Bible instruction is . . . constantly impressed on the pupils," boasted one of the seminary's supporters. Indeed, observed Sill's biographer, "pressure to make a profession of faith was intense."[9] In that pious environment, Jane Addams ceased wearing a crucifix as jewelry and steeled herself to defend against a religious fervor that she simply had not experienced back home.

Within the Addams family, Jane had seen an array of views on faith and religious practice, from Harry's sardonic disdain of churchgoers trying to "wheedle Jove" to Mary and John Linn's sincere devotion to a divine Christ.[10]

The mere existence of this Protestant continuum telegraphed to an observant adolescent that religion was an individual choice, not a universal dictate. Underscoring that message and standing at the center of the family continuum was Senator Addams, who was "not a professing Christian" but demonstrated his commitment to Christian ethics through dedicated participation in Cedarville church life.[11] We can glimpse the Senator's habitual reticence on doctrinal matters in Jane Addams's autobiographical tale about returning home from seminary and confronting her father with the question, "What are you? What do you say when people ask you?" Jane Addams misled readers by saying that her twinkling-eyed father responded by claiming a Quaker identity, but she did honestly convey in that story, and in others, that her father's tutelage consistently focused on responsible conduct, not obedient faith.[12]

So while she arrived at Rockford ill prepared for Miss Sill's evangelical onslaught, John Addams's teenage daughter was equipped to sniff out dogma. Even the phrenologist in Chicago had testified to Jane's skepticism on matters religious, noting: "Moral faculties very much larger than religious. Inclined to be skeptical, as, for instance, if someone was trying to make her believe a thing against her principle of right and wrong and even say that the Lord said so, she would begin to doubt if the Lord ever *did* say such a thing, whether it wasn't man that said it. She would never be a proselyte, not sectarian. Thinks everyone has the right to believe what they please."[13]

It would be years before Jane Addams could replace Sill's claim to "self-denying benevolence" with an honest expression of the "subjective necessity" for social service.[14] And years, too, before she could openly denounce the self-consciousness and self-righteousness that Addams came to associate with Sill's "primitive spiritual purpose."[15] But even at seventeen, Jane Addams knew her theological boundaries and correctly sensed that Anna Sill's presence would require that she guard those boundaries. "She does everything for people merely from love of God alone," Jane wrote in her notebook, "and that I do not like."[16]

It was obviously not the seminary's religiosity that inspired John Addams to send all three of his daughters to Rockford or to serve, in a ceremonial capacity, on the school's board of trustees. It was his pioneer pride in northern Illinois for having a seminary of Rockford's caliber at which to train the daughters of the steward class. It was, as well, his own personal pride in having the wealth to enhance a daughter's worth—and his own status—by investing in something so luxurious as female higher education. Only the rare family in northern Illinois could afford to spend $220 a year on a son's education, much less a daughter's.[17] So while Senator Addams probably shared the other seminary board members' view that Miss Sill was difficult to manage, he likely respected her for having built a highly respectable seat of female scholarship on the northern prairie.[18] Against the advice of pundits who warned of the physical and social dangers of too much female education, John and Anna Addams agreed with other upper-middle-class, Northern parents that college for daughters signified advancing civilization.

In an unfortunate bit of autobiographical simplification, Jane Addams recalled that at the time she entered Rockford, she had been "ambitious to go to Smith College" and indicated that she did not pursue that dream because her father preferred that she attend the nearby seminary.[19] In the biography her nephew later wrote of Addams (and that Addams approved), James Weber Linn embellished on that remark by claiming that the young Jane Addams had actually been admitted to Smith but was denied attendance by her father.[20] The story contradicts the overall thrust of Addams's autobiographical writings, which generally credit her father with encouraging her ambition, but it is consistent with her parallel effort to depict herself as an ordinary young woman of her day, subject to the same sort of constraints that other ordinary young women faced. Whatever Jane Addams's reasons for concocting this tiny shard of autobiographical fiction, the result has been decades of groundless speculation on Jane Addams's supposedly dramatic fight for independence from her supposedly domineering father. An examination of the evidence suggests a rather more prosaic reality.[21]

Smith College opened its doors in Northampton, Massachusetts, in 1875 when Jane Addams was fifteen years old. In the subsequent two years, just when she was preparing for college, three national magazines—*Harper's, Scribner's,* and the *Atlantic Monthly*—reported that Smith College had the most rigorous admissions requirements of any female college in the country. To be accepted at Smith, students had to pass entrance examinations in geometry and Greek.[22] Because she had attended only the village school in Cedarville, Jane lacked instruction in both those topics so she was automatically ineligible for admission to Smith. As Addams said in her autobiography, she arrived at Rockford "with such meagre preparation in Latin and algebra as the village school could afford."[23] Her nephew's claim that she traveled to Northampton before attending Rockford, passed the Smith entrance exam, and was admitted is pure fiction. Had Jane made any sort of application, she would have quickly learned that she did not meet the school's admissions standards, and she would certainly not have taken a train trip to Massachusetts to be examined in topics she had never studied. As *Scribner's* noted in May 1877, a month before Addams graduated from Cedarville's village school, Smith College received "large numbers of applications . . . from those who, not fully understanding the requirements for admission, were not sufficiently advanced in their preparation to enter."[24]

Within a few months of entering Rockford Seminary, Jane did start to think about transferring to an eastern school. Vassar was the first option she considered, but she soon turned her sights on Smith College, which not only boasted the most scholarly program for women in the United States but encouraged its students to "come into vital contact" with the surrounding community and swore off running "any theological machine in connection with the institution."[25] What a contrast to parochial, isolated Rockford, where Jane was required to attend daily chapel service and weekly prayer meetings, and had to memorize and recite a Bible verse each day. She faced there, as well, the informal evening devotions, the regular monthly fast days, the annual prayer week, and the frequent guest lectures from missionaries and temperance workers. Jane's only regular contact with the city of Rockford was obligatory attendance at a Sunday service at the church of her choice in order to provide the required written synopsis of the sermon on Monday morning.[26]

In one very practical way, John Addams helped Jane to prepare for a move from Rockford to Smith. He approved and probably paid for the special tutorials Jane took in Greek and geometry. This was not the sort of program she could have pursued without consulting her father; the Rockford system was so deferential to parental authority that Jane did not even know her grades until her Pa received them in the mail.[27] Jane settled into that "humdrum" system on the understanding that, after completing preparations at Rockford, she would move on to Smith and acquire the B.A. degree that Sill's seminary did not yet grant. The transfer was postponed year after year while Jane struggled with her command of Greek and geometry. Indeed, she looked upon her senior year at seminary as "a solid dig to make up all the odds and ends for Smith, such as little things like spherical trigonometry and the Memorabilia. My comfort," she explained to a friend, "is leisure next year and Boston to spend it in."[28]

Jane's acquiescence to the delay in attending Smith must be read in light of the family's experience with sons' schooling far from home and the family's concern over George, who was always Jane's academic partner. Jane's older brother Weber had failed when he tried to attend the University of Michigan, and Harry had also failed when he first moved away for his medical education. Meanwhile, ever-sensitive George was safe and comfortable at Beloit, the brother school to Rockford, and not ambitious to transfer to an Ivy League men's school comparable to Smith or Vassar. For Jane to head east without George, to attend a more prestigious school than George, would have constituted an unseemly abandonment, not the sort of thing a mediating sister did if she wanted to be loyal and solicitous to her fragile brother.[29]

There was the added fact that Jane's older sisters had been very happy at Rockford. Even the "strong-willed" Alice had glided over and around Miss Sill's sanctimony and emerged quite devoted to the headmistress. So enthusiastic was Alice about the domestic doctrine preached at Rockford that at the alumnae reunion in July 1878—two years into her own marriage with Harry Haldeman and a year into Jane's tenure at seminary—Alice delivered a speech extolling "the sacred influences" of home kitchens "such as our Alma Mater has endeavored to enable each of us to create and enjoy" and where "the wife, queen of the home, presides."[30]

Like so many other Rockford students, Alice could comfortably subscribe to Miss Sill's gender ideology, nodding in agreement when she described the "home circle" as woman's "heaven-appointed orbit," and could then follow that domestic path directly into loose-fitting identification with Christianity.[31] Jane could not follow her sisters, or her classmates, along that prescribed path. She did not identify the home circle as her likely "orbit," heaven-appointed or not, and felt none of the romantic urges that would impel her classmates into marriage. Jane Addams probably knew at seventeen that she was no more likely to take a husband in matrimony than to take Jesus Christ as her personal savior.

Jane's potential for alienation at Rockford was enormous. Her daily refusal to give in to that alienation (not some imagined melodrama with her father) is what deserves notice here. Looking back fifty years later, Addams bitterly critiqued Sill's pedagogy for deducing all its lessons from Christian dogma "instead of probing the foundations of knowledge."[32] When she wanted to mask her bitterness, Addams could jauntily claim that her resistance to Sill's evangelical pressure toughened her moral character for lifelong battles with "propagandists."[33] But the fact remains that at a time when Jane craved a sense of belonging to something larger than herself, she was distinctly outside the "heaven-appointed" orbits Sill extolled in all the school's sacred gatherings. As a child, Jennie Addams had been thrust outside the circle of her older siblings' memories of their dead mother, not to mention being thrust outside the circle of children who had mothers. Later, she had declined to compete for a central spot in the family circle. At Rockford, Jane's unsanctified status might easily have placed her on the margins. Instead, she claimed center position.

Though she was the youngest and the smallest girl in her class, and "trembly" on the first day, Jane Addams quickly carved out a popular—and elevated—position for herself at the seminary. Cedarville's one-room school had given her practice at asserting herself in an academic setting and, as luck would have it, the small group of girls who comprised her particular class at Rockford were notably independent, more inclined to be impressed by Jane's "direct and earnest eyes" than offended by her religious skepticism.[34] Within weeks of their arrival on campus, her classmates had secretly circulated and signed a pledge never to become missionaries and had also elected Jane president of the class.[35]

They would reelect her to that post for the subsequent three years. In contrast to her sister Alice, who belonged to Vesperians, the more social of Rockford's two debating societies, Jane was immediately recruited to join the more scholarly Castalian Society. She was the first member of her class to publish an essay in the campus magazine; by her second year, she was editor of the "Home Items" section; and in her third year she was editor of the "Clippings and Exchanges" section as well as class president and president of the Castalian Society. As a senior, Jane became editor in chief of the magazine, continued as class president, and concluded her Rockford career in the spring of 1881 as class valedictorian.

Never a campus socialite or a leader of dormitory high jinks, Jane was, instead, admired and influential because of her dignity and her intellect. She was, she later admitted, a girl "of serious not to say priggish tendency," and though unsanctified, she genuinely subscribed to many of Sill's high-minded values.[36] As well, she brought with her to Rockford a well-bred understanding of power, politics, and diplomacy that her more rebellious classmates lacked. So when the other girls complained about what a "fiend" and "an old cow" Miss Sill was, Jane remained silent; the girls "could never get" their discreet class president "to talk about Miss Sill." When classmates gossiped about each other, Jane warned them in print that "careless and insinuating remarks" could lead to "mean and hateful acts." When her peers worked themselves into heated competitions between classes or clubs, she used her best steward voice to remind them that the purpose of all such events was "the good of the whole" and cautioned that too much "rivalry and jealousy" might "spoil our private friendships and cooperation." For John Addams's daughter, harmony was the keystone of social intercourse, so when she saw Rockford students' "public-spirit swallowed up in class-spirit," she told them it would be "better to return to the old ground of humanity." Defeat, she argued, was preferable to being "little and petty."[37]

Jane complained to her parents about the seminary's monotonous diet but admonished her fellow students to raise their sights above "unwonted interest and discussion in things we have to eat." She eliminated all ruffles and curls from her own attire and advised her friends against silly vanities of dress and hair. She sweated for the best grades yet she wrote and staged a Faustian drama valorizing the pure "love of study" and disdaining the cheap bid for teachers' approval. She confessed in private to growing "perfectly restless . . . hemmed in by these four walls," but she publicly echoed Sill's belief that Rockford students should appreciate the "privileges we enjoy in being thus separated and set apart" and should relish having "a fire to ourselves and time to think."[38]

Amazingly enough, the girls at Rockford's seminary did not despise Jane Addams for these lofty preachments or regard her as the least bit sanctimonious. On the contrary, they applauded her "grand ideas and vast conceptions" and relished her precocious diplomacy.[39] Her friends certainly looked up to her, but they coupled respect with affection. In their letters, school chums addressed her as "dear Janie," "Darling Jennie," "my dear Jane," "dearly beloved," and (in an intriguing blend of intimacy and deference) as "dear little 'queen' Jane." Short items in the campus magazine teased her for her tardiness and for her "amateur" ventures into taxidermy, which invited jokes about her peculiar idea of fun and her fascination with glass eyes. Students were delighted when Addams appeared in a campus skit poking fun at her own well-known penchant for emphasizing the positive. And when the comic authors of her class prophecy looked at "the fate of Jane Addams," they declared "her brain is larger than her body."[40] But no one teased her for preaching the virtues of study and service.

As a public figure, Jane Addams would win wide praise for her secular sermons on virtue for three simple reasons: her audience saw reflected in Addams their own ambitions for themselves, they saw Addams striving to live by the values she espoused, and they saw that Addams produced tangible results with her virtuous ways. A similar, if juvenile, version of this dynamic seems to have operated at Rockford.

Jane Addams's school chums liked to think of themselves as part of the new wave of educated women, but they lacked the discipline and energy for all the reading that Jane pursued beyond the school's curriculum. They all made the occasional foray into Carlyle or Ruskin or Goethe, but none could keep pace with Jane's intellectual dedication. Still, her friends viewed Jane's exertions as a welcomed spur and as proof that their generation's ambitious dreams of female achievement might actually be realized.[41] At the same time, Jane's college sermons, published as editorials in the campus magazine, were redeemingly free of prideful claims to eternal salvation. Because she did not speak with the voice of a professing Christian, Jane Addams's admonitions to study hard and work for the common good carried no promise of and no bid for heavenly reward. Ironically, this made her motives seem even more pure. Jane's lack of religiosity at Rockford, as in her adult career, gave her the persuasive weight of disinterested sincerity.[42]

Finally, Jane's diplomatic ways bore the fruit of reform at Rockford as they would later in her career. Her classmates enjoyed grumbling in their rooms about Miss Sill, but when there was action to be taken, they had the good sense to "let Jane do it."[43] Life in Cedarville had trained her to take a calm and indirect approach over a loud and confrontational one, and her image at Rockford as a responsible, sober campus steward, above the fray of schoolgirl gossip, gave her leverage with Miss Sill. The seminary's headmistress was autocratic, but she was not stupid. She knew that at a school the size of Rockford—and with feisty students like Jane's classmates—she needed the cooperation of leaders like Jane Addams to maintain the sense of harmony and purpose requisite for a Christian education. Whatever their theological differences, Sill had "high expectations" of John Addams's daughter and good reasons to foster those expectations.[44] Jane understood equally well that she needed to win Sill's trust if she was to gain the authority that stewardship supposedly bestowed. The two women cultivated one another out of these mutual needs.

Rockford students' "chief complaint" in the late 1870s was their isolation from both real society and other colleges. Jane would reiterate this charge against the cloistered college for the rest of her life. During her last two years at Rockford, she directly addressed the isolation issue through practical reform of the campus magazine, whose insularity had come to symbolize Rockford's seclusion. During Jane's sophomore year, Miss Sill crushed the "disturbances" of some "revolutionists" who sought to open up the magazine to "progressive" influences. One year later, Jane quietly transformed the "Clippings and Exchanges" section from a page of dry quotations into a lively dialogue with the "exchanges" editors at schools like Harvard, Yale, Smith, Vassar, and Oberlin. Such expansion of the exchanges section exposed the seminary's girls to a whole array of worldly influences, but Sill did not object because this "innovation" also provided the sort of evidence she needed in her ongoing campaign to convince her board of trustees that Rockford Seminary had achieved collegiate status. Success made Jane worry that she might have compromised the rebels' original principles. A senior "revolutionist" had to assure her, using language that forecast the political future, "You *are* progressive, Jane, you have not disappointed my anticipations."[45]

Jane achieved her real coup the following year when she gained financial independence for the magazine by selling advertising to Rockford merchants.[46] Sill had allowed this shop-to-shop canvassing for money because it increased the seminary's visibility, and the seminary girls applauded the strategy as a bid for worldliness and editorial independence. Only Jane and one sturdy friend had actually ventured off campus to approach local businessmen for paid advertisements, however. Jane masked her pride in this small victory by complaining to Alice that she was "perfectly sick" of all the canvassing, but she cheerfully boasted to her stepmother that the campaign's success could be "attributed to our superior powers of talking" and declared the whole venture had been "quite an experience and I am glad I had it."[47] A year later, Jane felt secure enough in her triumph to tell Alice that "the magazine is the pride of Miss Sill's heart."[48]

Such assertive leadership of the *Rockford Seminary Magazine* might easily have translated into strong advocacy for women's rights on the pages that Jane wrote and edited during her senior year. In fact, quite the opposite occurred. During Jane's year as editor in chief, the Woman Question went on hiatus. Gone, for that one year, was the magazine's standard array of commentaries on the sacred duties of educated women in American society. The orthodox version of the Woman Question that had typically engaged Sill's students in the pages of the *Rockford Seminary Magazine* focused on whether women should serve God and Christianity at home or in the larger society, and on whether women should serve because of Eve's guilt or Mary's moral superiority. Under Jane's editorial hand, that religious approach not only disappeared but so, too, did the magazine's secular complaints about women's educational disadvantages, its regular paeans to women's traditional work as housekeepers and mothers, and its occasional bold claim to a woman's right to do whatever she wished with her life, independent of the church or family.[49]

Apart from one prosuffrage comment, Jane's editorship was notable for its inattention to women's roles and women's rights.[50] Since Jane could not discuss either subject in Rockford's standard Christian terms and was unwilling to attack them from a more radical angle, she simply did not discuss them at all. She actually engineered a structural change that facilitated this editorial policy by expanding eligibility for outside submissions beyond those alums active in the Sill-dominated Alumnae Association.[51] By replacing the pious "Alumnae Department" of the magazine with a liberal "Contributor's Department," Jane could avoid publishing articles on women's missionary work and maternal morality and could expand the number of articles on art, literature, travel, science, and U.S. politics. Privately, the young Jane Addams was struggling mightily with protofeminist questions of female nature and women's roles, but her reluctance to address these matters in the magazine gave tacit consent to the sanguine view that if female education was broad and rigorous, and women were interested in the wide world, then the question of women's future would simply take care of itself.[52]

The editorial record from the magazine makes clear that Jane Addams was far less bold and hearty on the Woman Question at Rockford than she indicated in her autobiography. There, she depicted herself as one of a merry band of nascent feminists with an uncomplicated agenda for women's rights. To achieve this literary image, Addams concocted an engaging story of having pioneered for "Woman's Cause" by venturing forth, miles and miles from

Rockford, as the first female to compete in the Midwest colleges' Interstate Oratorical Contest at Illinois College in Jacksonville, Illinois, in the spring of 1881. She then heightened the drama (and the irony) of the story by describing her friends' disappointment when she dealt "the cause of woman's advancement a staggering blow" by coming in fifth place to William Jennings Bryan's first.[53]

In real life, Jane did not participate in the Jacksonville oratorical competition that spring. She merely attended it as a representative of the collegiate press. Nor did William Jennings Bryan compete. As a graduating senior, Bryan was chair of local arrangements for the competition but was not a participant.[54] The only female competitor at Jacksonville, Miss Minnie Bronson of Upper Iowa University, came in third place with her speech on "Hypatia." In her autobiography, Addams claimed that she and her classmates had "assumed" that "moral earnestness . . . would be the unique possession of the feminine orator." At the time, however, Jane did not feel that sort of pride in female culture; on the contrary, she voiced disappointment that the "too dramatic" Minnie Bronson had not conformed more closely to men's rhetorical style. In a tone that smacked more of male-identified condescension than sisterhood, Jane attributed Bronson's loss to her "over-oratorical, almost theatrical" performance.[55]

Jane and her assistant editor from Rockford, Hattie Wells, counted themselves fortunate to have even heard Bronson and the winning orator from Indiana. Complications with the train had caused them to arrive late from Rockford and miss half of the contest. Still, as representatives of the college press corps, Addams and Wells were able to "share all the excitement" of the event. The two young women were squired around Jacksonville by two "gallants" from the Illinois College newspaper and "expressed themselves as being highly pleased with their visit."[56]

The long and newsy letter that Jane wrote to her father upon her return to Rockford apologized for not seeking his and Ma's approval before taking the trip. She explained that Miss Sill had been "anxious for some time to have Rockford enter the state contest," so she sent the two campus journalists to "open negotiations and likewise bring forward the institution by bringing forward the magazine."[57] This explanation for the trip squares with all the other contemporary evidence, but does nothing to explain why Jane was too rushed to gain parental permission before leaving. Perhaps she knew that her parents might not approve of a weekend away from campus in the last pressured weeks before graduation. Perhaps she understood that, even with her Pa, it was best not to ask an authority's approval if you did not want to be refused; it was more politic to apologize later for the oversight and graciously thank the authority for his understanding. Addams, the adult pacifist, came early to the skills of disarmament. So, too, Addams the negotiator came early to the notion of mutuality. In the Jacksonville case, as in other cases, Jane's ambition to expand her own and other students' outside contacts furthered Sill's collegiate goals. Whatever Sill's concern that coeducational activities would make female students "ambitious for a public life," she knew that inclusion in an interstate collegiate competition made one, ipso facto, a college.[58] So she sent Jane Addams and Hattie Wells to Jacksonville and, sure enough, Rockford was invited to participate in the collegiate contest the following year.

The Jacksonville story that Addams fabricated in her autobiography was perfectly suited to the audience she was writing for in 1910. It made her sound feisty and earnest, in an endearing sort of way. This construction of the debate as a chapter in "the cause of women's advancement" made her seminary self seem like a plucky college coed fighting one of those familiar turn-of-the-century battles for female access to men's world.[59] For Addams, a nontraditional, politically controversial female reformer in 1910, the immediate public relations benefit of depicting herself as Every Girl was obvious. The long-term cost of this depiction was that Addams erased the more complex, if more priggish, Victorian identity she was actually struggling with in the years between 1877 and 1881. Missing from the record was the aspiring steward anxiously searching her soul for harmonious ways to integrate women's private responsibilities with men's public duties without espousing Miss Sill's Christianity and without appearing (to her father or anyone else) to be "over-oratorical."

A significant moment in Jane's soul-searching, and one of the only two times during her seminary career that she spoke publicly about the Woman Question, was at the Junior Exhibition of 1880. Though the autobiography made light of the event, it was her speech there, not anything she did at the Jacksonville contest, that marked Jane Addams's greatest triumph with Miss Sill and her debut as a commentator on women's role in modern society.

Junior exhibitions had become popular at eastern women's colleges as a way of demonstrating to the public that educated daughters were still refined and feminine while also giving students precommencement experience in public display of their literary, linguistic, and oratorical skills. Addams, who had so relished opportunities for public performance of her academic abilities back in Cedarville, began lobbying for the institution of a Junior Exhibition at Rockford at the end of her sophomore year. She cleverly launched her campaign with a sermon to the students, not a demand to Miss Sill. Scolding her classmates for complaining about their isolation, Addams claimed that they had it within their own power to increase contact with the wider community; all they need do was obey school rules. In "a short time," she promised, they would be "free from restraints" and allowed to open the seminary to "occasional receptions" for Rockford citizens.[60]

By focusing her message on the students' responsibility instead of Miss Sill's repression, Jane Addams could simultaneously raise the students' expectations and corner Miss Sill into compliance. "If one holds . . . the broom which can sweep the cobwebs from the sky and does not use it," Jane exhorted her classmates, "she well deserves her misery." How could Sill deny such a righteous stance or argue with Jane's claim that "occasional social intercourse" was "essential" to those who "would be true ladies"? From this premise, Jane argued that it would be only logical (and thus in no way a rebellion against Miss Sill) to "throw open our doors . . . to the public" and allow Rockford citizens to witness campus programs and debates.[61] Once again, Jane's disarming stratagems coincided with Miss Sill's own purposes, and Sill was caught up in the momentum of the course she had charted. Orthodoxy argued against such public demonstrations by young ladies, but if one aspired to collegiate status in the 1880's, then public demonstrations of scholarly achievement were de rigueur.

Rockford Female Seminary's Junior Exhibition in the spring of 1880 attracted local newspaper coverage and a large audience to hear the members of Jane Addams's class (who now numbered sixteen) present musical offerings, a Latin oration, a historical dissertation, a French essay, a Greek oration, and both an ethical and a philosophical oration. To begin with, however, the audience heard from Jane Addams, class president. Standing in the seminary hall, which had been decorated with evergreens, flowering plants, and scarlet flags bearing a sheaf of wheat, Jane spoke on why the Class of '81 had taken the term "Bread Givers" as its class motto and the sheaf of wheat as its class symbol.[62]

Jane chose not to burden her audience with the source of the "Bread Givers" motto, which was John Ruskin's 1864 lecture "Lilies: Of Queens' Gardens," but her interpretation was consistent with Ruskin's thinking. Like Ruskin and the other Victorians Jane was reading in these years, she idealized the virtue of work above all others. Women's progress, she said, could be traced in their evolution from "the arts of pleasing" to their "capabilities for direct labor." In line with Ruskin, Jane asserted that women could perform their labor only if granted intellectual autonomy. "The ambition and aspirations of women," she said, required "independent thought and action."[63] Jane was quick to assure her audience, which undoubtedly included her Pa and Ma, that the power she sought for women was a distinctly female one. Woman, she insisted, "wishes not to be a man, nor like a man . . . we are not trying to imitate our brothers . . . we are not restless and anxious for things beyond us, we simply claim the highest privileges of our times, and avail ourselves of its best opportunities."[64]

In her claims for womanhood, the twenty-year-old Miss Addams was wise enough to avoid bold or unseemly demands. The special function of modern, educated women, she said, was to "retain the old ideal of womanhood—the Saxon 'lady' whose mission is to give bread unto her household. So we have planned to be 'bread-givers' throughout our lives, believing that in labor alone is happiness, and that the only true and honorable life is one filled with good works and honest toil." In this way, Jane dispelled fears that female education would yield radical results. On the contrary, she affirmed, female education would actually reinstate an "old ideal."[65] It was only in the wistful conclusion to her speech that she let slip her assumption, shared with Ruskin, that women's bread-giving labor should be public, not private, work. For Jane closed with the rather condescending hope that even those classmates who, "through some turn of fortune," were "confined" to the household would be able to rise above their narrow destiny and still provide sweet, if private, bread.[66]

Addams's breezy autobiographical dismissal of the "Bread Givers" motto as something "we must have found . . . in a book somewhere" deprived her readers of the real significance of her Junior Exhibition speech.[67] It was her maiden effort at finessing the conflict her generation faced between traditional female duty and educated female ambition. Jane would, we know, fall silent on the subject in her senior-year stint as magazine editor, but in this speech she deftly asserted that ancient womanly traits had modern civic value and, therefore, female ambition was consistent with performance of female duty. In making this argument, the speech also demonstrated Jane's precocious ability to assert lofty ideals without reference to established religion. "Bread Givers" was utterly secular, saying nothing about piety, Christianity, or female submission to God, much less to man. The speech put Miss Sill in the same sort of bind she always faced with Jane Addams: this poised and dutiful but unregenerate soul was infusing the seminary with the collegiate spirit Sill sought while threatening to abandon the godliness Sill cherished.

Miss Sill could not have been the least surprised by the "Bread Givers" speech. She had been reading Jane's classroom essays for the previous three years; she was familiar with her worldly approach to social ethics and individual destiny. The public face that Jane Addams showed to Sill, her other teachers, and many of the students at Rockford looked strong and certain in its devotion to public service without reference to eternal salvation. The private Jane Addams, inaccessible to most of those around her, was far more conflicted about matters of work and faith and womanhood than her public triumphs over Sill would suggest. At the heart of the matter lay the question of how she could possibly fulfill her desire to be a hardworking public servant like her father if she could not claim the mantle of Christian faith and divine inspiration.

How else could an American woman justify exertions in the public sphere? Jane drew on the cloak of dignity and self-assurance to shield her doubts from Miss Sill's prayers, but privately she yearned for an alternative source of faith and inspiration.

When, in later years, Jane Addams indicted sheltered Christian colleges for leaving students "unnourished," "oversensitive," and ill prepared for constructive participation in modern society, she was recalling Rockford Seminary's inability to help her resolve the genuine dilemmas she faced as a young, ambitious, idealistic woman. For all her public success at Rockford, Addams blamed the school and Sill for creating an "atmosphere of intensity" that left its graduates feeling "irresolute and timid."[68] It is hard to see timidity in Jane's posture as a seminary steward, but her long and bitter memory of the school's inadequacies suggests that her apparent confidence was, in part, youthful bluster. Jane's public strutting was a useful cover for the fears she felt for her future and her soul.

Chapter 5

My Relations to God and the Universe

In *The Spirit of Youth in the City Streets*, published in 1909 when Jane Addams was forty-nine years old, she described the "self-conscious walk, the giggling speech, the preposterous clothing" of the American factory girl. "And yet through the huge hat," wrote Addams, "with its wilderness of bedraggled feathers, the girl announces to the world that she is here. She demands attention to the fact of her existence, she states that she is ready to live, to take her place in the world. The most precious moment in human development is the young creature's assertion that he is unlike any other human being, and has an individual contribution to make to the world."[1] Thirty years earlier, as an officious young steward negotiating around Miss Sill, Jane Addams could not have drawn a connection between herself and the factory girl. Still, it is useful to view her philosophical posturings and emotional evasions at Rockford as the self-conscious walk and bedraggled feathers of a daughter of the steward class announcing that she was ready to take her place in the world, if only she could figure out what that place might be.

Jane's quest was bounded on the one side by her own self-protective need to meet sentimentality with reserve and to steady her inner tumult with an assured stance, thus inevitably putting distance between herself and the blushing schoolgirl culture of her day. Cut off from traditionally Christian or feminine routes to identity, she ventured toward worldly salvation through work and science, but sexism narrowed those paths, forcing Jane to carve out a private, secret passage to ambition with the aid of a cool, quiet, self-contained goddess figure. In the end, this seminary quest delivered her to no final destination but did leave clear tracks of her trajectory.

A careful social posture at Rockford served to balance Jane's dual desires for dignity and privacy with her desire to lead by occupying a group's emotional center. In adulthood, Addams would come to strike that balance with expert ease, but as a novice steward trying to define her individual place among schoolgirls, she was more earnest than easy. The fact that she attended seminary during the heyday of female boarding-school "smashes" only complicated her task.[2] All around her, Rockford's "sem girls" were playing out romantic fantasies with each other, usually in preparation for heterosexual marriage, but John Addams's self-possessed daughter never participated in the romantic life of her classmates. Such sentimental relations were not part of the identity she adopted for herself in this early moment of womanhood.

In her first six months at Rockford, Jane held her distance from seminary socializing through a lively exchange of letters with two off-campus friends, Vallie and Ida, who claimed to share her disdain for everything "school girl-ish" and her contempt for "the spooning malady."[3] The three correspondents clucked their disapproval of "obstreperous demonstrations" of affection and collectively scorned "the sweet girl" with the "sickly" smile who raced around dormitory hallways "hugging and kissing" everyone goodnight. While Jane announced her preference for "cold people," Vallie idealized those "who possess dignity, grace and minds of their own" and pointed to Jane as an exemplar of this "dignified style."[4]

The correspondence ended when Ida (who thought girls "disgusting" when they "actually *flirt* with *one another* in a way similar to the different sexes") suddenly tried to leverage a shared recoil from such attachments into a romance with Jane. Ida got nowhere in her jocular attempt to cast Jane as Pythias to her own Damon and was just as unsuccessful with simpering pleas that Jane "trust me with the secret of your heart." No further communication survived Ida's ostensibly unsentimental cry to Jane, "You don't love me for there can be no true love without perfect trust."[5]

Jane Addams never gave herself over to "true love" or "perfect trust" while she was at Rockford. In four years, she never expressed the slightest romantic interest in any seminary girl or college boy. Her stepbrother, George, and his Beloit roommate, Rollin Salisbury, corresponded with Jane, as did young male editors of more distant collegiate newspapers, but none of these men ever captured her attention.[6] Her adult writings expressed genuine sympathy for adolescents' flirtations and their hunger for love stories, depicting both as natural expressions of biological urges.[7] But whatever her own urges may have been at Rockford, Jane did not indulge them—or easily accept her classmates' indulgences in them—because, for her, the stakes were too high. She used her position as magazine editor to chastise her friends for sacrificing their study time to read trashy romance novels whose plots were "enervating and foolish." According to Jane's summary of such stories, "a hero and heroine are madly in love—it is not very clear to the reader why they are, for both are destitute of qualities eminently lovable—they have a misunderstanding, in which a dark rival figures, suffer untold trials, and are united with a dash of marriage bells. This story is repeated, with endless variations, and is hardly an ennobling theme to spend one's leisure hours over."[8]

Beneath all the prissiness in that preachment there echoes the determined voice of a young woman who believed that the "privilege" and purpose of education was to prepare for a life of the mind, not to prepare for sexuality. She earnestly wanted others to join her search for an alternative to the embodied path of private romance. Weeks after her editorial attack on romance novels, Jane advised her schoolmates to invest their affection in the seminary as an institution, not merely as a collection of personal friends: "Make unto yourselves friends of inanimate objects; see that you know definitely some unchangeable things, that you can love them . . . in future years."[9]

Such was the allure of her emerging persona that Jane's disdain for sentiment did not alienate her from her Rockford classmates. Such was the nature of that allure that Jane's school friends did not extol her kindness or generosity or playfulness. Praise always centered on her "intellectual vitality."[10] Jane's first-year roommate, Eva Campbell, derived intellectual stimulus "to press onward and upward" from Jane's mere "presence" and the "workings" of Jane's mind.[11] Another classmate, Maria Nutting, felt that "no one else" but Jane would understand her thoughts on the "weird" *Sartor Resartus,* one of Thomas Carlyle's most challenging texts, and yet another confessed to "almost wonder how one who writes as well as you can spend their time on a correspondent as dull as I."[12] Even though Jane had once scolded Corinne Williams for sloppy bookkeeping on the seminary magazine, Williams remembered Jane's room as the one that "was always crowded when the sacred 'engaged' sign was not hung out." As Williams recalled, "We just knew there was always something 'doing' where she was, and that however mopey it might be elsewhere, there was an intellectual ozone in her vicinity."[13] This is not to say that Jane Addams's room was typically the site of dormitory parties. She told her Pa of one "impromtu feast" to celebrate President James Garfield's inauguration, but just as happily reported to her sister Alice that she had "beat a graceful retreat" when her "energetic roommate" packed the room "full of girls having a regular good time." Jane liked to think of her room as a "sanctum . . . a delightful little haven . . . a cosy retreat." Helen Harrington certainly shared that view. Just weeks after graduation, Harrington waited anxiously for a letter from Jane "since your room is no longer an available refuge from all perplexities."[14] A Rockford "sem" girl went to Jane Addams's room if she was looking for intellectual conversation or campus organizing or a quiet haven from girlish gossip.[15] One did not go there for a siege of giggles, a heartfelt sob, or a romantic embrace.

Over the course of her Rockford years, only two friends—Ellen Gates Starr and Sarah Anderson—managed to sneak past Jane Addams's armor of dignity and self-possession. Significantly, neither woman was a seminary student. Sarah Anderson was an 1869 graduate of Rockford Seminary's Normal

Department, not its Collegiate Department. When Jane Addams was a student at Rockford, Anderson was nearly thirty years old and was teaching "English Studies" in the Preparatory and Normal Departments, as well as acting as the school's bookkeeper and gym teacher. No one at the time could have imagined that Anderson would serve as president of Rockford Female Seminary from 1891 to 1896, before she became Mrs. Henry Ainsworth of Moline.[16] Nor could anyone have predicted that Ellen Starr would partner with Jane Addams in founding the Hull-House settlement in Chicago in 1889. Starr had entered Rockford Female Seminary's Collegiate Department alongside Addams in the fall of 1877. Financial exigencies in the Starr family had forced Ellen to leave Rockford at the end of that year, however, and to begin earning her own living as a schoolteacher. It was from a distance, then, that Ellen initiated a deepening correspondence with Jane and Sarah Anderson.[17]

When Jane and Ellen were at seminary together, they, along with classmates Eva Campbell and Katie Hitchcock, formed an admiring circle around the pretty Miss Anderson. Within two years, Starr, Campbell, and Hitchcock had all departed Rockford for different reasons. Jane, not surprisingly, turned for solace and companionship to Anderson, the more permanent, mature member of her seminary community. Jane never gave herself over to a "schoolgirlish" crush on Anderson, but doubtless other girls at seminary swooned over the gym teacher's thick, coffee-colored hair, pink cheeks, and non-freckling white skin. Ellen herself admitted, after just three months away from Rockford, that she would "give a generous slice of my future happiness to see Miss Anderson's little round face."[18] It is easy to imagine the "sem" girls whispering among themselves when Jane, at the start of her junior year, was "forcibly torn from Miss Anderson's table" on a dictate from Miss Sill. In her report to Ellen, Jane dismissed the new table arrangements as the product of "some new theory about development and expansiveness." Jane would not whine or pout, even in private.[19] Nor would she curtail her contact with Anderson.

Jane Addams would probably have been less attached to Anderson if Ellen Starr had not left the seminary. Even as teenagers, Jane and Ellen had the makings of a substantive relationship. They shared a love of serious literature, a fascination with religion and science, and a dislike of Anna Peck Sill's evangelical style. Ellen had "contempt" for faults which she found "despicable in Miss Sill," and ruefully commented to Jane at the time of her departure, "my unsanctified feet will not pollute the sacred walks of the R.F.S. for the year 1878–79."[20]

Like Jane, Ellen had grown up in small-town Illinois. Her parents, Susan and Caleb Starr, along with her Aunt Eliza Starr, had moved from Deerfield, Massachusetts, to Laona, in northern Illinois, in 1855. Ellen later described her father as "a good farmer, though inclined to be a visionary." When farming in

Laona failed, he turned to the pharmacy business in nearby Durand in 1877, the same year Ellen went to Rockford Seminary. Caleb Starr had been a Civil War Republican, but his real political passion was the National Grange of the Patrons of Husbandry, and by 1900 he would be voting for William Jennings Bryan on the Democratic-Populist ticket and eyeing the Socialists. In his speeches at local Grange meetings in the 1870s, Starr railed at "middle men,

12. Sarah Anderson in the early 1880s. (Rockford College Archives)

manufacturers, merchants" who burdened Illinois farmers with "our present unjust basis of taxation." He gave full vent to his anger at "centralized government; wealth in the hands of a favored few; poverty, ignorance, oppression and degradation for the laboring many." If Cedarville's John Addams was a comfortable steward in his community, then Durand's Caleb Starr was a visionary democrat in his. Starr was the sort of feisty citizen who denounced the profits flowing from the railroad and banking systems John Addams had helped create.[21]

The different political and economic legacies that Jane Addams and Ellen Starr inherited from their fathers would ultimately create fissures in the women's relationship, but it was not paternal politics that mattered in their youth. As young women, they shared an understanding about beloved fathers. Both John Addams and Caleb Starr were great readers, both talked with their daughters about books and ideas, and both took a matter-of-fact approach to religion. Along with his wife, Susan, Caleb Starr imbued all of his children— Mary, William, Ellen, and Albert—with a love of the visual arts and a great respect for the family's New England, Unitarian lineage. Like Jane, then, Ellen came from a family that did not share Miss Sill's orthodoxy.[22]

Ellen Starr's most important female teacher was her maiden aunt, Caleb's sister, Eliza Allen Starr. Aunt Eliza was, in every respect, quite unlike Anna Haldeman Addams. After moving west with her brother and his family in 1855, she had established a painting studio in Chicago and made a name for herself as an artist, teacher, and lecturer. A convert from Unitarianism to Catholicism, she became active as an art historian in the Chicago Catholic community, and by the late 1870s, when Ellen and Jane became friends, Eliza Starr had begun work on the books of Christian art which would make her nationally known.[23] Ellen's own niece later claimed that it would be "impossible to overemphasize" Eliza Starr's influence on Ellen. She provided not only a model of independent womanhood and innovative artistry, but instilled in Ellen a hunger for the spiritual comfort that Eliza so obviously cherished. In 1879, on the eve of her move to Chicago for a new teaching position at a private girls' school, Ellen happily anticipated proximity to her impressive "Auntie," and made repeated, albeit unsuccessful, efforts to engage Jane's interest in this devout Catholic artist.[24]

History has so linked the lives of Jane Addams and Ellen Gates Starr that it takes effort to remember how easily their youthful friendship might have dissolved when Ellen left Rockford. Indeed, when a full year's absence confirmed that Ellen would never be returning to Rockford, Jane bluntly told her "beloved friend" that she was "disappointed to think . . . that our social intercourse is probably over for all time." Jane's expansion on this comment speaks volumes about her adolescent effort to inure herself to personal loss:

13. Ellen Gates Starr as a student at Rockford Female Seminary. (Swarthmore College Peace Collection)

It is queer, though, but a fact that I am glad when I know some people just so much and then stop. . . . not that I am afraid to go any further, but there is a sort of fascination to me. You remember them and retain the impression they leave, go steadily on your own way and meet someone else, who will sort of finish out what they began. Had you kept on with the same person, it would probably have been all right, but it is better and more variety so. I don't feel exactly that way in regard to your going away, but then I don't feel so very bad on the same principle that two people honestly going ahead are better if they don't meet too much—don't need to "descend" you know.[25]

Jane wrote this astonishing description of friends as interchangeable players in some impersonal human pageant on August 11, 1879, the second anniversary of her first meeting with Ellen. The year before, she had hurt Ellen by forgetting—or ignoring—the anniversary of their first meeting.[26] Now Jane included this calm resignation to the end of their friendship right in the middle of a long anniversary letter full of personal news, literary ponderings, and heartfelt introspection on religion. It ended with a warm, almost insistent, invitation to visit Jane in Cedarville.

So the relationship was to proceed, for years, with Jane drawing near and in the next instant pulling away, inviting Ellen to come close and then disappearing behind her cloak of reserve. A less persistent soul than Ellen Starr would have quit the whole business. But Ellen was drawn to the intensity of Jane's mind, her diligence, and probably her elusiveness—what a prize to be won.

Lots of young women loved Jane Addams, however, so the real question is not what drew Ellen, or Sarah Anderson, to Jane, but what drew Jane to them. There was the fact that both women were working for a living, which may have made them appear more solid and mature to Jane than her "sem" friends. There was the fact that they were not among the student constituents Jane had positioned herself to lead, so with these two women she could reveal some of her doubts. Then, too, there was the fact that they were both smart, articulate, serious about their reading, and not (yet) given to fawning over Jane. Finally, both Sarah Anderson and Ellen Starr were sufficiently reflective about their religious faith to be useful companions in Jane's own spiritual quest.

Recoiling from Miss Sill's plodding sermons on the literal authenticity of the Christian story, Jane and Ellen shared the significant core conviction that faith resided in the realm of the abstract. Both sought a spiritual leap of faith, chafed at the "barrier" that intellect posed, and longed for a time when "reason might become passive . . . or at least not quite so suspicious," so that they could enjoy faith "in peace."[27] From that common ground, however, the two young women took different directions. In Chicago, Ellen began to attend an Episcopal church and found that the aesthetic beauty of the service was "the only thing" that gave her spiritual satisfaction. Ellen saw "the unspeakable splendor" of faith encoded within Christian ritual and set about training herself to be transported beyond the tangible by the tangible, stretching her own capacity to accept mystery by struggling to accept the divinity of Jesus. Anticipating Jane's reaction, Ellen tentatively admitted that she felt "a kind of reality" in thinking of Jesus as divine, if only because that made God more of a reality for her and, thus, brought her nearer to salvation.[28]

Jane was "somewhat shocked" at Ellen's attraction to such traditional fare. She tried to be tolerant, agreeing that it was "absurd" to insist upon "seeing religion by the understanding instead of by faith," but Ellen's focus on finding transcendence through Jesus Christ irritated Jane.[29] She was convinced that belief in the divinity of Jesus fettered spirituality rather than releasing it. In response to Ellen's hopes for salvation through an embrace of Jesus, Jane mustered a smile for her "beloved friend" before declaring that the people of every nation, and every religion, could be "saved" if they would just be satisfied to experience the "mystery" of "the incomprehensible." Christians, like Jews and "Mohammedans," missed the whole point of religion by "lowering their ideal" to the most literal level. In Addams's clinical view, a fixation on Jesus was just the sort of concrete thinking that stifled any chance of transcendence. "Don't you see," beseeched Jane, "that you are all right? . . . Comprehending your deity . . . is to be saved. If you realize God through Christ, it doesn't make any difference whether you realize Christ or not, that is not the point."[30]

Assured as it sounded, this sort of pronouncement did not take Jane any closer to her own spiritual peace. She disdained the leaden use of intellect as a path to transcendent faith, but could not seem to get around her own intellectual view of religion as a human construct. In the same letter, she confessed to Ellen, "I wish I was where you are. Christ don't help me in the least. . . . There is a mystery and a beauty incomprehensible to me."[31]

Talks with Sarah Anderson failed to bridge the chasm between doubt and belief, even though Jane viewed those as "some of the best talks" she could "ever expect to have with anyone." When Jane voiced her respect for Anderson's religiosity, she said nothing about her teacher's profession of Christian faith. Rather, she praised Anderson for keeping "just as true to herself . . . as anyone could" and for having "built her religious principle right on from that." Try as she might to focus on faith in something above and beyond, Jane could not help but see religion as something one "built" from and for oneself. She told herself, and Ellen, that she would just "go ahead building up my religion wherever I can find it, from the Bible and observation, from books and people," but there was some bluster in that announcement.[32] Having strutted her spiritual certitude before a visitor to campus, she felt compelled to draft an apologetic note for the "unnatural" way she had spoken. "I see that my idea of embodying Truth in myself lacks much I could attract from other people," she conceded to "Mr. Smith." While claiming to agree with his notion that interaction with others could "bring out what was best in their lives as well as my own," Jane noted with a sigh that she would "never become" capable of such spiritual intercourse "unless I have the sacred flame to start with."[33]

Jane was sufficiently concerned, and sufficiently pressured, about her spiritual status to unburden herself to a liberal minister, T. H. Haseltine. In an intriguing reference to her reputation at Rockford, Haseltine tried to assure her that those who regarded her as "an atheist" simply did not understand that her lack of interest in Christianity meant she had moved on to a more abstract appreciation of the "greater Christ." His further advice, delivered at the end of Jane's junior year, that she "cease to blame" herself for "the rate" of her spiritual development suggests that she was not at all sanguine about her progress.[34]

The urgency in Jane's spiritual quest had nothing to do with gaining eternal salvation and everything to do with finding salvation in this life. Jane had fully absorbed the belief, popular among agnostic Victorian idealists, that faith in something beyond oneself was requisite to the pursuit of meaningful work. Untethered to any transcendent ideal or "sacred flame," work could too easily be sullied by egotism or greed. In the case of a female contemplating a life of work apart from domestic duties, the need for a spiritual calling, both for legitimacy and guidance, was obvious. With equal measures of confidence and doubt, Jane confided to Ellen that she feared she could not "use my best powers" without settling the religious question; "could I but determine *that*," she predicted, "and have it for a sure basis . . . I could train my powers to anything, it would only remain to choose what."[35]

As a seminary student, Jane was genuinely worried that her lack of faith meant that her life goals were bound to be prosaic and egocentric. She was caught between her intellectual view of religion as a human construct and her intimate belief that only an "expansiveness of soul" inspired people to do great work; without a leap of faith, she would never possess the expansiveness or the inspiration. "The great object of this age seems to be missionary works," Jane told Eva Campbell. As missionaries, Jane imagined that she and Campbell could "throw ourselves into the tide of affairs, feel ourselves swamped by the great flood of human action." Jane relished the idea of such vigorous endeavor, even going so far as to serve as vice president of the Home Missions Society at Rockford. But she saw herself as ineligible for the adventure because missionaries had to be believers. Left outside the circle of belief, she was "doomed" to a lifetime of "self-culture," and "self-culture," she sighed, "but impales a man on his personal pronoun," leaving "your soul spinning around on a great I."[36]

When Jane was feeling most isolated in her faithlessness, she bristled at Ellen's offerings to make common cause in the search for transcendence, bluntly pointing out the spiritual distance between herself and her more devout friend. "You long for a beautiful faith," wrote Jane, "I only feel that I need religion in a practical sense, that if I could fix myself with my relations to God and the universe and so be in perfect harmony with nature and deity, I could use my faculties and energy so much better and could do almost anything. *Mine* is preeminently selfish and yours is a reaching for higher things."[37] This complicated mix of self-flattery and self-deprecation aimed to be true to Jane's stated "creed" to "ever be *sincere*" about religion.[38] Even when she was feeling scratchy and alone, Jane did admire Ellen's "reaching for higher things." Though Jane could not shake the feeling that her friend's search for a "beautiful faith" within organized Christianity was a futile flirtation with superstition, she still longed for passage beyond the "great I."

Jane Addams's preoccupation with training her powers, transcending her ego, and thrusting herself full tilt into the flood of human action was not unique among Anglo-Americans of her era. The dual assault of Darwinism and industrialization in the Gilded Age caused many to doubt the saving power of the church and to seek, instead, the salvation of purpose through meaningful work that could be deemed a "calling." In post–Civil War America, faith in the saving grace of work was embedded in patriotic paeans to the blood-soaked victory of the free-labor North. It was vital to capitalists' defense of laissez-faire economics and just as vital to workers' claims to a larger share of the wealth they produced.[39]

Part of Jane's attraction to Sarah Anderson and Ellen Starr was that they were workers, and Jane applauded Anderson's announcement that "we are not put into the world to be religious, we have certain work to do, and to do that is the main thing."[40] Still, there was a gap. Sarah and Ellen embraced work as a pathway to the service and humility that would put them closer to the divine. Jane viewed work as a means of exertion and self-expression, as a way of adding the spark of her own divinity to the universe. In one of the last issues of the *Rockford Seminary Magazine* that she edited, Jane printed a maxim she had first copied into her private notebook: "A man will never feel at home in the world save through labor; he who does not labor is homeless."[41]

Unromantic though she was about friendship and religion, Jane fueled her faith in work by embracing the romantic ideals of Europe's greatest dreamers: Johann Goethe, William Wordsworth, Thomas DeQuincey, and John Ruskin. The social and aesthetic movements these men had launched were more than fifty years old when Jane Addams was at Rockford, but in her parochial setting, German romanticism and Victorian idealism were positively avant-garde.[42]

And no Victorian idealist was more avant-garde than Thomas Carlyle, the Scottish moralist whose decidedly undemocratic views had not yet lost favor in the United States. Jane, like many of her generation, was inspired by Carlyle's angry critique of industrialization for its destruction of creative work and its base perversion of mutual class obligations into the "cash nexus." She took a pre-industrial villager's joy in his claim that all work was ennobling, and drew an aspiring young steward's pleasure in his belief that those born to be heroic leaders could renew labor's dignity among the masses. John Addams's ambitious daughter thrilled to Carlyle's thundering cry: "Whatsoever of morality and of intelligence; what of patience, perseverance, faithfulness, of method, insight, ingenuity, energy; in a word, whatsoever of Strength the man had in him will lie written in the Work he does . . . Produce! Produce! Were it but the pitifullest infinitesimal fraction of a Product, produce it, in God's name!"[43] "Carlyle has a way of saying things that strikes me as it were my keynote," Jane declared with a tinge of pride over her grasp of his most demanding prose. The materials she planned to use in building her religion would come, she figured, "in no small degree from Carlyle."[44]

Carlyle's high-flying idealism spoke to Jane's youthful longing for a philosophy that could justify her ambition. He was critical of scientific materialism and modern rationalism without harkening back to Christian dogma; he extolled heroes, heroism, and heroic action in terms that valorized individual integrity and individual destiny; he was exuberant in his belief that each soul craved and deserved meaningful work and just as exuberant in his corollary belief that such work was the vehicle by which humans could discover their essence and transcend the material world. Moreover, and this was no small benefit, Carlyle did not pay particular attention to the Woman Question as such, nor did he write women out of his heroic script. This omission left Jane Addams free to imagine that when Carlyle said "man," he meant all individuals who possessed the strength and courage to seize "the pure ideal of a noble existence"—even adolescent females in backwater seminaries.[45] So great was Jane's sense of connection to Carlyle that when he died in 1881, during Addams's senior year at Rockford, she confessed to Ellen her despair over never meeting him and shared a moment of "personal bereavement" with Maria Nutting, a seminary friend.[46] Nutting would later "smile" over the "girlish enthusiasms and philosophizing" she and Jane had indulged in at Rockford, but recalled "it was all dead earnest" back then "and really we did touch upon some pretty deep subjects."[47]

Jane's "dead earnest" essays at Rockford were thick with the language of dramatic endeavor and heroic individualism that she absorbed from reading Carlyle. Over and over again, she extolled the world's heroes for their "terrible earnestness," for their willingness to come "face to face with stern unflinching reality," for their possession of that "primary condition of greatness: oneness of purpose," for their "daring to express an honest opinion," for "never deviating" from principle, for their "absorption" in real work, and for following Carlyle's maxim: "the end of life is an action, not a thought."[48] So while she was deriving a tremendous amount of pride and satisfaction from her intellectual achievements at Rockford, Jane was also adopting the view that scholarship was second best to direct engagement with the world. Even while reading *Sartor Resartus*, Carlyle's dense paean to the unseen essence, Jane told Ellen that her "admiration for a well-read person is mingled with just a little bit of contempt that they had to *read* to find out all about it."[49]

Ellen scrambled to keep up with Jane's philosophical spins and turns in these years. No sooner would Starr smooth over one disagreement than Jane would dart off in a new direction, announcing over her shoulder that "it would be better for us not to talk about religion any more."[50] Ellen often felt led in a discussion with Jane only to be abandoned when Jane up and decided it was "hopeless to express myself" because "my ideas are changing."[51] Rather than appear tentative in her thinking, Jane asserted that "I am not so unsettled as I resettle so often."[52] Ellen tried to strengthen the bond by noting how often their thinking coincided, but Jane ignored those cues.[53] Ellen responded warmly to Jane's remark that she often thought of Ellen when praying, but Jane then snapped back with the "awful" announcement that she no longer prayed. Ellen was left sputtering over the "harm" that "might" come to Jane's soul from losing that habit of mind.[54] As soon as Ellen tried to pick up the thread of connection by talking more about Carlyle, Jane suddenly ducked under the new cover of science. "Don't flatter yourself that I agree with you in your latent vein of hero-worship," Jane told her "dear girl." For the moment, Jane preferred "to get my inspiration from a dodecahedral crystal than even a genius," but with patronizing humor she congratulated Ellen's new interest in the heroic as an "unmistakable sign of advancement."[55]

The pursuit of science held, for Jane, Carlyle's promise of endeavor that would lead to transcendence, thereby avoiding the need to define spiritual principles before starting one's life work. Like so many others of her post-Darwinian generation, when Jane was forced to look beyond Christianity to legitimize and elevate her ambition, she turned to the precision and certitude of scientific materialism.[56] A childhood spent in the company of George Haldeman, "experimenting" with the flora and fauna along Cedar Creek, had instilled in Jane a lifelong appreciation for nature, as well as for experimentation. Many a Cedarville evening had been passed testing each family member's scientific knowledge by playing "natural history," and John Addams's library contained numerous volumes on chemistry, physiology, and "the connection of science and philosophy with religion."[57] A life devoted to science promised to satisfy Jane's taste for an unsentimental explanation of the origins of the universe and the purpose of life, and it certainly offered her an escape from perpetual "self-culture" by being swept up in a historic stream larger than herself.[58] Given the years at home with male relatives who willingly studied math and science with Jennie, it is not surprising that she looked to science as a likely site of active, meaningful work for an ambitious, unchurched female.

Addams never forgave Miss Sill for Rockford's woefully inadequate science program.[59] A committee assessing the school's readiness for collegiate status in the mid-1870s had recommended that the curriculum depend less on the literal "Biblical narrative" and more on critical study "of the results of modern research." Sill's half-hearted response was to begin using an 1863 text by Mark Hopkins, *Evidences of Christianity*, an utterly pedestrian attempt to employ contemporary science and history to prove the Christian story.[60] As a mild corrective to their school's curricular deficits, Jane and Ellen formed the Rockford Female Seminary Scientific Association in their first year on campus, and Jane stayed active in the club after Starr's departure.[61] Participation in the Scientific Association gave Addams regular exposure to *Popular Science Monthly*, a magazine the club used as the basis for its discussions every other Wednesday morning.

Jane did not embrace the monthly's enthusiasm for Herbert Spencer and social Darwinism. In her youthful search for a philosophy that would legitimize her ambition, she opted for Carlyle's elitist insistence on leaders' responsibility for the masses instead of the laissez-faire principle of "survival of the fittest."[62] Jane did, however, applaud the monthly's attacks on the "groveling anthropomorphism" of orthodox Christianity's deism and agreed with its claim that modern science had exposed the "duplicity" of religion.[63] Read within the walls of Miss Sill's seminary, such claims amounted to high treason.

The reports on research activity that filled the *Popular Science Monthly* gave Jane ammunition for an implicit critique of Rockford's stodgy curriculum. Her seminary essays are full of praise for "high priests of science" who had the devotion of medieval monks "to the grand total" but, unlike medieval monks, actually added "to the stores of human knowledge." She held such researchers in high esteem over the "pathetic," bookish "compilers" who merely studied "accumulated knowledge" and "dogmatic laws" but "produced nothing" and left the world "no richer."[64] Haunting Jane's recoil from "self culture," and fueling her geometry preparations for Smith College, was her fear that a seminary education fit her only for the dull life of a compiler.[65]

Regular exposure to the *Popular Science Monthly* could not assuage these fears. On the contrary, the magazine's content made clear that the world of science was hostile to intrusion by women. Try as she might to avoid the Woman Question and imagine herself as a disembodied, sexless hero, Jane could not presume to take up the powerful principles of science without being reminded that being female made her unfit for great work in this arena. Standard fare in the pages of the monthly were articles testifying to the biological inferiority of the female of the species. Modern, scientific theory of the day held that progress up the evolutionary scale was characterized by increased sexual differentiation and a widening gap between men's capacities and women's. This meant, of course, that females of the "civilized" "white" race had neither the physical stamina nor the intellectual acuity for the advanced science, politics, and engineering typical of the highly evolved Western society men had created.[66]

When the members of Rockford Seminary's Scientific Association met on the second Wednesday of December 1878, in the middle of Jane's sophomore year, to read the newest issue of the *Popular Science Monthly*, they learned that the prospect of "women's rights" threatened evolutionary disaster through a process of "unnatural selection" resulting in "a race of monstrosities." That particular article pointed to men's "superior cerebral and thoracic development," their "more intense and exuberant vitality," and their "bolder, more pugnacious, more adventurous nature" in order to argue for men's natural role as women's providers and defenders.[67] An article that appeared during Jane's junior year explained that the energy women expended in their "generative organs" naturally cost them intellectual energy.[68]

Serious young women like Jane Addams who wished to be modern and scientific had to expose themselves to a barrage of such testimonials on female inferiority. Over and over again, the day's scientists pointed with one hand to history to prove that men were "preeminent . . . in the highest qualities of mind, of reason, judgment, genius, inventive power, and capacity for acquiring and utilizing knowledge." With the other hand, they pointed to the physiological claim that "man, surpassing woman in volume of brain, must surpass her in at least a proportionate degree of intellectual power."[69] If a woman with scientific pretensions were to question such dogma, she would only be demonstrating the limitations of her mind.

While she was a seminary student, Jane did not have the luxury of grappling with orthodox Christianity, Victorian idealism, and Darwinian science in orderly sequence. She juggled them simultaneously, and with little intellectual guidance, while she matured from adolescence to young womanhood. It is not remarkable that a precocious student in the Gilded Age would be pondering these subjects. Intellectual upheavals at Harvard, Yale, Amherst, and even Smith occurred in these years precisely because students and faculty were reconsidering the foundations of knowledge, faith, and morality in light of new discoveries and developments. Jane's future compatriots in pragmatism, John Dewey and William James, were themselves grappling with the era's central question: how to preserve Christian ethics in a world turned upside down by Darwinian theory and industrial materialism.[70]

What is remarkable is that Jane Addams, secluded in a tiny, provincial, evangelical outpost in northern Illinois, was able to follow the general contours of this upheaval, tracing the logic of her father's latitudinarianism away from Cedarville and Rockford and out into the broader discourse of the day. Isolated as she was, her process inevitably produced contradictions and self-corrections, enthusiasms and disillusionments. But as she ricocheted between Christian orthodoxy and Darwinian science, Jane persistently challenged all theories that did not allow her to soar toward the heroic destiny she imagined residing within her.

When science bogged down in its petty proofs of female inferiority, Jane turned her critique of religion into a critique of science, charging it with being so literal that it lost sight of its own truth. Faced with exclusion from science as well as from religion, Jane scoffed at the shortsightedness in "this age of reason" when "we can account for the formation and growth of everything [but] life alone eludes our closest research."[71] Male scientists, like male theologians, were so preoccupied with their "swelling miscellany of facts" that they could not grasp "the incomprehensible" in nature—and nature in Jane's lexicon was always female.[72]

On only one occasion in their surviving correspondence did Jane share with Ellen the direction in which her thoughts on religion, science, and the heroic were taking her. In the summer before her junior year, just as she was admitting that "Christ don't help me in the least," Jane revealed her attraction to a rather different cosmology: "Lately it seems that I am getting back of all of it, superior to it I almost feel—Back to a great Primal Cause, not Nature exactly, but a fostering mother, a necessity, brooding and watching over all things, above every human passion and yet not passive, the mystery of creation. . . . The idea embodied in the sphinx—peace."

Jane felt she made "a botch trying to describe it," and Ellen did not try to follow this particular train of thought. Still, the whole notion of a "fostering mother" gave Jennie Addams "lots of comfort."[73] Though she never again spoke of it to Ellen, and never discussed it in any essay she wrote for a Rockford teacher or any editorial she ever printed in the seminary magazine, Jane continued to ruminate on this image. Finally, and quite privately, in the spring of her junior year, Jane took out an essay on "The Nebular Hypothesis" that she had once written for a mathematics class and reworked it into a private tribute to her "brooding" female goddess.

"Darkness vs. Nebulae," written in the same week that Rev. Haseltine assured her she was not an atheist, articulated Jane's belief in a female principle operating in the universe. The title alone signified an uncharacteristic willingness on her part to explicitly pit a feminine myth of creation—"the darkness"—against a masculine myth—"the nebulae." Just weeks earlier, in her "Bread Givers" speech at the Junior Exhibition, Jane had insisted that educated women did not want to be men, were not "trying to imitate our brothers." Now, in the privacy of "Darkness vs. Nebulae" she revealed why she did not aspire to be like her "brothers." Along the way, she revealed much about her anger at masculinized, modern science, and her reconciliation of divinity, heroism, and the feminine.[74]

In "Darkness vs. Nebulae," Jane contrasted masculine learning, quite unfavorably, to female intuition. Romola, the heroic "nature-goddess" in Jane's favorite George Eliot novel, possessed "a power deeper and more primordial than knowledge."[75] Traditional myths of creation acknowledged that primordial wisdom by reverencing the "life-giving power of moisture" offered by female goddesses dwelling in "silence and darkness." Jane, herself, wrote reverentially of the "calm invisible circle of peace" that surrounded such goddesses. She extolled the ancient statues of ideal women whose "coldness and quiet" announced "they could be alone in the world and need no other support." The "embodiment" of this ancient female ideal, Jane said, was the character of the Lady in John Milton's play *Comus*, wherein a young woman, "alone and unprotected, exercised her wonderful power" to resist temptations offered by a male, Comus, and bravely awaited rescue, not by her helpless brothers, but by a pagan river goddess.[76]

The dramatic turn in Jane's narrative came with the overthrowing of the peaceful, intuitive cultures that treasured goddess-centered creation stories. "Now, suddenly, we find ourselves in the midst of a revolution . . . [an] age of intellectual force and intensive living." Now, the men who were writing the tale of creation spurned "the Great brooding mother" and looked to a new, more masculine parent, the nebulae, "the dull heated mass extending throughout the universe in constant and frightful motion from which, by the very persistence of force man himself finally evolved."[77]

The sexual imagery in this private essay is extraordinary. The invidious comparison Jane drew between the "life-giving power of moisture" and the "dull heated mass extending throughout the universe" spoke loudly where her seminary editorials were silent and quite directly where her "Bread Givers" speech was oblique. There is confusion, however, in the essay's reappropriation of sex-linked traits. In 1880, every reader of every journal from *Popular Science Monthly* to *Godey's Lady's Magazine* knew that it was men who were quiet, calm, brave, dignified, self-reliant, even brooding, and cold. Men could stand unprotected. Men were self-sustaining. Jane Addams's father was certainly all of those things. But in Jane's private essay, these traits were reclaimed for women, at least in their "primordial" state, and modern men—men unlike Jane's father—were feminized as creatures of the mob, caught up, she said, in "the rush of events" and "false stimuli." Having rejected their fostering mother's "ancient power of solitude," the nebulae men were forever refashioning their ideas for popularity, wasting the potential of their youth because they lacked an inner core and because, unlike the ancient ideal woman, they could not stand alone in the world.

In reshuffling the deck of sex-linked traits so that she held her father's cards, Jane came very close to arguing that gender, like religion, was a cultural construct susceptible to human choice and historical change. Her ambition certainly required that she presume the possibility of greater gender fluidity than her society offered. She needed to believe in her capacity to claim male virtues for herself and the "fostering mother," and that belief fueled her embrace of Carlyle's heroic ideals, her commitment to work outside the home, and her assumption that she was destined for some sort of stewardship. But at age twenty, in a world of stark gender polarities, Jane Addams could not sustain an argument for gender fluidity. So her haughty retort to the sexist insults dealt out by Gilded Age Darwinians wound up defining as innately feminine those traits Jane coveted rather than boldly imagining that all traits were available to all people. In this retreat to fixed gender traits, Jane was as much a product of her time as she was a critic.

Emerging from Jane Addams's collegiate meanderings through Christianity, Victorian idealism, and evolutionary science came the outline of a philosophy that could both inspire and justify her ambitions. At the core of that philosophy stood the fostering mother, "the kindly bosom of mother Earth."[78] Missing entirely from this image was any hint of intimacy or interdependence. Jane Addams's ideal female provided nurturance—gave bread—but then stood alone. She was not embedded in an interdependent web of giving and receiving. She fed others' bodies but was herself disembodied. Her origins were moist, but she was "cold." She invited others' dependence but was sufficient unto herself. Having searched down numerous paths, the once-motherless Jennie Addams settled upon this figure to sustain her ambitions for stewardship.

Her attraction to this ideal was consistent with Jane's emotional style at Rockford. In her first semester at seminary, Addams had declared her admiration for "cold people."[79] Two years later, she had told Ellen she was "glad when I know some people just so much and then stop."[80] And two years after that, during her last semester at Rockford, Addams quoted Matthew Arnold (even

though she regarded him as "the limit of sentimentality") to convey to Ellen
her ideal of a "self-poised, mighty life":

Unaffrighted by the silence round them
Undistracted by the sights they see
These demand not that the things without them
Yield them love, amusement, sympathy.[81]

By constructing a collegiate image as a self-sufficient steward who demanded
not love, amusement, or sympathy, Jane managed to garner great quantities of
all three from those around her. She liked the idea of the fostering mother who
could "produce whatsoever is needful in each season of her course," and do
so "with perfect composure."[82] But she chafed at the emotional responsibility
of the position, often drawing tight when girlfriends pleaded for succor or
becoming self-righteous when they chastised her for inflicting hurt or disappointment.[83] Back and forth she went, inviting the intimacy of dependence and
then denying it. Long before Jane Addams could become a fostering mother,
her youthful impulse was to be a rather controlling one. Prior to her adult success at mediating conflict, her nascent tendency was to silence it.

The layers of emotional logic underlying this pattern of behavior had
been laid down from the time of Jennie Addams's earliest days in the big gray
house on Cedar Creek. A childhood marred by death had not only taught her
about loss but about stoicism as well. Her father's reserved dignity was a powerful example made more powerful when contrasted with her stepmother's
emotional extravagance. The need for autonomy—to stand "quiet" and "alone
in the world and need no other support"—only increased under Miss Sill's heavy
evangelical hand and the pubescent emotionalism in Rockford's dormitory.[84]

All around her, girls rehearsed for their heterosexual futures as wives and
mothers, blending crushes on each other and crushes on the boys at Beloit College into a blur of desire that everyone knew must end in the private world of
kitchen and nursery. These diversions never drew Jane away from her studies,
her stewardship of the female community at Rockford, or her spiritual quest.
For all her valorizing of Mother Earth, she responded to the corporeal reality
of sex much as she responded to spiritual demands of faith: with a bid for transcendence and the permanence of excellent work. "We can always think with a
body or without one," Addams insisted in one college essay. "So long as I continue to think I will survive the wrecks . . . and chaos. I thought and thought
can never die."[85]

There was some softening of the edges over the course of her years at
seminary. Addams was able to confess to Starr in the middle of her junior year

that she feared she had "laid too many of my plans simply for work."[86] And a year after telling Starr that their "social intercourse was probably over for all time," she could report to Helen Harrington that "the truest friendship . . . can annihilate time and space."[87] Jane Addams's real softening would come later, though, after being bruised by life outside the female cloister. Her seminary youth was spent idealizing a heroic, disembodied female independence, "brooding and watching over all things" and standing "above every human passion."[88]

Chapter 6
Cassandra

Every graduating senior at Rockford Female Seminary delivered a commencement address. So well before Jane Addams knew officially that she would be class valedictorian, she was pondering her graduation remarks. Three months before the event, she self-deprecatingly told her Pa of her "antiquarian efforts to dig up from my brain a deep and mature (?) graduating essay." And though she tried to reassure herself that there was "no haste," that she could "calmly wait for inspiration," she complained to Pa that "the result" of her effort on the essay "has not been extremely flattering." Weeks later, when the essay was "ready for the finishing touches," she confessed to George that she was "disappointed in it because I have had to cut it down over and over again, until it seems to me crude and a little obscure."[1]

The two-and-a-half page essay that Jane delivered on June 22, 1881, represented her valedictory attempt to resolve her seminary conflicts over spirituality, science, and womanhood. Rather than expose her primordial goddess to the harsh light of day, Jane chose to ground her public thoughts in the story of "Cassandra," the mythical Trojan princess whose prophecy of a Greek victory over the walled city of Troy was mocked and dismissed by her father's warriors. "This," said Jane Addams on the eve of her departure from the virtually walled community of Rockford Female Seminary, "was the tragic fate of Cassandra— always to be right, and always to be disbelieved and rejected."

From this text, Jane drew the lesson that women of her era were, mistakenly, being ignored because the modern age was so dazzled by the "power and magnificence" of scientific knowledge that it treated intuitive knowledge "with contempt." Her solution was to reassert the value of intuition, specifically female intuition, in modern life and to enhance that intuition by educating women in scientific theory and method. Once equipped with both intuition and scientific training, women would garner the very thing Jane most wanted: "what the ancients call *auethoritas,* the right of speakers to make themselves heard."[2]

Standing before the crowd of townspeople, trustees, teachers, and parents who had assembled for Rockford's commencement ceremonies, Jane threaded the needle of her brief argument very, very carefully. If she went too far in one direction, her speech would be just another sentimental paean to intuitive femininity; if she went too far in the other direction, it would be a diatribe against male supremacy; neither position was a comfortable one for the mediating Jane Addams. No wonder she struggled over this speech; its subject, so close to her heart, had to be navigated with some precision.

14. Jane Addams at the time of her graduation from Rockford Female Seminary, 1881. (University of Illinois at Chicago, University Library, Jane Addams Memorial Collection, neg. no. 5)

Jane's basic claim to the value of intuition was not particularly controversial in northern Illinois in 1881. The advent of Darwinian science in 1859
had sent both theologians and scientists into the arms of intuitionism, insisting that science could neither prove nor disprove God's existence; that sort
of knowing rested with intuition, feeling, emotions. Jane's insistence on an
abstract spirituality firmly aligned her with the intuitionists' finessing of the
debate between science and faith.[3] So, too, the notion that women were well
endowed with intuition was widely accepted; this was not a proposition that
would have astonished her audience. But references to "women's intuition" had
become hackneyed in the Gilded Age, evoking either whimsical or domesti-
cated images.[4]

On the eve of her graduation from Miss Sill's feminine cloister Jane set
about to translate respect for spiritual intuition into renewed respect for that
particular intuition which is "a feminine trait of mind." She then sought to
move female intuition out of the home and into the public world of knowledge
and action. "An intuitive perception committed to a woman's charge is not a
prejudice or a fancy," argued Jane against those who trivialized female insight.
No, she insisted, feminine intuition was "one of the holy means given to mankind in their search for truth." There were, she said, "discoveries to be made
which cannot come by induction, only through perception." But to realize
woman's social value in the search for truth, she "must take the active, busy
world as a test for the genuineness of her intuition."[5]

Thus, Jane navigated past the danger of sentimentalizing and privatizing
female intuition. But Rockford's studious valedictorian still had to explain why
women endowed with something so perceptive as intuition needed an education, especially a scientific education. For that was the hidden agenda in this
speech: to argue for precisely the thing Miss Sill had failed to provide and that
Jane still desired, training in modern science. The justification Jane offered in
the text befitted her role as campus mediator: the integration of intuition and
science offered an alternative to warring polarities; it was the way to cooperation and progress. Scientific research would be enhanced by a woman's "quick
recognition of the true and genuine," while training in the scientific method
would allow a woman to "detect all self-deceit and fancy in herself" by using
the tools of "logic" and "facts."

Nowhere in this careful speech did Jane suggest that those with scientific
knowledge, presumably men, be given any training in the use of intuition. The
mission here was not gender blending or even sex equity; it was finding a
practical way for ambitious females like Jane Addams to gain *auethoritas*, the
right to make herself heard. Her approach served to disarm the misogyny reflected in places like *Popular Science Monthly*. It made a virtue of the feminine

qualities that misogynists disdained and then embraced the scientific method that misogynists hoarded for men. In this way, the "Cassandra" address rose above diatribe as it skirted sentimentality.

The mediating, moderating skills that Jane displayed in this speech were all bent in the service of her own self-protective, self-advancing interests. Though she aligned with women's intuition, she did not align with women any more than she aligned against men. Anxious to avoid rancor, especially on the Woman Question, she could not bring herself to name the systemic constraints on women's access to men's *auethoritas*, whether they be scientific, economic, or political. As a young devotee of Thomas Carlyle, Jane was so enamored of the heroic ideal and so determined to believe that she could "train my powers to anything, it would only remain to choose what," that she focused on individual responsibility to take action, not on social barriers to that action.[6] In her valedictory, Jane placed no blame on men for the ascendancy of science over intuition. Instead, she faulted "a feminine trait of mind" which "rests contented in itself and will make no effort to confirm itself." She blamed women for having "failed to make themselves intelligible" to men. Just as she had righteously lectured her classmates, not Miss Sill, on the need for a Junior Exhibition, now she admonished "women of the nineteenth century" to see that "there is a way opened . . . by the scientific ideal."[7] It was up to women, apparently, to simply seize the day and engage in scientific study. Though she was a regular witness to the misogyny in *Popular Science Monthly* and designed her entire valedictory around women's need for scientific education, Jane uttered no public rebuke to the masculine scientific community for declaring women incapable of scientific work.

There was diplomacy at work here, to be sure, and a temperamental commitment to harmony and compromise. Her life with John Addams, Anna Haldeman Addams, and Anna Peck Sill had taught Jane that rewards were most likely to flow to those who nobly took the high road, not those who argued and accused. Jane's homegrown identification with her father, a man with public authority, and her difference from a stepmother, who lacked the tools to "detect all self-deceit and fancy in herself," enhanced these lessons. At the root of Jane Addams's claim to optimism about women's opportunities, however, lay the highly idealistic belief that those individuals, female or male, who possessed the intuitive spark of greatness could, with diligent effort and sincere purpose, gain *auethoritas*. This optimism coexisted with a good measure of youthful apprehension. But considered on its own, it looks like the smug fantasy of a privileged daughter of America's steward class whose school essays imagined leadership as a "latent force which could make itself felt without any visible means and could command respect from all mankind."[8] In her most romantic moments, and the valedictory address was certainly one of those moments, Jane Addams dreamt that she could bend gender rules and become a female hero without having to risk public scorn by ever appearing undignified, combative, or, heaven forbid, "over-oratorical."[9]

Speaking before the Rockford commencement audience on that "cool and pleasant" June day in 1881, Jane was a poised and dignified, albeit exhausted, young woman.[10] With her small frame dressed up in a new blue silk dress and her brown hair arranged, as always, in a small bun, Jane likely projected a rather charming mix of pride and humility, arrogance and self-doubt. In this, she was not so different from generations of American college graduates, though Jane was hardly typical in either her talents or her ambitions.

Before she stood up to deliver her "Cassandra" speech, fifteen other graduating seniors presented their essays in what the seminary magazine described as "the ordeal of a long programme."[11] Evident among these essays were many of Jane's ideals, though not her intellectual dexterity. Addie Smith criticized worship of heroes from the past and called upon her classmates to be heroes in the future; Kate Huey echoed Jane's notion that "every man has a vague belief in his destiny . . . [and] knows there is one thing he is capable of doing . . . which will command the respect and admiration of mankind." Annie Ellers argued that "we must be self-made," and this act of creation required great will; "without the will, no matter what the ability and genius of a person, he can never accomplish what he attempts." Phila Pope reminded her listeners that individuals with will and ability were to follow "wherever duty points the way . . . out into a world of noble deeds to be done." And Jane's good friend Helen Harrington chimed in with the claim that "happiness comes from . . . broad benevolence and helpfulness and charity." Other graduates spoke on topics ranging from free trade and the evils of monopoly to George Sand, George Eliot, and the beauty of the novel. None in this class of girls, who had begun at Rockford by swearing off missionary work, used her speech to testify to the importance of Christian faith.[12]

Just one other Rockford graduate that year spoke specifically about the Woman Question. Kate Tanner, not a member of Jane's circle of school chums, took a position that put her much closer to Miss Sill than to Jane Addams. Tanner asserted that "to be the center, the heart, the predicting and inspiring genius of such an institution as home" was a "high estate," one "worthy of the ambition of the most gifted and cultured woman in the world." She then warned that when a woman "neglects her own best interests in the home in order to reform the world and when political ambition leads her into worldly strife, she then is no more a lady and 'Bread Giver.'"[13]

All of the other graduates' admonitions—to fulfill destiny, to be self-made, to follow duty, to gain respect, to engage in benevolence—all of those charges could be fit into Kate Tanner's private, domestic version of womanhood. Even Jane Addams's "Bread Givers" speech, delivered the year before, had allowed for the possibility that those classmates who, "through some turn of fortune," were "confined" to the domestic sphere might still provide useful service to the world.[14]

Only Jane's "Cassandra" speech declared a domestic life insufficient; only her speech openly insisted on a more public, political life for the modern woman. This risky message was, again, gloved in a critique of women's insularity, not men's hostility. "Let her not sit and dreamily watch her child," chided Jane, "let her work her way to a sentient idea . . . to convert this wasted force to the highest use." It was silly, she argued, for a woman to imagine that "her child's every footstep is tenderly protected by a guardian angel." Instead, woman's intuitive mind needed to stiffen itself "with the strong passion of science and study." This, "more . . . than love" would make a woman "self-dependent" and "confident in errorless purpose." Having thus gained "accuracy," the intuitive female would be prepared for a public life in which she could "bring this force to bear throughout morals and justice."[15]

The word "justice" did not appear often in Jane Addams's writings at Rockford, so it is notable that Addams used "justice" several times in "Cassandra," especially in the few lines at the end of the speech which linked women's scientific training to the actual purpose of women's public role. The social benefit of expanding women's education, promised Jane, was that women would shift their sights from the personal to the political, from the private to the public. With scientific training, a woman's "sympathies" would be "so enlarged that she can weep as easily over a famine in India as a pale child at her door, then she can face social ills and social problems as tenderly and as intuitively as she can now care for and understand a crippled factory child."[16]

Such a brief comment about "social ills and social problems," amid a lengthy argument about scientific and intuitive forms of knowledge, is a reminder of Jane's evolution on the matter of "enlarged sympathies." Two years earlier, she had worried in a letter to Eva Campbell that she was "doomed to self-culture" because she found it "easier to pray for a million South Africans than for one."[17] By the time of her commencement, Jane had decided that this bent toward the impersonal was not so regrettable; she did not need the Christian's devotion to individual salvation in order to take on the mantle of steward. What she needed was the training and the character of a hero. Jane's youthful ambition to enlarge her sympathies was not fueled by any particular concern over individuals' suffering or social injustices; it was internally driven by a desire for *auethoritas*.[18]

Given her extravagant ideals, Jane Addams's seminary plan to gain public authority by becoming a physician looks quite pedestrian.[19] In fact, no idealism ever attached to this career plan. In all the romantic pages Jane wrote at Rockford about destiny, greatness, heroism, and creative genius, there is no surviving word about the heroism of the physician or the creativity of medicine. Still, the decision to become a doctor made sense. Notions of feminine intuition, and propriety, had created a small but respectable niche for female physicians in America (one that female lawyers, with their pretensions to logic, did not enjoy). A medical career was not as lofty a goal as George Haldeman's intention to become a research scientist, but it promised Jane equal standing in the family alongside Alice's husband, Dr. Harry Haldeman. Moreover, it accorded with Sarah Anderson's view that "at this stage in the woman question, one does the most good who does the most work in one of the professions . . . and yet maintains her true womanly way of helpfulness."[20] Though never excited about becoming a doctor, Jane may have persuaded herself that the female physician was the perfect, modern embodiment of the ancient goddess: respected, self-possessed, unsentimental, and able to provide tangible nurturance by using science.

The "Cassandra" argument for combining scientific training with feminine intuition might have been Jane's appeal to John and Anna Addams to continue her education beyond seminary, first by taking science classes and earning a bachelor's degree at Smith College, then by attending medical school. But there is no indication that an appeal was necessary, no indication that John and Anna in any way opposed Jane's postgraduate plans. In late April, two months before commencement, Jane spent her spring vacation at home in Cedarville and returned "refreshed and invigorated." After requesting from George a particular book she needed to aid her (persistent) preparations for the Smith geometry exam, Jane reported that her recent stay in Cedarville had afforded her "altogether . . . the most satisfactory visit of this year, I am not so cross and unsettled as I was during the winter I am thankful to say."[21] These are hardly the words of a daughter who was at odds with her parents, though they do suggest that she was experiencing normal anxieties about her future as commencement neared. During her "cross and unsettled" winter, she had declined Ellen Starr's invitation to spend spring vacation in Chicago on the grounds that she had to study for the Smith exams, and she had told her father in late March that she was beginning to feel "the hopes and fears of the 'last half' of the last term" that "one always finds a great deal [about] in books."[22] But spring vacation at home had settled her worries, not increased them, and Jane had returned to campus with renewed zeal to finalize her preparations for the entrance examination at Smith. The melodramatic theory that Jane

Addams's health broke down after commencement because her father, again, barred the door to Smith College ignores this record.[23]

It was the weeks at Rockford between spring vacation and commencement that left Jane in a state of complete exhaustion. Back in April, she had bragged to George that her restful stay in Cedarville had made her "quite equal to the eight weeks yet to come."[24] Just a month later she confessed to George that she was feeling "tired and rather worn out," but insisted that she still intended to "do all I can and go everywhere I can from now until Commencement and see if I can maintain respectable health and spirits."[25] She did not maintain "respectable health," but Jane certainly did everything and went everywhere she could that spring. In addition to completing her regular coursework, she wrote her "Cassandra" essay, edited the final issues of the campus magazine, studied for Smith's entrance exams, negotiated with her classmates over the commencement ceremony itself, and took her overnight trip to the Interstate Oratorical Contest in Jacksonville. It was during these same intense weeks in May and June 1881 that Miss Sill informed Jane that she would, indeed, be valedictorian and then utterly confounded Jane by inviting her to be the first Rockford student to receive the B.A. degree.

Jane's reaction to both the valedictory honor and the B.A. offer revealed her fear that her Rockford education was paltry preparation for realizing her ambitions. On the day she was officially told she would be class valedictorian, she wrote three letters—to Alice, George, and Pa—and in all three she hastened to assure her relatives that she was not "puffed up" about the distinction. To Alice, she insisted that she knew well "that it is but a transitory and vain honor," and to George she claimed that "it was never a passionate ambition . . . in strict, it appears of less consequence to me now than it ever did." She told George that she planned to "disclose" the news on an upcoming visit to Cedarville, but she could not resist announcing the honor to Pa, that same day, while writing to apologize for making the Jacksonville trip without his prior approval. In a well-placed postscript, she noted that the class valedictorian "is Your most humble servant and loving daughter." Then quickly added, "do not think I am puffed up. I too well realize how little it is worth or signifies. The only ground of satisfaction is that I hope the home folks will be pleased."[26]

There is the obvious element of feminine performance in these elaborate denials of pride and assertions of humility. Still, Jane's frequent expressions of concern about her preparation for Smith and her later criticisms of Rockford make clear that she really did not believe that success at Miss Sill's seminary counted for much. As a seminary student, she took four years of Latin and "natural science," two years of German, a year of civil government, a year of American literature, and the requisite four years of Bible history. Jane also took a year of rhetoric, four years of mathematics, four years of English history and literature, and a required, senior-year course with Miss Sill in Mental and Moral Philosophy.[27] Finally, she took her special tutorials in geometry, calculus, and Greek. She completed the course of study with a perfect 10 in deportment and a 9.86 in academics. Yet when Miss Sill offered her Rockford's first bachelor of arts degree, Jane told George that the whole idea made her uncomfortable because she knew "better than anyone else how little my scholarship is worth."[28]

Miss Sill's offer of the B.A. degree may have discomfited Jane, but it was, for Sill, a logical step in her longstanding campaign to win collegiate status for Rockford. Sill had been pressing for such status ever since the school's original charter in 1847 empowered the trustees to award bachelor's degrees, and she stepped up the campaign in the 1870s when she found herself increasingly competing with public high schools and eastern women's colleges. Shortly before Jane Addams's arrival on campus, Sill had watched some of her best students transfer to schools like Vassar.[29] Jane Addams's career at Rockford gave Sill an opportunity to convince the board of trustees that her school had, in fact, become a college. The Junior Exhibition, the oratorical contests, the exchanges with Eastern schools all supported her claim, but most important—and most ironic—was the fact that Rockford had been able to provide Jane Addams with the extra coursework she sought in order to enter Smith College. In the spring before Jane's graduation, Rockford's board agreed that the school was ready to add a fifth year to its program and, at the end of that fifth year, students could receive the baccalaureate degree. As Jane explained the situation to George, she already had the equivalent of an extra year of coursework, so Sill wanted her to accept the degree the following spring, at the first moment the school could offer it, in order to "bring forth the rank of the institution and incite other girls to try for it."[30]

The only problem was that Jane was not so sure she wanted a bachelor's degree from Rockford—or from Miss Sill. Confused by the offer, she wrote to George, swearing her childhood confidante to "eternal *secrecy*" on this "important" matter and asking for his "most mature and deliberate opinion" on the pros and cons of accepting the Rockford B.A. On the one hand, there was her worthless scholarship and the fact that it would be "awfully absurd" to have a Rockford B.A. "if I ever do take a degree at Smith." On the other hand, Jane knew that her classmates would want her to accept the offer; "it is natural to want to be the first class" with a bachelor of arts among its graduates. Finally, and not insignificantly, she thought the Rockford degree "would rather please Pa."[31]

Jane told George that she had already refused Sill's offer, but she had time to hear his thoughts and reopen the discussion.[32] George's opinions on the matter have not survived, but Jane made no firm commitments that spring. She agreed to write a letter to the board of trustees expressing her interest in the Rockford B.A.[33] She also included in her valedictory address a specific reminder that the seminary had possessed a college charter since its inception, and she encouraged the "wise" board of trustees to recognize Rockford's collegiate identity.[34] In this way, Jane supported Sill's campaign to have the bachelor's degree granted in the spring of 1882 to a member of the class of 1881 yet kept her own options open. After all, Jane had not yet taken the Smith College entrance exam, she harbored doubts about whether she would be accepted to the Eastern school or, once in, whether she could to earn a degree there, and she knew that she had nothing to lose by maintaining her degree candidacy at Rockford. She did not give Sill the satisfaction of enthusiastically embracing the B.A. offer, nor did she flatly reject it either.

In her autobiographical account of Rockford's adoption of the B.A. degree, Jane Addams completely erased Sill's agency from the record. Addams claimed that it was she and her classmates who "gravely decided" that collegiate status for Rockford ought to be their "driving ambition." The tale she constructed eliminated her preparations for the Smith College exam claiming, instead, that she and a classmate "took a course in mathematics, advanced beyond anything previously given in the school" with the conscious intention of earning B.A. degrees from Rockford.[35] Addams even claimed that the B.A. she received from Rockford, a year following her graduation, was a degree she and her classmates had "eagerly anticipated."[36]

Given the fact that Jane Addams's adult style was to bend magnanimously toward her enemies, this distorting erasure of Sill from the record is a stunning testimony to Addams's enduring resentment of Rockford's headmistress. It was not just that Addams banished Sill from the bachelor of arts story; she never once mentioned Sill's name in her chapter on Rockford, never acknowledged Sill's role in staging the Junior Exhibition or sending Addams to Jacksonville, and never paused to notice that the rigidly pious Miss Sill looked the other way when Jane studied through evening devotionals and allowed Jane to take a tutorial in the Greek New Testament instead of attending Sunday services.[37]

Addams was not alone in her anger at Sill. Five years after her graduation from the seminary, Helen Harrington reported on the tone of Rockford commencements under a fresh, young administration. The new headmistress offered "cheerful" words and created "a spirit of whole-hearted sincerity that we so sadly felt the want of." The graduates in 1886, said Harrington, heard "the message we waited for and did not receive."[38] This sense, encouraged by others, that Miss Sill's Rockford had withheld a vital life force from its young women fueled Jane Addams's bitterness toward her experience there and shaped all her memories of it. In 1897, sixteen years after her graduation, Addams uneasily acknowledged an invitation to include her name on an honor roll of America's college women. She was "afraid" that the college she attended "is such a humble one that I have no right to be on a list of representative college women." Addams assured the committee organizing the honor roll that it should "feel no embarrassment in case it seems wise to . . . substitute some other name in place of mine."[39]

The Rockford chapter in Addams's 1910 autobiography is a study in conscious and unconscious reconstruction. Titled rather disdainfully "Boarding School Ideals," it conveys in numerous ways Addams's contempt for Miss Sill's institution and for the girl she was there.[40] At the same time, the chapter performed an important function in Addams's self-presentation to the American public when she was forty years old and famous. It served Addams's adult purpose to capture on the page the sophomoric swagger and adolescent earnestness evident in her school papers and letters. But Addams's autobiographical agenda then collided with her self-protective memory and knocked the whole picture askew.

In *Twenty Years at Hull-House*, Addams presented her seminary self as far more democratic, and far more superficial, than she actually was at the time. She made herself appear ideologically progressive and socially girlish in ways that she had not been. Just as her autobiographical rendition of her childhood in Cedarville stripped away most of the interesting complexities in favor of narrative simplicity, political persuasion, and personal privacy, so, too, Addams's depiction of her college self was rather more charming, and evasive, than accurate. The elimination of Sill from the story was just one of many editorial devices.

The autobiography's seminary chapter depicted Jane as an equal member of a merry band of eager female intellectuals. In fact, she cast most of "Boarding School Ideals" in terms of "we" and described its writing as an "attempt to reconstruct the spirit of my contemporary group."[41] According to the picture Addams painted, Rockford's "ardent girls . . . discussed everything under the sun" and enjoyed intense interactions over books and ideas as well as good-natured competition for the academic limelight.[42] That image not only erased the fact that Jane's scholarly talent and spiritual angst sent her into the arms of Sarah Anderson and Ellen Gates Starr for companionship, it also ignored her history as a campus steward who scolded her classmates for reading "a good deal" of romantic "trash."[43] The autobiography claimed that Jane and her chums tackled tomes like Gibbon's *Decline and Fall of the Roman Empire* as their summer reading and then fell "upon each other with a sort of rough-and-tumble" examination when they regathered each autumn.[44] In fact, Jane had editorially chided her classmates for foolishly promising to read Gibbon over the summer, scolding those who could not honestly distinguish between their "present enthusiasm" and "what they can do when they are alone and self-dependent."[45] The girl Addams created in her autobiography did not wag such a reproving finger at her friends; rather, she skipped through great books alongside them.

To foster her sunny, collegial account, Addams told a humorous story about her participation in a dorm-room experiment with opium when she and four friends were reading Thomas DeQuincey, the British romantic who had described his opiate dreams. From there, she moved on to the equally humorous tale of her friends coaching her, "with brutal frankness," in preparation for the oratorical contest against William Jennings Bryan, on which rested the collective cause of "women's advancement." Finally, the chapter on seminary life claimed that the awarding of a B.A. degree at Rockford resulted from the students' scheming and dreaming.[46] While the veracity of her stories about the oratorical contest and the B.A. degree can easily be disproved, there is no surviving mention in any letter about a day of opium delusions in a seminary dorm room. There is an earnest essay on "The Poppy" in which Jane deviated from the assigned botany task in order to condemn opiate use, especially among Asians.[47] There is the record of Jane's distance from dormitory high jinks. And there is Jane's ego investment in her elevated status as the school's sober steward. Based on this persistent pattern of youthful rectitude, it seems far more likely that Jane scolded a clique of girls for experimenting with a bit of pilfered laudanum than that she actually joined in the opium experiment.[48]

The autobiography's endearing, if fictional, tales of a communal girlhood served the valuable purpose, in 1910, of making Jane Addams accessible to her readers and of suggesting that any coed could become a social reformer. They telegraphed that there was nothing unusual—or freakish—about Jane Addams. At the same time, these stories also made the young Jane Addams sound like a precocious version of her democratic adult self: tolerant of young people's interest in experimenting with drugs, willing to engage in public battle for women's rights, and ready to organize with others in reform efforts like the B.A. degree at Rockford. So even as she admitted in the autobiography that she was a girl of "serious not to say priggish tendency," she replaced the evidence of that priggishness with more appealing stories of a sociable schoolgirl who had intellectual pretensions.[49]

Readers of the autobiography met a naive scholar who looked at the world through "a rose-colored mist," full of "precious ideals" and "high purpose" but

15. Jane Addams with Rockford Seminary classmates. The fancy parasol Jane was given to hold only accentuated the difference in her style and demeanor. Seated are Helen Harrington, Phila Pope, Annie Sidwell, Ella Browning, and Mattie Thomas. In the back row are Nora Frothingham, Laura Ely, Kate Turner, and Jane Addams. (Rockford College Archives)

without any clue about how to translate her ideas into action.[50] This charming, if condescending, image of a young woman with her head in the clouds erased Jane's record of student leadership at seminary and ignored all signs that she knew quite well how to translate ideals into action. The essays, editorials, and letters that Addams reviewed in preparation for writing her memoir testify to her intense engagement with Ruskin and Browning, Emerson and Carlyle, Arnold and Goethe, but Addams made light of this part of her past. By writing that she and her classmates "must have found" the idea for the "Bread Givers" class motto "in a book somewhere," she did not simply ignore John Ruskin's influence on her life and thought, she made her Rockford self sound shallower and sillier than that girl had been.[51] The effect was to distance her adult self from the "absurdly inflexible" youth she saw etched in her own record.[52]

Twenty Years at Hull-House purported to tell a conversion story by tracing Jane's development from callow scholar to seasoned reformer. In constructing that story, Addams chose to edit out the real ideological conversion she underwent, in the decade after leaving Rockford, from Carlyle's ethic of heroic stewardship to an ethic of democratic humanitarianism. Addams avoided that history by simply covering up her devotion to Carlyle's decidedly undemocratic belief in the heroic leader. She claimed that she was only fifteen when she put aside Carlyle's *Heroes and Hero Worship*, having been inspired to a more democratic vision by the "public spirited" story of her pioneer neighbors pooling their resources to bring in the railroad.[53] By dismissing Carlyle so early from her story, Addams expunged the record of her seminary flirtation with elitist heroics and distorted the nature of her postgraduate struggle to fashion new ideals.

Had she chosen to, Addams could have quoted from several of her own seminary essays to show that she had once sincerely subscribed to Carlyle's notion that poor people needed the inspiration of truth and nobility more than they needed material goods. "Bread," wrote Jane at age nineteen, in the aftermath of the Paris Commune and the 1877 American railway strike, "is but the nominal object" of the "occasional uprising of the lowest dregs of society." Even if bread were provided, "they would still be unsatisfied," because what society's "followers" really longed for was a heroic faith that could lift them "above the commonplace."[54] A year before writing that essay, the young Jane Addams had inveighed against "Tramps" who roamed the countryside "expecting to be helped" without engaging in hard labor. In her future life, Addams would criticize philanthropists and would champion the rights of workers to strike, but as an idealistic young steward at Rockford she praised the "benevolent gentleman" who gave to the needy and described the unemployed who wandered the land asking for help as violators of "the laws of nature."[55]

Addams also could have shown that, as an adolescent, she resolved her concern over inequitable distributions of wealth by calling for wise, more heroic leaders who would restore responsible paternal relations with the "common people."[56] In 1881, she was "startled" by the assassination of Czar Alexander II because she expected "gratitude rather than barbarity" toward a leader who, she said, had done so much for his people. Jane Addams would later befriend countless Russian revolutionaries, but as a senior at Rockford, she could not understand the goals of "half-crazed fanatics trying to reform they know not what."[57]

Addams correctly recalled her interest in history while at Rockford, but she skipped over her youthful conviction that nations were best served when led by "a class of men wise and brave enough to impose their will on that of the people." She concluded from her Rockford studies of European and American history that it was ideal to establish a "hierarchy of the best and ablest" and create a "government to which all could loyally surrender themselves and in it find their welfare." Indeed, wrote John Addams's Republican daughter just three years after President Hayes removed the federal troops from the South, "we too often see an American statesman losing slowly his ideal in trying to please the people." But "the mass," argued Jane, in an echo of Carlyle, "are too often tainted with ignorance, prejudice, and passion." The "deepest convictions of a nation," had to be impressed upon the people "by their great men," not the other way around.[58] All of this from the pen of a young woman who would grow up to declare that "the cure for the ills of Democracy is more Democracy."[59]

In similar ways, the autobiography elided Jane's religious experience at Rockford, describing herself as simply "aloof" from the seminary's "evangelical appeal," and suggesting that her father and Ralph Waldo Emerson provided her with the armor of "rationalism" to fend off Christian dogma. Jane's appeal to intuition in the "Cassandra" speech was admitted, but her desperate desire for *auethoritas* vanished in her breezy dismissal of the speech as suffering from excessive "veneration of science." And, of course, nowhere in *Twenty Years at Hull-House* did she admit her readers into the deeper recesses of her adolescent fantasies about primal goddesses or bold, intuitive heroes.[60]

There are several plausible, and mutually reinforcing, explanations for Jane Addams's autobiographical construction of her Rockford self. There is the obvious need to persuade readers of the worthiness of her reform cause by convincing them that her nontraditional life was attractive, not eccentric. There is, as well, Addams's tendency as a writer to craft engaging narratives that sound personal but are actually less interested in self-revelation than in inspiring readers' commitment to social action. So even though a central theme in *Twenty Years at Hull-House* is that the reformer is ever in need of reform, and even though Addams openly critiqued her adult naivete about poverty, immigration, and politics, she still refrained from exploring the real depths of her seminary elitism. Instead, she created a picture of a happy, egalitarian collective of female scholars, one that evoked the settlement-house world her autobiography was intended to publicize.

When Addams published *Twenty Years at Hull-House* in 1910, she was already America's most famous reformer and most influential woman, which means she was already pushing political and gender boundaries. It is hardly surprising that she eliminated from her story those elements which could be construed as too masculine: her success as a steward at Rockford, for example, or her ambitious dream of individual heroic greatness. Nor, from a purely public relations standpoint, is it surprising that Addams declined to write a chapter on "Carlyle's Influence." Carlyle was greatly out of favor with the American public by 1910. It makes sense that she chose to write, instead, a chapter on "Lincoln's Influence," even though in her surviving college writings Lincoln is never mentioned. Lincoln had become an important figure for Addams in adulthood and in 1909, the year of Lincoln's centennial, he was a beloved (and much written about) symbol of both American patriotism and progressive reform.[61] Moreover, Lincoln could be politically linked to Addams's father, much as Emerson could be religiously linked to Pa. In both cases, Addams was able to use respected men to legitimize her own views. An autobiographical chapter on "Lincoln's Influence," placed immediately before her chapter on Rockford Seminary, allowed Addams to suggest that her democratic reform impulses were rooted in childhood and were inspired by two unassailable patriarchs, her Pa and Abe Lincoln.

Added to these politically pragmatic reasons for constructing the autobiography's treatment of Rockford as she did, there were important emotional reasons. Addams displayed, throughout her life, an inclination to step around those personal memories that were genuinely painful and move on to higher ground. In this case, there is the biographical fact that Addams's schoolgirl faith in her own heroic destiny set her up for disappointment and disillusionment in the years following graduation from Rockford. Looking back on that priggish valedictorian, Jane Addams saw a girl suffering from "sublime self-conceit" and "over-much conviction" and was moved to mock, if not erase, her memory.[62]

Several years after writing *Twenty Years at Hull-House*, Jane Addams commented on "that mysterious autobiographical impulse which makes it more difficult to conceal the truth than to avow it." Indeed, said Addams, there was always "the insistence of Memory upon the great essentials."[63] The fictions Addams fashioned for "Boarding School Ideals" and her dismissive tone of voice in the chapter ultimately revealed some essential truths about her Rockford experience and her memories of her Rockford self. They certainly revealed her abiding anger at Anna Peck Sill and at cloistered campuses that failed to prepare young people, especially young women, for real work in real life. Addams blamed Rockford's isolation and Miss Sill—as much as she blamed heroic individualism and Thomas Carlyle—for making her so "puffed up" that when she confronted real life she sank into self-doubt.

In the end, however, Addams displayed an uncharacteristic lack of charity toward her own youthful self in "Boarding School Ideals." A dismissive tone informs the chapter's recoil from her seminary fears, her gender conflicts, and her spiritual angst, and she demonstrated an unwillingness to explore or explain the ideology of heroism beneath her adolescent bravado. There were choices, conscious and not, in all of this. The "insistence of Memory upon the great essentials" evidently persuaded Addams to leave aside the earnest, questing, ambitious young woman of Rockford fame and mount a some-what patronizing portrait of her arrogant young self. Perhaps that girl was Addams's most striking evidence of the damage wrought by educators like Miss Sill. Perhaps she was the girl Addams remembered most clearly.

At the close of "Boarding School Ideals," Addams wrote that she and her classmates left Rockford thinking that the "difficulty in life would lie solely in the direction of losing these precious ideals of ours. . . . We had no notion of the obscure paths of tolerance, just allowance, and self-blame wherein, if we held our minds open, we might learn something of the mystery and complexity of life's purposes."[64] This was true of the young Jane Addams who graduated as valedictorian of her class in June 1881, but it was not the entire truth. In the magazine editorial she published in May of that commencement year, Addams revealed her fear that "these precious ideals" she had acquired from four years of study were not actually worth much. It was an indirect, impersonal revelation, to be sure. As a campus steward Jane Addams was no more self-revealing than she was as an autobiographer. But in a remarkably prescient public comment, made all the more interesting by the fact that she had originally included it in her "Darkness vs. Nebulae" essay, Addams looked ahead to a chilling future:

We remember Emerson's description of brilliant and talented young men who, during their college course, promise such great things, so impress one with their force and enthusiasm that their friends think they must win high honors in the world, become great and influential; but they always dodge the account, die young or become lost in the crowd. The reason of this disappointment is that they show a brilliancy not their own . . . but drawn from other sources; when these sources are removed their spirits flag, and they fail, for they possess not individual silent resources.[65]

Did the young Jane Addams comfort herself with the thought that her female intuition, the "fostering mother," would protect her from this sorry fate? If so, the older Jane Addams, looking back on that girl, could only shudder at her adolescent conceit.

Chapter 7
Claims So Keenly Felt

In the summer of 1901, exactly twenty years after graduating from Rockford Female Seminary, Jane Addams spoke to the Intercollegiate Alumnae Association about the Christian college woman's social responsibility. In that speech, she bluntly defined two key errors in her own postgraduate thinking: she had timidly thought that she needed more preparation before she could take any action in the world, and she had arrogantly thought that she was so special that any action she took would have to set an example for others. Looking back, Addams used criticism of her postgraduate self to chastise other Christian college women—including many sitting in her audience—for being such "moral prigs" that they postponed engagement in real life.[1]

This harsh self-assessment, while successful as a rhetorical ploy, was incomplete in its rendering of Jane Addams's own experience. It omitted the profoundly gendered demands of the postgraduate "family claim," which Addams would write about so insightfully in other contexts; it implied that Jane was more comfortably identified as a Christian at the time of graduation than was the case; and it suggested that, shorn of snobbish self-indulgence, she would have known what action to take in the world—an untestable but unlikely proposition. Graduation from Rockford had not solved Jane Addams's persistent dilemma: how to be an unconverted female with authority in American society? How to be a respected and respectable single woman with engrossing, satisfying work who could assert her authority with a fluid mix of Christian values, scientific principles, and spiritual intuition while fulfilling her family obligations and her friends' expectations? This dilemma was not caused by Jane's timidity or her arrogance. But she was right in recalling that she had to outgrow both tendencies before she would make any progress toward a living a resolute, vigorous life.

The months immediately following Rockford's graduation ceremony did not mark an auspicious beginning to Jane's journey. Her choice to "do all I can" in the weeks before commencement had sapped her energies and ignited a recurrent pain in what Sarah Anderson called Jane's "miserable back."[2] During the summer, at least one school friend wrote to inquire if Jane's health was "any better than when you left Rockford."[3] And in the subsequent months, other friends and former teachers scolded an ailing Addams for her "old habit of working altogether too hard," and credited her loss of "physical vigor" to the way she taxed her strength "both in study and in doing for others."[4] Jane had worked herself to such a frazzle in trying to prepare for the Smith College exams that she wound up with neither the physical strength nor emotional will to test herself in that daunting arena. Given a restful summer, she might have felt able to face Smith and its entrance exams in the fall, but there was to be no rest in the summer of 1881.

Ten days after the Rockford commencement, President James A. Garfield was shot in the back by Charles Guiteau. The assassin was the deranged son of Luther Guiteau, a long-time employee at Senator Addams's Second National Bank of Freeport. Up until his death a year earlier, Luther had been a devoted follower of John Humphrey Noyes's strict doctrine of perfectionism, which Noyes had unsuccessfully enacted at his Oneida community in New York. Now, in the hands of Luther's maniacal son, this zealotry had erupted into a dramatic act of public violence that offered an attentive young witness like Jane Addams some lasting lessons on the dangers of fanaticism.[5]

Seeking to shed the "odium" brought upon their community by the assassin Guiteau, Senator John Addams and ten other leading citizens of Freeport sent a formal message of condolence to Secretary of State James G. Blaine in the week after the shooting. At the same time, Freeport's leaders extended the community's sympathies to the family of the late Luther Guiteau, "whose standing in this city is second to none."[6] Included in the unfortunate Guiteau family was Flora Guiteau, Luther's daughter by his second wife, the assassin's stepsister, and Jane Addams's childhood friend. Jane's sympathetic attention to Flora in the years to come suggests that she was deeply affected by seeing the emotional devastation left in the wake of a calamity over which her friend had no control.[7] The whole upsetting episode only heightened Jane's exhaustion and spinal irritation.

It did not take long for word to reach Addams's seminary friends that their valedictorian's compromised health would prevent her from attending Smith College in the fall. "I am sorry for your disappointment about Smith's," wrote Ellen Starr, who was herself under a doctor's care for "nervous prostration caused partly by overwork." Starr was having to "admit it is a smash up," and friends urged Jane to confess to a similar condition.[8] "I know how you must beg off and say you . . . have not overworked," chided Nora Frothingham, but she hoped those charged with caring for Jane "will not believe you or let you alone," and Helen Harrington hoped Jane would "adopt the wise plan of resting for one year."[9] Even Sarah Anderson and Sarah Blaisdell, the two teachers at Rockford who had most supported Jane's ambition to attend Smith, counseled a hiatus from study: "You know I want you to go to Smith," wrote Anderson, "but not next year, Jane."[10] Jane's stepmother could only have echoed these sentiments; she viewed George's "steady delve into books-books-books" as "enough to sap all strength physically and take all the nerve force out of one."[11] Indeed, the fact that George entered Beloit College at the same time Jane entered Rockford, but graduated two years after Jane left Rockford, suggests that Anna's youngest son shared his mother's belief in regular recesses from study.

Disappointing as it must have been, there was nothing remarkable, in 1881, about Jane Addams's decision to postpone Smith College for health reasons. As an educated woman from a family that embraced modern scientific theory as an enlightened expression of God's wisdom, Jane was steeped in popular assumptions about the body's "nerve force" and its relative "vitality." She postponed Smith at a time when Americans in her social position were commonly diagnosed as "neurasthenic," a protean label for a long list of symptoms that could all be traced back to "nervous exhaustion." In the eyes of the neurologists who studied neurasthenia and published widely on the subject, Jane Addams's back pain was just one of many possible manifestations of fundamental somatic weakness in her physiological "nerve force." While neurologists conceded that mental disturbance and vicious habits could contribute to neurasthenia, they insisted that this was a physical ailment, not a psychological problem, and had to be cured through physical means: rest, food, regimented exercise, and the occasional surgical intervention.[12] In response to Ellen Starr's "smash up," Jane prescribed doses of malt and desiccated blood: "I know they will help build you up," she wrote in the health language of the day, "for I have wilted, tried them, and revived."[13]

Neurologists at the time did believe that female reproductive physiology, the demands of menstruation, pregnancy, and parturition, made women more vulnerable to neurasthenia, but this disease was by no means confined to women. It was, instead, called "the American disease" because experts believed that the industrialization, urbanization, and fast-paced civilization that had emerged since the Civil War placed a special tax on those Americans in the "brain-working class." The ironic assumption operating here was that the advanced evolutionary status of white, educated Americans endowed them with a valuable but vulnerable physiology. Their nerve force was simultaneously possessed of the intellectual genius to create American progress and the delicacy to be destroyed by it.[14] When Jane Addams's friends charged her with overwork, they were at once scolding her and admiring her. To them, her breakdown signaled her advancement as an intensely engaged "brain worker."

To her, it proved that she was far from her collegiate ideal of the "calm" and "peaceful" goddess standing aloof from this "age of . . . intensive living."[15]

As part of the standard, recommended cure for her condition, Jane went on vacation in August 1881, traveling with her father, her stepmother, and George to the Upper Peninsula of Michigan. At fifty-nine years old, John Addams seemed to be "a perfect specimen of physical vigor," showing no signs of ill health when he left Illinois in mid-August in the company of his ever delicate wife, ailing daughter, and oversensitive stepson.[16] But while climbing around a copper mine in Marquette, Michigan, Senator Addams reportedly "over-exerted" himself—put too much strain on his vital force—and collapsed. He was rushed 150 miles south to a hospital in Green Bay but died within thirty-six hours of acute appendicitis. As the *Freeport Weekly Journal* put it, "The brittle thread was sundered and the spark of life went out. . . . A good man has gone from among us."[17]

Jane wrote to Ellen at the time, "the greatest sorrow that can ever come to me has passed." In a poignant, private recollection some forty years later, Jane Addams observed that "the loss of my father changed the world for me for so many years."[18]

The minister at her father's funeral asked the mourners, "Upon whom shall his mantle fall? Who is there to take up this controlling principle of his life and embody it in their character and follow it as he did?" No one gathered in the yard outside the Addams's home that day for the county's largest-ever funeral would have looked to Senator Addams's grieving youngest daughter as the answer to the minister's question. But Jane might have read the letter that Rev. John Linn, her brother-in-law, wrote to her at the time as a testament to her capacity for taking up her father's mantle.[19]

In his extraordinary letter of condolence, Rev. Linn not only assured Jane that "your life aims were high enough and your plans broad enough" to provide Senator Addams with "delight" in preparing his daughter for her "mission." He went on to advise that Jane draw upon her memory of her father as a "foundation of joy and an incentive to work. You need not think," Linn added, "that because he is gone your incentive has perished." On the contrary, insisted this conservative Presbyterian minister, Jane could always rely on her father's approval to serve as her inspiration. "Your life work is before you," Linn promised. "His ideal and yours is to be reached. He did not desire you to live for him but for the world, for humanity."[20]

Jane wanted to believe that she could carry on the "permanence" of her father's "excellence." In addition to writing private tributes to the undying value of her father's civic record, she arranged to publish others' public tributes.[21] But in truth, as she told Ellen Starr, she felt "purposeless and without ambition."[22] However cheered she was by her brother-in-law's words, the fact remained that Jane's most powerful sponsor, if not her "incentive," had perished.

During what Addams later called the "black days" following her father's death, friends tried to comfort her, recalling simple things like the "happy, contented smile on his face as he talked of you." Ellen Starr assured Jane that she well knew "how large a part of your heart your father filled." Maria Nutting knew, too, how much Jane relied on her father's approval. Years later, she recalled meeting the Senator in Jane's room at Rockford "and having imbibed something of *your* ideas of him, how I drank in every word that fell from his lips!" Emma Briggs, a Rockford classmate, observed that Jane should be "glad ever to have had such a father . . . to have the memory of such a father." For while others had to "always be excusing" their father's "faults," thought Briggs, Jane had only "to glory in the good." As an endorsement of that view, Jane replied with the "kindest" letter Briggs had "ever received."[23]

Sarah Blaisdell, Jane's elderly Greek tutor at Rockford, also encouraged Jane to revel in the "wealth" her father "put into your own character." Blaisdell recognized that the death of Jane's father removed her "wall of defense," leaving her alone to "meet the responsibilities of life" as "her own person." But Blaisdell, a pious Christian, echoed Rev. Linn's view that Jane should draw upon her "recollection" of what her father "was and what his counsel would be if present to be consulted in the times when you feel the need of his counsel." Blaisdell felt "certain" that if Jane kept hold of her father's "high Christian principles" that "wisdom and strength will be furnished according to your need." She then added, at the close of this tribute to Jane's father and his abiding counsel, that she very much hoped that Jane would still be attending Smith College. Apparently, Rockford's Greek tutor had no reason to believe that Jane's attendance at Smith would contradict Senator Addams's wise wishes.[24]

During this time of intense grief, the ministers in Jane Addams's life counseled embrace of eternal life by accepting Christ as her personal savior; indeed, John Linn promised her "a much better" place in Heaven "because your life will be associated with such a father."[25] But Jane took no solace in Christianity at this time. Her life might have been easier, more peaceful, if she had been able to make a leap of faith, but she was not. Her father's legacy did not include the capacity to embrace the supernatural. Stricken by this rational man's sudden death, the young Jane Addams was left to draw comfort from her Pa's faith in the enduring value of labor. Sadly, that death greatly complicated Jane's efforts to define such labor for herself.

Before Senator Addams's death, Jane had been the daughter designated to spend time with him in his study, the one who discussed politics and religion with him, the one who, said Rev. Linn, gave her father "delight" with her "high aims."[26] After Pa's death, Jane's world, as she later observed, changed completely—and for many years. Her primary obligation now was to her stepmother. Anna was a woman who thought fondly of Jane, when she thought of her at all, as her "little housekeeper" and her "little student."[27] No longer John Addams's designated daughter, she was now expected to be Anna's dutiful daughter. With George still in school and all the other siblings married, it fell to Jane to serve as Anna's companion and to cheer her twice-widowed "Ma" out of her bleak ruminations on the "constantly foreboding sorrows that have filled my life."[28]

Before she went away to Rockford Seminary, Jane had served the Addams-Haldeman household as the accommodating youngest daughter. Her father's death thrust her back into that role. Four years spent honing an identity as a formidable seminary steward vanished, and no one in the family, with the possible exception of John Linn, even noticed. When Addams later described this abrupt transformation from college woman to dutiful daughter, in a depersonalized essay, she chose to emphasize the hidden, unspoken, repressed quality of the daughter's experience. There were no loud confrontations, no open debates; instead, the daughter's ambitions were rendered silent and invisible because the family had "absolutely no recognition" of any role for the daughter beyond the family role.[29]

Senator Addams died too soon after the Rockford commencement to allow for any certitude about how he might have influenced Jane Addams's postgraduate experience.[30] It was life as Anna's dutiful daughter that dominated Jane's recollections of her years following Rockford. In characterizing that life, Jane remembered that, for all the "tenderest affection," she was presumed to be a "family possession," and all possible paths leading away from the family went "wholly unrecognized."[31] Years later, Addams looked back with regret over not having been "better" or "wiser" in handling her father's death. But at the time she was mired in "such blackness" of grief and, at age twenty-one, she had few real choices in the situation, few ways to have been any wiser or any better.[32] Spinster daughters of Jane Addams's social class in 1881 were simply not free to leave their widowed mothers and strike out on their own—even if, as in Jane's case, the father left the daughter with the financial resources to do so.

The Senator never wrote a will, leaving it up to Illinois inheritance law, which he had helped draft, to divide Addams's impressive $350,000 estate. Anna received the standard widow's third of the estate, and John Addams's four biological children divided the rest. Senator Addams allowed the law to direct that nothing be left to either Harry or George. This meant Jane Addams ultimately came into ownership of a 250-acre farm, 60 acres of timberland, another 80 acres of land in the Dakotas, shares in the Second National Bank of Chicago and the Northern Pacific Railroad, along with $23,000 cash. A yearly income of 10 percent from this $60,000 inheritance promised Jane Addams an independent and comfortable life well into the next century.[33]

Jane was unable to make use of her economic independence because she faced other powerful constraints on her freedom. There was her own physical and psychological fragility, along with her moral obligation to her beloved father's needy widow. Jane allowed herself to be "quietly reabsorbed into her family" during this time of grief and illness because the pressing demands of her emotionally extravagant stepmother had cultural power; they were "concrete," they could be "definitely asserted." By contrast, a daughter's inchoate longings for individuality "as an integral part of the social order itself" carried no cultural legitimacy. Such longings, if expressed, could expose a daughter to charges of selfishness, ingratitude or, worse, unnaturalness.[34] That was certainly a concern in Jane Addams case; she could make no claim to a higher Christian calling and even the supportive Rev. Linn detected in his sister-in-law an unseemly desire for "praise" and "preeminence."[35] Addams's later self-criticism for timidly retreating into a self-indulgent "snare of preparation" overlooked the very strong web of cultural expectations that dictated her new role as a dutiful daughter.

Jane's enrollment in medical school in Philadelphia just weeks after Pa's death suggests that she was plowing ahead with her plan to become a physician. Addams did not remember it that way; indeed, she chose barely to remember it at all. The one semester she spent at the Woman's Medical College of Philadelphia earned one half of a sentence in her autobiography and was cast, uncharacteristically, in the passive voice.[36] It was not Jane's agency or her ambition that moved the family to Philadelphia that fall. The move was prompted by Anna's desire to escape Cedarville and Harry Haldeman's entrance into a postdoctoral surgery program at the University of Pennsylvania. Alice enrolled at the Woman's Medical College to prepare herself to serve as Harry's anesthetist.[37] Jane enrolled, alongside her sister, in lectures on anatomy and physiology and even took a course on dissection of the lower extremity.[38]

Despite her short stay at the medical school, Jane made an impression— at least on Dean Rachel Bodley, with whom Jane maintained a warm and affectionate relationship for several years.[39] But Jane was never committed to the endeavor. Even after she began classes in Philadelphia, Jane continued to tell friends that she would enroll at Smith College the following year, perhaps because she already knew that she was not cut out for a medical career.[40] George, for one, got the distinct impression that "dissecting was not the most interesting part of their studies," and in contrast to Jane's persistence in planning for

Smith, she never expressed the slightest interest in attending medical school after leaving Philadelphia in March 1882.[41]

Two lessons remained in Jane's memory from the Philadelphia experience: first, that trying to study when there were family members to attend to left her with an "uneasy consciousness." Second, that any attempt to divide her energies between family service and "selfish" studying was doomed to failure; "trying to fill too many objects at once" would only deplete her vital force.[42] In explaining her retreat from medical school, Addams's autobiography avoided (as it always did) the issue of family demands and emphasized the health issue by claiming both "a nervous affliction" and a "spinal difficulty."[43] Undoubtedly, the depleted energy and back pain that had plagued her since commencement and been exacerbated by her father's death factored into her departure from the Woman's Medical College; her former teacher, Sarah Blaisdell, responded to a letter from Jane by urging her to rest and "regain what you have lost of physical vigor."[44]

It is unlikely, however that Jane's condition in Philadelphia earned a full-scale treatment from Dr. S. Weir Mitchell, whose lengthy "rest cure" was vividly dramatized by Charlotte Perkins Gilman in *The Yellow Wallpaper* in 1899.[45] Though the autobiography claimed that she had entered Dr. Mitchell's hospital, it is much more likely that the hospital patient in this Philadelphia scenario was Anna, not Jane.[46] Whatever Jane's ailments that winter, she stayed in school until the end of the term in December. It was Anna who had an operation in February and Anna who had the "physicians of such rare skill, a professional nurse, and her own dear ones to notice her progress and anticipate every wish."[47] Writing to Jane from Beloit, George expressed great relief that Anna's health crisis had been resolved "so happily" and confidence that his mother's "restoration" would be "permanent."[48]

There is no doubt that Jane was in poor health while in Philadelphia, and possibly consulted with Dr. Mitchell, but her friends were more attentive to her situation than her family. The recuperative regimen that she pursued after finishing classes in December did allow her to write letters, but in those letters Jane complained of her boredom. In mid-January, Sarah Anderson encouraged her former pupil to "carry out your physician's instructions," but conceded that "one cannot lie abed nor sit with folded hands all day. . . . If you did everything everybody suggested you would surely kill yourself."[49]

Jane Addams's encounter with ill health in 1881 and 1882 lacks the elements of feminist melodrama that Gilman would later capture in *The Yellow Wallpaper*, but Jane's smash-up in Philadelphia was fraught with its own grave tensions. It introduced a persistent set of physical, emotional, and philosophical conflicts that would plague her for years. There was, at the most basic level, the aching in her back, which she came to call her "regulation pain." Competing with that was Anna's expectation that Jane would provide nursing care when Anna was ailing and would accompany her on horseback rides when Anna was well.[50] Overlaying it all was Jane's identification with the modern, rational world of science at a moment when science dictated rest and more rest for neurasthenic ailments like back pain. But that advice had to be balanced against her father's reverence for honest work and Carlyle's demand for heroic exertion, even if only by caring for sickly relatives.

Back in the safety of Rockford Female Seminary, Jane had gloried in Victorian prescriptions for bold, individual exertion and had dutifully written in her notebook, "he who does not labor is homeless."[51] But now science, the authority she had embraced as her path to social power, counseled rest, not exertion. In her schoolgirl dreams, the hero was virtually disembodied, acting on inner will, not outer muscle. Now she found herself in the real world of assassin's bullets, burst appendices, depleted nerve force, and boring dissections. Now she had to face the possibility that her destiny lay in a weak spine, not a strong will. And even if she could regain her health, what about her obligations to the family? In all her schoolgirl dreams, the hero was always alone, never bound to a family. But, here again, she found herself in the real world of dutiful daughters, needy stepmothers, and the social expectation that she would fulfill her obligations. Could a daughter who did not fulfill those expectations, could a daughter who abandoned her family, ever be taken seriously as a steward? Would she not carry with her the taint of shame and scandal?

When she chose to reflect sympathetically on these dilemmas from a distance of years, Addams concluded that daughters' ill health was the result, not the cause, of tensions over "the family claim" and "the social claim." "Her health," said Jane, "gives way under the strain" of the family's presumptions and the family's "indifference" to the daughter's ambition.[52] But that judgment, rendered in 1898, was shaped by changes in scientific thinking on the relationship between physical and mental health and physicians' growing recognition of the complex interaction between mind and body.[53] In the early 1880s, however, when Jane Addams was struggling to meet the demands of her spine and her stepmother, she was steeped in the day's orthodoxy: bodily ailments required rest. At twenty-one she had none of the confidence she would have at thirty-eight to say that the sickly college graduate needs not "to be put to bed and fed on milk. . . . What she needs is simple, health giving activity, which, involving the use of all her faculties, shall be a response to all the claims which she so keenly feels."[54] In her first years out of school, Jane Addams—Miss Sill's precocious scholar, Pa's designated daughter, Anna's "little housekeeper"—was totally unprepared for "all the claims" she so keenly felt. They came at her from every direction in a dizzying array of demands that denied her any opportunity to plan her own course. Whatever dreams Jane might have entertained at Rockford of the independent, heroic female standing alone in peaceful quietude were mocked by the cacophony of voices calling for her attention.

Loyalty to Anna involved more than shopping trips and horseback rides. There was the constant need to mediate between Anna and Harry and Alice and George, a duty that called up in Jane her most priggish voice, advising her older sister on the need to be more "just" in her "estimate of Ma," encouraging Anna's sons to write to their mother more often because "no one knows how these things affect her health," pleading with Alice and Harry to attend George's commencement at Beloit "for I think we would all enjoy [it] very much as a reunited family."[55] Jane typically took Anna's side in the family's regular squabbles. She shared Anna's disdain for Harry's drinking, and Harry's drinking was at the center of the family's tension. For many years after their stay together in Philadelphia, Anna refused to visit Harry and Alice's home and habitually included in her letters to them desperate preachments on the evils of drink.[56] Little wonder that Jane collapsed in Philadelphia under the strain of family service and medical studies; she was caught between an older sister loyal to an alcoholic husband and the husband's teetotaling mother, who was also the sister's stepmother.

According to family legend, an additional complication in this already complicated dynamic arose with Anna's desire that Jane rescue George from the life of an awkward, lonely recluse by marrying him—as Alice had married Harry. In James Weber Linn's biography of his aunt, he described a playful summer seance on the Maine coast in the 1920s when Jane "half whimsically and half in boredom" interpreted the rappings on the table as "my stepmother . . . reproaching me again for not having married George."[57] Alice and Harry's daughter, Marcet, went further, claiming that George actually fell in love with Jane, but Jane felt squeamish about romance with someone who had been her brother in every way since childhood and, ultimately, "did not love George enough to sacrifice the possibilities of usefulness that she hauntingly sensed in a larger field."[58]

If George made any overtures, they were likely quite oblique and likely occurred in the spring and summer of 1882, when Jane and Anna returned to Cedarville from Philadelphia. George proposed leaving school to join the two women in Cedarville, but when that notion evaporated, George wrote affectionate notes home to his still ailing stepsister. "It is strange, Jane, that the atmosphere affects you. I had always imagined that it was the reverse . . . at least on the home atmosphere."[59] Jane, for her part, avoided George and hated herself for it. "Clannishness," she wrote in her notebook—and then underlined—

after she chose to visit Mary but to omit an easy stop at Beloit en route. "The blunder of Beloit came from no other reason save that I did not enough *want* to see him—want of affection . . . am in danger of self-pity." By the summer, Jane was pondering "that terrible word—Forever" and weighing "thought and passion," "longing and constancy."[60]

Ultimately, Jane drew on the novelist George Eliot for her final word on the subject of George and marriage. She copied into her notebook a passage from *Middlemarch* in which a female character set aside as inappropriate her feelings for a male friend. "We can set a watch over our affections and constancy as we can over our other treasures," said Eliot's sturdy heroine. Below those words, Jane firmly defined George as one of her male siblings by writing, "Geo + Web—both," and then wrote with a large and unusual flourish: "Remember."[61]

Harry must have understood that any romantic fantasies his brother entertained (or his mother encouraged) in regard to Jane were foolish for he wrote a notably tender letter to George announcing a clear demarcation in the family's emotional geography: "I have given all to understand that from now on you and Ma will be together—It is my Dear Boy best—It is fitting that you and she should make a home for each other and I hope nothing will occur to separate you. Jane has Mary's and Weber's house to go to and Mother has no place except her own home which I hope she will always keep but keep alone."[62] Harry's thinking did not include the possibility that Jane would be anything but the maiden aunt in her siblings' homes answering to the family claim. He was wrong on that score, of course, and equally wrong to presume that Anna or George would want Jane out of their domestic sphere. But Harry's avuncular pronouncement does appear to have closed all discussion, however veiled, of George's matrimonial designs, and Harry was, in the end, correct in imagining Anna and George alone in the house in Cedarville "always."

At the very same time that Jane's relatives were imposing their family claims on Jane's present and future, Sarah Anderson, her former teacher at Rockford, was making a wholly different set of plans and demands. As Jane scrambled to find her footing in the world, Sarah made herself a devoted supplicant, pleading with Jane for time, attention, advice, and encouragement. Increasingly frustrated with her lowly position under Miss Sill at Rockford, Sarah turned to Jane for courage to change jobs, maybe careers. "I do need . . . *you* to make anything of myself," the teacher told the student a month after commencement.[63] Should she negotiate a different contract with Sill, Sarah asked the young and ailing Addams, or should she join Jane at Smith College or at medical school? Jane had barely enrolled in her anatomy and physiology classes when Sarah's "heart" began to fill "with plan upon plan" for their lives together as medical students. The thought of a future with Jane so excited the seminary teacher that she could "hardly maintain my natural composure."[64]

Sarah Anderson turned into a romantic, adoring fan just at the moment when Jane most needed an adult mentor to keep her from sinking under the competing weight of grief, dissection labs, and Anna's despair over Harry's drinking. Perhaps Anderson was trying to boost Jane's ego by insisting that she had "not learned to live without you, and I don't want to learn" or by taking no comfort in a visit to Jane's old room because "it is *you* I need and want."[65] But Sarah's declaration that she relied on Jane's help "as I do on divine help and feel just as confident of you never failing me" cannot have made Jane's burdens any lighter.[66] Jane reacted by cooling, but not ending, the relationship with her beautiful and beloved teacher. "Dear Childie," Anderson called Jane in some letters, "little woman" in others, and "my own dearly beloved" on occasion.[67] But even after inviting Jane to call her former teacher "Sarah," Jane clung to the formality of "Miss Anderson" for a while longer.[68]

Sarah Anderson proved to be little more help to Jane in these years than her other Rockford friends, who continued their seminary habit of placing Jane on a very high pedestal, out of range of normal human impulses. All of the letters Jane Addams received—or saved—from her friends in these years expressed deference to her wisdom or gratitude for her inspiration. Eva Campbell's announcement that Jane was "not one of my ordinary friends" echoed the views of those who found in Jane's company "strength and comfort," "wise counsel," and lessons in how to be "patient and cheerful."[69] At the very moment that Jane was withdrawing from medical school in Philadelphia, Helen Harrington looked to her for validation of her own efforts at the University of Michigan; only with Jane's approval could Helen count her year's work "in a measure successful."[70]

Among the entire cast of characters making claims on Jane Addams in these years, only Ellen Starr was an authentic peer; only Ellen referred to herself as Jane's "compatriot."[71] Their comradeship was not based solely on the intellectual and religious bonds already forged between them, though these bonds certainly continued to be important. Equally compelling in the postgraduate years was the shared zeal to find meaningful work. Family members chose not to recognize that this was even an issue in Jane's life, and school friends just sighed over their limited options, became "fatalistic," and figured to "marry a rich man" or become "an average schoolmarm."[72] Sarah Anderson burdened the quest with more adoring, romantic baggage than Jane could bear. Only Ellen engaged with Jane as an independent fellow seeker; over the years, she had learned how to express admiration for Jane without appearing to need her. As a result, only Ellen gained access to the fears, doubts, and ambitions that Jane concealed from everyone else.

It was to Ellen that Jane confessed when her Pa's death had left her feeling "purposeless" and, months later, in the worst throes of her "spinal difficulty," Jane admitted to Ellen her shame in revealing "even to my good friends" the "lassitude, melancholy and general crookedness" against which she had been "struggling."[73] Ellen responded with appropriate encouragements, assuring Jane that she could "never be disappointed" in her, that Jane was "too much like [her] father" to be "permanently shaken by anything, even the greatest sorrow," that Jane had a "beautiful disposition," and even that Ellen believed Jane's admirers made a "mistake" when they chose to "appreciate your good mind more than your good heart."[74] But, in contrast to Sarah Anderson's letters, Ellen's did not focus on her adoration of Jane; she flattered, instead, by saying Jane had "too little vanity to care for admiration."[75]

Whatever romance Ellen injected into these letters to Jane, it was by way of writing about visits with other female friends. Ellen gaily quoted one friend calling Ellen "a companionable little brute" as they "undressed and put on sacques to lie down and read."[76] She wrote, too, of her longing for a kindergarten teacher, Mary Runyan, who had moved from Chicago to St. Louis for work. Ellen made sure Jane knew that, before experiencing her "real pain" over Runyan's departure, Ellen had thought herself "incapable of that kind of feeling." She "felt inspired" to speak of it to Jane because others could only understand such sentiments "if it were a man."[77] Jane tried to commiserate with her friend's "grief," but then drew away from too much sentiment by claiming that such a feeling could attach "almost as much to places as it does to people."[78]

Given her friend's discomfort with sentimentality, Ellen wisely focused her letters on labor, not love. She admitted her desire for the vocational passion that she envied in teachers like Runyan and thought it would be "all very lovely" if people could "sacrifice themselves to the altar of a high calling." At the same time, Ellen worried about long hours and low pay and the effect of both on the health of a woman as "delicate" as Runyan—or herself.[79] Ellen spoke candidly to her wealthy friend about the pressures on those who had to "earn their bread," reminding Jane that women with jobs often felt cooped up and lonely in the city and often lacked the free time for intellectual self-improvement.[80] It was Ellen who taught Jane about the genuine conflict between working unreservedly, with a real "motive" among interesting people, and working "to save a little strength out of the race and amass enough of this world's goods to be comfortable."[81] More than five years before Jane and Ellen moved into Chicago's Hull-House, Ellen mused to Jane on "what happy people we might be" if "all the good things in the way of work and friends could be gotten together into one time and place."[82]

Whatever the friendship and adoration Jane received from her friends in these post-Rockford years, the fact remained that she was living every day with family members who simply never saw her in the same estimable light that struck her friends' eyes. The contrast produced a confused self-image. Jane's friends thought her a wise, humble, and kindly steward. But at home she was still the youngest daughter; her attempts at stewardship came off as awkward and clumsy. She chastised herself for "officiousness" with Harry when he came to care for an ailing Anna; she berated herself for "wishing to *do* and get credit for it."[83] She seems to have absorbed Rev. Linn's warnings about the "danger" of taking the "lower" path to "praise" and "preeminence" rather than the higher path to Christ.[84]

Jane fretted about "a selfishness eating out my very life" for "self-pre-occupation is but another symptom of selfishness." She told herself to "think of the people" around her and to strive to be the "highest, gentlest and kindli-est spirit." One minute she criticized herself for dwelling "too much on what I will do," for not going "quietly day by day," faithful to the family claim. But in the next breath she reared back against her obligation to care for Pa's widow or for George, announcing to her notebook, "it is contemptible to be idle while others are striving and working and there is so much to be done." That decla-ration was followed by two more comments: first, a quiet observation that "Sappho was a genius on the Island of Lesbos and liberated women formed a society;" second, a quotation from a novel by Dinah Maria Craik: "beyond the claims of any human being, father or lover, is God's claim to herself and her soul."[85]

Against the moral demands of the family claim, there still loomed the universal social claim, even for an unconverted soul like Jane Addams. Maybe she was officious, maybe she did seek praise and preeminence, maybe she was a moral prig, but Jane felt keenly the weight of her youthful stewardship at Rockford. "People expect certain things of me," she wrote in her notebook, "I have every chance to obtain them but fall short." Watching a maid labor in the kitchen, Jane felt "the responsibility of labor on all alike. I have no right to be idle . . . the very fact of her doing that for me increases my responsibility to do labor of a higher sort."[86] So the debate raged on in her mind in the spring and summer of 1882 until, finally, she convinced herself that answering the social claim was not rank selfishness, it was her moral duty. "People with wealth and a start of right ideas have no *right* not make the very highest use of life," she declared in her notebook: "Going to Smith College to start fresh. Make myself courteous and elegant. Be sure to be beautiful, accurate and careful in state-ments. . . . Definite in my study. Don't leave a thing until I have grasped it—

Sure of it."[87] Jane had already accepted the bachelor's degree from Rockford in the spring of 1882, just as Sill had originally proposed, and that degree may have served to qualify her for entrance at Smith without taking the dreaded entrance exams. She visited Northampton that summer and investigated off-campus housing, undoubtedly so that Anna could live with her in town.[88] On September 9, 1882, Sarah Anderson exclaimed, "So, you are going next month" and hoped Jane would not wear herself out in "getting ready."[89] But on September 10, Alice wrote a letter begging her younger sister to consult Harry at their home in Mitchellville, Iowa. Apparently, Harry had been thinking about Jane's aching back "night and day" and now had a plan for surgery to relieve his little sister's pain. To refuse to go would be to "disappoint" the two of them; Harry and Alice felt they "must help your back when we can and we can *now*."[90]

Jane's decision at that moment is a testimony either to the level of pain she felt in her back or the level of anxiety she felt over trying to succeed at Smith College with, or without, Anna. She canceled her plans to enroll at Smith and allowed her alcoholic brother to experiment on her spine. In September 1882, Harry injected an "irritant" into the tissue near Jane's vertebrae and then ordered her to lay on her back until March "while the scar tissue which formed supposedly pulled the spine straight."[91] As cockeyed as the whole treatment sounds, Jane would always insist that she was "amazed" at her improvement and "full of reverence" for Harry's work and Alice's "kindest" nursing.[92]

Jane was a "compliant" patient, but by the end of January, Harry was complaining about having Jane "still on my hands" though he was unwilling to "spoil the whole work" by letting her up too soon.[93] Confined to bed, Jane vacillated between "melancholy" and the optimistic belief that she was "emerging with a straight back and a fresh hold of life and endeavor."[94] Once he did let her get up, Harry prescribed a back brace, but Jane found it horribly uncomfortable and insisted she did not need it because she was free of the "regulation pain."[95] Her future bouts with sciatica suggest that Harry did less to cure his sister's back problem than to cure her of complaining about it to her family.

During her months of recuperation at Alice and Harry's home in Iowa, Jane found "more comfort and steadiness" in books than she had since leaving Rockford. With Alice, she read Sir Joshua Reynolds, whose eighteenth-century views on art as moral prescription were far more grounded in Christian orthodoxy than the views of John Ruskin, whom Jane always preferred. On her own, Jane tackled Thomas Carlyle's biography of Frederick the Great, his "voluminous" testament to the "lasting memory of such a hero as only Carlyle knows how to set forth."[96] Ellen was amazed and amused by her sickly friend's intellectual energy. "I don't know what I should feel adequate to reading under the circumstances," she exclaimed, "but I fear not Carlyle!" For Jane, however,

Carlyle's bracing paean to energetic leadership was just the tonic she needed when she was, as she said, "in trouble."[97] Thrown flat on her back, she found hope for her own resurrection in Carlyle's words.

Toward the end of her stay in Iowa, Jane penned a tribute to the value of hero worship in a short article for the *Rockford Seminary Magazine* in which she argued for the uplifting power of the post–Civil War sentiments evident at a "Village Decoration Day." In this, her first effort at capturing real people in small vignettes, Jane made her case that reverence for fallen war heroes could inspire "spiritual" feelings in village folk. The tone of the piece was condescending, for Jane was still the prig she would later disdain, but it was also loving, for John Addams's daughter sincerely envied and admired the "entire absence of self-consciousness" she saw in "simple-hearted people."[98] In the early 1880s, Jane's ambition, coupled with her mourning over her father, endowed hero worship with a satisfying resonance. Over time, she would lessen the undemocratic aspect of hero worship in her philosophy and would privilege the notion that nobility resided in even the most ordinary lives. Jane's own experiences as the dutiful spinster daughter managing the domestic routines—and crises—of family life certainly aided her in this ideological evolution.

A very real crisis called Jane out of her Iowa confinement in the spring of 1883, when her thirty-one-year-old brother, Weber, had a manic episode of sufficient magnitude to demand his immediate hospitalization. His wife, Laura, and six-year-old daughter, Sarah, stayed on the farm in Cedarville while Jane and Alice rushed to Jacksonville, almost two hundred miles downstate, where Weber was in a private asylum run by Dr. Andrew McFarland. Perhaps because the sisters recalled McFarland's unsavory association with an involuntary commitment case twenty years earlier, perhaps because the Illinois state asylum at Elgin was much closer to home, Alice and Jane moved Weber to Elgin as soon as they could, and he spent three months there recovering his sanity. According to the commitment papers filed in 1885, when Jane again had to hospitalize her brother, Weber's symptoms were acute, not chronic. His doctor believed that Weber's insanity was another manifestation of the era's rampant neurasthenia, as involuntary as Jane's spinal affliction and as likely (or unlikely) to be curable with rest.[99]

Just weeks before Weber's first commitment, the jury in the Charles Guiteau assassination trial had sentenced President Garfield's killer to hang for his crime, even though it agreed he was suffering from "moral insanity." The lengthy trial had pivoted around competing definitions of insanity. Thus, Jane's experience with Weber was played out against the backdrop of a heated national debate about whether insanity was the result of moral weakness and vicious habits, for which individuals should be held responsible, or was due to physiological disturbances over which the insane had no control.[100] In Guiteau's case, the American public wanted to hold the man responsible for his insanity. But in cases like Weber's, families preferred the neurologists' diagnosis of a somatic illness over which the loved one had no control and for which no one bore blame.

Jane's observations of her brother's treatment when he was "far from sane" show that she subscribed to the modern notion that his mental illness, like her back ailment, had a somatic base, but she, like most lay people and physicians, also carried the traditional belief that sufferers were responsible for advancing their own cures.[101] In the case of Weber's standard asylum treatment, Jane approved of the prohibition on his smoking or having "excitements of any kind."[102] And once he was declared cured and allowed to return home, Jane observed that Weber's willingness to "keep quiet without going out at all . . . speaks better for him than anything else."[103]

Weber's hospitalization had not been a restful three months for the still recuperating Jane Addams. There was, obviously, the worry about whether Weber would recover.[104] In addition, Anna was recuperating from a recent bowel attack of her own and had gone off to Green Cove, Florida, with George as her companion.[105] Alice stayed in Cedarville for a short while, but it was Jane, the unmarried sister, who moved into Weber's house to help Laura sort out the neglected finances for the farms and the mill. "I find myself becoming quite absorbed in business affairs and am afraid I shall lose all hold of the softer graces," Jane quipped to Ellen in an otherwise "dolorous" letter on Weber's breakdown, adding the tender note that she would "always come to you" to find those softer graces "and be cheered up."[106]

That bit of affection typified a new tone in Jane's relationship with Ellen in the spring of 1883. Having maintained but a meager correspondence with Ellen during her winter's recuperation in Iowa, Jane found that she missed her friend, missed knowing what Ellen was reading and thinking. The crisis occasioned by Weber's breakdown, or perhaps Jane's own return to health, pried open the emotional corners of their bond.[107] Jane admitted to being "delighted and comforted" by receipt of a photograph of Ellen, revealing that she had stationed the picture "where I can see you almost every minute."[108] That inviting comment set off a series of nearly sentimental exchanges in which both young women affirmed that they were elevated by the other's "view of things."[109] Jane did not run and hide when Ellen announced, "I love you more the longer and more I know you."[110] In fact, a visit from Ellen that June, before Weber was released from the asylum, made Jane "thankful" to have "received so much of you."[111]

The visit launched the two women on a new conversation about faith and Christianity, one in which Jane was far more humble than she had been at Rockford. "My experiences of late," she confessed to Ellen, "have shown me the absolute necessity of the protection and dependence of Christ." Jane not only admired Ellen for earning her own living but for coming into "the fullness" of what Jane called "the good cherishing mother church."[112] Absorbed as she was in Weber's health and business affairs, Jane was hardly free to indulge whatever sentimental or spiritual promptings she shared with Ellen that summer, but she did not close them off, either. Family duty continued to occupy Jane's time and attention, but something shifted in the emotional terrain she occupied with Ellen.

Jane took pride in helping Laura and the lawyers straighten out Weber's chaotic affairs and told Alice and Harry that she felt "splendidly from the exercise" involved with work around the farm. She was strained, however, by a two-week debate with Alice over how to pay Weber's asylum bills.[113] The proximate cause was Alice's refusal to honor the bill for the private asylum in Jacksonville on the grounds that Weber's care under Dr. McFarland's supervision had been poor. The hidden issue in the sisters' dispute was Jane's concern that "Dr. McFarland was an old friend of Pa's . . . and I hate to have anything disagreeable left over."[114]

The sisters' exchanges on this small matter reveal Jane's struggle to be less officious and more mediating with her siblings, especially with Harry's wife. Having been nursed by Alice for six months, Jane's manner was more intimate than it had been at Rockford when Jane alternated between humility and arrogance in her dealings with Alice.[115] Now, she claimed to share Alice's displeasure with the Jacksonville situation and promised to follow her older sister's lead in the matter, all the while coaxing Alice to just pay the bill.[116] When insulting letters from Jacksonville began to arrive in Cedarville, Jane announced that she would pay the bills herself but insisted that she missed Alice "more all the time."[117] Back and forth she tacked that summer, sounding more like a scold than a peacemaker in an unrelated spat between Alice and Harry and Anna and George ("there was," sniffed Jane, "sorrow and misunderstanding on both sides"). She assured Alice, however, that Weber did not at all fault her for the Jacksonville episode. He understood, said Jane, that "we were all at fault."[118] Taking the high road of conciliation with the students at Rockford Seminary had been easy compared to the stresses involved with diplomacy among Jane's less docile and more intertwined relatives.

Amidst all the other claims of this early postgraduate period, those that continued to come from her alma mater were welcome reminders to Jane of her capacity for stewardship. Even when ailing in Philadelphia, she answered Sarah Anderson's call to lead the alumnae fundraising campaign to buy scientific equipment.[119] And during the spring of Weber's insanity, she obeyed a personal summons from Miss Sill to attend an emergency meeting of the board of trustees. Aging and embattled, Sill was forced to turn to Jane, hoping that she could mount a persuasive defense of the "work of the teachers and the needs of the Seminary."[120] In telling Alice of her sudden need to make a trip to Rockford, Jane downplayed the honor implicit in Sill's request that such a recent graduate attend a trustees' meeting. "I feel quite powerless to effect anything," Jane told her older sister, one of Rockford's equally wealthy but less celebrated alumnae. Whatever Jane's influence as an advocate for the seminary at that historic meeting, it was the board, not she, who decided that Sill would take a six-month leave of absence, preparatory to her resignation six months later and the installation of Martha Hillard as Rockford's new—and far more liberal— principal.[121]

Jane spoke to these momentous changes when she delivered her notably candid alumnae address at the Rockford commencement ceremony in early June 1883. Speaking "To the Uncomfortableness of Transition," Jane made a public virtue of her own private, postgraduate struggles by preaching on the need to be patient with Rockford's transition from a seminary into a college. "The line of progress is a shaded line and never abrupt," Addams told herself and her listeners—who must have included Miss Sill. The hope that Rockford could shake off old "ideas and association" overnight and immediately embrace "freer and broader scholarship" was a "phantom."[122]

Sounding for all the world like someone who had actually achieved inner peace, Jane philosophized that it was "natural and inevitable" that in this "transitional period" the school would be "depressed and drawn back," would have "bitter experience," "misunderstandings and perplexing disappointments," and would feel "frightened" by the demands of this "new beginning." But, explained the twenty-three-year-old Jane Addams to Sill, the board of trustees, and many of her own schoolmates, this moment was no different than that time in the life of "every promising youth . . . when his friends are filled with disappointment and he himself with chagrin, a time when he traverses the uncertain region between roseate hopes and definite attainment." People feel "uncomfortable" in such times, confessed Rockford's star alumna, "because we are dimly conscious of sham and unfairness, because we bear a name which we do not duly represent and have raised vague expectations which we cannot fulfill." But every successful transition tested our "mettle," assured Jane Addams; all that was required was "courage and ambition," faith in the future, and determination to "make life uplifted and progressive."[123] If words alone could have hurled Jane through her own transition, this 1883 speech would have marked the end, not the beginning, of her postgraduate era of "chagrins" and "disappointments."

Within weeks of delivering that speech, however, Jane dove into her own "transitional period" by starting on a lengthy tour of Europe. The trip had long been part of Jane's plans; even in her junior year at Rockford, friends knew of her intention to "study medicine after . . . Smith College and that 'tramp' through Europe."[124] Three years later, medical school was off Jane's schedule and Smith College was never to be mentioned again. All that was left was the "tramp" through Europe. She persuaded five other women—including her stepmother—to accompany her and booked passage on the Cunard line's SS *Servia* for August 22, 1883. The initial plan was that they would be gone for at least one year, perhaps two.

Ellen was not in the traveling party since her schoolteacher salary could not support the luxury of a grand tour. In her discomfort over that inequity, Jane took refuge in a self-deprecating but always respectable medical excuse. "It seems absolutely essential for the establishment of my health that I have a radical change," she announced to her best friend six weeks before her departure. "So I have accepted the advice given to every exhausted American: 'go abroad.'"[125] At twenty-three, Jane could make fun of her privilege, especially if it served her relationship with Ellen, but she could not renounce it. She wanted this trip to Europe, she convinced herself she needed it, convinced others to join it, and convinced Ellen that she hated to leave her. But even as she prepared herself for a siege of European self-improvement, Jane could not shake the sense that this was a flight into self-indulgence. Ten days before departure, while stopping in Philadelphia, she paid a call on Dean Bodley of Woman's Medical College. They had a "beautiful talk," Jane told Ellen, but it left her feeling "quite . . . as if I were not 'following the call of my genius' when I propose to devote two years time to travel in search of a good time and this general idea of culture which some way never commanded my full respect. People complain of losing spiritual life when abroad, I imagine it will be quite as hard to feel earnestness of purpose."[126]

Chapter 8
Scenes Among Gods and Giants

In 1883, 600,000 Europeans emigrated to America to take up jobs and residences in booming industrial cities like Chicago. At the same time, thousands of Americans, many of them enriched by the labor of immigrants, traveled to Europe to absorb the continental culture, to define their own American identity against that culture, to display the wealth implicit in the luxury of travel, and—especially in the case of women—to enjoy the personal liberty that accompanied independent travel free of domestic duty.[1] Jane Addams was part of that stream of Americans who embarked on the European grand tour, but she was not a shallow or showy tourist. As her departing comment to Ellen Starr predicted, Jane spent much of her two years in Europe striving to "feel earnestness of purpose."[2]

Henry James, the expatriate American novelist, was a passenger aboard the SS *Servia* at the time of Jane Addams's first crossing. She observed him "most of the time between courses at table," concluding that the author of *Daisy Miller* did not appear "especially keen or intellectual."[3] Had the two of them met and conversed during those ten days on the Atlantic, Jane Addams might have changed her mind about the author's keenness and he, in turn, might have revised his view of the young American female traveling abroad. Jane Addams was entirely unlike Daisy Miller, the silly rich girl from Schenectady whom James had conjured up in his 1878 novella about Americans in Europe. Unlike Daisy, Jane was not in the market for romance or marriage. Her rare comments about her traveling companions' interest in men were as detached as her comments about their piano playing or studio painting; these were simply not of interest to her.[4] Nor did Jane share Daisy's uneducated boredom with European culture or her naive fascination with Euro-American "society."

If Henry James had spent one hour over coffee with Jane Addams during their crossing in August 1883, he would have encountered an earnest young American whose only boredom was with a life of leisure and whose naivete was evident in her self-important notions of social duty. Nearly three decades in the future, Henry James's brother, the psychologist William James, would declare that Jane Addams "simply inhabits reality," but the twenty-three-year-old woman who embarked on her first European tour in 1883 was very far from inhabiting reality.[5] Her highly romantic eye was focused on symbolic representations of heroism and transcendence. Though she enjoyed Wagner's operatic love stories, she did not like them "as well as his more tremendous scenes among gods and giants."[6] It was those scenes—on stage, in art galleries, at historical museums, on church frescoes, in the sculpture of public plazas—that Jane Addams went to Europe to study. Had Henry James been able to draw out Addams's youthful intensity, she might have revealed her hope that if she studied European culture intently enough, looked hard enough, listened long enough, the old masters would yield up the spiritual secret that inspired mere mortals to take bold action, and she would then possess the motive force she needed to follow "the call of my genius."[7]

Of course, if Henry James had spent any time at all with Jane's traveling companions, he might also have come away quite confirmed in his depiction of the frivolous female tourist from the American upper classes. "We are not," Anna Haldeman Addams told Harry, "a very intellectual" group.[8] Included in the "Addams party"—as the sextet was called—were Puss and Mary Ellwood, Rockford alumnae and the daughters of a wealthy family in DeKalb, Illinois; their aunt, Mrs. Alida Ellwood Young; Sarah Hostetter, Anna's niece and Jane's stepcousin from Mt. Carroll, Illinois; and, of course, Jane and Anna.

Jane had some reticence about traveling with the Ellwoods; she had hoped for a "more congenial, intimate party" and was perhaps put off by the fact that Mary Ellwood had decided to get married after the grand tour rather than continue her education. But once underway, Jane found that the sisters approached "everything in a good natured, happy go lucky sort of way."[9] Mrs. Young, the Ellwoods' chaperone, could become wearisome with her "insatiable thirst for dates" and other historical trivia, but her nieces were delightfully "unlimited as to time and money" and seemed to amuse Jane.[10]

Sarah Hostetter, Jane's cousin and childhood friend, was Jane's closest companion on the trip. She helped in caring for Anna on those occasions when Anna was ill, she gamely joined Jane on outings to all manner of historic and artistic sights and, in turn, she inaugurated Jane into the mysteries of fashion and shopping in Europe.[11] Anna Addams had less patience than Sarah for cultural sightseeing and was given to announcing that she was not "fond of art" and would not step foot inside another cathedral.[12] Still, Jane regarded her stepmother as a vital member of this party of American travelers and actively lobbied Anna to come along. In part, Jane did not want to be tied to the Ellwood party, so she needed her own chaperone. But Jane also believed that time away from "all disagreeable associations" would make her stepmother "better than she has been for a long time." Even when Anna's ill health caused her worried sons to call her home, Jane insisted that Anna was better off in her care and in Europe.[13] Rather than a plunge into self-indulgence, then, the European tour became an opportunity for Jane to minister to her stepmother and succeed where Harry and George had failed.

Three months into the trip, Jane was bragging to her sisters, Alice and Mary, about the compliments their group received on being so "good natured" and agreeing with each other "so well." Indeed, she told Alice in December, "the party meets in a room every little while to congratulate ourselves on the success of this winter."[14] By that time, the women had settled down for a six-week stay in a boardinghouse in Dresden, living under the same roof with two dozen other "American ladies," sixteen of whom were from Illinois.[15] Each member of the Addams party was taking private German lessons, Mary Ellwood had rented a piano, Puss Ellwood was painting in a studio every morning, Jane and Sarah and Anna were visiting art galleries and natural history museums, and all were attending the opera in the evening where Wagner kept Jane in a "continual state of shock and excitement."[16] In short, Jane told Mary in a characteristic mix of self-mocking and self-satisfaction, "we are all making desperate exertions toward knowledge."[17]

16. Jane Addams with her European traveling party. Seated are Alida Ellwood Young and Anna Haldeman Addams. Standing are Puss Ellwood, Jane Addams, Mary Ellwood, and Sarah Hostetter. (University of Illinois at Chicago, University Library, Jane Addams Memorial Collection, neg. no. 921)

Between the time of their first docking, in Ireland, at the end of August, and the start of their Dresden sojourn in early December, the Addams party had spent two weeks exploring Dublin and the surrounding Irish countryside and two weeks in Scotland, visiting the "enchanted city" of Edinburgh, as well as Glasgow and Stirling, and touring the Scottish highlands by carriage.[18] The group then headed down to Wordsworth's poetic Lake District in northwest England and devoted a month to exploring London, which Jane found, at first, "formidable" but later declared "a wonderful, wonderful spot on the earth's surface."[19] Their first stops on the continent were Amsterdam, "a tumble down town" which was too dirty to impress Jane, and Potsdam, which she preferred.[20] A similarly brief stop in Berlin before settling into Dresden allowed Jane to mount a detailed argument against George's opinion that the women should have planned to winter in Berlin, not Dresden. Berlin, she explained to her stepbrother, was too big, while Dresden offered better music, cheaper cab fare, and accommodations better suited to American standards of comfort. The choice, she admitted with the pride of the traveler who goes off the beaten track, was "a little eccentric," but the group was happy with it.[21]

The six-week stay in Dresden gave the Addams party time to rest and "read up" for the next leg of the journey.[22] In early 1884, they toured the German cities of Leipzig, Nuremberg, Munich, and Vienna before moving south for a month-long tour of Venice, Bologna, and Florence. Jane enjoyed the sunshine and the art in all three cities but laughed over Puss Ellwood's reaction to the "decayed grandeur" of Venice's Grand Canal: "I should think there would be lots of suicides here—the water is so convenient." Jane experienced this first month in Italy as a rehearsal for the next month, which was devoted to Rome. The ancient city was, for Jane, a microcosm of "the world itself," but also the spot where she sometimes shared Sarah Hostetter's desire "never to see another picture as long as I live."[23] At the end of the Roman holiday in April, the Ellwoods and Miss Young returned home to waiting family and Mary's "impatient lover," and Jane, Sarah, and Anna moved on to Athens and then to Naples—which was, "without exception, the filthiest place" Jane had ever seen—and then carriaged north to the welcomed sights of Milan and Turin.[24] The railway took them on to Lucerne, Geneva, and Paris before they met up with George Haldeman for summer hikes and horseback rides through the Swiss Alps. This was followed by an autumn return to Britain for a tour of Wales and a chance to show George the sights of London. So ended, for Jane, the "first chapter" of her European trip.[25]

After Sarah Hostetter and George Haldeman departed for the United States in the fall of 1884, Jane and Anna were left on their own, ostensibly with "no moorings on the other side of the ocean" and nothing compelling them to return home.[26] As Jane explained it to Alice, the first year in Europe had been "one of unmitigated pleasure and travel," so the second year "should have a little more study and profit in it."[27] The two women followed the crowd (and George's advice) to Berlin for the fall and winter, striving to master the German language but giving up "in despair" by the end of January.[28] They spent their final four months in Paris where, for the first time in the whole trip, they chose not to stay with an English-speaking host, instead taking rooms in the *pension* of a French family in hopes of improving their conversational French.[29] By the winter of 1885, both Jane and Anna looked forward to returning home, and in late May, after twenty-one months as "indominatable tourists," they reboarded the SS *Servia* for the trip back across the Atlantic.[30]

The Addams's tour of Europe was a notably energetic one for two women claiming to need a rest cure. Despite Jane's chronic back troubles and Anna's chronic bowel inflammation, they both demonstrated impressive capacities for sheer physical exertion. They took long carriage rides on bumpy roads through the Scottish Highlands and the Italian olive groves and covered miles of sights—from Hyde Park to Chelsea—in just one day of a whole month's worth of active days in London.[31] At one point, Jane and Sarah rode an overnight train from Paris to Geneva to meet Anna and George, then boarded a stagecoach for a nine-hour ride up into the Alps and awoke the next day to start hiking.[32] And just weeks before that, Anna, Jane, and Sarah had laid on their backs on the bottom of a boat to view the grottos on the Isle of Capri.[33] The party took care to avoid smallpox in Prague and cholera in Spain, but Jane went ahead with an overnight boat trip to Athens, fully knowing she would endure her familiar seasickness, and then took only one day to recuperate.[34] Anna, an experienced horsewoman, had looked forward to riding in the Alps. So even after she was thrown by her horse and had leeches placed on her bruises to reduce the swelling, she soldiered on, albeit in a chair carried by four porters. Meanwhile, Jane and Sarah, abandoned by a fast-walking (and self-absorbed) George, trudged together through a blinding rainstorm in the mountains near the Rhone glacier and emerged from that bit of "purgatory" with only mild colds. "Sarah declares that if I can stand that I am good for anything," Jane reported proudly to Alice, "and I think so too."[35]

Jane and Anna were healthiest on this trip when they were the most physically active and typically complained of various ailments when being tutored on German in cramped drawing rooms in Dresden or Berlin. If it suited her need to brag to her family about the marked improvements in Anna's health, Jane was happy to announce that "the outdoor life is just the thing for all of us."[36] But when considering her own situation, Jane took no solace in the fact that she felt strong when exercising her body but experienced those weak "feelings of the old sort" whenever she attempted rigorous brainwork.[37] A female with heroic ambitions could not plan for a life on horseback. Any future she could imagine for herself, whether as a scholar, a writer, or a community steward, inevitably involved brainwork; to engage merely in "unceasing activity," she observed to Ellen Starr, was "not, after all, industry."[38]

The fear that gnawed at Jane throughout this period in her life, when she was so much in Anna's company, was that she had used up all her capacity for productive mental work while at Rockford and was now an exhausted shell of a woman capable of only the most superficial thoughts and interactions. This worry reflected the era's assumption, which Anna subscribed to, that the body was a closed energy system, that each individual was endowed with just so much vital force. Once the supply was depleted, neurasthenia resulted and restoration was difficult if not impossible.[39] So even though her weight rose from 98 pounds to a healthy 115 pounds during the trip and she was constantly "reading up" on German history and Italian art, Jane ignored the evidence of health and fretted instead over her difficulty with foreign language.[40] She snapped at George when he wrote her a letter in German and later explained that her stepbrother's attempt at a friendly connection only made her feel "the old disappointment that I am not yet strong enough to study as I used to and enjoy it."[41]

It would have been entirely in keeping with the medical tilt of the day for Jane Addams to blame her exhaustion on her biological inheritance. She could easily have resigned herself to a permanent place in a line of weak constitutions: her sister Martha had died at age seventeen; her mother had died at forty-five and her father at fifty-nine, not notably early deaths but both surprisingly sudden; her sister Mary suffered—even while Jane toured Europe—from serious postpartum weakness after childbirth; Alice manifested her faulty constitution in being childless; and Weber's frail system had sapped his sanity. As well, Jane could have joined in the era's enthusiasm for blaming higher education as the cause of women's neurasthenia; she could have imagined herself the victim of an educational environment unsuited to the delicate constitution of the female.[42] But Jane Addams took the righteous route to understanding her postgraduate weakness: she blamed herself, she took individual responsibility. It was through her own foolhardiness that she had damaged her capacity for mental exertion, perhaps forever.

Addams revealed the depth of her own self-blame in the safe context of an authoritative lecture to Ellen Starr about Ellen's health, announcing there that she was "thoroughly convinced . . . that failure through ill-health is just as culpable and miserable as failure through any other cause." Writing from Geneva, on the eve of her strenuous hike through the Swiss Alps, Jane warned her friend to take heed and rest up lest she bring "failure" upon herself, as Jane had done by overworking at Rockford: "I have been idle for two years just because I had not enough vitality to be anything else and the consequence is that while I may not have lost any positive ground, I have constantly lost confidence in myself and I have gained nothing and improved nothing." Jane concluded, darkly, that she made this "confession" in order to "warn" Ellen "to take care while you can."[43]

Back in the United States when she was recovering from her collapse in medical school or flat on her back in Iowa, Jane had taken the uncomplicated scientific view that a somatic illness required a somatic cure; given proper rest, the body would probably heal. But now she was rested, now she was even vigorous, and her frailty in the face of brainwork seemed more culpable. It carried the threat of permanence if she could not find the secret others had found for transcending their limits and becoming productive.

In virtually every letter that Jane wrote to Ellen or George from Europe, she remarked on her envy of their engagement in serious work and her shame over her apparent idleness; their reports from home were "a constant reproach to my unproductiveness."[44] In notable contrast to the picture of activity she painted for the others, Jane's letters to Ellen and George were peppered with worry that the privileged life of the tourist offered "little chance for solid work." There was, she said, "a constant temptation . . . to play the dilettante," so that "you doubt whether any good is accomplished in placing yourself as a mere spectator to the rest of the world.[45] Jane was disappointed in the superficial conversation and "showy" information that passed between the tourists she encountered and told Ellen that she had learned to confine her conversation to "commonplace remarks" because people felt "you were really imposing on them" if you attempted anything more serious.[46]

In her autobiography, Jane Addams treated this condescending attitude toward her fellow travelers as proof that a rigid education had turned her into an overcultivated snob. And that was probably true. But it was equally true that Jane's education had imbued her with the conviction that only through substantive work could a person develop her highest powers and fulfill her duty to society. Being a snob did not protect Jane Addams from genuine fear that she would never achieve her high-toned ideals, and that fear made her impatient with the spoiled, superficial American traveler she knew she could become.

During the years that Jane was touring Europe, both Ellen and George were taking great joy in their work—Ellen as a teacher at Miss Caroline Kirkland's fashionable school for girls in Chicago, George as a graduate student in biology at Johns Hopkins University in Baltimore.[47] Back in college, Jane had been the stellar student among them, but now the tables were turned. In meeting her obligation to earn a living, Ellen was maturing as a teacher of Shakespeare and art history, "spiritedly giving out" to her students, as Jane observed, and thereby affirming her "powers." Through the lens of Ellen's letters, Jane saw her friend "doing things that you did not and possibly could not do when I knew you" and the long-distance effect was to leave Jane "haunted by the fear that I do not know you."[48]

As for George, his status as a male in the family meant that he was expected to leave his mother and go off to graduate school; his stepsister had no such career expectation clearing her path away from Anna and the family claim. So while Jane was struggling with poor concentration, George was chortling over study "as the grandest pleasure."[49] Jane figuratively peered over her former study partner's shoulder, into his microscope, finding his endeavors "broader both in principle and outcome" than her own and longing for his "absorption" because that, she knew, was "the one thing needful to industry."[50] So great was Jane's longing for absorbing work that, even as she toured Florence, she envied George his "skeletonizing" and "almost" envied Ellen her Greek lessons—momentarily forgetting that she had struggled with both those endeavors when she was in school.[51]

In constructing her autobiographical account of this trip and drawing from her diary's dry chronicle of sights seen, Jane Addams derided the grand tour as a "feverish search after culture."[52] But it was much more than that. This trip was Jane's search for ideals that could inspire her, heroes who could lead her out of her lethargy. Writing to her teacher, Sarah Blaisdell, Jane smartly observed that the entire tour had been devoted to "studying biography."[53] Indeed, from beginning to end, the trip was a veritable tour of dead heroes, every single one of whom was a man.

The tour of heroes began in Ireland, where Jane found "something inspiring" in the monument to Daniel O'Connell, the first Catholic in the British House of Commons and the Irish rebel who had opposed an armed uprising in Ireland because "one living patriot is worth a whole churchyard of dead ones."[54] From Ireland, Jane and her traveling companions moved on to Scotland to pay their respects to Rob Roy, Robert Burns, and Sir Walter Scott. They then visited Carlyle's home, as well as Horace Walpole's, in London before taking a bite of mulberries off Milton's tree in Cambridge.[55] (Addams made no effort to see George Eliot's home in England, but she did note in her diary that Susan B. Anthony had signed the guest register at Trinity College in Oxford, right above Jane's own signature.)[56] In Germany, they made pilgrimages to honor Frederick the Great, Goethe, Luther, and Liszt while, in Italy, they stopped at an "old Armenian monastery where Byron wrote his *Childe Harold*," saw the palace of the pro-constitution monarch Victor Emmanuel, and visited

Dante's house in Florence and Savonarola's cell in Rome.[57] Near the end of her tour, Jane attended a session of the Reichstag to hear Bismarck, "the great man," give a speech "without effort or haste but as if he had no idea in the world of meeting opposition."[58]

In tandem with this inspirational tour of political and artistic heroes came Jane's determined study of uplifting European art. She did not fancy herself well educated on the subject: "Works of art were always out of my line," she reminded Ellen, but Anna regularly reported home that Jane was so "wide awake" and "so enthusiastic" about her "steady museum work" that she was "inclined to overtax herself."[59] As preparation for all this effort, Jane had absorbed the Victorian view espoused by Matthew Arnold and John Ruskin that art and culture were expressions of a society's moral condition. Since the purpose of art was to capture God's creation and thereby inspire the viewer, then the success of artistic endeavor rested with the artist's interpretive vision which, in turn, rested with the artist's moral character. Jane carried these precepts with her through countless galleries and cathedrals, but because she was still unsure of her own conceptions of God and morality, she felt tentative about her ability to judge any work of art. She wound up squinting to see each painting's ennobling qualities, straining to understand how mere mortals translated their aspirations into tangible products that seemed to transcend human limitations.

The religious painter who most engaged Jane's attention in Italy was Fra Angelico, the fifteenth-century Florentine who painted on the walls of his cloistered monastery at San Marco, not caring if his work was "seen," not caring if they brought him fame. This made his paintings "sweeter," Jane thought, "unto themselves and peaceful that way."[60] After a day viewing Fra Angelico's frescoes, Jane told Ellen that artistic work performed for the sheer joy of the work itself gave her a "tremor and a corresponding desire for the power arising from mere goodness."[61] Carlyle, Ruskin, and Jane's own father had equipped her with enthusiasm for self-expanding, self-exceeding labor, but the question Jane carried into every European gallery, church, and workshop was how to engage in such labor "from mere goodness." What secret motivated such selflessness?

When she was a student at Rockford, Jane had told Ellen that her spiritual quest was to "get back of it all," beyond the layers of orthodoxy, to find what she imagined as an essential spiritual truth. She continued that effort in Europe, especially in Italy, where she consciously elbowed her way past the pomp and "glamour" of the Catholic Church and examined Catholic art for the "secret" of Christ and his most holy followers.[62] Jane brought a genuine disdain of Roman Catholicism with her to Europe, an attitude she shared with her stepmother and her sisters.[63] Like most Protestant Americans, she viewed Catholicism as slavishly hierarchical and suspiciously ritualistic.[64] This prejudice extended beyond her political alignment with Italian republicans and against the Vatican, expressing itself in a recoil from Catholic worship of "sacred relics" and "holy shrines."[65] In Jane's protesting eyes, worship of icons reified the very beliefs that ought to be abstract; the use of "impossible stories and miracles" pandered to people's superstitions rather than elevating their spirituality. Writing from Rome to her sister Mary, the Presbyterian minister's wife, Jane expressed amazement that "intelligent people" would kneel to kiss a wooden figure with supposedly supernatural powers or believe that water "miraculously" sprang forth from a dry bed when needed for baptism.[66]

Such attitudes might have put Jane in an awkward position with Ellen, for whom Episcopal ritual had become an uplifting avenue to spirituality. Ellen, in fact, had joined an Episcopal church in Chicago the same summer that Jane sailed for Europe.[67] But the two women shared a veneration for the spirituality of pure aesthetic beauty, and Jane admired Ellen for having found "the Peace that passeth understanding" in the "good cherishing mother church." In marked contrast to her earlier disdain for Ellen's Christian route to God, Jane now claimed that she prized Ellen's comprehension of the divine as "a new element in your character." After months spent peering into the painted faces of saints, the best Jane could offer back to Ellen by way of spirituality was the awkward admission that she had not found faith "but can see it not quite uncomprehendingly."[68] After still more months, and a Palm Sunday service at Notre Dame, Jane admitted to Ellen, "I believe more and more in keeping the events, the *facts* of Christ's life before us and letting the philosophy go."[69] Neither Ellen nor European art could make Jane a believer, but they could make Jesus a heroic figure in Jane's eyes; he was no longer "beside the point," as she had declared at Rockford. Some combination of historical facts and Christian aesthetics could, Jane hoped, propel her into meaningful labor with pure, unselfish motives, from "mere goodness."

So the grand tour was not merely a "feverish search after culture," as Addams later claimed; it was a quest for inspiration, motive, justification.[70] It was an opportunity, as well, for Jane to test her American identity against European assumptions about the privileges of wealth and hierarchy. Her observations on these matters situated her squarely in America's Northern, white, Republican middle class. She was at the upper end of that class, to be sure. She was blessed with the luxury of time to read the Victorian idealists' critique of an irresponsible, idle aristocracy and their idealization of pre-industrial labor.

Though not similarly blessed with any formal training in political economy, Jane was familiar with the Victorian idealists' denunciation of laissez-faire economics for its crass reduction of all social relations to self-interest and the cash nexus. As a privileged student and an aspiring steward, Jane Addams brought that philosophical background with her to Europe. She brought, as well, her experience as the daughter of a self-made grain miller from the Illinois prairie. Jane's vision of European social life was informed as much by her Republican father as by her reading of Carlyle, Ruskin, and George Eliot.

Wherever she went in Europe, Jane drew on her childhood spent watching the mill outside her Cedar Creek home. She was fascinated by industry and liked to see how things worked, how they were made.[71] This produced a paradoxical fascination with pre-industrial craftwork and with modern inventions. So whether she spent a day at the porcelain works in Dresden, observing Milan's field irrigation systems, or on a compressed air railway trip up into the Alps, Jane enthused over human inventiveness and productivity.[72] Her imagination leapt at the notion of the individual worker's access to both the joy of labor and social power. She wrote a long and celebratory description of the opera *Excelsior* in which "the good spirit of Civilization aided by Science" was represented by the inventor of the steamboat singly battling the forces of superstition and ignorance. The hero was rescued by the "Spirit of Progress" and all the good results of his individual genius were paraded across the stage in a special effects extravaganza depicting ocean liners, the Brooklyn Bridge, the freeing of the slaves, and the opening of Japan.[73] Just what the effects of all this progress would be on individual workers was beyond Jane's imagining in 1883. She was caught up in the romance of labor, not the reality.

At the center of Jane's European study of individual heroism and the goodness of pure labor lay her attention to the privileges—and responsibilities—of every society's stewards. Just as there was no question in the mind of this young American Republican that an orderly society had to have a ruling class, there was also no question that the members of that class were required to set an industrious example for those they ruled. She had no patience for a ruling class that squandered its power; when she saw Britain's "dingy and crowded" House of Commons, she was disappointed to find that the members of Parliament assigned "more space . . . to lunch and smoking rooms than to actual work."[74] Jane tended to be quite critical of the British aristocracy, in fact, finding fault with the "frightful extravagance" of everything from grouse hunting to Windsor Castle and the Albert Memorial.[75] She continually mocked the pretensions of "vanity fair" and noted, with disdain, the burden of high taxes on a productive middle class to support the leisure of an idle class. It was, she wrote resignedly to Mary, "the big fish living off the little fish over and over again," a comment inspired not by any images of exploited wage labor but by the number of taxes—including the taxes to support the poor—that her London boardinghouse keeper had to pay to the Duke of Portsmouth.[76]

She was impressed by Britain's seventeenth-century poet-priest George Herbert because he used his inherited wealth to build a church and parsonage "in order that his successor might have more to give to the poor."[77] In general, though, she thought British paternalism toward the poor did not accord with "American ideas of Republicanism."[78] The problem, as Jane reported it to Weber, was that those who labored on Britain's great estates could not own their own land.[79] The steward class in Britain was governing with a stacked deck, providing only alms, not opportunity, and protecting their position rather than earning their right to rule. Senator Addams's daughter could hardly approve.

Jane was curiously more tolerant of Continental royalty, which she viewed from a distance as an historical pageant comically enacted by some "flunky in a powdered wig."[80] In fact, once settled in Berlin for her second winter, Jane was quite bedazzled by the glamour and authority of the German monarchy. There, she forgave the "heavy-handed" state bureaucracy and high taxes because she was convinced that the German people were inspired by their love of the kaiser, and, after all, Carlyle said that the purpose of heroes and heroism was to uplift the people.[81] She even suspended her disdain for royal pomp long enough to be awed by the formal displays of imperial grandeur that were opened up to her and Anna by a letter of introduction from her father's friend, Elihu B. Washburne, a former Illinois congressman who served as U.S. ambassador to France during the Paris Commune.[82] Though she had been skeptical of a British duke's village school, Jane was remarkably impressed by the sight of the kaiser's nieces patting the heads of some four hundred children from "poor schools" who were guests at a Christmas party sponsored by the royal family in Dresden.[83]

Even more remarkable was Jane's reaction to the imperial valorization of Kaiser Wilhelm's mother, Queen Amalie Louise of Prussia, who was beloved for her patriotic, if futile, appeal to Napoleon in 1807 on the eve of France's takeover of much of her husband's kingdom. This maternal figure inspired Jane to write the only comments on an earthly female hero that appear in any of her surviving letters from Europe. Those comments were notably rapturous—and exclusively directed to Ellen and George, who usually received Jane's worries about her own future. What impressed Jane was the fact that there was "an entire literature" about Louise; her life was taught in the public schools, there were "great histories" as well as children's books devoted to the study of her life. She was a figure of intellectual and political substance, thought Jane, "and there is no doubt that her ideas were the largest and finest which could be conceived by an heroic soul." With language that harkened back to her seminary ideal of the goddess as a fostering mother, Jane rhapsodized about the public statue of Louise "erected by the citizens of Berlin and presented to the Emperor." The figure, she told George, "is so womanly and benign, the expression is so generous and mature that it is always an inspiration to me to walk by it." Indeed, she confessed to Ellen, she found the statue of Louise so "gracious" that she was "prone to pass by it even at the cost of some fatigue every time I take a walk."[84]

For all her Victorian idealism, Jane Addams did not habitually indulge in such florid outbursts of adoration, so it is worth noting that she directed her praise only in breathless tributes to Louise, in ecstatic celebration of the opera *Excelsior* and in a similarly enthusiastic celebration of Wagner's opera *Tannhauser.* Jane described that work as the "powerful" story of a man "who is down trying to work his way up." She omitted the fact that Tannhauser was saved not by his own efforts in his struggle against an unforgiving Catholic Church but by the selfless sacrifice of a woman who placed sacred duty above sensual love.[85] At age twenty-four, Jane Addams's passions were not excited by love stories but by "scenes among gods and giants" in which she perceived individuals, including strong females, struggling to advance human progress out of "mere goodness." Over the course of her European tour of heroes, she resonated most sympathetically with those privileged individuals—King Victor Emmanuel, George Herbert, Queen Louise—whom she associated with both aesthetic beauty and specific, practical aid to those they presumed to steward.

Fifteen years later, when writing her autobiography, Jane Addams would make the stylistic and political decision to greatly condense the story of her trajectory away from elite stewardship and toward democratic process. To achieve that narrative end, she had to cast her grand tour as not only a "feverish search for culture" but also, quite dramatically, as a time of mounting "distress" over the condition of the poor.[86] Jane's diary from the two-year tour, however, made only one reference to the working poor, and in the 115 surviving letters that Jane wrote home from Europe between 1883 and 1885 she made fewer than ten comments about the poor and most of those were casual references. The sight of "dirty, ragged children" in the streets of Dublin was "appalling," of course, but she told Mary and Alice that they had "bright complexions and straight strong mouths" and were "so impudent, jolly, and continually begging that it is hard to pity them."[87] Naples was notable for its streets "full of beggars," and the only drawback to the "delightful" ride out to Fiesole from Florence, she reported to George, was "the swarms of beggars which haunted the carriage constantly."[88] The "wretchedness" of the Irish, she pronounced, was "deeper than anything the government can reach," but rural poverty in Germany could hardly be called "wretchedness" since "everyone is warm and well fed" even if folks did have to share their homes with the cows.[89]

Addams devoted several pages of her autobiography to her memory of two encounters with the poor in Europe. The first described a group outing to London's impoverished East End one Saturday night soon after the *Pall-Mall Gazette*'s publication of the expose "Bitter Cry of Outcast London" had made "slumming" a popular activity for the quasi-concerned middle class.[90] The second recalled an encounter in Coburg, Saxony, where Jane saw women workers hauling casks of hot beer on their backs from the brewing site across the road to the cooling site.[91] It is true that Addams was a witness to both of these scenes, but the young woman who experienced them did not, to call on William James again, "inhabit reality" in the same way as the mature woman who later remembered them.[92]

In 1909, Jane Addams looked back on her 1883 visit to London's East End through the lens of twenty years lived intimately with the working poor who were her friends and neighbors at Hull-House. Her hindsight was aided by images acquired during interim trips to the East End. So she could vividly depict the scene, in her autobiography, of the hungry "clamoring" around "hucksters' carts" at the Saturday night sale of the week's discard meat and produce. At age thirty-nine, she could write movingly about the "pale faces" of the poor and their "workworn" hands "clutching forward for food that was already unfit to eat."[93] But in the single report she wrote to Weber at the time of her first visit to the East End, she described no faces, no hands, only "swarming thousands of people" in a "Dickens neighborhood."[94] And in her very brief, entirely private diary entry about the East End outing, Jane wrote several lines about the various transport modes used to reach the East End before noting, in one flat line, that "thousands of poor people were marketing at the booths and market stalls along the streets."[95]

Addams claimed later that her East End visit caused her to go about London "for the following weeks" obsessed with the reality of poverty and the unreality of everything else, but Jane actually left London just a few days after the outing. She remarked to Weber that her visit to the slum was "simply an outside superficial survey of this misery and wretchedness," though it was "enough to make one thoroughly sad and perplexed." Otherwise, her letters convey no hint of the "despair and resentment" which she later claimed "seized" her at the time.[96] Her letters at that moment do, however, contain her critique of Parliament for giving more space to "lunch" than to "actual work" and include her worried remark to Ellen that travel, while "it enlarges one's vision," gave "little chance of solid work."[97] In short, the visit to the East End caused her to focus less on the actual experience of the poor than on what those of the steward class, herself included, should be doing about poverty. This may seem like an awfully fine distinction, but it marks a world of difference between the distanced, elite stance Jane Addams held as a tourist in 1883 and the engaged, democratic stance she held as a veteran of real life at Hull-House by 1909.

The distinction emerges again in comparing her memory of the women with the beer casks on a "snowy morning" in Coburg and the record she made at the time of that rain-drenched scene. In her autobiography, Addams claimed that she was so indignant over the "cruel conditions" under which the women labored that she was "stung into action," making a futile effort at protest to the "phlegmatic owner of the brewery."[98] She recalled, too, that Saxe-Coburg was the home of Prince Albert, Queen Victoria's deceased husband, whose biography she was reading at the time. Indeed, Jane claimed that after the brewery incident she stopped reading the biography of Prince Albert because she could not fathom how the prince, or his teacher, could "ignore such conditions of life for the humble, hard-working folk."[99]

When the incident occurred, in January 1884, Jane did not record in her correspondence or in her diary any attempt to intervene on the brewery workers' behalf. She did comment to Alice on the "wretchedness among the poor women" but said the sight of them "became positively painful and so we were glad to get away."[100] Her letter to Weber ten days later and her atypically descriptive entry on the incident in her diary suggest, however, that the scene stayed with her. In both texts, Jane specified the brewery women's long hours and low wages, and in her letter to Weber she demonstrated unusual attention to the workers' experience by noticing how the hot beer spilled out of the "huge casks" that were strapped to the trudging women's backs, "often scalding their heads and shoulders."

Addams told Weber that she was surprised by the working conditions because Prince Albert "was such a philanthropist . . . one would naturally suppose his birthplace would be less degraded."[101] Writing in her diary about her reaction to the whole scene, Jane said that she was "impressed by the powerlessness." But it was not the powerlessness of the workers that struck her at the time, it was "the powerlessness of *one* man"—Prince Albert—"to do anything." Rather than feeling angry disillusionment with the prince for his ignorance, as she later claimed, Jane wrote sadly in her diary that "Prince Albert tried so hard and here was all this misery and hopeless work."[102]

When she was a young American touring Europe in the mid-1880s, Jane Addams bore no philosophical hostility to the poor. Yes, she was capable of a snooty characterization of Venice as "mainly flies and Italian beggars" and could, without a thought, turn away from a group of Turks because "their baggy trousers were too soiled and worn even to be picturesque."[103] But there was no social Darwinism or stern Protestantism informing her condescension; she never had to shed the assumption that the poor deserved their fate. Her Republican father had taught her that slaves were degraded by their situation, not their nature, and Carlyle and Ruskin had taught her to loathe employers who exploited labor for their own self-interest. She still had much to learn about the complexities of that exploitation in an industrializing, urbanizing world, but her assumption on the grand tour was that, in Europe at any rate, the poor existed because their betters had failed them.

As a result of this top-down philosophy, Jane Addams paid little attention to the subjective experience of the European poor. Their mere existence was all that mattered. It was the requisite backdrop for examining the motives and conduct of their stewards, especially those who had behaved heroically toward them. Jane spent her time gazing at representations of heroes to guide her path toward stewardship. She did not peer into the faces of the poor for signs of authentic human expression or search the eyes of beggars to discover heroic motives for rising above one's limitations. Nor did she listen to the individual voices or the stories of the poor. Instead, she made a study of the speaking styles of various preachers, teachers, and politicians, paying more attention to the qualities that made for effective delivery than to the actual content.[104]

Only a few years after this tour, Addams would distinguish herself by crafting—in essays and speeches—extraordinarily affecting profiles of her poor neighbors in Chicago, capturing in a few lines their highly individual personalities and life stories. Her letters from Europe included no such profiles, no indication that she ever directly looked at or spoke with any of the thousands of impoverished laborers whom she encountered all along the way. She was not yet searching the hearts of the poor for solutions to her own privileged problems.

Shortly before observing the brewery workers at Saxe-Coburg, Jane had confessed to George her doubt that "any good is accomplished in placing yourself as a mere spectator to the rest of the world."[105] Just a few days later, in the letter she wrote to Alice as soon as she could "get away" from the "painful" sight of laboring women, Jane devoted far more attention to Tannhauser's operatic struggles with good and evil than to the image of "humble, hard-working folk" of Saxe-Coburg.[106] She may have chafed at being a "mere spectator," but she still preferred to see her hardships on stage than in front of her hotel. While counting on aesthetics to guide her to spirituality, she allowed aesthetic idealism to divert her attention from humanity.

Whatever chronological liberties Addams later took in linking her anguish over the poor to her first trip to Europe, she never forgot the snobbish, hyper-cultured young woman she was in 1885. Addams wrote with disarming honesty when she described herself and her peers in the 1880s as scholars who allowed literature to "cloud the really vital situation spread before our eyes."[107] Just as she shuddered when she looked back on her arrogance in these years, so she disdained her attraction to artistic representation over human reality while in Europe. In her autobiography she even titled her chapter on these years "The Snare of Preparation," a phrase taken from Leo Tolstoy's critique of elite youth's self-indulgent postponement of genuine engagement with lived experience.

Lost in that charmingly candid self-criticism was the genuine depth and sincerity of young Jane's belief in art's uplifting power. During her stay in Florence, for example, when she was feeling particularly despondent about her own vitality and envying George's and Ellen's labors, Jane proposed to Alice that she have an Italian sculptor carve a bust or a medallion of her father, Senator John Addams, the central hero in her life. The unfulfilled plan came of Jane's sad hope that an artistically rendered, three-dimensional representation of "that best face of all" would "always be a help to us."[108] Art, for Jane, was not simply a pleasure, nor was it an escape; it was a "help," an inspiration to the best in ourselves.

As a well-read product of the late Victorian culture that legitimized the cultural philosophy of Ruskin, Arnold, Wordsworth, and Eliot, Jane's devotion to aesthetics was not intended as an escape from religious or social duties. Her aesthetic interest in these years was both an effort to find her soul's motive force and an effort to prepare for the only thing she was then equipped to do: become a steward of the arts. Of course, her dogged focus on aesthetics at the expense of humanity left Jane plagued with worry that she lacked any spiritual motive to act as a steward out of "mere goodness." To gain that motive, she would have to turn around and notice humanity. In retrospect, Addams was impatient with her young self for not understanding that. At the time, solutions were not quite so obvious, but she was considering some options.

Three months before sailing home, in a letter from Paris to her "good and talented friend" Ellen, Jane included a three-point paragraph that stands out from all her European correspondence as the single hint that she might have begun thinking about how to translate her artistic ideals into some sort of tangible action. The letter was written in her most cramped scribble, with virtually illegible words inserted here and there, as if she were just working out the idea on the page. She announced to Ellen, first, that she thought "every town and city in America" ought to have copies of great European masterpieces.

Next, she argued that those who had been privileged to see European art first-hand but made no effort to share that experience with their less privileged fellow citizens were "culpable." Finally, she took rather haughty issue with the "charge that art is so selfishly occupied with her own perfection" that she "has no desire to teach or improve."[109]

It was not much as a plan, perhaps, but it was certainly a position. At the very least, Jane's outburst represented an embrace of John Ruskin's essays in *Ethics of the Dust*, which she read while traveling. Ruskin argued against the false value society placed on beautiful, scarce objects that were "retained without a use." Such practices excited a false covetousness in human beings who were, by nature, generous. Only by putting beautiful objects of art to use, only by using them to communicate with others, could art realize its potential for improving human society.[110] This was solid ideological ground that Jane and Ellen could share. Whatever their differences over religious ritual, even religious faith, the two young women held in common a belief in the uplifting power of beautiful art. Jane did not, at that moment, see (or announce) the implications of this belief for her future. She was busy struggling with her French, looking forward to going home, and thinking "rather drearily," as she so often did, that she had "accomplished very little."[111] She was wrong about that, as she was about so many of her assessments of the grand tour. But it would be several years before the seeds planted during that trip would come to anything like fruition. Until then, there was home and the family claim to think about.

Chapter 9
Never the Typical Old Maid

Jane Addams celebrated her twenty-fifth birthday in the fall after her return from Europe. Coming off a grand tour of heroes and heroics and feeling "the full weight of a quarter of a century," Jane settled into a life that was notably prosaic.[1] She grounded herself in the practical business of daily living as the spinster daughter in an upper-middle-class, fatherless American family. In the two and a half years following her return, she divided her time between helping Mary, Weber, and Alice in their homes in the Midwest, living with Anna in Cedarville, and living with Anna and George in Baltimore, where George continued as a graduate student in biology at Johns Hopkins University. These were the last years when the agenda of Jane Addams's life would be regulated by her family's needs or expectations. They were also, ironically, the first years since her start at Rockford Female Seminary when Jane did not seem obsessed with enacting a heroic destiny.

In her autobiography, Addams described this period as "the nadir of my nervous depression and sense of maladjustment," but the surviving letters from the time masked that sentiment awfully well.[2] In her writings to Alice (the one correspondent who regularly kept letters from this moment in the life of her not-yet-famous sister), Jane projected an adult version of the self-possession she had cultivated at Rockford. The record she penned for her sister suggests greater emotional and physical stability than Jane had enjoyed since graduation. She gave the impression of maturity in fashioning a sensible, moderate life for herself, one that balanced family obligations with her own cultural and social interests. There was nothing heroic here, no risk-taking, and no more discussion of additional education or of preparation for a career such as medicine. By all appearances, Jane Addams was a young woman who had ceased chafing at the family claim and settled into her social position or, as some would have said, her destiny. She focused her diplomatic skills and logistical talents on caring for her relatives, young and old; she learned the decorative arts and became a tasteful consumer and efficient homemaker. She fulfilled the duties of her social station by entertaining at home, participating in women's cultural clubs, doing a bit of volunteer work, going to church, and taking passenger trains to visit friends and family around the country. All in all, she created a very stable, settled, comfortable spinster life in the years between 1885 and 1887, one that thousands of women of Jane Addams's class lived out in the late nineteenth century. In later characterizing these years as the "nadir of my nervous depression," Addams was not defining this as her time of outright angst; rather, she was recalling it as her time of greatest resignation to the family claim.

Jane's steadfast lack of skill at the household arts of cooking and sewing led her to announce to her stepmother that she would "never be the typical old maid," but the outward structure of her life in these years was precisely that of a typical old maid.[3] Indeed, the announcement to Anna may, itself, have been a veiled declaration of her sense of "maladjustment," a faint sign of resistance to the life settling in around her. Retrospect yields other clues to her discomfort, along with hints of what would draw her away from her conventional life and embolden her to invent a new space for women like herself, women who sought stewardship apart from formal academia, Christian orthodoxy, or organized feminism. But the overwhelming impression left from these years following her grand tour with Anna—and just prior to the life-altering European trip she would make with Ellen Gates Starr—is that Jane Addams was thoroughly immersed in a traditional social role that offered no prediction of the future she would create for herself but did significantly influence her shaping of that future.

Weber Addams suffered another manic episode at his Cedarville farm in August 1885, three months after Jane returned from Europe, and had to be removed from his home by the local sheriff.[4] Jane signed his commitment papers for the asylum at Elgin, where Weber stayed until early December. Throughout the fall, Jane shuttled between Cedarville, where she attended to Laura Addams, who was "more broken" by her husband's insanity than ever before, and Harvard, Illinois, some eighty miles east, where she helped care for her sister Mary and Mary's fifth baby, little Mary, who had been born the previous May.[5] Indeed, Jane and Anna returned from Europe in May instead of later in the summer because Jane was concerned about her pregnant sister's fragile health.[6]

Two years earlier, Jane had begged off returning from Europe to help Mary through her protracted recovery from the birth of her fourth child, Stanley. At that time, Jane had made fervent exclamations of concern and loyalty but left the caretaking to Alice and claimed her own frail health as an excuse.[7] Time and distance had given family life a new sweetness, however, and in her first autumn at home, Jane compensated for the missed years by throwing herself into the management of her relatives.[8] She moved Weber and Laura's eight-year-old daughter, Sadie, over to Harvard for an extended visit with her Linn cousins and then accompanied Laura to Elgin, where only Jane was allowed to visit with the "haggard" and "thoroughly homesick" Weber. Amidst all of this caretaking, Jane wrote gleefully to Alice that she "could never remember feeling so well." She was eating "voraciously" and, at 120 pounds, weighed "more than I ever had before." Her growth in "strength and size" was a happy sign, thought Jane, of "increasing health." In the full bloom of her season of family management, Jane reported to Alice on Weber's slow recuperation, chided her sister for being two letters "in debt" to Laura, and kept her abreast of developments at Mary's.[9]

Mary Addams Linn was forty years old in 1885. She had been married to Rev. John M. Linn for fourteen years, and he was still working for a presbytery that demanded frequent relocation. In the years between 1885 and 1887, Mary moved her young family from Harvard, Illinois, to Lake Forest, Illinois, and then to Geneseo, Illinois. These relocations were all within two hundred miles, and Mary's inheritance meant she could buy her way out of an inadequate parsonage, set the family up in nicer homes than many ministers could afford, and hire local immigrant girls to help out.[10] But they were difficult moves

17. Mary Addams Linn at the time of her marriage to Rev. John Linn in 1871. (Jane Addams Papers Project)

18. Rev. John Manning Linn at the time of his marriage to Mary Addams. (Jane Addams Papers Project)

nonetheless for a woman whose strength had been taxed by childbearing. When Jane returned from Europe, Mary was supervising—in addition to baby Mary—her son John, age thirteen; James Weber, age nine; Esther, age five; and Stanley, age two.

Jane delighted in Mary's children, whom she affectionately dubbed the "Linnets," and took great joy in watching Weber's daughter, Sadie, grow "jollier" and "more talkative than ever" among her "chatterin'" cousins.[11] Jane thought James Weber, her future biographer, a "remarkably clever boy," regarded the "thoroughly spoiled" Esther as "enthusiastic and charming," took heart from signs that baby Mary was "vigorous," and openly doted on the toddler Stanley, "a dear little morsel of humanity" whose constant attentions Jane found "so gentle and unobtrusive" that they were not "annoying."[12] Whenever Jane stayed at Mary's, she slept with Stanley, inspiring her to reflect to Ellen Gates Starr that "if you don't take charge of a child at night you can't feel a scared trembling hand grow confiding and quiet as soon as it lies within your own."[13] Ellen spent Thanksgiving of 1885 with Jane at Mary's home at Harvard and found the Linnets to be "ill mannered but immensely clever."[14] Ellen would later comment to her own sister on the importance of Jane's tie to the Linnets. Time with these children, explained Ellen, had taught Jane that she felt better after a day of childcare than after a day of socializing.[15]

John Linn was frequently absent from the household for stretches of time, taking the word of God to unchurched areas.[16] Alice railed at her brother-in-law's neglect of his wife and children and, from Europe's safe distance, Jane mediated between the two sisters, granting Alice her indignation while gently insisting that Alice's open disapproval of Rev. Linn would only "grieve" Mary, that Mary was "too weak and wretched . . . to improve anybody or anything."[17] Once back in the United States, Jane's regular visits to Mary's home allowed her to ease the family stress with more material help. Poised between feeling "helpless" in the company of expert housekeepers but "selfish" if she did not join in, Jane always rolled up her sleeves at Mary's to rock the baby or pack her brother-in-law's clothes for travel or cover a table with new baize or put on an ice-cream social for seventy-five parishioners.[18]

Jane provided substantial help during Mary's 170-mile move from Lake Forest to Geneseo in the spring of 1887. On the eve of that move, but before Jane's scheduled arrival from Baltimore, Mary gave birth to her sixth child, Charles. Mr. Linn's absence on that occasion gave Jane an angry "shiver" when she thought of Mary "all alone when the baby came." Unlike Alice, however, Jane did not direct her anger at the male in the situation; instead, she faulted Mary for not asking Jane to come sooner. By not telling Jane her troubles, Mary had created "an entire misapprehension of the state of affairs" in Lake Forest.

"I have no patience with the family mania for writing 'cheerful letters,'" Jane exclaimed to Alice in an unusual outburst of exasperation and guilt.[19]

Within the Addams family, of course, Jane was actually the master of the "cheerful letter." She had learned to skirt conflict in the house on Cedar Creek and at Rockford Seminary, and had proved precociously adept at finding the safety of high ground by rising above others' disagreements. Now, as the maiden aunt in a family that lacked Senator John Addams's unifying influence, Jane honed her performance of the conciliatory role with both cheerful letters and a calm presence intended to soothe family tensions. As the youngest female in the family, she had none of Pa's objective authority to maintain family harmony, so she had to refine her diplomatic strategies to influence her relatives. One unifying strategy Jane used in her letters was to rhetorically construct a family identity. She referred to the "mania" for "cheerful letters," for example, as a "family" trait. So, too, little Esther Linn's "impatience of all direction or command" was not simply impertinence, it was "an exaggeration of our family spirit." Holidays were described as more authentic and satisfying if celebrated "as we used to do at home" in Cedarville. And frequent letters from Alice were required because she represented "such an important branch of the family."[20]

Two sojourns in Baltimore in 1886 and 1887 allowed Jane to widen and deepen this sense of family identity by re-establishing regular contact with her father's extended family in Pennsylvania, as well as with her mother's family, the Webers and the Reiffs. Jane found these "dear people" to be warm and welcoming, making her feel fully a part of the clan.[21] After each of her three visits to Pennsylvania in these years, Jane wrote reports to Alice emphasizing the strength of family connection across time and space.[22] When Alice at age thirty-four finally gave birth to her only child, Jane reported in detail on the "exclamations of . . . triumph" when the Pennsylvania relatives pored over the baby pictures of Marcet Haldeman and discovered "one feature after another . . . to be an Addams, and her chin definitely pronounced like her grandpa's."[23]

Jane invested more time and emotional energy in her father's family than in her mother's on these trips. Even when she wrote of her visit to her mother's seventy-one-year-old sister, Aunt Elizabeth Reiff, she commented wistfully on driving "past the little public library Pa read through and Sanders Square where he bought wheat."[24] But when Aunt Elizabeth described Jane as knowing "nothing about your mother's family," Jane agreed to a tour of Sarah Weber Addams's birthplace and even took a trip with Aunt Elizabeth to New York City to visit her mother's brother Harry.[25] Neither excursion inspired Jane to pull her siblings together with new insights into their mother's life. Her attention was always on the warmth she drew from inclusion in a lively and affectionate paternal clan.[26]

In sharp contrast to Jane's Pennsylvania relatives, who resided within a few miles of one another and were affectionately entwined in each other's lives, Jane's own immediate family was geographically and emotionally fragmented. Back in the fall of 1884, Anna had announced from Berlin that the family was "now so scattered" and so lacking in "reseprosity" or "congenialities" that she had little hope for its unity. "When families have no deep centered love for each other," Anna told Harry, when there were "no deep eternal affections that will bind," well, then, there was "little hope" of any coming together in this life or the next.[27] The melodrama in this pronouncement was fueled by Anna's temperament and her "fevers," which may have been menopausal, but there was truth in what she said.[28] For her part, Anna seemed to regard this as a fate over which she had no control; she made no association between the family's fractured condition and her own choice not to function as an all-embracing matriarch in widowhood.[29] At age fifty-six, she thought of herself as a martyr living "more for others than for my poor self," as one whose life "held a gobletful of bitter mixtures" which she had "drunk to the dregs."[30] Rather than minister to Weber or Mary, she focused her emotional energy on George, her "manly baby boy," accepted Jane's filial ministrations as her due, and engaged in an intense but strained relationship with the determinedly alcoholic and feckless Harry and his determinedly sunny and competent wife, Alice.[31]

When she first returned from Europe, Jane was a bit "perplexed" about how to manage her competing obligations to her father's balkanized family, how to keep connected, if not united, this array of personalities and persons for whom she obviously felt sincere affection. She could have chosen to play out Harry's script in which Jane always had "Mary's and Weber's house to go to."[32] She could have devoted herself to commuting between those two households, serving as the beloved sister to siblings who needed her and the devoted aunt to children she adored. From that position, she could encourage visits between Weber, Laura, Mary, and Alice, shepherd Sadie up to Mary's for romps with her cousins, or ship John and Weber down to Alice's for a sharing of the childwatch. She could, in short, foster the family connections she desired, including her own connection to Alice, even if that meant time with Harry.

Jane did not reject this scenario, but she did give it clear boundaries. She was not, after all, the "typical old maid," so she never committed herself to a round of sibling domesticity that did not have a specific end date. In 1886 and 1887, she never spent more time with her siblings than she spent with Anna and George in Baltimore, and her whole pattern suggests a felt need to be in Baltimore—out of desire and duty. She regularly limited visits to Mary's and Alice's on the grounds that she was "due" in Baltimore, keeping to her schedule though "Stanley's pathetic little voice repeated with childish persistency, 'Aunt

Jane what's you going for?'" Even when Ellen Starr implored her for more time together than a stopover in a Chicago train station, Jane insisted on making her way to Anna's side.[33]

By situating herself in Baltimore for several months each year, Jane could attend to her father's widow and her ever awkward stepbrother while also gaining a respectable niche in the cultured society that was affiliated with Johns Hopkins, America's newest and most innovative university. Living with Anna and George meant living in the fashionable Charles Street neighborhood of Baltimore, within blocks of the Johns Hopkins University campus, the Peabody Institute, the Baltimore Academy of Music, the Walters Art Gallery, and the new Enoch Pratt Library.[34] It meant, too, living in a household in which she had a managerial position. When she was living with Mary or Alice or Weber's wife, Laura, Jane was always the maiden sister in another woman's house, subject to a sister's tastes and a brother's rule. In Baltimore, Jane had considerable influence and freedom in the business of daily living. She was certainly Anna's equal in "fussing with curtains and accessories" and enjoying "all the importance and dignity of housekeeping."[35] In fact, when Jane and George joined forces to convince a reluctant Anna to give up the conveniences of boardinghouse life for the privacy of an independent flat, Anna conceded to her adult children and left the decorating of the flat to Jane.[36]

Jane and Anna had learned to live compatibly together over the years. Anna missed her "little housekeeper" when Jane went to Rockford, and even allowing for the diplomatic bias in Jane's "cheerful" letters, there is every reason to conclude that the two women roomed together comfortably in Europe.[37] Jane often drew word pictures in her letters home depicting the two of them in a "cosy" room with the fire lit in the grate, Anna curled up in bed nibbling on arrowroot or the two of them at the writing table, Jane with pencil in hand, and Anna monopolizing the "family bottle of ink."[38] When Alice sent them checks as Christmas presents, Jane delayed shopping until Anna recovered from a cold because they wanted "the fun of going out to spend [the checks] together."[39] Jane's management of the daily logistics of the European trip, from luggage transport to duty payments to routing mail in and out, earned her that perch of control from which she could, with satisfaction, minister to Anna's ailments and appreciate her stepmother's traveling stamina.[40]

During their winter in Berlin, when Anna was experiencing "fevers" and was depressed about the "scattered" family, Jane confessed to Alice that she sometimes felt "very irritated and angry," but never named Anna as the cause for that anger.[41] By that point in her life, Jane had two decades of experience with Anna's ailments, exaggerations, manipulations, and obsessive orientation toward the menfolk in her life, but she may still have been capable of irritation

19. Jane Addams as a fashionable young lady in Baltimore, 1885. (Swarthmore College Peace Collection)

at her stepmother's emotional extravagances and insensitive focus on her biological sons. While Jane may not have known of Anna's letters to Harry wishing "I could have taken this tour with 'my boys,'" she surely knew of Anna's
excitement over George's impending visit with them in Europe.[42] Jane found
utterly "provoking" Anna's romantic fantasy that this absent-minded boy-child
would "take charge of us" when he arrived; in fact, Jane had to dictate exact
traveling instructions to George and then had to cut short a visit to Paris
because George misread those instructions.[43]

   In Anna Haldeman Addams's worldview, if she was not with a man—a
husband or a son—she was "quite alone."[44] Whether Jane was amused or hurt
by this effacement of her own company, she never dropped her public stance
as Anna's loyal companion. In the two years following their return from Europe,
Jane regularly worked alongside her stepmother on business and household
affairs in Cedarville in addition to spending months with her in Baltimore. When
describing the "round of modest gaiety" she and Anna enjoyed in Baltimore,
Jane never set herself apart from Anna.[45] They laughed, together, over the formal custom of visiting and "receiving" but participated in it—together; they
attended society luncheons and teas together, went to concerts and lectures
together, formed art and reading groups together, and attended "elegant" evening parties together (where Jane took "a great deal of pleasure" when "Ma took
the first prize" in euchre "for good playing and I took the booby prize for poor
playing").[46] Jane even took Anna with her on the first trip to Pennsylvania, and
Jane's maternal Aunt Elizabeth was "very much disappointed" when Anna
declined the chance to come along on the tour of Jane's mother's birthplace.[47]

   Jane did, of course, engage in social, cultural, and even charitable activities apart from Anna, and did so more frequently in her second Baltimore season than her first, but the rhetorical thrust of Jane's letters to Alice, Mary,
and Laura, whether writing from Europe or Baltimore or Cedarville, conveyed
the message that she and Anna were a team.

   The central focus of their joint effort was George, whose graduate work at
Johns Hopkins University gave both women a legitimate reason for living away
from Cedarville. George initially adored his work under W. K. Brooks, the
wunderkind of oyster studies in America. Brooks's innovative program of seaside fieldwork opened up opportunities for original graduate research that
most universities in the United States had not yet developed. Brooks was a pioneer in convincing state and federal government agencies to invest in scientific
research for economic development; his research helped to revive the oyster
business in Maryland and to establish research facilities such as the Woods
Hole Oceanographic Institute on Cape Cod.[48] During George's enthusiastic
first year at Hopkins, while Anna and Jane were in Europe, he had done little

but study. While he had delighted in the intellectual immersion, George appre-ciated the "new era" his mother and stepsister created for him with their arrival in Baltimore; they could provide "the enjoyment I had been deprived of by their absence."[49]

From Europe, both women had lectured the zealous young marine scien-tist on the need for a social life; Anna warned him against being "a snail in one's shell," Jane teased him about his inclination to be "an anchorite."[50] But both women knew the problem extended deeper than mere social graces; Anna gave voice to her worst (and most prescient) fears when she begged Harry to rescue his younger brother from becoming "a melancholy downcast [of] no use to the world and a burden to himself."[51] George himself admitted that he was "queer and everybody thinks so and usually avoid me because of my peculiarities."[52] Try as Anna might to convince herself that her son's "nervous depreciation" was a "safeguard to his talent and genius that otherwise would be *frittered* away in society," she worried terribly that her "pearl" of a son would drown in oyster studies.[53]

Any notion, however dim, that Jane could alleviate the situation by becoming George's wife had been completely squelched by 1885, but that did not diminish Jane's value in providing the ballast that kept Anna and George emotionally afloat. When, for example, Jane visited her maternal relatives in Pennsylvania in the fall of 1886, she promised Anna that she would "make a strenuous effort" to get back within a week.[54] When that week stretched to ten days, she came back to find George "sensitive" and "suspicious . . . of every-one" and "Ma and George both dreadfully depressed." Jane's "cheerful letter" to Alice on the episode refrained from comparing Haldeman possessiveness to her Pennsylvania relatives' generous efforts to reach out to both Anna and George.[55] Instead, her report described breaking Anna's spell with a "delightful afternoon" at the home of wealthy friends in the Baltimore suburbs and returning to their flat where George "had the family tea kettle boiling and sup-per almost ready and we ended up with a jolly evening."[56]

Jane's conduct with George in these years was alternately careful, candid, and clumsy. He was, at times, the warm and familiar partner she had grown up confiding in but he became, at other times, an awkward and alien male whose failings called up Jane's fury and then her pity. Jane always took the upper hand with George on practical matters but seemed to compensate for that by defer-ring to him on intellectual matters. For his part, George clung to the bit of masculine pride and privilege he could claim by being the family's scientist. He strained to enhance that status by unfairly stereotyping Jane as a partisan for the feminine world of the arts and as someone who was hostile to science. This gendered bit of sibling rivalry replicated the tension between masculine science and feminine intuition that had so vexed Jane at Rockford. Her tour of Europe and correspondence with Ellen Starr had advanced Jane's identification with art and intuition, but Jane did not appreciate the smug exclusivity George claimed for science. In their ongoing debates over the relative usefulness of art and science, Jane would concede to George for as long as she could and then blurt out that "modern science is a trifle esoteric and exotic in its relation to the world." Such charges brought forth a superior, self-satisfied tone from George, who would not even deign to participate in Jane's German reading group because they read novels instead of serious works. However infuriating her brother's intellectual bravado, Jane could not attack it too often or too directly because she knew the psyche under George's thin outer crust was so fragile.[57]

It would have been plenty taxing for any old maid, typical or not, to nurture filial connections between a captivatingly egocentric stepmother, a sensitive stepbrother who suffered from bouts of depression and paranoia, another brother who was periodically committed to an asylum for manic lunacy, a sister with six children who was weakened by too many pregnancies and too many relocations, and an ever expanding clan of aunts and uncles and cousins. But Jane faced the added diplomatic challenge of maintaining family harmony with Alice and Harry.

At issue, always, was Harry's drinking. Jane tiptoed around the problem in deference to her sister; she had, after all, advised Alice to respect Mary's affection for Rev. Linn. But Anna took the opposite approach with Harry, drawing a temperance lesson from every European sight, reminding her son that Ireland was a nation "cursed with whiskey" and that the "grape vine" climbing "over all and all" in Italy had produced a "beastly" people with "no intellect much less spirituality."[58] Hoping to coax her drunken, small-town son out of the bottle, Anna described Harry, with customary extravagance, as a "diamond" with "a genius for medicine."[59] Harry's response to his mother's inflated expectations was to leave the medical profession and depart Mitchellville, Iowa. While Anna and Jane were wintering in Berlin, he and Alice decamped to the eastern Kansas town of Girard, whose population of about 1,500 made it twice the size of Mitchellville. There, on the prosperous side of a state that averaged one mortgage for every two adults, Harry and his heiress wife became the proprietors of the Bank of Girard.[60]

Anna's initial reaction to this announcement was to pen her commentary on the fate of "scattered" families wherein "selfishness and all its evil train rule the soul," but she did summon the hope that "every association [in] your new home will be of the *highest*" and advised Harry to "never again" allow his life to be "disturbed by any circumstances that are under your control."[61] Jane, as always, avoided even the most oblique reference to Harry's vices, noting only her "dislike" of Harry's "giving up his professional work," and conceding to Alice's argument that "there are more ways than one of doing good" in the world.[62]

Once back in the United States, Jane and Anna both stayed in very close touch with Girard, but managed their relationships there in characteristically different ways. Jane tried to rise above the tensions with magnanimity, Anna opted for the withholding of affection. The resulting fault lines revealed themselves through terrain common to every family: how to allocate money and how to arrange visits. It fell to Jane to mediate the tensions that arose among Anna, George, Harry, and Alice over these mundane matters.

In the continuation of a practice begun in Europe, Jane seemed to be forever in the market for some fashionable item Alice had ordered from the hinterlands. Jane tried to make these "little friendly errands" a family enterprise by engaging Anna's expertise in selecting the right handkerchiefs, stationery, chess boards, statuary, illustrated prints, draperies, dresses, smoking jackets, bedroom slippers, bookcase curtains, or buffets for Alice's discerning eye.[63] But Anna, no stranger to shopping, was often disapproving of Alice's frequent requests for more goods. She saw Alice and Harry's zest for "things" as a childlike "love" for "toys with endless variety."[64] So great was Anna's disdain for the way Harry and Alice spent money that she once pushed beyond the pain of alcoholism and into the pain of childlessness by snidely congratulating Harry on being able to buy Alice "such a nice birthday gift" since he had "no children to save and plan for and educate."[65]

Meanwhile, Jane patiently scoured the shops of London and Rome, as well as Philadelphia and Baltimore, demonstrating both her devotion to her artistically inclined sister and her own determination to get the best product at the best price. Jane was tireless in her search for just the right item, going back and forth between stores, even between cities, before settling on a final purchase. In Europe, Jane fretted constantly over whether she had bought the right thing, but after a season among the refined citizens of Baltimore, she was more confident of her ability to find "something much prettier" than what Alice had ordered and even to advise that "something simpler would be in better taste." As always when trying to manage Alice, Jane begged off any desire to "influence you too much" and deflected blame by promising to consult Ma on the final purchase.[66]

From afar, it was possible to smooth over the tensions in Anna's relationship with Harry and Alice. Anna's persistent refusal to visit Harry and Alice in Girard, however, brought all the strains to the surface. Alice forced the issue by pressing Jane to bring Anna west in the summer of 1886 while George was busy with seaside research. After much stalling and dodging around false issues like "distance," Jane was, finally, able to assemble a family gathering with two

Pennsylvania cousins and two of Anna's nieces along for ballast. They met in Colorado—six hundred miles beyond Girard, Kansas, and Harry's liquor cabinet.[67]

Months later, Jane was still loudly protesting to Alice that "it *was* a delightful trip, wasn't it dear?"[68] But Jane's cheer could not conceal the fact that this was the last time Ma would visit her son and daughter-in-law for another two years. Even after Alice gave birth to their long-awaited child in the summer of 1887 and named that child Anna Marcet, Harry's mother stayed away from Girard and chose to spend the next summer with George in Florida. From there, she wrote to Harry of her constant prayers that he would be "cured" of his "sinful indulgences." She left no doubt about her resistance to visiting Girard: "When I return, if I ever do," she pleadingly threatened, "oh, meet me a cured and sober man."[69] Though Harry told George he wanted his mother's "guiding hand" and "loving heart" with them at the time of Marcet's birth, Anna did not appear. Though Jane lobbied George to persuade his mother to visit and then consoled Alice with tales of Ma dreaming of Marcet and "planning just a little, I think, to see her this fall," still, Anna did not budge.[70] The message was clear to those who cared to pay attention: if any of Anna's children moved too far beyond the range of her control, they could expect to be punished. Derelictions of the family claim bore consequences.

Jane scrambled to provide what Anna withheld. While requests from Girard for money could elicit a lecture from Anna on George's comparative frugality, Jane responded with assurances that Ma was "glad to have the opportunity of helping Harry" financially. Jane advised that Alice and Harry not upset themselves with bitter thoughts toward the "nervous" George or well-intentioned Ma.[71] Meanwhile, Jane began to invest quite liberally in the Bank of Girard. Since coming into her inheritance in 1881, she had engaged in a number of land transactions in the Cedarville area but when the need arose to help Harry and Alice, Jane adopted Girard as her "new banking place." During the difficult harvest of 1886, Jane hastily sent bank notes west in the hope of sparing the family "any mortifying appearances" and informed Alice of her willingness to invest another $6,000 note coming due "if you would like it dear."[72]

Eastern Kansas was not as drought burdened or debt ridden as the rest of Kansas in this period, but 1887 was a harsh year for that state, and it was in 1887 that Jane arranged for Alice to act as her agent in investing some $2,500 in Kansas farms, "an even amount," Jane thought, "and shapely."[73] The Girard bank would pay her 12 percent interest on the use of her money, better than the 7 percent she was earning at home in Stephenson County, and Jane insisted that Alice accept 2 percent of that as her agent's fee.[74] The arrangement helped both sisters. It gave Alice family support for a business enterprise in which she was clearly a full partner while giving Jane confidence, as she planned her next

European trip, that her money would be well tended. Anna might have thought Alice extravagant in her tastes, but Jane regarded her older sister as a shrewd businesswoman; indeed, it appears that Senator Addams had made sure that all three of his daughters knew how to invest and manage their money.[75] Beyond the business benefits, however, the Girard banking arrangement may have served to balance other sibling accounts. If Jane's choice to live with Alice's disapproving mother-in-law put Jane in emotional debt to Alice, or if Jane's decision not to encumber herself through marriage with a Haldeman son taxed the sisters' lifetime ledger, well, this investment of funds, coupled with Jane's regular, solicitous letters, represented an effort at repayment.

More than twenty years later, Jane sketched a story in her autobiography about investing money in "a western state" only to learn—to her horror—that she was profiting from conditions so "wretched" that the starved hogs on her farms were devouring one another.[76] It was an effective parable for illustrating Jane Addams's concern about "the big fish living off the little fish" and for depicting herself, as she was wont to do, as the average American making average American mistakes.[77] The story bore little relation to actual conditions around Girard, however, where Jane herself admitted to Laura Addams that the local farmers' "little bits of houses . . . and their apparent wealth are always a puzzle to me."[78] Harry was dead by the time Jane's melodramatic spin on her Kansas investments appeared in print. By then, Alice was president of the Bank of Girard and could, perhaps, accept the tale as fair revenge for Harry's disdain of Jane's efforts to do good in the family and, later, in the world.

Ellen Starr would, ultimately, partner with Jane in those worldly efforts, but in these two years, when Jane was shuttling between Baltimore, Cedarville, and her sisters' homes, Ellen saw precious little of her "darling" friend.[79] Though Jane felt she "could not afford to lose so much" of Ellen "in these years" of her life, she continued to privilege the family claim over spending time with Ellen.[80] They got "'visiting on the fly' reduced to an art," grabbing an hour here or there when a train of Jane's would pass through Chicago, and they managed a handful of visits lasting a few days, usually in conjunction with time at Mary's or in Cedarville.[81]

Their "ever increasing love and friendship," which had begun to intensify before Jane left for Europe, continued to evolve between the time of Jane's return in the spring of 1885 and the two women's tour of Europe together in the winter and spring of 1888.[82] Though few, their visits were crucial to the relationship's progress; they made Jane realize that she and Ellen enjoyed themselves "more each time," and they reminded Ellen that "it was quite the natural thing that we should be together and the unusual thing that we should not."[83] Still, Jane chose to reside far from Ellen, and though Ellen called Jane a "wretched girl" for not making more time for her, she supposed "on the whole it is better I can't see you very often. . . . I should get to depending on you, bod- ily, in a little while, and that would be quite sure to make trouble in the end."[84] For the time being, they played out the relationship in letters whose sweet sincerity can be traced up until the summer of 1886. Between that time and their trip to Europe, however, there is an eighteen-month gap in the surviving record, a silence that refuses to reveal if Jane was ever able to act on her resolve to write Ellen "more fearlessly," to deliver her of a "burning" letter.[85]

By the mid-1880s, they had been friends for nearly a decade. Jane was the "earliest" of Ellen's friends who had "remained anything" to her, the "one per- son" Ellen had "seemed to possess, absent or present."[86] Jane could become "disconcerted" by their separations and intense reunions; Ellen was capable of tears when they tried to "put so much into a few days" together.[87] Though she was "in deadly fear of being thought over sentimental," Ellen was increasingly open about her feelings for Jane, and Jane was increasingly accepting of her friend's expressiveness.[88] Slowly, they inched their way closer to each other along an emotional tightrope that was held aloft by their shared devotion to spiritual integrity and to finding work commensurate with that devotion.

In the last half of 1885, Ellen took to rereading Jane's old letters and essays from Rockford. "I had almost forgotten us," she claimed, but Jane's words and the "atrocity" of her spelling, brought back a shared youth. Even at seventeen, Ellen reminded Jane, "you *could* do lovely things." Such was Ellen's admiration for Jane's seminary work that she shared an essay of Jane's with her students at Miss Kirkland's school in Chicago and reported to Jane that the girls were so impressed, they thought surely Jane was now writing books. Of course, Jane was not writing books, and Ellen justified that contradiction of talent, expec- tations, and idleness by telling her students, "if my friend's body had been equal to her mind, and if a great many demands on the strength of both had not come to her which do not come to most people, she would have done a good many remarkable things which the Lord doesn't seem to have intended her to do."[89]

Back at Rockford, when Jane's heroic destiny seemed so bright, she had led Ellen on a merry chase through the thickets of her sophomoric philosophizing. Now, with the Lord's intentions blurred, Jane was more subdued and available. On the eve of her first European tour, Jane had admitted to Ellen that she felt the need of Christ, that "the good men and books I used to depend on will no longer answer."[90] Jane returned to that theme, after her tour of heroes, in announcing that she felt herself "approaching a crisis." For many years, she confessed, "it was my ambition to reach my father's moral requirement"; now, however, the unsanctified senator's designated daughter was "needing something more." Writing from her sister Mary's house in Harvard, Illinois, where she was both soothed and smothered in that pious family's love for "Aunt Jane," she looked "rather wistfully" to Ellen "for help."[91]

Jane saw in Ellen a woman who had successfully separated from her family, both geographically and religiously. "You were never so in rapport with Durand as I was with Cedarville," Jane observed, hinting at her growing realization of the dangers that lay in family devotion and in loyalty to a dead father's rationalism. Jane saw in Ellen, too, a woman whose faith was substantial while Jane felt her own religious life "has been so small."[92] There was a measure of flattery in all of this; religion was, after all, the language of their romance, as it was the language of so many women's romances in the nineteenth century.[93] Religious yearnings were no mere gloss, however; they constituted a compelling attraction for these fellow seekers. When Ellen told Jane, "I always think of *you* on special religious days," she was not, as Ellen might say, just "giving taffy."[94] She was saying that thoughts of Jane put her in a spiritual frame of mind; she was sanctifying the relationship as a true communion of souls.

Jane's assumption that Ellen had found the "peace that passeth understanding" was "wide of the mark," protested Ellen. It made her feel "fraudulent" to think that Jane imagined her at peace when she was not, so Ellen sat up late writing to Jane with a dying lamp and a "lame" eye. Joining the Episcopal Church was not, explained Ellen, "an indication of anything accomplished; only of a desire for something." Ellen was "shocked" by Jane's (prescient) thought that her friend might become a Catholic. Ellen herself felt "more like a floating island" and regarded Jane as "so much above me in goodness" that she could not bear to have Jane think Ellen the more religious. "You, outside the church, I within it, are simply trying to find the same thing, and you are much nearer it than I," insisted Ellen, because Jane's obedience to the family claim meant she, not Ellen, was living a "life of self-denial and of pleasing others and not one's self."[95]

In their youth, Jane had rejected Ellen's attempts to claim common spiritual ground. Now, she apologized to Ellen for her lack of understanding and religious "floundering."[96] Ellen met Jane's new attitude by recommending that her friend read religious writers whom Ellen admired. Her suggestions ran the gamut from the American Protestant Episcopal bishop, Phillips Brooks, through liberal Anglicans like Arthur Stanley, William Frederic Farrar, and Frederick Robertson, and on to the Anglican-turned-Catholic, Cardinal John Henry Newman.[97] For all of the theological (and political) differences that divided these Christians, the common attraction for Ellen was their willingness to give voice to their subjective experience with faith—and doubt.[98] The defining issue for Ellen at this point in her own religious development was not whether a particular theologian advocated Christian concern for social justice; some of her favorites did, some did not. The issue was whether they placed the essential spiritual character of Jesus above all considerations of church formality, hierarchy, or denomination, and whether they privileged faith over reason, aesthetics over science, the heart over the head.

Exposure to this approach to Christianity gave Jane a third alternative to her father's matter-of-fact "moral requirement" and Miss Sill's pseudo-modern attempts at proving Christian orthodoxy. Ellen provided a body of religious literature that could quench Jane's thirst for spiritual language while legitimating her sense that debates over doctrinal conformity, the evidence of miracles, or the promise of atonement were stupid diversions from the real task of keeping "the facts of Christ's life before us" and using the model of his spiritual character to inspire transcendence in ourselves.[99] For Ellen, and the theologians she recommended, faith in Christ's divinity was at the center of such an enterprise. Jane, however, could read these lyric testaments to the centrality of Jesus as proof that faith in a supernatural Christ was less important than faith in Jesus's moral example on earth. These texts held out the possibility that Jane's "practical" search for a religion to prepare her for good works (or works of "mere goodness") might not require the leap of faith that Ellen sought through holy prayer.

It appears that Jane began reading Leo Tolstoy's religious and social criticism in these years. His statement of faith, *My Religion*, was published in English in 1885 and Jane likely read it in the fall of 1886 during her second season in Baltimore.[100] Like the writers Ellen recommended, Tolstoy called for a focus on Jesus, not on the institutional trappings that had grown up around him. Tolstoy was more radical than Ellen's churchmen, however, because he insisted that true Christianity demanded faith in Jesus' message about human salvation on earth, not faith in a supernatural Jesus or promises of salvation after death. If Jane was reading *My Religion* in the fall of 1886, during that period when her correspondence with Ellen has not survived, she was encountering his argument that beyond the "mysteries of dogmatics, homiletics, patristics, liturgics, hermeneutics, apologetics," there was one, single "center of gravity" to Christ's teaching. That central message was "resist not evil," by which Christ meant "never do anything that is contrary to the law of love."[101]

The theologians Ellen was reading sought to clear wider spiritual pathways to experiencing faith in Jesus' divinity and thereby gaining individual, eternal salvation. By contrast, Tolstoy derided faith in a divine Jesus and in eternal salvation as myths that distorted the teachings of Jesus. Humans, he said, needed faith in the law of absolute, unconditional love of one another, not in the divinity of Jesus. Salvation was to be experienced only in this life and the path to that salvation came through collective, not individual, action. In the course of arguing that each individual's salvation came through ministering to others, Tolstoy called for a celebration of human reason and kindness as the route to human fellowship and the creation of heaven on earth.[102]

At the time that Jane was likely trying to integrate her reading in Tolstoy with her reading of Ellen's Anglicans, she was also sampling a variety of churches in Baltimore. Grace Episcopal was located closest to where she was living but she finally confessed to Ellen that it was "not quite what I want." Uplift, for Ellen, might have come through music, poetic liturgy, and ritual; for Jane, the sermon was "more to me than the service," so she was "rather afraid" she would "settle down" in the Unitarian Church.[103] The minister there, a descendent of the abolitionists Theodore Weld and Angelina Grimké, preached to a cross-class congregation on the individual's responsibility for what he called "the wholesome alleviation of the unfortunate."[104]

Whatever Jane's felt need for more than her "father's moral requirement" in these years, and however great her attraction to Ellen's emotional experience, the difference Jane identified at Rockford persisted: Ellen still longed for "a beautiful faith," Jane still sought religion "in a practical sense."[105] Ellen looked to those who said faith in the supernatural was required for worldly action; Jane was attending to the message that belief in human love would suffice. In Ellen's eyes, this difference only heightened her estimate of Jane's inner strength; she viewed Jane in the same positive light in which she viewed the novelist they both adored, George Eliot. Like Eliot, Jane adhered to Christian morals without reliance on the promise of eternal salvation.[106]

There were times, however, when Jane's rectitude was a source of exasperation for Ellen. In theory, she admired her friend's selfless loyalty to the family claim; in practice, it meant Ellen was continually neglected. The only surviving letter from the spring of 1887 includes an apology from Jane for having been so "ostentatiously virtuous" that she missed a date with Ellen in Chicago. At the time, Jane was staying with Mary in Lake Forest, just a few miles outside the city, and was to join Ellen for one of Aunt Eliza Starr's public lectures on Catholic art.[107] Jane failed to meet Ellen because she had gone on a "wild goose chase" in Chicago, looking for a nursemaid for Mary and a cradle for Alice.[108] As penance, she accepted Ellen's "estimate of my character" as it related to the "mania for self-sacrifice."[109] Extricating herself from the family claim to be at Ellen's side was not a simple proposition for Jane. Ellen could not "help wishing . . . that we could sometime be in the same place long enough to do some work together. I believe we should work well."[110] It was an inviting sentiment, but it begged the question: what work?

Chapter 10
Some Curious Conclusions

During the years between Jane's return from her first trip to Europe and her departure for her second trip, there appeared no clear path to doing good work in the world. Jane was not as openly anxious over her lack of direction as she had been at Rockford or in Europe. Instead, she seems to have begun eyeing the life choices that other women around her had made and considering her options in the context of her own experience and the experience of women she knew. Having spent six years trying to impose masculine theories of heroism on herself, Jane now turned the process around and began to create a model for female heroism out of the materials of her own life. The result of this empirical effort was not a discernibly different view of womanhood than Jane Addams had held before but, rather, a new embrace of the prosaic and the practical as a potential path to stewardship for a still unconverted and apparently nonscholarly female.

Jane Addams constructed her more commonplace heroism while living as the maiden stepsister of a biology graduate student at the country's newest and most ambitious research university in Baltimore, Maryland. The city and the Johns Hopkins University community were both lively centers of culture and politics in the mid-1880s even though Baltimore itself was lagging behind other major cities in the shift from a commercial to an industrial economy. With some 400,000 inhabitants, Baltimore's population in 1885 was not growing at nearly the rate of cities like Chicago, and its mix of black, native-born white, and immigrant workers struggled in these years with irregular employment and low wages. By 1886, the city had a well-organized Federation of Labor, a German Central Labor Union, and close to four thousand workers enrolled in the Knights of Labor. Jane Addams later claimed that she was in Europe at the time of Chicago's Haymarket riot, on May 1, 1886, when a bomb exploded at a Knights of Labor rally and police fired on workers demonstrating for the eight-hour day.[1] But she was actually living in Baltimore at the time, where streetcar workers went on strike in the month of April to gain a twelve-hour day, and skilled workers led a general strike on April 29, two days before Chicago's Haymarket demonstration. The purpose of Baltimore's general strike was to demand the eight-hour day and to protest against the very things that Jane Addams's beloved Carlyle so deplored: "the tasteless banality of machine production" and workers' increasing alienation from the product of their labors.[2] But Jane never mentioned these labor actions in her correspondence. Nor did she ever mention the rise of Baltimore's civic reform clubs that were intent on overthrowing the well-entrenched Democratic machine.[3]

Jane and Anna occasionally lunched on chicken salad at the Baltimore Women's Exchange, a site established by wealthy women to provide needy women with a respectable place to sell their wares on consignment.[4] But Jane expressed more amusement than respect for the philanthropic effort, noting that "the Bohemian manner of service rather enhanced the enjoyment" and that "all the fashionable people are patrons of it," so "no one dares criticize" the food or the wares. She never commented to Alice on the exchange's actual purpose.[5] And though she was attending various churches in Baltimore, no evidence suggests that she ever involved herself in their particular charitable works. She seemed unaware that Baltimore Unitarians like Mary Richmond, who would later be Jane's colleague in the settlement house movement, were teaching Shakespeare classes to workers under the church's auspices.[6] Nor did she seem to know that the women of Grace Episcopal had opened a daycare center for the children of black working women or that the rector of that church was calling out for more "places of innocent pastime and social intercourse" for those in the laboring class to share with the middle class.[7] Jane did not observe, either in her comments to Ellen on the Unitarians or in her mention to Alice of Tolstoy, that a new "social gospel" in Baltimore was calling on congregants to care as much about saving the community as saving their individual souls.[8] Jane described the Unitarians' socially conscious minister as "the finest minister in the city," but her only comment to Alice on reading Tolstoy was that he made her "more interested in Russia."[9]

Jane did involve herself in the city's cultural life, and Baltimore provided her with an impressive demonstration of what wealthy individuals could do with their money if they chose to be philanthropic. She lived close to and frequented the Peabody Institute, a private "institution for higher culture" founded by George Peabody, a successful merchant, in 1857.[10] The Peabody offered city residents of a certain class access to a reference library, various lecture series, musical concerts by its conservatory students, and an art gallery. Jane also frequented, though she complained it was always crowded, the brandnew Enoch Pratt Library, a privately funded public institution whose main branch opened just a few blocks south of where Jane and Anna were living in 1886.[11] What would become the Walters Art Gallery in later years was then housed at the rear of William Walters's home, also in Jane Addams's Baltimore neighborhood, and she visited that semiprivate gallery, as well as the semiprivate McCoy Collection of art history, at various times during her two seasons in the city.[12] When Jane was in Europe, she had been disturbed over how much fine art was still confined to private homes and had begun thinking about the duty of the privileged to share art with the general public. In Baltimore, though she never remarked upon it, she was exposed to the solutions that private cultural philanthropists were offering in their attempt, albeit limited, to make the fine arts more widely available.

Johns Hopkins University was the most impressive example of private philanthropy in the city of Baltimore. According to one 1881 report, the university was endowed with $3 million of the "hard earnings and careful savings of one of our greatest merchants." Though not yet five years old in 1881, Hopkins was already claiming to be "the best intellectual workshop in America" because of its focus on providing graduate students with experience in producing original work by studying under faculty members who combined teaching with an active research program.[13] By the time Jane Addams got to Baltimore in 1886, the university was a beehive of activity. G. Stanley Hall was investigating the ideas that would make him the founder of adolescent psychology in the United States; Woodrow Wilson had just earned his Ph.D. in political history and was now a lecturer pursuing his interest in British parliamentary government; and the young Richard T. Ely was shaking things up in the economics department, inculcating students like Thorstein Veblen, John R. Commons, Edward A. Ross, and Albion Small with his brash ideas on the need for government ownership of the railroads and the rights of labor to organize and strike.[14]

Ely wrote an editorial in support of the Baltimore streetcar workers' strike in March 1886, which appeared on the front page of the *Baltimore Sun*.[15] Jane Addams might have read it, just as she might have read the snide denunciation of Ely's prolabor position that Hopkins mathematics professor, Simon Newcomb, published in the *Nation* a few weeks later.[16] Given the faculty parlors and dining rooms Jane was visiting at this time, it seems probable that she would have overheard professors discussing this heated rivalry between Ely and Newcomb and might well have heard the scientists siding with Newcomb, the hardheaded mathematician. Though Jane gave Alice a detailed picture of the fine arts lectures, musical concerts, and social gatherings she and Anna were enjoying at the university, she never mentioned these university debates over political economy.

Nor did she ever comment on the fact that Daniel Coit Gilman, the vigorous president of Johns Hopkins, had attended a meeting of the Social Science Association in Albany, New York in 1881 where he heard about the Charity

Organization Society. The COS was an effort born in London, but now launched in New York, to rationalize the distribution of charitable funds. Gilman immediately founded a COS in Baltimore on the assumption that uncoordinated, decentralized private charity efforts and politically corrupt public charities perpetuated poverty by rewarding the lazy with direct relief and by not providing the deserving poor with the character education, job training, and subsidized housing they really needed.[17] Consistent with the mission of the university, the COS emphasized the collection of "social statistics" in order to base all charity on the "scientific method" and insure that the city's philanthropic efforts were efficient, effective, and uncorrupted by the chicanery of professional tramps.[18]

The introduction of COS theory into the discussion at Johns Hopkins' Seminary on History and Politics made philanthropy a virile new arena for reform activism among professors and their graduate students, who saw their scientific method as a way to wrest control of the poor away from "Lady Bountiful" and her "pet paupers."[19] Unfortunately, the COS's "fetish" with exposing frauds and harassing vagrants diverted its energies from developing genuine programs of aid in the years Jane Addams was living in Baltimore. Its general lack of progress was masked, however, in the city's 1886 report at the National Conference of Charities and Corrections where great emphasis was placed on one philanthropist's generous gift allowing the COS to offer coal, at cost, to the poor.[20]

Jane Addams was touring Colorado with Anna, Alice, Harry, and her cousins in July 1886, when this report on Baltimore's coal project was being delivered. But even when she was in Baltimore, Jane indicated no awareness of the National Conference of Charities and Corrections, the university's Seminary on History and Politics, or the Charity Organization Society. Nine months later, Jane was living at Mary's home in Geneseo, sitting up during those spring nights with the Linns' very sickly baby Charles.[21] As a result, she was not in Baltimore to hear Woodrow Wilson's history professor, Herbert Baxter Adams, deliver a talk on the fine work being done in a new charitable institution in London, Toynbee Hall, which called itself a "settlement house" because it had settled among its poor neighbors in the same East End Jane had once visited.[22] Jane was a regular reader of *Century* magazine in these years, so she may have seen its May 1887 article on Toynbee Hall and read the praise from Oxford University men for the settlement's enrichment of their lives.[23] Still, the family claim that spring left Jane little time for contemplating the social claim; eleven-week-old Charles Linn died on May 5 and, amidst that grief, Jane sped off to Girard to be on hand for the June birth of Alice's baby, Anna Marcet.

In the coming decades, Jane Addams would engage with virtually every one of the endeavors she seems to have missed in Baltimore. Though largely untouched by these movements in the mid-1880s, her life would soon be closely involved with everything from the labor movement to the social gospel movement, from cultural philanthropy to social science research. Toynbee Hall would be her touchstone; Richard Ely would be the editor of her first major book, *Hull-House Maps and Papers*; his student Albion Small would be her colleague at that other major research institution, the University of Chicago; she would be the first female president of the National Conference of Charities and Corrections and would play a role in reorienting that organization away from the early rigidities of the Charity Organization Society. Addams would develop and then revise her approach to machine politics, as well as her opinion of Woodrow Wilson; Hull-House would open both a lending library and an art gallery and would, in time, offer Shakespeare classes and cheap coal to the working poor. In fact, by the 1920s, graduate students in "social economics" at Johns Hopkins would be required to take a course that examined the lives and works of twelve leaders in human welfare, including Jane Addams.[24]

While she was living in Baltimore in 1886 and 1887, however, Jane traveled in circles entirely apart from those concerned with social justice and civic reform. The women and men with whom she and Anna socialized were connected to the university through George's world of science and mathematics. They were people who devoted their leisure time and civic energies to their own enjoyment of the arts, not to stewardship of the less blessed. The lectures Jane and her friends attended on campus were illustrated lectures on art history, literary studies of European writers, or popularized reports on zoological research.[25] Looking back, she recalled that the "lecture rooms at Johns Hopkins University" left her feeling "much disillusioned . . . as to the effect of intellectual pursuits upon moral development."[26] One measure of her disillusionment can be taken from the fact that she independently, quite apart from any social network of charitable women, began to make contact with the city's poor.

Jane launched her first stay in Baltimore by noticing the faces of the poor, which was the one thing she had not done in Europe. On Christmas Eve 1885, she and Anna and George had wandered through the city's outdoor markets, and Jane took sentimental comfort from the "shining faces of the Negroes over their wares."[27] Defining herself apart from two scholarly sisters in her boardinghouse who were "perfectly rabid on the Southern question," Jane chose to feel warmly toward Baltimore's "jolly" blacks and within just a few weeks of her arrival, she, along with Anna, visited a shelter for "about sixteen old colored women."[28] She found the women "interesting," and, without further mention of

Anna, decided she would "go to see them often."²⁹ A few weeks later, Jane visited "a sewing school for poor children" and, again, found them "very interesting, most of them patient and sick looking."³⁰

Charity work occasioned no further comment during that first winter in Baltimore. Jane's visits to the poor, however frequent or infrequent they may have been, protected her from feeling unproductive. During her first season in Baltimore, she tried to study French, Voltaire, Dante, and Ruskin but reported to both Alice and Ellen that her "faculties" were, once again, "paralyzed," all "perfectly inaccessible, locked away from me."³¹ When she compared her reading and attendance at lectures to Ellen's reports of strenuous, often burdensome, teaching duties, she felt that "with all my apparent leisure, I do nothing at all."³² An apology from Ellen for having to devote most of her time and energy to her students, "who seem to be my mission," caused Jane to reflect on her lack of mission and to conclude that she had "wasted time most shamefully this winter" due to her "natural indolence."³³ Once again, Jane was trapped between doing her duty to Anna by pursuing cultural life in Baltimore and realizing that such pursuits left her without the requisite energy to find any mission beyond her duty to Anna.

In one of her last letters to Ellen from Europe, Jane had mused on the responsibility of the privileged to take art to the masses. An utterly mundane experience reading poetry to a blind man in Girard, Kansas, in the summer of 1886 gave Jane "something phenomenal" to add to those musings. The connection she made with this "irritable old gentleman of seventy-seven" just by reading him Browning taught her that it was possible, with art as a vehicle, to push past presumptions and defenses and into an authentic human encounter. As she explained in a letter to Ellen, the cranky septuagenarian had been a professor of Greek and Latin, which surprised Jane, and he heard "a fine personality" in Jane's voice, which greatly pleased her. Jane insisted she was grateful that the blind man "could not see my face and how much I was below what he thought of me," but his praise for the personality in her voice resonated with her respect for Browning's belief that "each man owes to the world" the "power" of his personality.³⁴ The detail, the candor, and even the humorous self-effacement which Jane crafted into this vignette is strikingly similar to her later writings about daily encounters with neighbors in Chicago. This Girard experience (and perhaps others that went unrecorded or have not survived) allowed her to rehearse the role that her personality would play in others' lives and to see that knowledge of the arts might actually be of use and comfort to other human beings.

Within two weeks of her return to Baltimore in October 1886, Jane was reporting to Weber's wife, Laura, that she had "already gotten into a mission school, and I find all sorts of good works appealing for help."[35] She never mentioned the mission school again; its religious purpose may have been uncomfortable for her. But she did quickly return to the "old women at the Shelter," and reported to Alice, her summer companion in Colorado, that she "really got them excited and myself too telling them of our ascent of Pike's Peak."[36] A few weeks later she commented again on her "pleasant afternoon with the two old women in the Colored shelter. They are so responsive and confidential and begin to know me well enough now to be perfectly free." Jane said nothing about the organization and administration of the shelter, made no comment on the philosophy guiding this particular charity. The entire focus of her reports was on her direct, personal interaction with what appears to have been a handful of elderly black women living out their lives in an urban shelter. On only one occasion did Jane remark on charity policy and that was in the course of describing her Christmas day in 1886, when she delivered presents to the old women and then to "a little colored orphan asylum I have grown quite interested in." Jane reported that the asylum's practice was to "take little colored girls and keep them until they are fifteen, training them to be *good servants*." Lest this sound too accommodating to the Old South, Jane hastened to add that the children themselves were "expecting" to be servants and the training allowed them to be ambitious for "a good place." In her most officious tone she added, "I heartily approve of the scheme."[37]

The comments quoted here represent the sum total of Jane Addams's surviving remarks on her charity work in Baltimore in 1886—just a fleeting line here and there, tucked within paragraphs on wholly different subjects, interjected in a casual tone, repeated, as was her habit, in a letter to Alice and in the same day's letter to Laura.[38] Eight of the thirty-eight surviving letters written from Baltimore contain these brief references to Jane's contact with the city's poor.[39] Proportionately, that is twice as many comments as she made about the poor in Europe. More important, the whole thrust of the Baltimore comments differs from those she made in Europe. As a resident of Baltimore, Jane was no tourist distantly observing faceless symbols of foreign despair. Instead, she was a fully engaged citizen conversing with "interesting" individuals who had faces, names, confidences, and prospects. The difference in tone may have been due to Jane's discomfort with the languages in Europe, or to her sense of belonging in an American setting, or to fact that the poor she encountered in Baltimore were women and children (not drunks on the street), or to her maturing comfort with gentle intimacies. What is significant is the simple fact that Jane's first involvement with charity in America was through direct, hands-on, face-to-face human communication.

Jane was not attending Charity Organization Society meetings and theorizing about the "problem" of the poor, nor was she sitting in university seminars on history and politics, strategizing sweeping solutions to be enacted by an educated elite. And though she continued to be active in cultural clubs in this second season in Baltimore, her letters made no more despairing mention of French lessons or other regimented studies. She was, instead, having the experiences with "reality" she had dreamed of at Rockford, and she reported to Alice feeling "vigorous" and "happy" in a way which "I had imagined I should never feel again."[40] In her final comment to Alice on the subject, written in her last month in Baltimore, Jane said that she had been "investigating city charities this winter and have come to some rather curious conclusions."[41] She did not elaborate on whether her conclusions related to the objective organization and administration of charities or to her subjective experience participating in charities. Two years later, however, when Jane and Ellen were laying the plans for their settlement house in Chicago, Ellen reported to her sister that Jane "discovered . . . in Baltimore among the old colored people [that] after a lecture or social evening she would be quite exhausted and have to stay in bed, but after a morning with the colored people . . . she was actually physically better than if she had stayed in bed and been rubbed."[42]

Jane's references to "paralyzed" faculties and "natural indolence" in her letters to Alice and Ellen from Baltimore may have been code for lying in bed and being "rubbed," though it is hard to picture Anna doing the rubbing. What is quite clear from those letters is that Jane was not free, while living with Anna in Baltimore, to either stay in bed or to act on the logic of her experience and devote herself to old women and orphans. She and her stepmother were part of a network of women who kept them quite busy with social visits, university lectures, art clubs, gallery tours, and evening parties. None of the women in this circle offered Jane Addams a model for female stewardship, but they did represent various styles of womanhood against which Jane could test herself and here, as with the old colored women, she based her conclusions on experience, not theory.

Society in Baltimore—and Philadelphia—offered Jane two basic types of elite white womanhood: the gracious society matron and the professional intellectual. In her dealings with both types, Jane continued her search for that hybrid: the gracious intellectual. She recoiled from the caricature of what she called "the severe and terrible northern lady," an image reinforced in the public imagination by Henry James's novel *The Bostonians*, which was serialized in *Century* magazine at the time of Jane's move to Baltimore. Jane did not like James's depiction of Olive Chancellor, a stiff-necked Boston feminist, any more than she had liked his depiction of the silly Daisy Miller.[43] As an advocate of female intuition, Jane was sympathetic to the 1880s argument that advanced intellectual activity threatened to erode the feminine graces and peaceful inner calm that she had valorized in her Rockford tribute to the primordial mother goddess. As one who had dreamt of attending Smith College, Jane was familiar with the view, articulated in journals like the *Atlantic Monthly*, that the educated woman's face was "stamped with restlessness, wandering purpose, and self-consciousness," and that she earnestly set about to "'do' books as some travelers 'do' Europe."[44] Coming off her own restless, bookish grand tour, Jane squirmed to distance herself from that too serious, too severe caricature.

The distancing began even before Jane went to Baltimore. In her first months back from Europe, when she was serving as "Aunt Jane" in her siblings' households, she wrote an essay for the Rockford Seminary magazine about her grand tour. In it, Jane mocked those travelers so devoted to the fiendish "conceit" of literary "self-consciousness" that they could not appreciate the lived moment, the "subjective" experience. She chose as the moment to be experienced in her essay her very unromantic bout with seasickness on the Mediterranean. The lesson she drew for her readers was that intellectual complacency was useless in the face of our own or others' immediate suffering. One's character needed to be forged of sterner stuff to avoid quick descent into self-absorption. In its use of wry, self-deprecating humor to critique high-minded detachment from real life, this essay—written while she was helping her sister Mary care for the "Linnets"—was a marked departure from Jane's sonorous preachments in her seminary editorials and represented a new identification with the messy, bodily business of women's daily lives.[45]

Under Baltimore's southern sun, where the sentiment was "decidedly against college . . . for women," Jane thought the "typical New England school-teacher" style underwent a "charming" modification.[46] According to *Harpers' Monthly*, Baltimore society excluded "grim females"; the women in Baltimore's parlors were "the very reverse of anything offensive in the term 'strong-minded.'"[47] Jane found that she was entirely comfortable with these women, who had been "educated on the old fashioned plan" of fine arts and French, and that she admired their capacity to live "elegantly" but without "formality."[48] At a gathering at the home of one of George's professors, for example, the men sat around the dining table reading aloud from a biography of Louis Agassiz, the Harvard zoologist (and husband of the first president of Radcliffe College), while the ladies sat in the next room. So willing was Jane to participate in the genteel gender customs of the Southern intelligentsia that she described this segregation uncritically, noting only that the women "have their fancy work, listen, chat very delightfully."[49] The Baltimore women's apparent contentment, contrasted with the "self-consciousness" of the educated woman, "almost" caused Jane to doubt her "own convictions" on the value of female education.[50]

It is quite possible that Jane's comfort with less educated, less intellectual women is an index of her doubts about the worth of her own education—and intellect. That possibility must be entertained in view of her defensive dislike of Christine Ladd-Franklin, "the most intellectual woman" Jane had ever met and the person who best fit into Jane's taxonomy as "an anxious study of the higher educated woman of the modern type."[51] Ladd-Franklin or, as Jane noted parenthetically to Alice, "the famous Miss Ladd," was the only Vassar graduate in Baltimore and the sole woman allowed to engage in graduate study at Johns Hopkins, though only as a "special student" so her admission set no precedent.[52] The New England native was thirteen years older than Jane, had studied with the astronomer Maria Mitchell at Vassar, graduated in 1869, and taught science in Eastern female seminaries while publishing the sophisticated articles on mathematics that won her special treatment at Johns Hopkins. After completing her formal studies at Hopkins in 1882, Christine Ladd married Fabian Franklin, a professor in the university's mathematics department, and bore two children, one of whom died in infancy. By the time Jane met her in early 1886, Ladd-Franklin had already completed all the requirements for the Ph.D. in mathematics but would be denied the formal degree until 1926. She had moved from mathematics to symbolic logic and published work on the "algebra of logic" that Harvard's Josiah Royce regarded as the "crowning" achievement in the field. From there, she turned to her lifelong application of mathematics to the study of vision. Indeed, during the winter of 1886–87, when Jane was having most contact with Ladd-Franklin, the scientist was probably preparing her paper on binocular vision for the *American Journal of Psychology*.[53]

If Jane Addams had identified in these years with women who were professional intellectuals and also advocates for women's rights, then she would have delighted in her access to Christine Ladd-Franklin. The mathematician was clearly interested in Jane; she visited Jane's flat shortly after Jane and Anna returned to Baltimore for their second season, took the initiative to invite Jane to accompany her to the Peabody Institute's art gallery, and invited Jane to have lunch alone with her at her home.[54] But while Jane found conversation with Ladd-Franklin to be "like an education," she did not particularly relish the woman's company.[55] Jane felt like an unworthy intellectual imposter around Ladd-Franklin, conscious that she had not kept her valedictory promise to add scientific training to her feminine intuition. Jane was "alarmed beyond measure," for example, when Ladd-Franklin proposed that they view a Rembrandt exhibit together at the Peabody. Jane worried that the reputation she had earned among faculty wives for her knowledge of art would not withstand

Ladd-Franklin's scrutiny.[56] Worry over her own inadequacies combined with disdain for Ladd-Franklin's intellectual pretensions—and, perhaps, longing for the scholarly polish which Smith College could have given to Rockford Seminary's prize student. In reaction to such conflicted feelings, Jane dreaded time with the mathematician and looked forward to a "pleasant" meeting with the ladies in her art club.[57]

There may have been a political element to Jane's recoil from Ladd-Franklin, who was not only an outspoken suffragist given to calling men "the unfair sex," but was also a Democrat.[58] If she shared her husband's well-known enthusiasm for liberalism and laissez-faire capitalism, then it is likely that Ladd-Franklin based her prosuffrage claim on women's individual rights rather than on the Republican suffragists' claim to community welfare.[59] In a variety of ways, then, Ladd-Franklin confronted Jane with a set of cultural values that were alien to Jane's tastes and heritage. It was after one of her visits with Ladd-Franklin that Jane wondered about the "advisability" of higher education for women and confessed to Alice, for the second time, that "it is dreadful to be tortured by doubts on a subject you have been settled upon for years." With Ladd-Franklin, Jane detected "just a suggestion of strain . . . as if she was more intellectual than she really enjoyed."[60]

In years to come, Jane Addams would have the political vision to see that the joy of a woman with Ladd-Franklin's genius might well be strained if she earned, but was denied, a Ph.D. from the research institution that employed her husband. But that was not Jane's focus in 1886. She was looking for a style of womanhood that felt, to her, natural, gracious, authentic, and, probably, harmonious, and Christine Ladd-Franklin's style did not suit. After one encounter with her, Jane told Alice that she "used to believe it was only a matter of will to adapt yourself to anyone," but in her new zeal for sincerity in her relations, Jane was finding that "there are certain people to whom I cannot adapt myself and it sets each nerve askew to try."[61] And on the eve of another visit with Ladd-Franklin, Jane wrote to Laura, "It is equally difficult to be either overestimated or underestimated in this world, and in a city, people are always rushing to one extreme or another, they won't let you [go] quietly along and take you for what you are worth, they insist upon your declaring yourself."[62]

If Jane declared herself at all in these years it was as a woman who cared more about women's personal style and emotional authenticity than their education or occupation. In this, she was trying on a personal identity quite different from the detached one she had worn at Rockford. Her doubts about the effects of education on women did not harden into opposition, but they made her alert to signs that college need not destroy women's ability to notice people's faces, to be "bread givers," to preserve "the softer graces."[63]

Jane's visits to Philadelphia 1886 and 1887 afforded her the opportunity to visit with highly educated female friends there, including Rachel Bodley, Jane's former professor and Dean at the Woman's Medical College; Harriet Lewis, a former classmate at medical school who was now a physician; and Eva Williams, a former Rockford math teacher who had become a fellow at the new Quaker women's college, Bryn Mawr. Jane's reports on her "delightful" visits with these women reflect her emerging priorities.[64] She did not focus her comments on the women's learnedness but on their warmth and charm. Five years after leaving the Woman's Medical College, Jane said nothing of Bodley's medical pursuits but declared, "I love her sincerely and her affection for me I prize very highly." So, too, the fact that Dr. Lewis asked "affectionately" after Alice and had a "dear friend in Dr. Reed," another female physician, was as important to Jane as Dr. Lewis's supervision of an insane asylum with 375 patients.[65] And while an on-campus visit persuaded Jane that Bryn Mawr was destined to become the "finest woman's college in America," she was equally impressed that this "Johns Hopkins for women" could also provide the "jolliest" sort of encounters with "very pretty" girls in a "charming" atmosphere.[66]

As a student at Rockford, Jane Addams had claimed to admire the womanly ways of "bread givers," yet had rather disdained feminine sentiment and attachment. She had dismissed Ellen's departure from Rockford by claiming it was a "fascination" to know people "just so much and then stop."[67] Life experience since graduation had integrated Jane's theoretical praise for the feminine with her tangible embrace of female culture. Attachment to her sisters and to Ellen were vital in this transition. So, too, was the endurance of warm ties to several Rockford friends, including her teachers, Sarah Blaisdell and Sarah Anderson, and fellow alumnae like Helen Harrington, Nora Frothingham Haworth, and Laura Ely Curtis. By 1886, Jane had come to treasure the special "something" that made her seminary "associations . . . particularly genuine" and caused her to admire Bryn Mawr not for its academic ambitions but for "fostering the same" sense of affectionate community among the women students.[68]

Jane knew by this time that any heroism she aspired to would draw upon the connections that women fostered in their relationships. At her lowest points since leaving Rockford, it had been her classmates and former teachers who had reminded her of her strength; certainly her bond with Ellen Starr had kept alive her sense of herself and her talents apart from the family claim. And within the context of the family claim, her relations with Anna, Alice, Mary, and Laura, had given her a taste of the satisfactions to be gained from providing intimate and practical service to others. Her father had now been dead for more than five years, and she had learned to live without sympathetic male leadership in her life; neither Harry nor George—nor, for that matter, Weber or Rev. John Linn—made a compelling case for the wisdom of female dependence on men or male culture. Not even Thomas Carlyle and his heroic rhetoric had proved all that serviceable in ushering Jane through her darkest days. The "coldness" and "quiet" of the female goddess, which Jane had once revered, and the capacity to stand "alone in the world and need no other support" had lost their appeal.[69]

From her first days in Europe, Jane had been able to tell Ellen that "friendship with the mutual pities and responsibilities is, after all, the main thing in life."[70] But in repeating that notion two years later, her words sounded less like a speech and more like a sentiment, perhaps because she added, "I know my dear that I have often misunderstood you; it is the most discouraging view we can take of ourselves—our limitations in comprehension."[71] The emphasis in Jane's life had shifted away from standing alone, away from preachy self-assertions, and toward communion with others, both within and beyond the family. She was becoming someone for whom mediation was less about avoiding trouble and more about creating connection.

In her last editorial at Rockford, Jane had cautioned her classmates about the sorry fate of "brilliant and talented young men" who did not fulfill the promise of their college careers because their "brilliancy [was] not their own . . . but drawn from other sources." Those graduates became "lost in the crowd," warned Rockford's valedictorian, "for they possess not individual silent resources."[72] Five years later, after putting herself through a postgraduate course studying male heroics in the arts, politics, and sciences, and after two years comparing her experience in the lecture halls and parlors of Johns Hopkins University with her experience in Baltimore's shelters and asylums, Jane had come to feel that women risked their brilliancy and the silent resources of the goddess if they became too self-absorbed in intellectual pursuits. The issue for her was not that women were biologically unfit for such pursuits, it was simply that women's relational resources were too precious to the community—and to women themselves—to mortgage for any endeavor that was isolating.

On this point, Jane Addams's autobiographical memory was remarkably in line with the contemporary record. She recalled coming to the "conviction" that "the first generation of college women had . . . developed too exclusively the power of acquiring knowledge" but "in the process" had "lost that simple and almost automatic response to the human appeal, that old healthful reaction resulting in activity" when faced with "suffering or helplessness." She told her readers that, in these years, she came to regret that college women had "departed too suddenly from the active, emotional life led by their grandmothers and great-grandmothers," but she did not mention that this was the period in her life when she was most involved with her sisters and their children and was closest to her father's sister Harriet and her mother's sister Elizabeth, two women whose generosity of spirit she greatly admired.[73] Nor did she say how her convictions on female education were strengthened by her relationships with women in Baltimore.

Out of all the Baltimore women, from Christine Ladd-Franklin to the elegant socialites, the one Jane liked the best was Amelia Brooks, the wife of George's graduate adviser, W. K. Brooks. Dr. Brooks and "Mrs. Dr. Brooks" had been the hosts of the Agassiz reading in their home; indeed, Dr. Brooks was later recalled as one of the professors at Hopkins who regularly combined gracious entertaining with "scientific discussion."[74] Jane found Amelia to be "so genuine and simple" that she was "always more attracted to her."[75] Brooks was one of the five women, including Anna, with whom Jane formed an art study club that met weekly. Beyond that, Jane often spent time alone with Amelia Brooks, enjoying the informality of tea in each other's parlors, decorating the Brooks's Christmas tree, celebrating New Year's together when Dr. Brooks was out of town.[76] Jane enjoyed meeting prominent scientists at the Brooks's home, often remarking on her surprise at finding that "such learned men could be so agreeable."[77] The social network that ran through the Brooks's parlor could easily have afforded a young woman with ideal opportunities for meeting male graduate students with bright prospects, but Jane never evinced the slightest personal interest in any of the budding biologists she met at Amelia Brooks's home.[78]

While Jane's relationship with Dr. and Mrs. Brooks flourished, George's did not. He had encountered some difficulty with his seaside research the previous summer and disdained the academic socializing that occurred in the Brooks's parlor as simply "an opportunity" for "young men" to "display their asinine qualities." Jane thought of William Brooks, affectionately, as "the shyest man in Baltimore," so she was doubly embarrassed when Brooks's slide projector failed at a public lecture and George erupted in inappropriate laughter. For all his bluster, George was getting "so utterly discouraged" about graduate school that Jane pitied him, but George was already masking his discouragement by dismissing the importance of earning a Ph.D. degree.[79]

In her many comments to Alice about Amelia and William Brooks, Jane never mentioned that Dr. Brooks was a contributor to *Popular Science Monthly*, the journal Jane and her classmates had read for their science club at Rockford Female Seminary. It is possible, however, that Jane read a two-part article that Brooks published in *Popular Science* in the summer before her junior year, titled "The Condition of Woman from a Zoological Point of View."[80] In that article, the nation's expert on oysters argued that the human female brain had evolved for different functions than the human male brain. Unlike other contributors to the monthly in these years, Brooks did not crudely define women's intellect as inferior to men's, merely different.

The role of the female mind in human evolution and in human society, Brooks argued, was to serve as the "storehouse filled with the instincts, habits, intuitions, and laws of conduct which have been gained by past experience." The male mind, by contrast, had developed as the engine for expanding "our circle of experience." It was men who pursued "original trains of abstract thought," conceived new principles in science, created new poetry and art.[81] This assignment of duties, explained the "shyest man in Baltimore," was "not due to the subjection of one sex by another," it was simply "the means by which the progress of the sex is accomplished."[82] Thus, Brooks would have argued, Johns Hopkins University's decision to exclude women from graduate training (Christine Ladd-Franklin notwithstanding) was not a social injustice, it was a modern recognition of scientific reality.

The record is silent on whether Jane and Dr. Brooks ever discussed his "point of view" on the "condition of woman," a point of view he would reiterate in *Forum* magazine in 1896, seven years after his old friend Jane Addams had expanded Chicago's "circle of experience" to include settlement houses.[83] Such a discussion would have elicited differences between the two of them, to be sure, but also common ground regarding women's nature and role in society. As Jane deepened her embrace of lived experience over abstract theory, she might well have concurred with Brooks's view that women were more adept at learning from experience than theory. Based on her experience with her own siblings, especially George, she might also have agreed with Brooks that women, with their greater "common sense" and their special intuition, were more likely than men to take immediate and appropriate action "in actual practical life."[84] Even as a Rockford student aspiring to men's intellectual heroics, Jane had tried to carve out room for women's intuitive ability to grasp reality and take action. If Jane did read Brooks back in the summer of 1880, his argument may have assured her that science supported such female agency.

By 1886, Jane's new respect for women's capacity for care and affection might well have enhanced her sympathy with Brooks's argument that women not only understood other women better than men ever could, they also understood individual men better than men understood one another. Jane would not, however, have agreed with Brooks that this particular sex difference arose because women were pretty much all alike while men were so widely varied they needed women to provide a common base of translation.[85] Brooks certainly never persuaded Jane that women's style of thinking was ill suited to advancing human progress or made women unfit for scientific or artistic creativity. On the contrary, Jane had forthrightly asserted in "Cassandra" that the "intuitive perception committed to women's charge" was "one of the holy means given to mankind in their search for truth."[86] The five years since graduation had increased, not decreased, her certitude on this point. So while she stipulated the existence of a distinctive female intellect, Jane did not concede that this intellect was condemned to the life of a "compiler" who simply studied "accumulated knowledge" without adding to that knowledge.[87] Jane may have regarded Christine Ladd-Franklin's hyperintellectual "strain" as an unwise abandonment of womanly culture, but Ladd-Franklin's creative ability fit far better with Jane's assumptions about women's capacities than with W. K. Brooks's assumptions.

In the final months before she departed for a second tour of Europe, this time with Ellen Starr and Sarah Anderson, Jane took a few steps to "declare" herself on "the woman question." At the culmination of her two-year friendship with W. K. Brooks and her contact with Johns Hopkins's assertively male scientific community, Jane Addams presented the board of trustees of Rockford Seminary with a gift of $1,000, accompanied by a note stating that she "should be glad to have it expended upon the library and a preference given to scientific books."[88] Later that year, Jane reaffirmed her belief in medicine as a female career by giving away her medical school texts to a "poor minister's daughter," who was studying to be a "medical missionary" after she married.[89] And in December 1887, just a few days before boarding the ship that would take her and Sarah Anderson to Europe to meet up with Ellen, Jane donated twenty dollars toward the expenses of a Syrian student at Woman's Medical College in Philadelphia. It was a small gesture accompanied by an extraordinary remark. The young Syrian, said Jane, was "trying to study at the college" but was so "overcome by her eastern indolence that she has worn out everyone's patience."[90] The reference to "eastern indolence" was standard 1887 ethnocentrism. What was not standard was Jane's explicit, conscious choice to give money to an individual who did not conform to the "scientific" profile of the "worthy" poor. According to the Charity Organization Society, handouts to indolent Syrian girls would only encourage their lack of industry. Clearly, Jane did not intend her gift to have that outcome. Having recently criticized her own "natural indolence," Jane must have thought the aid would have an encouraging, not a corrupting influence.[91] Again, it was a very small act, almost casual, but taken in the context of Jane's experiences at the colored women's shelter, her exposure to Leo Tolstoy's doctrine of unconditional love for humanity, and her attention to bonds of affection and communion, it suggests an openness, on the eve of her second European trip, to alternative approaches to philanthropy.

Jane had linked her views on charity to her own "point of view" on the "condition of women," in an October 1887 speech to the Rockford Seminary

Alumnae Association meeting in Chicago. On that occasion, Jane was asked to speak on the topic "Our Debts and How We Shall Pay Them." One might expect that, two years before opening Hull-House, Jane Addams would tell the Rockford alumnae that it was their duty to use the privilege of their education on behalf of the less fortunate, to take art to the masses, to visit colored women in shelters, to read to the aged blind, even to aid the indolent. She did not say any of those things. She did not, in fact, deliver anything like the sort of sermon she had customarily delivered as editor of the seminary magazine. As in her essay on Mediterranean seasickness, Jane focused on the "subjective" aspects of her topic, on how individuals actually experienced their own charitable actions. In the process, she shed some light on those "curious conclusions" about charity work that she had once mentioned to Alice.

Jane's short, clever talk to the alumnae association, which she dismissed as "trite," posed a series of rhetorical questions intended to encourage her fellow alumnae to consider the possibility that the college woman, who belonged to "the most responsible cult of all," had become "a trifle morbid in her conscience, a little overzealous for action, a misdated Puritan seeking [peace] in good works."[92] Jane wondered aloud about the effect on college women of being "fed" on a "diet" of "subtle theories of heredity that [claim] our very nerve centres and muscle fibres have . . . predispositions for benevolence." She did not deny the existence or the value of these predispositions, she simply questioned whether college women, in their zeal to pay off their "enormous debt" for having received an education, were not taking their "long withheld . . . mathematics too seriously."

Whether Jane was thinking privately here about the mathematician Christine Ladd-Franklin or the ledger-driven proponents of "scientific" charity, the public message was clear: college women needed to cease straining, to stop fearing "insolvency" and to cultivate greater "ease" in their "beneficent conduct." Two years after her return from her European tour of heroes, Jane advised her audience of "kindly sisters" to "imagine the chagrin of the knight who was defeated because his armor was too heavy."[93] In 1901, Jane Addams would deliver a similar message, in rather more blunt terms, to an audience of Christian college women. Then she would have the authority to warn against undertaking any charitable effort out of a sense of duty to uplift others. Looking back on her own attitudes in college, Addams declared in 1901 that "to consider one's self as in any wise unlike the rank and file of human life is to walk straight toward the pit of self-righteousness."[94] Her speech in 1887 to Rockford alumnae marks her postgraduate effort to climb out of that pit.

It was in this frame of mind that Jane made her plans to revisit Europe in the company of her old friends, Ellen Starr and Sarah Anderson. Jane did not design the trip with any thought of finding a mission while abroad. On the contrary, she seems to have regarded it as a pleasant interlude before settling into a quiet life in northern Illinois after her return. A year earlier, while living in Baltimore and feeling the pressure to "declare" herself, Jane had told Alice that she felt she had "grown older . . . and have discovered among other things that it is well to hold fast to the place in which you were born."[95] She realized that "little towns are more exacting and trying than big ones."[96] Still, she claimed to have "all sorts of plans" for a life back home in Stephenson County, had imagined her own farmhouse there, and, shortly before leaving for Europe, even bought two horses.[97] Prior to departure, Jane spent an afternoon "calling" on old Freeport neighbors with Anna, friends like Flora Guiteau and Amelia Rowell, who were interested in art and literary pursuits. Afterward, Jane remarked to Alice, "there certainly are superior people in Freeport."[98] She had often noted the "superior" people in Baltimore, but Baltimore people insisted upon Jane declaring herself; in Freeport, her identity was unquestioned. Maybe, after all the years of doubt and wandering, life as Freeport's steward of the arts would be perfectly satisfying.

There was a discernible evolution in Jane's emotional and philosophical stance between her twenty-fifth birthday and her twenty-seventh. Since arriving back from her first European tour, she had simultaneously embraced female culture and rejected any claims to heroic action that smacked of the self-righteous or the spectacular. Though not a convert to Christianity, she had opened herself to Ellen and, therefore, to serious consideration of the mysteries as well as the morals of her society's dominant faith. She had, during this time, traded in Carlyle for Tolstoy; any heroism she sought now would come from a spiritual indwelling not a dramatic overcoming. If her second trip to Europe was to be anything more than a sojourn with dear friends, then it was a journey of spiritual and artistic appreciation, not another fevered search for more heroes among the continent's dead white men.

Jane had assumed that George would already be in Europe when she arrived. He was to be studying in Leipzig, Germany, as Harry had once done. There was some discussion of Anna joining the trip, in part to visit George. But on this occasion, in marked contrast to the first trip, Jane did not lobby for Anna's company. She left the whole matter up to Anna and George to decide.[99] Since Jane was now old enough to travel unchaperoned, she did not need Anna's company and, perhaps, did not want it. Anna, for her own reasons, chose not to go. Perhaps if Anna had accompanied George to Leipzig, things might have turned out differently. As it was, George came limping home in late October, weeks before Jane's scheduled January departure.

In her report to Alice, Jane treated the episode as a simple, if "unfortunate," case of "ill health" which caused George to look "so pale and thin" that Jane was "startled" when she first saw him.[100] George's letters to Harry at the time reveal a troubled young man trying to disguise his waning capacity to function in the world, but Jane chose to avert her eyes from yet another brother's break- down.[101] Instead, she took advantage of George's early return to book a pre- Christmas departure for Europe; with him at home, she told Alice, "there is not the same object in my staying until Christmas." She would spend Thanksgiv- ing with the Linns and leave immediately with Sarah Anderson to join Ellen, who was already in Germany visiting family friends.[102] Before departing, Jane assured Alice (and herself) that George was improving and pointed to the house's "new deep fire place . . . handsome lace curtains," and fresh paint and wallpaper as signs that he and Ma were "settled in for a very comfortable, cosy winter."[103]

George, meanwhile, was bragging to Harry that he would not be seeking employment because he was needed at home as Ma's companion, and this "unexpected turn of affairs" was a welcomed opportunity to "gain deeper insight" into biological and philosophical questions that the pressure of grad- uate school had forced him to regard "too superficially." The purpose of his studies, George boldly informed his older brother, was not to "astonish the world but to keep myself in a state of continual awe."[104] It occurred to no one, except, perhaps, Ellen Starr, that sister Jane was the only member of the Cedar- ville household who would ever astonish the world.

Chapter 11
The Subjective Necessity for the Social Settlement

"Don't worry about me," Jane told Alice on the eve of her ship's sailing for Europe in December 1887. "I expect to be well and happy all of the time."[1] It was a remarkably accurate prediction. Despite the trip's difficulties, which ranged from "beastly cold weather" to constant shifts in the makeup of the traveling party, to tragedies in Jane's family back home, to various illnesses, including Jane's own severe attack of sciatica, this seven-month tour with Ellen Starr and Sarah Anderson still gave Jane a chance to behave in accord with her own feminine ideals and to bask in her ability to do so. She remained, according to her companions, cheerful and optimistic throughout the journey, a model of patience and selflessness, and she recognized that she achieved such equanimity "more when I am away" from Anna and George "than at any other time."[2]

In the happy company of friends with whom Jane could read and talk, argue and laugh, she relaxed into her position as the center of affection. It was from that gentle angle of repose that she viewed Europe and, this time, the people of Europe, giving voice to her new appreciation for the human condition of which she now felt herself a part. Growing in tandem with Jane's capacity for affectionate regard of others was impatience with her own inaction on others' behalf. The farther she traveled away from old heroic haunts, however, the closer she came to a safe harbor that suited her subjective need for service.

Jane, Ellen, and Sarah formed the core of the traveling group, a core Jane referred to as "our ideal party of 'we three.'"[3] Months before they began, though, Jane decided it would be "rather selfish and ridiculous" to exclude others, so at different points along the way their party expanded to include a rotating cast of friends and acquaintances.[4] They began and ended the trip with Annie Kales, an acquaintance of the Starr family whom Jane initially praised as "quite self-reliant" but whom Ellen came to regard as annoyingly self-absorbed.[5] When Kales went her own way for a while, the party was "again supplied with a fourth spinster" in Helen Harrington, Jane's good friend from Rockford Seminary, who had since joined Sarah Anderson on the Rockford faculty. Along with Helen came Amelia Rowell, an older friend of Jane's family from Freeport, "an efficient, enthusiastic traveler" with whom Jane maintained a "natural" but "dignified, reserved relation."[6] Ellen found Helen's "dreadful whining voice" to be "rather wearing" and thought Mrs. Rowell lacked "any grace of manner," but she accepted the company as an inevitable result of Jane's inclusive spirit.[7] Indeed, during the very last stage of the trip, Jane brought her childhood friend Flora Guiteau from Freeport over to England, paying all of her expenses in the hopes that a summer in Europe would revive the exhausted schoolteacher.[8] Jane was also paying for much of Ellen's trip, but Ellen took on the responsibility for guiding two wealthy American girls around Italy in June 1888, thereby earning part of her own expenses and a stipend of $250.[9]

Jane announced early on that the traveling party "bids fair to be quite a model affair" and proceeded on that sanguine assumption.[10] After brief stops in Paris and Stuttgart, Jane and Sarah joined up with Ellen and Annie Kales in Munich by New Year's Day 1888, proceeding from there through the Bavarian Tyrol and into Italy on a route that took them along the Dolomite mountains. They spent ten very cold, hurried days walking on frostbitten feet around Verona, Parma, Mantua, Bologna, and Ravenna simply because they had not the "presence of mind" to change their plans in light of the bad weather.[11] Subsequent scheduling was much more responsive to climate, health, and their own impulses. Between the third week of January and early April, the party made two trips to Florence but spent most of its time in Rome. From Rome, Ellen and Sarah made side trips to Venice, Naples, and Monte Cassino while Jane nursed her sciatica. April and much of May were devoted to a tour of Spain that Jane and Ellen had been dreaming of since Rockford days, a tour that included a foray across the Straits of Gibraltar to Tangier, Morocco. In late May, the party headed for Paris to pick up Ellen's young charges. All then enjoyed a few days in Rheims and Amiens before Ellen headed back to Italy with her girls, and Jane, Sarah, Helen, Annie Kales, and Mrs. Rowell departed for a summer in England with Flora Guiteau.

A few serendipitous encounters on the journey had pointed Jane toward the World Centennial of Foreign Missions in London in early June as well as a tour of London's East End settlement, Toynbee Hall. Though Ellen did not visit Toynbee Hall on this trip, she did sign on to the "scheme" Jane proposed as a result of the European tour, thereby choosing to partner with Jane in a dramatic alteration of their individual and collective fates. Years later, Jane Addams would paraphrase George Eliot to say that "we prepare ourselves for sudden deeds by an infinite series of minor decisions we have previously made."[12] Jane's move to Chicago six months after her return from this second tour of Europe, and her creation of the Hull-House settlement nine months after that, probably looked like sudden, even brazen, deeds to her stepmother and other members of her family. Her relatives might have been spared the shock of it all if they had paid attention to the "series of minor decisions" Jane had been making all along the way.

Jane did have serious family worries while she was on this tour, the sort that tugged at the sleeve of her conscience, reminding her of her duties as a sister, aunt, and daughter. In the middle of February, while Jane was basking in Rome's "delightful weather" and beautiful countryside, she learned that Mary and John Linn's two-and-a-half-year-old daughter, Mary, had died of whooping cough at the end of January.[13] Six months later, Flora Guiteau brought the chilling news that twenty-seven-year-old George Haldeman had run away from home and that Harry Haldeman was out scouring Iowa, Wisconsin, and the Dakotas for leads to finding his depressed if not deranged brother, while Anna sat at home, frantic with worry.[14]

George's "melodramatic" act did not end in tragedy but in his sheepish return to Cedarville.[15] Jane cut short her summer in England with Flora in order to return to the United States and be available to her worried stepmother, but the crisis was resolved before she reached Illinois. By contrast, the Linns' family tragedy, occurring early in Jane's trip, was not amenable to resolution. Word of little Mary's death came as a shock to Jane; the sudden loss of this "sturdy and strong" toddler threw her back into all her own childhood fears of death, calling up in her a "genuine homesickness and longing" for the eldest sister who had been like a mother to her. Staring at the heartbroken letters from Mary and John Linn, Jane had "a little girl's feeling who is away from home at night" and became immediately "insecure for all of the children" in the family.[16] The Linn family had buried baby Charles less than a year before. Seven-year-old Esther Linn, whose impertinence Jane proudly viewed as a family trait, demanded to know what God wanted with so many children.[17]

For Mary and John Linn, the answer to that question was that God had wisely decided to take little Mary, who was "too good for this world," away to a "better world" and the warmth of Jesus's "bosom."[18] For Jane, who could never embrace the notion that there was a heaven beyond this world or that God selects certain individuals to enjoy immortality there, Esther's "very characteristic and natural question" had no answer.[19] Adopting the philosophical stance she later attributed to her father, Jane declined to explain the inexplicable.[20] Instead, she advised Esther's cousin Sadie to remember always little Mary's "baby individuality." She enclosed with that message a photograph of a Van Dyck painting of a little girl with an apple. The painting was admired, explained Aunt Jane, because it was "so honest and frank," because Van Dyck was "truthful" in his art and drew the little girl "exactly as she was" with no sentimental embellishment.[21] Seven years after her father's death, Jane was stronger in her belief that the only heaven worth working for came in this life, through love and "honest and frank" acceptance of the facts of lived experience.

During this sad interlude, Jane expressed great concern for her ailing sister Mary and told Alice she was "beginning to think it does not pay to put so much distance between yourself and the people you love best," but she made no moves to return home.[22] Knowing the theological distance between her own and the Linns' response to death, Jane may have welcomed the space to grieve independently.

The month prior to little Mary's death had impressed upon Jane the multiple joys of her new independence. "I am quite impressed with the difference in my age and dignity between this trip in Europe and the one before," she wrote to Alice after her first week with Ellen in Munich. At the age of twenty-eight, she relished being addressed as "Madame" instead of "Mademoiselle," as she inevitably had been in Anna's company; she noticed the respect she earned from hoteliers, customs agents, and taxi drivers by projecting a certain ease and competence.[23] As a veteran tourist, she delighted in being able to walk around without a guidebook and found she was "enjoying it all so much better than before" because she had "lost that morbid thirst for information and doing which simply consumes American travelers and certainly did me the last time."[24]

The real test of Jane's ability to sustain a joyful, honest, even heavenly, life began four days after she learned of little Mary's death. Coincident with her grief came an attack of sciatica that sent such shooting pain down her leg she could barely move. Whatever the mix of somatic and psychological causes for the attack, the result was that Jane was stuck in a rather drafty *pension* in Rome, in the "absurd position of a traveler who cannot travel."[25] The autobiography described this as a moment when Jane was forced to stay in Rome "with a trained nurse during many weeks" leading "an invalid's life once more."[26] It is true that Jane's bad leg laid her up and then slowed her down for close to three weeks, required the aid of a trained nurse for about a week so that Ellen and Sarah could continue their sightseeing in Rome, and then prevented Jane from accompanying Ellen and Sarah on a ten-day trip to Naples, Venice, and the Benedictine monastery at Monte Cassino. But she was strong enough to send her friends away, confident she could manage on her own without the nurse. Indeed, what is impressive about the entire Roman episode is not that Jane was thrust back into the role of invalid but that she so earnestly resisted that role and maintained the same cheerful, optimistic posture she had held before her leg gave way. Her English physician may have thought it improper for "so delicate a person, an invalid one might say" to be traveling around Europe on her own, but Jane brushed off his opinion. "He hasn't the remotest idea of the *toughness* of my constitution," she bragged to Alice, "and was very surprised by my rapid recovery."[27]

From Rome, Jane kidded with Weber that the city's damp, cold weather meant that "rheumatism and neuralgia" were widespread, so "I haven't even the satisfaction of being unique in my affliction."[28] Once separated from her stepmother, for whom illness was a mark of distinction, Jane defined her aches and pains as evidence of her common humanity. Rather than dwell on her disabled condition, Jane fairly chortled over her capacity to maintain a sunny disposition despite limping "in a manner alarming to my pride," and she took immense pleasure in her mature exercise of caution while tracking her own steady progress.[29] In constructing the episode at the time, Jane chose to depict herself not as an invalid but as a healthy woman with a "lame leg" who found the whole affair "provoking," not depressing.[30] Ellen offered independent confirmation of Jane's good nature throughout the ordeal, reporting back to her parents on Jane's little jokes and on the nurse's assessment of "Miss Addams" as a "most cheerful invalid."[31]

Jane passed an important test in Rome, both physical and mental, and came out of the experience knowing that she could isolate and treat an ailment without becoming an invalid.[32] Both Ellen and Sarah marveled at their friend's hearty attitude and their marveling was its own tonic.[33] It told Jane that she was performing as the person she wanted to be: stoic, but not cold; independent, but not aloof; "honest and frank" about lived experience, including lameness, but perseverant in her good-humored faith that humans are the architects of their own heaven. Mary Linn thought that her dead daughter was too good for this world; Jane was at work becoming good enough. "I have been self absorbed and priggish in my life," she told Alice after six hours of hot compresses on her leg, "and pray every day for redemption and beneficent goodness."[34]

Sarah Anderson, who had been applying the hot compresses, might have argued with Jane's self-criticism, but she would not have done so in the fawning tones she had used right after Jane left Rockford. Sarah was now older and wiser and considerably less needy. The replacement of Miss Sill with Martha Hillard as Rockford's principal had transformed Sarah's professional, spiritual, and social life. Unlike Sill, Hillard treated Sarah with professional respect and hired young, liberal teachers, including Helen Harrington, who brought a breath of fresh air to the seminary.[35] As much as Sarah Anderson treasured her continuing bond with both Jane and Ellen, she was not, in 1888, looking for a new life or looking for Jane to save her life (as she had been in 1881). She was, said Jane, "happy as a cricket" on the European tour.[36]

There seemed no question, from the start of the trip, that the bond between Jane and Ellen was a privileged one. When Jane and Sarah met up with

Ellen and Annie Kales in Munich, Jane moved into the double room Ellen had engaged for the two of them. There, they "*talked* and visited until we were exhausted." The confidences exchanged that week led Ellen to conclude that "Mr. Addams must have been a wonderful man."[37] Apparently, when Jane revealed herself, she revealed her continuing devotion to the memory of her Pa; apparently, too, she felt safe doing that with Ellen. Jane told Alice at the end of her Munich stay with Ellen, "I have seldom in my life had a happier week than we have had together."[38] And Ellen exclaimed to her parents, "Jeannie [*sic*] and I have such beautiful days together! We see things in the same way, except that she always sees them better than I do, and helps me very much, as she always has ever since I knew her."[39] Jane returned the sentiment by frequently reporting in letters home on some wise or witty remark of Ellen's. She was not charmed simply by the "cleverness" of "this friend of mine," Jane told Flora Guiteau, though that was "a constant source of pleasure to me." It was also Ellen's "persistent effort to get the *best* in the world, the highest and finest, and her efforts for patience to work it out in her own character."[40]

Travel with Ellen liberated Jane from slavish obedience to art authorities and dreary lessons in foreign language. On this tour, Jane embraced Ellen's subjective "method . . . of *ignoring* all the pictures she does not care for" and "enthusiastically" championing favorite artists "as she would personal friends."[41] Jane regarded Ellen as "the best possible influence in the world for me"; she believed that Eliza Starr's intuitive niece was the one person who could teach her to appreciate artistic works with her heart as well as her head.[42] So, too, Ellen lightened Jane's burden when learning foreign languages. In contrast to the painful struggles with German and French that Jane had endured while on the tour with Anna, her Italian and Spanish lessons with Ellen were marked by "jollity." Instead of guilt over not knowing as much German as she "should," Jane now laughingly reported to George that she could express herself in Italian "with some volubility, if not elegance."[43] Ellen's irreverence permitted Jane to prefer the Italian teacher who taught them street insults over the one who drilled their Latin foundation. "As abusive language is one of the first things a traveler in Italy requires," Jane joked with Alice, she and Ellen got on "famously" with their more "vivacious" tutor.[44] Jane even loosened up enough to jest, in Italian, with total strangers on a train.[45]

Laughter punctuated every aspect of this trip. When Anna sent a "warning against the subtle passions for mind and body," Jane (ignoring the body) sent back Ellen's playful assurance "that she has long been accustomed to the subtle passions for the mind and knows how to thrive on them." At the same time, Jane sent Anna a funny drawing of a balding Frenchman whom Ellen had secretly sketched, "with perfect nonchalance," while sitting across from him at

dinner. "Do not imagine we . . . were undignified at table," wrote the ever dutiful daughter; "no giggle was indulged in until we reached our rooms."[46] Later,
Jane teased Ellen for looking like a "funeral urn" when Jane was in the worst of
her sciatic pain, but Ellen retorted that cracking jokes and making "the precious child" laugh only increased her pain. For the sake of "the dearest girl in
all the world," Ellen resumed her "funereal aspect."[47]

Ellen initially resisted Jane's plan to hire a trained nurse in order to free
her traveling companions for sightseeing. "Jeannie is far more interesting to
me than Rome and all the Romans," Ellen announced to Alice, but she finally
agreed to the nurse in hopes that Jane would recover sufficiently to make the
planned trips to Naples and Monte Cassino.[48] When that did not happen, Ellen
was deeply disappointed because the trip to Monte Cassino, the birthplace of
the Benedictine order, was not easily arranged, especially for women. Ellen had
managed it through the good offices of her famous Catholic aunt. "It is very
hard for me to be reconciled to not being able to give you the one thing . . . that
you couldn't get as well for yourself," wrote Ellen from Monte Cassino, mind-
ful of Jane's status as Ellen's patron on this trip and heartbroken that she could
not share the simple beauty of the place and its holy inhabitants with her spiritual confidante.[49]

Ellen insisted to her parents that Jane was "so good, so dear and lovely in
every way" that she did not often "remember that I am using her money." In
fact, Ellen claimed, "I *like* to use it. There aren't many people that we could say
that of, are there?" So while Ellen referred to herself and Sarah Anderson, in
contrast to Jane, as "the impecunious," she continued to believe that by loving
Jane "so much," the money made "no difference."[50] For her part, Jane took
greater note of the price of lodgings and language lessons on this trip than on
the previous one. Her expenditures on travel for Ellen and, later, for Flora
Guiteau may have caused her to feel that Alice, her sister and banker, did not
approve of such largesse. After ordering a $500 bank draft for Flora's trip, Jane
added a disarming list of expenditures on goods Alice had requested and confided her worry over "the way I am spending money." She resolved to "certainly
save next year," wholly unaware that she was about to pour her inheritance into
a ramshackle mansion in a rundown Chicago neighborhood.[51]

Throughout the trip, it was Jane's generosity of spirit that Ellen exulted
over. "Jane is perfectly wonderful to me," she reported to Anna Haldeman
Addams from Florence; "I wish I could be like her . . . in her beautiful, unpretentious interest in everybody and voluntary taking of second place to give
others first."[52] Ellen and Jane had not lived together since their one year at
Rockford in 1878, and even then they were not roommates. In the two months
between their reunion in Munich on New Year's and Ellen's departure from

Rome with Sarah on March 7, Jane and Ellen were together day and night. On her trip to Monte Cassino, Ellen referred to Jane's Roman *pension* as "home" and did not sleep as well away from there, though Sarah seemed to sleep fine. The double bed in Pompeii was "even wider than ours," Ellen reported, but without Jane (or Jane's fur coat) to cuddle with in bed on chilly mornings, Ellen was left alone to wish she could "excite and tempt" Jane "by kissing you fifteen times this minute."[53]

Even as she wrote those words, Ellen was conscious of the cloud on the horizon: this trip together was an island in time and space.[54] In a matter of weeks Ellen would return to her life in Chicago, and Jane to hers, presumably in Cedarville. The new intensity and intimacy afforded by the trip would be ended. Jane herself remarked to Alice on missing Ellen and Sarah while they were away from Rome. Then, in an echo of her youthful detachment, she claimed to welcome their temporary absence as it allowed her "to get used to it a little before we separate in America."[55] Ellen knew better than anyone of Jane's capacity to steel herself against longing for what was gone, but Ellen no longer apologized for having a different emotional response. Writing to Jane from her lonely bed in Pompeii, Ellen allowed herself a "sentimental diversion" in order to reflect on just how much she missed Jane after only a few days apart. She bravely went on to name the heartache she knew she was inviting and had been inviting ever since their first week together in Munich: "I didn't know I was going to miss you so much. Yes, I *knew* it well enough, but knowing it isn't quite the same as experiencing it. I knew well enough in Munich that I was going to sacrifice our old relation and never get it back. [It] wasn't without a pang that I saw it going for it has been a great consolation to me for a good many years, but I am too old now to worry that I will never love anybody again as much as I can. It's about all there is worth doing and if it pulls you to pieces a good deal when you have to give up what you have and got dependent on—why let it!" Ellen quickly compensated for this outburst by remarking that she was "consumed with fleas," but humor could not mute the point: Ellen was choosing to break whatever rules of emotional restraint had governed her ten-year bond with Jane. She was letting herself love Jane as much as she could, even allowing herself to grow "dependent" on that love, knowing full well that she would have to give it up when they went home. It was worth it, she was willing to pay the price, and, at the age of twenty-nine, she was "too old now" to worry.[56]

Jane's response to Ellen, if there was one, has not survived. Jane may not have been able to match Ellen's devotion or her candor, but she did not flee from Ellen's emotional embrace as she might have in years past. Instead, she sought to fold Ellen into her family circle by writing often to Alice and Anna

20. Ellen Gates Starr in the late 1880s. (University of Illinois at Chicago, University Library, Jane Addams Memorial Collection, neg. no. 3566)

about her love for Ellen, reporting on Ellen's affection for Alice and Anna, and even sending to Alice the letters Ellen wrote to Jane from Naples and Pompeii.[57] Jane included along with them an apology for her friend's "demonstrative affection," demurring that Ellen "always overestimates my influence."[58] At the same time, Jane felt no need to conceal Ellen's longing for fifteen kisses or to explain why Ellen wondered "if I am wicked to wish that you were on one edge of [the bed] and I in the middle comme toujours."[59]

Jane, Ellen, and Alice inhabited a world where romanticized female friend-ships were commonplace, where women like Jane and Ellen identified them-selves as "spinsters," not "lesbians," and where demonstrations of physical and emotional affection between women were too ordinary to inspire curiosity about private sexual practices. It is maddening, of course, not to know whether sexual passion was included in Jane's developing capacity to be intimate, vul-nerable, and embodied, but the evidence of a tender, playful bond with Ellen offers poignant testimony to Jane's emotional maturity if not her erotic life.[60]

Throughout the European trip, Jane and Ellen engaged in a complicated dance around their religious similarities and differences. Together, they revered the "old Catholics," including the third-century monks who built Rome's catacombs and the fifth-century artists who captured the early faith's "gaiety, grace, and piety" in their mosaics at Ravenna.[61] Jane and Ellen shared the then-popular Protestant conviction that these pre-Byzantine Christians represented the most simple and authentic form of Christianity, a faith, said Jane, "we seem to have lost since."[62] Her autobiographical tribute to the beauty of the Greek Gospels, and her association of those texts to "Christian Ethics," is just one gesture Jane later made to her conviction that pre-institutionalized, under-ground Christianity, the faith shared by the early Roman poor before it became a symbol of power under Constantine, deserved its own resurrection.[63]

Along with this reverence for what Jane called "primitive Catholicity," she and Ellen also shared a "contemptuous opinion" of the Roman Catholic Church with its claims of papal infallibility and its "tawdry" displays of mate-rial wealth.[64] After letters of introduction from Ellen's Aunt Eliza gained them entry to a beatification ceremony at the Vatican, Jane told Alice that "the early church is as far as possible from any hint of this later depravity." Indeed, she declared, "nothing ever seems more absurd to me than to connect all this pageant and pride with the religion which Christ himself taught." She added, without much reflection on her own family's devotion to the Republican Party of Grant and Hayes, that she could not "see how Catholics stay devout amidst all the chicanery" at the Vatican.[65]

Ellen and Jane relished their shared disdain for Catholicism's lack of Christian humility. At the same time, however, Ellen attended Anglican church services in Rome that Jane thought "might almost as well be Catholic" and was irresistibly drawn to Catholic accounts of miraculous events that Jane regarded as preposterous.[66] Thus, when Ellen tried to determine if the cooling of St. Paul's executed head had really produced different temperatures in a trinity of fountains, Jane sighed over her "usually wise" friend's "naivete." When thinking about the Trinity made Ellen's head ache, Jane dryly advised her not to think about it. "That remedy" was not, Ellen explained, "applicable in my case," but it worked for Jane.[67] Offered the chance for spiritual uplift from an Anglican or Catholic ritual, Jane opted for the "stiffening" she received from a Scotch Presbyterian sermon.[68] And in a small sermon of her own on the message of Michelangelo's Medici Chapel, Jane told George that "endurance and determination are the sole recourses of life and not hopefulness and beneficence."[69] Her spiritual quest had brought Jane full circle, back to the permanence of excellence, only now she saw excellence with more humble, humane eyes.

Jane Addams claimed in her autobiography that she was reading the philosopher Auguste Comte during this trip and was "enormously interested in the Positivists" because of their belief in a supreme "fellowship" of all humanity based on lived experience rather than metaphysics.[70] No diaries remain from this moment in Jane's life and her surviving letters make no mention of Comte or the positivists. Those letters do, however, provide abundant evidence that by the time she took this European tour, Jane had settled firmly into an identity as a liberal Christian humanist. Her guides to that philosophy may have included the Positivists; they certainly included Leo Tolstoy, George Eliot, John Ruskin, Matthew Arnold, William Godwin, and Robert Browning.[71] Over the previous four years, those writers had provided Jane with the "stiffening" she needed to ignore speculation on atonement and salvation and to focus exclusively on humans' responsibility for Christian love of others in this life. Her conduct on this 1888 tour testified to her ideological and emotional progress toward the argument she would make in 1892 in "The Subjective Necessity for Social Settlements." "Christianity has to be revealed," Jane said, "in the way in which [man] connects with his fellows . . . the zeal and affection with which he regards his fellows. By this simple process was created . . . the wonderful fellowship, the true democracy of the early Church."[72] Traveling, now, as a student of human fellowship instead of a worshiper of heroes, Jane consistently directed her gaze at the people around her, and her letters are full of tiny vignettes aimed at capturing the sweetness of everyday connections.

In describing her solo visit to the cathedral at Ulm, for example, Jane told of becoming "intimate at once" with the tour guide and then chatting with "the dearest little old man watching for fire." Jane's missing notebooks from the time may have contained lengthy notes, as she later claimed, about the Ulm experience inspiring a Comtean vision of a "cathedral of humanity," but in her letter to Flora Guiteau Jane exulted over the cathedral's success at conveying both the "mystery" and the "humanity" of Christ.[73]

Ironically, Jane's commitment to an earthly Christianity and affection for her fellow humans worked to soften her attitude toward those who found solace in the metaphysical. Though she chafed at Ellen's mystical bent and sneered at the Vatican's materialism, Jane was fascinated by pure faith, respectful of "a sense of a religious life" in which she had "no part nor even a remote understanding."[74] It took no apparent effort for her to grasp the "intense interest" Italian peasants brought to an Easter ritual in Florence where the flight of a fiery dove predicted the year's harvest. Jane easily shared the crowd's relief when the dove took a propitious path.[75] This growing sympathy, which would serve her so well among her religious neighbors in Chicago, was evident in Jane's attitude toward priests and the poor on this second tour. She was quite impressed, even charmed, by the "learned" priests she met through letters of introduction from Ellen's Aunt Eliza Starr, and she became "very companionable" with a priest who visited with her while she was recuperating in Rome.[76] Jane took care to note that it was the priests who were behind Rome's "bread riots," which fully engaged her interest and sympathy. Grounded by sciatica, she declared herself "more anxious" to see the bread riots than to see the pope. Men were out of work, she explained matter-of-factly to Alice and to Anna, and they needed bread.[77]

Three years earlier, Jane had visited Italy without noticing the Italian people, except to remark on their dirtiness or dishonesty. Now she was "impatient to learn to speak [Italian] before we get among the country people" and editorialized on the "good breeding" and "delicacy" of Italian cab drivers.[78] On the eve of her move into an Italian immigrant neighborhood in Chicago, Jane walked the streets of Rome and Florence, convinced that the Italian people as a whole were "handsome no matter what they are doing" and gracious "as a matter of course without being vain or conscious of it."[79] During her first trip, Jane had focused her studious eye entirely on the heroes in Rome's paintings, now she visited the Sistine Chapel and looked past "the mighty prophets and sibyls" to find "fine relief" in the depictions of "true people."[80] No longer fascinated by warriors like Frederick the Great, Jane now bought a photograph of Albrecht Dürer's *Two Knights,* who were not fighting, she said, because "they realize how useless it was—that it must come in another way."[81]

On her first tour, Jane had been bored and irritated by dilettantish conversation among tourists in the boardinghouses. Now it was Ellen's turn to be exasperated over tablemates' stupid remarks on Ruskin while Jane sat back to "rather enjoy" the whole "funny" scene.[82] Ellen wrote to Anna at some length about Jane devoting "most of her time at table to an absurd old Missourian who wore a flannel shirt and a paper collar, speared his bread with his fork, and clicked his teeth." No one bothered to speak with him, reported Ellen, and yet Jane "talked to this man as she would have done to a man of the world." Ellen "never admired her more" and marveled at the "moral effort and self discipline" that made it "possible for her to act this way."[83] The record is silent on whether Anna Haldeman Addams shared Ellen's admiration for her step-daughter's increasingly democratic conduct.

Jane's happiness on this European trip, her growing confidence in her ability to operate independently of her family, and her deepening faith in the power of Christian humanism to chart a stable moral path to goodness all combined to revive her restlessness about her own future. Ellen tried to counter Jane's feelings of "uselessness" by proclaiming how much good Jane did for Ellen "every day of my life."[84] But Ellen, of all people, must have known that this was an irrelevant offering. Since Rockford days, Jane had longed to range beyond the private sphere. She had postponed, despaired, studied, prepared, all the while waiting to get her moral purposes straightened. Now they appeared to be straightened. The spiritual and ethical code she had adopted had moved her away from Carlyle's heroism and into humanism but then brought her right back to the Carlylean call to action. Love of humanity was meaningless as a passive faith; goodness existed only in the doing. Jane's Christian humanism could certainly justify a move away from the family and into wider service, but where would she go? What would she do? After a pleasant afternoon with an Englishwoman who lived in a villa in Florence, Jane tactfully mused to Anna: "It is always a source of wonder to me, seeing people in the midst of every cultivated and intellectual advantage, themselves studious Christians and cultivated, that they have not made more of it, although just exactly what I expect is hard to tell."[85]

In writing her autobiography, Addams faced the narrative challenge of explaining just how it was that she shook herself out of this paralysis. The conversion story she constructed recalled the afternoon in Madrid in late April 1888 when she, along with Ellen and Sarah and a male escort from their hotel, attended the "Testa del Toros," which, as Jane explained to Anna at the time, "certainly sounds better than bullfight."[86] Addams used that brutal, bloody event as the crisis that ostensibly galvanized her to take social action, to cease pretending that she was "in preparation for great things to come," and to realize that she was mired in privileged "self-seeking" with all of her travels and galleries and books and concerts. It was at this moment, she wrote, that she

revealed to Ellen her plan to rent a house in the neediest part of a city and provide useful employment there for women like herself who had "been given over
too exclusively to study" and needed to "learn of life from life itself."[87]

There is no need to dismiss this story simply because Addams exaggerated
its details and used it to accelerate the history of her planning for a settlement
house. As with all the embellished stories Addams constructed for her autobiography, this one conveyed a deeply felt truth about her experience. She
claimed, for example, that she alone stayed to watch all of the day's bullfights
while her companions retreated in horror. That was not true; the detailed
descriptions of the day that Jane wrote to her relatives say that Ellen and Sarah
were just as transfixed by the bullfights as Jane, just as admiring of their "magnificence." Still, Jane may have felt quite alone in her later thoughts about the
event. Her subsequent horror over being "brutal enough" to tolerate the wan-
ton killing of six bulls and almost twenty-five horses for the sake of splendid
pageantry did, undoubtedly, strengthen her inner resolve to renounce art for
art's sake and place art in the service of life.[88]

Jane's most telling comment about her bloody afternoon in Madrid came
at the end of a long letter to Weber's wife, Laura. There, Jane confessed that she
would "rather not have the children of the family know of the bullfight."[89] It
was this powerful sense of shame that Addams later drew upon to craft her
bullfight story and to make her point that aesthetics divorced from morality,
art separated from life, corrupts the audience. "So much does skill and parade
go towards concealing a wrong thing," wrote Jane to Anna, that it was only "the
suffering of the horses" that forced her to realize that this was not just another
thrilling opera.[90] She had progressed far from the priggish girl who preferred
artistic representation to human experience, but her "own brutality" at the bullfight convinced her that she had not progressed far enough.[91] In crafting her
conversion around that event, Jane neatly captured her difficult transition from
a life of abstract, bloodless representation to a life of concrete, embodied reality.

A week after the bullfight, Jane was stranded in a train station writing to
Anna. "I still have time to 'read and write,'" she wryly observed, "apparently the
two sole occupations open to people of unlimited leisure."[92] Her restlessness
was palpable; she was fed up with her privilege. When they went back to the
United States, Ellen, Sarah, and Helen Harrington would all return to teaching
jobs in which they felt stretched and challenged. Jane would return to a fractured, fractious family headed by her anxious, lonely stepmother whose life
was now circumscribed by George's depression and paranoia. From where Jane
sat in May 1888, it looked as if this second European tour had illuminated her
joy when operating as a sturdy and cheerful female friend and revealed her
despondency when faced with a life apart from women friends or engaging

endeavor. The trip had not yet, however, showed her a permanent path to the friends or the endeavor.

In the time that was left to them, Jane and Ellen basked in the Spanish sun, and the entire party took a boat from Cadiz to Tangier for two days in the "enchanted air" of northern Africa. Jane's double delight in her friends' company and in encountering the "good looks and intelligence" of the "Moors" turned her reports of general seasickness in the Straits of Gibraltar into comic sketches in which she and her fellow travelers were a bedraggled assemblage in pathetic contrast to the "tall, dignified Moor men" they encountered on shore.[93]

A visit to an English missionary hospital in Tangier, combined with a visit to a Protestant evangelical school in San Sebastian, Spain, ten days later, afforded Jane an important introduction to women who were using their education to engage in direct service. Jane had disdained missionary work when she was at Rockford, and neither medical work nor evangelical education was attractive to Jane in the spring of 1888. But in the aftermath of the bullfight and at the approach to her voyage home, Jane was at a receptive crossroads in her life and was noticeably impressed by the missionary women she met on these tours.[94] Just two weeks after her visit to San Sebastian, Jane suddenly announced to Alice that her itinerary was now aimed at reaching London by June 10, in time for the World Centennial of Foreign Missions.[95] Before her encounters in Tangier and San Sebastian, none of Jane's earlier discussions of schedules had mentioned this missionary meeting, much less her interest in attending it.

On her way to the London meeting, Jane said goodbye to Ellen in Rheims, France. Ellen turned back to Italy with her novice art history students; Jane and Sarah crossed the English Channel, planning to rest in Canterbury before taking on London and the meeting of the world's missionaries. It was by sheer chance that Jane and Sarah crossed paths with the wife of the bishop of Dover on the day they were touring the cathedral at Canterbury. That stroke of serendipity led to an invitation to tea, which led to a meeting with Canon William Fremantle and his wife, which led to a dinner invitation at the Fremantles' home, which led to Canon Fremantle encouraging Jane and Sarah to visit the Toynbee Hall settlement when they were in London.

Jane took Fremantle's suggestion to visit the settlement because she was "charmed" by the sight of her hosts' home, "filled with scholarly things," and equally charmed by their "simple hospitality" and their "sympathy with all questions and people." Jane liked the fact that Fremantle was "the second son of a lord, his wife the daughter of a baronet."[96] Her commitment to Christian humanism had not turned John Addams's daughter against the "finest" people.

It had simply caused her to define the "finest" people as those with education and refinement, those with spirituality but not dogma, those who cared about the less blessed and who manifest that concern in direct, personal ways. Canon and Mrs. Fremantle more than qualified.

Canon Fremantle had served from the mid-1860s until the early 1880s as the rector of St. Mary's Church, the mother church of the St. Mary's parish in that section of London bounded by Marylebone Road and Baker Street. There, he had aligned himself with the "broad church" movement, which took a very different approach to revitalizing the Anglican church than had the churchmen toward whom Ellen Starr inclined. For broad churchmen like Fremantle, the future of the Church of England lay not in a renaissance of near-Catholic ritual and metaphysics but, rather, in an ecumenical embrace of all religious sects within a national church that unified Britain's moral and cultural life on the principles of love, fellowship, and service. According to broad churchmen, these were the essential features of all Christianity.[97]

Jane Addams was well prepared for her unplanned meeting with Canon Fremantle. Her reading for the previous five years had made her fluent in liberal Christian arguments for emphasizing the similarities, not the differences, between Christian and non-Christian, secular and religious movements for spiritual humanism and social justice. Just before encountering Fremantle, Jane had been reading a church history by Arthur Stanley, one of Fremantle's teachers.[98] She was wholly unaware at the time of the influence of Fremantle's own writings on American social gospel advocates like Graham Taylor and Richard Ely, but her isolation was about to end, and when it did, she would emerge well versed in the spiritual canon from which her American reform colleagues drew their inspiration.[99]

Samuel Barnett was Canon Fremantle's prize protege. As a young curate in Fremantle's London parish, Barnett had helped create a cross-class parish council that included Jews as well as Christians as community representatives, and he had assisted with the parish's social work.[100] In 1873, Barnett and his energetic wife, Henrietta, moved to the vicarage at St. Jude's Church in Whitechapel, at the heart of London's East End. They spent a frustrating decade trying to serve their religiously diverse and religiously skeptical community from within the confines of the Anglican Church. Finally, in partnership with reform-minded, broad church friends at Balliol College in Oxford, the Barnetts designed a secular institution to settle among and serve the people of the East End. Their goal was to unite people across denominational lines through Christian ethics and to harmonize across class lines by sharing what the British poet Matthew Arnold once called "the best that has been said and thought in the world."[101]

The Barnetts named their new institution "Toynbee Hall" in honor of Arnold Toynbee, the Oxford political economist who had originated the term "the industrial revolution" and then called for a fundamental change in modern class relations. Two years before his death at age thirty-one in 1883, Toynbee had delivered a speech on "Industry and Democracy" in which he compared Carlyle's nostalgic demand that the rich "govern and protect the poor as they did in the past," with the poor's modern demand for self-government. "Who was right, Carlyle or the people?" asked Toynbee. He quickly answered, "The people!"[102] Inspired by Toynbee's belief that relations across classes needed to move away from patronizing stewardship and toward democratic mutuality, the Barnetts opened their East End settlement house in 1884. Four years later, William Fremantle directed Jane Addams to their doorstep.

"The most interesting thing we have done in London," Jane reported to Alice after just five days back in the city, "was to visit Toynbee Hall in the East End." The World Centennial of Foreign Missions had been interesting; Jane came away from it "ashamed" of her "former ignorance" about the opium traffic in China and the liquor traffic in the Congo.[103] But it was Toynbee Hall in the Whitechapel parish that captured her imagination. The settlement's stately red brick building, with its university-style residence hall, public rooms, and quadrangle, sat amidst narrow streets and crowded old buildings that housed a diverse and growing population of the working poor, almost 20 percent of whom were Irish, Russian Jews, or Germans.[104] The majority of the area's inhabitants had steady employment, enough to eat, and adequate if not desirable housing, but almost 40 percent of East Enders lived in poverty because the area's economic patchwork of small shops, dock work, and specialty trades offered only irregular employment. The schools were wholly inadequate to the size and needs of the population, medical care was poor when it could be had, sanitation standards were ignored, crimes (including those committed by Jack the Ripper) were rampant, and though property-owning members of the British working class had won the franchise in 1867, the political voice of the East End was often muted by disorganization and alienation.[105]

On this, her second tour of the East End, Jane got more than the "superficial survey" of the "misery and wretchedness" she had glimpsed five years earlier at the Saturday night market stalls, and she did not come away, this time, "thoroughly sad and perplexed."[106] Instead, she came away inspired by the work which Samuel and Henrietta Barnett were directing at Toynbee Hall. "It is a community of University men," she explained to Alice, "who live there, have their recreating clubs and society all among the poor people. Yet in the same style they would live in their own circle."[107] Among the sixteen Oxford and Cambridge graduates who lived at Toynbee Hall at any given time, some worked in the city during the day, others did social service work in the East End, but all did community service in the evenings, either by offering free classes, giving music and art lessons, sponsoring clubs and lectures, providing meeting space to labor organizations, or working with local residents on issues of housing, sanitation, and education.[108] "It is so free from 'professional doing good,'" Jane enthused to Alice, "so unaffectedly sincere and so productive of good results . . . that it seems perfectly ideal."[109]

Whatever her prior, inchoate notions about taking art to the people or somehow replicating her direct service experience in Baltimore, Jane's encounter with Toynbee Hall brought into focus her thoughts and plans. It gave her a way to picture herself engaged with women friends in useful, secular endeavor. In a speech to the Chicago Woman's Club three years later on "Outgrowths of Toynbee Hall," Jane revealed her own experience by describing young people returning "from college, and Europe, and Wagner operas and philosophical lectures." Some were "listless" with "indecision," but others, she said, had "had a vision." Jane then employed Samuel Barnett's favorite axiom to define that vision; it was the belief that "the things that make us alike are stronger than the things that make us different."[110]

The Barnetts' vision, which they held in common with a vigorous and influential reform subculture of the late Victorian period, drew from both feudal and democratic assumptions, Carlyle and Toynbee. On the one hand, the Barnetts held to the belief that every community, in order to thrive, had to be led by a refined, cultivated, leisured gentry class equipped to model Christian ethics and provide an Anglo-centered education in "the best that has been said and thought in the world." This was the image of harmonious paternalism in the village parish that guided broad churchmen like Canon Fremantle. On the other hand, the Barnetts and their reform friends assumed—and this was no small assumption in the age of Herbert Spencer—that every member of the society was intellectually capable of appreciating "the best." They further assumed that members of the working class deserved an education in "the best" and that such an education would prepare them for democratic political action that would improve their economic status, whether individually or collectively. When one Liberal MP proclaimed in Parliament in 1888, "we're all socialists now," he was not endorsing Marx. He was aligning himself with men like Samuel Barnett and against the industrial revolution's ruthless competitive individualism.[111] In this way, Britain's ancient paternalism coalesced with modern notions of Christian ethics and democratic access in places like Toynbee Hall.

By the time Jane met the Barnetts, in 1888, they had already shifted their own thinking away from paternalist control and toward more democratic strategies. This was most evident in their separation from their secular mentor in social work, Octavia Hill. Hill was one of the originators of the notion of "scientific charity" and a founder of the Charity Organization Society that Daniel Coit Gilman had imported to Baltimore when Jane was living there. Under Hill's tutelage, the Barnetts had begun their parish social work with Canon Fremantle at St. Mary's on the presumption that poverty represented a failure of moral character, that direct aid only weakened the poor further, and that all charities needed to carefully separate the deserving from the undeserving poor.[112] Years of living in Whitechapel had convinced the Barnetts that Hill's view assigned too much blame to the victims of a harsh economic system. As they evolved toward what they called "practicable socialism," they aligned themselves with those who argued that an impoverished environment itself produced material and moral poverty, and they joined with their working-class neighbors in direct labor and legislative action to attack environmental problems. The Barnetts continued to devote themselves to educational and cultural activities in the settlement, partly out of the belief that artistic and spiritual nourishment were vital to fuel the political and economic fight.[113] As a result, Toynbee Hall featured classes in Shakespeare as well as meetings of the Sanitary Aid Society, lectures on natural history as well as speeches by labor leaders like Ben Tillett on "The Future of the Dockers' Union."[114]

The East End settlement house that Jane Addams visited in June 1888 was not a radical institution by any means. The Barnetts maintained a working relationship with the local Charity Organization Society and, like most "enlightened" Victorians of the day, were skeptical about direct aid to the poor and pretty much blind to the independent working-class culture surrounding them. But while burdened by the class biases and stiff formalities endemic to the steward class in Victorian Britain, Toynbee Hall did not project a harsh, evangelical ethos. To Jane Addams's eyes, the settlement was refreshingly free of "professional doing good."[115] Of course, her vision had been rubbed a bit rose-colored by reading the romantic novels of Walter Besant, which celebrated the philanthropic rich while valorizing the noble poor. Jane read Besant's popular 1882 novel, *All Sorts and Conditions of Men*, the same week she visited Toynbee Hall.[116] The novel's heroine, Angela Messenger, was a wealthy heiress who felt useless after graduation from Newnham College, took herself to East London to live and learn (and fall in love) among the working classes, and built there a People's Palace as a haven for recreation and culture.[117] After reading *All Sorts and Conditions of Men*, Jane visited the real "People's Palace," a new East London youth center built with private and public funds.[118] The Palace's classrooms, meeting rooms, billiard rooms, music and dance rooms, and library were an important model for Hull-House, which would be more alive with the sounds of youth than Toynbee Hall. The Palace, claimed Besant in the month after Jane left London, fostered an understanding that "everything that is done in and for the place must be supported and carried through by the people for the people." Though the East London People's Palace ultimately fell short of this lofty goal, Besant's aspirations likely resonated with Jane's Lincolnesque heritage.[119]

In *Twenty Years at Hull-House*, Jane Addams devoted just three autobiographical sentences to her pivotal encounter with the "missionary side of London" and the Barnetts at Toynbee Hall. She quickly moved on to recall her relief that, at long last, her period of "passive receptivity," "ever-lasting preparation," and "curious inactivity" had come to a close and she was finally going to begin work too long delayed. In her zeal to argue that Miss Sill's Rockford Seminary had ill prepared her for useful action in the real world, Addams strongly implied that the years she lived after leaving Rockford and before opening Hull-House had been wasted. By eliminating her family from the story (in deference to the tensions attendant upon Jane's move into public life), she also eliminated all reflection on the ways in which her filial duties, her experiences in Baltimore, and her sojourns in Europe had contributed to her education and maturity. So great was Addams's residual sense of time wasted that she created, in her memoir, the impression that she could have appreciated, embraced, and successfully undertaken something like the Barnetts' project years earlier if only she had not been caught up in that stupid "snare of preparation."[120]

It is true that Senator John Addams's daughter, fresh out of Rockford Seminary, could have endorsed Toynbee Hall's paternalistic model of a harmonious village, led by wise stewards, in which mutual interests and a shared identification with the nation's "best" culture united all. She could even, in theory, have accepted the proposition that all members of the community, properly led, were capable of appreciating, if not exemplifying, the nation's best culture. As a student of Carlyle, Ruskin, Wordsworth, George Eliot, and Matthew Arnold, the young Jane Addams was well schooled in the Victorians' antimaterialist, anti-industrial, pro-paternalist counterculture. This cultural coalition of tutors in British stewardship had reinforced Senator Addams's American example, delivering to Jane a powerful message about the duty of the privileged to serve and to lead. It was a message she had long resonated to and one that had inspired her nongendered, non-Christian dreams of heroic stewardship while at Rockford.[121]

Had Jane's seminary been less orthodox, had her father not died, had she gone to Smith College, had Anna been more encouraging, she might well have begun her career as a steward earlier, but almost certainly with less success.

Her postgraduate years were vital for humbling Jane and humanizing her understanding of spirituality and artistic expression. Those years of "ever-lasting preparation" taught her to value the caring and intimacy fostered by female culture, directed her eye away from the hero on stage and toward the individual on the street, and forced her to realize that in a world of bent backs, dying children, filthy factories, and selfish power, heroism was not a romantic flight of the disembodied will but a daily decision to show up and hold on. She knew none of this when she left Rockford, and without the intervening years she could not have grasped, replicated, or—most important—improved upon what she saw at Toynbee Hall.

The essence Jane was able to extract from Toynbee Hall was not its paternalist assumptions, which were ubiquitous in charity work, nor its democratic ideals, which she could have found in numerous political and labor organizations. What she grasped there, beneath all the British propriety, was an enduring faith in every individual's capacity to live by Christian ethics and to parlay those ethics, collectively, into the active creation of a civil society that dignified labor, culture, and religious diversity.[122] Samuel Barnett's motto was "one by one," by which he meant that social reform and moral regeneration had to be rooted in direct and daily human encounters in which lives became entwined and from which grew a shared commitment to the common good. When he spoke of "the best," Barnett meant not only Matthew Arnold's cultural best, but the spiritual best envisioned by Balliol College's T. H. Green, a devout Christian ethicist who disavowed Christian dogma. Green's philosophy infused Toynbee Hall with the idea—so similar to Leo Tolstoy's—that individuals found their "best selves" and their greatest joy when they identified their happiness with that of the commonweal. This meant that service to others was not a sacrifice, it was a choice to pursue happiness along a deeper, surer path; it was, as Addams would later explain, "a subjective necessity."[123]

Back in 1882, when Jane's heroic ambitions were chafing against her duty to Anna, she had worried that she might "begin a life of self-sacrifice" but lack "strength enough to carry it on."[124] The intervening years had stripped away the need to cover ambition in the weighty cloak of sacrifice, revealing an authentic desire for joyful engagement. Without those years preceding her encounter with Toynbee Hall, it is unlikely that Jane Addams would have grasped that the settlement's promise of earthly salvation applied to her—and to the members of her class—as much as it applied to those in the working classes. It is certainly unlikely that she would have grasped that idea with such zeal. For while Barnett and his Oxford and Cambridge residents claimed that they were as uplifted as their neighbors by settlement work, Addams placed at the very center of her American project the insistence that rich, idle, educated women needed settlement salvation as much as, if not more than, the poor. It was an older and wiser Jane Addams, a veteran of the Baltimore Colored Women's Shelter, who defined her enterprise as a cross-class partnership, not a heroic rescue mission.

Jane debuted some of her new ideas in the eulogy she delivered at the memorial service for Anna Peck Sill a year after her return from Europe. There, Jane described Toynbee Hall by tracing its roots back to Balliol College and defining the Balliol ethic as "rational godliness, and a certain passion for doing good." When Jane graduated from Rockford, she had all the rationality and none of the passion; lacking faith in her own nondogmatic spirituality, she had not trusted that her impulse to serve was anything but selfish ambition. In her backhanded eulogy to Sill, Jane proclaimed that a college education was nothing more than a "mountain of mere straw and stubble" if it did not give graduates "a moral purpose."[125] Since that was the very thing she lacked when she left Miss Sill's Rockford, Jane's postgraduate education in humanity and humility was hardly a self-indulgent waste of years.

By the time Jane delivered her eulogy to Anna Sill in July 1889, she was already living in a Chicago boardinghouse with Ellen, and the two of them were busy with the social and material preparations attendant upon opening their own settlement house on Halsted Street. Getting there had not been easy; it had taken months after returning from Europe to extricate herself from the family. Jane had returned to the United States in July 1888, earlier than planned, after learning of George's disappearance and the family's frantic efforts to locate him. But even while doing her filial duty, Jane had begun distancing herself from the situation. She was, she wrote to Alice from England, "dreadfully sorry" for George and for "his mother" too.[126] She repeated this rhetorical separation from her stepmother in a second letter to Laura. Jane insisted that she was "not in the least afraid" that George would commit suicide; "he is too good a man for that." She was fearful for his safety, though, and begged Laura to keep her informed. "You know I take things quietly," she told her sister-in-law, as if to say that she could handle the worst news.[127] For ten days aboard ship, Jane had no way of knowing what the worst news might be. Harry was out looking for George, and Anna fretted alone, still resistant to all pleas that she visit Girard.[128] If George had killed himself or died during his weeks on the road, Jane's plans for starting a settlement in Chicago and living with Ellen might well have been destroyed. Faced with another family tragedy, her place would have been with Anna.

As it was, George's adventure ended all possible pretense that he was in his right mind or would ever have a career as a research scientist. Anna's dreams for her two sons, her "diamond" and her "pearl," were now dust. She had preached to both of them a gospel of service. "To do good to our fellow beings. That is all the *religion* worth one Christian thought," she told Harry. "It is our mission every day to do some use or good," she insisted, and George had tried to obey. "The only way in which I can repay you," he had written his mother from Baltimore, "is by making myself of worth and service." Though Anna had not, herself, ever engaged in community service, she firmly believed it was the duty of men with her sons' talents to instill in others "the mutual interests of humanity . . . and help lift up the downtrodden."[129]

It does not seem ever to have occurred to Anna that Jane might be the only one of her children capable of fulfilling these calls to public service. Nor does it appear that Anna ever took pride or pleasure in her stepdaughter's enactment of these ideals. Anna's sense of abandonment was too great. After all, Anna was left trapped in Cedarville with an increasingly peculiar son while Jane escaped to the city and a life of her own choosing. The depth of Anna's resentment over Jane's departure to Chicago can best be measured by the breadth of the silence that surrounds it. Six years later, when Anna learned from Ellen that Jane was stricken with appendicitis, she wrote to Harry, "Tis only the beginning of the end that you have long prophesied. Every selfish end, no matter how it takes the form of an 'angel of light,' meets its downfall. Surely it is no fault of ours if they sow the wind and reap the whirlwind."[130]

It was not as though Jane had made a sudden exit from Cedarville. In September following her return from Europe she promptly became president of the Cedarville chapter of the Woman's Christian Temperance Union.[131] That move was followed by her decision, in October, to join the local Presbyterian church.[132] This act was not, she later explained, the result of any "emotional conversion"; when Jane read the testament of the Scottish believer Henry Drummond, she "felt more than ever before the vast difference between one who has once felt the inspiration and one who has not." Still, she longed for "an outward symbol of fellowship, some bond of peace," and had given up all "conceit" that she could achieve goodness on her own.[133] Jane looked upon her life as "tangled" when it was "far from Christ" and was uncomfortable with Alice's praise of her for "always" doing right. No, Jane replied, "it is only the narrowest escape from great wrong and weakness all the time with me."[134] Jane's exposure to an earnest, devout, but nondogmatic view of Christianity had convinced her, however, that her affiliation with a church could be both authentic and useful. And her plan to cultivate support for her settlement project in Chicago's charitable community certainly made church membership prudent.

Visits with Alice, Harry, and Marcet in Girard, Kansas, and with the Linns in Geneseo, Illinois, limited Jane's involvement with affairs in Cedarville or Freeport in that fall after her return from Europe. She knew by then that she was moving to Chicago and so did Anna. Perhaps that explains Jane's stay with Mrs. Guiteau in Freeport in September and her longer visits farther away from home. Forty-five years later, Jane would write of the "family difficulties" that are "easily developed when children are grown up and begin to find their individual interests. . . . In a household composed of parents and adult children," she noted, "it is much more difficult to maintain a warm and understanding family affection than it is during an earlier period of family life."[135]

By January 1889, even Jane's old teacher, Sarah Blaisdell was asking when the "Chicago plan" was to be entered upon, and Ellen was impatient for Jane to break free of the family claim and launch their settlement "scheme."[136] January dragged on for Ellen and still Jane was enmeshed in the family, unable to leave Mary Linn, to whom "I owe so much," or little Stanley, who was sick. "I know you disapprove dear heart," wrote Jane to Ellen, "and I appreciate your disapproval. I disapprove myself in a measure, but 'God as make me so,' I suppose."[137] Just a year earlier, in a gushing tribute to Jane's "beautiful, unpretentious interest in everybody," Ellen had confided to Anna that she realized any effort toward making Jane "less generous" with other people was entirely "futile."[138] By early 1889, Anna and Ellen were both exasperated with Jane's magnanimity. Anna wanted Jane to be more generous at home; Ellen wanted her to focus on their new life in Chicago. Ellen, of course, won out. "Have patience for a few days longer," Jane wrote to her in late January. There was to be a meeting of Rockford alumnae in Chicago the last week of that month. Jane thought that would be a good place to begin enlisting support for their scheme. She would be there soon, Jane promised Ellen. Until then, she begged, "don't scold me, dear. I am awfully sorry about the delay. Let's love each other through thick and thin and work out a salvation."[139]

21. Jane Addams at the time of her move to Chicago in 1889. (University of Illinois at Chicago, University Library, Jane Addams Memorial Collection, neg. no. 2795)

Chapter 12
Power in Me and Will to Dominate

In July 1889, two months before Jane Addams and Ellen Starr opened their settlement house on Halsted Street, a local Congregational newspaper announced the pair's intention to provide a gracious meeting place where the "rich and cultured" could associate with the "less largely endowed." The article acknowledged that the plan was notable for its "elasticity" and might "extend in many directions," but was confident that "the beginnings will be small, easily controlled and involving no great risk."[1] Indeed, Ellen herself envisioned just "one large room in which to have classes, lectures, or whatever we may wish." There was, she said, to be "no organization and no institution." She and Jane "simply intended to *live* there and get acquainted with the people and ask their friends of both classes to visit them."[2]

Just two years later, the women's once modest home had become Hull-House, nationally known as "a noted institution" whose "social and educational work . . . has grown beyond the anticipation of those who have been interested in it."[3] By the time they celebrated their second anniversary at 335 South Halsted Street, in the fall of 1891, Jane and Ellen were welcoming eight hundred to a thousand friends and neighbors into their home every week, offering twenty classes, sponsoring dozens of clubs, lectures, and concerts, and all the while running interference between their neighbors and the court system, the local hospitals, landlords, and city hall. With the aid of just a few other residents and scores of volunteers, they were operating a kindergarten and a branch of the Chicago public library, mounting art exhibits in the Butler Gallery they had built next to their house, managing a day nursery in a cottage down the street, and celebrating the transformation of the saloon next door into a gymnasium. Ellen was acknowledged in press reports as Jane's "associate," her friend, her co-host, her able assistant, even her "second self."[4] But there was no doubt in anyone's mind, including Ellen's, that "the moving spirit in this novel philanthropy is Miss Addams," or that it was "Miss Jane Addams, the head of Hull House, to whom its success is largely due."[5]

This was a meteoric rise in stature for a woman who had spent most of her twenties "absolutely at sea so far as any moral purpose was concerned," fretting that she had "gained nothing and improved nothing," and fearful that she lacked the physical stamina for sustained labor.[6] But from the moment she arrived in Chicago in February 1889 and moved into a boardinghouse with Ellen at 4 Washington Place, Jane worked with a vengeance. She spent those first seven months on her feet, meeting with potential allies, speaking to interested groups, investigating neighborhoods, visiting various of the city's private charities, searching for the right house in the right place. After the settlement opened in September of that year, Jane naively imagined that the pace would relax, once there were "fewer letters to answer and fewer people to see," but that never happened. She relished the "astonishing pace" of the work, diving into it like a demon and proposing one new project after another, month after month, as if to prove her theory that "nervous people do not crave rest but activity of a certain kind."[7] She was in full rebellion against Anna, the medical community, Harry, and anyone else who had ever told her to recline her way through life. After eight years of self-doubt, Jane was now sure of her strength and purpose.

In an unusual burst of self-revelation, written just a few weeks after leaving Anna and George behind in Cedarville, Jane told Alice that it had become "impossible" to behave as someone she was not. She was her father's designated daughter, after all, and could no longer deny her "inherited powers and tendencies." Turning to a Robert Browning poem for help in explaining herself, Jane wrote to Alice:

There's power in me and will to dominate
Which I must exercise, they hurt me else:
In many ways I need mankind's respect
Obedience *else*[8]

Jane had long worried that her ambition for a public life was selfish and egocentric. But she now approached her thirtieth birthday with the Tolstoyian conviction that the only escape from selfishness and egocentrism was active engagement in the common life of the most common people. With Ellen whispering encouragement in her ear, Jane was now unapologetic about her ambitions and unafraid in her pursuit of them.

Just as her father had settled in northern Illinois at a propitious moment in the 1840s, so Jane Addams settled in Chicago at a propitious moment in 1889. The city's economy was booming, its population had grown from 100,000 to over a million in just three decades, and its civic leaders were about to win their national campaign to be named as the site for the 1893 World's Columbian Exposition, celebrating the four hundredth anniversary of Columbus's voyages to the Americas. Chicago's booster pride could not mask the city's inequities, however. A white, native-born elite was prospering on the backs of an exploited working class that was overwhelmingly foreign born; in fact, three-quarters of Chicago's population in 1889 was of foreign parentage. While new mansions glistened on Prairie Avenue and Lake Shore Drive, neighborhoods to the south and west struggled against filth, neglect, poverty, and the continual swirl of newcomers moving all over the urban map and all up, and down, the economic ladder.[9]

Those who had been in control of the city since the Civil War were justifiably proud of their triumph in rebuilding Chicago after the disastrous fire of 1871, and proud as well of the numerous charitable institutions they supported with generous, if impersonal, donations. According to the logic of social Darwinism, however, it made little sense for the successful to spend time with the failed. The mere fact of poverty was taken as evidence of incompetence or, worse, moral depravity. What was to be gained by communion with the unfit? Philanthropic checks were written out of a sense of Christian duty or noblesse oblige; staffs were hired to run the asylums, orphanages, and charity hospitals; gala charity banquets and elegant benefit concerts were staged in the name of civic virtue while the neighborhoods of Chicago's working poor continued to sink under the weight of their own muddy, garbage-laden streets.[10]

At the very time that Jane Addams and Ellen Gates Starr arrived in Chicago, however, the smug insularity of the city's Gilded Age leadership was giving way to a new generation of men and women. These sons and daughters of the Gilded Age would usher in a "progressive" era in American life, an expansive period of social experimentation and political redefinition, a time when the relationship between public welfare and private property would be reformed, if not revolutionized, to fit the needs of an urban, industrial, multiethnic society. It was a time, as well, when individual economic failure (and success) came to be viewed as evidence of an unjust economy more than as proof of individual "fitness." Jane Addams arrived in Chicago, then, when economic prosperity and civic pride were being mocked by widespread poverty and urban blight, and concerned citizens were hungry for innovative ways to meet the responsibility they felt for the city's shames. It was an ideal moment for her to step out as a pioneering figure in Chicago's bid to become America's most forward-looking city.[11]

"Jane's idea," wrote Ellen to her sister, "which she puts very much to the front and on no account will give up, is that [the settlement] is more for the benefit of the people who do it than for the other class." This, explained Ellen, was a concept that Jane had fashioned "out of her own experience and ill health."[12] She had fashioned it, as well, out of her contact with Toynbee Hall and her continued reading of Tolstoy. His book, *What Then Must We Do*, which appeared in English in 1887, had built upon his argument in *My Religion* that work on others' behalf was the only true source of happiness. Contact with his powerful prose had persuaded Jane that individual productive labor alongside the masses was, in and of itself, "an anodyne" for the "misery" of pampered luxury.[13] Thus, in pitching her settlement notion to potential allies in Chicago, Jane made no appeals to Christian duty, extolled none of the virtues of self-sacrifice, and said nothing about a fundamental redistribution of society's wealth. She focused instead on the need among individual women of her class and education to find useful outlets for their energies and their intellectual training.[14]

Jane combined this new attention to the needs of women like herself with Toynbee Hall's well-rehearsed focus on the need to build bridges of communication and cooperation between the classes. Out of the mix of these two impulses, the need to serve and the need to communicate, Jane hoped to re-create a sense of shared community amid the urban chaos and class separation that accompanied industrialization. Jane formulated an argument that was, for many people, utterly original: there was not one "needy" class in the city, she said, but two. The argument gained national attention in 1892, when *Forum* magazine published her suggestion that "over-accumulation at one end of society" be placed right alongside "destitution at the other" as twin problems "engendered by the modern conditions of life."[15] Jane formulated that argument well before 1892, however. Newspaper reports from her first summer in Chicago in 1889 make clear that she had insisted from the start that her settlement was to be a place where the two classes "may find help from the other."[16]

Ellen was stunned by the warm reception that greeted their settlement plan in Chicago. "I had no idea in my most sanguine moments that people were going to take it up as they do," she exulted to her sister just weeks after she and Jane began their efforts to enlist public support. "The thing is in the air," she explained, "people are coming to the conclusion that if anything is to be done toward tearing down these walls . . . between the classes . . . it must be done by actual contact and done voluntarily from the top."[17] In fact, an 1887 report on "Methods and Machinery of the Organization of Charity" in Chicago had announced that the "social gulf between the rich and the poor is widening rapidly" and the rich could not close that gap simply by donating to their favorite mission. Like Protestant charity organizations in other cities, those in Chicago were insisting that "the cure of pauperism is a social question . . . not one of alms . . . but of genuine neighborhood." The report concluded that only by actually spending time with the poor could prosperous citizens hope to do their "share of the world's deeds of mercy."[18]

The superficial similarity between Jane's plan to live among the poor and the Protestant charities' call for direct neighborhood contact served to mask, momentarily, the huge philosophical difference between Jane's earthbound interest in cross-class Christian love and the heaven-bound motives of those who set out to do "deeds of mercy." But because Jane had been genuinely impressed by Samuel Barnett's practical application of Christianity in London's East End, she was willing to pursue the possibility of affiliation with the Chicago missionary community, taking full advantage of Rev. Linn's connections in that community.[19] In a sincere bid for family connection at the start of her Chicago adventure, Jane reported to Mary on "similar undertakings," such as the Neighborhood Guild in New York City, but assured her pious sister that her idea, with its emphasis on fluid mutuality with neighbors, "is more distinctly Christian and less Social Science."[20]

Between February and May 1889, Jane happily trotted about the city, introducing herself and her settlement idea to the devout volunteers at the Armour Mission and the Clybourne Street Mission, getting advice from Chicago's premier Protestant clergymen, volunteering to teach an art class for school-age boys at the Moody Bible Institute and to supervise a girls' social club in a rough area of town for the Woman's Christian Temperance Union.[21] Jane's letters to her family describing her contacts with the city's prominent churchfolk glowed with pride over their interest in her settlement scheme, their "vast promises," of "money or moral support," and their conviction that her plans were "eminently Christian."[22] In characteristic fashion, Jane did not directly confront her relatives' suspicion that her Chicago scheme was harebrained. She simply wrote cheerful letters about her meetings with famous preachers like David Swing and Frank Gunsaulus, making clear between every line that these patriarchs thought Miss Jane Addams from Cedarville had something to contribute to the life of the city.[23] Indeed, Swing—a minister so popular that his congregants followed him out of the Presbyterian church and into a nondenominational church of his own—published one of the first articles on Jane and Ellen's project in June 1889. There, he publicly praised the women's "eloquent tongues," "enthusiasm," and "vivacity."[24]

These early contacts with Chicago's leading Protestants may have served to legitimize Jane's project, and ministers' hearty promises of financial support may have helped Jane temporarily assuage Alice's worries that her little sister was about to squander her inheritance.[25] But there was no future for Jane and Ellen in that male-dominated, faith-based missionary community. It was not only that the power in that community centered around men or that those men, however kindly, were inevitably patronizing toward young women like Jane.[26] Nor was it simply that affiliation with an operation like the Armour Mission put the new settlement at risk of being "swallowed up in a great organization."[27] It was their fundamental difference in assumptions that made a partnership impossible.

Missionaries presumed themselves to be a saved people taking the gift of eternal salvation through Christ to the masses. Jane and Ellen assumed that they would not be saved, in any sense of the word, until they lived and worked among the masses, offering fellowship and whatever earthly gifts their education had given them. As Ellen explained to her sister, "Jane feels that it is not the Christian spirit to go among these people as if you were bringing them a great boon." It was, instead, Jane's belief "that one gets as much as one gives."[28]

The Protestant men who embraced the settlement scheme as a vehicle for aiding the poor could not seem to grasp Jane's goal of rescuing the rich from their own sloth. Jane was "grateful" to the superintendent of the Armour Mission for his zeal in publicizing her endeavor, but she was "never quite sure that he has the idea *exactly*."[29] Similar doubts must have accompanied Swing's article, for while he lauded the settlement as a "new social movement" on behalf of the city's "forlorn homes," he also patronized Jane and Ellen as "smooth talkers" who espoused the "astonishing proposition" that "society girls" might be helped by this endeavor as much as "the humbler classes." Swing openly doubted that a project staffed by idle females in Chicago could ever "equal in size" the Toynbee Hall settlement run by Oxford's Anglican men.[30] So, too, the Rev. M. W. Stryker, who took over the prestigious Fourth Presbyterian Church after Swing left, told an amused Jane and an outraged Ellen that "the 'modern fashionable young lady'" was too "hard-hearted" to serve the settlement scheme.[31]

Jane's experience with the Chicago Women's Club (CWC) stood in marked contrast to her experience with the Protestant men. At a club member's reception just a week before the encounter with Rev. Stryker, for example, Jane's presentation of her plan to provide useful female occupation was greeted with grateful tears. It elicited, as well, the weighty endorsement of Helen Ekin Starrett, an author known for publishing her own concerns about idle female youth.[32] A series of similarly successful meetings and receptions with "the Women's Club people" resulted in a newspaper article by Dr. Leila Bedell, a former CWC president, which explicitly recognized that "the chief aim" of the proposed settlement was to serve as a "retreat for other young women." Exposure to "the poverty and struggles of half the people," explained Bedell, "will beget a broader philanthropy," leaving less time for "selfish ambition" and "real or fancied invalidism."[33] Unlike Swing or Stryker, Bedell and her colleagues in the Women's Club grasped what Jane and Ellen were about.[34]

It was Ellen who provided many of the initial contacts with the Chicago Women's Club by calling on friends, such as Bedell, whom she knew from her years of teaching at Miss Caroline Kirkland's private school. Additional introductions were provided by Allen Pond, a young architect Jane met at the Armour Mission and the one man in that community who fully grasped the significance of her concern for young women. Thanks to Ellen and Pond and those mission-affiliated women who also belonged to the CWC, Jane gained early access to that impressive group of Chicago women who would be her key supporters and closest friends in the coming decades.[35] Once she connected with women like Lydia Avery Coonley, Mary Wilmarth, Ellen Henrotin, and Julia P. Harvey, Jane's trajectory in the city was set. She and Ellen were promptly welcomed into the Chicago Women's Club as new members, and their appointment to the Philanthropic Committee exposed them to the decidedly secular and determinedly "practical" aims of the organization.[36]

As advocates for compulsory education, prisoners' rights, industrial arts, and a wide array of other similarly concrete measures, the members of the Chicago Women's Club energetically pursued their stated aim to expand women's civic influence and usher in "A Better Chicago," as Mary Wilmarth put it in a speech she delivered in 1889.[37] Many CWC members with whom Jane and Ellen affiliated were the wives and widows of Chicago's leading businessmen; Henrotin was married to the president of the Chicago Stock Exchange, and Wilmarth was the widow of the founder of Chicago's First National Bank. Rather than blind them to the city's problems, these women's elevated status seemed to give them a broader, even bolder, vision. Indeed, the club's motto, "Humani nihil a me alienum puto" (Nothing human is alien to me), announced the CWC members' intention to push past class and gender boundaries in addressing civic needs. By the time Jane arrived in Chicago, the CWC was on the cutting edge of the city's shift from Gilded Age philanthropy to Progressive Era reform, and its secular orientation toward saving the community rather than individual souls guaranteed the club's sympathy with Jane's agenda and secured its enduring support for her settlement's ever expanding programs.[38]

Beyond the institutional affiliation provided by the Women's Club, there was also the opening it offered Jane to develop lifelong friendships. The women Jane met through the Chicago Women's Club were different from the women she had known in Baltimore. They were more politically aware and more socially engaged than Amelia Brooks but not as hard-edged as the daunting mathematician and suffragist, Christine Ladd-Franklin. Having matured into an appreciation of the importance of female friends, Jane was gifted (virtually upon her arrival in Chicago) with a circle of women who represented her feminine ideal. In a eulogy to Mary Wilmarth in 1919, Jane praised her for being the "perfect antithesis" to the "self-assertive public woman." Unlike Ladd-Franklin, Wilmarth stored her mind "not with knowledge that 'puffeth up' but with wisdom that brings humility." Wilmarth, Jane said, looking back over thirty years of shared activism, was "never a fanatic, exacting moral rules at the expense of human nature"; she gave aid to others "quite without a suggestion of condescension, pushing aside gratitude with a gracious intimation that it was always a privilege to help a forward-looking public effort."[39] This was the blend of feminine compassion and masculine confidence that Jane had aspired to since her days at Rockford; she felt she had found it in her Women's Club friends, and she credited them with helping her to achieve that balance in herself as the head resident of Chicago's first settlement.[40]

Before she could lead a settlement, though, Jane had to find a building in which to house such an operation. By mid-March she was a "little tired of talking about" the project and felt she "should quite prefer beginning."[41] But it was not until April or May that she entered into negotiations with Miss Helen Culver to rent part of the dilapidated old mansion on South Halsted Street that Culver's deceased uncle, Charles J. Hull, had built in the 1850s.[42] When it was new, the gracious brick structure with its broad veranda on three sides and its Corinthian wood pillars overlooked a spacious, tree-shaded yard in one of the city's wealthy suburbs. The house had survived the Great Fire, but by 1889, it squatted in the middle of an impoverished industrial quarter of the Nineteenth Ward alongside some 10,000 Italians and a generous mix of Bohemians, Poles, Russian Jews, Germans, Irish, and French-Canadians.[43]

Jane's initial shock at the crowded, filthy conditions in the neighborhood serves as a strong reminder that she did not begin this enterprise as an expert on urban poverty. She confessed to Mary that the people living in Chicago's immigrant "slums" were "more crowded than I imagined people ever lived in America." Still, she was drawn to the Italian district because her visits there brought back fond memories of her own travels in Italy.[44] And she was drawn to the Hull mansion because it was large and "hospitable" and, perhaps, because the landlord, Helen Culver, was an unmarried businesswoman who had inherited her uncle's wealth as well as his penchant for combining an interest in real estate with an interest in social welfare.[45]

Charles Hull believed that home ownership was key to good citizenship, and he had created much of his fortune by building affordable homes in new subdivisions and selling them to working people on the installment plan. Culver came into the Hull fortune, which included 224 Chicago lots and was estimated at some $3 million in February 1889, the same month Jane moved to Chicago. A few years later, the *Chicago Evening News* described Culver as a "refined" silver-haired lady and "sound businesswoman" whose wise investments had doubled the size of her uncle's estate and who was, at the time, "one of the richest maiden ladies in America."[46]

Whether Jane acquired Helen Culver as her landlord by design or luck, the indisputable fact is that Culver played a vital role in the economic survival and physical expansion of the settlement. Because Culver owned most of the property around the Hull mansion, Jane was dependent on her approval—and sub-sidy—whenever she wanted to expand the operation. In the decades between 1889 and her death in 1925, Culver donated rent-free space, rent-free land, and sizable cash grants to the settlement house that bore her beloved uncle's name. Though never a member of Jane's inner circle of female friends, she was the first member of that small group of wealthy Chicago women who made it pos-sible for Jane, eventually, to expand her operations across thirteen buildings covering an entire city block. This was a level of physical growth that no other settlement house in the United States ever matched and that neither Jane Addams nor Helen Culver could have imagined when they started negotiating their relationship in 1889.[47]

All of the diplomatic skills that Jane had developed over her years with Miss Sill and with Anna Haldeman Addams came into play in her dealings with Culver. But now Jane was more assertive and more determined—and the woman she was dealing with was more generous and more reasonable. During

22. The Hull mansion as it appeared in its first years as a settlement house, before Jane Addams coaxed improvements and expansions out of Helen Culver. (University of Illinois at Chicago, University Library, Jane Addams Memorial Collection, neg. no. 146)

the first two years of their unusual partnership, Jane applied gentle but constant pressure on Culver to pay for improvements on the building as part of her duty as the landlord. Culver pressed back with pointed references to the terms of the lease and to her hope that "others interested in what you are trying to do will lend a hand." Jane retreated into claims that she was new to the business of fundraising while coyly noting that philanthropists could not be expected to "play the part of landlord." Culver, in return, agreed to play landlord by paying for things like new furnaces and by approving structural changes that Jane financed, but Jane pressed on with yet more requests in her never-ending campaign to make her landlord play the part of philanthropist.[48] Though Jane lost many of those battles, she did win the war. Within a year, Jane and Ellen had expanded beyond their original tenancy in half of the house to take possession of the entire house, and Culver was both so exhausted and so impressed by her tenant that she gave Jane a free four-year lease, thereby saving the settlement sixty dollars a month. In reporting this "great news" to her sister, Ellen dryly noted that they would henceforth call the settlement "Hull-House" and invited her sister to "connect these two facts in any way your refined imagination suggests."[49]

Culver did not think Jane was a very good businesswoman. In 1891, she described Jane's accounts as an "interesting . . . mingling of economy and lavish expenditure." She suspected that Jane "must have paid mechanics enormous prices for repairs" in order to have spent $3,000 of her limited inheritance on refurbishing a house she did not even own. But Culver did think Jane was one of the world's "unselfish workers . . . largeminded, largehearted . . . ready to spend and be spent and not wanting one jot of credit . . . but only to make the world happier and better."[50] In her own youth, Culver had observed that our one duty in life was to love our neighbors but admitted she thought that task would be easier "if we could only choose our neighbors."[51] In Jane Addams, Culver encountered a woman who had actually chosen her neighbors, but not from the cast of characters wealthy Chicagoans typically loved.

In all of the work Jane did on the Hull mansion and, later, in all of the buildings she erected around the original house, she always had the kind counsel and architectural expertise of Allen Pond and his brother, Irving Pond. Over the years, Allen Pond supervised everything from the remodeling of the first kitchen and installation of the first two extra bathrooms on the ground floor to the later design of a first-class gymnasium and a multilevel childcare center.[52] He looked upon Jane and Ellen as women who were following "the Christ method" by giving "not alms" but themselves, and he believed that the "enmity of class against class" could be eliminated in Chicago if every bored and idle youth would follow the Hull-House example.[53]

For Jane, a key element in the Hull-House example was the creation of physical beauty; she labored to have the interior of the Hull mansion reflect the domestic aesthetic she had been cultivating since Anna let her decorate their Baltimore flat.[54] Thanks to her seasons in Baltimore, and in Europe, and thanks to Alice's voracious appetite for material goods, Jane was already an experienced shopper when she and Ellen set up housekeeping on Halsted Street in the late summer of 1889. She knew how to find "real artistic furniture," how to ingratiate herself with artisans and shopkeepers, how to keep looking for just the thing she wanted, even how to negotiate for the best price on the best terms.[55] In the past, even when using Alice's money, Jane had been hesitant to spend; she always seemed caught between her father's disdain for extravagance and Anna's pleasure in beautiful objects. So while Jane bragged to Alice that renovation of the Hull house was "coming out beautifully," she quickly assured her sister-turned-banker that it was the practical repairs on the building, not anything so frivolous as furnishings, that were soaking up the bank drafts Jane requested from Girard.[56]

In truth, interior decoration at Hull-House was not at all frivolous; it was fundamental to the whole settlement purpose. Both Jane and Ellen were drawn to the "new aestheticism" of their day. As devotees of John Ruskin, they were part of the counterculture that disdained machine-made furnishings and idealized hand craftsmanship. They also subscribed to the au courant belief that an artistic interior could be therapeutic for the soul as well as a delight to the eye, and they coupled that belief with the more traditional notion that tasteful surroundings were culturally, even morally, uplifting.[57] Jane's expenditure of $1,800 on furniture, therefore, could be justified as an investment in the neighbors' well-being and a dramatic way of advertising her Ruskin-inspired conviction that "all luxury is right that can be and is shared."[58] Reporters' descriptions of the Hull-House decor suggest Jane's and Ellen's identification with the progressive tastes of their day. They shared the desire to create artful interiors whose color schemes, cozy niches, and eclectic mix of cosmopolitan styles could produce a harmonious effect. Thus, the *Chicago Times* reported in the summer of 1890:

The halls were done in delicate terra-cotta tints and the rooms in ivory and gold. The floors were polished and laid with rugs from the orient. There was the music room with its classic simplicity, the dainty piano, and soft etchings and water colors on the walls. The library blossomed forth with rows of books in scented leather bindings and in dusky niches flashed the snowy marble of bits of rare statuary. . . . A chord of quiet, almost severe, elegance had been struck, and the whole house joined in the harmony.[59]

It was, Jane announced to Alice just five days before opening the doors of

Hull-House to the public, "by *far* the prettiest house I have ever lived in."[60] She was not even interested in a discussion with her sisters about who was to inherit which lamps or tables from Cedarville; "I really don't care for the things at home when I think of them."[61] Now she and Ellen were settled "in our own home of which we are growing so fond."[62]

After announcing to Alice that there was "power in me and will to dominate," Jane never returned to the subject of her choice to liberate herself from

23. An interior view of Hull-House as it looked in the mid-1890s. (University of Illinois at Chicago, University Library, Jane Addams Memorial Collection, neg. no. 202)

Cedarville, Anna, and George. In characteristic fashion, Jane avoided any conflict over this choice by rhetorically assuming that everyone accepted, even endorsed, her position. In the case of the Linns, this was a reasonable assumption. The close bond Jane had built with her eldest sister, with Rev. Linn, and with each of the children did not suffer from her move to Chicago. Though they lived 150 miles away, the entire family joined Jane and Ellen for their first Thanksgiving on Halsted Street, and over the course of the subsequent twenty years, all three of the Linns' sons spent some time as residents of Hull-House. In fact, their eldest son, John Addams Linn, entered college in Chicago the same fall that Jane launched the settlement. So just as she was adjusting to the dizzying onslaught of boys' clubs, kindergarteners, and art classes, Jane was also lugging her nephew's bicycle and guitar across the city to his new dormitory.[63]

Weber and Laura seem to have been similarly accepting of Jane's life choices. Whenever Jane visited Cedarville, she stayed in their home rather than with Anna, and Jane continued to manage Weber's medical care when he required hospitalization.[64] Laura even moved into Hull-House in the early twentieth century, during one of Weber's periods in the asylum, and the couple's daughter, Sadie, followed her aunt's footsteps to Rockford College and into settlement work.

With Alice, as always, the relationship was more complicated. Their sisterhood was shot through with an unstable mix of love, respect, jealousy, longing, and resentment, and all of those elements were on full display during Jane's first years at Hull-House. While Jane was being toasted in the press for "doing more to prevent despair and relieve the sorrow of sad lives than many immense organizations," Alice was managing farm mortgages—and Jane's investments—in Girard, Kansas.[65] At the same time, she was raising Marcet, her toddler daughter, and probably enduring Harry's dyspeptic tirades against social reformers who fancied themselves "the way and the light." The truth, proclaimed Harry, two months after Hull-House opened, was that such reformers' "longing for disciples" merely represented "a longing for power and . . . its own method for abhorring it." The whole game of "revolutions, delusions and dogmas, hopes and disappointments . . . progress and retrogress" was simply "beastly," sighed Harry, "tiresome beyond expression, very little short of awakening disgust ad nauseam."[66]

For years, Jane had been caught between Anna and George, on the one side, and Harry and Alice on the other. Now it was Alice who was caught between Jane, on the one side, and Harry and Anna on the other. While the two sisters adjusted to this new emotional landscape, some standard themes in their relationship persisted. There was the matter of money, of course. Because Alice continued as Jane's banker in these early years, she knew exactly how much money Jane was pouring into Hull-House, and Jane felt the need she had always felt to explain her expenditures to her sister.[67] Then there was the shopping, an urban service Alice continued to request and Jane continued to provide. Alice now had to wait longer for Jane to find time for such errands and had to repeat instructions that Jane mislaid among her mounting piles of Hull-House papers.[68] But the mutual provision of material goods was a tangible display of love that carried the sisters past hurt feelings over letters not written and visits not paid.

Perhaps that was why Jane was "so sore" when Alice refused to loan Hull-House a sideboard that Jane had taken great pains to find for Alice in Baltimore. Jane claimed to be "ashamed" of her anger, but that did not stop her from making sure Alice knew that the wife of a former Chicago mayor had been willing to contribute an elegant old oak sideboard; "she was not afraid," sniffed Jane, that the settlement's furniture would be neglected. Indeed, added Jane, landing a final blow, "everybody seems to trust me more than my most beloved sister."[69]

Jane's fear that she would lose her family's love if she displayed too unfeminine a desire for "preeminence" had dogged her since her days at Rockford when she promised she was "not puffed up" by being named valedictorian.[70] At the same time, she longed to have her relatives see her in the same estimable light in which others saw her. She managed these twin impulses with a double-edged strategy: she campaigned to change her relatives' view by regularly reporting on others' high opinion of her, and she guarded against their resentment by couching these reports in declarations of humility. Even with Mary, Jane concluded her glowing reports of prominent Chicagoans' interest in her project with the assurance that "our heads are not in the least turned by the first flush of success"; she and Ellen fully realized "that the first enthusiasm won't last," that "the slough of despond may be near," that "the ardor may all disappear."[71] To ward off the pride that might precede a fall, Jane mocked the settlement idea for having become "something of a fashionable fad" and mocked herself for "playing the role of philanthropist."[72]

With Alice, the mix of pride and humility had more of an edge to it. In thanking Alice for a birthday check large enough to buy a few books, she commented on having just received $110 "from a lady whom I had never seen," then quickly added, "if we don't succeed after all this help, we will deserve to fail."[73] Jane repeated that phrase two months later after noting all the "sympathy and money from a great many people," and this time adding, "I often wish that you were doing this thing instead of me, you would do it so much better."[74] Jane even tried to win Alice's identification with her move to Chicago by claiming that she saw the "power" and "will to dominate" in Alice as much as in herself.[75]

All of Jane's self-promotional self-effacement would seem shamelessly manipulative were it not accompanied by so many poignant comments about missing Alice, longing for Alice to visit, worrying when Alice did not write, begging that Alice not let Marcet forget her Aunt Jane. In June 1890, Alice wrote a codicil to her will stipulating that, should she die, it was her "most earnest, sincere desire" that Marcet "be given into the entire care of my sister Jane Addams."[76] That was certainly an act of trust on Alice's part (as well as a comment on Harry's reliability as a father). Jane was touched by it but disturbed by the thought of Marcet losing her mother. Jane recalled her own "childish experiences" with a mother's death and her "horrible dream every night" that the death of Mary—Jane's mother figure—would leave "no one to love me."[77]

At the end of 1891, after two years at Hull-House, Jane told a reporter for the *Chicago Tribune*, without evincing "the slightest sense of sacrifice," that settlement work "is the work I must do because it is the work I love."[78] But that same month she wrote to Alice, "I get very anxious some times. I wake up in the night with a great longing for you."[79] Jane had chosen the social claim over the family claim and was happier for it, but that did not release her from the pull she felt toward her family. A public life promised Jane access to many, many more people who could love her. Still, she had forged strong bonds with her relatives, Haldemans and Addamses alike, and had suffered too much loss in her life to treat those bonds lightly. Added to that emotional reality, there was the fact of Jane's embrace of the philosophy of unconditional love for others. If she could not abide by that principle with her relatives, all other claims would be fraudulent. She did not have to sacrifice her life for them—Jane's Christianity did not include that drama—but she did have to love them.

Over the years, the situation in Cedarville worsened, George grew more withdrawn from the world and reality, and Anna found herself growing old in a situation that actually warranted the martyred stance she had cultivated throughout her life. All of this placed new burdens on Alice. Jane praised Alice for being a "dear patient woman" with Anna and George and defined Harry as the "only person" who could do anything to improve things in Cedarville. She never once hinted at the possibility of abandoning her settlement project to resume her place as the caretaking spinster daughter.[80]

Just three months after Jane first moved to Chicago, George staged another runaway, this time to Colorado. He stayed in touch during this episode by writing manic letters to Anna full of theories about how science could not help "human happiness or misery" and how technology was "stealing the muscles from thousands of healthy legs," killing the "souls" of children in factories, and creating "more combinations of capital." After noting his own "feminine trait of character," George asked Anna for news about Jane and settled down for a "careful pondering of [a] host of contradictions."[81] Within a month he was back home, living off of Anna's inheritance and using the opium his brother prescribed to calm his nerves.[82]

Jane tried to normalize her relations with both Anna and George, writing friendly reports about progress at Hull-House, occasionally sharing her views on social reform, regularly inviting them to visit.[83] But the letters she received back and the brief visits she made to Cedarville left her with a "helpless, bewildered feeling about them."[84] Near the end of her second year at Hull-House, Jane detected a softening in Anna's attitude toward her. Fresh flowers from Cedarville arrived at Hull-House in May, delighting Jane with this "piece of the yard," and a trip home in August 1891 marked the second time Jane had visited without any sort of "outbreak" from Anna. By that time, too, George seemed to be making "great progress;" he was able to go whole weeks without any opium.[85]

The sad irony in the family's history is that Anna was unable to enjoy the fact that many of the skills Jane drew upon at Hull-House were skills she learned through Anna: how to create a gracious domestic space, entertain, make small talk, play games, enjoy music and drama, even be a bit coy and beguiling when it suited her purpose. Instead, it continually grated on Anna that a daughter who had abandoned her duty to her family was publicly praised for

24. George Haldeman reading at home in Cedarville. (University of Illinois at Chicago, University Library, Jane Addams Memorial Collection, neg. no. 1106)

being "noble" and for opening the "broad doors of her beautiful and spacious home . . . like a true woman."[86]

Jane had, finally, been able to finesse her womanhood into a secular stewardship that others saw as eminently feminine. She generated, within assertively domestic space, a bold and energetic public program and then presided over it with maternal calm and gentleness.[87] Jane had kept that cloak of dignity—that "large man's doublet"—which she had once pulled around herself for protection at home and at Rockford. By the time she moved to Chicago, it had aged and softened into a cloak of composure, or what one reporter called "high bred serenity."[88] Visitors to Hull-House might comment on Miss Addams's fatigue, or on her funny habit of constantly rearranging the furniture and straightening pictures, but no one ever reported seeing her lose her temper, speak in a raised voice, or break down in frustrated tears.[89] Years of training in her family had produced in Jane the habit of equanimity. Her conversion to Tolstoy's belief that a true Christian was one who loved every person unconditionally gave that habit philosophical weight. And the opportunity to devote her life to productive work that drew on the power she knew was within her provided Jane with such an abundance of joy, such a lifelong sense of salvation, that she fairly radiated peace and good cheer.

On the eve of her move into Hull-House, the *Freeport Daily Journal* had sent Jane "good wishes" because she was selflessly embarking on a "great field of denial and labor."[90] Years later, Jane would publicly dismiss such sentimentality as "the twaddle of heroism."[91] She knew that she had not chosen denial; she knew that true denial would have been a life in Cedarville. She knew, too, that Tolstoy was right: in choosing what looked like sacrifice, she had chosen happiness.

Chapter 13
The Luminous Medium

When Leila Bedell, former president of the Chicago Women's Club, wrote her May 1889 article for the *Woman's Journal* announcing Jane's settlement plans, she declared that "Miss Addams's rarest attraction . . . is her wonderful spirituality." Bedell claimed, "One cannot spend much time in her presence without wondering by what processes she has attained to such remarkable growth of the soul; how she has at so early a period of life grown 'out of her little self into a larger self.'"[1] Jane cringed with embarrassment when she read those words. "I positively feel my callers peering into my face to detect 'spirituality,'" she complained to Ellen.[2] And though Ellen usually agreed with Jane's low opinion of newspaper sentimentality, it is likely that Ellen had talked with her friend Leila Bedell about Jane and was partially responsible for what Bedell wrote.[3] During these early Chicago days, Ellen herself was enraptured with Jane. "Everybody who comes near her is affected by her," Ellen told her cousin three days before opening the doors to Hull-House. "It is as if she simply diffused something which came from outside herself, of which she is the luminous medium."[4]

Ellen's long search for a spiritual home had, by the fall of 1889, delivered her to Hull-House and to the bed she shared there with Jane.[5] So etherealized had Ellen's view of Jane become that she refused to even consider her cousin's warnings about "the weaknesses of the flesh." All Ellen could think about was this "beautiful spiritual life" beside her. Theirs was, she insisted, "an ordinary relationship as friends who live together." At the same time, however, Ellen viewed her own "attacks of peevishness and obstinacy" in stark contrast to Jane's "unattainable character" and concluded that Jane represented the "high ideal," the "outside brace" that Ellen required. Having once feared dependence on Jane, Ellen now wholly submitted to it in the belief that she was "obeying God" by yielding to "this fine thing." It was Jane, after all, who had conceived of the settlement scheme that seemed to be saving Ellen's life; "I could not do *this* without her," Ellen explained to her cousin, "and I couldn't very well *not* do it."[6]

Apparently unaware that Jane saw "power" in herself and a "will to dominate," Ellen imagined that Jane merely strengthened others' "weak knees" and "feeble hands" but had "no sense of strength herself."[7] Playing Sancho Panza to Jane's Don Quixote, Ellen initially relished her public image as the "petite" and "sparkling" complement to Miss Addams's matronly calm.[8] When Jane objected to Ellen taking a back seat, Jane appeared yet more noble in Ellen's eyes—and more worthy of Ellen's deference.[9] This was not an unfamiliar dance; Ellen had been praising Jane's nobility for years, and, for just as many years, Jane had been encouraging and deflecting that praise. Months before they opened Hull-House, Jane assigned Ellen the job of "bugbear" to prevent Jane's indulgent expenditure of either time or money on anything but the settlement. "I need you, dear one, more than you can realize," Jane confided.[10] The implicit intimacy of the "bugbear" assignment was sufficiently attractive to mask its inherent inequality: Ellen's responsibility was to take care of Jane so that Jane could shoulder the responsibility of the house.

It was one thing to toy with the romance of dominance and subordination in letters, even on a European sojourn; it was quite another to sustain such a romance under the daily pressures of Hull-House. The partners maintained the fiction of independence insofar as Jane did not assume financial support for Ellen, but that arrangement only underscored their obvious inequality: Jane had money and Ellen did not. Jane recognized the sacrifice Ellen made by giving up her teaching career and trusting her future to the settlement; Jane even instructed Alice to provide Ellen with $1,500 in the event of Jane's death.[11] But the fact remained, day in and day out, that Ellen was forever broke, forever searching for ways to earn some extra income.[12] It might not have mattered; indeed, they might have altered the arrangement in time had their relationship prospered at Hull-House, but it did not. During their first year of work together, Jane frequently mentioned Ellen in her letters to her relatives. By the second year, Ellen's name appeared (and then only perfunctorily) just once in the surviving letters. Within only a year, the very things Jane and Ellen loved about each other had become sources of tension.[13]

Jane had always delighted in Ellen's wry impudence, but once Hull-House was launched, Ellen's attitude conflicted with Jane's desire to cultivate the rich and well placed. When a connection with Mrs. Joseph Medill, the wife of the publisher of the *Chicago Tribune*, promised a measure of control over press coverage of the settlement, Ellen scoffed at Jane for stooping to conquer Medill. "I've no use for Mrs. M. or any of her tribe," she bragged to her parents, thereby claiming back a share of the nobility she too often conceded to Jane.[14]

Ellen's posture toward the elite was born of her experience as the student who could not afford to stay at Rockford Seminary, the teacher who served fashionable girls at Miss Kirkland's school, the friend who had to be subsidized around Europe, and, of course, the daughter of a rural anticapitalist. Ellen's intellectual ambitions drew her toward society's elites, including Jane, but her own poverty then tugged her back, reminding her to stay loyal to her father's distrust of the rich. Ellen initially felt that Jane's commitment to cross-class understanding was admirable in one whose class privilege was so clear, but Ellen's genteel poverty and radical bent ultimately grated against her admiration for Jane's philosophy. As Jane's nephew observed many years later, "Hull House stood for tolerance," but there was a militancy deep in Ellen that "found tolerance difficult."[15]

Their temperamental differences proved overwhelming. Ellen acted out her angers, her frustrations, her fears; Jane did not. Nor did Jane like close association with those who did. Twenty years with Anna had provided Jane with quite enough histrionics for a lifetime. However endearing Ellen's emotionalism had been in the past and at a distance, it became an annoyance to Jane in the close quarters of Hull-House. Traces of Jane's cold intolerance for Ellen's outbursts are evident in Ellen's self-recrimination. "I have thrown away all," she feared, "by losing my hold one minute."[16] Her promises that "my temper is improving" mounted alongside her disappointment with Jane for tolerating everyone's shortcomings but hers.[17] Still, Ellen continued to admire Jane's public talents. She marveled, for example, when Jane—with whom Ellen had giggled through Italian lessons—was able to serve as a courtroom translator for Italian immigrant neighbors, providing the judge with words that Ellen "didn't suppose one human being ever said to another." That particular court proceeding left Ellen fuming over injustice while "Miss Addams," as Ellen now referred to her, proceeded "with dignity and decency."[18]

Unlike Ellen, Jane found life at Hull-House to be a perfect fit between her temperament, her training, and her environment; she relished the storm, in part, because she relished being the calm at its center. After years of leisure and family diplomacy, Jane was ready to glide through their unremittingly busy days without blowing up, but Ellen's nerves were frayed by what Jane herself described as the "unending activity" and the "confusion of a house constantly filling and refilling with groups of people." Looking back, Jane recalled that any hope of sitting with a book by the fire had to be abandoned: "All one's habits of living had to be readjusted."[19] The settlement's "strenuous routine" was a tonic for Jane's soul but an assault on Ellen's senses.[20] By the end of the first year, Ellen longed for "some sort of moderation." But there "is no moderation where Jane is—can't be."[21]

A mere glance at the Hull-House weekly program for the "term" begun in January 1891 provides some hint of the number of plates Jane kept spinning at any one time. Not that Jane actually ran many of the clubs, taught many of the classes, or delivered many of the lectures. In fact, she taught none of that term's eighteen daytime classes, ran only two of the twenty-seven clubs and classes that met in the evening, and delivered just one of the lectures in the two lecture series mounted that season. Contrary to Tolstoy's theory that true fellowship required one to engage in manual labor in the fields, Jane's work was largely administrative. She delegated the housework to Mary Keyser, whom Jane had hired away from her sister Mary Linn, but did acquire the hands-on habit of rearranging furniture because every room in the house was continually being reconfigured to suit the next club, the next class, the next meeting.[22]

As the "head resident" of Hull-House, Jane served as the director of programming, the director of development, the volunteer coordinator, the cohostess —with Ellen—at all social gatherings, a "friendly visitor" for the neighborhood, and the coordinator of outreach to the courts, the schools, the hospitals, and the local charities. In these early years, it was she who coaxed Women's Club members like Ellen Henrotin to give a lecture, encouraged society maidens like Harriet Trowbridge to run the Jolly Boys' Club, and persuaded Mary Wilmarth not only to pay for the art teacher from the Art Institute but to come down, herself, and teach French on Saturday evenings.[23] Though Frank Gunsaulus and David Swing contributed the occasional lecture, it was Rev. Jenkin Lloyd Jones, the decidedly nonevangelical pastor of All Souls' Unitarian Church (and uncle of the architect Frank Lloyd Wright), who became Jane's closest friend among the city's clergy.[24]

The regular, short notes Jane and Rev. Jones exchanged in these early years reveal the sort of working partnerships Jane cultivated with allies. By using a mix of charm, gratitude, flattery, and playful intimacy she delicately cemented collegial bonds. Could Jones and his wife come to Hull-House for dinner, Jane wondered in the fall of 1891. Miss Culver would be there and, "you know that you are the one member of the 'faculty' that she thoroughly approves of."[25] Months earlier, by way of apology for asking Jones to deliver more lectures at the Hull-House Summer School than he had planned, on topics different from those he had suggested, Jane confided, "you have been a member of the 'Hull-House faculty' for so long that we treat you quite as one of ourselves."[26] Rev. Jones claimed to find Jane's confidence in him "appalling," but nonetheless agreed to serve out of "respect for the good work and the right spirit you put into it."[27]

The "good work," as Jones called it, was forever piling up on Jane's desk. Before she learned to delegate, or had many residents to delegate to, it fell to Jane to make sure that course materials were on site including a stereopticon for Rev. Jones's talk on Millet, ingredients for the cooking class, fabric and thread for the sewing class, books for the Fairy Story Club, brushes and easels for the painting class, and endless refreshments for the social gatherings.[28]

Hull-House Weekly Program for January-March, 1891

Kindergarten in Hull-House Drawing Room, every morning, 9:00 A.M.–12:00 P.M.
Day Nursery at 326 South Halsted Street, Monday through Saturday

Monday

3:30–5:00 Calisthenics . . . Miss Savage
Sewing (for Italians only) . . . Misses Barnum, Solner, Lewis, Cutter,
Swett, Smith, Kirkland, Mrs. Delano, Mrs. Walker

7:30–9:30
Library: History of Art (College Extension) . . . Miss Starr
Octagon Room: Mathematics (College Extension) . . . Mr. Arnold
Drawing Room: Girls' Club . . . Miss Addams
Drawing Room: Embroidery Club . . . Miss Forstall
Kitchen: Cooking . . . Miss Gary
Dining Room: Drawing . . . Miss Barnum
Upper Hall: Victor Hugo reading party for young men . . . Mr. Noyes
Library hours for working girls

Tuesday

3:30–5:00
Octagon Room: Knights of the Round Table . . . Miss Starr
Dining Room: Jolly Boys' Club . . . Miss Trowbridge
Library: Hero Club . . . Miss Stone
Upper Hall: Fairy Story Club . . . Miss Farnsworth
Drawing Room: Red Stars . . . Miss Dodge
Class lessons on Piano . . . Mrs. Hilton
Library hours for Schoolboys . . . Miss Head

7:30–9:30
Upper Hall: Latin (College Extension) . . . Miss Miller
Octagon Room: English Literature . . . Miss Starr
Dining Room: Drawing class . . . Miss Price
Library: Travelers' Club: "London" . . . Miss Addams
Drawing Room: Young Citizens' Club . . . Mr. Ryerson
Library hours for working boys

Wednesday

3:30–5:00
Kitchen: Cooking . . . Miss Gary
Class lesson on Piano . . . Mrs. Hilton

7:30–9:30

 Library: English History (College Extension) . . . Miss Howe

 Octagon Room: Bookkeeping (College Extension) . . . Mr. Greeley

 Dining Room: Drawing (College Extension) . . . Mrs. Beggs

 Drawing Room: Working People's Social Science Club:

  December 3: "Progressive Taxation of Estates" . . . Col. Jacobson

  December 10: "Outgrowths of Toynbee Hall" . . . Miss Jane Addams

  December 17: "Conservative View of Radical Movement" . . .
   Mr. Henry D. Lloyd

  January 7: "The Forgotten Man" . . . Mr. Calvin C. Dickey

  January 14: "Christian Socialism" . . . Mrs. Lucinda B. Chandler

  January 21: "Influences Which Have Shaped American
   Jurisprudence" . . . Mr. David J. Wile

  January 28: "The Problem of the Unemployed" . . .
   Mr. William M. Salter

  February 4: "Municipal Government" . . . Mr. John H. Hamline

  February 11: "The Negro Problem" . . . Mr. Edwin Burritt Smith

  February 18: "Woman of the Twentieth Century" . . .
   Mrs. Ellen Henrotin

  February 25: "The Divine Law of Service" . . . Rev. L. P. Mercer

Thursday

3:30–5:00

 Afternoon Teas: Talks on Domestic Economy and the Care of Children

 Embroidery classes . . . Miss Anthony

 Class lessons on Piano . . . Miss Lyon

7:30–9:30

 Library: Roman History (College Extension) . . . Mr. Howland

 Kitchen: Clay Modeling . . . Signor Guerini

 Drawing Room: 7:30–8:00: Music . . . Miss Root

 Drawing Room: 8:00–9:00: Lectures in connection with College
  Extension classes

  January 15: "Rome, Ancient and Modern" (Illustrated with
   stereopticon) . . . Mr. Howland

  January 22: "The Wonder World" (with experiments) . . .
   Prof. William Richards

  January 29: "Birds" . . . Mrs. Sara Hubbard

  February 5: Concert . . . Miss Root

  February 12: "Jean Francois Millet" (Illustrated with stereopticon) . . .
   Rev. Jenkin Lloyd Jones

February 19: "Washington Irving" . . . Rev. James Frothingham
February 26: Concert . . . Prof. C. B. Cady
March 5: "Monte Casino" (Illustrated) . . . Miss Eliza Allen Starr
March 12: "Architecture" (Illustrated) . . . Mr. Irving K. Pond
March 19: "The Cost of an Idea" . . . Rev. Jenkin Lloyd Jones

Friday
3:30–5:00
Housekeeping, Sick-room cooking, and Kitchen Garden classes . . .
    Misses Williamson, Cook, Antisdel, Winston, Clapp, Manning, Smith,
        Foote, Howe, and Runnels
7:00–10:00
Library: Rhetoric (College Extension) . . . Mr. Underwood
Octagon Room: Zoology (College Extension) . . . Dr. Hardin
Dining Room: Drawing (College Extension) . . . Mr. Beggs
Drawing Room: Needlework (German method) . . . Fraulein Honnig
Upper Hall: 7–8: German (College Extension) . . . Fraulein Neuschafer
Upper Hall: 8–9: Singing . . . Miss Eleanor Smith
Drawing Room: German Social Reception

Saturday
3:00–5:00 Classes in Italian . . . Signor Alfieri
7:00–10:00
Octagon Room: French . . . Mrs. Wilmarth
Kitchen: Clay Modeling . . . Signor Guerini
Drawing Room: Italian Social Reception

Source: Hull-House Weekly Programs, January–March, 1891, JAMC.

Though she certainly never taught a music class, Jane acquired a second piano from somewhere and persuaded Lydia Avery Coonley to loan Hull-House her new pipe organ for a year.[29] And while she delegated scheduling of the college extension classes to her resident Alice Miller, it was Jane who made sure that the guest lectures on Thursday evenings coordinated with those classes. After 1892, it was Jane who negotiated with the new University of Chicago to elevate the status of some of those classes to "University Extension" classes for which students earned credits toward a B.A. degree.[30]

In the seven months following publication of the January 1891 "Programme," Hull-House enlarged its day nursery into a new cottage, built and opened the Butler Art Gallery, and launched a Summer School program on the campus of Rockford Seminary, where Sarah Anderson was now the president and Jane was on the board of trustees.[31] Jane negotiated all of the arrangements for these expansions, including the protracted dealings with Miss Culver over donating the land on which the businessman and philanthropist Edward Butler had agreed to build a $5,000 art gallery, studio, and reading room.[32] The gallery was to be, as one newspaper announced, a "new educational home where pictures and books may be enjoyed by those who are not accorded the privileges of more pretentious institutions."[33]

News coverage of the opening of the Butler Gallery in June 1891 makes clear it marked the arrival of Hull-House as a secure and successful feature of the Chicago landscape.[34] This was as close as Jane would get to a formal installation

25. In 1891, Jane Addams launched a summer school for Chicago working women at Rockford Seminary. Jane Addams is in the third row from the top, with her nephew Stanley Linn. Another nephew, John Linn, is at the top of the stairs on the left, and Esther Linn is perched at the end of the left-hand bannister, holding a fan. Julia Lathrop is leaning against the right-hand bannister, third from the front, and Ellen Starr is standing behind Jane Addams, looking in the opposite direction. The other early summer school students in the photograph could not be identified. (Swarthmore College Peace Collection)

ceremony at Hull-House and though none of her siblings attended, Samuel and Henrietta Barnett crossed the Atlantic to join in the celebration of the gallery's completion.[35] The *Chicago Herald* noted that Jane "looked her best in violet crepe with velvet trimmings." Despising hats as she did, Jane finessed the custom with a "gracefully poised bunch of wood violets" in her hair.[36]

Just a few days after the gallery's gala opening, Jane raced off to Rockford to launch the first of many sessions of the Hull-House Summer School at her alma mater. She was exhausted, but it did not seem to matter.[37] "I find myself very loathe to leave," she confessed to Alice amid packing for Rockford. "I grow fonder of this place all of the time."[38]

Whether negotiating with donors, volunteers, residents, or neighbors, Jane's effectiveness lay in her acquired ability to personify in daily life the principle of unconditional love that she had come to espouse. Freed from the family dynamic, her rhetorical mix of pride in the Hull-House enterprise and humility about her own worth lost its manipulative edge and took on an authenticity that disarmed wealthy businessmen and surly teenagers alike. As a young woman, Jane Addams had fretted that her officious conduct betrayed a loathsome self-righteousness. By the time she was in a position to be truly officious, her own dark nights of self-doubt had transformed a priggish stance into an empathic one. Having turned away from strong-arm heroics, Jane could enact her youthful ideal of the "fostering mother."[39]

As head resident at Hull-House, Jane satisfied her "will to dominate" not by imperious command but through the seduction of direct, egalitarian comradery. When, for example, the residents voted to charge a small fee for college extension courses, a dissenting Jane Addams knew she was "in the minority in my belief and willingly yielded the point."[40] Frances Hackett, a Hull-House resident in the early twentieth century, "always had the feeling I did not do enough," yet recalled that "Miss Addams" never used "reproof" to ignite activity; instead, "she elicited goodwill in a common cause."[41] "The durable fact about Miss Addams," wrote Hackett, "was that people were not *objects* outside herself. They were persons with wills to be respected, attitudes to be considered, consent to be gained."[42] Jane, as head resident, found her early satisfaction in providing volunteers and residents with the opportunity for direct, daily, hands-on service. "As to what their work shall be," explained one reporter for the *Unitarian*, "that is decided by the worker herself. Each elects that for which she thinks herself best fitted." Supervision by the settlement's head resident was "felt not as in any sense a chain hindering freedom, but rather as a spur to one's own freest, and therefore best, work."[43]

Jane's unswerving belief that Hull-House merely reflected "the goodness and kindness which most people feel toward everyone else, but don't act out" was so matter-of-fact, so free of sanctimony, that even the most jaded found her hard to resist.[44] Using language remarkably similar to that of Jane's former classmates at Rockford Seminary, Frances Hackett claimed that people were drawn to Jane because their "personalities gained value through contact with hers." Another resident, Madeline Wallin, defined Jane's genius as the ability "to get into relation with every sort of person by instinctively giving him what he wants and can assimilate." She won a loyal following because she consistently demonstrated a "disinterested . . . solicitude" for every person she encountered.[45] Given a temperament already bent toward equanimity, Jane found that she could embrace and enact a philosophy of even-handedness and open-mindedness without much strain. For her, universal acceptance of humanity proved emotionally much easier than partisanship and was by far the most comfortable way of exercising the power within her.

Though this "depersonal and disinterested" quality of Jane's conduct doomed her relationship with someone as passionate and partisan as Ellen, it was the central secret to the success of Hull-House. Donors and volunteers, residents and neighbors were alternately surprised and impressed by Jane's "boundless" acceptance of humanity, especially as it was manifest in the settlement's flexible, responsive program.[46]

She and Ellen began, of course, by offering lectures and classes on the arts and literature along with social evenings centered around German and Italian music. They did this, first, because they honestly believed it was all they were equipped to offer their neighbors and all that their volunteer clientele of educated society girls could be recruited to provide. They did it, as well, because they believed that art and literature and music were the best instruments for cutting across class and reaching into the universal human experience. For both Jane and Ellen, the message of Victorian reformers like Ruskin and Arnold was that "the best" products of any culture were those whose technique was so fine, whose imaginative impulse was so truly realized that they spoke to every person who encountered them. Tolstoy taught Jane that great art was that which "breaks through the individual point of view," broadens the individual's perspective, and invites identification with the human race. As Jane tried to explain to George during her second Hull-House Christmas, the purpose of art, music, and drama was not to "stem the poverty" nor to provide "merely social pleasure." The purpose was to "fortify people, who need fortitude above all others, with the best we can procure for them."[47]

Jane and Ellen were not students of immigration before they opened Hull-House. When they first looked upon the Italians and Russian Jews on Halsted Street they saw people who were picturesque and needy. They did not realize, in the beginning, just how many of the impoverished foreigners in Chicago's Nineteenth Ward had been artisans, professionals, or political activists in their homelands; they did not calculate that emigration alone was testament to resources—or resourcefulness.[48] It was thanks to the cultural programs they offered that Jane and Ellen learned this valuable sociological lesson. The neighbors who attended lectures and literary groups and art classes—or showed up just to read one of the seventy-five English and foreign language periodicals that the Hull-House library subscribed to—were individuals who had once gone to school, taken a drawing class, sung in a chorus, marched with a band or with an army, listened to speeches, and enjoyed books and paintings.[49]

By addressing their own need to teach art, literature, and music, Jane and Ellen accidentally tapped into a feature of immigrant life which too often went unrecognized: that immigrants had not only ambition for their future lives but deep connections to their past lives which were often culturally, if not materially, rich. Having traveled in Europe, Jane and Ellen could picture their neighbors' homelands and could sometimes speak in their neighbors' languages.[50] So even though they often idealized the immigrants' histories, they did not make the mistake of ignoring those histories.

At the same time, Jane and Ellen learned that the neighborhood housed a population of native-born residents, "people of former education and opportunity" who, "because they lack the power of making money, because of ill health, because of an unfortunate marriage, or for various other reasons which do not imply criminality or stupidity," were living in "untoward circumstances." Describing this population in 1892, Jane noted that for such people—both native-born and immigrant—the settlement was a "refuge," a way to "keep up some sort of intellectual life." Jane and Ellen had the imagination to see these neighbors in the context of their past—and their future. The cultural program at Hull-House attracted those who were "bent on self-improvement," hungry for an education, determined to be among that mobile portion of the working class which moved through the Nineteenth Ward and beyond.[51]

Right from the start, however, Jane and Ellen also offered services that addressed more immediate needs in the neighborhood. Because one of their first volunteers from the upper class was Jenny Dow, a trained kindergarten teacher, Hull-House was immediately able to mount a kindergarten program. Virtually overnight that program spun off a day nursery program for working mothers. So Hull-House was, very soon, teaching thirty kindergarteners and caring for thirty to forty infants and toddlers every day.[52] As one reporter noted, "the first residents made friends with the children, and through them with the mothers." The rapid addition of clubs and classes for schoolage children and adolescents, many of whom were in the workforce, meant that the new settlement was providing tangible benefits to neighborhood families who might not have been attracted to a lecture on Washington Irving.[53]

For many of these families, Holy Family Catholic Church or St. Francis of Assisi Catholic Church or one of the neighborhood's numerous Orthodox Jewish temples and chevras occupied the center of their spiritual lives and their children's educational lives; the church or temple was certainly the first place they turned to in times of trouble. Two unmarried Protestant women like Jane and Ellen had to prove themselves useful before earning a welcome among those neighbors. One way they did so was by never proselytizing: "I should say that the religious questions should be neither avoided nor urged," Jane explained in a letter to a fellow settlement worker in New York at the end of 1891. If neighbors did not have to "fear" evangelism, it became "more possible to discuss frankly religious problems and differences."[54]

In place of prayer, the settlement house offered more material forms of neighborly support. In the early years, that meant opening up for public use three baths (which soon expanded to five baths and then twelve) and providing laundry facilities for any woman in the neighborhood who wanted to use them. The press described this as "inculcating the habits of cleanliness," but Jane and Ellen lived in the neighborhood so they knew better.[55] The ward's residents did not need "inculcating," they needed washing facilities. Neighbors were dirty because their homes had no baths, no laundries, no running water. So while the line of neighborhood bathers on a hot day could so reduce water pressure in the upstairs part of the house that residents had to forego their own baths, Jane and Ellen maintained this valuable service until they could persuade the Chicago City Council to build a public bathhouse nearby.[56]

Whatever service Hull-House provided, from dancing to diapering, the goal in these early years was, always, to be a good neighbor. Jane was delighted, for example, when "a number of girls at the Western Electrical Works" expressed enthusiasm over the settlement's provision of "a social time" for them on Friday evenings. She thought some classes for the girls might grow out of that, but only "if"—and "if" was the key word here—"the girls like." If not, then "let them keep to the social time."[57] As Jenny Dow, the kindergarten teacher, put it, the settlement's workers wished to prove to those "who have found so inhospitable a welcome in this country . . . that there is such a thing as a kindly American."[58]

Kindliness toward immigrants was not an uncontroversial stance in 1890. Just as Jane was crafting a speech about her Italian neighbors for the Chicago Women's Club, *Popular Science Monthly* published an article denouncing the "dago" as such a lazy and depraved creature that he actually welcomed a term in a U.S. prison so he could enjoy the creature comforts provided by soft-hearted prison reformers. The article made Ellen "*very* mad" and she fired off a retort to the magazine.[59] Jane, meanwhile, included in her speech a beguiling story about an Italian neighbor who attended the unveiling of a statue of Garibaldi at Hull-House and, with a "cracked, out-of-door voice," launched into a song he had sung while marching with Garibaldi. "He had come into the house with more or less a hang-dog look," she told her audience. "In the opinion of the Americans he knew, he was a 'dago,' unwashed and unskilled, fit only to sweep the streets and dig with a shovel. He had gone out straightened by the memory that he had been a soldier under the most remarkable leader of modern revolutions. He had once served a noble cause; he could again become a valuable citizen. Americans had taken his hand, not with condescension, but honor."[60] Stylized parables such as these were far more effective than Ellen's angry letters when it came to softening American hearts toward the immigrant.

After spending a week at Hull-House, a reporter for the *Chicago Tribune* wrote a profile of the settlement's neighbors that was so much more generous in its view of the immigrant poor than standard journalistic fare of the day that one suspects Addams's influence. Describing one home visit by a settlement resident, the reporter contrasted the "poor room of a swarming tenement" with the "evidences of family life that is happy and content and trustful in spite of conditions," the "highly-colored prints on the walls," the "savory mess of meat and vegetables simmering on the stove," and the "successful efforts" at cleanliness. There was a "hearty welcome" for the Hull-House resident, according to the reporter who accompanied the resident, along with "light-hearted chatter." But there was "much practical assistance" in these visits, too. "By reporting nuisances, by giving advice about physicians and instruction in regard to hospitals, by giving . . . sympathy and sincere affection," the Hull-House residents both befriended and aided their hard-working immigrant neighbors.[61]

Neighborliness required sensitivity to an array of ethnic and gender customs, as well as class prejudices. Jane and Ellen would not bow to their German neighbors' demand that all of the Italian children be kicked out of the kindergarten because they were "so dirty and had bugs." Still, they had to respond to such concerns, if only by reminding the Germans that kindergartners were bathed at Hull-House twice a week.[62] So, too, they had to react quickly when they realized that Italian women "got embarrassed" if Hull-House invited both men and women to evening receptions. Once the evening was designated for women and children alone, a "good many" came to play dominoes, checkers, and jackstraws. In time, fathers joined those Italian social nights, but on their terms, not the settlement's.[63]

First-time visits to neighbors' homes also required sensitivity to gender, as Jane and Ellen quickly learned. Daytime calls interrupted the housewife's work; evenings, Ellen explained to her parents, were the best time to call because "'he' is at home and they are all sitting about, rather bored with each other." It was advisable, however, to bring a male volunteer along on such introductory calls because male neighbors "were more likely to respond" to male visitors.[64] The easy availability of numerous male volunteers and residents at Hull-House serves as a reminder that men as well as women thrived under Jane Addams's leadership.[65] Hull-House was not a female space in the sense that only women worked there; it was female space in the sense that a nonpatriarchal style of management governed there and none of the settlement's many male volunteers ever thought to doubt or challenge it.

Though Jane and Ellen launched their scheme with the explicit purpose of providing meaningful work for idle society girls, they enlisted relatively few from that category who were sufficiently direct, independent, and creative to

26. Unidentified settlement volunteer (left) visiting a Hull-House neighborhood family. (University of Illinois at Chicago, University Library, Jane Addams Memorial Collection, neg. no. 1001)

make the necessary contribution to the endeavor. Anna Farnsworth, an early resident who precisely fit the profile of the bored society girl escaping self-involvement through labor, never quite met Jane's standards. Though a "cheerful resident" who did her "duty bravely" for over two years, Farnsworth lacked the "inward resources" needed to generate her own projects.[66] So while Farnsworth won Ellen's and Jane's affection, she never earned the same respect that Jane gave to Alice Miller, a Vassar graduate whom Jane could count on to handle correspondence and the college extension program.[67]

Jane's ideal resident turned out to be not a refugee from debutante balls but Julia Lathrop, a fiercely smart graduate from Vassar with a quick wit and equally keen eye. Lathrop had grown up in Rockford under the tutelage of a strong and loving father and had even attended Rockford Seminary for a year before Jane arrived on campus.[68] Within two months of Lathrop's first appearance at Hull-House in October 1891, Jane declared her "the best resident we have had."[69] Jane greatly respected the business acumen Lathrop had acquired by managing her father's law office and other businesses in Rockford. What she most admired about Lathrop, though, was the way her "disinterested virtue" gave her "freedom from egocentric preoccupations"—the very quality Frances Hackett associated with Jane herself. Jane also credited Lathrop with assuring Jane that the settlement's residents need not, indeed, could not refuse calls for humanitarian help from neighbors simply because they were inexpert in areas as basic as midwifery. Lathrop understood that traditional charity was not Hull-House's mission, but she became an early advocate for the view that direct, human assistance, neighbor to neighbor, was the foundation for any broader community organizing the settlement hoped to inspire.[70]

The practical wisdom of the settlement's early attention to neighborhood needs is so impressive that it is easy to forget that the original theory behind that wisdom was deeply flawed. Jane Addams went to Hull-House presuming that cross-class mutuality meant that the upper-class volunteers would provide education to the needy neighbors and the neighbors, in return, would provide a sense of usefulness to the volunteers. In that scenario, the neighbors were fairly passive players, serving primarily as an occasion for others' utility. It took remarkably little time for Jane and Ellen, and the volunteers and residents they attracted to Hull-House, to figure out that the neighbors were going to provide far more than an occasion for the educated class to feel useful. Education would be flowing in both directions on Halsted Street, and Jane Addams became, once again, a student. As such, she quickly grasped that her neighbors had a past and aspired to a future and saw that Hull-House educational programs could address both. It took a bit longer for Jane to recognize that the settlement had to be engaged in the neighbors' present lives, and not just by providing

27. Jane Addams's neighbors near Hull-House in Chicago's Nineteenth Ward. (University of Illinois at Chicago, University Library, Jane Addams Memorial Collection, neg. no. 285)

childcare and baths and hospital referrals. Gradually, Jane's neighbors educated her about pressing issues that had to be addressed: sweatshop labor, housing and factory conditions, inadequate schools, woeful sanitary standards, child labor, and exploitive wage levels, to name just the most obvious.

Hull-House sponsored, right from the start, the classroom in which Jane took her key lessons on these matters of political economy. Allen Pond and "some rather clever men" started up a "Social Science Club" during the settlement's first month.[71] This was to be a place where labor activists, businessmen, civic leaders, and working people could openly debate the merits of capitalism, socialism, the single tax, the tariff, the still lively matter of the Haymarket Riot, and anything else that engaged their interest.[72] "We ourselves have little to do with that," Jane demurely reported to Alice in October 1889, but within two years she was one of three members on the Executive Committee of the Working People's Social Science Club, and was arranging for talks on "The Problem of the Unemployed," "Christian Socialism," and "The Negro Problem." She was also making new alliances with men like Henry Demarest Lloyd, a leading Chicago journalist, reformer, and labor advocate.[73]

Affiliation with the Chicago Women's Club in 1889 had signified Jane's initial step toward broader social reform, but Jane had thereafter cautiously defined the settlement's agenda in line with Tolstoy's emphasis on individual salvation for the rich through labor with the poor. Life in the Nineteenth Ward, however, taught Jane that her personal choice to live a life engaged with harsh social reality was not enough. Looking back on her evolution away from Tolstoy's focus, Jane would later write, "a righteous life cannot be lived in a society that is not righteous."[74] As she celebrated her first Thanksgiving at Hull-House, Jane told George that she felt so "overpowered by the misery and narrow lives of so large a number of city people" that she understood the "movement toward Christian Socialism."[75] Just a few weeks later, she attended a speech on "The Emancipation of Labor" by the radical Episcopal priest Father James O. Huntington and reported to Alice that it was "like a spiritual revelation to me."[76] For the next two years, however, Hull-House stood "not so much for a solution of problems as a place of exchange" for ideas.[77] It was engaged with its neighbors but not yet activist on their behalf.

The press amply rewarded Jane and Hull-House for this noncombative stance. Reporters could comprehend a benevolent institution that was housed in a "pretty little structure" and insisted it was not a "charity"; they could categorize this female-led endeavor as thoroughly domestic and homelike. The endless repetition of the tale of the Hull mansion's redecoration and breathless descriptions of its new beauty and elegance served to reinforce the nonthreatening femininity of the settlement.[78]

Jane deeply distrusted the press, as her attempts to influence publishers and reporters, and even to write stories herself, testifies.[79] But that distrust arose, in part, from her understanding of how important the press was to her success. She recoiled from moralistic sentimentalizing about self-sacrifice but not from endearing images of herself as a little girl dreaming of owning a big house among little houses or as a refined and gracious hostess welcoming her working-class neighbors into her parlor.[80] A number of newspaper articles in the early years made a straightforward appeal to readers to contribute funds to the homey enterprise, and Jane looked kindly upon such articles, even if they did describe her as a good Christian "offering practical lessons of cleanliness."[81]

In its fascination with Hull-House as a thoroughly feminine, domestic institution, the press couched the settlement's positive effects in personal, therapeutic terms. Residents sought refuge from private boredom and self-indulgence while visitors to the house were blessed with "gentle companionship" and their lives "brightened and refined."[82] This characterization was in contrast to descriptions of the male-run Toynbee Hall, where the residents were said to be motivated by a "public spirit," by their sense of their "duty as citizens," and by the need to improve their neighbors' capacity to act as responsible citizens.[83] For the first two years of its existence, in fact, Hull-House lived in the paternal shadow of Toynbee Hall. Of the dozen articles on the Chicago settlement for the months between May 1889 and January 1891, seven used "Toynbee Hall" in the headline while only one referred to "Hull House." Five headlines referred to the "house on Halsted Street." When Samuel Barnett came to Chicago for the opening of the Butler Gallery, he was actually asked if he thought an enterprise like his could succeed in Chicago. Barnett's response left no doubt that he understood the gendered subtext of the question. "If the ladies can organize such an institution," he replied, "then surely the men can." Those reporting on this interview interpreted Barnett to mean that something more than a female auxiliary to Toynbee Hall was needed in Chicago and that a half-dozen good men were required to run it.[84]

Within six months of the grand opening of the Butler Gallery, references to Toynbee Hall in Chicago headlines disappeared and Hull-House stood on its own as the signifier of Jane Addams's womanly settlement in Chicago. The Hull-House identity was, by then, a comfortable one for Chicago's elite. The Butler Gallery itself appealed to the most cautious philanthropic impulses in the city. Supporters like Charles Hutchinson, president of the Chicago Board of Trade and of the Chicago Art Institute's board of trustees, liked to imagine that art alone could eliminate the most harsh features of industrial life, and they saw the Butler Gallery in terms of that belief. These philanthropists took their Ruskin in measured doses, focusing solely on the Victorian reformer's argument that art is uplifting and humanizing. Beyond their view lay Ruskin's point that serious social criticism and ethical debate is required to produce great art. This blinkered approach allowed cultural philanthropists to concentrate on art as the solution to Chicago's poverty, ignoring the economic structures that produced both poverty and the wealth of art patrons.[85]

Jane and Ellen heard Ruskin's call to social critics, but in their early years at the settlement, they did more to cultivate benefactors like Hutchinson than to challenge them. Hull-House gained its stature in Chicago and around the nation as a homey site for cultural uplift, and Jane did not protest that press construction. It conformed to her initial definition of the enterprise, it protected her nonreligious approach from close scrutiny, and it gave the settlement a sheltered cocoon in which to evolve. In all its detailed and glowing reports of the settlement's decor and day nursery, its baths and social evenings, its art exhibits and college extensions classes, the press paid very little attention to the Working People's Social Science Club. It was mentioned in passing as a site for lively debate, but no reporter paused—or was encouraged to pause— over the social criticisms being launched from Hull-House's well-appointed drawing room.[86] Even as the settlement was securing for itself a warm spot in the hearts of philanthropic Chicagoans, it was moving toward a more challenging role in the city's political life.

At the end of Hull-House's second year, Jane hosted Grace Dodge, the daughter of an elite New York family who had launched "Working Girls' Societies" in the early 1880s as a vehicle for educating young working women. Dodge was hardly radical in her views on the rights of labor, bur she articulated a crucial point about cross-class mutuality in a speech she gave to some three hundred working women crowded into the downstairs of Hull-House one October evening in 1891. Dodge conceded that educated women's culture and leisure were useful to working women. But, she quickly added, working women possessed equally useful "practicality and common sense." The two groups needed to "combine forces," she said, in recognition of "the great sisterhood of women."[87] A *Tribune* report on Dodge's speech noted that Hull-House was its appropriate site "since no one can have more at heart the interests of working girls than its founders," and then listed all the clubs and classes available to Chicago working women at the settlement.[88] The *Tribune* reporter did not notice that Jane Addams had, as yet, done nothing to help working women address the immediate problems they faced on the job; she had given them culture but taken little advantage of their practicality.

Less than a month after Dodge spoke at Hull-House, Jane wrote a letter to Mary Kenney, an Irish bookbinder who was organizing women workers from her perch as a delegate to the Chicago Trades and Labor Assembly. Jane invited

Kenney to have dinner at Hull-House with some British visitors interested in the labor movement. Having given up on the sort of working girls' clubs that Dodge fostered, Kenney doubted that Jane Addams had anything useful to offer, but she went to Hull-House at her mother's urging. Looking back on that first dinner, several decades later, Kenney recalled how Jane disarmed her skepticism by directly asking if there was anything she could do to help with Kenney's union work. Kenney asked for a room in which to meet. She got it. She asked for help with paying for and distributing fliers. Jane paid—and Jane herself distributed fliers.[89] At the same time, Jane acted on Kenney's behalf to persuade her new colleague, Henry Demarest Lloyd, to speak at Kenney's meeting to organize women shirtmakers. Kenney thought it would be "utterly impossible to secure" a labor activist as busy and famous as Lloyd, but Jane did not hesitate to use her connections for the cause.[90]

Jane and Hull-House were stepping out onto new terrain by the end of the second year. In December 1891, she told Katherine Coman, a colleague from the College Settlement in New York, that "we find ourselves almost forced into the trades unions" because there were so few for women in Chicago. Whether to assure herself or Coman, Jane added, "we hope to help them on a conservative basis."[91] For a natural mediator like Jane Addams, unions looked uncomfortably partisan. But there was an undeniable logic to the lessons the neighborhood taught about the injustices of working-class life in Chicago, and those lessons convinced Jane to accept a greater responsibility for advocacy than anyone would have predicted at the settlement's opening. Her next challenge was to integrate cross-class mutuality and working-class advocacy.

Meanwhile, Hull-House was becoming known as much as a place of refuge for the socially conscious and the slightly marginal as for the idle rich. By June 1891, Henry Standing Bear, the son of the Sioux Chief Standing Bear, was living at the settlement and serving as a handyman and occasional greeter at the front door. Young Standing Bear was a recent graduate of the government-run, intensely assimilationist Carlisle Indian School in Pennsylvania. Apparently, the school had not killed the Indian in him, for he took his diploma and headed home to the reservation. A forced stop in Chicago when he ran out of travel money led him to Hull-House. As Ellen explained to her family, with wry pride, "If there were one single Indian in the city, or in the state, we would get him."[92] Henry Standing Bear was still working at Hull-House six months later.

Chapter 14
Unity of Action

Henry Standing Bear and Jane Addams were the figures Florence Kelley called to mind when she thought back on her first moments at Hull-House. She remembered a "snowy morning between Christmas 1891 and New Year's 1892" when she appeared on the doorstep at 335 South Halsted, seeking whatever aid or advice the settlement could offer.[1] Her three "chicks"—Nicholas, age six; Margaret, age five; and John, age four—had been left back at the Women's Christian Temperance Union nursery while their mother tracked down this lead to possible work, possible shelter. Kelley's one friend in Chicago, an editor for the WCTU's *Union Signal*, had thought Hull-House might have use for someone with Kelley's college training, European experience, and record of labor activism among working women in New York and Philadelphia. The fact that she was the thirty-three-year-old daughter of a recently mourned U.S. Congressman, the mother of three, and the runaway wife of an abusive husband certainly gave Kelley a different profile from the typical Hull-House resident, but not an unattractive one.[2]

Looking back, Kelley recalled being "welcomed" as though she had been "invited."[3] To her host, Jane Addams, Kelley represented an opportunity to move Hull-House more purposefully in the direction of labor activism. The fact that Addams chose to take that opportunity deserves notice. Addams could have easily, and graciously, declined settlement residency to this destitute mother of three whose 1887 translation of Friedrich Engels's *The Condition of the Working Class in England in 1844* had put Kelley on the socialist map in America. Her first breakfast with Kelley would have told Addams that she was dealing with a strong-minded, blunt-spoken, and ambitious political activist. Had Addams wanted to avoid the partisan associations that inevitably followed in Kelley's wake, she could have done so. Instead, Addams moved into high gear to get Kelley settled at Hull-House.

The solutions she devised to Kelley's financial and childcare difficulties testify to the kinds of relationships Addams forged during her first two years in the Chicago reform community. Through her friends in the Chicago Women's Club, Addams raised funds to pay Kelley to run a nonprofit placement bureau for those seeking employment as domestic servants.[4] She then turned to Henry Demarest Lloyd, her new colleague in the labor movement, to provide a warm and welcoming home for Kelley's three children. Lloyd and his wife, Jessie, lived a comfortable life on their spacious "Wayside" estate in Winnetka, fifteen miles north of Chicago, even though their shared commitment to radical politics had pulled them away from Henry's secure editorial post at the *Chicago*

28. Florence Kelley (University of Illinois at Chicago, University Library, Jane Addams Memorial Collection, neg. no. 404)

Tribune and had cost the couple Jessie's inheritance.[5] The Lloyds immediately absorbed Kelley's children into their extended household, accepting the struggling mother's payments for room and board while providing a well-subsidized place for Kelley and her "chicks" among the various labor activists, social reformers, and political rebels who gathered around their dining table. Proof of a stable home for the children assured Kelley a victory in her 1892 custody battle with her estranged husband, Lazare Wischnewetzky, a Russian Jewish physician who had tracked her down and was constantly "prowling about." Less than a month after her arrival in Chicago, Kelley was celebrating her new, "dear" friends "whose generous hospitality astonishes me."[6] At the same time, the press was hailing Kelley's "admirable preparation and fitness" for bringing order out of the chaos that reigned in the household labor market and was quoting her unusual aim to "register" and "grade" the qualifications of employers as well as employees, to ensure that "both sides" understood their obligations to the other.[7]

The failure of the idealistic placement bureau mattered less in the long run than the successful partnership it launched between Jane Addams and Florence Kelley. From the winter of 1892 until Kelley's death in 1932, whether living in the same city or thousands of miles apart, the two women regarded themselves as the best of friends, the closest of colleagues, the most formidable of political teams. The superficial similarities Addams and Kelley shared—precocious, privileged childhoods under the tutelage of powerful Republican fathers whom they adored and tried to emulate, youthful struggles with ill health, even familial duty to care for unstable brothers—hardly suffice to explain how they overcame their impressive differences. While Jane studied literature and moral philosophy at evangelical Rockford Female Seminary, closing her career there with writings on the primordial goddess and Cassandra, Florence studied political economy at Cornell University, finishing up with a thesis on "The Legal Status of the Child Since Blackstone" which was published in the *International Review*. While Jane studied Christian art in Italy, read Ruskin in France, and praised Bismarck in Germany, Florence explored England's industrial cities and enrolled at the University of Zurich, read Marx, converted to socialism, and denounced Bismarck. While Jane was dabbling in charities in Baltimore, reading Tolstoy, and worrying that education was the bane of femininity, Florence was marrying a socialist Jew from Russia, translating Engels, bearing babies, and fighting for the rights of women to be taken seriously within the Socialist Labor Party. And while Jane was moving closer to Ellen, discovering Toynbee Hall, and developing her own, gendered theory of the subjective need for cross-class mutuality, Florence was escaping a violent, oppressive marriage and establishing herself in Philadelphia and New York as an articulate critic of the capitalist class and defender of the rights of working-class women. In the decade before they met, both Addams and Kelley had agonized over their place as elite women in the class struggle, but Addams had grappled with the question in theological terms while Kelley had been focused on historical materialism.

Alongside their experiential and ideological differences lay the temperamental ones. Addams exuded a dignified calm; Kelley gave off a "bursting vitality" and a "dismaying energy." Addams maintained a steady decorum; Kelley swung between "genial kindliness" and intimidating ferocity. Addams emotionally and philosophically recoiled from conflict; Kelley was, according to Jane's nephew, "the finest rough-and-tumble fighter for the good life for others that Hull House ever knew."[8] In the end, Addams was a mediator and Kelley was an advocate. Yet Samuel Barnett's dictum, "the things that make us alike are finer and stronger than the things that make us different," was nowhere more true in Addams's life than in her relationship with Florence Kelley.[9]

What drew them together, right from the start, was the shared conviction that salvation in this life came through immersion in labor that expanded and exceeded the self. Kelley was every bit as passionate and histrionic as Ellen Starr, but unlike Ellen, Kelley's outbursts were not about herself, they were about the work. It was that zeal for work that cut through all the apparent differences between Addams and Kelley and revealed both women at their core. Their shared joy in channeling passions outward, in making the human condition their personal business fueled their friendship for four decades and created around them a climate of mutual acceptance that allowed diversity to flourish at Hull-House.

By the time she arrived on Halsted Street, Kelley had broken with the Socialist Labor Party over its disdain for American labor unions, women, and the English language. She had not, however, abandoned her fundamental assumption that class arrangements under capitalism represented an injustice demanding redress, nor had she given up her training in the use of empirical evidence to craft legislative remedies for the social ills wrought by capitalism.[10] Kelley's whole being was wired for targeted action aimed at specific social outcomes; good intentions counted for little in her world—it was results that mattered.

By contrast, Jane Addams's initial focus at Hull-House had been on process, not specific outcomes. Her fluid project was intended as a corrective to charity workers' obsession with order, and it was supposed to be a symbol of cross-class mutuality, not an outpost for class conflict. Even before Kelley's arrival, however, Addams's faith in process had meant that Hull-House evolved in response to the needs and impulses of neighbors and residents alike. She had been willing to follow the logic of the process toward greater involvement with labor organizing and direct engagement with the governing class on behalf of her neighbors. Increasingly, cross-class mutuality at Hull House had come to mean not only that the working poor were exposed to the educated views of the rich but that the rich used their education to articulate what the world looked like from the point of view of the poor. "Perhaps the greatest value of a settlement," Addams told Chicago's Sunset Club just weeks after Kelley's arrival at Hull-House, "is its service as an information and interpretation bureau."[11]

Florence Kelley's orientation toward class struggle and reform victories did not alter the daily internal operations at Hull-House. In her first months, those operations drove Kelley mad with impatience. In response to the typhoid epidemic of the summer of 1892, for example, Kelley immediately lobbied the municipal sanitation board for reforms in street cleaning and garbage collection that would avert future epidemics. Ellen, by contrast, devoted her energies to visiting the stricken, finding burial gowns, and arguing with "obstinate" health officers about the handling of specific cases in the neighborhood. An exasperated Florence Kelley warned "Sister Starr" that to "bring about a change in this country *peaceably*" meant facing the harsh political fact that individual casework was "mighty incidental!"[12] Six years later, however, Kelley had come around to the settlement view that hands-on neighborly assistance was the foundation for all political organizing. "Although at times the House may seem to exist chiefly for its mass of detail work," Kelley wrote in 1898, "yet as the years go by the truth grows clearer, that much of this has been chiefly valuable for the fund of experience it yields as a basis for wider social action."[13]

Addams's embrace of Kelley in the winter of 1892 is a clear sign of her desire to expand the settlement's involvement in "wider social action," to move her operation into those arenas of civic duty and public citizenship that the press had so far assigned to masculine settlements like Toynbee Hall. Within weeks of Kelley's arrival, when it became clear that the city was not responsive to the idea of a household labor bureau which protected workers' interests, Addams began "wirepulling" to secure alternative employment for Kelley as an investigator for the Bureau of Labor Statistics of Illinois.[14] Over the course of the next two years, Kelley used her official position within the government to doggedly gather data on the wages and conditions in Chicago sweatshops and to dramatically expose her findings to the public.[15] In one blistering speech after another, Kelley drew on her eyewitness accounts and incontestable statistics to awaken the public and the legislature to the need for greater state regulation of the workplace.[16] As Addams later recalled, Kelley's investigations "galvanized us all into more intelligent interest in the industrial conditions around us."[17]

The result was landmark Illinois legislation in 1893 banning child labor, mandating an eight-hour day for women workers, and prohibiting the production of garments in sweatshops. The *Chicago Post* scoffed that the new law was so sweeping, the state legislature might as well have outlawed poverty.[18] But as the state's newly appointed chief factory inspector (and the only female with such authority in the nation), Florence Kelley set out to prove that legislation could alter the conditions of capitalism.[19]

Support for the labor law that Kelley and her allies in the labor movement crafted was not a philosophical stretch for Addams. The legislative approach and the campaign's thrust were entirely consistent with Addams's focus on cross-class mutuality and state-sponsored mediation of economic interests. The campaign itself linked concerns about child labor and women's working conditions with fears that contagious diseases were being sewn into the seams of "every kind of wearing apparel" and that the well-to-do were dressing "in the cast-off scarlet fever skins of the poor."[20] The language was not what Addams would have used, but the notion that the classes were irrevocably stitched together was right in line with her own thinking. So, too, the campaign's focus on state intervention rather than labor-union organizing not only recognized the practical impossibility of organizing sweatshop labor, it satisfied Addams's desire to "appeal to all elements of the community" for support.[21]

The legislative focus conformed to Addams's Republican belief in the state's duty to regulate economic conditions for the common welfare. In public, Addams was still far more diffident than Kelley in regard to women's place in this political process, conceding before the all-male Sunset Club that there were "thus far" some "duties of citizenship" that a "woman's settlement must perforce leave unperformed."[22] Philosophically, however, Addams supported suffrage for women and agreed with Kelley's political assertiveness. These two women, one bent toward socialism, the other toward mediation, occupied common ground as the daughters of mid-nineteenth-century Republican politicians who had actively legislated for prosperity and firmly believed in the state's role as the guarantor of economic opportunity.[23]

But while Jane Addams served on the lobbying committee for the new factory legislation, she was not prominent at the mass meetings and labor rallies that demanded its passage. She did not make the investigative rounds of sweatshops with Kelley and the legislators. Nor did she join in the chorus of hot rhetoric that denounced merchants like Marshall Field for selling disease-ridden garments made by children. Rabble-rousing was not Addams's forte; she had to carve out her own position on sweatshop labor, one that would explain to her neighbors how someone claiming their friendship could campaign to shut down their shops and eliminate their children's wages.[24]

The stance Addams adopted was a tough one but utterly consistent with her maturing view of her neighbors. In her eyes, they were not passive victims but active agents with their own responsibility for civic life. So while most antisweatshop campaigners, including Kelley, focused their angry rhetoric on downtown shops and wealthy consumers, Addams reminded her neighbors that their duty to "universal social relations" meant they should protest work that "lowers the wage standard."[25] Risking the charge that she was blaming the victims for their poverty, Addams insisted that workers were intelligent social actors who made moral and economic choices every day; to assert their status as full participants in social and economic decisions, they had to demonstrate their concern for community welfare.

Addams stood her ground on this position against hostile questioning from an audience of workers who gathered at the Chicago Music Hall during the antisweatshop drive. Would she advise a woman with a dependent family to reject work that offered poor wages, one worker asked. No, said Addams; she would advise the woman to work but to also agitate with fellow workers for better wages. Wasn't the best way out of the workers' exploitation simply to confiscate wealth from the rich, another asked. No, Addams countered; the best way out was for all to maintain a "unity of action," working together for both labor unions and pro-labor legislation to democratize the economy. According to the sympathetic newspaper reporter who witnessed these exchanges, Addams stayed calm and cool amidst a chaotic meeting, satisfying her questioners and proving herself to be "an eminently wise and well-balanced woman."[26] Having thrown off Carlyle's heroic paternalism and adopted Arnold Toynbee's call for self-governance among the working-class, Addams was steadfast in insisting that her neighbors act responsibly in the face of social problems.

Jane Addams was not actually in Chicago at the height of the antisweatshop campaign. In mid-February 1893, she left for a speaking tour on the East Coast—expenses paid, she assured Alice, by the 19th Century Club of New York City. In the same week that Florence Kelley publicly denounced Marshall Field for exploiting garment workers, Addams was speaking at Smith College, where her youthful deficiencies in Greek and geometry no longer seemed to matter. Included on this tour, along with Smith, were Bryn Mawr, Wellesley, and Vassar—the founding schools of the College Settlement Association. Their alumnae were encouraged to pursue settlement work at the Rivington Street Settlement in New York City. Jane wrote to Alice about the tour with so much pride she had to mask it in parentheses: "(I find I am considered quite the grandmother of American settlements)," she whispered. It was, she said, a "beautiful trip" and "a good thing to break into the winter's grind." Jane's satisfaction was due, in part, to being greeted so warmly by college women whose education, she felt, was so far superior to her own. But the eastern trip marked, as well, the first of many happy journeys Jane would make with Mary Rozet

Smith, a Hull-House volunteer whose work with neighborhood children Jane so admired that she claimed it infused "more of the Christian spirit that we hoped the house would stand for than anything that has been done."[27]

By the time they traveled east together, Jane had known Mary for three years, virtually since the opening of Hull-House, when Mary began to assist her friend Jenny Dow in the kindergarten. Early in 1891, almost a year before Florence Kelley's arrival, Jane acknowledged that Mary's "interest and friendship" had already "come to mean a great deal" to her.[28] But as Jane recounted in a poem in 1895, it took her awhile to see Mary as far more than just a volunteer:

One day I came into Hull House
    (No spirit whispered who was there)
And in the kindergarten room
    There sat upon a childish chair
A girl both tall and fair to see,
    (To look at her gives one a thrill).
But all I thought was, would she be
    Best fitted to lead club or drill?
You see, I had forgotten Love,
    And only thought of Hull House then.
That is the way with women folks
    When they attempt the things of men . . .
So I was blind and deaf all those years
    To all save one absorbing care
And did not guess what now I know—
    Delivering love was sitting there.[29]

Before Jane allowed herself to feel a "thrill" over Mary, her cordial notes to the wealthy "Miss Smith" always included regards from "Miss Starr." Mary, who was eight years younger than Jane, had been a student at Miss Kirkland's school where Ellen once taught fashionable girls from Mary Smith's social set.[30] When Ellen left Chicago, in the summer of 1892, to spend three months in England, relations between Jane and Mary intensified and future correspondence made no mention of Ellen or her regards.

It was not as if Jane and Ellen were estranged by 1892. Their history was much too deep, and whatever their tensions, disappointments, and resentments, Jane would never have permitted the sort of emotional outburst that might spark an estrangement. In fact, Jane assured the homesick Ellen that "I miss you all the time and never wanted you more than the last few days when everything seemed to be moving at once." But amidst her description of beds being shifted about the house, Jane added, "of course, Mary and I slept together."[31]

Women friends in the nineteenth century customarily slept together—in the same room, in the same bed; it was as often an expression of everyday intimacy as romantic sexuality. Before Mary, however, that expression had been reserved for Ellen. Now, Jane expected Ellen to understand that, "of course," her intimate arrangements included Mary. That matter-of-fact quality of Jane's, which so charmed audiences weary of sentimentality, could wound a friend—and silence her. There was nothing to be done for it; Jane was who she was, willfully sensitive in so many ways and willfully obtuse in others. As Ellen's Episcopal mentor, Father Huntington, observed, there was no point in taking offense at the things Jane said: "One might as well be affronted by the multiplication tables."[32]

Ellen's cousin had warned her, back in 1889, about the "weaknesses of the flesh," and Ellen returned home from England in the summer of 1892 full of reflections on "how much the spirit is fettered by the flesh and compelled to communicate through it." She was full of longing, as well, for a time past, a time "lost," when friendship with Jane had been independent of any physical tie, when they did not live together and seldom even saw each other. The spiritual and the physical, Ellen now realized, "are two different kinds of affection, and they interfere with each other almost."[33] The spiritual love Ellen and Jane had felt for one another could not survive daily embodiment in Hull-House.

By contrast, the love that grew between Jane and Mary Rozet Smith took root in the settlement's soil and thrived on it. Rather than compete with Hull-House for Jane's time and affection, Mary made herself indispensable to Jane's work there. For over forty years, Mary Rozet Smith devoted herself entirely to "making life easier for Jane Addams. That," recalled Jane's nephew, "was her career, her philosophy." A few months before she died, Mary thanked Jane for having "made my life. All its meaning and color come from you." And at the time of Mary's death in 1934, just a year before Jane's, one mourning friend wrote that Jane was "the one through whom Mary found herself."[34]

Mary Rozet Smith would actually play a trio of roles in Jane Addams's life, and all three were evident in the early 1890s. Her first, and continuing, role was as an active participant at Hull-House. Mary never became a resident there, but as a volunteer she taught in the kindergarten, oversaw the nursery, managed a variety of clubs along with musical and dramatic activities, and just "looked after things"—especially things related to children. Remembering his own youth at Hull-House, James Weber Linn insisted that no timid child or gawky teen "ever knew Mary Smith without falling in love with her" because she offered safety and serenity. His aunt's life partner was, he suspected, "as tolerant as Jane Addams herself" and "unquestionably gentler." Another long-time Hull-House friend concurred in the opinion that Mary was "the most

29. Mary Rozet Smith (Jane Addams Hull-House Museum, University of Illinois at Chicago)

universally beloved person" at the settlement.[35] Unlike wry and jagged Ellen, sweet-natured Mary could serve as a surrogate in Jane's absence and successfully bestow as much good will as her adored partner.

During the summer of 1892, Jane began to refer to Mary as "my sweet nurse," and whether they were at Hull-House, traveling in Europe, Asia, or the Middle East, staying at Mary's lovely Chicago home on Walton Place, or at the summer home they later shared in Bar Harbor, Maine, Mary always served as Jane's caretaker.[36] One friend recalled that "Mary was in the habit of following her around with a shawl, pocket handkerchief, crackers if she thought Miss Addams might be hungry, or anything else she might want, and was always ready to supply Miss Addams's needs, whatever they were."[37] After a five-speech week, Jane told Alice that Mary was feeding her raw oysters and providing "delightful rubbings," and in Alice's own attempt to be as satisfactory a traveling companion as Mary, she promised to wash Jane's hair on a trip en route to San Francisco.[38]

Along with the physical care came emotional support. Mary was Jane's personal sounding board, that person in her life who did not attend residents' meetings or committee meetings, the one whose only agenda was to assure Jane of the wisdom of her dreams and schemes. Jane spoke more familiarly about various neighbors' daily lives with Mary than with other correspondents, but when the two were apart, Jane never had time to write up all the day's business. As a result, letters to Mary are peppered with Jane's longing to "tell you so many things," to "talk to you of so many things," to "talk over a plan which has occurred to me to see if you approve." Ideas "flashed" into Jane's mind throughout the working day, but she was convinced "a great deal many more things would flash if you were here to help talk about it."[39]

Whether Jane and Mary expressed their love for each other sexually is a secret that was buried with them. Jane saw to that by destroying those letters she regarded as "much too intimate to be used" in any biography of her, a caution she did not feel moved to take with Ellen's letters.[40] Despite that effacement, what survives is a record of tenderness and affection, the sort of mutual admiration and devotion that typifies any strong marriage. As Mary's niece wrote to Jane at the time of Mary's death, "what fineness has passed between you two."[41] Relatives on both sides acknowledged the bond, but it was Mary's parents, Charles Mather Smith and Sarah Rozet Smith, who took Jane into their gracious home, treated her and her work as their own, and became for Jane not just Mary's parents but "the dear parents." They provided Jane with the parental approval she could never win from her own deceased father and bitter stepmother.[42]

Familial support proved to be important because it allowed Mary to play a third significant role in Jane's life, that of philanthropist. By the fall of 1893, Jane had spent almost $15,000 of her $60,000 inheritance on Hull-House. Over the course of those four years, the settlement's budget had more than doubled, from over $8,500 a year to almost $21,000, and while Jane's share of those expenditures declined, her absolute outlay continued to increase. She was not subsidizing actual programs; the classes and the clubs, the summer school at Rockford, and the kindergarten were all self-sustaining. Jane's money went to house repairs, maintenance, and expansions and to subsidizing residents' room and board—including Ellen's and Florence Kelley's.[43] Helen Culver continued to make a substantial contribution with both additional land and her rent-free lease, which she extended to 1920 in 1894. Two years after Edward Butler funded the art gallery, businessmen William Colvin and Allison Vincent Armour put up $14,000 for another two-story brick building to house recreational activities.[44] In addition, various donors, like Nettie Fowler McCormick, could be counted on for annual contributions of $50 or $100.[45] Jane felt "grateful to all of them," but confessed to feeling "more than that" to Mary.[46] As idea after idea for settlement projects "flashed" into Jane's head, she needed a steady and ready source of funds, and as early as Christmas 1890, well before Ellen's trip to England, Mary and her family served as a source of such funds.[47]

Whatever inequality inhered in Mary's deference to the pace of Jane's career, it was balanced by Jane's dependence on Mary's financial support of that career. Surviving records show that between 1906 and 1934, Mary and her family contributed more than $4,000 a year to the settlement, and every indication from earlier correspondence suggests that Hull-House benefited just as much from the Smiths' generosity in the 1890s and early 1900s.[48] In 1894, when it was clear that childcare needs in the neighborhood far exceeded what a nearby cottage could provide, Mary's father, the wealthy owner of a paper company, funded a three-story children's building, later called the Smith Building.[49] But there were more prosaic contributions all along the way. When the new coffeehouse was floundering, Charles Smith donated the funds to keep it afloat, and Jane looked forward to "reading him the accounts." When the summer school needed start-up cash, Mary sent a check.[50] When the addition of a men's settlement in a building across Halsted Street involved $1,000 in structural repairs and then created an additional $400 deficit in residents' board payments, Smith funds saved the day. Indeed, when Florence Kelley could not afford boarding school tuition for her children in the late 1890s, Mary stepped in.[51]

As James Weber Linn explained, it was Mary's "constant overcoming of deficits here and there . . . that literally kept the work going."[52] Project costs inevitably exceeded predictions and Jane could not endlessly tap the proceeds of her own limited investments, but Mary and her father regularly made up the difference. In the fall of 1892, after their first intense summer together, Mary sent $300 and Jane claimed that "nothing ever touched me so much or relieved me so much." Two years later, when settlement accounts were $888 in arrears, Jane felt "a lump in my throat to think of the round thousand dollars" Mary sent along. Early on, she worried that their "very dear" friendship would be "jarred by all these money transactions," but Jane Addams never shrank from Mary's generosity and grew to enjoy the intimacy that such sharing bespoke.[53] In an undated poem written later in their life together, Jane defined their material bond as evidence of a distinctive love that set them apart from both "married" people and "single" people:

The "mine" and "thine" of wedded folk
Is often quite confusing
And sometimes when they use the "ours"
It sounds almost amusing

But you and I may well defy
Both married folk and single
To do as well as we have done
The "mine" and "thine" to mingle.[54]

Clearly, Jane did not feel as economically dependent on Mary as women in traditional heterosexual marriages, nor did she view herself as a "single" person. Just as she innovated in her social reform, so, too, Jane Addams innovated in the intimate, domestic, and material arrangements in her life. However queer it may have been to "defy" convention as she and Mary did, Jane Addams quietly embraced her defiance and delighted in the spiritual and material support it brought to her.

Thanks in part to the Smith family's contributions, Hull-House continued to expand its facilities and programs in the years between 1892 and 1894. The settlement added a playground, a new gymnasium with shower room, and a men's club with billiard table; it opened a "coffee house" and a working women's cooperative boarding house called the "Jane Club," as well as the men's settlement house across the street, which was subsequently colonized by a group of young male printers who named it the Phalanx Club. Clubs and classes continued to proliferate, and unions continued to meet at the settlement, especially women's unions—the shirtmakers, the shoemakers, the bookbinders, and the cloakmakers—because members did not want to meet in local saloons. The settlement's increasing commitment to civic reform is evident in Ellen Starr's creation of the Public School Art Society, dedicated to placing visual art in classrooms; the appearance of the "Eight Hour Club," comprised of working women committed to enforcing the state's new work rules for women; the "Arnold Toynbee Club," devoted to the promotion of legislation on economic and social reform; as well as the creation—at Jane's urging—of the Nineteenth Ward Improvement Club, which lobbied for municipal reforms, like the ward's public bathhouse, and established a coal cooperative to reduce neighbors' heating costs.[55]

By 1892, Jane served as the "chief" of an intensely busy beehive of an operation with some eighteen residents—twelve women and six men—and over a hundred volunteers. Settlement life allowed Jane, Ellen, and Florence occasional private evenings in the parlor, eating apples and bananas with other residents and entertaining each other with stories from the day.[56] Typically, though, the residents lived out their lives in public space, constantly interacting with neighbors and volunteers, constantly rearranging rooms for different uses, constantly answering the doorbell and "never doing one thing without being interrupted to tend to half a dozen others."[57] Those who were prickly, high strung, or irritable seldom survived the settlement's pace and lack of privacy. Not surprisingly, the head resident placed a high premium on harmony; with the notable exception of Ellen, "certain thorny people were not admitted" to settlement work on Halsted Street.[58]

It was not Jane's style to openly dictate what the settlement's platoon of workers should do or to scrutinize their daily work. Instead, each individual who volunteered was expected either to take charge of some existing class, club, or neighborhood service or to identify an unmet local need and invent a way to meet it.[59] Jane was on hand to advise and encourage, in her kindly but matter-of-fact, of-course-you-can-manage way. At the dawn of each day, though, everyone at Hull-House was trusted to meet individual obligations or candidly seek help. Those who could not handle the responsibility, or the independence, were advised (in the residents' meeting) to leave after their six-week trial period ended; those who displayed a capacity for harmony, initiative, good judgment, and the all-important sense of humor were invited (by the residents' meeting) to stay on.[60]

As Hull-House evolved beyond its initial focus on the process of cross-class contact and became more committed to achieving real goals in the neighborhood, the notion that it might serve as a site of spiritual renewal for idle, sickly society girls completely vanished. The institution that Jane was building on Halsted Street was no place for sissies. Increasingly, the settlement attracted residents with specific talents rather than independent wealth. Though Jane told others in the settlement world that residents should not be paid for being good neighbors, she effectively arranged for residents' pay by persuading wealthy donors to sponsor fellowships to pay the living expenses of specific residents.⁶¹ The result, as Clifford Barnes, himself a resident, explained in an 1893 article, was that those volunteering to live at the settlement "represented among them a great divergence of special interests, such as law, medicine, journalism, theology, teaching, dietary cooking, tenement-house investigation, charity relief, and the study of various social and economic problems."⁶²

Even so, Jane fought to maintain the settlement's responsiveness and flexibility, to keep a featherweight's balance between "conviction" and "tolerance."⁶³ In a speech to the Wisconsin Conference of Charities and Corrections in 1894, she claimed that the key to settlement work was to "feel your way first. You find what your neighborhood likes and respond. You are not a reformer," she insisted, "not a straight reformer." By this she meant that settlement workers were not to impose their own ideas on neighbors. They were to take their cues from those around them: "If you are sure you are supplying a demand you are bound sooner or later to succeed."⁶⁴ A glance at Jane's experience with the playground, the coffeehouse, and the Jane Club proves the wisdom of that rule.

So great was the local enthusiasm for a playground—the first public facility of its kind in Chicago—that no one protested the demolition of decrepit housing to make space behind Hull-House. Perhaps the evicted tenants took vengeful pleasure in knowing the way in which the property was secured: Florence Kelley publicly humiliated its owner for profiting off slum housing, and Jane Addams then graciously offered to relieve the owner of his embarrassment by taking over the land rent-free and replacing his firetraps with play equipment. Or perhaps the anger of those tenants who were displaced by this bit of urban renewal was simply drowned out by the din of two hundred neighborhood children playing on swings and jungle gyms.⁶⁵

The rule was that local demand ensured success, and the signal failure of the settlement's modern, scientific "New England Kitchen" abundantly proved that rule. No Hull-House neighbor ever demanded hermetically steamed or efficiently baked "American" meals and, much to Jane's surprise and disappointment, no crowds lined up for the settlement's takeout health food in the spring of 1893. Demand was all, and when it became clear that the neighbors were not about to give up their spaghetti and piroshgi for barley soup designed in a Boston home economics lab, Jane quietly borrowed some money from Mary's father and turned the space into a profitable coffeehouse, one that served community demand both as a restaurant and as a source of hot lunches and coffee that could be delivered to nearby factories.⁶⁶

The cooperative boardinghouse known as the Jane Club met more than one demand in the neighborhood. It represented Jane's direct response to the needs of the working women whose unions met at Hull-House. After just a few months of meeting with those women Jane grasped how their fear of lost rent money constrained their freedom to protest labor conditions. The Jane Club's cooperative housing plan succeeded because Jane funded the start-up costs, enlisted Mary Wilmarth's aid in furnishing each new flat, and then left the women to manage their own affairs. Every news article on the early Jane Club gushed over the boardinghouse's refined tone and genteel decor. A few remarked that it was unique among women's boardinghouses insofar as it had no curfew and each resident carried her own key. As Jane explained to one reporter, "Any girl who can come into the city and earn an honest living knows enough to run her own evenings."[67]

Unnoticed at the time was how this particular success not only proved the rule of neighborly demand but conformed, as well, to the settlement's guiding principle of cross-class mutuality. The Jane Club ran on a system of self-governance that paralleled the one residents used at Hull-House. In both buildings on the settlement "campus," residents voted in new members and held weekly meetings to distribute household duties, settle financial accounts, and air concerns or grievances. In both, a high premium was place on civility toward everyone, from the cook to the rotating "chair." And in neither building were there any rules constraining residents' freedom of movement, day or night, except for the requirement that all attend the weekly meeting. The rules were the same across class, and by according the women of the Jane Club that respect, Hull-House met its neighbors' most basic demand.[68]

Press coverage of Hull-House in these years was pretty much consumed with the settlement's continual growth, its thousand visitors a week, and its perpetual addition of "one form of activity to another . . . in seemingly the most natural way." Indeed, wrote one reporter, "there seems scarce a month but some new feature is added." It was the sheer magnitude of the operation that impressed observers; "few charitable schemes are as far-reaching as this one," said one paper; "Hull House," declared another, offered the most "diversified social and intellectual activity" in Chicago.[69] But Ellen worried that the "success of Hull House outwardly and visibly is sometimes like a snare! When people praise it and us," she feared, that praise served "as an excuse for the things we ought to do and be and don't and aren't."[70] While Ellen fretted that the settlement was not doing enough, especially in opposition to industrial capitalism, Samuel Barnett wrote from London to caution Jane against allowing the settlement to become a "platform" for any particular interest while also warning her against such incessant "doing" that "faith in our Lord" gets obscured.[71]

These two old friends, both so vital to Jane's creation of Hull-House, now represented the two ideological poles tugging at her. With increased prominence came increased pressure, from Christians and capitalist critics alike, for Jane to hoist their flags and march in their parades. Jane's responses to these pressures, both in her conduct and her writings between 1892 and 1894, reveal the extent and the direction of her education, illuminating where she was now firm in her commitment to principles already forged and where she was open to accommodating those principles to the realities of the world she inhabited. They show her further drift away from organized Christianity and her increased willingness to stand on a "platform" with the critics of capitalism, but always on her terms, to contribute her message of mutuality and mediation to the era's economic debate.

Jane articulated her early settlement philosophy in two public addresses— "The Subjective Necessity for Social Settlements" and "The Objective Value of the Social Settlement"—at a conference in Plymouth, Massachusetts, in the summer of 1892. So effective were these two speeches, and the published articles they quickly became, that they have acquired iconic status, frozen in time as Jane Addams's signature statements, quoted as though she never revised her thinking beyond the age of thirty-two. While, in truth, she was revising her thinking even as she delivered the speeches, they still serve as eloquent samples of the ideas and prose she had been rehearsing in Chicago gatherings since 1890.

Both talks were delivered in the fourth week of the summer session of the School of Applied Ethics, which met in an old high school building on a hillside overlooking Plymouth Bay. The school's organizers invited Jane because they regarded her as "the guiding spirit of . . . the most influential Settlement in the country." Her lectures were part of the series offered by the school's Department of Economics not, interestingly, its Department of the Science of Ethics nor its Department of Comparative Religion. Her charge, like that of the other speakers in the series that week, was to address the question of "philanthropy and social progress."[72] She had adapted the first of her two talks from her earlier talk, "Outgrowths of Toynbee Hall," and had dictated the final version to Edward Burchard, a Hull-House resident, while juggling settlement duties, the Rockford Summer School, and her intensifying bond with Mary Rozet Smith.[73] It was not Mary who accompanied Jane to Plymouth, however; instead, Julia Lathrop went along. That left Ellen and Florence Kelley to manage Hull-House and swelter in the Chicago heat. The worst days found Ellen vying with the neighbors for bath time and Florence soaking her feet, which were swollen from door-to-door collection of data for the Illinois Bureau of Labor Statistics.[74]

Meanwhile, cooled by the breezes that blew off Plymouth Bay that late July, Jane opened her two-day appearance at the School for Applied Ethics by explaining "The Subjective Necessity" for founding social settlements. She identified three "motives"—the humanitarian, the Christian, and the democratic

—which impelled the movement of educated young people away from their "unnourished, over-sensitive lives" and into "the great opportunities for helpfulness" offered by full engagement with life's unadorned "starvation struggle." Jane's most familiar theme—young people's need to escape the deadening grasp of luxury—was incorporated here as the "humanitarian" motive, which she defined as the "primordial" need to "share the race life," to partake of "the great mother breasts of our common humanity, with its labor and suffering and its homely comforts."[75]

Accompanying that humanitarian motive, she claimed, was the second motive, a "renaissance" of early Christian ideas. Jane specifically refrained from calling this a "religious" motive because, she said, "we have no proof" that Jesus or his first followers regarded his teachings as a set of fixed truths comprising a religion. Rather than heavenly dogma, she argued, Jesus' teachings were a call to action motivated by "a deep enthusiasm for humanity," a "zeal and affection" for "his fellows." The "constant revelation" promised by Jesus could come only through "the joy of finding the Christ which lieth in each man, but which no man can unfold save in fellowship."[76]

Standing before her audience that day, Jane probably wore, at the neck of her dress, the same round brooch that she wore in most of the surviving photographs from the 1890s. This aesthetic representation of the first two Greek letters in Christ's name, known as a Chi-Rho cross, announced Jane's identification with that early moment in Christian history when, in Jane's mind, followers of Jesus' teachings comprised a democratic counterculture. The starkly simple Chi-Rho that Jane wore did not incorporate the alpha omega symbol, a later assertion of Jesus's divinity. Nor did her Chi-Rho cross gesture to Constantine, who carried the symbol into battle as a sign of conquest. As a student of Tolstoy, Jane regarded Constantine's legalization of Christianity, and his violent use of it, as a tragic distortion of "the spirit of the whole doctrine" which Jesus meant to convey. For her, the brooch was symbolic of the pre-Constantinian era, as well as a pre-crucifix era, when Jesus was a guide to peaceful love in this life, not disembodied salvation in the next.[77]

The influence of Tolstoy was evident throughout the Christian portion of "Subjective Necessity" but was made explicit in Jane's discussion of the key principle of "non-resistance." There, for the first time in her career, she devised language that set forth her concurrence with Tolstoy's belief that Christ taught "the futility of opposition." Evil, Jane explained, "can be overcome only with good and cannot be opposed." "If love is the creative force of the universe," she declared, "the principle which binds men together, and by their interdependence on each other makes them human, just so surely is anger and the spirit

30. Jane Addams wearing the Chi-Rho cross in early 1890s. (University of Illinois at Chicago, University Library, Jane Addams Memorial Collection, neg. no. 13)

of opposition the destructive principle of the universe, that which tears down, thrusts men apart, and makes them isolated and brutal."[78]

It is unfortunate that this did not become the most quoted phrase in "Subjective Necessity" because greater attention to this stubborn pacifist principle might have saved Jane Addams's friends and foes a lot of trouble in their struggles to align her with partisan causes. As it was, however, the most quoted passage from the speech came from her discussion of the "democratic" motives for the settlement movement. There Jane wrote the lines that reporter after reporter would cite in the coming years to describe her Chicago project: "Hull House," she explained, "endeavors to make social intercourse express the growing sense of the economic unity of society. It is an effort to add the social function to democracy."[79]

These two sentences had the benefit of endowing Hull-House with a secular, civic mission in countless press profiles, but just how much real sense readers could make of those phrases when extracted from the whole speech is hard to say. Jane's point, in the context of "Subjective Necessity," was that universal male enfranchisement was not, alone, sufficient to create a democracy in which participation by each citizen had genuine meaning. "To make the entire social organism democratic," she argued, "to extend democracy beyond its political expression," required the experience of social intercourse across class, race, sex, religion, and ethnicity. The necessity for such intercourse was heightened in modern industrial life where a complex national economic system meant that disparate peoples were truly dependent upon one another for survival but were increasingly isolated from one another by culture and wealth. Since social relations were inherently reciprocal, Jane reasoned, and since modern life demanded that people grasp their essential interdependence, the creation of social spaces in which people from different backgrounds could come to know one another was the optimal method for addressing the alienation of modern life. Hence the need to "add the social function to democracy."[80]

In an earlier speech to the Chicago Women's Club, Jane had attempted to gender this analysis by suggesting that women mistakenly assumed that, because they were disenfranchised, their command over social life had no bearing on democracy.[81] In another speech before the Sunset Club she had argued that women's assignment to social life specially fitted them for this key role in democracy.[82] These lines of argument, of course, served to justify women's participation in nongovernmental but avowedly prodemocratic work, such as social settlement work, but Jane chose not to mount that justification in Plymouth or to say much at all about the woman question. In discussing "civic life" at Hull-House, she made a nod to those who doubted "women can be said to perform civic duties," but it was a very slight nod.[83] Even her discussion of youth's disaffection with wealth and leisure expanded beyond the plight of daughters to include all "young people" of the privileged class.[84] In a rhetorical bit of nonresistance to sexism, Jane followed the same strategy in these Plymouth speeches that she had used in her "Bread Givers" speech a dozen years earlier: she affirmed what women were doing; she did not argue over what they were denied.

Read as a statement of principle, "The Subjective Necessity for Social Settlements" was an exquisite piece of work. Each part of the speech lyrically captured ideas that Jane had been working over for years, and she took this opportunity to fit them together into a conceptual whole that was consistent, accessible, and engaging. The speech represented, as well, the final Americanization of the settlement concept. Jane moved it from Samuel Barnett's Anglican interest in establishing a "broad church" and asserted its logic as a political instrument in a democratic nation with universal, albeit male, enfranchisement. Almost two decades later, she was still pleased enough with the speech to include it as a chapter in her autobiography, offsetting the appearance of pride by remarking that it was "too late in the day to express regret for its stilted title."[85]

In the summer of 1892, Jane delivered the speech to an audience of about seventy people, the average number that had been attending the Plymouth lecture series. Its impact can be measured by the fact that one hundred and fifty people showed up the next day to hear her second address. According to one reporter covering the applied ethics lectures, "the modest and sensible, yet inspiring lecturer from Chicago" proved to be "the most attractive"of all the speakers in the course. "The impression she makes as you hear her unemphatic but convincing tones," wrote another audience member, was of someone with both "the quiet force of her sex, but also with the invincible energy for which Chicago is noted."[86]

The crowd that turned out for "The Objective Value of a Social Settlement" was not gifted with as coherent a speech as the one delivered the day before. This second speech, hastily crafted and conceptually awkward, bears the strained sound of Jane Addams in transition. Just six months after Florence Kelley's arrival at Hull-House, Jane could not rest easy with what Ellen called the "snare" of their success; she honestly shared Ellen's sense of "just how painfully too little of the real thing . . . there is in it."[87] To address that problem, Jane devoted the first part of "Objective Value" to a bleak portrait of that segment of the Nineteenth Ward population which her settlement was only beginning to serve. Jane drew on Kelley's new research to describe the ward's filth, disease, and poverty, using terms and details she had never before used in a public address. To drive home the terrible human effects of those conditions, she tried out an uncharacteristically dismal portrayal of the drunken, sordid, ignorant types roaming the streets of her neighborhood.[88] In the mouth of a Florence Kelley or Henry Demarest Lloyd, such grim descriptions served as an effective prelude to attacking the greed of exploitive capitalists. Attack was not Jane's mode, however, so a third of the way into the talk, she was rhetorically and conceptually stranded between her description of an outrageous set of circumstances and her publicly stated belief that "anger" and the "spirit of opposition" are "destructive."

Life at Hull-House did not leave Jane much time to devise either the positive language or the constructive solutions that would be both responsive to the toughest problems on Halsted Street and consistent with Jane's own ethical convictions. So "Objective Value," a speech that may well have been written on the eastbound train, fell back from its dark opening onto familiar, sunny terrain: an engaging, upbeat description of Hull-House classes and clubs and the sober, hard-working, ambitious neighbors who took advantage of them.[89] Jane had delivered versions of that part of the speech around Chicago many times before; it captured the settlement she had set out to create: a gracious comingling of those possessing culture and education with those who were anxious to have culture and education.

Her audience at Plymouth did not grasp the disconnect between the two parts of the speech, but Jane did. She tried to return to those neighbors "who are too battered and oppressed" to care about clubs and classes by noting that the settlement "acts between" the ward's most needy and the charity world that "is apt to lace itself up in certain formulas . . . forgetting the mystery and complexity of life."[90] But neither charity, nor Jane's critique of it, was an answer to the problems she had laid out. "I am sorry we have not more to present in the line of civic activities," she confessed to her Plymouth audience in the summer before the antisweatshop campaign and the passage of the Illinois factory law.[91] All she could offer was a halting discussion of the settlement's relationship with the trade union movement, one that revealed, again, the conflict between Jane's desire to be true to her neighbors and to her own convictions about mutuality. Though proud that the settlement was known as a place that "stood by working people," Jane still held back from fully aligning with partisan labor unions against employers. After describing the urban industrial horrors that surrounded her on Halsted Street, all she could bring herself to say, in the summer of 1892, was that it was "logical that a Settlement should have a certain value in labor complications, having from its very position sympathies entangled on both sides."[92]

Jane had welcomed Florence Kelley on board to increase the settlement's "value in labor complications" and she shared Florence's outrage, and Ellen's

31. In her second lecture at the School for Applied Economics in 1892, Jane Addams struggled to express the "objective value" of a settlement in the Hull-House neighborhood, where immigrant families such as this one labored to make ends meet. (University of Illinois at Chicago, University Library, Jane Addams Memorial Collection, neg. no. 275)

outrage, at the wage exploitation underlying those complications. But her voice was more relaxed and authentic in "Objective Value" when she spoke of the "tolerance" gained through cross-class dialogue in the Working People's Social Science Club than when she tried to strike chords of anger better suited to other vocal temperaments.[93] The muddiness of "Objective Value,"compared with the clear message of love and interdependence in "Subjective Necessity," testifies to the challenge Jane faced in reconciling her daily contact with economic oppression and her philosophical commitment to loving fellowship and nonresistance as instruments for social change.

No one at the time pointed out these problems. *Forum* magazine, a prominent Eastern journal, published Jane Addams's two speeches in its October and November issues in 1892, and that exposure catapulted her to national prominence.[94] There was a large and growing population of Americans, stretching across a continuum of classes, ethnicities, and ideologies, who resonated to arguments for interdependence and cooperation. This population of working-class and middle-class people were tired of the smug individualism of the Gilded Age, feared that the harsh rigidities of social Darwinism would produce class warfare, and admired those taking concrete steps to reinvigorate democracy in urban, industrial America. Even with a flawed speech, Jane Addams spoke to that population in more practical, accessible terms than the vast majority of those who shared her philosophy. On the eve of the great depression of 1893 and the Pullman strike of 1894, the dual events that would galvanize this restive population to launch a progressive "era" in America, Jane Addams appeared to be one of the most appealing stars in the reform firmament.

Chapter 15

What We Know Is Right

Writing against the record of her growing fame and popularity, Jane Addams recalled the 1890s as a time of such heated debate between labor and capital that her advocacy of tolerant mediation satisfied no one. In a counter to those who dismissed hers as the easy success of the temporizer, Jane described how her "desire to bear independent witness to social righteousness often resulted in a sense of compromise difficult to endure, and at many times it seemed to me that we were destined to alienate everybody." Rather than argue with the critics of her nonpartisanship in her 1910 autobiography, Jane confided that she had "longed for the comfort of a definite social creed" in the 1890s and that she would have "been most grateful at that time to accept the tenets of socialism." It was conscience, not the desire to please, that held her back; she felt "compelled to defend the confusion arising from the clashing of free wills as an alternative to acceptance" of any deterministic doctrine.[1] And if her partisan critics, reading the autobiography, felt the rhetorical impact of that nonresistant punch, then her point was made.

This compulsion to "bear independent witness" proved as vexing for Jane's colleagues in Chicago as it had for Miss Sill at Rockford Seminary. In both places, Jane's work was unassailable, her commitment to the common good was unimpeachable, her charisma as a leader undeniable. But in both places, she declined to line up ideologically, preferring to place her faith in process rather than outcomes. Ever since Rockford, Jane had suffered for her disinterestedness, always feeling that she had her nose pressed up against the window of faith, destined to watch others celebrate their partisan creeds and victories. As she would confess after World War I, pacifism gave her a crushing sense of "aloneness," a sense that she was "curiously outside the enchantment given to any human emotion when it is shared by millions of others."[2] Against all the pressure to join one camp or another, and that pressure was considerable, Jane held fast to her humanistic Christianity, her nonresistant method, and her democratic commitment to finding common ground on which all contestants could stand in mutual agreement on peaceful process.

Jane's stance, which appeared cowardly to some, drew on all her reserves of courage. At Rockford, after she had worked out a compromise with Miss Sill over the campus magazine, her friend Mary Downs assured her, "You *are* progressive, Jane, you have not disappointed my anticipations."[3] But she did disappoint the anticipations of dedicated partisans in the early 1890s, at the start of the "progressive era." It took the crucible of the depression of 1893 and the Pullman strike of 1894 to forge in Jane the language she needed to confront those disappointments and demonstrate that her position resulted not from political timidity but philosophical toughness. The firm line Jane adopted made clear that she regarded no one, including herself, as blameless for the social and economic problems America faced, and that she exempted no one from finding democratic, peaceable solutions. In the rough and tumble of events in the early 1890s, her stubborn even-handedness was at once admirable and immensely irritating.

Jane's autobiography included socially conscious Christians among those to whom Hull-House offered a neutral meeting ground "to consider the social question," but press reports from the time suggest that these Christians hoped Jane Addams was anything but neutral about their cause.[4] Adherents to the emerging "social gospel" movement, that effort to expand religious attention beyond individual salvation and toward social salvation, sought to include Jane in their ranks.[5] The Hull-House scrapbooks from this moment are full of glowing articles by liberal Christians intent on persuading their coreligionists that Jane Addams was "an earnest Christian" and, therefore, Christians could learn "some exceedingly important lessons" from her work about how to make the gospel "a manifestation as well as a word."[6] In opposition to those conservatives who dismissed Hull-House because it did not preach the gospel, Jane's Christian defenders pointed to the Plymouth speeches in the *Forum* as proof that she stood for "the same idea which the carpenter of Nazareth first uttered," that she represented "what our Lord meant by being a neighbor," that her living sermon was the deed of love, "the ultimate mission of the New Jerusalem."[7]

Traditional Christians insisted that secular settlements like Hull-House were "necessarily antagonistic to Christianity and religion" because they aimed "at worldly results only" and did not bring their neighbors to Christ.[8] But Protestants and Catholics who wished to move their congregations toward greater engagement with social problems pointed to Jane Addams as an exemplar of Christ's teaching on "the cosmic force of Love" and insisted that she was a true Christian precisely because she did not proselytize. One Presbyterian minister pointed approvingly to Jane's claim that "it would simply be a foolish and unwarrantable expenditure of force to oppose or antagonize any individual or set of people in the neighborhood" by preaching a specific faith; the settlement's value, he argued, depended on the residents living in "opposition to no man, with recognition of the good in every man."[9]

While many advocates of the social gospel accepted the practical wisdom of this latitudinarian policy in the operation of settlements like Hull-House, they still wanted to believe that Jane Addams herself, in her heart of hearts, was a believing Christian. A writer for the Congregational journal, *Advance*, understood, in 1892, that Hull-House had to mute its sectarian leanings out of deference to the neighbors, but predicted that once local trust was gained, Christ would perform a more prominent role in the life of the settlement. "It is hardly likely," thought the *Advance* reporter, "that such persons as Miss Addams" would be "permanently satisfied with any play of Hamlet with Hamlet left out."[10]

Such was Jane's reputation that Christian proponents of the social gospel thought it benefited their cause to claim her as one of their own. But wishing could not make it so. Jane did not simply refuse to impose Christian beliefs on her neighbors, she declined to identify with organized Christianity herself, even questioning whether Jesus intended his humanistic philosophy to become a religion.[11] Had Jane identified with organized Christianity in these years, the record would be very different than it is—and her relationship with Ellen, and with other Christian women in the national settlement movement, would have been less strained.

Vida Scudder, for example, was Jane's colleague in the settlement movement, but never her friend or ally. Scudder, the Boston-based founder of the College Settlement Association, aligned much more closely with Ellen in both her earthly and spiritual devotions. As members of the Episcopal Order of the Holy Cross who shared a commitment to Christian Socialism, Ellen and Vida Scudder inhabited a philosophical universe that was light years away from Jane's.[12] Like other believing Christians, their language was rich with obedient references to "Him," "His will," and "the Master," terminology that Jane never employed because she followed a teaching, not a teacher. Scudder, like Ellen and most other Christians of the time, set the spiritual world apart from, and above, the physical world, while Jane presumed one inhered in the other. In fact, Scudder conceded to the social Darwinist view that the laws of nature were "inexorable" in their cruelty but offered up the mystical mercy of Christ to reverse those laws. By contrast, Jane believed that kindness and cooperation were "primordial" and that Jesus set about to remind people of the goodness of their own nature, not to rescue them from the clutches of an enemy nature. So while Ellen and Scudder sought to transcend human nature through prayer and ritual, Jane struggled to become fully human through unconditional love of her fellows, believing that achievement would be transcendence enough.[13]

Surprisingly enough, Jane led private religious observances at Hull-House, perhaps in deference to Ellen and other Christian residents like Clifford Barnes. As late as November 1893, the Residents' Minutes included an announcement by "Miss Addams" that "devotions would be held as usual at nine o'clock on Sunday evening and that attendance would not be obligatory."[14] Edward Burchard, a resident in the early 1890s, could recall those Sunday evening meetings of "Bible and prayer with every one on their knees." Rummaging around in his memory over forty years later, however, Burchard made a telling error: he assumed that the Bible meetings ended before Florence Kelley arrived in late 1891, suggesting some association in his mind between a decline in Christian observance at Hull-House and a rise in Kelley's influence.[15] Religious expression was not, however, ended by Kelley; other influences muted the prayers at Hull-House.

The United States went into the most serious economic depression it had ever known in the fall of 1893, and the experience registered in Jane's religious life as it registered in the lives of others who felt the church responded inadequately to this crisis. Rather than inspiring her to follow Ellen into Christian Socialism, Jane's reaction was to distance herself further from organized Christianity.[16] Technically, she was a member of the Ewing Street Congregational Church, but the scant evidence of her participation is a survey from the depression year 1894 in which she voiced the "desire to have the work of the church more closely cooperative with Hull House"—not the other way around.[17] That same year, she joined with Rabbi E. G. Hirsch, William Salter of the Ethical Culture Society, and Jenkin Lloyd Jones of the All Souls' Unitarian Church in calling for a Congress of Liberal Religions—dedicated to the "great law of life and love"—to meet at Chicago's Sinai temple.[18]

It was also in the spring of 1894, after she had witnessed months of bitter hardship living in a ward devastated by the depression, that Jane attended a meeting of Congregational ministers in Oak Park, a comfortable Chicago suburb. There she dealt rather sharply with those clergymen who were "not satisfied" with her answers on "the religious attitude of Hull House." Asked by one of the "more orthodox of her hearers" if she thought a church could successfully undertake settlement work, she replied, "that all depends upon what kind of people comprise the church." Asked if Hull-House took the place of the church, Jane had to "confess that there is in my mind a little ecclesiastical confusion with regard to the meaning of the word church."[19] Rescued from further self-incrimination when an admiring minister from Quincy, Illinois, closed off questioning to praise Hull-House, Jane departed the tree-lined streets of Oak Park and returned home to the bustling decay of Halsted Street, where she faced absolutely no demand to align herself with any religious organization.

Back at Hull-House, Jane was free to contemplate the words of her new friend and colleague William T. Stead, the flamboyant British journalist and social gospel advocate whose book *If Christ Came to Chicago* had just been published.[20] Stead had mounted a harsh attack on the city's wealthy industrialists, corrupt politicians, and leading clergy for so neglecting civic health that Chicago's masses were vulnerable to the devastation wrought by the depression of 1893. Stead spoke of the need for a "Civic Church" with a "determined worker" at its nucleus who could "resolve that he or she, as the case may be, will never rest until the whole community is brought up to the standard of the most advanced societies." In Stead's judgment, Jane Addams's Hull-House represented Chicago's best hope for such a "civic church."[21]

The depression of 1893–94 had begun at the end of a dizzying year that opened with millions of tourists pouring into Chicago for the World's Columbian Exposition and closed with tens of thousands of unemployed workers wandering the city's streets. It was a year that tested Jane's commitment to nonpartisanship; she chose to stand firmly "on the side of unions" but insisted on independence in that alignment.[22]

Chicago's leaders were thrilled when the city won the bid to host the four hundedth anniversary celebration of Christopher Columbus's journey to the "New World." That victory made official Chicago's status as a major American metropolis, and the city made the most of the opportunity to show off for the 27.5 million admissions to the Columbian Exposition between May and October 1893. With its ornate, immaculate "White City" of two hundred white plaster buildings in neoclassical style on 600 acres along Lake Michigan, the "fair" stylistically evoked an imagined past of European empire. Inside the buildings, manicured exhibits of scientific, technological, and industrial innovation proclaimed the triumph of the New World's wealth and social order.[23] For Jane Addams, however, the fair was less about celebrating industrial triumph than about reaching for unrealized democratic ideals.

Her memory of the fair was forever colored by the economic hardships that followed in its wake, but Jane's focus before the event was on mundane logistical preparations for an onslaught of visitors. Hull-House had become "a kind of Mecca for philanthropists," and thousands toured the settlement while visiting the fair in the summer of 1893.[24] In addition, Jane wished to house colleagues from East Coast settlement houses, even opening up new flats in the Jane Club to meet the demand.[25] She was anxious, as well, for her family to partake of the excitement of the fair. Anna claimed to Harry that she was "glad" not to have received "the least hint of an invitation" to the fair from any of her stepdaughters, but it seems just as likely that she brushed off invitations because she could not leave George alone in Cedarville without any household help. For the previous two years, George had taken private refuge in a deafening silence that was, according to Harry, "absolute and without reason," making it "impossible to give relief and assistance." Anna's relief when George broke his silence that summer was offset by her despair over his refusal to bathe and his "turns of bilious diarrhea."[26]

Excursions to the fair were equally hard for Laura to arrange since Weber Addams had been readmitted to the Elgin Asylum for the Insane in late 1892 and would remain there until the Exposition festivities were almost over.[27] Squeezing visits to Weber between publication of her *Forum* articles and her speaking tour of Eastern women's colleges, Jane negotiated with Alice about when she and six-year-old Marcet might come to the fair. Ever since Jane had snapped at Alice's "fussiness" about exposing Marcet to the filth on Halsted Street—telling her that "the idea of its not being sanitary" was "perfectly absurd"—the whole matter of visits from Alice and Marcet had been delicate.[28] Perhaps Alice was moved by Ellen's letter wishing "we might have a long beautiful visit like those Mrs. Linn pays us" and hoping she could get the chance to know Marcet as well as she knew the "Linnets."[29] However clumsy that lobbying effort, it certainly testifies to the difference between the Linn family's regular involvement with Hull-House and Alice's infrequent appearances there.

In June 1893, a month after the fair's official opening, Alice and Marcet did join the Linns at Hull-House while Harry stayed home in Kansas writing bitter letters to Anna about "Miss Jane Addams" giving lectures "on god knows what."[30] Anna's real or imagined exclusion from her stepdaughters' reunion at the fair left her complaining that she could not go unless Harry "should open your heart to come and go with me and take care of me."[31] He did not oblige and, once again, travel plans provided a map of filial fault lines.

Family tensions, however, were the least of Jane's problems in the run up to the fair. There were other conflicts to be negotiated—or avoided. Indeed, Jane's experiences with the fair's Congress of Social Settlements, its World's Congress of Representative Women, and its Labor Congress reveal her talent for dodging skirmishes over gender discrimination, settlement ideology, and labor politics. By 1893, journalists were already referring to the head of Hull-House as "Saint Jane."[32] It was a title that captured her ability to rise above the fray but one that had the potential to annoy those fractious colleagues who could well resent Jane's diplomatic neutrality.

Unlike scores of her friends in the Chicago Women's Club, including Ellen Henrotin and Mary Wilmarth, Jane was not deeply involved in the female bureaucracy established by the fair's male directors to manage the exhibits of women's industrial and cultural accomplishments.[33] As a result, Jane avoided the fierce wrangle between the official Board of Lady Managers, led by the wealthy socialite Bertha Honore Palmer, and the unofficial Queen Isabella

Association, led by suffragists like Eliza Starr, Ellen's aunt. Jane took no part in their debate over whether women's exhibits should be displayed alongside men's, which was the suffragist position, or segregated in a separate woman's building, which was Bertha Palmer's position.[34] It was not the physical exhibits but the educational conferences run by the World's Congress Auxiliary that engaged Jane's attention. There, she sidestepped the sexism that clouded other women's participation at the fair by focusing on the Congress of Social Settlements, where Jane Addams was officially recognized as the chair of the congress and where women and men were notably integrated in their committee work and on all panels. Jane enjoyed immunity from the fair's patriarchal rules about where women could speak and how many women could speak simply because of her status in the then-small, predominantly female world of social settlements, where no man in the country outranked Jane Addams.[35]

The Congress of Social Settlements was intended to advertise to the world the promise and achievements of this nascent social movement in America, and no one challenged Jane Addams's authority—or home court advantage— in organizing the Chicago event. Robert Woods, the head resident of Andover House in Boston, and the man Jane later defined as "the natural leader" of the young settlement movement, deferred to Jane's planning on the grounds that she was "doing the best piece of social work that is being done anywhere in the country."[36]

Woods, along with Vida Scudder, had shared the platform with Jane at the Plymouth meeting and, along with Scudder, had witnessed the excitement over Jane's talks in contrast to the polite reception for their less engaging lectures.[37] Scudder nursed a lifelong jealousy toward the popularity of the unsanctified, nonsocialist Jane Addams, who had opened her "social" settlement weeks after Scudder opened her "college" settlement but was still regarded, even among Scudder's own students, as "quite the grandmother of American settlements." Woods, on the other hand, recognized the value of having Jane's attractive public face associated with the settlement movement and respected her talents.[38]

As a Christian, Woods admitted that he was anxious to show "that settlement work is itself religious," but he was careful to "merely suggest" to Addams that the fair's settlement conference begin with a Sunday evening church service led by a member of the social gospel clergy. Jane was amenable to the plan, even helpful, and Woods was reciprocally encouraging of secular parts of the program.[39] By contrast, Scudder, who claimed that the "religious aspect" of settlement work "has always been primary with me," made the unchristian assumption that Jane would think religion "an unwise subject to handle" at the fair. The professor from Wellesley then begged off discussing college women and settlement work at the Chicago congress—the very topic Jane had discussed at Scudder's campus—because, sniped Scudder, the subject "rather bores me."[40] Jane was willing to have Scudder discuss anything she wished, but, in the end, Scudder managed Jane's irritating unflappability by not attending the fair at all.[41]

So it was that the Christian Socialist Vida Scudder missed hearing other Christian settlement workers argue against in-house Christian proselytizing. She missed, as well, the "delightful" evening when "socialistic" labor unionists embarrassed Jane by collectively singing her "earnest praise." In one tribute, Mary Kenney, who had become an American Federation of Labor organizer, joked that "during her residence at Hull House she would have had to *consider* the proposition to leave it for heaven."[42] Having risen above potential conflicts within the Congress of Social Settlements, Jane reigned over the event, serving "as one," said Woods, "who stands in responsibility to the various phases of settlement activity."[43]

The Social Settlement Congress occurred in July, between Jane's participation in the World's Congress of Representative Women in May and her appearance at the Labor Congress in late August. At these two other fair congresses, Jane chose not to be "confined" to the subject of social settlements but to speak, instead, on the issue of female labor—specifically on the question of domestic servants and their employers.[44] Even as Harry was sourly musing to Anna about what "Miss Jane Addams" could possibly be lecturing on at the fair, Jane was drawing on her experience as the stepdaughter of a woman who was ever in search of "a good housekeeper" to mount an argument for more businesslike, mutual, democratic relationships between household employers and employees. In calling for a more modern organization of household work, Jane used this pair of congress speeches to address issues raised by the failure of Florence Kelley's Household Labor Bureau and the failure of the New England Kitchen.

In these two speeches, Jane was, at last, able to resolve her multiple desires to present workers as agents (without blaming them for their plight), to insist on mutuality in all economic relations, and to strike a note that was unsentimental but not bitter. In contrast to her "Objective Value" speech at Plymouth, where Jane's voice got caught between grim anger and sunny nostrums, her discussion of the outdated organization and "belated ethics" governing household labor was pitched in the middle range of matter-of-fact tones that suited her temperament and philosophy.

With an ethnographer's eye, Jane sketched a three-dimensional, life-size portrait of the "working girl," something that was largely missing from all of the fair's sappy tributes to female labor.[45] This young working woman was a rational actor calculating the difference between autonomy and sociability in modern factory work and servility and isolation in "feudal" domestic work. Pitted against the working girl was the household employer, who Jane diagnosed as "curiously" unable to see that her own desires for family life, privacy, and dignity were held as dear by domestic servants. Employers were equally blind to fact that live-in service was an antiquated practice of a pre-industrial, predemocratic era. Jane was diplomatic in defining only live-in service as outdated in her talk to the Women's Congress and more direct about the need for public, communal kitchens from which women could purchase ready-made meals at the Labor Congress, but the two talks shared a clear, authentic articulation of one overarching labor principle: that employers look at the world from the workers' standpoint and understand that the same ethical rules and human desires govern the behavior of all human beings, regardless of class.[46]

In all of the backstage battles that accompanied the World's Columbian Exposition, the one fight Jane could not avoid was that between the labor activists, including Henry Demarest Lloyd and Florence Kelley, who wanted a hard-hitting Labor Congress, and the fair's elite directors, who did not. In solidarity with her friends, Jane did sign an angry letter of protest, but when the dust settled and a compromise was worked out, she joined Lloyd and Kelley on the Labor Congress program. Later, Jane obliquely exacted revenge by feigning ignorance when Bertha Palmer sought her help in reaching Terence Powderly of the Knights of Labor. Jane was not about to use her labor contacts to aid the antilabor, antisuffrage Mrs. Palmer. It was one of those very small acts in Jane's life that blurred the distinction between her belief in nonresistance and her capacity for passive aggression.[47]

The year 1893 marked both the Columbian Exposition and passage of Illinois's landmark Factory and Inspection Act. In her enthusiasm over this tremendous victory, Florence Kelley predicted that "a year hence," the beautiful fair would be "only a charming memory," but decades into the future people would remember 1893 as the start of a new and better day for American workers.[48] Even as she spoke those optimistic words in late summer, the economic collapse that began with overleveraged businesses in the East was already rolling toward Chicago. Before the fair was over, economic troubles were evident everywhere. The city's mayor, Carter Harrison, pleaded with the U.S. Congress to keep the fair open beyond October 30 in order to avert massive unemployment, but to no avail. Thousands of workers demonstrated just outside the fairgrounds, demanding food and jobs, and 25,000 protesters attended a labor rally on the lakefront. The assassination of Mayor Harrison on October 29 heightened the sense of crisis in a city where 20 percent of the citizens were without work. By the end of summer, homeless mothers were starting to bed down with their babies in the Hull-House nursery school, and by December the settlement had opened a shelter for domestic servants "left stranded" when the fair closed down.[49]

Jane wrote to Mary Rozet Smith, who had embarked for Europe, that "it takes something of an effort in these hard times to keep up our spirits, our neighbors are so forlorn and literally flock to the house for work." Hull-House had long resisted the role of "relief station," but in the waning days of 1893 the situation was dire and the residents expended "a good deal of effort" just to keep their neighbors "from going under." Jane now participated on citywide charity committees, hoping to "do things more systematically this winter than is usual in Chicago."[50] As the lean winter dragged on into spring, Jane confessed to Alice that she felt "pressed" as never before: "We have known nothing like it in the history of Hull House."[51] Grateful to her old friend Sarah Anderson for sending an extra check in June, Jane observed that they had suffered a budgetary "leak" that year because of "the huge amount given in relief to our neighbors."[52] And just as she was moved by Sarah's thoughtfulness, she was "touched by the goodness of our neighbors to each other and their sweet attitude toward us." The effect of the depression, Jane thought, had been to draw the neighbors together, "like trouble in a family."[53]

That sense of close connection to her neighborhood was palpable in November 1893 when Jane appeared before the all-male Sunset Club to answer their question: "What Shall We Do for Our Unemployed?" After explaining that the residents of Hull-House had always known people who were unemployed, people who were destitute, Jane observed that it was an altogether different matter when "the majority of your acquaintances are out of work," when people who had sent their children to Hull-House clubs, enjoyed settlement social gatherings, participated in classes, lectures, and art gallery events were suddenly paupers, made desperate in a matter of weeks. What should the governing class do with such people? Jane's answer was consistent with everything she had seen and learned and said in the previous four years: "Take them into our confidence. . . . They are men; they have practical ideas; they would be glad to do their share to remove the trouble, of which they are the chief victims. We ought to come together and regard it as a common trouble, and we should consider not what shall we do with the unemployed, but what shall we and the unemployed do together, that we may all as brothers grow out into a wider and better citizenship than we have ever yet had."[54]

The Gilded Age gentlemen of the Sunset Club were not uniformly hostile to this message. Just days after hearing Jane's words, a number of the club members attended a revival-like mass meeting called by British journalist William Stead in the Central Music Hall. Throughout the afternoon and into the evening, the most enlightened members of the city's business elite sat alongside workers, club women, socialists, anarchists, temperance workers, saloonkeepers, lawyers, judges, clergy, ward bosses, and Hull-House residents. Together, they listened to speech after speech denouncing the moral corruptions and economic inequities laid bare by the depression and demanding democratic reforms in civic life.[55]

As a result of that tumultuous gathering, at which Jane spoke to the crowd on "Life in the Social Depths," forty leading figures in Chicago formed the Civic Federation. The Federation was a sincere, if genteel, attempt to energize "the public conscience of Chicago" and apply "new ideas" from "the great Exposition" to urban, industrial problems.[56] Henry Demarest Lloyd shunned the organization because of its probusiness respectability, but Jane could not resist the Federation's promise to "serve as a medium of acquaintance and sympathy" between the diverse members of the Chicago community.[57] She promptly joined her friends Jenkin Lloyd Jones, Ellen Henrotin, Mary Wilmarth, Frank Gunsaulus, even Bertha Palmer, in a federation of interlocking committees assigned to specific civic issues.[58] Jane chose not to join the Federation's Philanthropic Committee, whose immediate concern was relief for those devastated by the winter's economic depression. Nor did she join the Municipal Committee, whose focus was corruption in city hall, or the Moral Committee, whose concern was urban vice. By February 1894, Jane had enrolled with the Civic Federation's Industrial Committee, whose task was to harmonize labor relations in Chicago by encouraging cooperation and arbitration between workers and employers. Within three months, she was serving on the Federation's Conciliation Board, a special body created to encourage arbitration of the springtime strike that had erupted down at George Pullman's railway car manufacturing plant, just south of Chicago.[59]

Reports of labor trouble at the Pullman Palace Car Company drew particular attention in Chicago because George Pullman had cultivated a reputation as an enlightened employer. Alongside the plant he had built in the early 1880s to manufacture his famous sleeper cars, Pullman had also built a town with over 1,400 residences to house much of the plant's workforce. His paternalistic retort to the fatalistic social Darwinists was that sober, reliable, productive labor could be molded by a good environment. Like the Whig stewards of Senator John Addams's generation, Pullman intended to prove that an employer could do well and do good; he could achieve harmony with his workers, guarantee his investors an 8 percent annual dividend, and still earn a 5 percent profit on rents from company housing.[60]

The Pullman Company was not immune to the effects of the nationwide depression of 1893. Having built 300 extra cars to transport tourists to, from, and around the Columbian Exposition, the company was left with a glutted inventory and few orders for new cars. Between July and November of 1893, Pullman laid off 3,400 of its 4,500 workers and cut the wages of those remaining by as much as 40 percent. A few contracts early in 1894 allowed the company to begin hiring again, but wages stayed at depression levels. The sticking point for the workers was that Pullman refused to reduce rents in company housing to reflect either the wage decline or the rent reductions in adjacent towns. Instead, the company's layoff and rehiring policies gave preference to those who agreed to live in Pullman town and pay Pullman's high rents out of Pullman's low wages. Because George Pullman had postured as such a benevolent employer, these policies left the workers feeling doubly exploited and doubly betrayed. In desperation, they turned to the American Railway Union (ARU) for aid in organizing a union that could negotiate with Pullman over the workers' grievances.[61]

On May 9, 1894, the day that the local ARU delegation met with George Pullman to discuss wages and rents, Jane was in Madison, Wisconsin, speaking before the university's School of Economics.[62] Her host for the day was Richard Ely, the prolabor economist and social gospel Christian whom Jane had not met at Johns Hopkins University, back in their overlapping Baltimore days, but who was now her friend and colleague. There was no one better equipped to give Jane a tutorial on the Pullman Company and on George Pullman's company town than Ely. He had written "Pullman: A Social Study" for *Harper's* in 1885 in which he carefully praised the physical accoutrements that George Pullman provided for his workers but criticized the town's "benevolent, well-wishing feudalism," which denied workers the right to own homes in Pullman much less the right to any form of democratic government or labor organizing.[63] Riding in a comfortable Pullman car from Madison to Chicago on May 10, Jane had time to ponder Richard Ely's view that the good intentions of George Pullman constituted a paternalistic intrusion on American workers' democratic freedoms.[64] Arriving home, Jane learned that the company had fired the members of the ARU delegation who had met with Pullman, and three thousand angry workers had promptly walked off the job.

As a member of the Civic Federation's special Board of Conciliation, Jane devoted her energies from mid-May through mid-June to investigating arbitration possibilities. She met with workers down in Pullman and learned that they were "very friendly toward the notion of arbitration."[65] During her meeting with the ARU's local officers, her tour of the workers' homes, and her supper with some of the female employees, Jane learned that the company houses that looked so pretty on the outside were crowded with families who took in boarders to pay the rent, that the management of the Pullman Company had taken no cut in salary during the depression, and that the stockholders had received their full dividend payment in that year of economic disaster.[66] Surely there was a way to negotiate a more equitable distribution of the pain among all the Pullman players.

Jane's one experience successfully negotiating a two-day labor walkout by a few young women at a neighborhood knitting works had not prepared her for the likes of George Pullman.[67] He may have shared her father's faith in doing good while doing well, but he did not agree with Senator Addams that the community had a legitimate role to play in regulating business. Pullman held firm to his Gilded Age belief that no one—not workers, not civic reformers, not the state—had any right to tell him how to manage his company.[68] By June 1 the *Chicago Mail* was reporting that George Pullman had ignored Jane's letters asking for arbitration. And when Jane attempted to visit with the company's vice president, Thomas Wickes, on June 1, she was rudely snubbed and left to cool her heels in the company's foyer. When Wickes finally received Jane the next day, he flatly informed her that there was "nothing to arbitrate."[69]

The strike had become not only a struggle between "one of the great monopolies on earth and the most powerful organization in railway labor," but a test, as well, of the "moral force" of bodies like the Civic Federation to intervene in such struggles and negotiate a peace. Jane labored mightily to justify the existence of her Board of Conciliation, meeting once with Eugene Debs, the president of the ARU, and traveling again, alone, to Pullman for an evening meeting in mid-June with sixty delegates from the local union. But George Pullman was intransigent, and Jane's efforts were all for naught. As she said in her August testimony before the presidentially appointed United States Strike Commission, it was "impossible to come to any understanding with the Pullman company" on the matter of arbitration, "and it was dropped." In the end, said Addams, "we considered the effort a failure."[70]

In the months following the Pullman strike, the Civic Federation would try to redeem itself by sponsoring a two-day Congress on Industrial Conciliation and Arbitration and then persuading the Illinois General Assembly to establish a state Board of Conciliation and Arbitration. It was a purely symbolic victory since the state board could mediate disputes only when both parties agreed, but the establishment of the board represented progress for the principle of voluntary, civilized arbitration between workers and employers, and that represented movement away from the Gilded Age's assertion of individual power and toward the Progressive Era's assertion of collective will.[71]

As the Pullman strike contorted into those violent spasms that often signal the shift from one era to another, Jane watched helplessly. Events in late June and early July unfolded with dizzying speed and tragic results. In response to George Pullman's intransigence, the ARU, on June 21, launched a national boycott of all trains carrying Pullman cars. Within days, the U.S. rail system was stalled and snarled, the government charged the ARU with blocking mail service, and fourteen thousand armed federal agents were deployed to Chicago alone. Masses of unemployed workers battled with troops at railway yards, a dozen people were killed, hundreds were arrested, the U.S. attorney general under President Cleveland issued injunctions, the ARU was effectively immobilized, and Eugene Debs was jailed. By July 11, the workers in Pullman were no better off than when the whole upheaval began eight weeks earlier. Through it all, George Pullman maintained a stony silence behind the walls of his vacation retreat on the New Jersey shore.[72]

Just a week before the rail boycott made train travel treacherous, Jane journeyed to Cleveland to deliver the commencement address to the female graduates of Western Reserve University. Her disappointment over failing to end the Pullman strike rings through that speech's sharp censure of both the rich and the poor who lacked an "industrial conscience," whose "narrow individuality" and "selfishness" blinded them to concern for "those around them." Jane was increasingly comfortable with such harsh language as long as she could apply it across class in positive service to the commonweal. Indeed, this graduation speech—to college girls and their parents—was much more pointed than "Subjective Necessity" in its criticism of "mothers" who failed to "recognize the humanitarian claim upon their educated daughters."[73]

At the very moment that she was insisting on the "humanitarian claim," Jane was also coping with the most grave of family claims. On the eve of the Pullman strike, Jane's beloved sister Mary Linn became seriously ill, and Jane swung into action, making all of the arrangements for Mary's care. In April, when Mary's unnamed illness became "quite serious," Jane lobbied hard for Mary to convalesce near her, rather than with Alice in Girard. She then arranged for Mary to move fifty miles from her home in Storm Lake, Iowa, to the Pennoyer Sanitarium in Kenosha, Wisconsin, fifty miles north of Chicago. Jane dispatched Mary Keyser, the settlement's housekeeper and Mary Linn's former employee, back to Storm Lake to take care of Rev. Linn, Esther, and Stanley; and she hired a Jane Club resident to attend Mary at all times in Kenosha. Years earlier, Jane had deferred to Alice in dealings related to Weber's hospitalization, but now she dictated the terms and pressed hard on Alice to help pay for the sanitarium of Jane's choice, reminding her sister that the year's economic burdens weighed as heavily on a settlement worker in Chicago as on a banker in Kansas.[74]

Public success had not removed Jane from the family; it had made her the head of the family. Her fame, her confidence, her competence, and her close ties with the Linn children gave her logistical and emotional leverage that her older siblings lacked. Having attended college in Chicago while his aunt was establishing Hull-House, John Linn was so integrated into her life that he even had a love affair with a kindergarten teacher at the settlement and talked candidly with Jane about his inner conflicts over pursuing a career in the Episcopal ministry and leading a celibate life. John regarded Jane as "a second mother to me . . . the one who would back me up in any good thing or be the first to turn me from a wrong faith." Though he spent more hours at Hull-House talking with Ellen, the settlement's resident Episcopalian, John relied on his Aunt Jane for real wisdom and direction.[75] Jane responded by taking seriously John's doubts about his future and by putting John in touch with her new friend, Dr. John Dewey at the University of Chicago, to discuss career plans.[76] No one else in the family could take the sort of action, no one else could provide the next generation with the experiences, the contacts, or the worldliness that Aunt Jane offered.

The arc of the family story had curved in such a surprising direction that Harry and Anna never got over the sense that they been tricked into playing bit parts when they meant to be leads and that Jane had stolen all of silent George's lines. Alice, given the most awkward role in the family scenario, trooped on, proud of Jane's success and her own fidelity.[77] In one of her typically, and touchingly, extravagant displays of attachment to her sister, Alice commissioned a portrait of Jane in 1894 from the Chicago artist Alice Kellogg Tyler and managed to pay for it while complaining about Mary's medical bills.[78] For Anna's amusement, Harry described this classic painting as a study of "Miss Laura Jenny Addams—now called Jane." He said it showed his famous sister-in-law with "hands clasped over coccyx . . . breast flat . . . chin well stuck forward . . . and a little too much on the jaws to be perfectly satisfactory." The image, he said, was of an "aggressive" woman whose features were "gentle, alive" but "tinged with sweat glands." In all, he drily concluded, "an excellent picture of Miss Addams."[79]

Jane called up all her reserves of both public and private optimism in the spring of 1894. While Harry was dissecting the Kellogg portrait with alcoholic precision, and Weber languished, "blue and depressed," at his Cedarville farm estranged from his equally forlorn neighbors Anna and George, and while Mary lay gravely ill in a sanitarium in Kenosha, separated from her husband and children by miles of vulnerable railway lines, Jane told Alice of her dream that the family would "all rendezvous . . . at some beautiful spot that would be good for Mary."[80] By the Fourth of July, when federal troops marched into Chicago to shut down the American Railway Union, Jane was consumed with Mary's steady decline and feeling "like a brute when I think of the days I have not been here."[81]

32. The Alice Kellogg Tyler portrait of Jane Addams, which Alice Addams Haldeman commissioned in 1894. (Jane Addams Hull-House Museum, University of Illinois at Chicago)

The chaos of the railway boycott undoubtedly complicated Rev. John Linn's attempts to reach Mary before she died of heart failure on July 6, leaving Jane—not Rev. Linn—as the legal guardian for the four children. The unmarried head of Hull House was now the "second mother" to John, age twenty-two; James Weber, age eighteen; Esther, age fourteen; and Stanley, age eleven. In the coming years, it fell to her to manage their schooling, supervise their health, plan their vacations, and generally "monitor" their lives, as young John Linn put it.[82] Whatever marital resentment lay beneath the assignment of guardianship to Aunt Jane instead of Rev. Linn, it was masked by acquiescence to Jane as the head of the family and as the person best equipped to manage the children's affairs. In her new role as guardian to "the Linnets," Jane was aided by material support from the wealthy and gentle Mary Smith and loving concern from the good-hearted but ill-paid and ever-mobile Rev. Linn.[83] On the eve of the first Christmas after Mary's death, Jane solemnly pledged to Alice that "you may be sure I will perform as long as I am on earth."[84]

In her autobiography, written fifteen years later, Jane recalled Mary Linn's death in the context of the Pullman strike and the family's struggle to reach her bedside when twenty major railroads were shut down. Jane described her own "profound apprehension lest her last hours should be touched by resentment toward those responsible for the delay," but she claimed that Mary pronounced absolution on the warring parties before she passed away. "I don't blame any one," Jane quoted her sister saying, "I am not judging them." Jane chose to immortalize her pious sister in this Christlike role in order to make the point that violent conflict inevitably creates "lasting bitterness" in the hearts of those less devout than Mary Linn, and that even a righteous cause is sullied if it adds to human woe or violates human connection.[85]

In the weeks and months following Mary's death and the workers' defeat in the Pullman strike, Jane drew on her grief to craft the valedictory that captured her social philosophy and marked the completion of her first five years at Hull-House. She was compelled to create something of value out of the "cruelty and waste" of the summer of 1894. The memory of the strike could "only be endured," she felt, "if we learn from it all a great ethical lesson." For Jane, the lesson of the summer was that one historical era was over and a new era was beginning. "The virtues of one generation are not sufficient for the next," she declared, and while "individual striving" may have been the virtue of the previous generation—of George Pullman's generation—that virtue was "certainly too archaic to accomplish anything now. Our thoughts," said Jane, speaking for her own generation, "cannot be too much directed from mutual relationships and responsibilities."[86]

Jane framed that lesson in her speech, "A Modern Lear," which she apparently premiered at a Chicago Women's Club meeting in the fall of 1894 before delivering it at the meeting at the United Charities Building in New York City in May 1895.[87] It was in this speech comparing George Pullman to King Lear that Jane wove her personal and political history into a strategically optimistic vision of social progress based on cooperation, not conflict. It was here, too, that she refined her voice as a fair-minded but plainspoken mediator whose role was to remind all contestants that the goal of a democratic society was "human affection" and "common consent," not bloody revenge or even total victory.[88]

The speech was written in the tones of a confident adult authority; at thirty-four years old, Jane could call up a child's perspective but she had achieved parental status. Mary's death marked the passing of Jane's last sentimental link to childhood. She had once suffered the "childish" fear that when her sister Mary died, there would be "no one to love me," but now that fear was banished.[89] Jane was no longer the orphan toddler; she was the head of the family and had Mary Rozet Smith by her side to care for the Linn children.

Resolution of her own conflict between the "family claim" and the "social claim" is evident in the fact that Jane Addams had first invoked the notion that "our thoughts cannot be too much directed from mutual relationships and responsibilities" back in 1882, when she was still grieving over her Pa's death and chastising herself into accepting her private duty to Anna.[90] Now the phrase appeared in "A Modern Lear" as a clear reference to political life, and now Jane took adult control by depicting the "barbaric" end to the Pullman strike as the last gasp of a dying generation of "dictatorial" leaders. "In later years," she predicted, Americans would "look back upon the industrial relationship in which we are now placed as quite incomprehensible." Her generation, the generation poised to take power in the United States in 1894, was caught up in "the sweep of a world-wide moral impulse." Jane had no doubt that the "genuine feeling of the age" demanded "fair play," "social adjustment," and evolution beyond the "commercial standpoint" to the "social standpoint." Jane chose to believe that this "great accumulation of moral force" need not build toward a bitter and violent class revolt. Instead, it could head toward "sane and strenuous progress" if her fellow citizens would devote themselves to "mutual interest in a common cause." Jane admitted that finding the "rhythm of the common heart-beat" was "no easy task." But, she insisted, "progress is impossible without it."[91]

Jane used the King Lear story to illuminate the Pullman situation because "we have all shared the family relationship" and could all draw on that experience to understand "the industrial relationship." There is no question that

33. Jane Addams reading to her nephew, Stanley Linn, around 1894. This photograph is more revealing than the Tyler portrait of the aging effects of life at Hull-House when Addams was thirty-four years old. (University of Illinois at Chicago, University Library, Jane Addams Memorial Collection, neg. no. 1703)

Jane's analysis of Lear and Pullman was informed by her own memory of her beloved father. By thinking of Pullman as an "indulgent parent," she said, her judgment of the industrialist was "modified and softened."[92] This approach gave Jane the even-handedness she sought; the speech required its audience to look at the world from Pullman's point of view and sympathize with his confusion. He thought of himself as an "unusually generous employer," and everyone in his world confirmed that. He was "feted throughout Europe . . . as the friend and benefactor of workingmen," and his colleagues in the United States made fun of the care he lavished on his workers. To be then publicly rebuked by those same workers was, in Pullman's view, a betrayal by those who should have been grateful.[93]

Jane's ability to mount such a human portrait of Pullman was rooted in her loving relationship with her father. She bore fundamental respect for pioneering elders who had built the wealth from which she benefited, and she had seen how generational change in John Addams's own career had rendered him obsolete in Springfield, despite his Republican service. In "A Modern Lear," Jane treated the emancipation of labor as her generation's natural progression beyond the last generation's emancipation of the slave, and she saw her father as Lincoln's servant in that earlier struggle.[94] This fundamental bond with her father imbued Jane with generosity for Pullman and dozens of other businessmen in Chicago; she was neither intimidated by them nor rebellious against them. Senator Addams had made it possible for her to speak candidly and even kindly about such men without feeling dishonest.

It was Jane's experience with Anna that fueled her more pointed criticisms of Pullman's inability to "perceive himself in the wrong" or to grow beyond the controlling habits of an egocentric parent who saw children's—and workers'—independence as a "personal slight."[95] In her commencement address in Cleveland at the time of the Pullman strike, Jane had explicitly criticized "mothers" who did not recognize their daughters' interest in human issues beyond the family claim.[96] In "A Modern Lear," she confined herself to masculine imagery, but when she wrote that "lack of perception is the besetting danger of the egoist" and that those who refuse to see another's viewpoint imagine themselves "more sinned against than sinning," Jane was sketching a profile of Anna. When she sighed over "one will asserting its authority through all the entanglement of wounded affection, and insisting upon its selfish ends at all costs," she was sighing over Anna. And when Jane wrote that King Lear had been "insufficiently wise" to forge a bond with an adult child in which the family claim and the social claim were not in conflict, she was speaking of her own stepmother.[97] Anna had refused to see Jane's move to Chicago as anything but rejection and had refused to renegotiate the relationship on new, more adult, more egalitarian terms. All of that history was poured into Jane's critique of King Lear and George Pullman in the months after Mary Linn's death, when Jane found herself unnecessarily motherless.

Autobiography only goes so far in explaining "A Modern Lear," however. Fundamentally, Jane's speech argued that the parental analogy does not fit the industrial relationship; even with the kindest parent, "we are forced to challenge the ideal itself" because workers had to be able to stand independent of their employers in order to associate with them as economic and social partners. Though Jane characterized "the simple rights of trade organization" as "the merest preliminary" to the sort of cooperation she envisioned in a future economy, she left no doubt in this speech about her support for the labor movement. She conceded the mistakes made in the Pullman strike but insisted that it started from "an unselfish impulse" and that the workers who risked all for the sake of a larger social principle bore a "touch of nobility."[98]

Jane's partisan friends in the labor movement would have been happy had she rested the argument there, but she stubbornly pushed on to what, for her, was higher ground by turning a critical eye on the "fatal lack of generosity" that marked the movement's attitude toward employers. She warned her union allies that theirs was a "narrow conception of emancipation" if they adopted the capitalist principle of "possession" and continued to use material wealth as the sole measure of social value. She also urged her unionist and socialist friends to abandon the heroic romance of class conflict, just as men like Pullman had to abandon the heroic romance of philanthropy. Democratic progress and the rule of "common consent" required that all members of the community—including employers—have a place at the governing table.[99]

Jane did not carry away from the Pullman strike any illusions about the readiness of capitalists to sacrifice personal wealth and power for the common good. On the contrary, that experience taught her that powerful men of George Pullman's generation were bent on resistance, even violent resistance. The "barbaric instinct to kill, roused on both sides" in the summer's conflagration, and the "distrust and bitterness" that followed only confirmed Jane's belief that her generation had to invent alternatives to violent class conflict.[100] Such confrontations served only to further rend the social fabric, making Jane's goal of peaceful mediation and universal tolerance more distant. The "sane and strenuous progress" that Jane offered as a substitute involved, she admitted, a ponderously slow process of touching "those who think they lose, as well as those who think they gain," building relationships across class, pressing for legislation that recognized workers' rights to organize, and creating alliances with sympathetic employers in order to isolate the recalcitrants. This crablike path to progress would be "slower perpendicularly," she knew, but the results would be "incomparably greater because lateral."[101]

In a characteristic ploy to minimize debate with her audience, Jane declared in "A Modern Lear" that "we are all practically agreed that the social passion of the age is directed toward the emancipation of the wage-worker." She then warned her capitalist listeners that "nothing will satisfy the aroused conscience of men short of the complete participation of the working classes in the spiritual, intellectual, and material inheritance of the human race." But she warned her friends in the labor movement, as well, that their endeavors would fail lest "we hold the mind open, to take strength and cheer from a hundred connections" and learn to "look all men in the face, as if a community of interest lay between."[102]

Jane had wandered the streets of Europe for two years in the early 1880s before she learned to "look all men in the face." Now she hoped others would follow her lead and renounce the individual heroism of overcoming for the collective daring of cooperation. It was a difficult thing Jane Addams asked of her friends and colleagues, both uptown and downtown. Any one of them could point to tangible evidence showing that a community of interest did not unite the classes, and no Jamesian leap of faith, no acting "as if," could change that. As Jane said in her autobiography, she often seemed "destined to alienate everybody."[103] In her four decades of public service following the Pullman strike, Jane would come under censure from labor activists and socialists—including Ellen—who found Jane's persistent calls for cross-class cooperation naive at best, reactionary at worst.[104] Though they admired her consistency in granting to others the ideological respect and autonomy that she demanded for herself, Jane's associates in reform did not always see that her insistence on cooperation over conflict arose from tough-minded philosophy, not weak-kneed sentiment. For them, the ethical imperative of the day necessitated constant, combative assertions of industrial capitalism's evils, not conciliatory gestures to common ground. At the same time, conservative members of the business community viewed Jane's repeated calls for democratic relations in the economy and for mediation in all labor conflict as evidence that she was an anticapitalist partisan disguised as a moderate.

Jane explained how she withstood the pressures to define herself in more openly partisan terms during a series of conversations she had with John Dewey just weeks after the Pullman strike. Dewey had recently moved to Chicago to head the philosophy department at the new University of Chicago and had found Hull-House to be one of the more lively intellectual centers in the city. As Jane was beginning work on "A Modern Lear," she and Dewey were discussing the role of conflict in social progress. Dewey began that exchange with the assumption that "antagonism was necessary to an appreciation of the truth and to a consciousness of growth"; it was a requisite step toward "the reconciliation of opposites." Jane, however, made him think he had "the dialectic wrong end up." She was steadfast in her view that "antagonism was not only useless and harmful, but entirely unnecessary." Opposites, she argued, were never really opposites; they were merely "unity in its growth." Antagonism interfered with the natural growth of unity, endowing personal animosity with a philosophical legitimacy that served no good end.[105]

It was an extraordinary position, one that caused Dewey to shake his head and confess that Jane had "converted me internally, but not really, I fear." In the aftermath of the Pullman strike, Dewey simply could not bear the thought that "all this conflict . . . has no functional value."[106] But two years later, when Jane was circulating a revised version of "A Modern Lear" among her friends, Dewey was effusive in his praise. He found nothing to criticize in the text, declaring it "one of the greatest things I have read both as to its form and ethical philosophy."[107] Not everyone agreed. When Jane failed to find a publisher for the speech, she joked that she had received rejection letters from "the most illustrious magazines in the country."[108] Editors in the 1890s, including Vida Scudder's conservative uncle at the *Atlantic Monthly*, found the speech too personal in its critique of Pullman or too radical in its suggestion that philanthropic relationships be replaced by democratic ones.[109]

By the time "A Modern Lear" was published in 1912, Jane's success had grown far beyond Hull-House and she was widely recognized as one of the most articulate voices for progressive reform on the American scene. Publication of the essay was affirmation of a prodemocratic and promediation position for which she was, by then, well known and widely respected. In fact, when Jane claimed in her 1910 autobiography that she longed for "a definite social creed," she seriously underestimated her own achievement in fashioning—out of the bits and pieces of a scattered, self-directed education—a coherent, consistent social philosophy of democratic mediation that suited her temperament, caught the spirit of her time, and gave her the authenticity for which she had longed.[110]

At the height of the Pullman strike and the depths of Mary Linn's illness, a female reporter for the *Chicago Herald* went to Hull-House to interview Jane. The reporter found Jane's face too pale and her body too frail to qualify as beautiful, and confessed to her readers that Jane was "a woman whom at first you are inclined not to like, who after short acquaintance you admire and with less than a month of daily intercourse might dearly love." The reporter also indicated that Jane was a slippery interviewee, quickly glancing off "socialistic topics" and on to "humanitarianism." But when asked if, after five years, she was discouraged by the slow progress on Halsted Street, Jane looked the reporter dead in the eye and replied: "Of course not. Why should I be? Do we ever tire of what we know is right?" In the midst of one of the worst weeks of her personal and professional life, Jane met despair with optimism. "I could never flag in this," she announced, "I love it better every day and hope I may live a hundred years to carry it forward."[111]

Epilogue

Jane Addams did not, of course, live another hundred years beyond 1894. She lived another forty-one years, never abandoning her post as head resident at Hull-House but continuously expanding her sphere of influence beyond Chicago, beyond Illinois, and, ultimately, beyond the United States. Over the course of those four decades, she became more confident of her belief that "affectionate interpretation" was essential to dignified conduct of all human relations and became more adept at articulating her conviction that, whatever perplexities we faced, the key to a peaceful, democratic outcome lay in all parties rising above dogma and self-interest and embracing flexible solutions out of mutual concern for a common good. Addams's enactment of these principles at Hull-House and in the Women's International League for Peace and Freedom certainly deserve an honorable mention in any American history, but it is the amplification of her activism through her published writings that make the most compelling argument for Addams as a blue-ribbon figure in the history of the Progressive Era, in the history of American pragmatism, in the history of international pacifism, and in the history of democratic campaigns for the rights of workers, women, ethnics, and nonwhites. Amid the din of competing voices that cried out for peaceful, democratic reform in the decades following the Pullman strike, Jane Addams both acted and spoke in a singular, consistent, trustworthy tone that often served as the conscience of the nation and has seldom been heard with such clarity since.

It is perfectly possible, and highly recommended, to read Addams's major works—*Democracy and Social Ethics* (1902), *Newer Ideals of Peace* (1907), *Spirit of Youth and the City Streets* (1909), *Peace and Bread in Time of War* (1922)— and encounter there a coherent, cohesive body of political and social theory that places Addams squarely in the ranks of America's leading advocates for democratic, pacifist pragmatism. In all of her writings, she weighed social practice by social outcomes. Did the practice enhance the capacity of all the world's citizens to participate in the governing process? Did the practice encourage a peaceful process for negotiating to consensus? If so, she was open to all manner of social experiment; if not, she cared little for immediate gain.

On these matters of process and outcome, Addams was every bit as tough and as principled as the phrenologist had predicted in 1876. To her dying day she held firm to the nonresistant philosophy with which she astonished John Dewey: all forms of hostility were inherently undemocratic because they precluded the process of participatory dialogue and interfered with the natural evolution toward a unity of belief and action; no single cause merited a rancorous fight for the simple, pragmatic reason that the pain and bitterness resulting from the fight would trump the value of any victory.

These were not elusive concepts in Jane Addams's writings. They were woven into the seams of every parable, tucked into pockets of every human profile, threaded through the fabric of every sermon. For millions of readers in the Progressive Era, these messages offered a peaceful, practical route out of the spoiled and contentious Gilded Age and held the enormously attractive promise of a better day. Even after World War I, when Addams's pacifist convictions were smeared by charges of treason, she continued to have a loyal following, and the ranks of her following grew in the thirties when her equation of social justice with common sense had such immediacy. But since her death in 1935, history has not been particularly kind to Jane Addams or to her social theory. Hitler's campaign of genocide seemed to mock her faith in humanity, and postwar Freudianism found more to pity than admire in her nonheterosexual life.

Disillusioned radicals in the 1970s applauded her war resistance but rejected the rigors of an all-forgiving pacifism that smacked of liberal cooptation in the waning days of Vietnam, Watergate, and the War on Poverty. The women's movement ignited a feminist interest in Addams's achievements followed quickly by embarrassment over her harmonizing, unifying language on women's role and rights. Indeed, any nonpacifist movement that attempts to enlist Addams as its advocate winds up disappointed because her words are never as angry, as exclusionary, as damning of the other side as our partisan passions desire. It is only recently that philosophers, historians, and sociologists have found ways to admire Addams as a serious practitioner and stubborn theorist for whom pacifism and democratic process could not be fashioned to fit the rancor of the day.

With increased interest in Jane Addams's philosophy inevitably comes renewed interest in her biography. This is, in part, because she grounded her social theory so firmly in lived experience that we seek more about the experience in order to better grasp the theory. But it is also because the theory itself is so rigorous, demanding so much charity, so much trust, so much faith in the inevitable triumph of unity that we must wonder if Addams herself really lived it, and that curiosity fuels our biographical quest. Focused as it is on the first half of her life, *The Education of Jane Addams* offers one set of answers to the biographical questions we bring to her life and philosophy. There remains four decades' worth of letters, speeches, and published writings to explore if we want to watch Addams enact her theories, if we want to study when and why she stumbled over them or where and how she succeeded with them.

A foundation in the first half of her life launches us into that study with some key concepts in hand. We can watch her operate as a negotiator knowing that Jennie Addams came early and honestly to impartial mediation; taking the high ground won her psychic safety in the conflicted Haldeman-Addams household and earned Pa's grateful approval as well. Addams was not putting on saintly airs when she counseled understanding of all points of view; she was inviting her listeners to don the cloak of peace and protection that had sheltered her through life. The early biography tells us, too, that when Addams allowed, first, Ellen Starr and, later, Mary Smith, to peer beneath her equanimity, she was opening herself to the vulnerability required for any sort of empathic social action. Starr and Smith remind us just how frozen and haughty Rockford's bread-giving goddess might have been and how much her public life owed to the influence of these two women. So, too, Addams's prosuffrage celebration of womanly ways appears almost defiant, certainly not acquiescent, once we know that the young Jane Addams had to shed her arrogant identification with male heroism and her priggish recoil from female friendship before she could, in maturity, embrace the prosaic embodiment of women's lives.

It makes a difference that Jane Addams sought a steward's elite responsibility for others long before she grasped her equal interdependence with all. That biographical sequence means that her public demands on all citizens, across class, to share responsibility for solving social problems arose not out of an insensitive desire to hold victims responsible for their plight but out of a genuine, emotional recoil from the imposition of heroic action from above. It means, too, that her insistent demands on the state to replace philanthropy by redistributing wealth was deeply rooted in her belief that the political process offered more democratic control than could private charity. Jane Addams's particular evolution away from heroism and toward democracy does not resolve our contemporary debate on this subject, but it does allow us to understand why John Addams's daughter, an emerging democrat with republican roots, chose to believe in the state's ability to generate an ethic of mutuality.

Finally, and most poignantly, the early biography teaches us that Jane Addams's unswerving faith in humanity was no polite camouflage for tepid religiosity; it was a hard-won and deeply felt spiritual conviction from which arose all her other convictions. Her leap to faith in humanity gave Addams the spiritual peace and calm dignity that she had imagined when she wrote of the primordial goddess, but it replaced the chill of that stoic icon with the warmth of nieces and nephews and neighbors. Once she shifted her gaze from the heroes to the masses, Addams found the motive force needed to justify the public career she had yearned for. Democratic service among Chicago's working class bore no stamp of sacrifice in Addams's life, no hint of duty, no expectation of gratitude. That is the secret her early biography reveals: life on Halsted Street was a life freely chosen and exuberantly embraced. Jane Addams carried out of her education and into her career the certain knowledge that democracy—as daily practice—was the path to joy, and it was the experience of joy that guided the next forty years of her democratic endeavor.

Notes

The following archival abbreviations appear in the notes.

CHS   Cedarville Historical Society, Cedarville, Illinois
EGSP   Ellen Gates Starr Papers, Sophia Smith Collection, Smith College
HHScrapbooks Hull-House Scrapbooks, Hull-House Association Records, University of Illinois, Chicago
HJFP   Haldeman-Julius Family Papers, University of Illinois, Chicago
JAMC   Jane Addams Memorial Collection, University of Illinois, Chicago
JAPP   Jane Addams Papers Project on microfilm
RCA   Rockford College Archives
SAH   Sarah Alice Haldeman Papers, Lilly Library, Indiana University
SCHS   Stephenson County Historical Society, Freeport, Illinois
SCPC   Swarthmore College Peace Collection

Introduction

1. "Pullman Follows Lear: Miss Addams, of Chicago, Traces Their Histories in a Speech," n.p., May 4, 1895; "Likens Him to Lear: Miss Addams's Striking Characterization of Pullman," n.p., May 3, 1895; neither newspaper title noted in HHScrapbooks.

2. "Settlement of Hull House: Miss Jane Addams Explains Its Plan to Berkeley Students," n.p., February 8, 1894; "Miss Jane Addams of Chicago Explains the Socialistic Settlement Idea," n.p., May 19, 1894; "The Cool Reasoning at Plymouth," *Springfield Republican*, July 1892; Isabella Judd, "A Social Settlement" n.p., n.d., summer 1892; B. F. Underwood, untitled editorial, *Religio-Philosophical Journal*, Mar. 29, 1893; HHScrapbooks. According to Hilda Polacheck, a Hull-House student and volunteer at the turn of the century, "Jane Addams was not a forceful speaker. She spoke with conviction and sincerity and always held her audience." Hilda Satt Polacheck, *I Came a Stranger: The Story of a Hull-House Girl* (Urbana: University of Illinois Press, 1989), p. 102.

3. Bertha Damaris Knobe, "Lighthouses of Chicago: Hull House," *Union Signal*, July 26, 1894, HHScrapbooks.

4. Mary Josephine Onahan, "A Social Settlement," *The Citizen*, n.d., end of 1894, HHScrapbooks.

5. Complete bibliographies of Jane Addams's publications can be found in *The Jane Addams Papers: A Comprehensive Guide*, ed. Mary Lynn McCree Bryan (Bloomington: Indiana University Press, 1996), pp. 129–75, and John C. Farrell, *Beloved Lady: A History of Jane Addams's Ideas on Reform and Peace* (Baltimore: Johns Hopkins University Press, 1967), pp. 217–41.

6. Mary Jo Deegan, *Jane Addams and the Men of the Chicago School, 1892–1918* (New Brunswick, N.J.: Transaction Books, 1988).

7. "1,200 Pay Tribute to Jane Addams," *New York Times*, May 3, 1935, p. 7.

8. JA to Sarah Anderson, Feb. 20, 1894, RCA.

9. Jane Addams, "A Modern Lear," *Survey* 29 (Nov. 2, 1912), pp. 132, 134. Addams wrote this essay in 1894, but was unable to get it published until 1912. A close comparison of surviving drafts indicates that what she wrote in the mid-1890s was virtually identical to what she published in 1912, SCPC.

10. Ibid., p. 134, 132, 136.

11. Ibid., p. 134; JA to Eva Campbell, July 25, 1879, SCPC.

12. Allen F. Davis, *American Heroine: The Life and Legend of Jane Addams* (New York: Oxford University Press, 1973); G. J. Barker-Benfield, "'Mother Emancipator': The Meaning of Jane Addams' Sickness and Cure," *Journal of Family History* 4 (Winter 1979): 395–420; Daniel Levine, *Jane Addams and the Liberal Tradition* (Madison: State Historical Society of Wisconsin, 1971); Farrell, *Beloved Lady*. Recent works have done little to alter this standard story: Gioia Diliberto, *A Useful Woman: The Early Life of Jane Addams* (New York: Simon and Schuster, 1999); Barbara Garland Polikoff, *With One Bold Act: The Story of Jane Addams* (Chicago: Boswell Books, 1999); Jean Bethke Elshtain, *Jane Addams and the Dream of American Democracy* (New York: Basic Books, 2002).

13. Jane Addams, *Twenty Years at Hull-House* (New York: Macmillan, 1910), p. 197.

14. "The Only Saint America Has Produced," *Current Literature* 40 (April 1906).

15. Jane Addams, *The Long Road of Woman's Memory* (New York: Macmillan, 1916), p. xii. The analysis of Jane Addams's autobiography has been informed by the work of various literary critics. See, for example, James Olney, *Metaphors of Self: The Meaning of Autobiography* (Princeton: Princeton University Press, 1972); John Sturrock, "The New Model Autobiographer," *New Literary History* 9 (Autumn 1977); Susan Stanford Friedman, "Women's Autobiographical Selves: Theory and Practice," in *The Private Self: Theory and Practice of Women's Autobiographical Writings*, ed. Shari Benstock (Chapel Hill: University of North Carolina Press, 1988); Nancy K. Miller, "Changing the Subject: Authorship, Writing and the Reader," in *Feminist Studies/Critical Studies*, ed. Theresa deLauretis (Bloomington: Indiana University Press, 1986); and Patricia Meyer Spacks, "Selves in Hiding," in *Women's Autobiography: Essays in Criticism*, ed. Estelle Jelinek (Bloomington: Indiana University Press, 1980).

16. For a contrasting view, see Louise W. Knight, "Biography's Window on Social Change: Benevolence and Justice in Jane Addams's 'A Modern Lear,'" *Journal of Women's History* 9 (Spring 1997): 111–38.

17. James Weber Linn to Ellen Gates Starr, May 4, 1935, and Caroline F. Urie to Ellen Gates Starr, May 25, 1935, EGSP.

18. Davis, *American Heroine*, pp. 110–11. Like Davis, Jill Conway enriched the Addams literature by treating her as a complex figure, but she stopped short of fully examining the philosophical evolution that drove her particular approach to social reform. See Conway, "Jane Addams: An American Heroine," *Daedalus* (1964): 761–80; "Women Reformers and American Culture, 1870–1930," *Journal of Social History* (Winter 1971–72): 164–77.

19. William L. O'Neill, *Everyone Was Brave: The Rise and Fall of Feminism in America* (Chicago: Quadrangle Books, 1969), pp. 118–20; Polikoff, *With One Bold Act*, pp. 121–22; Elshtain, *Jane Addams*, pp. 23, 173–74.

20. Knight, "Biography's Window on Social Change."

21. Charlene Haddock Seigfried, ed., *Feminist Interpretations of John Dewey* (University Park: Pennsylvania State University Press, 2002); Charlene Haddock Seigfried, ed., *Democracy and Social Ethics* by Jane Addams (Urbana: University of Illinois Press, 2002); Marilyn Fischer, *On Addams* (Belmont, Calif.: Wadsworth, 2002); Kathryn Kish Sklar, *Florence Kelley and the Nation's Work: The Rise of Women's Political Culture, 1830–1920* (New Haven: Yale University Press, 1995); Dorothy Ross, "Gendered Social Knowledge: Domestic Discourse, Jane Addams, and the Possibilities of Social Science," *Gender and American Social Science: The Formative Years*, ed. Helene Silverberg (Princeton: Princeton University Press, 1998).

22. Caroline F. Urie to Ellen Gates Starr, May 25 and June 13, 1935, EGSP.

23. Charlotte Perkins Gilman, *The Living of Charlotte Perkins Gilman* (New York: D. Appleton-Century, 1935), p. 184.

24. Addams, "A Modern Lear," p. 137.

Chapter 1. Self-Made Man

1. Rev. John Linn to JA, Aug. 26, 1881, SCPC.

2. Ibid.

3. Jane Addams, *Twenty Years*, dedication page and p. 1.

4. For the view that Jane Addams's career was in defiance of her father, see Barker-Benfield, "'Mother Emancipator,'" and Knight, "Biography's Window on Social Change." For the contrary view that nontraditional daughters in the late nineteenth century tended to have supportive fathers, see Patricia Palmieri, "Patterns of Achievement of Single Academic Women at Wellesley College, 1880–1920," *Frontiers* 5 (1980): 63–66. In a study of twenty-nine female reformers born between 1850 and 1870, Catherine Nisbett found that the fathers of twenty-two of them were either actively supportive of women's right to a nondomestic life or were sufficiently devoted the American principles of individual rights that they supported their daughters' ambitions. "Father-Daughter Relationships in Reform Era Women," capstone paper, Grinnell College, September 1999.

5. Addams, *Twenty Years*, p. 1.

6. Jane Addams notebooks, JAMC; Davis, *American Heroine*, p. 26.

7. Addams, *Twenty Years*, p. 53. Jane Addams, *The Excellent Becomes Permanent* (New York: Macmillan, 1932). There is no independent confirmation that Jane was actually introduced to this Platonic thought at the time, but the concept squares with her tributes to her father's "purest integrity" and "stern honesty." Jane Addams notebooks; JAMC.

8. Mary X. Barrett, *History of Stephenson County, 1970* (Freeport, Ill.: County of Stephenson, 1972), pp. 63, 489. M. W. Bailey, *Freeport City Directory* (Freeport, Ill.: Steam Book and Job Print, 1868), pp. 117–18.

9. Jane Addams's full name was Laura Jane Addams, but she was always called "Jennie" or "Jane." She referred to her father's "high and shining silk hat" in *Twenty Years*, p. 9.

10. John Addams Diary, Oct. 5, 1844, SCPC. "The Court House Crowded Full,"

Freeport Journal, Jan. 5, 1870. The *Journal* story makes clear that John Addams moved easily among his neighbors when pouring "oil on troubled waters," typescript, SCPC. Daniel Walker Howe, The Political Culture of the American Whigs (Chicago: University of Chicago Press, 1979). "Biographical Sketch" of John Addams, in M. H. Tilden, The History of Stephenson County (Chicago: Western Historical, 1880), p. 1. For assistance in research on John Addams's life and career, I am indebted to Jon Minkoff's independent study, "John Huy Addams: Steward of Stephenson County, Illinois," Grinnell College, spring 1993.

11. Census Population Schedules: Illinois (Washington D.C.: National Archives of the United States, Microfilm Publishing, 1934), film 8357, reel 69.

12. Addams, *Twenty Years,* p. 12.

13. James Weber Linn, *Jane Addams: A Biography* (New York: D. Appleton-Century, 1935), pp. 1–2. Linn traces the paternal family line back to Robert Adams who, though not a Quaker, was granted 500 acres of land in the Quakers' Pennsylvania colony in 1681. Robert's nephew, Isaac, adopted the "double d" spelling of his last name to avoid confusion with a family cohort, also named Isaac.

14. Selden J. Coffin, *The Men of Lafayette, 1826–1893: Lafayette College, Its History, Its Men, Their Record* (Easton, Pa.: George W. West, 1891), p. 145.

15. Marcet Haldeman-Julius, "The Two Mothers of Jane Addams," unpublished, undated typescript, pp. 1–2, SCPC. Haldeman-Julius was the daughter of Jane's sister, Alice, and her stepbrother/brother-in-law, Harry Haldeman. While it is impossible to verify all of the stories Marcet told in this brief family history, one can assume that accounts such as these represent the family history as Jane Addams and her siblings knew it.

16. John Addams Diary, Aug. 13–Dec. 19, 1844, SCPC.

17. John Addams to Enos and Elizabeth Reiff, Jan. 12, 1845, SAH. For others' impressions of the land, see *Prairie State: Impressions of Illinois, 1673–1967, by Travelers and Other Observers, ed.* Paul M. Angle (Chicago: University of Chicago Press, 1968). John Addams did not share Charles Dickens's view that the "vast expanse of level ground . . . left nothing to the imagination," p. 214.

18. See John Addams diary entries in October 1844, for the correlation between his mood fluctuations and his uncomfortable dependence on his father's financing, SCPC; Linn, *Jane Addams,* p. 9.

19. John Addams Diary, Dec. 18 and Nov. 30, 1844, SCPC. I am grateful to Mary Lynn Bryan for assistance in sorting out the details of this loan arrangement.

20. John Addams to Enos and Elizabeth Reiff, Jan. 12, 1845, SAH; John Addams Diary, November 28, 1844, SCPC. Pennsylvanians and German immigrant farmers dominated the population in Stephenson County in the 1840s and 1850s. Barrett, *The History of Stephenson County, 1970,* pp. 25–26, 64. This source states that Addams paid $4,400 for the mill and the land, but in his letter to the Reiffs, Addams said he paid $4,600.

21. John Addams Diary, Oct. 12 and Dec. 18, 1844, SCPC.

22. Sarah Addams to Enos and Elizabeth Reiff, Apr. 14, 1845, and John Addams to Enos and Elizabeth Reiff, Jan. 12, 1845, SAH.

23. Alexander Davidson and Bernard Stuve, A Complete History of Illinois from 1673 to 1873 (Springfield: Illinois Journal Company, 1874); Marguerite Jenison Pease and Theodore C. Pease, The Story of Illinois, 3rd ed. (Chicago: University of Chicago

Press, 1965); Robert P. Howard, *Illinois: A History of the Prairie State* (Grand Rapids, Mich.: Eerdmans, 1972); John H. Krenkel, *Illinois Internal Improvements, 1818–1848* (Cedar Rapids, Ia.: Torch Press, 1958); George W. Dowrie, *The Development of Banking in Illinois, 1817–1863*, vol. II, no. 4, University of Illinois Studies in the Social Sciences (Urbana: University of Illinois Press, December 1913); William V. Pooley, "The Settlement of Illinois from 1830 to 1850," *Bulletin of the University of Wisconsin*, History Series, vol. 1, no. 4 (Madison: University of Wisconsin Press, May 1908): 287–595; Henry Brown, *The History of Illinois from Its First Discovery and Settlement to the Present Time* (New York: J. Winchester, New World Press, 1844).

24. Addison Fulwider, *History of Stephenson County, Illinois*, vol. 1 (Chicago: S. J. Clarke, 1910), p. 119.

25. Patrick E. McLear, "The Galena and Chicago Union Railroad: A Symbol of Chicago's Economic Maturity," *Journal of the Illinois State Historical Society* 73 (Spring 1980): 17–24; Robert J. Casey and W. A. S. Douglas, *Pioneer Railroad: The Story of the Chicago and North Western System* (New York: McGraw-Hill, 1948); Paul Wallace Gates, *The Illinois Central Railroad and Its Colonization Work* (Cambridge: Harvard University Press, 1934); *History of Stephenson County, Illinois* (Chicago: Western Historical, 1880), p. 273; Fulwider, *History of Stephenson County, Illinois*, 1:119; *History of Stephenson County* (Mt. Morris, Ill.: Kable Printing, 1972), p. 272.

26. Casey and Douglas, *Pioneer Railroad*, p. 54.

27. John Moses, *Illinois Historical and Statistical*, vol. 2 (Chicago: Fergus Printing, 1892), p. 1138; Linn, *Jane Addams*, p. 14.

28. Gates, *Illinois Central Railroad*, p. 86. Fred Gerhard reported that the Galena and Chicago Union Railroad was paying dividends of 21 percent, *Illinois As It Is* (Chicago: Keen and Lee, 1857), p. 135.

29. Judson Fiske, *Transportation as a Factor in the Development of Northern Illinois Previous to 1860* (Chicago: University of Chicago Press, 1917), p. 41; Barrett, *History of Stephenson County, 1970*, pp. 70, 472; *In the Footprints of the Pioneers* (Freeport, Ill.: Pioneer, 1900), pp. 19–20.

30. Census Population Schedules: Illinois. Typescript for Buckeye township, including John Addams's worth in 1850, in SCPC. 1860 Census Population Schedules: Illinois; film 8356, Reel 50.

31. Addams helped negotiate an arrangement by which the Illinois Central Railroad and the Galena and Chicago cooperated on rail service through Freeport by cutting out a planned western line to Galena. This harmonious deal may have caused "a slight feeling between the Addamses and the Webers" because John's father-in-law had established a milling business in western Illinois in 1851. Still, when Col. Weber died in the 1850s, he left John and Sarah their share of his "considerable estate." Linn, *Jane Addams*, p. 23; McLear, "The Galena and Chicago Union Railroad"; Casey and Douglas, *Pioneer Railroad;* Fulwider, *History of Stephenson County*, 1910, p. 119; Gates, *Illinois Central Railroad*, pp. 25, 93; "Election of Railroad Directors," *Freeport Journal*, Jan. 28, 1853, typescript in SCPC.

32. *Preliminary Report on the Eighth Census for 1860* (Washington, D.C.: Government Printing Office, 1862), p. 177. The new mill was a three-and-one-half story frame building where Addams could grind wheat he had purchased in bulk and then shipped on the railroad and could do custom grinding for the farmers in the area. *History of Stephenson County*, p. 64.

33. Haldeman-Julius, "The Two Mothers of Jane Addams," p. 6; Linn, *Jane Addams*, pp. 28–29. Alice's full name at birth was Sarah Alice Addams, but she was always called "Alice" or "Allie."

34. Haldeman-Julius, "The Two Mothers of Jane Addams," p. 5; John and Sarah Addams to Mary Addams, Oct. 15, 1858, SCPC; *History of Stephenson County, 1970*, p. 66; *Freeport Bulletin*, July 8, 1858.

35. Sarah Addams to Enos and Elizabeth Reiff, Apr. 14, 1845, SAH. Sarah Weber Addams's obituary did not state any church membership. See untitled clipping from Freeport newspaper, Jan. 21, 1863, SCPC; George Weber to Elizabeth Weber Reiff and DeVault Weber, Jan. 17, 1863, SCPC. In regard to John Addams's religious status, Jane Addams was unequivocal: "my father was not a 'professing Christian'; he never belonged to any church." JA to James Weber Linn, Feb. 2, 1935, SCPC. In his 1844 diary, John Addams occasionally commented on "good" sermons he had heard and professed his commitment to Christian ethics and to faith in God. But he noted on Nov. 24, 1844, that he had "spent the evening not becoming a Christian." It appears he spent the rest of his life not becoming one, though he was a loyal servant of his community's religious institutions. See the eulogy delivered by the local Presbyterian minister at the time of John Addams's death: "Hon. John H. Addams," *Freeport Budget*, Aug. 27, 1881.

36. Haldeman-Julius, "The Two Mothers of Jane Addams," p. 8.

37. For evidence of his strong Whig affiliation, see John Addams to Enos and Elizabeth Reiff, Jan. 12, 1845, SAH; John Addams Diary, Aug. 8, Nov. 1 and 4, 1844, SCPC. "For State Senator" and "Whig Meeting," *Freeport Journal*, Sept. 7, 1854.

38. In 1860, Stephenson County citizens would cast 60 percent of their votes for Lincoln. Arthur Cole, *The Era of the Civil War, 1848–1870*, vol. 3 of *Centennial History of Illinois* (Springfield: Illinois Centennial Commission, 1919), p. 200. John Moses, *Illinois Historical and Statistical*, vol. 2 (Chicago: Fergus Publishing, 1892). Stephen L. Hansen, *The Making of the Third Party System: Voters and Parties in Illinois, 1850–1876* (Ann Arbor: UMI Research, 1978); Donald E. Fehrenbacher, "Illinois Political Attitudes, 1854–61," Ph.D. diss., University of Chicago, 1951; J. O. Cunningham, "The Bloomington Convention of 1856 and Those Who Participated in It," *Transactions of the Illinois State Historical Society* 10 (1905): 101–10. Cunningham noted the "frequent citations from speeches of Henry Clay."

39. Addams, *Twenty Years*, chapter 2, "The Influence of Lincoln"; Merrill D. Peterson, *Lincoln in American Memory* (New York: Oxford University Press, 1994).

40. In 1861, when his daughter Alice was just seven years old, she sent a message to her Pa in Springfield to "fetch Mr. Lincoln up" their way, and family lore always claimed that Addams cherished a packet of letters from Lincoln to "My dear Mr. Double-D'ed Addams." Alice's message to her Pa is included in Mary Addams to John Addams, Jan. 9, 1861, SCPC. In response to an inquiry about the packet of Lincoln letters, which she had mentioned in her autobiography, Jane Addams replied, "My brother had those Lincoln letters, together with other papers belonging to my Father, but I am sorry to say they were mislaid or lost years ago." Addams, *Twenty Years*, p. 31; JA to Gilbert Tracy, June 23, 1914. Gilbert Avery Tracy Papers, Newark, New Jersey Historical Society.

41. John Addams to Enos and Elizabeth Reiff, Jan. 12, 1845, SAH; John Addams Diary, Aug. 8, Nov. 1 and 4, 1844, SCPC. "For State Senator" and "Whig Meeting," *Freeport Journal*, Sept. 7, 1854.

42. "Anti-Nebraska State Convention," *Daily State Journal*, Sept. 25, 1856; "The Republican State Convention Meets in Springfield, June 16," *Illinois State Journal*, May 24, 1858, and "Republican State Convention: Official Proceedings," *Illinois State Journal*, June 17, 1858; *Proceedings of the Republican State Convention Held at Springfield, Illinois, June 16, 1858* (Springfield: Bailhache and Baker, 1858).

43. Addams, "A Modern Lear," p. 137. Paul Selby, "Genesis of the Republican Party in Illinois," *Transactions of the Illinois State Historical Society* 11 (1906): 270–83; George T. Palmer, "A Collection of Letters from Lyman Trumbull to John M. Palmer, 1854–1858," *Journal of the Illinois State Historical Society* 16 (1923): 20–41; and Cunningham, "The Bloomington Convention of 1856." The moderate platform adopted at the Bloomington Convention is reprinted in Davidson and Stuve, *A Complete History of Illinois*, pp. 652–53.

44. "Speech of Hon. John H. Addams," *Freeport Journal*, Oct. 23, 1872, typescript, SCPC.

45. JA to James Weber Linn, Feb. 2, 1935, SCPC. In this letter, Addams said that she did not think her father was a pacifist, more a "nonresistant." Thus, she tried to discern in her father's behavior and workaday philosophy signs of his agreement with Leo Tolstoy whose notions of "nonresistance" in the face of evil were so influential in Jane Addams's later development. For the roots of John Addams's Whig influence on his daughter's later view of the relationship between government and the economy, see Howe, *The Political Culture of the American Whigs*, and Hansen, *The Making of the Third Party System.* "Whig principles," notes Hansen, "were based on a general concept that the federal government should take an active part in fostering national development," p. 8.

46. Jane Addams said that her father had "Quaker tendencies" and claimed that his "his eyes twinkled" when she asked him "what are you?" but then he "soberly" replied that he was a Hicksite Quaker. Addams, *Twenty Years*, pp. 2, 16. John Addams did own the *Journal of the Life and Religious Labors of Elias Hicks as Written by Himself*, 2nd ed. (New York: Isaac T. Hopper, 1832), and may well have admired the reform Quaker's views on enacting one's faith in society, but his was a philosophical affinity at best, not a denominational commitment. Addams Family Library, JAPP, reel 28, frames 0857–0869.

47. Jane Addams told her nephew, "the Addams family was not Quaker," and she responded to a "query" from Prof. William I. Hull, her colleague in the peace movement, by saying that she wished "with all my heart" that she could trace a Quaker heritage but regarded her one Quaker grandmother on her mother's side as "too slight a claim." JA to James Weber Linn, Feb. 2, 1935, SCPC; JA to William I. Hull, Jan. 16, 1916, Swarthmore College Friends Historical Library. Regarding the family's Union loyalty, see Addams, *Twenty Years*, pp. 23–32.

48. Mary Addams to John Addams, Feb. 3, 1865, SCPC.

49. *Daily Illinois State Journal*, Sept. 14, 1861; Addams, *Twenty Years*, p. 23. Though formal lists of Civil War units from Illinois do not include the "Addams Guards," the family displayed a poster in the Cedar Creek house with this honorary designation and the names of all the local members of the unit. My thanks to Mary Lynn Bryan for this information.

50. *Freeport Journal*, Aug. 3 and 10, 1864, SCPC. Marcet Haldeman-Julius deposited typescripts of official letters and newspaper articles along with a narrative about Senator Addams's success at exempting Stephenson County from the 1864 draft in the Swarthmore College Peace Collection.

51. George Weber to Elizabeth Weber Reiff and DeVault Weber, Jan. 17, 1863, SCPC.
52. Ibid.
53. Addams, *Twenty Years*, p. 11.

Chapter 2. The Predominant Elements of Her Character

1. Addams, *Twenty Years*, pp. 39–40; JA to Alice Addams Haldeman, Feb. 17, 1884, JAMC; JA to Alice Addams Haldeman, Aug. 20, 1890, SAH.
2. In her biography of Emily Greene Balch, Jane's colleague in both settlement and peace activism, Mercedes Randall noted, "It is significant that so many of that notable group of women, Emily's friends and contemporaries, who in the last generation lent distinction to American public life, also received such encouragement while growing up. Jane Addams and Julia Lathrop of Illinois, Florence Kelley of Pennsylvania, Mary Kingsbury (Simkhovitch) of Massachusetts, Alice Hamilton of Indiana — all had fathers of brilliance and forceful personality, and all, like Emily, acknowledged their intellectual indebtedness to these farsighted parents." Randall, *Improper Bostonian: Emily Greene Balch* (New York: Twayne, 1964), p. 33. See, too, Nisbett, "Father-Daughter Relationships in Reform Era Women."
3. Anna Haldeman Addams to John Addams, Jan. 2, 1869, SCPC. Addams, *Twenty Years*, pp. 8, 9, 2–3, 20.
4. Stephen M. Frank, *Life with Father: Parenthood and Masculinity in the Nineteenth-Century American North* (Baltimore: Johns Hopkins University Press, 1998); Shawn Johansen, *Family Men: Middle-Class Fatherhood in Early Industrializing America* (New York: Routledge, 2001).
5. John Addams Linn to JA, Dec. 21, 1910, SCPC.
6. William Wolfe to JA, Sept. 17, 1904; David James Burrell to JA, Jan. 10, 1910, and Andrew Zimmerman to JA, Apr. 20, 1931, SCPC.
7. "The Last Call," *Freeport Daily Bulletin*, Aug. 18, 1881.
8. All surviving letters from John Addams to Mary, Alice, and Weber Addams are archived in SCPC.
9. John Addams to Alice Addams, Jan. 6, 1872, SCPC.
10. John Addams to Alice Addams, Apr. 16, 1872, SCPC.
11. Untitled obituary for Sarah Weber Addams from unnamed Freeport, Illinois, newspaper, Jan. 21, 1863, SCPC.
12. JA to John E. Watkins, Apr. 3, 1914, JAMC. Questionnaire on "heredity" from James W. Fawcett to JA, Nov. 9, 1925, University of Virginia Library, James Waldo Fawcett Collection, item no. 9831.
13. Addams, *Long Road of Woman's Memory*, pp. 154, 158.
14. Addams, *Twenty Years*, pp. 23–27.
15. Addams, *Long Road of Woman's Memory*, pp. 146, 149, 155; Addams, *Twenty Years*, pp. 2, 19.
16. Addams, *Long Road of Woman's Memory*, pp. 160–62. Here, the fifty-six-year-old Addams described her girlish self as "defiant" against "the theology of the entire community" because it doubted that an unconverted person, however "righteous,"

could go to heaven. George Weber took the occasion of his sister's death to express self-righteous disapproval of the Addams family's lack of piety and worldly success: "Sarah had a very fine and no doubt expensive coffin and was dressed in a black taffeta dress she used to wear. I should liked to have seen a white shroud and things more plain. We hope she died in peace." George Weber to Elizabeth Weber Rieff and DeVault Weber, Jan. 17, 1863, SCPC.

17. Addams, *Twenty Years*, p. 20.

18. For the explicit description of John Addams as "not a professing Christian," see JA to James Weber Linn, Feb. 2, 1935, SCPC; Addams, *Twenty Years*, p. 15. In his 1844 diary, John Addams wrote, "firmly impressed that 'honesty is the best policy' and hope that I may by all means and through all hazards stick to the above Proverb. Come what may let me stick to the above. . . . Spent the evening not becoming a Christian." John Addams Diary, Nov. 24, 1844, SCPC. When his brother-in-law "enlisted under the banner of Christ," John Addams hoped George Weber would "not become too much excited but keep within bounds that he may not get prejudice against him in his enthusiasm and prevent him from doing good amongst his fellow beings." John Addams Diary, October 4, 1844, SCPC.

19. Mary Addams to Elizabeth Reiff, Aug. 1, 1863, SAH; John Addams to Anna Haldeman Addams, Aug. 1, 1869, SCPC.

20. Uncle George Weber viewed his sister's death as "chastisement" for her own and her husband's support of the inherently unchristian Civil War, but Jane never identified her version of pacifism with his. Linn, *Jane Addams*, p. 24.

21. Haldeman-Julius, "The Two Mothers of Jane Addams," p. 10. Christopher Lasch, *The New Radicalism in America, 1889–1963: The Intellectual as Social Type* (New York: Alfred A. Knopf and Vintage Books, 1965), p. 25. Lasch cites an interview Carrie Chapman Catt conducted with Alice Addams Haldeman in 1894, which was quoted at a meeting of the Women's International League for Peace and Freedom on Sept. 6, 1935; Addams, *Twenty Years*, pp. 6–7.

22. Mary Addams to John Addams, Feb. 1, 1865, SCPC.

23. Sarah C. T. Uhl to JA, Nov. 16, 1896, SCPC.

24. Alice slept with her stepmother when John Addams left for Springfield, making "amends for her Father's absence by being so warm and lovingly twining her arms about me." Mary exulted because she "has *no more care* and feels so *much younger.*" Anna Haldeman Addams to John Addams, Jan. 2 and 10, 1869, SCPC.

25. John Addams to Anna Haldeman Addams, Jan. 6, 1869; Anna Haldeman Addams to John Addams, Jan. 2, Jan. 9 and 10, 1869, SCPC. Both Alice's daughter, Marcet, and Mary's son, James, reported that Jennie made a quick adjustment to Anna's control because her stepmother's "domination" was not "harsh" and was applied equally to George and to Jane. Haldeman-Julius, "The Two Mothers of Jane Addams," p. 17; Linn, *Jane Addams*, p. 31.

26. Anna Haldeman Addams to John Addams, Jan. 2, 9, and 10, Feb. 25, and Mar. 6, 1869, SCPC.

27. Haldeman-Julius, "The Two Mothers of Jane Addams," p. 17. Marcet Haldeman-Julius, "Jane Addams as I Knew Her," *Reviewer's Library* (Girard, Kan.: Haldeman-Julius Company, 1936), p. 4.

28. Haldeman-Julius, "Jane Addams as I Knew Her," pp. 4, 6, 9. Marcet's frank

comments about Anna's temper and egocentrism confirm what others said about Anna, and her abiding affection for her grandmother give her remarks added credibility.

29. Linn, *Jane Addams*, p. 29.

30. *History of Stephenson County, 1970*, pp. 70–71.

31. Paul E. Fry, "Generous Spirit: The Life of Mary Fry," privately published family reminiscence, 1992, p. 35, SCHS; Haldeman-Julius, "The Two Mothers of Jane Addams," pp. 10–14.

32. Anna Haldeman Addams to Harry Haldeman, Feb. 7, 1884, HJFP. Anna referred to Harry in this letter as her "*Dimond*" and George as her "*Pearl.*" "I have never owned jewels to 'plash out in gay attire. But God made me the mother of *two sons* more precious and of more real value with *their talents improved* than all the jewels that refract the rays of the sun."

33. Mary Addams to John Addams, Jan. 25, 1865, SCPC.

34. Census Population Schedules: Illinois, film 8356, reel 50.

35. Mary Addams to John Addams, Jan. 25, 1865, SCPC.

36. Anna Haldeman Addams to Harry Haldeman, Dec. 24, 1884, HJFP. Thirty years earlier, Anna had told her first husband that she feared her "sensibilities will prove my death some day." Anna lived to be ninety-one. Anna Haldeman to William Haldeman, Feb. 15, 1855, HJFP.

37. Census Population Schedules: Illinois, film 8357, reel 69. In 1871, Harry Haldeman indicted a Haldeman relative for his "shameful negligence in running our affairs," but that very typical tendency to blame others served to efface his mother's own role in mismanaging the William Haldeman estate. Harry Haldeman to Anna Haldeman Addams, date illegible, 1871, SAH; personal communication with Mary Lynn Bryan, editor, JAPP.

38. John Hostetter to Anna Haldeman, May 26, 1866, SAH.

39. Haldeman-Julius, "The Two Mothers of Jane Addams," pp. 10–13.

40. John Addams to Anna Haldeman, June 30, 1868, SCPC.

41. John Addams to Anna Haldeman, June 5 and 30, 1868; Oct. 31, 1868, SCPC.

42. Anna Haldeman Addams to John Addams, Mar. 6, 1869, SCPC; John Hostetter to Anna Haldeman, Nov. 16, 1868, SCPC. Marcet Haldeman-Julius claimed that her grandmother "had qualms" about the marriage but "thought he would make a good father for my sons and I *knew* I would make a good mother for his children." "The Two Mothers of Jane Addams," pp. 12, 16.

43. Anna Haldeman Addams to Harry Haldeman, Nov. 30, 1882, HJFP.

44. John Hostetter to Anna Haldeman, Nov. 16, 1868, SCPC. There is no record of Anna ever joining any female service organization.

45. Daniel T. Rodgers, "Socializing Middle-Class Children: Institutions, Fables, and Work Values in Nineteenth-Century America." *Journal of Social History* 13 (Spring 1980): 354–67; Jacob Abbott, *Gentle Measures in the Management and Training of the Young* (New York: Harper and Brothers, 1871). Abbott stayed in print until 1913.

46. John Hostetter to Anna Haldeman, Nov. 16, 1868, SCPC.

47. Anna Haldeman Addams to John Addams, Jan. 10, 1869, SCPC.

48. Jane Addams Diary, 1875, SCPC. See, for example: Jan. 7, 18, and 23, Feb. 7 and 28, Mar. 8 and 30, Apr. 19 and 20, May 4, 1875. Jennie and George formed the "Science Almanacs Association" on Dec. 27, 1873, with George B. Haldeman as "Chief." Jane Addams's childhood jottings, CHS. JA to Vallie Beck, Mar. 16, 1876, SCPC.

49. Frances B. Cogan, *All-American Girl: The Ideal of Real Womanhood in Mid-Nineteenth-Century America* (Athens: University of Georgia Press, 1989); David Tyack and Elizabeth Hansot, *Learning Together: A History of Coeducation in American Schools,* (New Haven: Yale University Press, 1990); Sharon O'Brien, "Tomboyism and Adolescent Conflict: Three Nineteenth-Century Case Studies," in *Woman's Being, Woman's Place: Female Identity and Vocation in American History* (Boston: G. K. Hall, 1979), pp. 351–72; Jane H. Hunter, *How Young Ladies Became Girls: The Victorian Origins of Girlhood in the United States* (New Haven: Yale University Press, 2003); Annette Atkins, *We Grew up Together: Brothers and Sisters in Nineteenth-Century America* (Urbana: University of Illinois Press, 2001); Karen V. Hansen, *A Very Social Time: Crafting Community in Antebellum New England* (Berkeley: University of California Press, 1994); Victoria Bissell Brown, "Golden Girls: Female Socialization in Los Angeles, 1880 to 1910," Ph.D. diss., University of California, San Diego, 1985. For the reality of childhood life among Jane Addams's peers and future colleagues, see Helen Lefkowitz Horowitz, *The Power and Passion of M. Carey Thomas* (New York: Alfred A. Knopf, 1994); Ruth Bordin, *Frances Willard: A Biography* (Chapel Hill: University of North Carolina Press, 1986); Robert Booth Fowler, *Carrie Catt: Feminist Politician* (Boston: Northeastern University Press, 1986); Barbara Sicherman, *Alice Hamilton: A Life in Letters* (Cambridge: Harvard University Press, 1984); Lela B. Costin, *Two Sisters for Social Justice: A Biography of Grace and Edith Abbott* (Urbana: University of Illinois Press, 1983).

50. Anna Haldeman Addams to Alice Addams, July 6, 1871, and Apr. 2, 1872, SAH.

51. Jane Addams Diary, 1875. The entries for Jan. 28 through Feb. 12 are typical in recording George's participation in parlor games with Jane and her girlfriends. On Feb. 12, "Pa, Kate, George, Ma and I played proverbs and enjoyed ourselves in doing so until bed time. Kate spent the night," SCPC. Jane mentioned George entertaining a male friend in only two surviving letters, six years apart. JA to Alice Addams, Dec. 3, 1871, SAH; JA to Vallie Beck, Mar. 30/Apr. 2, 1876, SCPC. Addams mythology often suggests that Anna, George, and Jane spent their evenings reading poetry and Shakespeare aloud to one another. While these readings may well have occurred, Jane did not mention them in her 1875 diary.

52. JA to Vallie Beck, Mar. 16, 1876, and May 3, 1877, SCPC.

53. Jane Addams Diary, 1875: Feb. 24, Mar. 23, Aug. 4, SCPC.

54. JA to Vallie Beck, May 3, 1877, SCPC; Jane H. Hunter, "Inscribing the Self in the Heart of the Family: Diaries and Girlhood in Late-Victorian America," *American Quarterly* 44 (March 1992): 51–81.

55. Francis Adams, *The Free School System of the United States* (London: Chapman and Hall, 1875), p. 106.

56. Jane Addams Diary, Apr. 9 and 26, 1875, and May 31, 1875, SCPC. On the evening of Mar. 19, Mr. Moore and Mrs. Moore "came down just as we were having a nice time and then we didn't." She was "provoked" in natural philosophy class on Feb. 10 and got her "dander up" in Latin on Feb. 23. Expressions of frustration with Mr. Moore's teaching are scattered throughout the school year's entries.

57. Jane Addams Diary, Jan. 26, May 13, 17, 20, and 31, 1875, SCPC.

58. Tyack and Hansot, *Learning Together*; Victoria Bissell Brown, "Fear of Feminization: Los Angeles Schools in the Progressive Era," *Feminist Studies* 16 (Fall 1990): 493–518.

59. Jane Addams Diary, Mar. 2, 1875, SCPC.

60. Jane Addams Diary, Jan. 26, Feb. 5, Mar. 5 and 26, and May 7, 1875, SCPC.

61. Jane Addams Diary, Jan. 5, 12, 14, 25, and 26, Feb. 5, Mar. 3, 1875, SCPC. Jane Addams's handwritten translation of Caesar's *Commentaries* from October 1876 are on file at SCPC.

62. Anna Haldeman Addams to Alice Addams, Apr. 2, 1872, SAH.

63. Jane Addams Diary, Jan. 14, Feb. 1 and 16, 1875, SCPC.

64. JA to Vallie Beck, Apr. 2, 1876, SCPC.

65. Jane Addams Diary, Feb. 24, Mar. 3, 5, and 23, May 24, Aug. 15, 1875, SCPC.

Chapter 3. Sober, Serious, and Earnest

1. John D. Davies, *Phrenology: Fad and Science* (New Haven: Yale University Press, 1955). Eugene Taylor, *Shadow Culture: Psychology and Spirituality in America* (Washington, D.C.: Counterpoint, 1999). David Bakan, "The Influence of Phrenology on American Psychology," *Journal of the History of the Behavioral Sciences* 2 (1966): 200–220. Davies reports that Nahum Capen, who appears to have been John Capen's father, published a series, *The Phrenological Library*. Davies, *Phrenology*, p. 26.

2. John L. Capen, phrenologist, untitled and undated analysis of Anna Haldeman Addams's head; Detzer Collection, UIC.

3. John L. Capen, phrenologist, "The Contents of Jane Addams's Head," July 28, 1876, Detzer Collection, UIC.

4. Jane Addams Diary, Apr. 24, 1875, SCPC. The Addams family library included *Lectures on Phrenology*, 3rd ed., with Corrections and Additions, by George Combe (New York: Edward Kearny, 1846), and *Etherology or the Philosophy of Mesmerism and Phrenology* by J. Stanley Grimes (New York: Saxton and Miles, 1845). These stood alongside writings on moral philosophy by Combe, a prominent phrenologist, and shared shelf space with *Chemistry as Exemplifying the Wisdom and Beneficence of God* by George Townes (New York: Wiley and Putnam, 1844) and Thomas Dick's *The Connection of Science and Philosophy with Religion* (Hartford: Sumner and Goodman, 1847). Books such as these indicate Senator Addams's interest in contemporary efforts to move beyond biblical descriptions of the natural world and to treat scientific investigation as another path to understanding God's universe. Addams Family Library, JAPP, reel 28, frames 0857–0869.

5. Haldeman-Julius, "Jane Addams as I Knew Her," p. 4.

6. Mary Addams Linn to Alice Addams, Nov. 11, 1871, SAH; JA to Anna Haldeman Addams, October 11, 1872, SCHS. Jane Addams Diary, Jan. 16, Feb. 22, Mar. 8, May 1, 17, 20, and 28, June 7, Aug. 4, 1875, SCPC. John Addams to Alice Addams, July 19, 1875, SCPC. Linn, *Jane Addams*, p. 29.

7. Weber Addams to John Addams, Jan. 7 and 16, 1868, Dec. 1 and 6, 1869, SCPC. Anna pointedly reported to her new husband that Weber smiled upon hearing that she was writing to the senator. Anna Haldeman Addams to John Addams, Jan. 1, 1869; Mary Addams to John Addams, Oct. 16 and Dec. 16, 1869; John Addams to Alice Addams, Nov. 4, 1869, SCPC.

8. Mary Addams to John Addams, Dec. 16, 1869, SCPC. Tilden *History of Stephenson County* (Chicago: Western Historical, 1880), p. 741. 1870 Census Population Schedules: Illinois, film 8357, reel 69.

9. Weber's visits tended to correlate with times when either Alice or Mary were at home visiting. In addition to taking Jennie to Lena, Weber also took her to visit Mary in Durand. Jane Addams Diary, Jan. 15, Feb. 16 and 19, Mar. 10 and 28, Apr. 12, May 23, 1875, SCPC. When Weber was still unmarried and became sick with a fever and cold, his father nursed him at Weber's house rather than bringing him to the Addams homestead. John Addams to Alice Addams, Apr. 16, 1872, SCPC. Anna's displeasure with Weber was sufficient to prompt Harry to write, "Weber is an ass and you cannot expect anything of him." Harry Haldeman to Anna Haldeaman Addams, Jan. 18, 1870, SAH.

10. Harry Haldeman to Anna Haldeman Addams, Nov. 16, 1875, SAH.

11. Jane Addams Diary, Feb. 6, 1875, SCPC.

12. Linn, *Jane Addams*, p. 31; Paul Fry, *Generous Spirit: The Life of Mary Fry* (privately published in cooperation with the Cedarville Historical Society, 1992), p. 38.

13. Harry Haldeman to Anna Haldeman Addams, Nov. 16, 1875, SAH.

14. John Addams to Alice Addams, July 19, 1875, SCPC.

15. Harry Haldeman to Anna Haldeman Addams, Jan. 18, 1870 and Feb. 16, 1873, SAH.

16. Anna Haldeman Addams once told Harry, "You are like me in many ways." Anna Haldeman Addams to Harry Haldeman, Jan. 10, 1884, HJFP.

17. Linn, *Jane Addams*, pp. 31–32.

18. Jane Addams Diary, Mar. 21, May 2 and 16, 1875, SCPC.

19. JA to Vallie Beck, Mar. 16 and Mar. 30/Apr. 2, 1876, SCPC; Hunter, "Inscribing the Self," pp. 51, 58, 64; Jane Addams Diary, June 21, 1875, SCPC; Capen, "Contents of Jane Addams's Head."

20. Capen, "The Contents of Jane Addams's Head."

21. John H. Addams to Anna Haldeman Addams, Feb. 23, 1869, SCPC; Jane Addams Diary, Jan. 6, Feb. 8 and 11, Apr. 3 and 28, May 18, Aug. 1, 2, and 5, 1875, SCPC; Fry, "Generous Spirit: The Life of Mary Fry," p. 34. Mary Fry, a Cedarville native, knew Anna Haldeman Addams's reputation as a difficult employer but became her housekeeper and companion in 1889 and stayed on until Mrs. Addams's death in 1919. Paul Fry quotes a ditty that made the rounds in Cedarville (the term "lake front" refers to the Addams's mill pond): "Down on the lake front / where troubles do brew, / The hired girls are leaving / and the men are quitting too." It appears that Polly Beer, the family's housekeeper at the time of Sarah Addams's death, was not working for the family in 1875. In *Twenty Years*, Addams incorrectly places Beer's death in 1875. In 1877, John Weber, her cousin, thanked Jane for giving him "an account of Polly's last moments." Addams, *Twenty Years*, pp. 19–21; John Weber to JA, Jan. 24, 1877, JAMC.

22. Haldeman-Julius, "The Two Mothers of Jane Addams," p. 13. According to her granddaughter, Anna "declared that in her earlier years she did too much of her own housework," so while "she was admittedly deft and sympathetic in a sickroom," Anna avoided other domestic work.

23. Rev. John Linn to JA, Aug. 26, 1881, SCPC.

24. John Addams to Anna Haldeman Addams, Feb. 23 and 27, SCPC. Linn, *Jane Addams*, pp. 17, 30. Linn repeated Anna's characteristically egocentric belief that Senator Addams's retirement was linked to "social wars" involving Anna the previous winter in Springfield. Surviving letters show only that, following Anna's visit to the state capital ten weeks after her wedding, John claimed that he was receiving more social invitations, was "growing in favor," and heard many "kind inquiries concerning you."

Anna's letters give no hint of "social wars." Anna Haldeman Addams to John Addams, Feb. 18, 1869, and John Addams to Anna Haldeman Addams, Feb. 24, 1869, SCPC.

25. Addams, *Twenty Years at Hull-House*, p. 30.

26. For Addams's vote on the Black Laws, see *Journal of the Senate of the Twenty-Fourth General Assembly of the State of Illinois* (Springfield: State of Illinois), p. 877. For his votes on the U.S. constitutional amendments, see John Moses, *Illinois Historical and Statistical*, vol. 2, p. 720, and *Journal of the Senate of the Twenty-Fifth General Assembly of the State of Illinois* (Springfield: State of Illinois), p. 76.

27. Arthur Charles Cole, *Era of the Civil War, 1848–70*; Howard, *Illinois: A History of the Prairie State*, pp. 329–37; Michael Robinson, "After Lincoln: The Transformation of the Illinois Republican Party, 1865–1872," *Selected Papers in Illinois History, 1982*, ed. Bruce D. Cody (Springfield: Illinois State Historical Society, 1983), pp. 51–56.

28. *History of Stephenson County, 1970*, pp. 63, 489, 497; M. W. Bailey, *Freeport City Directory*, p. 116. According to the city directory, the board of trustees of the Protection Life Insurance Company, led by John Addams, was "composed of some of the very best, most reliable men in Illinois" whose "names in this community are a perfect guaranty of honorable and successful management." This language captures the prewar faith in doing business based on local reputation. Senator Addams, however, introduced legislation designed to "surround [insurance companies] with proper restrictions," "New Departments," *Daily Illinois State Journal*, Jan. 23, 1865. See *Journal of the Senate of the Twenty-Fifth General Assemby of the State of Illinois*, p. 79, for Addams's introduction of a bill to regulate corporations.

29. Pease and Pease, *The Story of Illinois*, p. 145; Richard Jensen, *Illinois: A Bicentennial History* (New York: W.W. Norton, 1978), p. 73; Janet Cornelius, *Constitution-Making in Illinois* (Urbana: University of Illinois Press, 1972), p. 83.

30. John Eilert, "Illinois Business Incorporations, 1816–1870," *Business History Review* 37 (Autumn 1963): 169–81. Out of seventy-three special acts for banking institutions in the 1869 legislative session, Senator John Addams voted "no" on sixty-five of them. On fourteen of those votes, he voted entirely alone. *Journal of the Senate of the Twenty-Sixth General Assemby of the State of Illinois*. Addams had begun voting against bills of incorporation in 1867. See, for example, Feb. 4 and 6 of the *Journal of the Senate of the Twenty-Fifth General Assembly of the State of Illinois*.

31. John Addams to Anna Haldeman Addams, Mar. 9, 1869; see also John Addams to Anna Haldeman Addams, Feb. 27, 1869, and John Addams to Alice Addams, Feb. 11, 1869, SCPC. Addams's committee assignments in the 1869 session may have contributed to his burdens. As the dean of the senate, he not only chaired the finance committee but also served on the railroad committee and the public accounts committee. Given the tenor of the times, these were difficult committee assignments. Minkoff, "John Huy Addams: Steward of Stephenson County, Illinois," p. 30.

32. "For Congressman," *Freeport Journal*, Mar. 24, 1869, typescript in SCPC.

33. John Huy Addams was not included in the early, book-length histories of the Republican Party: Charles Church, *History of the Republican Party of Illinois, 1854–1912* (Rockford, Ill.: Wilson Bros., 1912), or Green B. Raum, *History of Illinois Republicanism* (Chicago: Rollins, 1900). Nor was Addams named in any surveys of leading political actors of the period. D. W. Lusk did not include Addams on his list of the "prominent members" of the Illinois Senate; Jeriah Bonham, a former newspaper editor from Peoria, profiled 77 leading figures in the state's history but did not mention Addams,

and Gen. Usher F. Linder profiled of 102 Illinois "men of politics" but did not list Addams among them. D.W. Lusk, *Politics and Politicians of Illinois, 1856–1884* (Springfield: H. W. Rukker, 1884); Jeriah Bonham, *Fifty Years: Recollections with Observations and Reflections on Historical Events Giving Sketches of Eminent Citizens—Their Lives and Public Service* (Peoria, Ill.: J. W. Frank and Sons, 1883); Gen. Usher F. Linder, *Reminiscences of the Early Bench and Bar of Illinois* (Chicago: Chicago Legal News Company, 1879). Addams is similarly absent from both autobiographies by and biographies of prominent Illinois politicians of the era.

34. Jane Addams Notebooks, JAMC.

35. "Speech of Hon. John H. Addams: Senator Trumbull Reviewed, Handled Fairly, but Without Gloves. Democratic Slander Refuted," *Freeport Journal*, October 1872, typescript, p. 8, SCPC.

36. JA to Vallie Beck, Mar. 21, 1877, SCPC.

37. Jane Addams, "The Present Policy of Congress," Dec. 5, 1877, Rockford Seminary essay, Detzer Collection, UIC.

38. Addams, *Twenty Years*, p. 22.

39. Ibid. Elizabeth Barrett Browning, *Aurora Leigh and Other Poems* (London: Women's Press, 1978), p. 60. Addams slightly misquoted the verse to read "He wrapt me" instead of "He wrapt his little daughter." The error may suggest the degree to which Addams identified with that line in the poem, as well as with the line that read, "I am like, / They tell me, my dear father." See *Aurora Leigh*, book 1, lines 727 and 198. I am grateful to Dorothy Mermin of Cornell University for guiding me to the correct verse in Barrett's work. See Angela Leighton, *Elizabeth Barrett Browning* (Bloomington: Indiana University Press, 1986), for a discussion of the father-daughter relationship in *Aurora Leigh* and of fathers rather thoughtlessly preparing daughters for intellectual lives that challenge society's expectations.

40. Rev. John Linn to JA, Aug. 26, 1881, SCPC.

41. Addams, *Twenty Years*, p. 5. This story began to appear in profiles of Jane Addams in Chicago newspapers in the early 1890s. Reporters and Addams alike used it to make her nontraditional actions appear to be the result of childhood instincts not adult ambition. It served to mask those years of her life in which Addams was not particularly interested in the poor. See, for example, "Our Lady of the House," *InterOcean*, May 20, 1892, and Isabella Judd, "A Social Settlement," *Boston Transcript*, July 30, 1892.

42. Anna Haldeman Addams to John Addams, Jan. 10, 1869; John Addams to Anna Haldeman Addams, Feb. 20, 1869, SCPC. Patricia Palmieri notes that "the daughters of the 'public aristocracy of benevolence'" were "encouraged to get a higher education and to use it in service to community," "Patterns of Achievement of Single Academic Women," p. 64. See, too, Lori Ginzberg, *Women and the Work of Benevolence: Morality, Politics, and Class in the Nineteenth-Century United States* (New Haven: Yale University Press, 1990); Karen J. Blair, *The Clubwoman as Feminist: True Womanhood Redefined, 1868–1914* (New York: Holmes and Meier, 1980); Barbara Epstein, *The Politics of Domesticity: Women, Evangelism, and Temperance in Nineteenth-Century America* (Middletown, Conn.: Wesleyan University Press, 1981).

43. Haldeman-Julius, "The Two Mothers of Jane Addams," p. 14. Jane Addams Diary, Apr. 23, 1875, SCPC. On Apr. 24, 1875, Jane accompanied her father into Freeport where they spent five dollars on new furnishings for Jane's room. Jane Addams Diary, Apr. 24, 1875, SCPC. For a discussion of the role of household furnishings in establishing class

status in a community, see Katherine C. Grier, *Culture and Comfort: People, Parlors, and Upholstery, 1850–1930* (Rochester, N.Y.: Strong Museum, 1988), chapter 2, "The Comfortable Theater: Parlor Making in the Middle-Class Household, 1850–1910," pp. 19–58.

44. Mary Addams to Martha and Alice Addams, Jan. 9, 1867; Mary Addams to Martha Addams, Mar. 9, 1867; Mary Addams to Alice Addams, June 5, 1867, SAH.

45. Anna Haldeman Addams to John Addams, Jan. 9, 1869, Feb. 25, 1869, SCPC. Haldeman-Julius, "The Two Mothers of Jane Addams," p. 14. Jane Addams Diary, Jan. 20, Feb. 8, Mar. 17 and 20, Apr. 21 and 24, May 29, 1875, SCPC.

46. John Addams to Anna Haldeman Addams, Feb. 21, 1869, SCPC.

47. *History of Stephenson County, 1970,* p. 26.

48. JA to Alice Addams, Dec. 3, 1871, SAH.

49. Addams, *Twenty Years,* pp. 13–14.

50. JA to Vallie Beck, Mar. 21, 1877, SCPC.

51. Capen, "Contents of Jane Addams's Head."

Chapter 4. Bread Givers

1. Lucy F. Townsend, "Anna Peck Sill and the Rise of Women's Collegiate Curriculum," Ph.D. diss., Loyola University of Chicago, 1985, pp. 216–217, 283. Though later published as *The Best Helpers of One Another: Anna Peck Sill and the Struggle for Women's Education* (Chicago: Educational Studies Press, 1988), the pages from the uncut dissertation are cited herein.

2. Carrie Longley Jones to Rockford Alumni Association, Feb. 16, 1925, RCA; "Home Items," *Rockford Seminary Magazine* 5 (October 1877): 186–87.

3. Linn, *Jane Addams,* p. 41.

4. *Annual Catalogue,* Rockford Female Seminary, 1877–78, RCA; Roberta Wollons, "The Impact of Higher Education on Women: The Case of Rockford College, 1870–1920," unpublished qualifying paper, University of Chicago, 1974, p. 6, cited in Mary E. Cookingham, "Bluestockings, Spinsters, and Pedagogues: Women College Graduates, 1865–1910," *Population Studies* 38 (1984): 353.

5. For the twenty-seven students in the "collegiate" course in which Jane Addams was enrolled, there were only six faculty. *Annual Catalogue,* Rockford Female Seminary, 1877–78, RCA.

6. Addams, *Twenty Years,* p. 44.

7. Townsend, "Anna Peck Sill," includes biographical information on Rockford's headmistress; see p. 104 for quote; "Chicago Alumnae Reunion," *Rockford Seminary Magazine* 6 (April 1878): 113.

8. Rev. H. M. Goodwin to Beloit College president, Rev. A. L. Chapin, June 20, 1852. RCA; *Memorials of Anna Peck Sill* (Rockford, Ill., 1889), pp. 5–20, RCA; J. O. C. Phillips, "The Education of Jane Addams," *History of Education Quarterly* 14 (Spring 1974): 50; "Chicago Alumnae Reunion," *Rockford Seminary Magazine* 6 (April 1878): 113. Townsend, "Anna Peck Sill," pp. 18, 234–35. Sill kept track of the number of graduates who became missionaries. Of the 282 women graduated by 1882, 37 had become missionaries and 8 had served the Freedman's Bureau. These numbers do not include the many graduates who had married missionaries. Anna Peck Sill, "A Letter to Our Old

Girls and to Them Only," in "Miss Sill's Scrapbook," RCA; "The Progress of Foreign Missions and the Reflex Influence upon Women," *Rockford College Magazine* 8 (January 1880): 6–8.

9. Townsend, "Anna Peck Sill," p. 235; Hattie Smith to JA, Aug. 28, 1878, SCPC.

10. Harry Haldeman to Anna Haldeman Addams, Feb. 16, 1873, SAH.

11. JA to James Weber Linn, Feb. 2, 1935, SCPC.

12. Addams, *Twenty Years*, p. 16.

13. Capen, "Contents of Jane Addams's Head."

14. *Memorials of Anna Peck Sill*, pp. 5–20. Phillips, "The Education of Jane Addams," p. 50.

15. Addams referred to Miss Sill's "primitive spiritual purpose" and her "primitive Seminary energy" in *Memorials of Anna P. Sill*, pp. 70–75. Addams was explicit in her disdain for self-conscious, self-righteous charity efforts and supportive of authentic, personal "motive power" to fuel social service in "The College Woman and Christianity," *Independent* 53 (Aug. 8, 1901): 1852–55.

16. Jane Addams Notebook, 1878–1879, SCPC; JAPP, reel 27, frame 0160.

17. For a more general discussion of the debates about and trends in female higher education in the second half of the nineteenth century, see Barbara Miller Solomon, *In the Company of Educated Women: A History of Women and Higher Education in America* (New Haven: Yale University Press, 1985); Patricia Graham, "Expansion and Exclusion: A History of Women's Higher Education," *Signs: A Journal of Women in Culture and Society* 3 (Summer 1978): 759–73; Patricia Palmieri, "From Republican Motherhood to Race Suicide: Arguments on Higher Education of Women in the United States, 1820–1920," in *Educating Men and Women Together: Coeducation in a Changing World*, ed. Carol Lasser (Chicago: University of Illinois Press, 1987); Helen Lefkowitz Horowitz, *Alma Mater: Design and Experience in the Women's Colleges from Their Nineteenth-Century Beginnings to the 1930s* (Boston: Beacon Press, 1984); and Lynn D. Gordon, *Gender and Higher Education in the Progressive Era* (New Haven: Yale University Press, 1990), especially chapter 1, "From Seminary to University: An Overview of Women's Higher Education, 1870–1920."

18. Thomas Woody compared Rockford Seminary's catalogue for 1854 with the catalogues of more than 160 other female seminaries and concluded that Rockford was one of the two women's institutions in the West that was of collegiate rank, *The History of Women's Education in the United States* (New York: Science Press, 1929), p. 160. Evidence of the board of trustees' occasional exasperation with Sill is abundant in Townsend, "Anna Peck Sill." I am indebted to Lucy Townsend for pointing out that Senator Addams seldom attended board of trustee meetings during his tenure.

19. Addams, *Twenty Years*, p. 43.

20. Linn, *Jane Addams*, p. 40.

21. The total of Jane Addams's autobiographical remarks on this subject amounted to two sentences in the first paragraph of the third chapter of *Twenty Years at Hull-House*. There Addams wrote, "I was very ambitious to go to Smith College, although I well knew that my father's theory in regard to the education of his daughters implied a school as near at home as possible, to be followed by travel abroad in lieu of the wider advantages which an eastern college is supposed to afford. I was much impressed by the recent return of my sister from a year in Europe, yet I was greatly disappointed at the moment of starting to humdrum Rockford." *Twenty Years*, p. 43.

Bold use of these two sentences as evidence for the theory that Jane Addams struggled against paternal domination is evident in Barker-Benfield, "'Mother Emancipator,'" and Knight, "Biography's Window," p. 123. See, too, Rebecca Sherrick, "Their Fathers' Daughters: The Autobiographies of Jane Addams and Florence Kelley," *American Studies* 27 (Spring 1986): 46, and Sarah H. Gordon, "Smith College Students: The First Ten Classes, 1879–1888," *History of Education Quarterly* 15 (Summer 1975): 155. In *American Heroine*, Davis claimed that Addams was "determined to go to Smith" before she left Cedarville, but Davis stuck close to the autobiography in claiming only that her father "insisted that she stay closer to home," p. 10.

22. "Liberal Education for Women," *Harper's Monthly Magazine* 54 (April 1877): 695. "Education," *Atlantic Monthly* 38 (September 1876): 383. "Smith College," *Scribner's* 14 (May 1877): 17. According to the *Atlantic Monthly*, Smith's high admission standards meant it "could muster but fifteen for its Freshman class."

23. Addams, *Twenty Years*, p. 43.

24. "Smith College," *Scribner's* 14 (May 1877): 17. Sarah Gordon found that the trustees were concerned about the effect of their tough requirements on enrollment and did, for one year, in 1877, relax the Greek requirement and waive tuition for those "indigent" applicants who were otherwise qualified for admission. As a result of this policy change in 1877, the very year Jane Addams was applying to college, the size of the entering class at Smith did increase from fifteen in 1876 to forty-six in 1877. Addams still lacked requisite training in geometry, however. Gordon, "Smith College Students," pp. 150–51.

25. "A New Woman's College," *Scribner's* 6 (October 1873): 749.

26. Linn, *Jane Addams*, p. 40; Addams, *Twenty Years*, pp. 44–45; Townsend, "Anna Peck Sill," pp. 79, 231–35.

27. JA to John Addams, Mar. 6, 1881, SCHS.

28. Addams, *Twenty Years*, p. 43. Vallie Beck to JA, Feb. 5, 1878; Hattie Smith to JA, Aug., 28, 1878; Mary S. Downs to JA, May 23, 1880; Eva Campbell to JA, June 1, 1880, and Helen Harrington to JA on July 15, 1880, SCPC. JA to Ellen Gates Starr, Feb. 13, 1881, EGSP.

29. Linn, *Jane Addams*, describes Jane and George as "inseparable companions," p. 32. Though Linn is not reliable on specific events, his lengthy discussion of the tenor of this sibling relationship in childhood fits with the tone of caring and affection in the stepsiblings' correspondence in their twenties.

30. Alice Addams Haldeman, "The Studio and the Kitchen," *Rockford Seminary Magazine* 6 (July 1878): 167.

31. Anna Peck Sill quoted in Townsend, "Anna Peck Sill," p. 67.

32. Jane Addams, "The New Challenge of the Scholar," Alumnae Address, Seventy-Fifth Anniversary of Rockford College, 1924, typescript, RCA.

33. Addams, *Twenty Years*, p. 57.

34. Linn, *Jane Addams*, p. 41. At age eighteen years, seven months, Jane Addams was the youngest in her class at Rockford (the oldest in her class was twenty-three years, six months). At 5'3", she was not the shortest girl but, at 98 pounds, she was the lightest, even though she gained three pounds during her first year at Rockford. The average weight of the "sem girls" was 120 pounds; the average height was 5'4". "Home Items," *Rockford Seminary Magazine* 6 (July 1878).

35. Linn, *Jane Addams*, p. 48. Sill never learned of the subversive pledge, but when she was later slighted in an alumnae letter written for the class of 1881, Sill remarked that the offense was "quite characteristic of the class." Martha Thomas to JA, Apr. 27, 1882, SCPC.

36. Addams, *Twenty Years*, p. 49.

37. Jane Addams, "Editorial," *Rockford Seminary Magazine* 9 (April 1881): 114; Jane Addams, "Editorial," *Rockford Seminary Magazine* 9 (May 1881): 153–55. Mary Elwood to JA, Sept. 25, 1881, June 8, 1882, and Mattie Thomas to JA, Apr. 27, 1882, SCPC.

38. JA to Anna Haldeman Addams, Jan. 14, 1880, SCHS; JA to Anna Haldeman Addams, Mar. 7, 1880, Frances Woodhouse Papers, Freeport, Illinois; Jane Addams, "Editorial," *Rockford Seminary Magazine* 9 (April 1881): 113; Jane Addams, "Five New Year Resolves and Their Outcomes," *Rockford Seminary Magazine* 9 (January 1881): 4–9; Jane Addams, "The Chivalry of Study," *Rockford Seminary Magazine* 8 (February 1880): 63–64; "Home Items," *Rockford Seminary Magazine* 7 (May 1879): 130; JA to Ellen Gates Starr, Jan. 29, 1880, EGSP; Jane Addams, "Editorial," *Rockford Seminary Magazine* 9 (February 1881): 89.

39. "Sage and Sibyl," *Rockford Seminary Magazine* 9 (July 1881): 194; "Home Items," *Rockford Seminary Magazine* 9 (July 1881): 209.

40. Ellen Gates Starr to JA, Aug. 20, 1879, and Feb. 29, 1880; Clara Lutts to JA, Aug. 25, 1878; Mary Down to JA, Nov. 14, 1880; Mattie Thomas to JA, Sept. 21, 1881; Eva Campbell Goodrich to JA, June 1, 1880; and Katie Hitchcock to JA, Sept. 30, 1879, SCPC. For evidence of campus affection for Addams, see: "Home Items," *Rockford Seminary Magazine* 8 (June 1880): 181; "Home Items," *Rockford Seminary Magazine* 8 (March 1880): 85; "Sage and Sibyl," *Rockford Seminary Magazine* 9 (July 1881): 194; "Home Items," *Rockford Seminary Magazine* 9 (July 1881): 209; and "Sage and Sibyl," p. 193.

41. "Sage and Sibyl," p. 194; Hattie Smith to JA, Aug. 28, 1878; Eva Campbell to JA, June 18, 1879; Maria Nutting to JA, July 2, 1880; Eva Campbell Goodrich to JA, Aug. 31, 1880; Maria Nutting to JA, Mar. 7, 1881; Helen Harrington to JA, Apr. 15, and June 8, 1882, SCPC. Patricia Palmieri finds college women of the 1870s and 1880s distinctive for their sense of "daring, bravado, and adventure." Palmieri, "From Republican Motherhood to Race Suicide," p. 54. Palmieri's focus is on women in Eastern colleges and coeducational universities. It would be a mistake to exaggerate these qualities in Jane Addams's class-mates; they were more constrained in their ambitions than their eastern counterparts, but they did have fantasies of outstanding female achievement. See, for example, "Home Items," *Rockford Seminary Magazine* 5 (October 1877), in which the anonymous author expressed the hope that Rockford's literary stars would one day "stand out in the firmament," p. 188. Similarly, the class prophecy for 1878 imagined that all of the grad-uates would refuse marriage in order to be "devoted to the elevation and bettering of the entire race of mankind." "Home Items," *Rockford Seminary Magazine* 6 (July 1878): 141. These sorts of comments carried a humorous, self-deprecating air, but they indicate that women at Rockford, like female students everywhere in the United States in these years, were beginning to consider the possibility of public female achievement as a con-sciously chosen life course.

42. James Turner, *Without God, Without Creed: The Origins of Unbelief in America* (Baltimore: Johns Hopkins University Press, 1985), chapter 8, "A More Excellent Way."

43. Linn, *Jane Addams*, p. 48.

44. Maria Nutting to JA, July 2, 1880, SCPC.

45. For a list of all the schools with which Jane established an exchange during her year as editor of this section of the magazine, see "Clippings and Exchanges," *Rockford Seminary Magazine* 8 (April 1880): 123. It appears that Jane did more than simply tap into an existing network of elite colleges; she may have actually created that network. The editor from Vassar told Jane that the plan she proposed "certainly has the merit of novelty." Myra Reynolds to JA, Oct. 24, 1879; Mary Downs to JA, May 23, 1880, SCPC.

46. Jane Addams, "Editorial," *Rockford Seminary Magazine* 9 (February 1881): 86.

47. JA to Alice Addams Haldeman, Jan. 23, 1880, SCHS; JA to Anna Haldeman Addams, Jan. 14, 1880, SCHS; "Home Items," *Rockford Seminary Magazine* 7 (February 1879): 23–24.

48. JA to Alice Addams Haldeman, Jan. 19, 1881, JAMC.

49. For examples of *Rockford Female Seminary Magazine* treatment of the Woman Question in the years just preceding Jane Addams's tenure as editor, see: Jerusha Jones (a pseudonym), "The Woman's Pavilion," 4 (October 1876): 197–207; "Individuality," 6 (January 1878): 46–47; "Study," 6 (April 1878): 64; Louise Hinkley, "Let the Woman Rule Under the Roof," 6 (July 1878): 150–57. An editorial calling for more funding for female education argued that woman "moulds the character of the nation." "Editorial Notes," 5 (October 1877): 201. See, too, "Clippings and Exchanges," for the view that an education will make a woman a "better household manager," 7 (May 1879): 33. In "George Eliot," Marie T. Perry, a graduate of the class of 1863, harkened back to "simpler ages" when "genius was divine, unsexed . . . age and sex were ignored, the power was acknowledged, the pre-eminence granted," 8 (March 1880): 66. A prosuffrage editorial asked why a woman "of strong ruling mind" should not be U.S. president. "Editorial," 8 (May 1880): 159. Regarding the important Christian work women could do, see Mary Ella Huey, "Woman Commissioned," 7 (June 1879): 143–47, and "The Progress of Foreign Missions and the Reflex Influence upon Women," 8 (January 1880): 6–8.

50. Jane Addams, "Editorial," *Rockford Seminary Magazine* 9 (May 1881): 155.

51. Mary Downs to JA, Nov. 14, 1880, SCPC. Downs was a former "revolutionist" who wrote to express her "great admiration for the powers which have succeeded in quenching that bothersome 'Alumnae Department.'"

52. The characterization of the editorial content of the *Rockford Seminary Magazine* under Jane Addams's editorship is based on an analysis of the contents of each issue of the magazine for the years between 1874 and 1882. There were educators at the time who took the optimistic view that women would be most likely to progress if they concentrated on matters other than the "Woman Question." Rev. L. Clark Seelye, for example, argued that the wisest course was to focus college woman's thoughts on the "purely ideal and intellectual" and thereby "elevate all her employments and qualify her better for any station to which she may be called." "The Need of Collegiate Education for Women," paper read before the American Institute of Instruction, North Adams, Massachusetts, 1874.

53. Addams, *Twenty Years*, pp. 54–55.

54. "Inter-State Collegiate Oratorical Contest," *College Rambler* of Illinois College, Jacksonville, Ill., Apr. 30, 1881, p. 1.

55. Ibid. JA to John Addams, May 8, 1881, JAMC; "Personals," *Rockford Seminary Magazine* 9 (June 1881): 173.

56. JA to John Addams, May 8, 1881, JAMC. "Inter-State Collegiate Oratorical Contest," *College Rambler* (May 7, 1881): 57.

57. JA to John Addams, May 8, 1881.

58. Townsend, "Anna Peck Sill," p. 263.

59. The public image of the "coed" to which Addams was appealing in 1910 is evident in Shirly Marchalonis, *College Girls: A Century in Fiction* (New Brunswick, N.J.: Rutgers University Press, 1995).

60. Jane Addams, "Editorial," *Rockford Seminary Magazine* 7 (July 1879): 205.

61. Ibid., pp. 204–5.

62. Jane Addams, "Opening Address of Junior Exhibition," *Rockford Seminary Magazine* 8 (April 1880): 110–11. Newspaper report on "Class Day Exercises" in Sill Scrapbook cited in Townsend, "Anna Peck Sill," p. 250. Jane Addams's class of 1881 had grown from its original seven members to sixteen members because a number of girls transferred in or moved over from the seminary's preparatory school. The class would graduate with seventeen members.

63. John Ruskin, "Lilies: Of Queens' Gardens," in *Sesame and Lilies: Two Lectures Delivered at Manchester* (New York: John Wiley and Son, 1864); Addams, "Opening Address of Junior Exhibition," pp. 110–11.

64. Addams, "Opening Address of Junior Exhibition," p. 110.

65. Ibid., pp. 110–11. Three months before delivering this speech, Addams wrote to her sister Alice: "You know of course that Breadgivers is the primitive meaning of the word lady, and there are sixteen girls in RFS who mean to do all they can to restore the word to its original sense—probably because they are so far off now from the accepted meaning." The wording of this private correspondence suggests that Jane Addams was not conscious of any manipulation of tradition in her Junior Exhibition speech. It suggests, as well, that Addams was using the bread givers image as a vehicle for establishing some common ground on the Woman Question with her sister, who had valorized the "sacred influences of home kitchens" in a speech two years earlier. This desire to be in harmony with family members would, for years, influence Addams's thinking. JA to Alice Addams Haldeman, Jan. 23, 1880, SAH; Alice Addams Haldeman, "The Studio and the Kitchen," *Rockford Seminary Magazine* 6 (July 1878): 167.

66. Addams, "Opening Address of Junior Exhibition," p. 111.

67. Addams, *Twenty Years*, p. 48.

68. Jane Addams, "The Subjective Necessity for Social Settlements," in *Philanthropy and Social Progress* (New York: Thomas Y. Crowell, 1893), p. 6. This essay was Addams's first, and most famous, statement of the "want of harmony . . . the lack of coordination" between college students' "theory and their lives." See, too, Addams *Twenty Years*, p. 44; Jane Addams, "The College Woman and Christianity," pp. 1852–55. This article was a strong indictment of cloistered education. Near the end of her life, Addams attributed to her friend Julia Lathrop a youthful wish that colleges might "cease to dig that ancient chasm which yawns so wide between the preparation for life and actual life itself." Addams, *My Friend, Julia Lathrop* (New York: Macmillan, 1935), p. 46.

Chapter 5. My Relations to God and the Universe

1. Jane Addams, *The Spirit of Youth and the City Streets* (New York: Macmillan, 1909), p. 8.

2. Nancy Sahli, "Smashing: Women's Relationships Before the Fall," *Chrysalis* 8 (1979): 18–27; Martha Vicinus, "Distance and Desire: English Boarding-School Friendships," *Signs: Journal of Women in Culture and Society* 9 (1984): 602–12.

3. Ida May Carey to JA, Dec. 5, 1877; Vallie Beck to JA, Oct. 4, 1877, SCPC.

4. Ida May Carey to JA, Dec. 5, 1877; Vallie Beck to JA, Nov. 3 and Dec. 6, 1877, SCPC.

5. Ida May Carey to JA, Dec. 5, 1877, SCPC.

6. In an effort to neutralize his aunt's lifelong association with women, James Weber Linn concocted a tale of romance between Jane and Rollin Salisbury, but the record of their casual contact does not support Linn's claims. Linn, *Jane Addams*, pp. 49–50; Rollin Salisbury to JA, Jan. 15, 1881, SCHS; JA to Rollin Salisbury, Jan. 18, 1881, SCHS; Rollin Salisbury to JA, June 11, 1881, SCPC. For other girls' involvement with Beloit students, see "The Tale of the Beloit Boys Told," *Rockford Seminary Magazine* 7 (February 1879): 12–15. As "Clippings and Exchanges" editor for the seminary magazine, Jane received a personally complimentary, even flirtatious, letter from a male student at Colby College. Even though he wrote one letter on Valentine's Day, this did not lead to further contact. J. T. MacDonald to JA, Nov. 18, 1879, and Feb. 14, 1880, SCPC.

7. Addams, *Spirit of Youth and the City Streets*. Addams anticipated a number of her arguments in this book in an article for the *Ladies' Home Journal*, "Why Girls Go Wrong," 24 (September 1907): 13–14. There, she wrote sympathetically of "that exuberant stream of youthful spirit which wanders up and down the streets of a summer evening, giggling and shoving and shouting from sheer joy of life. . . . we know that it is the same surging energy that produces the song of the bird in the mating season, that is the joy of life anticipating its continuation."

8. Jane Addams, "Editorial," *Rockford Seminary Magazine* 9 (February 1881): 88.

9. Ibid.; Jane Addams, "Editorial," *Rockford Seminary Magazine* 8 (May 1880): 158–59. One departing seminary friend admitted to Jane that she would miss her Rockford friends far more than she would miss the academic work. Katie Hitchcock to JA, Sept. 30 and Dec. 23, 1879, SCPC.

10. Linn, *Jane Addams*, p. 47.

11. Eva Campbell Goodrich to JA, Aug. 31, 1880; Eva Campbell to JA, June 18, 1879, SCPC.

12. Maria Nutting to JA, Mar. 7, 1881, SCPC; Vallie Beck to JA, Nov. 3, 1877, SCPC.

13. JA to Ellen Gates Starr, Jan. 29, 1880, EGSP; Maria Nutting to JA, July 2, 1880, SCPC; Corinne Williams (Douglas) to James Weber Linn, n.d., quoted in Linn, *Jane Addams*, p. 47.

14. JA to John Huy Addams, Mar. 6, 1881; JA to Alice Addams Haldeman, Jan. 23, 1880, SAH; Jane Addams, "Editorial," *Rockford Seminary Magazine* 9 (November 1880): 256; Helen Harrington to JA, July 23, 1881, SCPC.

15. Addams's aversion to gossip is evident in an exchange with her former roommate, Eva Campbell. When Campbell inquired about "the trouble with the senior class," Addams responded that she was "disgusted with the whole thing" and refused to talk "about that fuss for it is over so long ago and sounds so stale." Eva Campbell to JA, June 18, 1879; JA to Eva Campbell, July 25, 1879, SCPC.

16. For the scant biographical information that exists on Sarah Anderson Ainsworth see Rockford College catalogues and an undated, anonymous undergraduate paper, "President Sarah Anderson," RCA.

17. Miss Sill had never been able to realize her dream of offering scholarships to the "less favored classes of young women." Townsend, "Anna Peck Sill," p. 69; *Memorials of Anna Peck Sill,* p. 14.

18. "President Sarah Anderson," RCA; Ellen Gates Starr to JA, Aug. 11, 1878, EGSP.

19. JA to Ellen Gates Starr, Nov. 22, 1879, EGSP.

20. Ellen Gates Starr to JA, Aug. 11, 1878, EGSP.

21. Ellen Starr, "In Memoriam: Caleb Allen Starr," a eulogy written on the occasion of his death in 1915. The eulogy expressed pride in her father's sympathy for socialism. Caleb's letters to his son Albert and his daughter Mary testify to his disdain for the temporizing in traditional party politics and his belief that the capitalist owners of the railroads conspired to blacklist workers and to control the government. Caleb Starr to Bert Starr, Oct. 11, 1900; Caleb Starr to Mary Starr, Jan. 30, 1899; Caleb Starr to Bert Starr, July 16, 1907, EGSP. Caleb Starr's handwritten speeches for the local Grange are also in this collection. Elizabeth Carrell, "Reflections in a Mirror: The Progressive Woman and the Settlement Experience," Ph.D. diss., University of Texas at Austin, 1981, pp. 38–53; Jennifer Bosch, "Ellen Gates Starr," in *Women Building Chicago, 1790–1990: A Biographical Dictionary*, ed. Rima Lunin Schultz and Adele Hast (Bloomington: Indiana University Press, 2001), pp. 838–42.

22. Starr, "In Memoriam," EGSP.

23. Kathleen Banks Nutter, "Eliza Allen Starr," in *Women Building Chicago*, pp. 836–38; Carrell, "Reflections in a Mirror," pp. 46–47.

24. Josephine Starr, "Notes by Miss Josephine Starr on Ellen Gates Starr," EGSP; Ellen Gates Starr to JA, July 27, 1879, SCPC; Ellen Gates Starr to JA, Aug. 11, 1878, EGSP; Ellen Gates Starr to JA, Oct. 12, 1879, SCHS.

25. JA to Ellen Gates Starr, Aug. 11, 1879, EGSP.

26. Ellen Gates Starr to JA, Aug. 11 and Aug. 18, 1878, EGSP.

27. Ellen Gates Starr to JA, Dec. 25, 1879, EGSP.

28. Ellen Gates Starr to JA, Mar. 6, 1881; Dec. 28, 1879; and July 27, 1879, EGSP.

29. JA to Ellen Gates Starr, Jan. 29, 1880 and Nov. 22, 1879, EGSP.

30. JA to Ellen Gates Starr, Aug. 1, 1879, EGSP.

31. JA to Ellen Gates Starr, Nov. 22, 1879, EGSP.

32. Ibid.

33. Jane Addams included an undated draft of these comments to "Mr. Smith" in a notebook she kept at Rockford. It is not clear if she ever sent the comments to "Mr. Smith." See Jane Addams Diary, Dec. 5, 1875, SCPC. Jane took the 1875 diary with her to Rockford and continued to write in it though the preprinted dates at the top of the page bore no relationship to when she wrote in the diary. These post-1875 entries will hereafter be referred to as "Jane Addams Notebooks."

34. T. H. Haseltine to JA, June 13, 1880, SCHS. Jane Addams's letter to Haseltine did not survive.

35. JA to Ellen Gates Starr, Nov. 22, 1879, EGSP.

36. JA to Eva Campbell, July 25, 1879, Eugene Goodrich Papers, York, Nebraska.

37. JA to Ellen Gates Starr, Jan. 29, 1880, EGSP.

38. JA to Ellen Gates Starr, Aug. 11, 1879, EGSP.

39. Daniel T. Rodgers, *The Work Ethic in Industrial America, 1850–1920* (Chicago: University Press of Chicago, 1974); Walter Houghton claimed that "except for the 'God,' the most popular word in the Victorian vocabulary must have been 'work.'" *The Victorian Frame of Mind* (New Haven: Yale University Press, 1957), pp. 243–44.

40. JA to Ellen Gates Starr, Nov. 22, 1879, EGSP.

41. *Rockford Seminary Magazine* 9 (May 1881): 155. Addams copied the quote once again into the notebook she kept in the summer of 1882. See entry for July 15, 1882, SCPC and JAPP, reel 27, frame 0370. For seminary essays testifying to her youthful commitment to the work ethic and her belief in work as spiritual salvation, see: "Hannibal," n.d.; "High Trees Take the Wind," n.d.; "Resolved: That the Invention and Use of Machinery Is a Hindrance to the Increase of Wealth in a Country," n.d.; "The Study of Nature," June 1879; "Resolved: the Civilization of the Nineteenth Century Tends to Fetter Intellectual Life and Expression," February 1880; "The Chivalry of Study," February 1880; "Compilers," 1881; all are Rockford Seminary essays, Detzer Collection, UIC.

42. Raymond Williams, *Culture and Society* (New York: Columbia University Press, 1958); Houghton, *The Victorian Frame of Mind*; *Victorian America*, ed. Daniel Walker Howe (Philadelphia: University of Pennsylvania Press, 1976); *The Gilded Age*, revised edition, ed. H. Wayne Morgan (Syracuse: Syracuse University Press, 1970); Avrom Fleishman, *Figures of Autobiography: The Language of Self-Writing in Victorian and Modern England* (Berkeley: University of California Press, 1983); George P. Landow, *Ruskin* (Oxford: Oxford University Press, 1985); A. L. LeQuesne, *Carlyle* (Oxford: Oxford University Press, 1982); Bernard Schilling, *Human Dignity and the Great Victorians* (New York: Columbia University Press, 1946); Walter Waring, *Thomas Carlyle* (Boston: G. K. Hall/Twayne, 1978); Philip Rosenberg, *The Seventh Hero: Thomas Carlyle and the Theory of Radical Activism* (Cambridge: Harvard University Press, 1974); Reed Whittemore, *Whole Lives: Shapers of Modern Biography* (Baltimore: Johns Hopkins University Press, 1989); Frederick Kirchhoff, *John Ruskin* (Boston: G. K. Hall/Twayne, 1984).

43. Thomas Carlyle, *Past and Present* (1843; New York: Charles Scribner's Sons, 1918), p. 183. Quoted in Rodgers, *The Work Ethic in Industrial America*, p. xiv.

44. JA to Eva Campbell, July 25, 1879, Eugene Goodrich Papers, York, Nebraska; JA to Ellen Gates Starr, Aug. 11 and Nov. 22, 1879, EGSP.

45. Jane Addams, "Follow Thy Star," Rockford Seminary essay, Feb. 26, 1879, Detzer Collection, UIC; Barbara Sicherman, "Reading and Ambition: M. Carey Thomas and Female Heroism," *American Quarterly* 45 (March 1993): 73–103; Helen Lefkowitz Horowitz, "'Nous Autres': Reading, Passion, and the Creation of M. Carey Thomas," *Journal of American History* 79 (1992): 68–95.

46. JA to Ellen Gates Starr, Feb. 13, 1881, EGSP; Maria Nutting to JA, Mar. 7, 1881, SCPC. Jane's letter to Ellen reveals her presumption that she was entitled to access to men of Carlyle's status. "Carlyle is dead," she announced, "and if I don't get to Massachusetts before [Ralph Waldo] Emerson dies, and don't have the opportunity of seeing him, I shall have to give up on the one experiment I would like to try above all others. Alas! Time is fleeting, experiments slippery, judgments difficult, and art continually appears longer and longer." Though her "experiment" is undefined, her words make clear that she saw herself sitting at the feet of these masters.

47. Maria Nutting to JA, Nov. 17, 1887, SAH.

48. Jane Addams, "George Eliot's View of Savonarola," n.d.; "Follow Thy Star,"

Feb. 26, 1879; "Hannibal," n.d.; "High Trees Take the Wind," n.d.; "The Notion of Conscience," n.d.; all are Rockford Seminary essays, Detzer Collection, UIC.

49. JA to Ellen Gates Starr, Aug. 11, 1879, EGSP.

50. Ellen Gates Starr to JA, Feb. 29, 1880, SCPC; JA to Ellen Gates Starr, May 15, 1880, EGSP.

51. Ibid.

52. JA to Ellen Gates Starr, Aug. 11, 1879, EGSP.

53. Ellen Gates Starr to JA, Dec. 25, 1879, Feb. 29 and June 5, 1880, SCPC.

54. Ellen Gates Starr to JA, Dec. 25, 1879, SCHS; JA to Ellen Gates Starr, Jan. 29, 1880, EGSP; Ellen Gates Starr to JA, Feb. 29, 1880, SCPC; JA to Ellen Gates Starr, May 15, 1880, EGSP. Jane's comments to Ellen about her "awful experiment" in not praying are a characteristic mix of conceit and self-deprecation, candor and coyness. She bragged to Ellen that not praying freed her to "think about a great many other things that are noble and beautiful," allowing her to settle upon "a very simple creed" extolling "the Good and the Beautiful." But she also flattered Ellen by claiming that Ellen's insistence on prayer signified her spiritual advancement while Jane's comfort without prayers "show how shallow my religion is."

55. JA to Ellen Gates Starr, Feb. 13, 1881, EGSP.

56. Turner, *Without God, Without Creed*; Paul F. Boller, Jr., "The New Science and American Thought," in *The Gilded Age*, pp. 239–57; D. H. Meyer, "American Intellectuals and the Victorian Crisis of Faith," in *Victorian America*, pp. 59–80; Paul Carter, *The Spiritual Crisis of the Gilded Age* (DeKalb: Northern Illinois University Press, 1971).

57. Jane Addams Diary, Feb. 1 and Mar. 10, 1875, SCPC; Addams Family Library, JAPP, reel 28, frames 0857–0869. In December 1873, when Jane was thirteen and George Haldeman was twelve, they formed the "Science Almanacs Association," of which George was listed as the "Chief," and George and Jane were listed as the only members. The club's password was "Quinaxgimoto," and its goal was to "get a collection of Almanacs," childhood jottings, CHS; Addams Family Library, JAPP, reel 28, frames 0857–0869. In the summer between Addams's sophomore and junior years at Rockford, she and George took up the subject of comparative anatomy and became "very interested." JA to Ellen Gates Starr, Aug. 11, 1879, EGSP.

58. Turner, *Without God, Without Creed*, p. 174. JA to Eva Campbell, July 25, 1879, Eugene Goodrich Papers, York, Nebraska.

59. Almost fifty years later, Addams took the occasion of Rockford's seventy-fifth anniversary to criticize Sill's curriculum for deducing all its lessons from Christian dogma. "Instead of probing the foundations of knowledge," she lamented, "Rockford students reasoned from premises. There were exact definitions in our minds and we were examined on them." Jane Addams, "A New Challenge to the Scholar," typescript of Alumnae Address, Seventy-Fifth Anniversary of Rockford College, 1924, RCA.

60. Townsend, "Anna Peck Sill," pp. 237–38; *Annual Catalogue*, Rockford Seminary, Senior Year, "Mental Philosophy," 1878–79, p. 21, 1880–81, p. 22.

61. "Home Items," *Rockford Seminary Magazine* 6 (April 1878): 81; "Home Items," *Rockford College Seminary Magazine* 7 (March 1879): 64.

62. The members of the Scientific Association "use mainly for their textbook 'The Popular Science Monthly,' and justly pride themselves on being well-informed on the latest scientific investigations." "Home Items," *Rockford Seminary Magazine* 8 (November

1880): 266. Robert C. Bannister, *Social Darwinism: Science and Myth in Anglo-American Social Thought* (Philadelphia: Temple University Press, 1979); Charles S. Rosenberg, *No Other Gods: On Science and American Thought* (Baltimore: Johns Hopkins University Press, 1976); Boller, "The New Science and American Thought"; Merle Curti, *Social Ideas of American Educators*, 2nd ed., (Paterson, N.J.: Pageant Books, 1959); Gilman Ostrander, *American Civilization in the First Machine Age, 1890–1940* (New York: Harper and Row, 1970).

63. Edward L. Youmans, "The Accusation of Atheism," *Popular Science Monthly* 11 (July 1877): 369; Edward L. Youmans, "Morality and Evolution," *Popular Science Monthly* 15 (May 1879): 126.

64. Jane Addams, "Compilers," Rockford Seminary essay, 1881, Detzer Collection, UIC.

65. JA to Eva Campbell, July 25, 1879, SCPC; JA to Ellen Gates Starr, Aug. 11, 1879, EGSP.

66. Janice Law Trecker, "Sex, Science and Education," *American Quarterly* 26 (October 1974): 352–66; Elizabeth Fee, "The Sexual Politics of Victorian Anthropology," in *Clio's Consciousness Raised: New Perspectives on the History of Women*, ed. Mary S. Hartman and Lois Banner (New York: Harper and Row, 1974): 86–102; Jill Conway, "Stereotypes of Femininity in a Theory of Sexual Evolution," in *Suffer and Be Still: Women in the Victorian Age*, ed. Martha Vicinus (Bloomington: Indiana University Press, 1972): 140–55; Flavia Alaya, "Victorian Science and the Genius of Woman," *Journal of the History of Ideas* 38 (April–June 1977): 261–80.

67. "Biology and 'Woman's Rights,'" *Popular Science Monthly* 14 (December 1878): 210–13.

68. A. Hughes Bennett, "Hygiene in the Higher Education of Women," *Popular Science Monthly* 16 (February 1880): 521.

69. Bennett, "Hygiene in the Higher Education of Women," p. 523; "Biology and 'Woman's Rights,'" p. 204. For additional examples of this viewpoint see W. K. Brooks, "The Condition of Women from the Zoological Point of View," *Popular Science Monthly* 15 (June–July 1879): 145–55, 347–56; G. T. W. Patrick, "The Psychology of Woman," *Popular Science Monthly* 47 (June 1895): 209–25, and Olivia Fernow, "How Does Higher Education Unfit Women for Motherhood?" *Popular Science Monthly* 66 (April 1905): 573–75.

70. George Marsden, *The Soul of the American University: From Protestant Establishment to Established Nonbelief* (New York: Oxford University Press, 1994); Julie A. Reuben, *The Making of the Modern University: Intellectual Transformation and the Marginalization of Morality* (Chicago: University of Chicago Press, 1996); Jon H. Roberts and James Turner, eds., *The Sacred and the Secular University* (Princeton: Princeton University Press, 2000); Louis Menand, *The Metaphysical Club: A Story of Ideas in America* (New York: Farrar, Straus and Giroux, 2001); Howard Feinstein, *Becoming William James* (Ithaca, N.Y.: Cornell University Press, 1984); Robert W. Westbrook, *John Dewey and American Democracy* (Ithaca, N.Y.: Cornell University Press, 1991).

71. Jane Addams, "An Allegory," n.d.; "Teeth," n.d.; "We Miss the Abstract When We Comprehend," Jan. 6, 1879; "The Study of Nature," June 1879; see also Addams's "Affirmative" argument in the Rockford debate, "Resolved: The Civilization of the Nineteenth Century Tends to Fetter Intellectual Life and Expression," Feb. 18, 1880; all are Rockford Seminary essays, Detzer Collection, UIC.

72. Addams, "The Study of Nature."

73. JA to Ellen Gates Starr, Aug. 11, 1879, EGSP.

74. Jane Addams, "The Nebular Hypothesis," Jan. 28, 1880, and "Darkness vs. Nebulae," June 14, 1880, Rockford Seminary essays, Detzer Collection, UIC; "Opening Address of Junior Exhibition," *Rockford Seminary Magazine* 8 (April 1880): 110.

75. George Eliot, *Romola* (1863; New York: Thomas Y. Crowell, 1891), p. 88; Turner, *Without God, Without Creed*, pp. 180–87.

76. Addams, "Darkness vs. Nebulae." For background on John Milton's *Comus*, I am indebted to Michael Cavanagh of the English Department at Grinnell College.

77. Addams, "Darkness vs. Nebulae."

78. Addams, "The Study of Nature."

79. Vallie Beck to JA, Dec. 6, 1877, SCPC.

80. JA to Ellen Gates Starr, Aug. 11, 1879, EGSP.

81. JA to Ellen Gates Starr, Feb. 13, 1881, EGSP.

82. Addams, "The Study of Nature."

83. JA to Ellen Gates Starr, Aug. 11, 1879, EGSP; JA to Eva Campbell, July 25, 1879, Eugene Goodrich Papers, York, Nebraska.

84. Jane Addams, "Darkness vs. Nebulae"; Turner, *Without God, Without Creed*, pp. 208–11.

85. JA to Ellen Gates Starr, Jan. 29, 1880. Addams claimed the ability to think as well without a body as with one and thought of the soul as regrettably "imprisoned" in "puny" and "perishable flesh." Jane Addams, "What I Think, That I Am" and "Teeth," Rockford Seminary essays, Detzer Collection, UIC.

86. JA to Ellen Gates Starr, Jan. 29, 1880, EGSP.

87. JA to Ellen Gates Starr, Aug. 11, 1879, EGSP; Helen Harrington to JA, July 15, 1880, SCPC.

88. JA to Ellen Gates Starr, Aug. 11, 1879, EGSP.

Chapter 6. Cassandra

1. JA to John Addams, Mar. 20, 1881, SCHS; JA to George Haldeman, May 29, 1881, JAMC.

2. Jane Addams, "Cassandra," in *Essays of Graduating Class, Thirtieth Commencement, Rockford Seminary*, June 22, 1881, p. 37, RCA.

3. Turner, *Without God, Without Creed*, pp. 187–202.

4. Dorothy Ross, "Gendered Social Knowledge: Domestic Discourse, Jane Addams, and the Possibilities of Social Science," in *Gender and American Social Science: The Formative Years*, ed. Helene Silverberg (Princeton: Princeton University Press, 1998), pp. 235–64.

5. Addams, "Cassandra," pp. 37–38.

6. JA to Ellen Gates Starr, Nov. 22, 1879, EGSP.

7. Addams, "Cassandra," pp. 37–38.

8. Jane Addams, "Hannibal," Rockford Seminary essay, Detzer Collection, UIC.

9. JA to John Addams, May 8, 1881, JAMC. In numerous college essays, Addams fashioned a heroic ideal that emphasized quiet autonomy and the ability to lead with

"terrible earnestness" but without violent bluster. See "Unknown Quantities," n.d., SCPC; "An Allegory," n.d.; "Goethe," n.d.; "George Eliot's View of Savonarola," n.d.; "Hannibal," n.d.; "High Trees Take the Wind," n.d.; "Savonarola," n.d.; "The Study of Nature," June 1879; "The Gipsies of Romance," Oct. 15, 1879; "Cicero and Caesar," Nov. 10, 1879; "The Magnificence of Character," Oct. 5, 1880; all are Rockford Seminary essays, Detzer Collection, UIC.

10. "Class-Day Exercises," *Rockford Seminary Magazine* 9 (July 1881): 211.

11. Ibid.

12. All of the graduation essays were published in *Essays of Graduating Class, Thirtieth Commencement*, pp. 37–38.

13. Kate Tanner, "'Too Many Gates to Swing On,'" in *Essays of Graduating Class, Thirtieth Commencement*, pp. 37–38.

14. Jane Addams, "Opening Address of Junior Exhibition," *Rockford Seminary Magazine* 8 (April 1880): 111.

15. Addams, "Cassandra," p. 38.

16. Ibid., pp. 38–39.

17. JA to Eva Campbell Goodrich, July 25, 1879, Eugene Goodrich Papers, York, Nebraska.

18. Jane's report to Pa on hearing an Italian revolutionary-turned-missionary indicated little interest in his "statements and statistics" about those he was serving. She wrote, instead, about her sense that the Italian was "a hero after all, for his manner was peculiar and impressive." JA to John Addams, Mar. 6, 1881, SCHS.

19. Mary Downs inquired at the end of Jane's junior year if she still expected "to study medicine after a course of study at Smith and that 'tramp' through Europe." Mary Downs to JA, May 23, 1880, SCPC.

20. Sarah Anderson to JA, July 14, 1881, SCPC.

21. JA to George Haldeman, Apr. 26, 1881, JAMC.

22. JA to Ellen Gates Starr, Feb. 13, 1881, EGSP; JA to John Addams, Mar. 20, 1881, SCHS.

23. Barker-Benfield, "'Mother Emancipator,'" pp. 395–420, and Diliberto, *A Useful Woman*, pp. 77–81. These arguments rely entirely on Addams's autobiographical remark that she wanted to attend Smith when her father wished her to attend Rockford in 1877 at the start of her college work.

24. JA to George Haldeman, Apr. 26, 1881, JAMC.

25. JA to George Haldeman, May 29, 1881, JAMC. In January of her senior year, Addams had reported to her sister that she was having some eye trouble due to overuse and fatigue and described herself as "a little run down." JA to Alice Haldeman Addams, Jan. 19, 1881, JAMC.

26. JA to Alice Addams Haldeman, May 8, 1881, JAMC; JA to George Haldeman, May 8, 1881, SCHS; JA to John Addams, May 8, 1881, JAMC.

27. Course of Study for "Collegiate Course," *Annual Catalogue*, Rockford Female Seminary, 1877–1881, RCA.

28. JA to George Haldeman, May 8, 1881, SCHS.

29. Townsend, "Anna Peck Sill," p. 236; Addams, *My Friend, Julia Lathrop*, pp. 36–37.

30. JA to George Haldeman, May 8, 1881, SCHS.

31. Ibid.

32. Ibid.

33. Townsend, "Anna Peck Sill," p. 265.

34. Jane Addams, "Valedictory," *Rockford Seminary Magazine* 9 (July 1881): 219–20.

35. Addams, *Twenty Years*, p. 54.

36. Ibid., p. 63.

37. JA to Ellen Gates Starr, Jan. 29, 1880, SCPC; Addams, *Twenty Years*, p. 51.

38. Helen Harrington to JA, July 25, 1886, SCPC. Harrington's assessment of Rockford's progress may have been affected by her position on its faculty in 1886. Still, her sense of an earlier deprivation resonated with Addams's own memory.

39. JA to Ellen Hayes, May 22, 1897, Vassar College Library.

40. Addams, *Twenty Years*, pp. 43–64.

41. Ibid., p. 45.

42. Ibid., p. 48.

43. Addams, "The Chivalry of Study," pp. 63–64; Jane Addams, "Editorial," *Rockford Seminary Magazine* 9 (February 1881): 88.

44. Addams, *Twenty Years*, p. 48.

45. Jane Addams did not read Gibbon's *Rise and Fall of the Roman Empire* until six years after graduation from Rockford. JA to Laura Shoemaker Addams, June 30, 1887, SCPC. Jane Addams, "Editorial," *Rockford Seminary Magazine* 9 (May 1881): 152–53.

46. Addams, *Twenty Years*, pp. 46, 55, 53.

47. Jane Addams, "The Poppy," Rockford Seminary essay, 1878, Detzer Collection, UIC.

48. It is not at all inconceivable that seminary girls in the 1880s experimented with opium stolen from a mother's dressing table or secured from a trusting physician. The point here is that it is very difficult to spend years reading Jane Addams's seminary letters, essays, and editorials and then imagine her consuming "small white powders at intervals during an entire long holiday." In the absence of any direct evidence on the incident, we are left with all of the other evidence on the "priggish" Jane Addams and that evidence, combined with the demonstrable other fictions in the autobiography, suggest that the opium story was included for effect, not for historical accuracy.

49. Addams, *Twenty Years*, p. 49.

50. Ibid., p. 63.

51. Ibid., p. 48. Throughout the first four chapters of her autobiography, Addams employed quotes from Rockford essays and from letters she wrote from Europe, suggesting that she did have direct access to these materials when she was writing the memoir. She often chose, however, to alter the context and even the meaning of a quotation; in one case, she actually revised the phrasing in a Rockford speech to make herself sound less enamored of Carlylean heroism than she had, in fact, been. See note 58. This suggests that Addams had a clear political purpose in constructing the story of her life before Hull-House and that she was willing to craft the materials of her life in service to that purpose.

52. Addams, *Twenty Years*, p. 56.

53. Ibid., p. 36.

54. Addams, "Follow Thy Star."

55. Jane Addams, "Tramps," Rockford Seminary essay, Apr. 10, 1878, Detzer

Collection, UIC. Jane began the essay by saying, "The country is flooded with tramps but where they come from and whither they go is a conjecture, we only know they are trying to evade the principle set down from the foundation of the earth, that a man must give a full equivalent for everything he receives; by disregarding this principle [tramps] render themselves abject and mean and merit their universal contempt." If Jane was reading national magazines at Rockford, she would have heard similar attitudes articulated. See J. G. Holland, "Once More the Tramp," *Scribner's* 15 (April 1878): 882–83; "Crime and Tramps," *Harper's* 58 (December 1878): 106–9. Perhaps it was her rereading of this essay that prompted Addams to write in *Twenty Years*, "there were practically no economics taught in women's colleges—at least fresh-water ones—thirty years ago," p. 47.

56. Jane Addams, "Resolved: That the Invention of Machinery Is a Hindrance to the Increase of Wealth in a Country," Rockford Seminary debate, Detzer Collection, UIC.

57. Jane Addams, "Editorial," *Rockford Seminary Magazine* 9 (April 1881): 115.

58. Jane Addams, "Resolved: That the British Form of Government Tends to Develop Better Statesmen than the American Form," argument for the affirmative, Rockford Seminary debate, Nov. 19, 1880, Detzer Collection, UIC. Jane recycled these exact views when she was editor of the campus magazine. In her final editorial she wrote: "The tyranny of the mob is worse than the tyranny of a Caesar. So the wise Englishmen do not talk so much of Democracy, but begin to preach organization, and a hierarchy of the best and ablest. They conclude that brave, simple, honest life is best attained under a strong, controlling government to which every man can loyally submit himself." Jane Addams, "Editorial," *Rockford Seminary Magazine* 9 (June 1881): 181.

59. Addams, *Democracy and Social Ethics*, pp. 11–12.

60. Addams, *Twenty Years*, pp. 50, 61. For her seminary disdain of "rationalism," see her Rockford essays: "We Miss the Abstract When We Comprehend," "Follow Thy Star," "Compilers," and "Goethe," Detzer Collection, UIC. In the autobiography, Addams quoted a paragraph that she attributed to a speech delivered at an "oratorical contest." She used the quotation, which argued against justice being won by "the strong arm of the hero" and in favor of more methodical progress, in order to claim possession of "premature pragmatism." Jane did deliver an oration at Beloit College in the summer of 1880, but the text has not survived. A year later, however, in "Cassandra," Jane explicitly favored the "intuition's "quick recognition of the true and genuine" over the "patient adding one to one." Maria Nutting to JA, July 2, 1880, SCPC; Addams, "Cassandra," p. 37.

61. Peterson, *Lincoln in American Memory*, pp. 175–94.

62. Addams, *Twenty Years*, pp. 61, 63.

63. Addams, *The Long Road of Woman's Memory*, pp. xii, xiv. Addams's remark squares with current literary theory on autobiography, which holds that whether an autobiographer is conscious or not of her role in constructing a public version of her past life, the story she produces will inevitably convey authentic emotional messages about her sense of that life. As John Sturrock said, "Whatever an autobiographer writes cannot but count as testimony . . . The untruth [an autobiography] tells may be as rich, or richer in significance, than the truth," "The New Model Autobiographer," p. 52. See note 17 in Introduction for references to the theoretical literature on autobiography.

64. Addams, *Twenty Years*, p. 63.

65. Jane Addams, "Editorial," *Rockford Seminary Magazine* 9 (May 1881): 153.

Chapter 7. Claims So Keenly Felt

   1. Addams, "The College Woman and Christianity," p. 1853.
   2. JA to George Haldeman, May 29, 1881, JAMC; Sarah Anderson to JA, Aug. 21, 1881, SCPC.
   3. Mary Ellwood to JA, Aug. 28, 1881, SCPC.
   4. Sarah Blaisdell to JA, Dec. 24, 1881. Mary Ellwood to JA, June 8, 1882; Helen Harrington to JA, July 23, 1881, SCPC.
   5. Charles S. Rosenberg, *The Trial of the Assassin Guiteau: Psychiatry and the Law in the Gilded Age* (Chicago: University of Chicago Press), pp. 15–23, 81. See also Allan Peskin, *Garfield: A Biography* (Kent, Ohio: Kent State University Press, 1978), pp. 583–96.
   6. Untitled, *Freeport Journal*, July 13, 1881, p. 4. The Freeport newspapers continued to draw a clear distinction between Charles Guiteau and his father, Luther. Later in the summer of 1881, in an article unrelated to the assassination, the *Freeport Daily Bulletin* listed Luther Guiteau alongside John Addams as among the "prominent citizens and leading men in the banking business" whom the community had recently lost to death, Aug. 19, 1881, p. 1.
   7. JA to Alice Addams Haldeman, Jan. 10, 1887, JAMC. JA to Alice Addams Haldeman, October 9, 1887, SAH; JA to Alice Addams Haldeman, Apr. 6 and 7, 1888, SAH. For the view that Flora Guiteau "has had such a hard life," see A. M. Rowell to JA, Feb. 5, 1887, SCPC.
   8. Ellen Gates Starr to JA, June 1881, EGSP.
   9. Nora Frothingham to JA, Sept. 22 and 24, 1881; Helen Harrington to JA, July 23, 1881, SCPC.
   10. Sarah Anderson to JA, July 14, 1881, SCPC; Sarah Blaisdell to JA, Dec. 24, 1881, SCPC.
   11. Anna Haldeman Addams to Harry Haldeman, Jan. 6, 1884, SAH.
   12. F. G. Gosling, *Before Freud: Neurasthenia and the American Medical Community* (Urbana: University of Illinois Press, 1987); Anita Clair Fellman and Michael Fellman, *Making Sense of Self: Medical Advice Literature in Late Nineteenth-Century America* (Philadelphia: University of Pennsylvania Press, 1981); Barbara Sicherman, "The Uses of Diagnosis: Doctors, Patients, and Neurasthenia," *Journal of the History of Medicine* 32 (January 1977): 33–54; David M. Rein, *S. Weir Mitchell as a Psychiatric Novelist* (New York, International Universities Press, 1952), pp. 37–46. Gosling notes that "spinal weakness" was one of the ten most cited symptoms of neurasthenia, p. 34.
   13. JA to Ellen Gates Starr, Sept. 3, 1881, SCPC.
   14. Gosling, *Before Freud*, pp. 22, 83. Fellman and Fellman, *Making Sense of Self*, pp. 14, 119. Regina Morantz, "The Lady and Her Physician," in *Clio's Consciousness Raised*, p. 47.
   15. Addams, "Darkness vs. Nebulae." In *Making Sense of Self*, the Fellmans note that, in the face of neurasthenia, "a calm equilibrium was the desired norm," p. 45.
   16. Wilder Smith to JA, Oct. 5, 1881, SCPC.
   17. "Gathered to His Fathers: Death of Hon. John H. Addams," *Freeport Weekly Journal*, Aug. 24, 1881. News articles on John Addams's death in the *Freeport Daily Bulletin*, Aug. 18 and 19, 1881, quoted the physician's certificate to the effect that "death was caused from congestion of lungs." In his biography of his aunt, however, James Weber Linn stated that the cause was appendicitis. Since Jane Addams approved this portion

of the biography, and there would be no reason to dissemble on this point, it seems likely that the newspaper was incorrect. Linn, *Jane Addams*, p. 65.

18. JA to Ellen Gates Starr, Sept. 8, 1881, EGSP; JA to Myra Linn, Jan. 3, 1922, Stanley R. Linn Family Papers, JAMC.

19. "Gathered to His Fathers," *Freeport Weekly Journal*, Aug. 24, 1881; "Dead: Hon. John H. Addams of Cedarville, Died at Green Bay, Wisconsin, on Wednesday Last," *Freeport Budget*, Aug. 20, 1881. The *Freeport Budget* carried the transcript of the Rev. Irvine's eulogy along with formal resolutions of condolence published by the bankers of the city of Freeport and the board of directors of the Second National Bank of Freeport. *Freeport Budget*, Aug. 27, 1881.

20. Rev. John Linn to JA, Aug. 26, 1881, SCPC.

21. Ibid. Jane Addams Notebook, summer 1881, JAMC. For evidence of Jane's competent efforts to make public her father's civic leadership, see: Rev. Isaac Carey to JA, published in *Freeport Budget*, Aug. 27, 1881; L. H. Mitchell to JA, Aug. 29, 1881, SCPC.

22. JA to Ellen Gates Starr, Sept. 3, 1881, SCPC.

23. S. Kendall to JA, Aug. 24, 1881, SCPC; Ellen Gates Starr to JA, Aug. 21, 1881, SCPC. Maria Nutting to JA, Nov. 17, 1887, SAH. Because Nutting's comment was made six years after John Addams died, not for condolence purposes but as part of Nutting's spontaneous recollections of her relationship with Jane at Rockford, it strikes an authentic note. Sarah Anderson to JA, Nov. 23, 1881, SCPC. Emma Briggs to JA, Dec. 30, 1881, SCPC.

24. Sarah Blaisdell to JA, Dec. 24, 1881, SCPC.

25. T. H. Haseltine to JA, Aug. 29, 1881; J. C. Irwin to JA, Apr. 5, 1882; John Linn to JA, Aug. 26, 1881, SCPC.

26. John Linn to JA, Aug. 26, 1881, SCPC. Patricia Palmieri coined the term "designated daughter" in "Patterns of Achievement of Single Academic Women," p. 64.

27. Anna Haleman Addams to JA, June 11, 1878, SAH; Anna Haleman Addams to Harry Haldeman, Dec. 12, 1884, SAH. In the fall of Jane's junior year at Rockford, she had offered to go home "for a couple of weeks" to take care of the house and "initiate the new girl" so that Anna could go visit Harry and Alice. JA to Anna Haldeman Addams, October 21, 1879, JAMC.

28. Anna Haldeman Addams to Harry Haldeman, Dec. 5, 1884, SAH.

29. Jane Addams, "The College Woman and the Family Claim," *Commons* 3 (September 1898): 3. Four years later, Addams reorganized the paragraphs in this essay and placed more emphasis on the role of social and political attitudes in legitimizing daughters' extrafamilial interests when she republished it as "Filial Relations" in *Democracy and Social Ethics* (New York: Macmillan, 1902), pp. 71–101.

30. Addams wrote that an educated daughter's "delicacy and polish were but outward symbols of her father's protection and prosperity," but it is not clear that she identified "delicacy and polish" with her own father's educational goals. Addams, "The College Woman and the Family Claim," p. 3.

31. Ibid., pp. 3, 5.

32. JA to Sarah Anderson, undated, RCA. Letter written when Sarah Anderson's father died. Because she used Rockford College stationery, Addams likely wrote the letter during one of the summer school sessions that Hull-House and Rockford jointly sponsored on the college's campus in the 1890s.

33. Report of the Administrator of the Estate of John Addams, filed Jan. 5, 1885,

Stephenson County Courthouse, Freeport, Illinois. Cited in Levine, *Jane Addams and the Liberal Tradition*, p. 27. Though this report was not filed until four years after Senator Addams's death, his survivors clearly had the right to earn from and dispense with the property before 1885. Jane Addams, for example, sold eighty acres in Stephenson County for $4,400 in March 1883, and engaged in two other land transactions in May and August 1883. See warranty deeds on file in Stephenson County Courthouse and JAPP, reel 27.

34. Addams, "The College Woman and the Family Claim," pp. 3–4.

35. Rev. John Linn to JA, Aug. 26, 1881, SCPC.

36. Addams, *Twenty Years*, p. 65. Addams began the chapter by writing, "The winter after I left school was spent in the Woman's Medical College of Philadelphia."

37. Draft of biographical sketch of Alice Addams Haldeman for the *National Cyclopedia of American Biography*, written after Alice's death in 1915, SAH.

38. Woman's Medical College of Philadelphia was one of the finest women's medical colleges in the country, having graduated 276 women in its first thirty years of operation. Jane knew about the college while she was at Rockford. When she was "Clippings and Exchanges" editor, she included this slightly inaccurate note: "Woman's Medical College of Pennsylvania has already graduated over 300 women as physicians and these graduates are now doing successful work in private practice, clinics and hospitals," *Rockford Seminary Magazine* 8 (February 1880): 57. The quality of the work done at the college had worn down the opposition of male physicians in Philadelphia. By 1881, the college's students were allowed to attend various clinics in the city, and the all-male Philadelphia County Medical Society no longer excommunicated members who associated with the college. Gulielma Fell Alsop, M.D., *History of the Woman's Medical College of Philadelphia, 1850–1950* (Philadelphia: J. B. Lippincott, 1950); Regina Morantz-Sanchez, *Sympathy and Science: Women Physicians in American Medicine* (New York: Oxford University Press, 1985), pp. 64–89; Mary Roth Walsh, *"Doctors Wanted: No Women Need Apply": Sexual Barriers in the Medical Profession, 1835–1975* (New Haven: Yale University Press, 1977), p. 72. Jane Addams expressed her high opinion of the college near the end of her stay there. Emma Briggs to JA, Dec. 30, 1881, SCPC.

39. Rachel Bodley to JA, July 11, 1885, JAMC. When Jane returned from two years abroad in the summer of 1885, she brought Dean Bodley a handmade gift of flowers that Jane had gathered in various localities in Europe, then mounted and labeled. In her delight over the very personal gift, Bodley told Jane, "I prize your love and trust that it may long be mine! I reciprocate all that you so generously lavish upon me. Do not wait to come to Philadelphia to say to me some of those things you 'saved' to say. Write them to me in some quiet hour at home and I shall be delighted to read and to reply." Given the sentimental style in which women communicated with one another in this era, this letter—the only surviving one of their correspondence—is not remarkable. But the strength of the attachment is noteworthy given Jane's very short tenure at the medical school.

40. Sarah Blaisdell to JA, Dec. 24, 1881; Emma Briggs to JA, Dec. 30, 1881, SCPC.

41. George Haldeman to Anna Haldeman Addams, Dec. 21, 1881, SAH.

42. JA to Alice Addams Haldeman, Oct. 23, 1885, JAMC.

43. Addams referred to her Philadelphia breakdown as a "nervous affliction" in "The World Is Better That This Woman Lives," by A. L. Bowen, *New Age Illustrated* 11 (November 1927): 27. She called it a "spinal difficulty" in *Twenty Years*, p. 65.

44. Sarah Blaisdell to JA, Dec. 24, 1881, SCPC.

45. Gosling, *Before Freud*, p. 37; Ann Douglas Wood, "The Fashionable Diseases: Women's Complaints and Their Treatment," *Journal of Interdisciplinary History* 4 (1973): 25–52; Ernest Earnest, *S. Weir Mitchell: Novelist and Physician* (Philadelphia: University of Pennsylvania Press, 1950), pp. 81–85. Charlotte Perkins Gilman, *The Yellow Wallpaper* (Boston: Small and Maynard, 1899).

46. Addams, *Twenty Years*, p. 65. Addams received a certification of her completion of the dissection course in December 1881 and enrolled in an anatomy course in the winter session, SCPC and JAPP, reel 27, frame 0472.

47. Laura Malburn to JA, Feb. 11, 1882, SCPC. Malburn was a friend of Anna's from Freeport who was writing in response to a note from Jane reporting on the success of Anna's operation and the quality of care Anna was receiving. Malburn expressed relief that Anna was in Philadelphia, where she could get the finest care, and commented on "how admirably all was arranged for her convenience."

48. George Haldeman to JA, Feb. 12, 1882, SAH.

49. Sarah Blaisdell to JA, Dec. 24, 1881; Sarah Anderson to JA, Jan. 11, 1882, SCPC.

50. JA to Alice Addams Haldeman, Aug. 8, 1883, JAMC; George Haldeman to JA, June 1, 1882, SAH; Linn, *Jane Addams*, p. 49.

51. Jane Addams Notebook, July 15, 1882, SCPC and JAPP, reel 27, frame 0370.

52. Jane Addams, "The College Woman and the Family Claim," pp. 3, 5.

53. Gosling, *Before Freud*, pp. 165–75. In his Introduction to *Before Freud*, Alfred M. Freedman, M.D., comments that "Gosling demonstrates the transformation of etiological concepts of neurasthenia from a somatic disorder with a variety of physical and mental manifestations to the realization that neurasthenia was basically a disorder of the mind. Many physicians, particularly after 1900, spoke of the mind and body as inseparable and that perturbations of the mind could produce serious physical symptoms," p. 4.

54. Addams, "The College Woman and the Family Claim," p. 5.

55. JA to Alice Addams Haldeman, July 11, Oct. 8, and June 15, 1883, JAMC.

56. Virtually every letter Anna Haldeman Addams wrote to Harry Haldeman in the years between 1883 and 1885 includes some reference to the evils of drink.

57. Linn, *Jane Addams*, p. 33.

58. Marcet Haldeman-Julius, "Jane Addams as I Knew Her," p. 5.

59. George Haldeman to JA, Feb. 12, 1882, SAH; George Haldeman to Harry Haldeman, Feb. 12, 1882, HJFP; George Haldeman to Anna Haldeman Addams, Feb. 14, 1882, HJFP; George Haldeman to JA, June 1, 1882, SAH.

60. Jane Addams Notebook, April 1882 and July 15, 1882, SCPC and JAPP, reel 27, frames 0367, 0370.

61. George Eliot, *Middlemarch* (1871–1872; London: Zodiac Press, 1982), p. 561. The female character in this passage was Mary Garth, who was reaffirming her loyalty to Fred Vincy by setting aside her fondness for Mr. Farebrother. Jane Addams Notebook, July 15, 1882, SCPC and JAPP, reel 27, frame 0370.

62. Harry Haldeman to George Haldeman, Jan. 30, 1883, HJFP.

63. Sarah Anderson to JA, July 14, 1881, SCPC. Regarding emotional role reversals in nineteenth-century teacher-student relationships in Britain's female schools, see Martha Vicinus, "Distance and Desire," pp. 600–622.

64. Sarah Anderson to JA, Dec. 19, 1881, SCPC. For additional examples of Anderson

seeking job advice from her star student, see Sarah Anderson to JA, Jan. 11, Apr. 11, June 4 and 6, 1882, SCPC.

65. Sarah Anderson to JA, Jan. 11, 1882, and Sept. 11, 1881, SCPC.

66. Sarah Anderson to JA, Apr. 11 and June 6, 1882, SCPC.

67. Sarah Anderson to JA, Apr. 27 and Aug. 13, 1882, SCPC.

68. Sarah Anderson to JA, Oct. 26, 1881, SCPC. Jane and Ellen Gates Starr both continued to refer to Anderson as "Miss Anderson." See JA to Ellen Gates Starr, Mar. 19, 1882, EGSP; Ellen Gates Starr to JA, Apr. 9, 1882, SCPC. The first use of "Sarah" to refer to Sarah Anderson appears in a letter from Ellen remarking that she hoped a particularly excellent student of hers would become, to Ellen, "something of what you were to Sarah." Ellen Starr to JA, Apr. 28, 1885, EGSP.

69. Eva Campbell Goodrich to JA, Mar. 4, 1882; Ida May Carey to JA Oct. 5, 1881; Helen Harrington to JA, Aug. 17 and Oct. 1, 1881, SCPC.

70. Helen Harrington to JA, Mar. 9, 1882, SCPC.

71. Ellen Gates Starr to JA, May 14, 1882, SCPC.

72. Helen Harrington to JA, October 1, 1881; Mary Downs to JA, Nov. 14, 1880; Helen Harrington to JA, Aug. 17, 1881; July 25, 1882, SCPC. See, too, Eva Campbell Goodrich to JA, Sept. 28, 1882, in which the now-married young woman with two stepchildren explained that she "still" taught music to thirty students but found little time for reading or study as her main work was "the care of these boys," SCPC.

73. JA to Ellen Gates Starr, Sept. 3, 1882, SCPC; JA to Ellen Gates Starr, Jan. 7, 1883, EGSP.

74. Ellen Gates Starr to JA, Sept. 10, 1881, and Oct. 22, 1882, SCPC.

75. Ellen Gates Starr to JA, Apr. 25, 1883, SCPC.

76. Ellen Gates Starr to JA, June 5, 1880, SCPC.

77. Ellen Gates Starr to JA, Oct. 22, 1882, SCPC.

78. JA to Ellen Gates Starr, Jan. 7, 1883, EGSP.

79. Ellen Gates Starr to JA, Jan. 12, 1883, SCPC.

80. Ellen Gates Starr to JA, May 14 and Apr. 19, 1882, and Jan. 12, 1883, SCPC.

81. Ellen Gates Starr to JA, Jan. 12, 1883, SCPC.

82. Ibid. In this letter, Ellen noted that "the only thing I regret about my work is that I get very little time for 'improving my mind' and the work I do does not require much reading except on artistic subjects."

83. Jane Addams Notebook, undated but the entry refers to the summer of 1882, SCPC and JAPP, reel 27, frame 0357.

84. Rev. John Linn to JA, Aug. 26, 1881, SCPC.

85. Jane Addams Notebook, entries undated but internal comments indicate spring and summer of 1882, SCPC and Jane Addams Microfilm, reel 27, frames 0366, 0368, 0364, 0373, 0374.

86. Jane Addams Notebook, Apr. 27, 1882, and undated entry from 1882, SCPC and Jane Addams Microfilm, reel 27, frames 0367, 0368.

87. Jane Addams Notebook, undated entry from 1882, SCPC and JAPP, reel 27, frame 0357.

88. Mary Ellwood to JA, July 30, 1882, SCPC. Jane's report on investigating off-campus housing elicited Ellwood's warning, "boarding in town . . . is not near as nice and you don't get acquainted as easily."

89. Sarah Anderson to JA, Sept. 9, 1882, SCPC. Mary Ellwood wrote to Jane on

Sept. 1, 1882, expressing the wish that she could see Jane before Jane left for Smith. Ellwood had decided not to return to the Massachusetts college. Mary Ellwood to JA, Sept. 1, 1882, SCPC.

90. Alice Addams Haldeman to JA, Sept. 10, 1882, SAH.

91. Davis *American Heroine*, p. 30.

92. JA to Alice Addams Haldeman, Apr. 24, 1883, JAMC; JA to Ellen Gates Starr, Jan. 7, 1883, EGSP; JA to Alice Addams Haldeman, May 3 and 29, 1883; JA to Alice Addams Haldeman, Dec. 22, 1883, JAMC. In this last letter, written a year after the procedure, Jane assured Alice that she remembered her sister's "devotion and goodness" during the recuperative period "with warmest gratitude."

93. Harry Haldeman to George Haldeman, Jan. 30, 1883, HJFP.

94. JA to Ellen Gates Starr, Jan. 7, 1883, EGSP.

95. JA to Alice Addams Haldeman, Aug. 8, 1883, JAMC.

96. JA to Ellen Gates Starr, Jan. 7, 1883, EGSP.

97. Ibid.; Ellen Gates Starr to JA, Jan. 12, 1883, SCPC.

98. Jane Addams, "A Village Decoration Day," *Rockford Seminary Magazine* 11 (March 1883): 75–79.

99. Jury verdict in commitment proceedings regarding John Weber Addams, Stephenson County Courthouse, Freeport, Illinois, Aug. 3, 1885, Records of Stephenson County Courthouse. In the 1860s, Dr. McFarland had complied with the involuntarily commitment of Elizabeth Packard, whose husband had viewed her dalliance with spiritualism as evidence of insanity. The case inspired the passage of Illinois' landmark "personal liberty bill," which created safeguards against unwarranted, involuntary commitments and spurred creation of the Illinois Board of Public Charities, which was supposed to oversee the management of the state's various asylums. Andrew McFarland was "an old friend" of Senator Addams, but that did not prevent the Senator from supporting both laws. JA to Alice Addams Haldeman, Apr. 25, 1883, JAMC; Minkoff, "John Huy Addams: Republican Steward of Stephenson County." Thomas J. Brown, *Dorothea Dix: New England Reformer* (Cambridge: Harvard University Press, 1998), pp. 338–39; Gerald Grob, *Mental Illness and American Society, 1875–1940* (Princeton: Princeton University Press, 1983), pp. 10–11, 47–48.

100. Rosenberg, *The Trial of the Assassin Guiteau*. The *Freeport Journal* anticipated this debate over the nature and meaning of insanity in its commentary on Charles Guiteau just four days after the shooting. The editorial distinguished between true insanity, "the dethronement of the reasoning faculties," and Guiteau's status which was "*non compos mentis*—not of sound mind." In the judgment of his hometown neighbors, young Guiteau had been predisposed to fanciful thinking "from boyhood up" but was sane enough to "coolly calculate the chances of danger and take the precautions for escape." *Freeport Journal*, untitled editorial, July 6, 1881, p. 4. Five months later, during Guiteau's trial, the *Freeport Journal* reported that the defendant had promised to make the late Senator John Addams governor of Illinois in exchange for a loan to buy the Chicago *InterOcean* newspaper. According to Guiteau, Senator Addams was "a man of reputation and character" who declined Guiteau's offer because "he did not have any political aspirations . . . he preferred his old, simple way of living." *Freeport Journal*, Dec. 7, 1881.

101. Grob, *Mental Illness and American Society*, pp. 13–33. In "The Paradox of

Prudence: Mental Health in the Gilded Age," Barbara Sicherman argues that physicians from across a broad spectrum of experience and theoretical orientations agreed that mental health was achieved through a life of moderation and stability. In *Madhouses, Mad-Doctors, and Madmen: The Social History of Psychiatry in the Victorian Era,* ed. Andrew Scull (Philadelphia: University of Pennsylvania Press, 1981), pp. 218–40.

102. JA to Alice Addams Haldeman, May 7 and 3, 1883, JAMC.

103. JA to Alice Addams Haldeman, July 11, 1883, JAMC.

104. People in the last quarter of the nineteenth century were pessimistic about recovery from even acute mental illness, fearing that a manic episode destroyed a critical amount of vital force. Grob, *Mental Illness and American Society,* p. 39. For Jane's worry that Weber's recovery would "never" occur or would "not be permanent," see JA to Alice Addams Haldeman, May 22, 1883, JAMC.

105. Anna Haldeman Addams to Harry Haldeman, Nov. 30, 1882, HJFP. No letter from Anna to Jane survives from this spring, and Anna did not rush home to help. JA to Alice Addams Haldeman, Apr. 24 and May 3, 1883, JAMC; George Haldeman to Anna Haldeman Addams, May 20, 1883, HJFP.

106. JA to Ellen Gates Starr, Apr. 24, 1883, EGSP.

107. JA to Ellen Gates Starr, Jan. 7, 1883, EGSP.

108. JA to Ellen Gates Starr, Apr. 24, 1883, EGSP.

109. Ellen Gates Starr to JA, Apr. 25, 1883, SCPC. JA to Ellen Gates Starr, Aug. 12, 1883, EGSP.

110. Ellen Gates Starr to JA, Apr. 25, 1883, SCPC.

111. JA to Ellen Gates Starr, July 11, 1883, EGSP.

112. Ibid.

113. JA to Alice Addams Haldeman, Apr. 24 and May 1, 1883, JAMC.

114. JA to Alice Addams Haldeman, Apr. 24 and 25, May 1 and 3, June 5, July 24, 1883, JAMC.

115. JA to Alice Addams Haldeman, Jan. 23, 1880, SAH; Jan. 19, 1881, JAMC. As a seminary student, Jane had delivered a lofty "little preach" to Alice about treating Anna with greater care and remembering that "the responsibility of tolerance lies with those of deepest insight."

116. JA to Alice Addams Haldeman, July 24 and Apr. 25, 1883, JAMC.

117. JA to Alice Addams Haldeman, May 3, 1883, JAMC.

118. JA to Alice Addams Haldeman, July 11 and 24, 1883, JAMC.

119. Sarah Anderson to JA, Nov. 16, 1881, SCPC.

120. Anna Peck Sill to JA, May 3, 1883, RCA.

121. JA to Alice Addams Haldeman, May 7, 1883, JAMC; Townsend, "Anna Peck Sill," pp. 283–85.

122. Jane Addams, "To the Uncomfortableness of Transition," alumnae address printed in *Rockford Seminary Magazine* 11 (July 1883): 215–17.

123. Ibid.

124. Mary Downs to JA, May 23, 1880, SCPC.

125. JA to Ellen Gates Starr, July 11, 1883, EGSP. It does appear that Starr considered joining Jane in Europe in the spring of 1885 but could not manage it. See Ellen Gates Starr to Mary Blaisdell, Mar. 14, 1885, EGSP.

126. JA to Ellen Gates Starr, Aug. 12, 1883, EGSP.

Chapter 8. Scenes Among Gods and Giants

1. Mary S. Schriber, *Writing Home: American Women Abroad, 1830–1920* (Charlottesville: University Press of Virginia, 1997), and William W. Stowe, *Going Abroad: European Travel in Nineteenth-Century American Culture* (Princeton: Princeton University Press, 1994).

2. JA to Ellen Gates Starr, Aug. 12, 1883, EGSP.

3. JA to Alice Addams Haldeman, Aug. 27, 1883, JAMC. Henry James, Jr., *Daisy Miller* (New York: Harper and Brothers, 1878).

4. JA to Alice Addams Haldeman, Nov. 21 and Dec. 26, 1883, JAMC. At an early point in the trip Jane apologized for not even opening a book Ellen had mailed to Cedarville as a going-away gift. She had thought it was from "a certain youth who has been sending so many books, etc., that I have been obliged to return them." Her "suspicion" that the gift came from a young man overcame any "temptation" to open the package. JA to Ellen Gates Starr, Nov. 3, 1883, EGSP.

5. Upon reading *Spirit of Youth and the City Streets,* William James wrote that the book was "simply great. Hard not to cry at certain pages! The fact is, Madam, that you are not like the rest of us, who *seek* the truth and *try* to express it. You *inhabit* reality; and when you open your mouth truth can't help being uttered." William James to JA, Dec. 13, 1909, SCPC.

6. JA to Alice Addams Haldeman, Nov.16, 1884, JAMC.

7. JA to Ellen Gates Starr, Aug. 12, 1883, EGSP.

8. Anna Haldeman Addams to Harry Haldeman, Feb. 7, 1884, HJFP.

9. JA to Ellen Gates Starr, July 11, 1883, EGSP; JA to Alice Addams Haldeman, Dec. 14, 1883, JAMC.

10. JA to Anna Haldeman Addams, Jan. 28, 1888, and Dec. 14, 1883, JAMC.

11. When Anna was bedridden in Dublin with her recurrent bowel inflammation, Sarah was "such a fine nurse" that Jane felt like "the lady of leisure." JA to Harry Haldeman, Sept. 7, 1883, JAMC. Jane and Sarah bought "tony" traveling dresses and then laughed at "the idea of two country girls coming to Paris and getting dresses that they are only comfortable in when they sit perfectly 'quiet.'" JA to Alice Addams Haldeman, June 22, 1884, JAMC. After Sarah returned to the U.S., Jane wrote for her cousin's "hearty approval" of the new clothes she and Anna had purchased in London: "We go to the continent a shade less shabby than a year ago." JA to Sarah Hostetter, Sept. 23, 1884, JAMC.

12. Anna Haldeman Addams to Harry Haldeman, Jan. 29, 1884, HJFP.

13. A few weeks before departing the U.S., Jane told Alice that she was "trying very hard to persuade Ma to go and she thinks seriously of it." Jane told Ellen, "If Ma goes we will be more or less independent of [the Ellwoods]." When Anna and Sarah Hostetter agreed to go, Jane was "delighted" and "sure we are going to have a happy, healthful, and profitable time." JA to Alice Addams Haldeman, July 11, 1883, JAMC; JA to Ellen Gates Starr, July 11, 1883, EGSP; JA to Alice Addams Haldeman, July 18, 1883, JAMC. For Jane's belief that Anna would benefit from the trip, see JA to George Haldeman, Oct. 8, 1883, SCPC; JA to Alice Addams Haldeman, Oct. 8, 1883, JAMC. Anna welcomed the opportunity to get away. In a letter to Harry from Europe, Anna commented on feeling no ties "to the other side of the ocean . . . tis not much attraction to think of empty Cedarville and call it home without anything to bind us to it except a world of care and unfriendly people, most of them at least." Anna Haldeman Addams to Harry

Haldeman, June 29, 1884, HJFP. When Anna became ill in Dublin, their first stop, Harry, Alice, and George argued that she should return home immediately to recuperate, but Jane lobbied hard against the idea by arguing, "Sarah and I both feel it is a privilege to have Ma with us and that we could hardly keep on without her." JA to Alice Addams Haldeman, Oct. 8, 1883; JA to Harry Haldeman, Sept. 7 and 12, 1883, JAMC. JA to George Haldeman, Oct. 8, 1883, SCPC.

14. JA to Mary Addams Linn, Dec. 6, 1883, JAMC; JA to Alice Addams Haldeman, Dec. 14 and Dec. 22/23, 1883, JAMC.

15. "Personals," *Rockford Seminary Magazine* 12 (February 1884): 68; JA to George Haldeman, Jan. 20, 1884, SCHS.

16. JA to Mary Addams Linn, Dec. 6, 1883, JAMC; JA to Alice Addams Haldeman, Nov. 21, and Dec. 22/23, 1883, JAMC.

17. JA to Mary Addams Linn, Dec. 6, 1883, JAMC.

18. JA to Alice Addams Haldeman, Sept. 30, 1883, JAMC.

19. JA to George Haldeman, Oct. 8, 1883, SCPC. JA to Alice Addams Haldeman, Oct. 23, 1883, JAMC.

20. JA to Ellen Gates Starr, Nov. 3 and. Dec. 2, 1883, EGSP; JA to Mary Addams Linn, Nov. 4, 1883, JAMC; JA to Alice Addams Haldeman, Nov. 18, 1883, JAMC.

21. JA to George Haldeman, Nov. 30, 1883; SCPC. George was a bit stung by Jane's retort to him on the Dresden matter; he wrote to his mother that he was "sorry I have disseminated heretical opinions and am glad indeed you find Dresden so pleasant." George Haldeman to Anna Haldeman Addams, Dec. 22, 1883, HJFP.

22. JA to Alice Addams Haldeman, Sept. 30, 1883, and Jan. 17 and Mar. 6, 1884, JAMC.

23. JA to Sarah Blaisdell, Apr. 26, 1884, SCPC. JA to Weber Addams, Mar. 20, 1884, JAMC.

24. JA to Mary Addams Linn, Mar. 31, 1884; JA to Weber Addams, May 19, 1884; JA to Alice Addams Haldeman, May 25 and 31, 1884, JAMC.

25. JA to Alice Addams Haldeman, Oct. 24, 1884, JAMC.

26. It appears to have been Harry who volunteered the notion that Jane and Anna had "no moorings." In a letter to Harry announcing their final decision to stay another year, Anna wrote: "As you say, we have no moorings on the other side of the ocean (at least not I)." Anna Haldeman Addams to Harry Haldeman, June 29, 1884, HJFP.

27. JA to Alice Addams Haldeman, Nov. 16, 1884, JAMC. Jane told Mary that the purpose of this second year was to "study some, and see some things over again more slowly in order to digest and make the trip more complete than one year can make it." JA to Mary Addams Linn, Mar. 31, 1884, JAMC.

28. JA to Alice Addams Haldeman, Dec. 28, 1884, JAMC.

29. JA to Alice Addams Haldeman, Feb. 1, 1885, JAMC. After two months in Paris, living with a French family and attempting to speak French every day, Jane Addams was still unable to figure out even the subject of the debate underway in the French Senate on the day she and Anna attended. But in April, Jane reported to Alice that she and Anna were able to order their meals in French and conduct limited conversation. JA to Mary Addams Linn, Feb. 1, 1885; JA to Alice Addams Haldeman, April, n.d., 1885, JAMC.

30. George Haldeman to Anna Haldeman Addams, June 20, 1886, HJFP.

31. JA to Alice Addams Haldeman, Sept. 30 and Oct. 19, 1883; JA to Weber Addams, Oct. 19, 1883, JAMC.

32. JA to Alice Addams Haldeman, June 29, 1884, JAMC.

33. JA to Weber Addams, May 19, 1884, JAMC.

34. JA to Alice Haldeman Addams, Jan. 8, 1884, JAMC. In her second December in Europe, when she was alone with Anna, Jane wrote to Ellen Starr that she shared Ellen's "regard of Spain and were it not for the cholera we would probably have spent this winter in the south of France and Spain." The situation in Spain was severe enough to have prompted official travel quarantines. JA to Ellen Gates Starr, Dec. 7, 1884, EGSP. Jane and Anna made numerous accommodations to the cholera situation in Europe in 1884. Given Anna's bowel condition, cholera held special terrors in her mind. Though Jane insisted that, thanks to travel, Anna's "bowels have never been better than the last six months," still, she admitted to Alice that her stepmother was "sometimes inclined to be afraid of" cholera. JA to Mary Addams Linn, July 12, 1884; JA to Alice Addams Haldeman, July 14, 1884; JA to Mary Addams Linn, Aug. 10, 1884; JA to Weber Addams, Aug. 17 and Sept. 14, 1884; JA to Alice Addams Haldeman, Nov. 16 and Dec. 20, 1884, JAMC. The fear about cholera was much more Anna's issue than Jane's. Anna told Harry that "Jane has been restless and anxious to go to Spain amidst earthquakes, cholera, and warlike uprising of the people," but Anna was sure she would "not venture further." Jane wrote rather playfully to Alice about the merits of putting themselves in danger for the sake of spending a month in Spain in the spring. "Is it less ignominious to perish by an earthquake than to be blown up by dynamite or succumb to cholera?" she asked her sister. Anna Haldeman to Harry Haldeman, Feb. 13, 1885, HJFP; JA to Alice Addams Haldeman, April, n.d., 1885, JAMC. Seasickness was a real and constant problem for Jane Addams; she was even seasick on the "calm" boat ride from London to Hamburg. But she was determined not to give in to this particular ailment. JA to Mary Addams Linn, Aug. 30/Sept. 1, 1883, JAMC; JA to Sarah Blaisdell, Apr. 26, 1884, SCPC; JA to Mary Addams Linn, Apr. 26, 1884, JAMC; JA to Alice Addams Haldeman, May 7, 1884, JAMC.

35. JA to Mary Addams Linn, July 12, 1884; JA to Alice Addams Haldeman, July 14 and 20, 1884; JA to Mary Addams Linn, July 29, 1884, JAMC. Jane wrote disparagingly of the vast numbers of tourists in the Alps who did not hike or ride horseback but passively stared at "'the view.'" JA to Weber Addams, July 4, 1884, JAMC.

36. JA to Alice Addams Haldeman, July 14, 1884, JAMC; JA to George Haldeman, Jan. 4, 1884, SCHS. Jane was so influenced by her era's assumptions about the dangers of overexertion that she did not recognize that she and Anna felt lethargic only when they resumed a sedentary schedule. When Anna was running a fever in Berlin, Jane was completely puzzled, insisting to George, "This has not been the result of overdoing for we have been very quiet and regular and very glad to settle into the pleasant hum-drum of life." JA to George Haldeman, Oct. 24, 1884, SCHS.

37. JA to Alice Addams Haldeman, Dec. 22–23, 1883, JAMC. In Dresden, Jane limited herself to German, instead of trying to take French as well, because she did not want to "run any risks of overwork." JA to Alice Addams Haldeman, Nov. 21, 1883, JAMC.

38. JA to Ellen Gates Starr, Dec. 2, 1883, EGSP. In her 1898 essay "The College Woman and the Family Claim," Addams recalled her impression of "energy misapplied" when she saw fashionable young men and women engaged in Alpine hiking because they had nothing useful to do. "They did not, of course, thoroughly enjoy it," wrote Addams, "for we are too complicated to be content with mere exercise." Addams, "The College Woman and the Family Claim," pp. 3–7.

39. Gosling, *Before Freud*; Fellman and Fellman, *Making Sense of Self*; Trecker,

"Sex, Science, and Education"; Anna Haldeman Addams to Harry Haldeman, Jan. 6, 1884, HJFP.

40. JA to Alice Addams Haldeman, Oct. 1, 1884, JAMC; JA to Ellen Gates Starr, June 8, 1884, EGSP. Jane told Alice that they were spending a lot of time "reading up" because they had discovered that they were "painfully ignorant" and it was "hard work to be intelligently prepared for Italy." She approached "the old life of Florence" as "such an intense, intellectual affair that it takes more than usual effort to get into the spirit of it." Similarly, she told George that they were spending a lot of time on maps and guidebooks "in order to see intelligently" and because "it is utterly impossible to transport yourself back into the time of Dante and Giotto . . . without a certain amount of effort and distinctive reading." JA to Alice Addams Haldeman, Sept. 30, 1883, Feb. 10 and Mar. 6, 1884, JAMC. JA to George Haldeman, Feb. 2 and Mar. 8, 1884, SCHS.

41. JA to George Haldeman, Mar. 8, 1884, SCHS. Jane compensated for the scholarly imbalance in their relationship by scolding George severely for an absent-minded failure to send his letters through the American Exchange service, which they were paying for. Jane admitted to being "excessively annoyed" that several family members "*will not* obey explicit instructions" and excused her outburst with George on the grounds that he was "the most patient victim" to whom she could "express" herself. JA to George Haldeman, Jan. 20, 1884, SCHS.

42. Gosling, *Before Freud*; Trecker, "Sex, Science, and Education"; Alaya, "Victorian Science and the Genius of Woman"; Patricia Smith Butcher, "More Than Just a Parlor Ornament: Women's Rights Periodicals and Women's Higher Education," Ph.D. diss., Rutgers University, 1986; Edward Clarke, *Sex in Education; Or a Fair Chance for the Girls* (Boston: James R. Osgood, 1873).

43. JA to Ellen Gates Starr, June 8, 1884, EGSP. Jane's mood at this point of her European tour was likely influenced by the fact that she was spending "every day" at the dentist's office. "My teeth have never been so miserable," she told Alice. "Do not be dreadfully surprised if you see me come home with a new set!" JA to Alice Addams Haldeman, June 10, 1884, JAMC.

44. JA to George Haldeman, Nov. 15, 1884, SCPC.

45. JA to Ellen Gates Starr, Nov. 3 and Dec. 2, 1883, EGSP; JA to George Haldeman, Jan. 4, 1884, SCHS.

46. JA to Ellen Gates Starr, June 8, 1884, EGSP.

47. Ellen Gates Starr to Mary Starr Blaisdell, Mar. 14, 1885, EGSP. Blaisdell was Starr's sister and no relation to Sarah Blaisdell, Jane's Rockford teacher. Ellen turned down a teaching job at Rockford Female Seminary because she felt she would be "bored" there and "the difference in money isn't worth that." Ellen felt great affection for the headmistress at her school, Caroline Kirkland, and told Blaisdell, "My work this year has been so satisfactory and pleasant. . . . It is the nicest year on the whole that I have ever had." George, meanwhile, was writing letters to his mother in which he assured her that his "health and spirits" were good, that he was enjoying his work "and try to think that I am useful if I study and that it does good as much as if I were in some other active employment." George described himself as "in love with the University" and felt he "would be content to stay here always and think it would be a good way to pass existence." George Haldeman to Anna Haldeman Addams, Jan. 6 and Feb. 3, 1884, HJFP.

48. JA to Ellen Gates Starr, Dec. 2, 1883, and Feb. 21, 1885, EGSP.

49. Just when Jane had given up German "in despair," George announced that "the exercise of the mind in study" was doubtless the "grandest pleasure" and "everything else is cheap in comparison." JA to Alice Addams Haldeman, Dec. 28, 1884, JAMC; George Haldeman to Anna Haldeman Addams, Jan. 25, 1885, HJP.

50. JA to George Haldeman, Feb. 2, 1884, SCHS; JA to George Haldeman, Nov. 15, 1884, SCPC.

51. JA to George Haldeman, Mar. 8, 1884, SCHS; JA to Ellen Gates Starr, Mar. 9, 1884, EGSP.

52. Addams, *Twenty Years*, p. 75.

53. JA to Sarah Blaisdell, Apr. 26, 1884, SCPC.

54. D. J. Hickey and J. E. Doherty, eds., *Dictionary of Irish History Since 1800* (Dublin: Gill and Macmillan, 1980), pp. 419–22.

55. JA to Alice Addams Haldeman, Sept. 30 and Oct. 19, 1883; JA to Weber Addams, Sept. 14, 1884, JAMC.

56. Jane Addams Diary, Sept. 16, 1883, JAMC.

57. JA to Alice Addams Haldeman, May 31, 1884, and Nov. 18, 1883, JAMC; JA to Mary Addams Linn, Jan. 13, 1884, JAMC; JA to Weber Addams, Jan. 27, 1884, JAMC; JA to Alice Addams Haldeman, Feb. 20, 1884, JAMC. JA to Ellen Gates Starr, Mar. 9, 1884, EGSP; JA to Sarah Blaisdell, Mar. 15, 1884, SCPC. Though Addams later claimed a distinct memory of her father grieving over the death of Joseph Mazzini, the leader of the pro-republican forces in Italy, she made no pilgrimage to Mazzini's birthplace in Genoa. Instead, she admired Victor Emmanuel, the man whose constitutional monarchy Mazzini could not accept. Addams, *Twenty Years*, pp. 21–22. In her November 1883 letter to Alice about visiting Frederick the Great's palace at Potsdam, she allowed for the possibility that it was Carlyle's depiction, as much as the "greatness of [Frederick] himself," that gave her such a feeling for the palace. JA to Alice Addams Haldeman, Nov. 18, 1883, JAMC. Jane visited Savonarola's cell because of her affection for George Eliot's historical novel *Romola*, which treated the rebel monk as a great man brought down by his own hubris. Jane reflected Eliot's view in writing to Ellen, Mar. 9, 1884, that "intense political life . . . overcame Savonarola's larger aims and made him confuse God's cause with Florentine government," EGSP.

58. JA to Ellen Gates Starr, Dec. 7, 1884, EGSP.

59. JA to Ellen Gates Starr, Nov. 3, 1883, EGSP; Anna Haldeman Addams to Harry Haldeman, Feb. 7, 1884, Mar. 23, 1884, and Jan. 29, 1884, HJFP. Anna was of the opinion that "to stretch one's neck" to view paintings and frescoes all day was "the hardest work for the back and shoulders in the world." JA to Weber Addams, Oct. 29, 1883, JAMC.

60. JA to Alice Addams Haldeman, Mar. 6, 1884, JAMC. JA to Ellen Gates Starr, Mar. 9, 1884, EGSP.

61. JA to Ellen Gates Starr, Mar. 9, 1884, EGSP.

62. JA to Ellen Gates Starr, July 11, 1883, EGSP.

63. JA to Alice Addams Haldeman, Apr. 6, 1884, JAMC, and JA to Mary Addams Linn, Aug. 10, 1884, and Mar. 29, 1885, JAMC, all expressed her disapproval of the grandeur of St. Peter's Basilica in Rome. From Bologna, Anna described Italians as people with "no intellect much less spirituality," and categorized the "old nations" like Italy as "far behind us" in their religion. Writing from Florence, Anna observed that Italians had wasted a lot of money on "tributes to God" and sacrificed "progress." But Anna reserved her final comment on Italian Catholicism for a retrospect written from Paris

in which she declared that the Italian privileging of crucifixes over the Bible had "sunk" the people in "superstition" and resulted in "a nation of fetish practices . . . and fearful habits . . . leaning more toward the beastly side of their instincts than to any spirituality." Anna Haldeman Addams to Harry Haldeman, Feb. 24, Mar. 11, and June 14, 1884, HJFP.

64. Anti-Catholicism was an unremarkable attitude among American Protestants, even liberals like John Addams, who were not notably hostile to immigrants; it was simply an everyday assumption. See Jay Dolan, *The American Catholic Experience: A History from Colonial Times to the Present* (Garden City, N.Y.: Doubleday, 1985); Jenny Franchot, *Roads to Rome: The Antebellum Protestant Encounter with Catholicism* (Berkeley: University of California Press, 1994).

65. Jane expressed partisan support for Victor Emmanuel and disdain for Pope Pius IX in various remarks. JA to Weber Addams, Mar. 20, 1884; JA to Alice Addams Haldeman, May 31, 1884, JAMC.

66. JA to Mary Addams Linn, Mar. 31, 1884 JAMC.

67. Carrell, "Reflections in a Mirror," pp. 100–101. Carrell argues that in the summer of 1883, "as Jane Addams prepared to sail for Europe,, Ellen tried valiantly to recover her equilibrium. Still seeking a religious solution to her problems she decided somewhat impulsively to join the Episcopal Church." With good support from Ellen's correspondence, Carrell claims that Ellen joined the church as a way of preparing herself for faith, not because she had achieved it. Initially, Jane did not grasp that this was Ellen's process.

68. JA to Ellen Gates Starr, June 8, June 22, and July 11, 1883, EGSP. Jane's struggle for inspiration from religious art is evident in a letter to Mary from Dresden. Jane reported to her sister, the minister's wife, on one beautiful chapel where the "divine faces" make you feel as if "you would never do a mean thing again." The unconverted Jane immediately added, "of course, you . . . probably do something trifling on the way home but it never fails to make the same impression." JA to Mary Addams Linn, Dec. 10, 1883, JAMC.

69. JA to Ellen Gates Starr, Mar. 30, 1885, EGSP.

70. Addams, *Twenty Years*, p. 75.

71. In a letter to Weber on the beauties of Switzerland, Jane paused to describe Swiss-style haymaking and to explain how seven horses were rotated every ten miles on their lengthy stagecoach ride in the Alps. JA to Weber Addams, July 4, 1884, JAMC.

72. JA to Mary Addams Linn, Dec. 10, 1883, JAMC; JA to Alice Addams Haldeman, Dec. 14, 1883, Feb. 20 and May 31, 1884, JAMC. Addams was so impressed by the actual production process at the Dresden porcelain works that she devoted an entire page to a similar description in her diary. This is notable because Jane's travel diary tended to be just a list of sights seen each day. Jane Addams Diary, Dec. 2 and 9, 1883, JAMC.

73. JA to Alice Addams Haldeman, Nov. 16, 1884, JAMC. Her unusually lengthy description of this one opera went into one of her "circular" letters, which were addressed to Alice but then made the rounds to each member of the family. It was in this letter that Addams told her relatives that she preferred "scenes among gods and giants" to love stories.

74. JA to Weber Addams, Oct. 29, 1883, JAMC.

75. JA to Alice Addams Haldeman, Sept. 30, 1883; JA to Weber Addams, Oct. 14, 1883; JA to Alice Addams Haldeman, Oct. 19, 1883; JA to Weber Addams, Sept. 14, 1884, JAMC.

76. JA to Mary Addams Linn, Nov. 4, 1883, JAMC. Jane mentioned taxes again to Mary when she was in Dresden, noting that the people were "proud of the Emperor in a way but complain bitterly of the higher taxes since Prussia has taken all of the telegraph and post taxes." JA to Mary Addams Linn, Jan. 4, 1884, JAMC.

77. JA to Mary Addams Linn, Aug. 31, 1884, JAMC. Jane indicated her familiarity with Herbert by commenting that he "wrote such fine religious poetry" and she always associated him with her teacher Miss Blaisdell.

78. JA to Weber Addams, Aug. 17, 1884, JAMC.

79. JA to Weber Addams, Oct. 14, 1883, JAMC. Jane reported to Weber the average wages for male and female laborers and the cost of land rentals. She noted workers' wages on only one other occasion, in a letter to Weber about the women workers in Coburg, Saxony. JA to Weber Addams, Jan. 27, 1884, JAMC.

80. JA to Alice Addams Haldeman, Jan. 15, 1885, JAMC. Jane's view of the servants of the aristocracy as "lackeys" was consistent with her tendency at this age to objectivize people as representations rather than seeing them as individuals in their own right. In describing the display of wealth at Hyde Park, London, she saw a scene of ladies and lackeys, everyone playing a social role. She was not yet able to discern the economic exploitation of the "lackeys." JA to Mary Addams Linn, Jan. 28, 1885; JA to Alice Addams Haldeman, Oct. 19 and Nov. 18, 1883, JAMC.

81. JA to Alice Addams Haldeman, Nov. 16 and Oct. 24, 1884, JAMC; JA to George Haldeman, Feb. 2, 1884, SCHS; JA to Mary Addams Linn, Jan. 4, 1884, JAMC; JA to Alice Addams Haldeman, Nov. 5, 1884, JAMC; JA to Ellen Gates Starr, Dec. 7, 1884, EGSP; JA to Mary Addams Linn, Jan. 28, 1885, JAMC.

82. JA to Alice Addams Haldeman, Nov. 5, 1884, and Jan. 15, 1885, JAMC; JA to Mary Addams Linn, Jan. 28, 1885, JAMC. Washburne's letter allowed Jane and Anna to attend the very elaborate "Orders Fest," at which the Crown Prince and Princess of Prussia appeared in full regalia, and a "great boar hunt," which Jane thought "very pretty."

83. JA to Alice Addams Haldeman, Dec. 22/23, 1883, JAMC. Jane was utterly uncritical of this affair. She told Alice she "would not have missed the sight for a good deal" and noted that there was "great enthusiasm and admiration" for the royals who turned up to pat heads and hand out cake.

84. JA to George Haldeman, Nov. 15, 1884, SCPC; JA to Ellen Gates Starr, Dec. 7, 1884, EGSP. Official Prussian history celebrated Queen Louise as an iconic maternal figure, heralded for her patriotic devotion to Prussia in the face of danger and defeat during the conflict with Napoleon. Following her death in 1810, her husband established the Order of Louise, and the Louise Foundation for the education of girls was created in her honor. The statue that Jane Addams admired in Berlin was erected in the Tiergarten in 1880.

85. JA to Mary Addams Linn, Jan. 4, 1884; JA to Alice Addams Haldeman, Jan. 17, 1884, JAMC. Jane told Alice that *Tannhauser* was "the most powerful thing I ever heard or thought could be represented" because it was about "the great moral struggles of a human soul who is trying to regain everything he has lost with everything against him." Victor Hugo's Jean Valjean, added Jane, "was the only character that ever expressed it in just the same force before to me."

86. Addams, *Twenty Years*, p. 71.

87. JA to Mary Addams Linn, Aug. 30/Sept. 1, 1883, JAMC. JA to Alice Addams Haldeman, Sept. 10, 1883, JAMC.

88. JA to Weber Addams, May 19, 1884, JAMC. JA to George Haldeman, Mar. 8, 1884, SCHS.

89. JA to Alice Addams Haldeman, Sept. 16, 1883, JAMC. JA to Alice Addams Haldeman, Feb. 10, 1884, JAMC.

90. *The Bitter Cry of Outcast London; by Andrew Mearns, with Leading Articles from the "Pall Mall Gazette" of October 1883*, ed. Anthony S. Wohl (Leicester: Leicester University Press, 1970). *Bitter Cry* was just one of several sensationalistic accounts of poverty in England in the 1880s. For a discussion of the context in which these accounts were written and received, see Gertrude Himmelfarb, *Poverty and Compassion: The Moral Imagination of the Late Victorians* (New York: Knopf, 1991) and Anthony S. Wohl, *The Eternal Slum: Housing and Social Policy in Victoria London* (Montreal: McGill-Queen's University Press, 1977). In *Twenty Years at Hull-House*, Jane Addams said that her missionary guide on the London outing referred the impoverished in the slums as "the submerged tenth," p. 67. But that phrase was not introduced into the lexicon on poverty until 1890 when the Salvation Army's "General" William Booth published *In Darkest England and the Way Out* (London: International Headquarters, Salvation Army, 1890). Gertrude Himmelfarb noted this discrepancy in Addams's memory in "Victorian Philanthropy: The Case of Toynbee Hall," *American Scholar* 59 (1990): 373. "General" Booth is not to be confused with Charles Booth, the author of *Life and Labour of the People of London*, a seventeen-volume study whose first volume appeared in 1889.

91. Addams, *Twenty Years*, pp. 73–74.

92. William James to JA, Dec. 13, 1909, SCPC.

93. Addams, *Twenty Years*, pp. 66–68.

94. JA to Weber Addams, Oct. 29, 1883, JAMC.

95. Jane Addams Diary, Oct. 27, 1883, JAMC and Jane Addams Microfilm, reel 28, frame 1721.

96. Addams, *Twenty Years*, pp. 68–69; JA to Weber Addams, Oct. 29, 1883, JAMC.

97. JA to Weber Addams, Oct. 29, 1883, JAMC. JA to Ellen Gates Starr, Nov. 3, 1883, EGSP. In her letter to Ellen, Jane summarized her three weeks in London as "the most remarkable of the trip" and declared the city to be possessed of "the best of all nations, times, and peoples." She said nothing about the poverty in the East End.

98. Addams, *Twenty Years*, pp. 73–74. In the paragraph she wrote to Alice about the incident, she mentioned that "it was raining" in Coburg so "we did not see much of the town." JA to Alice Addams Haldeman, Jan. 17, 1884, JAMC. In her autobiography's vivid rendition of the scene, Addams gave the story immediacy by saying the "innkeeper" accompanied her to see the brewery owner but then "slunk away" in the face of the "great magnate of the town" (who was, just a sentence earlier, "phlegmatic"). It is a testimony to Addams's mature talents as a writer that she was able, in 1909, to craft this bit of fiction out of the materials at hand. For example, her diary entry included no comment about an innkeeper but did include a scribbled margin note that the waiter at the hotel reminded her of Uriah Heep. This characterization was followed by two exclamation points indicating that she and her traveling companions had found him to be as hilariously oily and ingratiating as the character in Dickens's novel *David Copperfield*. Though it is highly doubtful that Coburg's "Uriah Heep" accompanied JA to any brewery owner's office on a January morning in 1884, it is likely that she drew on her note about this unsavory waiter to create the character of her slinking innkeeper in the autobiography.

99. Addams, *Twenty Years*, pp. 74–75. Her criticism of Prince Albert's teacher, Baron Stockmar, for failing to "make princely the mind of his prince," was just one more subtle critique of Miss Sill and Rockford Seminary for failing to prepare Jane better for realistic social service. In the autobiography, Jane said she was reading "Gray's *Life of Prince Albert*." This was probably meant to be a reference to *The Early Days of the Prince Consort*, a volume Queen Victoria commissioned and that her secretary, General Henry Grey, compiled and published in 1867.

100. JA to Alice Addams Haldeman, Jan. 17, 1884, JAMC.

101. JA to Weber Addams, Jan. 27, 1884, JAMC. Jane made no mention to Weber, Alice, or in her diary of actually reading Grey's biography of Albert at the time, she merely commented that the scene did not square with her general impression of the prince's philanthropic efforts.

102. Jane Addams Diary, Jan. 15, 1884, JAMC. In the same letter in which she told Weber about the experience at Coburg, Jane also mentioned that Munich, where they were then staying, was their "first large Catholic City." The traveling party had just visited Martin Luther's home in Wartburg, Germany, a few days earlier and Jane commented that seeing the power of Catholicism in Munich gave her "new respect for Luther" and caused her to "wonder how one man could do so much." JA to Weber Addams, Jan. 27, 1884, JAMC.

103. JA to Alice Addams Haldeman, Feb. 16, 1884, JAMC; JA to Sarah Blaisdell, Apr. 26, 1884, SCPC.

104. When she heard the English Nonconformist minister Charles Spurgeon speak, she judged the sermon itself quite ordinary but was fascinated by the oratorical methods he employed to "sway" the crowd. When she attended a two-hour lecture on Julius Caesar by the Scottish novelist George Macdonald, she was impressed by his ability to say "shocking things" but still hold an audience with his "kindly and pleasant" manner. Still, Jane found MacDonald to be "a little dramatic and given to attitudes." Her report on the sermon by the famous Nonconformist preacher Joseph Parker emphasized his large size and her sense that his head looked "like a lion." Though she found the content of Russell Forbes's lecture on the history of Rome to be terribly useful, she remarked to Weber that it was "rambling" in its style and organization. She was impressed by the voice, but not the appearance nor the "dreary and poor" chapel of a French preacher (and lacked the language skills to judge his text). Overall, she was most impressed by Donald Fraquier, a British preacher who, she thought, gave a "very fine sermon." Jane's attention to the effectiveness of the talks she heard is evident in her comparison of two British preachers, Fraquier and Spurgeon. She concluded that Fraquier was superior because he offered both an effective style and substantive text, whereas Spurgeon was "nothing but magnetism." JA to Mary Addams Haldeman, Oct. 3/6/7, 1883; JA to Alice Addams Haldeman, Oct. 19, 1883; JA to Weber Addams, Oct. 29, 1883, and Mar. 20, 1884; JA to Mary Addams Linn, Mar. 8, 1885 and Aug. 10, 1884, JAMC.

105. JA to George Haldeman, Jan. 4, 1884, SCHS.

106. JA to Alice Addams Haldeman, Jan. 17, 1884, JAMC.

107. Addams, *Twenty Years*, p. 70.

108. JA to Alice Addams Haldeman, Mar. 16, 1884, JAMC. She was so serious about this plan that she had Alice mail particular photographs of her father to her so she could show potential artists more pictures of Pa than the one Jane always carried with her. This was a risky venture since there were no copies of these photographs and the

mail was fallible. Still, Alice acceded to her younger sister's sentimental request. Jane gave up the plan after finding "the sculptors in Rome would put no heart into a portrait bust as they much prefer the ideal." An ironic turn of events for a young woman who was, herself, preferring the ideal to the real. JA to Alice Addams Haldeman, sometime during her stay in Rome, May 7–19, 1884, JAMC.

109. JA to Ellen Gates Starr, Feb. 21, 1885, EGSP. Very early in her trip, when she was first touring England, Jane told Alice, "we are continually surprised to find so many fine paintings in private collections, I had imagined that all the finest things had been long ago collected in public museums." JA to Alice Addams Haldeman, Oct. 19, 1883, JAMC.

110. John Ruskin, *Ethics of the Dust: Ten Lectures to Little Housewives on the Elements of Crystallization*, 2nd ed. (New York: Thomas Y. Crowell, 1893), p. 30; JA to George Haldeman, Feb. 2, 1884.

111. JA to Ellen Gates Starr, Feb. 21, 1885, EGSP.

Chapter 9. Never the Typical Old Maid

1. JA to Alice Addams Haldeman, Sept. 13, 1885, JAMC.

2. Addams, *Twenty Years,* p. 77.

3. JA to Anna Haldeman Addams, Oct. 16, 1885, SCHS.

4. Order to bring the Person before the Judge . . . in commitment proceedings regarding John Weber Addams, Stephenson County Courthouse, Freeport, Illinois, Aug. 3, 1885, Records of the Stephenson County Courthouse.

5. JA to Alice Addams Haldeman, Oct. 7, 1885, JAMC.

6. JA to Ellen Gates Starr, Mar. 30, 1885, EGSP; JA to Alice Haldeman, May 7, 1885, SAH. Between March and May, Jane and Anna decided to move up their departure from July to May 30. When Jane told Alice that "a letter from Mary was the turning point in our plans," she implied that Alice had not kept her sufficiently informed on Mary's health.

7. JA to Alice Addams Haldeman, Jan. 17, 1884, JAMC. Jane believed that Mary, who had cared for Jane after her mother died, "has every claim on me" and "a right to demand everything." Jane also worried that Alice would not stay by Mary's side long enough and would not alert Jane to hurry back "before it may be too late." Still, Jane handed over all responsibility to Alice, much as Alice had left care for Weber with Jane. Deflecting guilt through self-deprecation, Jane reminded her former nurse of her own health deficiencies, adding, "If one sister puts the ocean between and seems to shirk her duty, you know, dear, that you must do enough for two." Even after Mary's health crisis passed, Jane continued to promise that a word from either sister would "have us on the next steamer." JA to Alice Addams Haldeman, Mar. 6, 1884; JA to Mary Addams Linn, Mar. 31, 1884; JA to Alice Addams Haldeman, June 10, 1884, JAMC. For Jane's desire to play a long-distance role in managing Mary's health care, see JA to Mrs. James Goddard, June 23, 1884, SCPC.

8. For her family sentiment while overseas during the holidays, see JA to Mary Addams Linn, Dec. 10, 1883, JAMC; JA to Alice Addams Haldeman, Dec. 22 and 23, 1883, and Nov. 30, 1884, JAMC. As if in denial about how long she was away, Jane constantly expressed surprised at reports of the children's growth and development. JA to Mary Addams Linn, Aug. 10, 1884, JAMC; JA to Alice Addams Haldeman, Feb. 24, 1885, JAMC.

9. JA to Alice Addams Haldeman, Sept. 17, Oct. 7 and 23, Nov. 12 and 20, 1885, JAMC. The inability to "fatten" was viewed as a sign that education had sapped all of a woman's vital force. T. D. Clouston, "Female Education from a Medical Point of View," *Popular Science Monthly* 24 (January 1884): 327.

10. Mary sold the family home in Harvard, Illinois, for $4,000, a considerable sum for a home in a small town in the Midwest in 1886. Rather than live in the "small and cramped" parsonage in Geneseo, "Mary bought a very comfortable pleasant place for $2500." Mary Addams Linn to JA, Feb. 16, 1886, SCPC; JA to Alice Addams Haldeman, Feb. 25 and Mar. 31, 1887, SAH; JA to Laura Addams, Apr. 11, 1887, SCPC. For evidence of Jane's involvement in Mary's attempts to secure household help, see JA to Alice Addams Haldeman, Sept. 17, 1885, JAMC; JA to Anna Haldeman Addams, Oct. 16, 1885, SCHS; JA to Alice Addams Haldeman, Oct. 23, 1885, JAMC; Mary Addams Linn to JA, Aug. 19, 1886, SCPC; Mary Addams Linn to JA, Aug. 23, 1886, JAMC; JA to Alice Addams Haldeman, Apr. 11, 1887, SCPC.

11. JA to Alice Addams Haldeman, Sept. 17 and Nov. 20, 1885, JAMC.

12. JA to Alice Addams Haldeman, Sept. 17, Oct. 23, and Dec. 4, 1885, JAMC; JA to Ellen Gates Starr, Dec. 6, 1885, EGSP; JA to Alice Addams Haldeman, Mar. 2 and Feb. 25, 1887, SAH.

13. JA to Ellen Gates Starr, Apr. 3, 1887, EGSP.

14. JA to Alice Addams Haldeman, Dec. 4, 1885, JAMC; Ellen Gates Starr to JA, Nov. 28, 1885, EGSP.

15. Ellen Gates Starr to Mary Starr Blaisdell, Feb. 23, 1889, EGSP.

16. JA to Alice Addams Haldeman, July 23 and Sept. 17, 1885, and Mar. 6, 1886, JAMC.

17. JA to Alice Addams Haldeman, Jan. 17 and Dec. 20, 1884, JAMC. Against Jane's long-distance counsel, Alice (who was always protecting her own husband from criticism) told Mary just what she thought of Mary's husband. This ignited a transatlantic triangle of sisterly correspondence in which Jane assured Alice that Mary understood Alice's "motives," and Mary's affection for Alice was "unchanged." Jane diplomatically admitted to Alice that she was "by no means sure I could have kept silence so long had I seen and heard what you report in your letter," but still expressed regret that Alice had spoken out when Mary was so weak.

18. JA to Alice Addams Haldeman, Oct. 23, 1885, JAMC; JA to Ellen Gates Starr, Dec. 6, 1885, EGSP; JA to Alice Addams Haldeman, Sept. 17, 1885, JAMC; JA to Alice Addams Haldeman, Apr. 24, 1887, SAH.

19. JA to Alice Addams Haldeman, Feb. 25, 1887, SAH.

20. Ibid.; JA to Alice Addams Haldeman, Oct. 23 and Dec. 26, 1885, Oct. 17, 1884, JAMC; JA to Weber Addams, Nov. 28, 1887, SCPC.

21. JA to Alice Addams Haldeman, Mar. 20, 1886, JAMC.

22. JA to Alice Addams Haldeman, Mar. 31, Apr. 11, and Nov. 4, 1886, JAMC; JA to Alice Addams Haldeman, Dec. 10, 1887, SAH.

23. JA to Alice Addams Haldeman, Dec. 10, 1887, SAH.

24. JA to Alice Addams Haldeman, Mar. 31, 1886, JAMC.

25. JA to Alice Addams Haldeman, Oct. 18, 1886, SCPC; JA to Anna Haldeman Addams, Oct. 24, 1886, JAMC; JA to Laura Addams, Oct. 24 and Nov. 4, 1886, SCPC; JA to Alice Addams Haldeman, Feb. 15, 1887, SAH.

26. Jane was "delighted" when her second cousin on her father's side, General James Addams Beaver, was elected the Republican governor of Pennsylvania while she was visiting there in November 1886. After dining with him in January 1887, Jane reported that he was "a very *attractive* sort of man." JA to Alice Addams Haldeman, Nov. 4, 1886, JAMC; JA to Alice Addams Haldeman, Feb. 9, 1887, SAH. Jane made one genetic connection to her mother's family when she associated Alice's rheumatism with their Aunt Elizabeth Reiff's rheumatism and predicted "we are all coming to rheumatism sooner or later, my dear." JA to Alice Addams Haldeman, Dec. 28, 1886; undated from late January or early February 1887; Feb. 9, 1887, SAH.

27. Anna Haldeman Addams to Harry Haldeman, Nov. 7, 1884, HJFP.

28. Both Jane and Anna were completely puzzled by Anna's "fevers" in the fall of 1884. Jane reported, "she is not sick in any way except for this tremendous fever," and asked for Harry's opinion on fevers that were unaccompanied by any bowel, stomach, or chest problems but did have companion headaches and exhaustion. JA to George Haldeman, Oct. 24, 1884, SCHS; JA to Alice Addams Haldeman, Oct. 24 and Dec. 20, 1884, and Feb. 1, 1885, JAMC. During this feverish period, Anna made specific references to aging, to the impending crossing of the "chasm," amid her regular litany of "the sorrows that have filled my life." Anna Haldeman Addams to Harry Haldeman, June 29, 1884, HJFP; Anna Haldeman Addams to Harry Haldeman, Dec. 5, 1884, SAH.

29. In reflecting on her own life while in Europe, Anna was inclined to believe that "destiny has tossed us just where it wanted us" and that "all my life has been so strangely planned . . . it seems to have been all arranged for me." Yet, when she was commenting to Harry on his path, she took the position, "we can't blame Father in Heaven for the life we choose to make for ourselves." Anna Haldeman Addams to Harry Haldeman, Jan. 10, Feb. 17, and May 29, 1884, HJFP.

30. Anna Haldeman Addams to Harry Haldeman, Sept. 15, 1883, and n.d., 1884, SAH.

31. Anna Haldeman Addams to Harry Haldeman, June 14, 1884, HJFP. Though reputedly competent in a sickroom, Anna did not attend Jane's recovery from back surgery in Iowa. Instead, she beseeched Harry not to be "neglectful" of his brother because she thought Harry's "blood tie" should have "first claim" on his attention. Anna Haldeman Addams to Harry Haldeman, Nov. 30, 1882, HJFP; Anna Haldeman Addams to Harry Haldeman, Apr. 28, 1883, SAH; Anna Haldeman Addams to Harry Haldeman, May 12, 1883, HJFP. Anna aided Mary at the time of Stanley's birth, when Jane was busy with Weber and Laura, but does not appear to have stepped in to help with subsequent births or illnesses in the Linn household or in Weber's household. Anna Haldeman Addams to Harry Haldeman, Feb. 7, 1884, HJFP.

32. JA to Alice Addams Haldeman, Sept. 13, 1885, JAMC; Harry Haldeman to George Haldeman, Jan. 30, 1883, HJFP.

33. JA to Alice Addams Haldeman, Oct. 6, 1886, JAMC; Ellen Gates Starr to JA, Dec. 6, 1885, and Dec. 9, 1886, EGSP.

34. During their first stay in Baltimore, between late December 1885 and June 1886, Jane and Anna lived in a boarding house at 144 Washington Place. When they returned in October 1886, they lived with George in a four-room flat in the same central neighborhood at 413 North Charles Street. This area, encircling the city's Washington Monument and just two blocks west of the university and the Peabody Institute, was regarded as "more distinguished" than the neighborhood to the east, known as the

Latin Quarter, where students like Woodrow Wilson rented rooms. John C. French, *History of the University Founded by Johns Hopkins* (Baltimore: Johns Hopkins University Press, 1946), p. 76.

35. JA to Laura Addams, Oct. 18, 1886, SCPC; JA to Alice Addams Haldeman, Oct. 23, 1886, JAMC.

36. JA to Alice Addams Haldeman, Apr. 11 and Oct. 6, 1886, JAMC; JA to Laura Addams, Oct. 18, 1886, SCPC.

37. Anna Haldeman Addams to JA, June 11, 1878, SAH.

38. JA to Alice Addams Haldeman, Sept. 10 and 30, 1883, JAMC; JA to George Haldeman, Jan. 4, 1884, SCHS; JA to Alice Addams Haldeman, Nov. 16, 1884, JAMC.

39. JA to Alice Addams Haldeman, Dec. 28, 1884, JAMC.

40. JA to George Haldeman, Jan. 20, Feb. 2, and Mar. 21, 1884, SCHS; JA to Alice Addams Haldeman Feb. 16, May 7, and Dec. 15, 1884, JAMC.

41. JA to Alice Addams Haldeman, Oct. 24, 1884, JAMC.

42. From London, Anna told Harry of a woman in their boardinghouse who was traveling with her five daughters. She made no mention of traveling with her daughter, writing instead, "I wish I had two sons . . . in this old world with me." Later, she wrote of wishing she could have "taken this tour with 'my boys' . . . [but] I cheerfully plod on." Anna Haldeman Addams to Harry Haldeman, Oct. 26, 1883, HJFP; Anna Haldeman Addams to Harry Haldeman, n.d., 1884, SAH.

43. Anna Haldeman Addams to Harry Haldeman, n.d, 1884, SAH; JA to George Haldeman, Jan. 20 and Mar. 21, 1884, SCHS; JA to Alice Addams Haldeman, June 22 and 29, 1884, JAMC. Jane used her familiar mix of self-deprecation and blame when she wrote that the mix-up destroyed their "conceit" that the trip up to that point had been smooth and trouble-free due to "superior planning."

44. Anna Haldeman Addams to Harry Haldeman, June 29, 1884, HJFP.

45. JA to Alice Addams Haldeman, Oct. 23, 1886, JAMC.

46. JA to Alice Addams Haldeman, Feb. 10, 1886, JAMC; JA to Alice Addams Haldeman, Jan. 3, 1886, SCPC; JA to Alice Addams Haldeman, Jan. 25, Feb. 17 and 28, Mar. 7, Oct. 23, and Dec. 15, 1886, January, n.d., and Jan. 10 and 22, 1887, undated letter from late January or early February 1887, JAMC. See, too, JA to Laura Addams, Oct. 18, 1886, SCPC. In the Jan. 22, 1887, letter to Alice, Jane joked that she and Anna had been at home for only one "quiet evening this week, quite too dissipated for country folk."

47. JA to Anna Haldeman Addams, Oct. 24, 1886, JAMC.

48. French, *History of the University Founded by Johns Hopkins*, pp. 227–28.

49. George Haldeman to Harry Haldeman, Jan. 10, 1886, HJFP.

50. Anna Haldeman Addams to George Haldeman, Jan. 15, 1884, HJFP; JA to George Haldeman, Jan. 4, 1884, SCHS.

51. Anna Haldeman Addams to Harry Haldeman, Jan. 6, 1884, HJFP.

52. Anna claimed to be quoting George in a letter to Harry Haldeman, Apr. 2, 1886, HJFP.

53. Anna Haldeman Addams to Harry Haldeman, Apr. 2, 1886, HJFP. Anna referred to George as her "pearl" in a letter to Harry Haldeman, Feb. 7, 1884, HJFP.

54. JA to Anna Haldeman Addams, Oct. 24, 1886, JAMC.

55. For efforts by the Philadelphia clan to include both Anna and George in their circle, see JA to Anna Haldeman Addams, Oct. 24. 1886, JAMC; JA to George Haldeman, Jan. 4, 1884, SCHS.

56. JA to Alice Addams Haldeman, Nov. 4, 1886, JAMC.

57. George Haldeman to Anna Haldeman Addams, Mar. 2, 1884, HJFP; JA to George Haldeman, Mar. 8, 1884, SCHS; JA to Ellen Starr, Mar. 9, 1884, EGSP; JA to George Haldeman, Dec. 19, 1884, SCPC; JA to Laura Shoemaker Addams, Dec. 1, 1886, SCPC. After George's visit with Anna and Jane in Europe, during which he was quite irritating, Jane wrote that George should "not think too much" upon their conversations. "I was more often in the wrong than right," she insisted, "and then trying to excuse the weakness of my position." JA to George Haldeman, Oct. 24, 1884, SCHS.

58. Anna Haldeman Addams to Harry Haldeman, Sept. 15, 1883; Feb. 24 and June 14, 1884, HJFP. See, too, Anna Haldeman Addams to Harry Haldeman, Oct. 26 and Dec. 23, 1883, Jan. 29, Feb. 7, Nov. 7, and Dec. 24, 1884, HJFP. In all of these letters, Anna preached temperance to her eldest son.

59. Anna Haldeman Addams to Harry Haldeman, Jan. 29, 1884, HJFP.

60. JA to Alice Addams Haldeman, Sept. 17, 1884, JAMC. William F. Zornow, *Kansas: A History of the Jayhawk State* (Norman: University of Oklahoma Press, 1957), pp. 165–67.

61. Anna Haldeman Addams to Harry Haldeman, Nov. 7 and Dec. 24, 1884, HJFP.

62. JA to Alice Addams Haldeman, Sept. 17, 1884, JAMC.

63. JA to Alice Addams Haldeman, Feb. 9, 1887, JAMC. The shopping theme is a constant in the correspondence between Jane Addams and Alice Addams Haldeman; the majority of the surviving letters from Jane to Alice between 1883 and 1887 contains some reference to an item Jane was seeking for Alice, had bought for Alice, or had shipped to Alice.

64. Anna Haldeman Addams to George Haldeman, Dec. 30, 1884, HJFP. Anna did indulge Harry in a twenty-five-dollar dressing gown one Christmas when Jane sent an eight-dollar smoking jacket. JA to Harry Haldeman, Dec. 12, 1886, JAMC; JA to Alice Addams Haldeman, Dec. 15, 1886, JAMC.

65. Anna Haldeman Addams to Harry Haldeman, June 6, 1884, HJFP.

66. JA to Alice Addams Haldeman, Nov. 12 and 14, 1886, JAMC. A year later, Jane was an even more confident shopper. She vetoed the purchase of a "perfectly horrid" mantlepiece that Rev. Linn had picked out for Alice in Chicago and prescribed a "simple slate mantle of one color." JA to Alice Addams Haldeman, Oct. 9, 1887, JAMC. By that time, Jane was trying to persuade her relatives to adopt the more modern styles of furnishings that would soon distinguish Hull-House.

67. JA to Alice Addams Haldeman, Apr. 11, 1886, JAMC.

68. JA to Alice Addams Haldeman, Dec. 28, 1886, SAH.

69. Anna Haldeman Addams to Harry Haldeman, Aug. 11, 1887, HJFP.

70. Harry Haldeman to George Haldeman, May 28, 1887, SAH. Jane stayed in Girard for the two months surrounding Marcet's birth, and suggested that Anna arrive near the end of her visit in order to extend family aid to Alice. In coaching George to plead Alice's case, Jane wrote, "It seems to me Ma would be willing to come if she knew the great pleasure it would afford." JA to George Haldeman, July 5, 1887; JA to Alice Addams Haldeman, Sept. 30, 1887, SAH. Harry commented, sarcastically, that Anna "ought to see Anna Marcet," then six months old, "before she is a young lady." In that same letter, Harry remarked that he was in a "complete state of Melancholia and Dipsomania." Harry Haldeman to George Haldeman, Jan. 18, 1888, HJFP. See, too, Harry Haldeman to Anna Haldeman Addams, Jan. 18, 1888, SAH.

71. Anna Haldeman Addams to Harry Haldeman, Apr. 2, 1886, HJFP; JA to Alice Addams Haldeman, Sept. 23, 1886, JAMC.

72. JA to Alice Addams Haldeman, Aug. 19 and Sept. 23, 1886. JAMC. Evidence of Jane Addams's land transactions in Stephenson County in the early to mid-1880s can be found on Jane Addams Microfilm, reel 27, frames 542–601.

73. JA to Harry Haldeman, Jan. 13, 1887, SCPC. Zornow, *Kansas: A History of the Jayhawk State*; Jeffrey Ostler, *Prairie Populism: The Fate of Agrarian Radicalism in Kansas, Nebraska, and Iowa, 1880–1892* (Lawrence: University Press of Kansas, 1993); James C. Malin, *Winter Wheat in the Golden Belt of Kansas* (Lawrence: University Press of Kansas, 1944).

74. JA to Alice Addams Haldeman, Jan. 22 and Feb. 9, 1887, SAH; JA to Harry Haldeman, Jan. 13, 17, and 25, 1887, SCPC.

75. An article appeared in the *Atlantic Monthly* eight months before John Addams died declaring that no man had the "right" to leave behind family members "without doing his uttermost to assure them not only a competence but the requisite knowledge to keep and expend it wisely." "The Contributor's Club: Need of Financial Education for Women," *Atlantic Monthly* 47 (January 1881): 139. Based on the record of transactions undertaken and discussed by John Addams's daughters in the years following his death, it appears he had prepared his daughters to manage their inheritances. See, for example, JA to Alice Addams Haldeman, Jan. 25 and Aug. 19, 1886, JAMC; JA to Harry Haldeman, Jan. 13, 1887, SCPC; JA to Alice Addams Haldeman, Feb. 15, Sept. 24 and 30, 1887, SAH.

76. Addams, *Twenty Years*, p. 79.

77. Jane Addams had first commented on "big fish" living off "little fish" when she observed the British system for taxing the middle class to support the aristocracy. JA to Mary Addams Linn, Nov. 4, 1883, JAMC.

78. JA to Laura Addams, June 30, 1887, SCPC. Jeffrey Ostler found that farmers in eastern Kansas "escaped the severe economic crisis that occurred on the Great Plains," and had more in common with the farmers of Iowa and Nebraska, which is to say that their economic hardship was "moderate." Ostler, *Prairie Populism*, p. 35.

79. Ellen Gates Starr to JA, December n.d., 1885, EGSP.

80. JA to Ellen Gates Starr, July 17, 1886, EGSP.

81. JA to Alice Addams Haldeman, Oct. 6, 1886, JAMC. Jane and Ellen visited with each other in Cedarville and Chicago in the summer of 1885, following Jane's return from Europe; over Thanksgiving of 1885 at the Linns' home in Harvard, Illinois; and in the summer of 1886. Ellen Gates Starr to JA, Nov. 28, 1885; Ellen Gates Starr to JA, Dec. 3, 1885, EGSP. Regarding hasty or postponed visits, see JA to Alice Addams Haldeman, Dec. 26, 1885, JAMC; Ellen Gates Starr to JA, Dec. 6, 1885, JA to Ellen Gates Starr, Dec. 9, 1885, EGSP; JA to Alice Addams Haldeman, Nov. 20, 1885, JAMC.

82. Ellen Gates Starr to JA, December n.d., 1885, EGSP.

83. JA to Alice Addams Haldeman, Dec. 4, 1885, JAMC; Ellen Gates Starr to JA, Nov. 28, 1885, EGSP. See JA to Ellen Gates Starr, Dec. 6, 1885, EGSP, for her comment, "my visits with you this summer have been much to me."

84. JA to Ellen Gates Starr, Dec. 6, 1885; Ellen Gates Starr to JA, Nov. 28, 1885, EGSP.

85. JA to Ellen Gates Starr, Dec. 6 and 9, 1885, EGSP. Six months before Jane's departure for the European tour with Ellen, she mentioned "all sorts of letters from

Ellen and Miss Anderson about 'the party,'" referring to negotiations over which other women might join them on the trip. This reference proves that Jane and Ellen were actively corresponding in these months despite the gap in the surviving record. JA to Laura Addams, June 30, 1887, SCPC.

86. Ellen Gates Starr to JA, Apr. 28 and Nov. 28, 1885, EGSP.

87. Ellen Gates Starr to JA, Nov. 28 and Dec. 3, 1885, EGSP. Jane was Ellen's "'disconcerted' person" because of the time that had passed between their visits. According to Ellen's recollection, she had not noticed Jane's discomfort and that had upset Jane further. "I laugh whenever I think of it," Ellen confessed to her now charmingly vulnerable friend. Ellen Gates Starr to JA, Jan. 31, 1886, SCPC.

88. Ellen Gates Starr to JA, Dec. 3, 1885, EGSP.

89. Ibid.

90. JA to Ellen Gates Starr, July 11, 1883, EGSP.

91. JA to Ellen Gates Starr, Dec. 6, 1885, EGSP.

92. Ibid.

93. Martha Vicinus, *Independent Women: Work and Community for Single Women, 1850–1920* (Chicago: University of Chicago Press, 1985); Carroll Smith-Rosenberg, "The Female World of Love and Ritual," *Signs: Journal of Women in Culture and Society* 1 (Autumn 1975): 1–29.

94. Ellen Gates Starr to JA, December n.d., 1885, EGSP; Ellen Gates Starr to JA, Jan. 12, 1883, SCPC.

95. Ellen Gates Starr to JA, Dec. 3, 1885, EGSP.

96. JA to Ellen Gates Starr, Dec. 6, 1885, EGSP.

97. Ellen Gates Starr to JA, Dec. 3 and 8, 1885, and Jan. 31, 1886, EGSP. Ellen Gates Starr to JA, Mar. 10 and 13, 1886. SCPC.

98. For discussion of these theologians' use of the subjective in discussing religious experience, see: Phillips Brooks, "The Essential in Religion," *Christian Union* 21 (June 9, 1880): 528–29; John Woolverton, *The Education of Phillips Brooks* (Urbana: University of Illinois Press, 1995); *Life and Letters of Frederick W. Robertson*, vols. 1 and 2, ed. Stopford A. Brooke (Boston: Ticknor and Fields, 1865); George G. Bradley, *Recollections of Arthur Penrhyn Stanley* (New York: Charles Scribner's Sons, 1883); Desmond Bowen, *The Idea of the Victorian Church* (Montreal: McGill University Press, 1968); Owen Chadwick, *The Spirit of the Oxford Movement* (Cambridge: Cambridge University Press, 1990); Frank M. Turner, *Contesting Cultural Authority* (Cambridge: Cambridge University Press, 1993); William E. Buckler, "The *Apologia* as Human Experience," in *Newman's Apologia: A Classic Reconsidered*, ed Vincent F. Blehl, S.J., and Francis X. Connolly (New York: Harcourt, Brace and World, 1964).

99. Jane first indicated her desire to keep the "facts" of Christ's life at the center of her quest in a letter to Ellen from Europe. JA to Ellen Gates Starr, Mar. 30, 1885, EGSP.

100. JA to Alice Addams Haldeman, Nov. 24, 1886, JAMC. In this letter, Jane referred to "the two Tolstoi's we read," but did not specify which two they were. Her only additional comment in that letter was that this reading had ignited an interest "in Russia." She said nothing to Alice about the religious or ethical interests she might have had in Tolstoy. The assumption that *My Religion* was one of the Tolstoy books she read in the fall of 1886 is based on changes in her conduct and attitude, such as increased pleasure in charity work and reduced worry about studies. Addams did not specifically refer to any of Tolstoy's opinions about the individual's ethical duty to society until over

a year after this first mention to Alice. See JA to Flora Guiteau, Jan. 7, 1888, JAMC. The absence of letters to or from Ellen Gates Starr between the summer of 1886 and the winter of 1888 complicates the task of tracking Addams's thinking on Tolstoy. In her autobiography, Jane Addams claimed that she had read *My Religion* "immediately after I left college," but there was no English translation until 1885, four years after her graduation. Addams's lack of training in French and struggles with German make it doubtful that she tackled this text in any other language but English. This error in the autobiography is consistent with Addams's pattern of accelerating the pace of her coming to consciousness about social injustice. Addams, *Twenty Years*, p. 261; Count L. N. Tolstoy, *My Religion*, trans. from the French by Huntington Smith (New York: Thomas Y. Crowell, 1885).

101. Leo Tolstoy, *My Religion*, vol. 17, *The Novels and Other Works of Lyof N. Tolstoi* (New York: Charles Scribner's Sons, 1899), pp. 77, 85.

102. Tolstoy, *My Religion*. These ideas are repeated throughout the text. See, especially, pp. 183–84, 233–37, in Scribner's 1899 edition.

103. JA to Ellen Gates Starr, Feb. 7, 1886, EGSP.

104. Elizabeth N. Agnew, "Charity, Friendly Visiting, and Social Work: Mary E. Richmond and the Shaping of an American Profession," Ph.D. diss., Indiana University, 1999, p. 64.

105. JA to Ellen Gates Starr, Jan. 29, 1880, EGSP.

106. Ellen Gates Starr to Mary Starr Blaisdell, Aug. 28, 1884, EGSP. Ellen told her sister in this letter that Eliot's practice of all that a Christian "could practice, without its motive" was "to me . . . very grand." Ellen's belief that Jane was more religious than she reflects a similar view. Ellen Gates Starr to JA, Dec. 3, 1885, EGSP.

107. JA to Ellen Gates Starr, Apr. 3, 1887, EGSP.

108. JA to Alice Addams Haldeman, Mar. 31, 1887, SAH.

109. JA to Ellen Gates Starr, Apr. 3, 1887, EGSP.

110. Ellen Gates Starr to JA, Nov. 28, 1885, EGSP.

Chapter 10. Some Curious Conclusions

1. Charles Hirschfeld, *Baltimore, 1870–1900: Studies in Social History* (Baltimore: Johns Hopkins University Press, 1941), pp. 32–41, 54, 66–67. See, too, Patricia McDonald, "Baltimore Women, 1870–1900," Ph.D. diss., University of Maryland, 1976, pp. 17–21; George DuBois, "The Search for a Better Life: Baltimore's Workers, 1865–1916," Ph.D. diss., University of Maryland, 1995. Addams, *My Friend, Julia Lathrop*, p. 47.

2. Clayton Colman Hall, *Baltimore: Its History and Its People* (New York: Lewis Historical Publishing, 1912), p. 267; Hirschfeld, *Baltimore, 1870–1900*, pp. 66–68.

3. Hall, *Baltimore*, pp. 253–76; Geoffrey Blodgett, "Reform Thought and the Genteel Tradition," in *The Gilded Age*, p. 74. Blodgett identifies the civic reformers of the 1880s as men who came of age in the post–Civil War world from which John Addams had retired. Senator Addams might have applauded their reform goals but not their bolting from the Republican Party to achieve them. The reform effort began in Baltimore in 1885 and culminated in the National Municipal League in 1894. Jane Addams was a founding member of the Chicago Civic Federation in 1894, another nonpartisan expression of this national movement.

4. Kathleen Waters Sanders, *The Business of Charity: The Women's Exchange Movement, 1832–1890* (Urbana: University of Illinois Press, 1998). When the Women's Exchange movement began in the 1830s, there was greater stigma attached to women's genteel poverty and a pressing need to provide such women with a "respectable" way to earn money by selling their decorative arts projects (pp. 49, 51). By the time the Baltimore Woman's Industrial Exchange began in 1880, the effort had broadened to include a wider range of women selling a wider range of products. In 1887, the Baltimore exchange purchased a building with five boarding units on North Charles Street, near where Jane Addams had lived, and rented those units to working women.

5. JA to Alice Addams Haldeman, Feb. 28, 1886, JAMC.

6. Agnew, "Charity, Friendly Visiting, and Social Work," p. 70.

7. McDonald, "Baltimore Women," p. 141. Richard Ely, *Social Aspects of Christianity and Other Essays* (New York: Thomas Y. Crowell, 1889), p. 112. Ely, the progressive economist and advocate of the social gospel, quoted a letter from Dr. Leeds, the pastor of Grace Episcopal, written in March 1885, about a year before Jane joined Anna and George in Baltimore.

8. Agnew, "Charity, Friendly Visiting, and Social Work," pp. 64–70. In her discussion of Baltimore's emerging social gospel movement, she says Charles Weld, the Unitarian minister of the church Jane was attending, believed that "salvation entailed a social process, in which people came together in the spirit of Christ 'not to save their own souls' but to 'raise the bottom of society,' through working to destroy 'poverty, viciousness, and wrong.'" Agnew embeds these views within Robert Wiebe's argument that the social gospel's endorsement of community caring and mutuality drew upon "small town virtues as the cornerstone of a future cooperative society." These virtues were familiar to Cedarville's Jane Addams. Robert Wiebe, *The Search for Order, 1877–1920* (New York: Hill and Wang, 1976), pp. 136–40; Susan Curtis, *Consuming Faith: The Social Gospel and Modern Culture* (Baltimore: Johns Hopkins University Press, 1991).

9. JA to Ellen Gates Starr, Feb. 7, 1886, EGSP; JA to Alice Addams Haldeman, Nov. 24, 1886, JAMC. Jane referred to "the two Tolstoi's we read," but did not specify which two they were. There is an assumption being made here, based on the 1885 publication date of the first English translations of *My Religion* and Jane's later claim to have read it, that *My Religion* was one of the two Tolstoys she read in Baltimore in the fall of 1886.

10. Hall, *Baltimore*, pp. 218, 266.

11. JA to Alice Addams Haldeman, Nov. 24, 1886, JAMC. Hall, *Baltimore*, pp. 649–50. The Pratt Library was opened at Mulberry Street, near Cathedral Street, just a couple of blocks south of Jane's living quarters at Washington Place and, later, on Charles Street.

12. JA to Alice Addams Haldeman, Apr. 11, 1886, and January, n.d., 1887, JAMC. Hall, *Baltimore*, p. 638.

13. *Memorial Volume: An Account of the Municipal Celebration of the One Hundred and Fiftieth Anniversary of the Settlement of Baltimore, October 11th–19th, 1880*, ed. Edward Spencer (Baltimore: Mayoralty Historical Committee, 1881), p. 289. For a sense of the ethos of the institution in its founding years, see: Hugh Hawkins, *Pioneer: A History of Johns Hopkins University, 1874–1889* (Ithaca: Cornell University Press, 1960).

14. Benjamin Rader, *The Academic Mind and Reform: The Influence of Richard T. Ely in American Life* (Louisville: University of Kentucky Press, 1966), pp. 20–25.

15. Rader, *The Academic Mind and Reform*, p. 24.

16. Simon Newcomb, "An Economist's Advice to the Knights of Labor," *Nation* 42 (Apr. 8, 1886): 292–293. The "economist" referred to in the title was Richard T. Ely. Newcomb described his colleague's letter supporting the labor movement as a "curious admixture of sense and nonsense" reflecting both "naivete" and "simple-minded faith." Newcomb equated Ely's support of labor unions with support of "the stoppage of trains, the mobbing of scabs and the expulsion of the Chinese."

17. Hall, *Baltimore*, p. 670. Fabian Franklin, *The Life of Daniel Coit Gilman* (New York: Dodd, Mead, 1910), p. 268. For an array of assessments of the Charity Organization Society see Michael B. Katz, *In the Shadow of the Poorhouse: A Social History of Welfare in America* (New York: Basic Books, 1986); Lori Ginzberg, *Women and the Work of Benevolence: Morality, Politics, and Class in the Nineteenth-Century United States* (New Haven: Yale University Press, 1990); Walter Trattner, *From Poor Law to Welfare State: A History of Social Welfare in America* (New York: Free Press, 1974); Robert Bremner, "Scientific Philanthropy, 1873–1893," *Social Service Review* 30 (June 1956): 168–73; Robert Bremner, *American Philanthropy*, 2nd ed. (Chicago: University of Chicago Press, 1988); Roy Lubove, *The Professional Altruist: The Emergence of Social Work as a Career, 1880–1930* (Cambridge: Harvard University Press, 1965); James Leiby, "Charity Organization Reconsidered," *Social Service Review* 58 (December 1984): 523–38; Joan Waugh, *Unsentimental Reformer: The Life of Josephine Shaw Lowell* (Cambridge: Harvard University Press, 1997).

18. Hirschfeld, *Baltimore, 1870–1900*, pp. 136–41; Baltimore 1881 *Memorial Volume*, ed. Spencer, pp. 305–6, praised the increasing efficiency and coordination of the city's charitable efforts and endorsed aid to the "deserving poor" but not to "imposters."

19. Marvin E. Gettleman, "John H. Finley and the Academic Origins of American Social Work, 1887–1892," *Studies in History and Society* 2 (1970): 13–28. Johns Hopkins University used the term "seminary" to mean "seminar."

20. Hirschfeld, *Baltimore, 1870–1900*, pp. 139–41. *Proceedings of the National Conference of Charities and Correction, Thirteenth Annual Session Held in St. Paul, Minnesota, July 15–22, 1886*, ed. Isabel C. Barrows (Boston: Press of George H. Ellis, 1886), p. 401. See, too, Amos G. Warner, "The Charities of Baltimore," report reprinted from the Conference on Charities and on Other Subjects Pertaining to the Prevention of Suffering, Pauperism and Other Crime, Baltimore, Maryland, Apr. 15–16, 1887.

21. JA to Laura Addams, Apr. 11, 1887, SCPC.

22. Farrell, *Beloved Lady*, p. 42. Herbert Baxter Adams was one of the leaders of the Seminary on History and Politics at Johns Hopkins University. Under the auspices of the seminar, Hopkins students were undertaking internships out in the city of Baltimore to gain experience working with the poor. This was similar to, but far less intense than, the work of Oxford University students at London's Toynbee Hall. Gettleman, "John H. Finley and the Academic Origins of American Social Work," p. 15.

23. "Toynbee Hall, London: An Interesting Social Experiment," *Century* 34 (May 1887): 158–59.

24. French, *History of the University Founded by Johns Hopkins*, pp. 237–39.

25. JA to Alice Addams Haldeman, Jan. 25, Feb. 10 and 28, 1886, Mar. 7, Dec. 8, 1886, January, n.d., Jan. 10, 1887, JAMC; JA to Ellen Gates Starr, Feb. 7, 1886, EGSP; JA to Laura Addams, Dec. 1, 1886, SCPC. Midway through her second season in Baltimore, Jane confessed to Alice that she was "just a little sated with illustrated lectures." JA to Alice Addams Haldeman, Dec. 15, 1886, JAMC.

26. Addams, *Twenty Years*, p. 77.

27. JA to Alice Addams Haldeman, Dec. 26, 1885, JAMC.

28. Ibid.; JA to Alice Addams Haldeman, Feb. 10, 1886, JAMC.

29. JA to Alice Addams Haldeman, Feb. 10, 1886, JAMC.

30. JA to Alice Addams Haldeman, Mar. 7, 1886, JAMC. Jane tried to participate in the children's sewing class but found she "could not make button holes very well myself." On this one the charity visit, Jane mentioned a female companion, Mrs. Bradford.

31. JA to Ellen Gates Starr, Feb. 7, 1886, EGSP; JA to Alice Addams Haldeman, Feb. 17, 1886, JAMC.

32. JA to Ellen Gates Starr, Feb. 7, 1886, EGSP. Ellen had apologized for not writing better, longer letters on the grounds that she was "a good deal 'handicapped' by a mere mass of drudgery in the way of huge piles of worthless compositions to correct weekly, consuming evening after evening; and my best material is a good deal drawn upon by the individual needs, ethical and otherwise, of the girls who seem to be my mission, and whom I wouldn't dare to neglect for anything." Mirroring Jane's facility for self-serving self-deprecation, Ellen reminded her wealthy friend that "it is astonishing how much is involved . . . in the mere honest pursuit of one's daily bread," adding that such pursuit involved "the best things, really." Ellen Gates Starr to JA, Jan. 31, 1886, SCPC.

33. Ellen Gates Starr to JA, Jan. 31, 1886, SCPC; JA to Alice Haldeman, Mar. 7, 1886, JAMC.

34. JA to Ellen Gates Starr, July 17, 1886, EGSP. Ellen had recommended Browning to Jane because of his liberal approach to Christianity. Jane, for all her insistence on the abstract in religion, had found Browning's ideas "a trifle obscure and mystical." Still, she applauded his emphasis on the power of personality in shaping human society. JA to Ellen Gates Starr, Feb. 7, 1886, EGSP.

35. JA to Laura Addams, Oct. 18, 1886, SCPC.

36. JA to Alice Addams Haldeman, Oct. 23, 1886, JAMC.

37. JA to Alice Addams Haldeman, Dec. 28, 1886, SAH. The Johns Hopkins Colored Orphan Asylum opened in 1873 at 519 West Biddle Street, just a few blocks northwest of Jane's apartment. Endowed by Johns Hopkins, it was run by the local Quakers. Hall, *Baltimore*, p. 669; Farrell, *Beloved Lady*, p. 41. Jane's comfort with Negro confinement to domestic service was not unusual among Northerners who thought of themselves as nonracist. Richard Ely, a progressive, prolabor economist, argued in these years that "to-day, and for a long time to come, perhaps, the majority of our negroes will find in the condition of servants in really superior families precisely the best possible opportunity for personal development which they are able to use." Ely, *Social Aspects of Christianity*, p. 126.

38. JA to Alice Addams Haldeman, Feb. 10, 1886, JAMC; JA to Alice Addams Haldeman, Dec. 28, 1886, SAH; JA to Laura Addams, Dec. 28, 1886, JAMC.

39. JA to Alice Addams Haldeman, Feb. 10 and Mar. 7, 1886, JAMC; JA to Laura Addams, Oct. 18, 1886, SCPC; JA to Alice Addams Haldeman, Oct. 23 and Nov. 24, 1886, JAMC; JA to Laura Addams, Dec. 28, 1886, JAMC; JA to Alice Addams Haldeman, Dec. 28, 1886, and Jan. 22, 1887, SAH.

40. JA to Alice Addams Haldeman, Nov. 4, 1886, JAMC.

41. JA to Alice Addams Haldeman, Jan. 22, 1887, SAH.

42. Ellen Gates Starr to Mary Blaisdell, Feb. 23, 1889, EGSP.

43. JA to Ellen Gates Starr, Feb. 7, 1886, EGSP. Henry James's *The Bostonians*, was first serialized in *Century* 29 (February 1885) to 31 (February 1886). Jane reported to Ellen in this letter that a "cultivated" Baltimore acquaintance of hers had "said with all seriousness" that she "thought northern people always talked about books and I have been waiting to have you ask me about Henry James' last novel." Jane viewed this remark as "only a phase of the misconception they have of the severe and terrible northern young lady."

44. Kate Gannett Wells, "The Transitional American Woman," *Atlantic Monthly* 46 (December 1880): 818, 821.

45. Jane Addams, "Three Days on the Mediterranean Subjectively Related," *Rockford Seminary Magazine* 14 (January 1886): 11–17.

46. JA to Alice Addams Haldeman, January, n.d., 1887, JAMC.

47. "The Social Athens of America," *Harper's New Monthly Magazine* 65 (June 1882): 35–36.

48. JA to Laura Addams, Oct. 18, 1886, SCPC.

49. JA to Alice Addams Haldeman, Feb. 1, 1886, JAMC.

50. JA to Alice Addams Haldeman, Feb. 17, 1886, JAMC.

51. JA to Alice Addams Haldeman, January, n.d., 1887, and Nov. 4, 1886, JAMC.

52. JA to Alice Addams Haldeman, Feb. 17, 1886, JAMC. Christine Ladd-Franklin entry, *Dictionary of American Biography*, vol. 10 (New York: Charles Scribner's Sons, 1933), pp. 528–30; *Notable American Women, 1607–1950: A Biographical Dictionary*, ed. Edward T. James, Janet Wilson James, and Paul S. Boyer, vol. 2 (Cambridge: Belknap Press, 1971), pp. 354–56.

53. *Dictionary of American Biography*, 10:528–30; *Notable American Women*, 2:354–56. See, too, Ladd-Franklin's obituary, *New York Times*, Mar. 6, 1930, p. 23.

54. JA to Alice Addams Haldeman, Nov. 4, 1886, JAMC; JA to Laura Addams, Dec. 1, 1886, SCPC; JA to Alice, January, n.d., 1887, JAMC.

55. JA to Alice Addams Haldeman, January, n.d., 1887, JAMC.

56. JA to Laura Addams, Dec. 1, 1886, SCPC. In telling Laura about her "alarm" over the invitation from Mrs. Franklin, Jane said that she was "unfortunately getting a reputation for knowing more about art than I do."

57. JA to Alice Addams Haldeman, Nov. 4, 1886, JAMC.

58. *Dictionary of American Biography*, 10:530; *Notable American Women*, 2:354.

59. Dr. Fabian Franklin was so devoted to Democratic politics and laissez-faire principles that he resigned his position at professor of mathematics at Johns Hopkins University in 1895 and became editor of the *Baltimore News*. From there, he moved on to an associate editorship at the New York *Evening Post* and at the *Nation*. He was an advocate of liberalism, low tariffs, world peace, and women's rights. *Dictionary of American Biography*, vol. 22, supplement 2 (New York: Charles Scribner's Sons, 1958), pp. 206–7.

60. JA to Alice Addams Haldeman, Nov. 4, 1886, JAMC.

61. JA to Alice Addams Haldeman, February, n.d., 1887, SAH.

62. JA to Laura Addams, Dec. 1, 1886, SCPC. More than a quarter of a century later, in 1914, Christine Ladd-Franklin visited Chicago and made contact with Jane Addams. Jane claimed to "remember with the greatest pleasure and minuteness our acquaintance in Baltimore," expressed regret at missing Ladd-Franklin's lecture on logic, and attempted to squeeze Ladd-Franklin into her busy schedule by including her

in a luncheon she was already holding. It is impossible to know if Jane derived any satisfaction from having to tell Ladd-Franklin that the luncheon was their only opportunity to visit as "I don't seem to have a minute this week and it is very difficult for me to get away." JA to Christine Ladd-Franklin, May 12, June n.d., and June 12, 1914. Christine Ladd-Franklin and Fabian Franklin Papers, Columbia University Libraries.

63. JA to Ellen Gates Starr, Apr. 24, 1883, EGSP.

64. JA to Alice Addams Haldeman, Mar. 20, 1886, JAMC.

65. JA to Alice Addams Haldeman, Dec. 10, 1887, SAH; JA to Alice Addams Haldeman, Mar. 31, 1886, JAMC.

66. JA to Alice Addams Haldeman, Mar. 20, 1886, JAMC.

67. JA to Ellen Gates Starr, Aug. 11, 1879, EGSP.

68. JA to Alice Addams Haldeman, January, n.d., 1887, JAMC.

69. Addams, "Darkness vs. Nebulae."

70. JA to Ellen Gates Starr, Nov. 3, 1883, EGSP.

71. JA to Ellen Gates Starr, Dec. 6, 1885, EGSP.

72. Jane Addams, "Editorial," *Rockford Seminary Magazine* 9 (May 1881): 153.

73. Addams, *Twenty Years*, p. 71.

74. JA to Ellen Gates Starr, Feb. 7, 1886, EGSP; JA to Alice Addams Haldeman, Feb. 1, 1886, JAMC. French, *History of the University Founded by Johns Hopkins*, p. 79.

75. JA to Alice Addams Haldeman, January, n.d., 1887, JAMC.

76. JA to Laura Addams, Oct. 18, 1886, SCPC; JA to Alice Addams Haldeman, Feb. 10, Oct. 23, Nov. 4 and 24, Dec. 21 and 28, 1886, January, n.d., Jan. 10, 1887, JAMC; JA to Alice Addams Haldeman, Jan. 22, Feb. 9, 1887, SAH.

77. JA to Alice Addams Haldeman, Feb. 10, Apr. 11, Oct. 23, 1886, JAMC; JA to Laura Addams, Dec. 1, 1886, SCPC.

78. JA to Alice Addams Haldeman, Feb. 17, Apr. 11, 1886, JAMC; JA to Alice Addams Haldeman, Dec. 28, 1886, and Jan. 22, 1887, SAH.

79. JA to Alice Addams Haldeman, Nov. 24, 1886, JAMC; George Haldeman to Anna Haldeman Addams, June 26, 1886, HJFP; JA to Alice Addams Haldeman, Dec. 15, 1886, JAMC; JA to Alice Addams Haldeman, Feb. 9, 1887, SAH.

80. William K. Brooks, "The Condition of Woman from a Zoological Point of View," *Popular Science Monthly* 15 (June-July 1879): 145–55, 347–56.

81. Ibid., pp. 154–55.

82. Ibid., p. 155.

83. William K. Brooks, "Woman from the Standpoint of a Naturalist," *Forum* 22 (November 1896): 286–96.

84. Brooks, "The Condition of Woman," pp. 155, 353.

85. Ibid., pp. 348–349.

86. Addams, "Cassandra," pp. 37–38.

87. Addams, "Compilers."

88. JA to Rockford College Board of Trustees, June 20, 1887, RCA.

89. JA to Anna Haldeman Addams, Dec. 10, 1887, SAH.

90. Ibid.

91. JA to Alice Addams Haldeman, Mar. 7, 1886, JAMC.

92. Jane Addams, "Our Debts and How We Shall Pay Them," unpublished speech before Rockford Alumnae Association, Oct. 9, 1887, Detzer Collection, UIC.

93. Ibid.

94. Addams, "The College Woman and Christianity," p. 1853.

95. JA to Alice Addams Haldeman, Jan. 10, 1887, JAMC.

96. JA to Laura Addams, July 23, 1887, SCPC.

97. JA to Alice Addams Haldeman, Jan. 10, 1887, JAMC; JA to Alice Addams Haldeman, Sept. 30, 1887, SAH.

98. JA to Alice Addams Haldeman, Nov. 4, 1887, SAH. Amelia Rowell had asked Jane for advice on setting up a small "art library" in her home in Freeport. Amelia M. Rowell to JA, Feb. 5, 1887, SCPC.

99. JA to Alice Addams Haldeman, Jan. 10, 1887, JAMC.

100. JA to Alice Addams Haldeman, Nov. 4, 1887, SAH.

101. George Haldeman to Harry Haldeman, Nov. 12, 1887, HJFP. George was sarcastic and defensive with Harry. "It is pleasant to know that my return meets with your approval," he wrote to his older brother, "I hope it may prove advantageous to mother. I did not realize how deeply she seemed to feel my absence nor how inadequate your sympathy was to alleviate the situation." George made no reference to any role Jane might have played in Anna's care or happiness. Turning his failure into a virtue, he set himself up as the more dutiful son.

102. JA to Alice Addams Haldeman, Nov. 4, 1887, SAH.

103. JA to Alice Addams Haldeman, Nov. 4 and 28, 1887, SAH.

104. George Haldeman to Harry Haldeman, Dec. 2, 1887, HJFP. George rejected Harry's offer of a share in the banking business taking it "more as a token of good will than serious earnest." He declined to seek employment because his mother had "use for me here as a companion."

Chapter 11. The Subjective Necessity for the Social Settlement

1. JA to Alice Addams Haldeman, Dec. 13, 1887, SAH.

2. JA to Alice Addams Haldeman, Weber and Laura Addams, and Mary Addams Linn, Jan. 20, 1888, SAH; Ellen Gates Starr to Anna Haldeman Addams, Jan. 30, 1888, EGSP; Ellen Gates Starr to Anna Haldeman Addams, Feb. 23, 1888, SCPC; Sarah Anderson to JA, Mar. 14, 1888, SCPC; Amelia Rowell to Anna Haldeman Addams, July 17, 1888, SAH; JA to George Haldeman, June 9, 1888, HJFP.

3. JA to Alice Addams Haldeman, Jan. 29, 1888, SAH.

4. JA to Laura Addams, June 30, 1887, SCPC.

5. JA to Anna Haldeman Addams, Jan. 7, 1888, JAMC; Ellen Gates Starr to Caleb and Susan Starr, Feb. 19, 1888, EGSP. In regard to Annie Kales, Ellen assured her parents, "We are all remarkably patient with her, and her perceptions are too blunt to see how trying she is."

6. JA to Anna Haldeman Addams, Apr. 7, 1888, JAMC; JA to Alice Addams Haldeman, Apr. 6, 1888, SAH. Jane admired Rowell's ambition to set up an art library in her Freeport home and her humble sentiment that "sometimes we can do things in a small way very satisfactorily from ideas we gain from others." Still, Jane shared Ellen's desire for independence from Rowell; she would have been "tempted" by Rowell's plan to spend two months in Spain, rather than the one month Jane and Ellen had budgeted "if I loved Mrs. Rowell more and Sarah and Ellen less." Amelia M. Rowell to JA, Feb. 5, 1887, SCPC; JA to Alice Addams Haldeman, Jan. 6, 1888, SAH.

7. Ellen Gates Starr to Susan and Caleb Starr, Apr. 8 and May 2, 1888, EGSP. Ellen knew that she was "sometimes fault-finding." Ellen Gates Starr to Susan and Caleb Starr, Oct. 30, 1887, EGSP.

8. JA to Alice Addams Haldeman, Apr. 6, 1888, SAH; JA to Alice Addams Haldeman, Apr. 6, 1888, JAMC; JA to Alice Addams Haldeman, June 5, 1888, HJFP.

9. It appears that Jane paid for Ellen's expenses when they were actually traveling together. Ellen Starr's niece claimed that Jane paid "half of E.G.S.'s expenses" on this European tour. Josephine Starr, "Notes," EGSP. Ellen felt she would "not have money enough" for trips off on her own, though "Jeannie offers to lend it to me." Ellen Gates Starr to Caleb and Susan Starr, Feb. 19, 1888, EGSP. Ellen's arrangement with the two young "charges," Matilda Peasley and Mary Breckenridge, hints at her connections in Chicago, probably through Miss Kirkland's school. Peasley and Breckenridge were escorted over to Europe by Bertha Honore Palmer, the wife of Potter Palmer, one of Chicago's leading developers, and herself a prominent force in Chicago civic life with whom Jane would later have many dealings. Peasley later married into the wealthy Delano family and volunteered at Hull-House. Breckenridge, the niece of Kentucky Colonel William C. P. Breckenridge, was the cousin of Sophonisba Breckenridge, who would become a close colleague of Jane's in the creation of the field of social work at the University of Chicago. JA to Anna Haldeman Addams, May 11 and 12, 1888, JAMC; JA to Alice Addams Haldeman, June 5, 1888, HJFP.

10. JA to Weber Addams, Jan. 11, 1888, SCPC.

11. Jane quoted Ellen on this point in two letters: JA to Alice Addams Haldeman, Mary Addams Linn, Weber Addams, and Laura Addams, Jan. 20, 1888, SAH; and JA to George Haldeman, Jan. 21, 1888, JAMC. George was not included in the letter that "circulated" to the sisters and to Weber even though he and Weber were neighbors in Cedarville.

12. Jane Addams, "My Experience as a Progressive Delegate," *McClure's* 40 (November 1912): 14. In *Romola*, Eliot wrote that "we prepare ourselves for sudden deeds by the reiterated choice of good and evil that gradually determines character," p. 204.

13. JA to Alice Addams Haldeman, Feb. 8 and 16, 1888, SAH.

14. JA to Alice Addams Haldeman, July 3, 1888, HJFP; JA to Laura Shoemaker Addams, July 4, 1888, SCPC.

15. Jane used the word "melodramatic" to describe George's alarmingly uncharacteristic behavior. JA to Alice Addams Haldeman, July 3, 1888, HJFP.

16. JA to Alice Addams Haldeman, Feb. 16, 1888, SAH; Mary Addams Linn to JA, Jan. 31, 1888, SCPC; JA to Alice Addams Haldeman, Mar. 5, 1888, SCHS.

17. Mary Addams Linn to JA, Feb. 23, 1888, SCPC; JA to Anna Haldeman Addams, Mar. 15, 1888, SCHS.

18. Mary Addams Linn to JA, Mar. 6 and 7, Jan. 31, Feb. 8 and 23, and Mar. 2, 1888; John Linn, Jr., to JA, Jan. 31, 1888; Rev. John Linn to JA, Jan. 31, 1888, SCPC. Amid her heartrending grief, Mary Linn ruminated on the evidence that her daughter's pious baby soul was heaven-bound. She took maternal solace in the thought that little Mary's death, though devastating to the other children, "makes them think of heaven." Echoing language she had used when her own mother died, Mary wrote to Jane that "I know our Father doeth all things well." Mary Addams to Elizabeth Reiff, Aug. 1, 1863, SAH.

19. JA to Anna Haldeman Addams, Mar. 15, 1888, SCHS.

20. Addams, *Twenty Years*, pp. 14–15. Addams attributed to John Addams the opinion that "it was very important not to pretend to understand what you didn't

understand and that you must always be honest with yourself inside, whatever happened."

21. JA to Sadie Addams, Feb. 21, 1888, SCPC.

22. JA to Weber Addams, Feb. 17, 1888, SCPC. JA to Alice Addams Haldeman, Feb. 27, 1888, SAH.

23. JA to Alice Addams Haldeman, Jan. 6, 1888, SAH. Logistics at the start of the trip necessitated that Jane stay alone in Ulm, Germany. She reported to Alice, with great pride, on taking a hotel room for herself and feeling "perfectly at ease and dignified the whole time."

24. JA to Alice Addams Haldeman, January, n.d., 1888, SAH; JA to George Haldeman, Jan. 21, 1888, JAMC; JA to Alice Addams Haldeman, Jan. 26, 1888, SAH; JA to Anna Haldeman Addams, Jan. 28, 1888, JAMC.

25. JA to Laura Addams, Mar. 11, 1888, SCPC.

26. Addams, *Twenty Years*, p. 84.

27. JA to Alice Addams Haldeman, Feb. 27, 1888, SAH.

28. JA to Weber Addams, Mar. 1, 1888, SCPC. Jane had sounded a similar note in describing her inevitable seasickness during the Atlantic crossing. She emphasized that "we were all violently seasick at once," which meant that she was not unusually frail. JA to Alice Addams Haldeman, Dec. 23, 1887, SAH.

29. JA to Alice Addams Haldeman, Feb. 27, 1888, SAH; JA to Laura Addams, Mar. 11, 1888, SCPC; JA to Anna Haldeman Addams, Mar. 9, 15, and 27, 1888, SCHS; JA to Alice Addams Haldeman, Mar. 15 and 18, 1888, SAH.

30. JA to Laura Addams, Mar. 11, 1888, SCPC; JA to Alice Addams Haldeman, Apr. 6, 1888, SAH.

31. Ellen Gates Starr to Susan and Caleb Starr, Feb. 26, 1888, EGSP.

32. JA to Alice Addams Haldeman, Mar. 22, 1888, SAH.

33. Sarah Anderson to JA, Mar. 14, 1888, SCPC.

34. JA to Alice Addams Haldeman, Mar. 3, 1888, SAH.

35. JA to Alice Addams Haldeman, Dec. 27, 1887, SAH; JA to Anna Haldeman Addams, Jan. 28, 1888, JAMC.

36. JA to Weber Addams, Dec. 22, 1887, SCPC. Despite the advent of Martha Hillard, Sarah Anderson had gone through a difficult time in the fall of 1885. She was "threatened with nervous prostration" and checked into an "invalid home" in Kenosha, Wisconsin. JA to Alice Addams Haldeman, Oct. 23, 1885, JAMC.

37. Ellen Gates Starr to Caleb and Susan Starr, Feb. 19, 1888, EGSP. In the month before Ellen made this remark, Jane had raised with Alice, once again, the idea of having a "bust or bas relief" made of their father's head, even asking that Alice send a greater array of photos of Pa than Jane had with her on the trip. JA to Alice Addams Haldeman, Jan. 26, 1888, SAH.

38. JA to Alice Addams Haldeman, Jan. 6, 1888, SAH.

39. Ellen Gates Starr to Caleb and Susan Starr, Feb. 19, 1888, EGSP.

40. JA to Flora Guiteau, Jan. 7, 1888, JAMC. Jane repeated the notion that Ellen was "a constant source of delight for me" in a letter to her stepmother. JA to Anna Haldeman Addams, Mar. 15, 1888, SCHS.

41. JA to Anna Haldeman Addams, Jan. 28, 1888, JAMC.

42. JA to Alice Addams Haldeman, Jan. 26, 1888, SAH.

43. JA to Anna Haldeman Addams, Jan. 28, 1888, JAMC; JA to George Haldeman, Jan. 21, 1888, JAMC. JA to George Haldeman, Mar. 8, 1884, SCHS.

44. JA to Anna Haldeman Addams, Jan. 28, 1888, JAMC. JA to Alice Addams Haldeman, Jan. 26, 1888, SAH. Jane repeated the remark about the utility of "abusive" language in Italy in her letter two days later to Anna.

45. Stuck on a stalled train, Jane uttered Galileo's words, "it does not move for all that," and the delighted Italian passengers immediately peppered her with questions, in Italian, which were way beyond her vocabulary, thereby illustrating, she told her siblings, "the evil results of showing off." JA to Alice Addams Haldeman, Weber and Alice Addams, Mary Addams Linn, Jan. 20, 1888, SAH.

46. JA to Anna Haldeman Addams, Feb. 5, 1888, SCHS.

47. Ellen Gates Starr to Alice Addams Haldeman, Feb. 23, 1888, SAH; Ellen Gates Starr to Anna Haldeman Addams, Feb. 23, 1888, SCPC.

48. Ellen Gates Starr to Alice Addams Haldeman, Feb. 23, 1888, SAH.

49. Ellen Gates Starr to JA, Mar. 14, 1888, SCPC.

50. Ellen Gates Starr to Caleb and Susan Starr, Feb. 19, 1888, EGSP.

51. JA to Alice Addams Haldeman, Apr. 6, 1888, SAH.

52. Ellen Gates Starr to Anna Haldeman Addams, Jan. 30, 1888, EGSP.

53. Ellen Gates Starr to JA, Mar. 17 and 18, 1888, SAH; Sarah Anderson to JA, Mar. 14, 1888, SCPC. Ellen Gates Starr to JA, Mar. 14, 1888, SAH. Jane told Alice of awakening early one morning in Ravenna to find Ellen crying because she was so cold. "Upon inviting her to share my fur cloak (in which I always slept), she stopped crying and the tears dried on her cheeks like a child." JA to Alice Addams Haldeman, Mar. 22, 1888, SAH.

54. Ellen was acutely conscious of the fact that she had quit her job at Miss Kirkland's school in order to tour Europe with Jane, and she felt pressure to "make arrangements for next year's bread and butter." At the same time, Ellen noted to her parents, "there are only about six weeks more" of time with Jane. Ellen Gates Starr to Caleb and Susan Starr, Feb. 19, 1888, EGSP.

55. JA to Alice Addams Haldeman, Apr. 6, 1888, SAH.

56. Ellen Gates Starr to JA, Mar. 17 and 18, 1888, SAH.

57. "Ellen is growing very fond of you through me," Jane told Alice. "She always heartily concurs in your opinions when I quote them, which is often my dear." JA to Alice Addams Haldeman, Jan. 26, 1888, SAH. See also JA to Alice Addams Haldeman, Jan. 29 and 6, Feb. 8 and 27, Apr. 6, 1888, SAH.

58. JA to Alice Addams Haldeman, Mar. 18 and 22, 1888, SAH.

59. Ellen Gates Starr to JA, Mar. 17 and 18, 1888, SAH.

60. Whether the surviving evidence warrants assigning to JA or Ellen Starr an identity as a "lesbian" depends entirely on how one defines "lesbian." If we adopt Blanche Wiesen Cook's argument that lesbians are "women who love women, who choose women to nurture and support and to create a living environment in which to work creatively and independently," then Jane Addams and Ellen Gates Starr were lesbians. If, however, we employ the term "lesbian" to mean a female who has genital contact with another female and who self-identifies as belonging in a different sexual category from women who have intercourse with men, then we must decline to define either Addams or Starr as lesbians simply because we do not have evidence of genital contact or conscious self-identification based on sexual behavior. Caution is advisable because it serves to remind modern readers that sexual identity is historically constructed and that individuals can live emotionally satisfying lives without defining themselves in terms of sexual activity. Both Lillian Faderman and Leila Rupp have

argued that female socialization away from sexual expressiveness in the nineteenth century makes it likely that most intense, intimate female partnerships did not include genital sexuality. Their arguments built upon the concept which Carroll Smith-Rosenberg articulated in 1975: "Sexual and emotional impulses [are] part of a continuum or spectrum of affect gradations strongly affected by cultural norms and arrangements." Smith-Rosenberg's argument was intended to move our thinking beyond rigid dichotomies and place relationships in the context of their own culture. Thus, romantic expressions of love between women might not signal an erotic lesbian relationship in every culture. Some have used this cultural constructionist argument to diminish the significance of nineteenth-century women's words to and about a beloved other woman. That is not the intended message here. This analysis takes very seriously the centrality of Ellen Gates Starr in the story of Jane Addams's development. The assumption here is that Ellen's expressiveness, her sentimentality, her desire for emotional intimacy and physical affection all played a crucial role in liberating Jane's sensibilities and providing Jane with an emotional home away from her family. Knowledge of these two women's erotic expression is not necessary to establish the vital role Ellen Starr played in Jane Addams's life in the late 1880s and early 1890s. Leila Rupp's formulation of the need to "make distinctions among different sorts of women's relationships in the past without denying their significance or assigning fixed categories" has been particularly helpful in this analysis. See: "'Imagine My Surprise': Women's Relationships in Historical Perspective," *Frontiers: A Journal of Women's Studies* 5 (Fall 1980): 61–70, and *A Desired Past: A Short History of Same-Sex Love in America* (Chicago: University of Chicago Press, 1999). See, too, Blanche Wiesen Cook, "Female Support Networks and Political Activism: Lillian Wald, Crystal Eastman, Emma Goldman," *Chrysalis* 3 (Autumn 1977): 43–61; Carroll Smith-Rosenberg, "The Female World of Love and Ritual," *Signs* 1 (Autumn 1975): 1–29; Lillian Faderman, "Boston Marriages as a Possible Lesson for Today," *Boston Marriages: Romantic but Asexual Relationships Among Contemporary Lesbians*, ed. Esther D. Rothblum and Kathleen A. Brehony (Amherst: University of Massachusetts Press, 1993), pp. 29–42; Noel Riley Fitch, "The Elusive 'Seamless Whole': A Biographer Treats (or Fails to Treat) Lesbianism," *Lesbian Texts and Contexts: Radical Revisions*, ed. Karla Jay and Joanne Glasgow (New York: New York University Press, 1990); Nancy S. Landale and Avery M. Guest, "Ideology and Sexuality Among Victorian Women," *Social Science History* 19 (Summer 1986): 147–70; Karen Lystra, *Searching the Heart: Women, Men, and Romantic Love in Nineteenth-Century America* (New York: Oxford University Press, 1989); Steven Seidman, "The Power of Desire and the Danger of Pleasure: Victorian Sexuality Reconsidered," *Journal of Social History* 24 (Fall 1990): 47–67; Estelle Freedman, "Sexuality in Nineteenth-Century America: Behavior, Ideology, and Politics," *Reviews in American History* (December 1982): 196–215.

61. JA to George Haldeman, Jan. 21, 1888, JAMC.

62. JA to Laura Malburn, Jan. 26, 1888, SCPC; JA to George Haldeman, July 5, 1887, SAH. In *My Religion*, Tolstoy depicted pre-Constantine Christians as better adherents to Jesus' message than their descendents, p. 102. Ellen's beloved Cardinal Newman encouraged his fellow Catholics to "keep their minds open to the old principle of primitive Catholic faith." Owen Chadwick, *Newman* (Oxford: Oxford University Press, 1983), p. 58. At the time of Marcet's birth, Jane and Alice read Edward Gibbon's *Decline and Fall of the Roman Empire* and Frederic William Farrar's *Early Days of Christianity* "and kindred books." There, they encountered a thoroughly historicized view of Christianity.

Though Gibbon was a skeptic and Farrar an Anglican, both men treated the church as a socially constructed institution subject to historical influences. J. G. A. Pocock, "Gibbon and the Primitive Church," in *History, Religion, and Culture*, ed. Stefan Collini, Richard Whatmore, and Brian Young (Cambridge: Cambridge University Press, 2000), pp. 48–68.

63. Addams, *Twenty Years*, pp. 51–53.

64. JA to Flora Guiteau, Jan. 7, 1888, JAMC; JA to Weber Addams, Feb. 17, 1888, SCPC; JA to Mary Addams Linn, Feb. 5, 1888, SAH.

65. JA to Alice Addams Haldeman, Feb. 12, 1888, JAMC; JA to Weber Addams, Feb. 17, 1888.

66. JA to Mary Addams Linn, Feb. 5, 1888, SAH.

67. Ellen Gates Starr to Anna Haldeman Addams, Jan. 30, 1888, EGSP. Spiritual struggles caused Ellen other physical discomforts. She reported to her parents, "I celebrate the Lord's day pretty regularly by having a diarrhea." Ellen Gates Starr to Caleb and Susan Starr, Feb. 19, 1888, EGSP.

68. JA to Alice Addams Haldeman, Feb. 8, 1888, SAH. JA to Weber Addams, Jan. 21, 1888, SCPC.

69. JA to George Haldeman, Jan. 21, 1888, JAMC.

70. Addams, *Twenty Years*, pp. 82–83.

71. Jane referred to William Godwin's *Essays*, his posthumously published plea for belief in Christian ethics not supernatural dogma, in a letter from Europe to her stepmother's friend, Laura Malburn, Jan. 26, 1888, SCPC. William Godwin, *Essays* (London: Henry S. King, 1873).

72. Addams, "The Subjective Necessity for Social Settlements," p. 18.

73. JA to Flora Guiteau, Jan. 7, 1888, JAMC. Jane told Flora that the iconography there made her think of "Matthew Arnold's idea of culture" because the images of the saints "are but the embodiment of fine action." Since fine action "is what we are all trying" to achieve, we perpetuate the saints "in stone and glass, anything that will *last*" and thereby provide an inspiration to others. JA to Flora Guiteau, Jan. 7, 1888, JAMC. Addams quoted this sentence about the saints embodying "fine action" in *Twenty Years*. She said it was from her "smug notebook" from the time and claimed it accompanied a lengthy entry on her hope for a "cathedral of humanity," p. 83.

74. JA to Alice Addams Haldeman, May 12, 1888, JAMC.

75. Jane described this Florentine ritual, conducted on the Saturday between Good Friday and Easter, in three letters home. JA to Alice Addams Haldeman, Apr. 7, 1888, SAH; JA to Weber Addams, Apr. 6, 1888, SCPC; JA to Anna Haldeman Addams, Apr. 7, 1888, JAMC.

76. JA to Alice Addams Haldeman, Feb. 12, 1888, JAMC; JA to Laura Addams, Mar. 11, 1888, SCPC.

77. JA to Laura Addams, Mar. 11, 1888, SCPC; JA to Alice Addams Haldeman, Mar. 3, 1888, SAH; JA to Anna Haldeman Addams, Mar. 9, 1888, SCHS.

78. JA to Alice Addams Haldeman, Mar. 22, 1888, SAH.

79. JA to Weber Addams, Jan. 21, 1888, SCPC; JA to Alice Addams Haldeman, Mar. 22, 1888, SAH.

80. JA to Alice Addams Haldeman, Mar. 22, 1888, SAH.

81. JA to Flora Guiteau, Jan. 7, 1888, JAMC.

82. JA to Anna Haldeman Addams, Jan. 28, 1888, JAMC.

83. Ellen Gates Starr to Anna Haldeman Addams, Jan. 30, 1888, EGSP.

84. Ellen Gates Starr to JA, Mar. 17 and 18, 1888, SAH.

85. JA to Anna Haldeman Addams, Jan. 28, 1888, JAMC.

86. JA to Anna Haldeman Addams, Apr. 27, 1888, JAMC.

87. Addams, *Twenty Years*, pp. 85–86.

88. JA to Sarah Hostetter, Apr. 24, 1888, JAMC; JA to Laura Shoemaker Addams, Apr. 25, 1888, JAMC. Shortly before opening the settlement, Ellen told her cousin that she was "tired to death of art for art's sake, words for words' sake, music for music's sake." Ellen Gates Starr to Mary Allen, Sept. 15, 1889, EGSP.

89. JA to Laura Shoemaker Addams, Apr. 25, 1888, JAMC.

90. JA to Anna Haldeman Addams, Apr. 27, 1888, JAMC. Jane was not alone among Americans in her recoil from the violence of the bullfight. In an article for *Century* magazine, Charles Dudley Warner described the "cheap barbarity" of the whole scene and claimed he later sought refuge in a church to soothe his "bruised nerves." Jane was with Anna in Europe when the article first appeared. It is impossible to know if she read it. Charles Dudley Warner, "The Bull Fight," *Century* 27 (November 1883): 3–13.

91. JA to Sarah Hostetter, Apr. 24, 1888, JAMC.

92. JA to Anna Haldeman Addams, Apr. 27, 1888, JAMC.

93. JA to Anna Haldeman Addams, May 11, 1888, JAMC; JA to Alice Addams Haldeman, May 12, 1888, JAMC.

94. JA to Alice Addams Haldeman, May 12, 1888, JAMC; JA to Sadie Addams, May 21, 1888, SCPC. Six months earlier, Jane had received a letter from a Rockford seminary friend who had become a missionary in Turkey. She reported feeling "more deeply satisfied and happy in my work than I can tell you," and then asked if Jane were carrying out "any regular line of work." Maria Nutting to JA, Nov. 17, 1887, SAH.

95. JA to Alice Addams Haldeman, June 5, 1888, HJFP.

96. JA to Alice Addams Haldeman, June 14, 1888, HJFP.

97. Lois Ellen Shankman Nettleship, "The Settlement Rationale: A Comparative Study of Samuel Barnett and Jane Addams, 1870 to 1914," Ph.D. thesis, University of Sussex, England, 1976, pp. 7–43; L. E. Nettleship, "William Fremantle, Samuel Barnett and the Broad Church Origins of Toynbee Hall," *Journal of Ecclesiastical History* 33 (October 1982): 564–79.

98. JA to George Haldeman, June 9, 1888, HJFP; Ellen Gates Starr to JA, Dec. 3, 1885, EGSP. For Stanley's controversial stance in the Anglican Church in the 1860s, see George Granville Bradley, *Recollections of Arthur Penrhyn Stanley: Three Lectures Delivered in Edinburgh, November, 1882* (New York: Charles Scribner's Sons, 1883).

99. Both Graham and Ely were influenced by Fremantle's *World as the Subject of Redemption: Being an Attempt to Set Forth the Functions of the Church* (London: Longmans, Green, 1895); Mina Jane Carson, *Settlement Folk: Social Thought and the American Settlement Movement, 1885–1930* (Chicago: University of Chicago Press, 1990), pp. 15–17.

100. Nettleship, "The Settlement Rationale," pp. 7–43; Nettleship, "William Fremantle, Samuel Barnett and the Broad Church Origins of Toynbee Hall," pp. 574–75.

101. Matthew Arnold, *Culture and Anarchy*, ed. J. Dover Wilson (Cambridge: Cambridge University Press, 1963), p. 6. Carson, *Settlement Folk*, pp. 1–9. For earlier treatments of the settlement's religious and intellectual context, see K. S. Inglis, *Churches*

and the *Working Classes in Victorian England* (London: Routledge and Kegan Paul, 1963), and Nettleship, "The Settlement Rationale." Other treatments of Toynbee Hall have failed to take seriously its roots in the broad church movement.

102. Arnold Toynbee, "Industry and Democracy," an address delivered in early 1881 before an audience of workers and employers at Newcastle. Published in *Lectures on the Industrial Revolution of the Eighteenth Century in England* (London: Longmans, Green, 1884).

103. JA to Alice Addams Haldeman, June 14, 1888, HJFP.

104. Asa Briggs and Anne Macartney, *Toynbee Hall: The First Hundred Years* (London: Routledge and Kegan Paul, 1984), pp. 22–23.

105. Briggs and Macartney, *Toynbee Hall: The First Hundred Years*, pp. 1–3, 16–22; Gertrude Himmelfarb, *Poverty and Compassion: The Moral Imagination of the Late Victorians* (New York: Alfred A. Knopf, 1991); Gareth Stedman-Jones, *Outcast London: A Study of the Relationship Between Classes in Victorian Society* (London: Oxford University Press, 1971). It was a shocking description of the district in 1883 that had stimulated the sort of "slumming" trips that Jane herself took to the East End during her first visit to London. Samuel Barnett argued that such sensational exposés brought forth quick infusions of ill-spent funds while doing nothing to create long-term change in the district's economic, cultural, and social life. Mearns, *The Bitter Cry of Outcast London*; Samuel Barnett, "Sensationalism in Social Reform," *Nineteenth Century* 19 (February 1886): 280–90.

106. JA to Weber Addams, Oct. 29, 1883, JAMC.

107. JA to Alice Addams Haldeman, June 14, 1888, HJFP. In her biography of her husband, Henrietta Barnett incorrectly recalled the Barnetts' initial contact with Jane Addams. According to Mrs. Barnett, Jane first visited Toynbee Hall in 1887 and then made a second visit in 1889, at which time, said Mrs. Barnett, she and her husband recognized that Jane had a "great soul." In fact, the only visit Jane made before founding Hull-House was in June 1888. Whether the Barnetts thought, at the time, that Jane had a "great soul" cannot be determined, but the three did make an important and lifelong connection. Henrietta Barnett, *Canon Barnett: His Life, Work, and Friends by His Wife* (New York: G. P. Putnam's Sons, 1921), p. 422.

108. For daily operations at Toynbee Hall, see Barnett, *Canon Barnett*; Briggs and Macartney, *Toynbee Hall: The First Hundred Years*, pp. 30–35; Standish Meacham, *Toynbee Hall and Social Reform, 1880–1914: The Search for Community* (New Haven: Yale University Press, 1987), pp. 24–62; Nettleship, "The Settlement Rationale," pp. 152–91.

109. JA to Alice Addams Haldeman, June 14, 1888, HJFP.

110. Jane Addams, "Outgrowths of Toynbee Hall," unpublished speech delivered to the Chicago Women's Club Board, Dec. 3, 1891, SCPC.

111. Himmelfarb, *Poverty and Compassion*, p. 75. See Daniel T. Rodgers, *Atlantic Crossings: Social Politics in a Progressive Age*, for a discussion of this diffuse, ethical understanding of the term "socialism" and its use as an "antonym of competitive individualism" (Cambridge, Massachusetts: Belknap Press of Harvard University Press, 1998), p. 100. See, too, Edward Norman, *The Victorian Christian Socialists* (Cambridge: Cambridge University Press, 1987).

112. For a positive view of Hill's work, see A. F. Young, *British Social Work in the Nineteenth Century* (London: Routledge and Kegan Paul, 1956), and Himmelfarb, *Poverty and Compassion*, chapter 14. For a more critical view, see Beatrice Webb, *My Apprenticeship* (London: Longmans, Green, 1926).

113. Amidst their insistence that Toynbee Hall was a thoroughly elitist institution intent on social control, both Standish Meacham and Emily K. Abel provide considerable evidence of Samuel Barnett's evolution away from Octavia Hill's harsh assumptions and toward a more critical view of the elite's control of the economy and political system. Meacham, *Toynbee Hall and Social Reform, 1880–1914*; Emily K. Abel, "Middle-Class Culture for the Urban Poor: The Educational Thought of Samuel Barnett," *Social Service Review* 52 (December 1978): 596–620; Emily K. Abel, "Toynbee Hall, 1884–1914," *Social Service Review* (December 1979): 606–32. For even stronger evidence of this transition, see Webb, *My Apprenticeship*, pp. 200–209; Samuel and Henrietta Barnett, *Practicable Socialism: Essays on Social Reform*, 2nd ed. (London: Longmans, Green, 1894); Donald O. Wagner, *The Church of England and Social Reform Since 1854* (New York: Columbia University Press, 1930), pp. 177–82.

114. For lists of Toynbee Hall speakers, see *The Toynbee Record*, University of Illinois–Chicago, Special Collections, and Barnett, *Canon Barnett*, pp. 370–71. These lists support the argument that Toynbee Hall sought to impart a particular form of British literary culture, but they also support the argument that the settlement was friendly to labor unions, legislative activism to reform British society and regulate the British economy, and expansion of British educational and political opportunity.

115. JA to Alice Addams Haldeman, June 14, 1888, HJFP. A new look at Barnett and Toynbee Hall could usefully combine greater attention to his particular position within Christianity, his—and his wife's—unique personalities, more evidence of change in his political thinking, and more evidence of persistence in his inability to grasp the working-class culture than modern scholars have retrieved. Such a study could capture settlement work as a charged encounter between various cultures, all of which must be respected so that the ironic, tragic, well-intentioned, unintentioned, and even beneficial results of the encounter can be appreciated. The study that has come closest to achieving that goal is Carson, *Settlement Folk*.

116. JA to Alice Addams Haldeman, June 14, 1888, JAMC.

117. Walter Besant, *All Sorts and Conditions of Men: An Impossible Story* (London: Chatto and Windus, 1882).

118. JA to Alice Addams Haldeman, June 14, 1888, JAMC; Addams, *Twenty Years*, p. 87.

119. Walter Besant, "The People's Palace," *North American Review* 147 (July 1888): 63. For the problems that bedeviled the People's Palace, see *The Autobiography of Sir Walter Besant* (New York: Dodd, Mead, 1902), pp. 243–46.

120. Addams, *Twenty Years*, pp. 87–88.

121. Norman Vance, *The Sinews of the Spirit: The Ideal of Christian Manliness in Victorian Literature and Religious Thought* (Cambridge: Cambridge University Press, 1985); W. C. Lubenow, *The Cambridge Apostles, 1820–1914: Liberalism, Imagination, and Friendship in British Intellectual and Professional Life* (Cambridge: Cambridge University Press, 1998); Desmond Bowen, *The Idea of the Victorian Church: A Study of the Church of England, 1833–1889* (Montreal: McGill University Press, 1968); Norman, *The Victorian Christian Socialists*; Peter d'A. Jones, *The Christian Socialist Revival, 1877–1914* (Princeton: Princeton University Press, 1968).

122. Henry Bradford Washburn, *The Religious Motive in Philanthropy* (Philadelphia: University of Pennsylvania Press, 1931), pp. 31, 40–41. In his essay on Samuel Barnett, Washburn, the dean of the Episcopal Theological School of Cambridge, Massachusetts,

referred to Jane Addams as one who believed, like Barnett, "in the capabilities of human nature." Washburn argued that "the secret" of Barnett's philanthropic work lay in his belief that "God was within himself and others, and, in some mystical way, Christ was to be found in the inner life of all men," p. 40.

123. Addams, "The Subjective Necessity for Social Settlements." Regarding T. H. Green, see James T. Kloppenberg, *Uncertain Victory: Social Democracy and Progressivism in European and American Thought, 1870–1920* (New York: Oxford University Press, 1986). Addams did not articulate her familiarity with Green until she fist delivered the speech "Outgrowths of Toynbee Hall," December 1890, SCPC. Her familiarity with Tolstoy's fierce, lyric tribute to these ideals prepared her for an appreciation of Green's less accessible philosophical defense of them. There is a discrepancy in the records regarding when Jane wrote the "Outgrowths" speech and actually delivered it to the Women's Club. The minutes of the Chicago Women's Club date her delivery as Dec. 3, 1891, and Jane delivered a lecture at Hull-House in December 1891 titled "Outgrowths of Toynbee Hall" according to the *Comprehensive Guide to the Jane Addams Papers.* But correspondence indicates the speech was written and delivered in December 1890 and the *Comprehensive Guide* notes that Jane's cover note for "Outgrowths" dates the speech in December 1890. Given Jane's propensity for recycling speeches, it is possible she delivered versions of the speech twice, a year apart.

124. Jane Addams Notebook, Summer, n.d., 1882, SCPC and JAPP, reel 27, frame 0371.

125. Jane Addams, "Alumnae Essay," *Memorials of Anna Peck Sill* (Rockford, Ill.: Rockford College, 1889), pp. 71–75.

126. JA to Alice Addams Haldeman, July 3, 1888, JAMC.

127. JA to Laura Addams, July 4, 1888, SCPC.

128. Harry Haldeman to Anna Haldeman, June 18, 1888, SAH; Alice Addams Haldeman to Harry Haldeman, June 19 and June 20, 1888; Alice Addams Haldeman to Anna Haldeman Addams, June 25, 1888; Alice Addams Haldeman to Harry Haldeman, June 26, 1888, SAH.

129. Anna Haldeman Addams to Harry Haldeman, Nov. 30, 1882, Oct. 26 and 29, 1883, Jan. 27, 1884, HJFP; George Haldeman to Anna Haldeman Addams, Jan. 6 and Mar. 2, 1884, HJFP.

130. Anna Haldeman Addams to Harry Haldeman, Sept. 10, 1895, SAH.

131. "Cedarville," *Freeport Daily Journal,* Sept. 26, 1888.

132. Jane Addams's certificate of baptism, Oct. 14, 1888, JAMC. Addams's later claim that she had joined the Presbyterian church after her first trip to Europe is consistent with her tendency to accelerate the ideological process that led her to found Hull-House. Addams, *Twenty Years,* pp. 77–78.

133. Addams, *Twenty Years,* p. 78; JA to Alice Addams Haldeman, Mar. 22, 1888, SAH.

134. JA to Laura Malburn, Jan. 26, 1888, SCPC; JA to Alice Addams Haldeman, July 3, 1888, HJFP. Jane made her comment to Alice when she was feeling torn between returning home to Anna and staying in England with Flora Guiteau.

135. George Haldeman to Harry Haldeman, Sept. 14, Nov. 30, and Jan. 30, 1888, HJFP; JA to Anna Haldeman Addams, Jan. 2, 1889, SCPC. Addams, *My Friend, Julia Lathrop,* p. 43. Due to his own confusion, or Jane's dissemblance, George thought Jane would be returning to Cedarville after a "stay" in Chicago.

136. Sarah Blaisdell to JA, Jan. 5, 1889, SCPC; JA to Ellen Gates Starr, Jan. 24, 1889, EGSP.

137. JA to Ellen Gates Starr, Jan. 24, 1889, EGSP.

138. Ellen Gates Starr to Anna Haldeman Addams, Jan. 30, 1888, EGSP.

139. JA to Ellen Gates Starr, Jan. 24, 1889, EGSP.

Chapter 12. Power in Me and Will to Dominate

1. Mary H. Porter, "A Home on Halsted Street," *Advance*, July 11, 1889, HHScrapbooks.

2. Ellen Gates Starr to Mary Starr Blaisdell, Feb. 23, 1889, EGSP.

3. "Hull House: A Visit to a Noted Institution," *Philadelphia Public Ledger*, Aug. 5, 1891; "In the Butler Gallery," *Chicago Tribune*, May 31, 1891, HHScrapbooks.

4. Though some early newspaper articles depicted Jane and Ellen as equal partners in the enterprise, the press typically placed Jane at the head of the enterprise and Ellen at her side. See Leila Bedell, "A Chicago Toynbee Hall," *Woman's Journal*, May 5, 1889; "A Social Reformer: Miss Jane Addams's Efforts to Elevate the People Socially," *Troy Daily Press*, May 15, 1889; David Swing, "A New Social Movement," *Evening Journal*, early June 1889; "She Gave Up Her Home: Noble Work Being Done Among the People of the West Side," *Evening Journal*, May 17, 1890; "Two Women's Work," *Chicago Tribune*, May 19, 1890; "Art for the Masses: What Miss Addams Desires to Make her West Side Home Complete," *Evening Journal*, May 27, 1890; "Work of Two Women," *Chicago Times*, July 8, 1890, HHScrapbooks.

5. Bedell, "A Chicago Toynbee Hall"; *Chicago Tribune*, headline and date illegible, HHScrapbooks.

6. Addams, *Twenty Years*, p. 64; JA to Ellen Gates Starr, June 8, 1884, EGSP.

7. JA to Alice Addams Haldeman, Feb. 19, 1889, SCHS; Ellen Gates Starr to Mary Starr Blaisdell, Feb. 23, 1889, EGSP.

8. JA to Alice Addams Haldeman, Feb. 19, 1889, SCHS. These lines were taken from Robert Browning's 1855 poem "Bishop Blougram's Apology," in which Browning's bishop struggled to "reconcile" his desire for "power and influence with the spiritual and idealistic values that still" inspired him. Scholars argue whether Bishop Blougram was sincere in his faith or merely using it for self-aggrandizement. Frank Charles Allen, *A Critical Edition of Robert Browning's "Bishop Blougram's Apology"* (Salzburg: University of Salzburg, 1976). In writing the word "else" after "Obedience," Addams was either misquoting the poem in an interesting way or using "else" as the equivalent of "et cetera." In Browning's poem, the line is "In many ways I need mankind's respect,/Obedience, and the love that's born of fear." In her management of Hull-House, Jane Addams sought to inspire willing cooperation, not fear. I am grateful to Patricia O'Neill of Hamilton College for guiding me to the source of these lines of poetry.

9. Harold M. Mayer and Richard C. Wade, *Chicago: Growth of a Metropolis* (Chicago: University of Chicago Press, 1969); Bessie Louise Pierce, *The Rise of a Modern City, 1871–1893*, vol. 3 of *A History of Chicago* (New York: Alfred A. Knopf, 1957); Donald Miller, *City of the Century: The Epic of Chicago and the Making of America* (New York: Simon and Schuster, 1996); Melvin G. Holli and Peter D'A. Jones, *Ethnic Chicago:*

A Multi-Cultural Portrait, 4th ed. (Grand Rapids: Eerdmans, 1995); Perry R. Duis, *Challenging Chicago: Coping with Everyday Life, 1837–1920* (Urbana: University of Illinois Press, 1998); James Gilbert, *Perfect Cities: Chicago's Utopias of 1893* (Chicago: University of Chicago Press, 1991); Carl Smith, *Urban Disorder and the Shape of Belief* (Chicago: University of Chicago Press, 1995).

10. Kathleen D. McCarthy, *Noblesse Oblige: Charity and Cultural Philanthropy in Chicago, 1849–1929* (Chicago: University of Chicago Press, 1982).

11. The literature on the Progressive Era is vast. Among those works that provide useful discussions of the philosophical and programmatic changes that characterized the years between 1890 and 1918, see Arthur Link and Richard L. McCormick, *Progressivism* (Arlington Heights, Ill.: Harlan Davidson, 1983); Richard L. McCormick, *The Party Period and Public Policy: American Politics from the Age of Jackson to the Progressive Era* (New York: Oxford University Press, 1986); Kathryn Kish Sklar, *Florence Kelley and the Nation's Work* (New Haven: Yale University Press, 1995); David B. Danbom, *"The World of Hope": Progressives and the Struggle for an Ethical Public Life* (Philadelphia: Temple University Press, 1987); Daniel T. Rodgers, "In Search of Progressivism," *Reviews in American History* 10 (December 1982): 113–32; Rodgers, *Atlantic Crossings*; Steven J. Diner, *A Very Different Age: Americans of the Progressive Era* (New York: Hill and Wang, 1998); Thomas R. Pegram, *Partisans and Progressives: Private Interest and Public Policy in Illinois, 1870–1922* (Urbana: University of Illinois Press, 1992); Andrew Feffer, *The Chicago Pragmatists and American Progressivism* (Ithaca: Cornell University Press, 1993); Stephen Skowronek, *Building a New American State: The Expansion of National Administrative Capacities, 1877–1920* (New York: Cambridge University Press, 1982); Kloppenberg, *Uncertain Victory*; Dorothy Ross, *The Origins of American Social Science* (Cambridge: Cambridge University Press, 1991).

12. Ellen Gates Starr to Mary Starr Blaisdell, Feb. 23, 1889, EGSP.

13. There is no record of when Addams read this particular Tolstoy work, though Addams's recollection of the effect on her of Tolstoy's *What Then Must We Do?* squares with the explanations she offered, between 1889 and 1891, for settlement work. She recalled that she read it "in the late eighties," implying it was after opening Hull-House. The analysis herein assumes that Addams read the book shortly before beginning her settlement work. She could not have read it in English until 1887 and probably did not read it until 1888. The English copy that Addams had Tolstoy autograph when she visited him in Russia in 1896 had been published in 1888 in London by W. Scott and is the copy that was in her personal library at the time of her death. It seems plausible that Addams purchased it in London during the summer she visited Toynbee Hall. The first English translation by Isabel F. Hapgood appeared in 1887 as *What to Do?* (New York: Thomas Y. Crowell). Jane Addams, "A Book That Changed My Life," *Christian Century* 44 (Oct. 13, 1927): 1196–98; Jane Addams, "Introduction," *What Then Must We Do?* by Leo Tolstoy (London: Oxford University Press, 1934); Jane Addams, "Tolstoy's Theory of Life," *Chautauqua Assembly Herald* 27 (July 14, 1902): 2–3. Five months before Addams opened Hull-House, the *North American Review* printed a letter expressing anger at "those church dignitaries" who disdained Leo Tolstoy's belief that humble labor, shared with one's fellow citizens, was the route to becoming a true Christian and to dissolving class differences. See Alfred H. Peters, "Count Tolstoi and His Critics," *North American Review* 148 (April 1889): 524.

14. Porter, "A Home on Halsted Street"; Bedell, "A Chicago Toynbee Hall."

15. Jane Addams, "A New Impulse to an Old Gospel," *Forum* 14 (November 1892): 356. This article was the magazine version of Jane's speech "The Subjective Necessity for Social Settlements," in *Philanthropy and Social Progress*, ed. Henry C. Adams (New York: Thomas Y. Crowell, 1893), pp. 1–26.

16. Porter, "A Home on Halsted Street."

17. Ellen Gates Starr to Mary Starr Blaisdell, Feb. 23, 1889, EGSP.

18. W. Alexander Johnson, "Methods and Machinery of the Organization of Charity," *Annual Report of the Charity Organization Society of Chicago*, Oct. 11, 1887. Johnson represented Chicago's defunct Charity Organization Society (COS), whose four-year effort at hands-on case management was taken over by the well-established business elite from the Chicago Relief and Aid Society (CRA) in 1887. The CRA advocated centralized control, professional staffs, and businesslike financial management over the COS's decentralized system of "friendly visiting" and case-by-case referrals. Jane Addams was fortunate that Chicago did not have an active COS when she began. She could advocate for neighborhood-based programs without having to fear association with a localistic COS that shared the CRA's assumption that moral depravity was the cause of poverty. McCarthy, *Noblesse Oblige*, p. 129.

19. JA to Alice Addams Haldeman, June 14, 1888, HJFP; JA to Ellen Gates Starr, Jan. 24, 1889, EGSP. Writing from the Linns' home in Geneseo, Illinois, Jane assured Ellen (who was waiting impatiently for her in Chicago) that she had "not been idle. I have made friends with a Mrs. Beveridge who works in the Armour Mission and will do what she can for us." Subsequent correspondence with Mary suggests the Linn's familiarity with Beveridge and indicates Jane's gratitude for providing a valuable contact. JA to Mary Addams Linn, Feb. 12, 1889, SCPC.

20. JA to Mary Addams Linn, Mar. 13, 1889, SCHS.

21. JA to Mary Addams Linn, Feb. 12, 1889, SCPC; JA to Alice Addams Haldeman, Feb. 19, 1889, SCHS; JA to Mary Addams Linn, Feb. 19 and 26, 1889, SCPC.

22. JA to Mary Addams Linn, Feb. 26 and Apr. 1, 1889, SCPC. See, too, JA to Mary Addams Linn, Feb. 12 and 19, 1889, SCPC.

23. JA to Mary Addams Linn, Feb. 19 and 26 and Apr. 1, 1889, SCPC. Ellen Gates Starr to Mary Starr Blaisdell, Feb. 23, 1889, EGSP. Rev. Frank Gunsaulus was a talented, liberal, and relatively young minister who had taken over the pulpit of the Plymouth Congregational Church in 1887. Jane and Ellen found Gunsaulus to be the least patronizing of all the ministers they met. He was "tickled to death" that the two young women "repudiated" the idea of building yet another philanthropic "institution" and had no intention of joining the "saintly drivellers who go out harpooning for souls." Julia Beveridge, Jane's first Protestant contact in Chicago, was a member of Gunsaulus' congregation, and the Sunday School division of Gunsaulus's Plymouth Congregational Church managed the Armour Mission, which was the largest and best-funded mission in Chicago. In 1894, Gunsaulus took over direction of the secular Armour Institute, which was dedicated to technical and industrial education for young men. Harper Leech and John C. Carroll, *Armour and His Times* (New York: D. Appleton-Century, 1935), pp. 207–16. William T. Stead, *If Christ Came to Chicago* (Chicago: Laird and Lee, 1894), pp. 78–85.

24. David Swing, "A New Social Movement," *Evening Journal*, n.d., HHScrapbooks. Writing from Cedarville, Jane asked Ellen to send her a copy of "a *Journal* with Swing's article." JA to Ellen Gates Starr, June 4, 1889, EGSP; Ellen Gates Starr to JA, Oct.

12, 1879, EGSP. In the mid-1870s, Swing's battle with the Presbyterian Church over his nontraditional theology was a cause celebre that landed him in the new, $50,000 non-denominational Central Church which met in the city's Central Music Hall. Among Swing's congregants was Mary Wilmarth, who would become both Jane's and Ellen's great friend through the Chicago Woman's Club. Ellen had attended several Swing sermons in 1879 but came away unimpressed. Joseph Fort Newton, *David Swing, Poet-Preacher* (Chicago: Unity Publishing, 1909); Bessie Pierce, *A History of Chicago*, 3: 429–32. Ellen Gates Starr to JA, Oct. 12, 1879, EGSP.

25. Shortly after her move to Chicago, Jane asked Alice to send her a draft from her bank account in Girard. It arrived along with a "warning in regard to spending too much money." Jane assured Alice, "I mean to be careful." Six weeks later, Jane reported to Mary and Alice that Dr. Gunsaulus had promised to "see to the rent" and that two "wealthy men have offered to become 'associates' on the paying bills question." Whether Jane ever seriously considered allowing Protestant male philanthropists to gain so much control of her project is unknown. Clearly, she wanted to assure her sisters regarding the "financial basis" of her scheme. JA to Alice Addams Haldeman, Feb. 19, 1889, SCHS; JA to Mary Addams Linn, Apr. 1, 1889, SCPC.

26. After one memorable encounter, Jane wrote to Mary: "I met the entire board of the Armour Mission last Sunday at four, about twenty gentlemen including some of the head teachers with Mrs. Beveridge to chaperone for me. Dr. Hollister himself introduced me, sat beside me and petted my shoulder encouragingly when I said anything that pleased him." JA to Mary Addams Linn, Feb. 12, 1889, SCPC. Jane often seemed amused by her encounters with missionaries, as if she saw a secret joke in these earnest believers' interest in her and her project. JA to Mary Addams Linn, Apr. 1, 1889, SCPC.

27. Ellen Gates Starr to Mary Starr Blaisdell, Feb. 23, 1889, EGSP.

28. Ibid.

29. JA to Mary Addams Linn, Feb. 19, 1889, SCPC.

30. Swing, "A New Social Movement."

31. JA to Mary Addams Linn, Feb. 26, 1889, SCPC. Ellen claimed that Rev. Stryker promised he would help, as long as she and Jane agreed to locate where Stryker wanted them to locate. Ellen Gates Starr to Mary Starr Blaisdell, Feb. 23, 1889, EGSP.

32. Jane offset her pride in the fact that "some of the older ladies cried" by adding Ellen's sardonic comment, "surprises never cease." JA to Mary Addams Linn, Feb. 19, 1889, SCPC. Helen Ekin Starrett, *After College, What?* (New York: Thomas Y. Crowell, 1896); Joyce Antler, "'After College, What?' New Graduates and the Family Claim," *American Quarterly* 32 (Fall 1980): 409–34. Antler used Starrett's question to discuss Addams's views but was unaware of Starrett's early support of the settlement scheme.

33. Bedell, "A Chicago Toynbee Hall."

34. Even Sarah Sears, who was both a Women's Club member and a volunteer at the Clybourne Mission (and the mother-in-law of a Vassar graduate), lobbied against affiliating the settlement with a mission. She wanted it, instead, to be a "child of the Woman's Club." JA to Mary Addams Linn, Feb. 12, 1889, SCPC. In the political culture of the day, the Women's Club designation of public projects as their "children" represented an assertion that women's work extended beyond the home, not a patronizing attitude toward those projects. The club changed its name from the Chicago Women's Club to the Chicago Woman's Club in 1895 to signify its affiliation with the woman suffrage movement. Henriette Greenebaum Frank and Amalie Hofer Jerome, *Annals of*

the *Chicago Woman's Club for the First Forty Years of Its Organization, 1876–1916* (Chicago: Chicago Woman's Club, 1916), p. 74. Anne Forsyth, "What Jane Addams Has Done for Chicago," *Delineator* 70 (October 1907): 493–97, 619.

35. JA to Mary Addams Linn, Feb. 12 and 19, 1889, SCPC. After her meeting with the Armour Mission's Board of Trustees, where some of the older men thought her project "sheer nonsense," Allen Pond assured Jane that she had "*voiced* something hundreds of young people in the city were trying to express . . . [but] are dying from inaction and restlessness." JA to Mary Addams Linn, Feb. 12, 1889, SCPC.

36. As part of her effort to persuade her family that sophisticated people were excited about her project, Jane exaggerated the story of her acceptance into membership with the Chicago Women's Club. She told Mary that the 360-member club was "trying to restrict" itself to the addition of just "one new member a year" but that Julia Harvey was so influential she had promised to make sure that Jane was that one new member. In fact, the club's members had rejected the idea of a cap on membership just the year before. They had agreed, instead, to submit the names of all proposed members to a committee for review in order to ensure that each new member could be assigned to an appropriate standing committee. The club voted in more than forty new members between 1888 and 1890. Frank and Jerome, *Annals of the Chicago Woman's Club*, pp. 64–69.

37. Ibid., "Chapter III: 1887–1892"; Lila Weinberg, "Mary Hawes Wilmarth," in *Women Building Chicago, 1790–1990*, pp. 982–86.

38. Maureen Flanagan, *Seeing With Their Hearts: Chicago Women and the Vision of the Good City, 1871–1933* (Princeton: Princeton University Press, 2002), pp. 29–34.

39. Jane Addams, "Mary Hawes Wilmarth," in *The Excellent Becomes Permanent*, pp. 97–109.

40. For an example of Jane's continuing respect for women who combined masculine scholarship with "a woman's quick, sympathetic grasp of a situation," see Jane Addams, "Remarks on Mrs. Humphrey's Lectures on 'The Plan of Redemption as Fulfilled in the Old Testament,'" unpublished essay, Detzer Collection, UIC; JA to Mary Addams Linn, Feb. 12, 1889, SCPC. The twenty-six-page handwritten essay reads as if Jane were intending to publish it.

41. JA to Mary Addams Linn, Mar. 13, 1889, SCHS.

42. JA to Anna Haldeman Addams, May 9, 1889, JAMC.

43. Addams, *Twenty Years*, pp. 92–94; Linn, *Jane Addams*, pp. 92–94.

44. JA to Mary Addams Linn, Mar. 13, 1889, SCHS. In what reads like a bit of feigned naivete, Jane claimed to find it "incomprehensible" that people would not visit Chicago's Italian quarter.

45. Addams, *Twenty Years*, p. 93.

46. Peggy Glowacki, "Helen Culver," in *Women Building Chicago, 1790–1990*, pp. 202–5. "Is a Woman of Business: Something About Miss Helen Culver, Who Is Worth $5,000,000 or More," *Chicago Evening News*, undated but reference to upcoming "Fair" suggests 1892 publication, HHScrapbooks.

47. Glowacki, "Helen Culver"; Kathryn Kish Sklar, "Who Funded Hull House," in *Lady Bountiful Revisited: Women, Philanthropy, and Power*, ed. Kathleen D. McCarthy (New Brunswick, N.J.: Rutgers University Press, 1990), pp. 94–115.

48. See, for example, Helen Culver to JA, Mar. 3, 1890; JA to Helen Culver, Mar. 7, 1890; Helen Culver to JA, Mar. 9, 1890; JA to Helen Culver, Mar. 11, 1890; Helen Culver

to JA, Mar. 15, 1890, SCPC. When Jane and Ellen moved into the house, they occupied all of the second floor and half of the ground floor. The other half was being used by Mr. Sherwood, a furniture dealer, as a storage area, but Jane expected to "have all of the house" by "next year." JA to George Haldeman, Nov. 24, 1889, HJFP.

49. JA to Anna Haldeman Addams, June 3, 1890, JAMC; Ellen Gates Starr to Mary Starr Blaisdell, May 18, 1890, EGSP. Ellen admitted that the name made sense since older residents in the neighborhood already referred to the "Hull house" and was grateful the name "though not musical," was less "nauseating" than some of the other names that had been proposed. The whole arrangement reminded Ellen of the manufacturer of castor oil who offered to fund the pedestal for the Statue of Liberty "in exchange for the privilege of having 'Castoria' on it, in huge letters, for a year."

50. Helen Culver to cousin Nelly, Jan. 19, 1891, Hull-Culver Papers, UIC. When she was younger, Culver served as a nurse in the Civil War and taught at the "office night school" her uncle, Charles Hull, established for street-trade boys in Chicago. Glowacki, "Helen Culver," pp. 202–3.

51. Glowacki, "Helen Culver," p. 203.

52. Mary Lynn McCree Bryan and Allen F. Davis, *100 Years at Hull-House* (Bloomington: University of Indiana Press, 1990), pp. 7, 20, 266.

53. Allen B. Pond, "Personal Philanthropy." Talk given at Plymouth Congregational Church, Nov. 10, 1890, HHScrapbooks. Jane's comfort with involving men in the enterprise is evident in her pleasure that men comprised over half of those who attended one of their early organizational meetings. She joked that this allayed their fears that they would be founding a "home for single women and widows." JA to Mary Addams Linn, Apr. 1, 1889, SCPC.

54. JA to Alice Addams Haldeman, Oct. 18, 1886, SCPC, and November, n.d., 1886, SAH. The stylistic touches Jane discussed with Alice were characteristic of the "new aestheticism" of the day. Mary Warner Blanchard, *Oscar Wilde's America: Counterculture in the Gilded Age* (New Haven: Yale University Press, 1998).

55. JA to Alice Addams Haldeman, Nov. 14, 1886, JAMC.

56. JA to Alice Addams Haldeman, Aug. 6, 1889, SAH.

57. Blanchard, *Oscar Wilde's America*, chapter 3. Blanchard's descriptions of the use of unusual colors and foreign ornamentation to evoke an "exotic" sense that the interior was a world away from the exterior conforms precisely with Jane and Ellen's goal of transporting their neighbors away from their difficult daily lives. I am indebted to Kirsten Swinth, Fordham University, for suggesting this connection and guiding me to Blanchard's work.

58. Helen Culver to cousin Nelly, Jan. 19, 1891, Hull-Culver Papers, UIC. Culver noted Jane's expenditure of $1,800—"wholly her own money"—on furniture as evidence of her new tenant's "lavish" tendencies. John Ruskin's *Ethics of Dust* had introduced Jane to the notion that luxury was fine as long as it was shared. This idea was referred to in at least three of the early newspaper reports on Hull-House. See Nora Marks, "Two Women's Work: The Misses Addams and Starr Astonish West Siders . . . What a Visit to the Place Disclosed," *Chicago Tribune*, May 18, 1890; "Work of Two Women: Philanthropic Feminine Efforts in the Way of West-Side Moral Elevation," *Chicago Times*, July 8, 1890; Eva Brodlique, "A Toynbee Hall Experiment in Chicago," *Chautauquan*, September 1890, HHScrapbooks.

59. "Work of Two Women."

60. JA to Alice Addams Haldeman, Sept. 13, 1889, SAH.

61. JA to Alice Addams Haldeman, Jan. 8 and 22, 1890, SAH. Jane diplomatically explained that she would be shipping "my long curtains" to Alice by saying, "we have decided not to use them in the house . . . they are very handsome but am sure that the moral effect of them down here is not good." Given the expenses Jane incurred to make Hull-House quite stylish, it is likely that the curtains represented her family's traditional taste and ill suited the particular "moral effect" Jane was trying to achieve with her more modern aesthetic.

62. JA to Alice Addams Haldeman, Oct. 8, 1889, SAH.

63. JA to George Haldeman, Nov. 24, 1889, HJFP; JA to Alice Addams Haldeman, Oct. 8, 1889, SAH. In her letter to Alice, Jane mentioned that Mr. Linn was in town for a "Moody Convention." Though Jane and Rev. Linn did not end up in the same missionary circle, they did share an interest in humanitarian service.

64. Marcet Haldeman-Julius, "Jane Addams as I Knew Her," p. 5; JA to Alice Addams Haldeman, Aug. 12, 1891, SAH.

65. "Art for the Masses: What Miss Addams Desires to Make Her West Side Home Complete," *Evening Journal*, May 27, 1890, HHScrapbooks.

66. Harry Haldeman to George Haldeman, Feb. 2, 1890, HJFP.

67. Near the end of her second year at Hull-House, Jane asked Alice to send two hundred dollars "at once if possible." She explained that she had been "helping" John Linn, Jr., with his expenses and "doing all sorts of things, outside of the regular expenses." But she assured her sister, "whenever we get settled down it ought to be easy to keep within our income." JA to Alice Addams Haldeman, June, n.d., 1891. For other letters in which Jane discussed money matters with Alice in these first two years at Hull-House, see JA to Alice Addams Haldeman, Feb. 19, 1889, SCHS; JA to Alice Addams Haldeman, Aug. 6, 1889, SAH; JA to Alice Addams Haldeman, Jan. 5, 1890, JAMC; JA to Alice Addams Haldeman, Mar. 6, July 5, Aug. 20, 1890, SAH.

68. JA to Alice Addams Haldeman, Jan. 22 and Mar. 23, 1890; Sept. 6, November n.d., and Dec. 6 and 28, 1891, SAH.

69. JA to Alice Addams Haldeman, Sept. 13, Aug. 6, Oct. 8, 1889, SAH. In first mentioning the "pretty oak sideboard" from Mr. and Mrs. Roswell B. Mason, Jane commented that "people are so good about everything." She later remarked, "Ellen and I live here alone with one servant," a pointed reminder that Jane was not living luxuriously and that Jane was doing some share of the housework.

70. JA to Alice Addams Haldeman, May 8, 1881, JAMC; JA to George Haldeman, May 8, 1881, SCHS; JA to John Addams, May 8, 1881, JAMC; John Linn to JA, Aug. 26, 1881, SCPC.

71. JA to Mary Linn, Feb. 12 and 19, 1889, SCPC; JA to Anna Haldeman Addams, May 9, 1889, JAMC.

72. JA to Anna Haldeman Addams, May 9, 1889, JAMC; JA to Mary Linn, Feb. 19, 1889, SCPC.

73. JA to Alice Haldeman, Sept. 13, 1889, SAH. Jane took a similar swipe at Anna at the time of her first Christmas at Hull House. She thanked Anna for sending ten dollars, which Jane said would be used to purchase dinner knives, "something the household needs very much." She then reported, "We have had a very happy Christmas and a generous one certainly. Our first caller on Xmas morning left three twenty dollar gold pieces, apparently waiting for the day that he might do it gracefully." JA to Anna Haldeman Addams, Dec. 26, 1889, JAMC.

74. JA to Alice Addams Haldeman, Nov. 23, 1889, SAH.

75. JA to Alice Addams Haldeman, Feb. 19, 1889, SCHS.

76. S. Alice Haldeman, custody provision for Marcet Haldeman, filed in Girard, Kansas, June 5, 1890, JAMC. For additional examples of the exchanges of both hurt and tenderness between the sisters, see JA to Alice Addams Haldeman, Aug. 20, 1890, and Nov. 9, 1891, SAH.

77. JA to Alice Addams Haldeman, Aug. 20, 1890, SAH.

78. *Chicago Tribune* headline and date illegible, probably late 1891, HHScrapbooks.

79. JA to Alice Addams Haldeman, Dec. 6, 1891, SAH.

80. JA to Alice Addams Haldeman, Jan. 8, 1890, and Nov. 23, 1889, SAH. When Alice, Harry, and Marcet paid a visit to Cedarville in 1890 to help out, Anna complained about "all the comings and goings" and the expense and work of feeding extra people. Alice and Harry offered to take George into their care, but Anna refused, preferring to complain to Alice about the burden of George. George did go to stay with Harry and Alice for a few weeks in the spring of 1891 and the spring of 1892. Alice Addams Haldeman to Anna Haldeman Addams, June 20, 1890, SAH; Harry Haldeman to Anna Haldeman Addams, Apr. 15, 1891, Apr. 19, 1892, SAH.

81. George Haldeman to Anna Haldeman Addams, May 3, 4, 6, 7, 10, 12, 13, 14, 15, 16, 17, 18, and 20, 1889, HJFP.

82. George Haldeman to Anna Haldeman Addams, May 13, 1889, HJFP; Harry Haldeman to Anna Haldeman Addams, Apr. 15, 1891, SAH.

83. There is no indication that Anna visited Hull-House between its opening in September 1889 and Christmas 1891. JA to Anna Haldeman Addams, May 9, 1889, JAMC; JA to George Haldeman, Nov. 24, 1889, HJFP; JA to Anna Haldeman Addams, June 3, July 4 and 17, Aug. 11, Dec. 9, 1890, JAMC; JA to George Haldeman, Dec. 21, 1890, SCHS; JA to Anna Haldeman Addams, May 14, 1891, JAMC; JA to Anna Haldeman Addams, May 20 and Dec. 28, 1891, SCHS.

84. JA to Alice Addams Haldeman, July 5, 1890, SAH.

85. JA to Anna Haldeman Addams, May 20, 1891, JAMC; JA to Alice Addams Haldeman, Aug. 12, 1891, SAH; Harry Haldeman to Anna Haldeman Addams, Apr. 15, 1891, SAH.

86. "She Gave up Her Home," and "Art for the Masses." Alice's daughter, Marcet, claimed that Jane resented the fact that Anna "steadfastly refused to give any financial assistance to Hull House" and always felt that her father "would have been interested in helping her" had he lived. Haldeman-Julius, "Jane Addams As I Knew Her," p. 5.

87. For examples of newspaper articles that emphasized the womanliness and domesticity of Hull House, see Jenny Dow, "The Chicago Toynbee Hall," *Unity*, Mar. 15, 1890; see also "Art for the Masses," "Work of Two Women," Brodlique, "A Toynbee Hall Experiment," and Emily Kellogg, "Hull House," *Union Signal*, Jan. 22, 1891, HHScrapbooks.

88. Marks, "Two Women's Work."

89. Sarah Blaisdell to Sarah Anderson, Sept. 21, 1891. Diary of Helen Gow's Visit to the United States, vol. 3, Apr. 11, 1897. H. J. Gow Papers, Special Collections, William R. Perkins Library, Duke University. Gow was stunned by the fatigue she saw etched on Jane's face; "I have never seen one so deathlike moving about." Linn, *Jane Addams*, p. 119. Nicholas Kelley, "Early Days at Hull House," *Social Service Review* 28 (December 1965): 426. Kelley was the son of Florence Kelley, who became a Hull-House resident in

early 1892. Nicholas Kelley did not live at Hull-House but did spend a great deal of time there. He recalled, "I never saw Miss Addams angry and never heard of her being angry. My mother once asked her how she could be so calm. Miss Addams replied that she had had a great struggle to master her temper when she was young." Addams may have been thinking back to her childhood struggles when Anna first came on the scene in Cedarville. No record on any youthful fits of anger has survived.

90. *Freeport Daily Journal,* July 3, 1889, p. 2.

91. Jane Addams, "Tolstoy's Theory of Life," *Chautauquan* 27 (July 11, 1902): 2.

Chapter 13. The Luminous Medium

1. Bedell, "A Chicago Toynbee Hall." May 5, 1889.

2. JA to Ellen Gates Starr, May 3, 1889, EGSP. Part of Jane's embarrassment may have derived from the fact that Bedell's article was reprinted in the *Freeport Daily Journal* while Jane was visiting in Cedarville and George was writing manic letters from Colorado. Anna not only saw the article, she had the immediate opportunity to make Jane feel uncomfortable about such puffery.

3. Ellen Gates Starr to Mary Starr Blaisdell, Feb. 23, 1889, EGSP.

4. Ellen Gates Starr to Mary Allen, Sept. 15, 1889, EGSP.

5. Ellen Gates Starr to Mary Allen, Dec. 24, 1893, EGSP. In this letter, Ellen told her cousin about a little Italian boy who was staying with Ellen at Hull-House for the week. "I took him to my bed and board the first day and night, Miss A. retiring to Miss Farnsworth, whose hospitality received her." The fact that Ellen and Jane were still sharing a bed in 1893, when their relationship had definitely cooled, suggests their sleeping arrangements were more practical than romantic.

6. Ellen Gates Starr to Mary Allen, Sept. 15, 1889, EGSP.

7. Ibid.

8. Bedell, "A Chicago Toynbee Hall."

9. Ellen Gates Starr to Mary Starr Blaisdell, Feb. 23, 1889, EGSP. Ellen claimed that Jane "resents it" whenever Ellen credited Jane with the settlement scheme, but Ellen said she would never have worked out the idea on her own and was only writing out a description of the settlement plan to be circulated among both families because "I am anxious to save her the fatigue." Jane would "do the subject far more justice than I," Ellen insisted, because Jane had "done all the working out of it save a little I happen to know about girls."

10. JA to Ellen Gates Starr, June 7, 1889, EGSP.

11. JA to Alice Addams Haldeman, Aug. 31, 1889, JAMC.

12. Ellen Gates Starr to Caleb and Susan Starr, Nov. 3, 1889, SCPC. Ellen Gates Starr to Eliza Starr, March n.d., 1890, Ellen Gates Starr to Mary Allen, Dec. 7, 1890 (in which Ellen wrote that she wished she were not "penniless"), Ellen Gates Starr to Mary Blaisdell, Dec. 19, 1890, Ellen Gates Starr to Mary Allen, Dec. 30, 1890, EGSP. By giving lectures and getting gifts from wealthy Chicago friends, Ellen told Allen, she hoped to "pay my debts and be an honest woman."

13. JA to Alice Addams Haldeman, Dec. 28, 1891, SAH. While Ellen's father shaped her anticapitalist bent, her mother's example likely influenced Ellen's self-described

tendency toward "fault-finding." Before Hull-House opened, Ellen predicted that it would be mothers who would throw "cold water" on their daughters' desire to work at the settlement. Though Susan Starr at least visited Hull-House, while Anna Addams did not, she did not grasp the enterprise's spirit. Ellen Gates Starr to Mary Blaisdell, Oct. 30 and Feb. 23, 1889, and Dec. 19, 1890, EGSP; JA to Anna Haldeman Addams, June 3, 1890, JAMC.

14. Ellen Gates Starr to Caleb Starr and Susan Gates Starr, Nov. 3, 1889, SCPC; JA to Ellen Gates Starr, June 4, 1889, EGSP.

15. Linn, *Jane Addams*, p. 132. Ellen's class identity was complicated by early press depictions of her as an elite woman who, like Jane, had given up a life of leisure and luxury. Among all of the write-ups in the Hull-House scrapbook for the first three years of the settlement's life, only Alan Pond's speech acknowledged that Ellen was "self-supporting." Brodlique, "A Toynbee Hall Experiment in Chicago"; Eva Bright, "Work of Two Women: Philanthropic Feminine Efforts in the Way of West-Side Moral Elevation," *Chicago Times*, July 8, 1890; "Art for Poor People: Formal Opening of Hull House," *Chicago Herald* June 21, 1891; Nora Marks, "Two Women's Work"; Allen Pond, "Personal Philanthropy," Nov. 10, 1890, HHScrapbooks.

16. Ellen Gates Starr to Mary Allen, Dec. 30, 1890, EGSP. Ellen often lost her temper amid busy holidays when Jane's relatives were most likely to be on the scene. She apologized for having been "peevish and disagreeable" during a visit from Alice and lost her temper "out and out" in front of the Linns. She suspected the "devil was in it in every sense" and punished herself with the "public humiliation" of apologizing to everyone at dinner. Ellen Gates Starr to Anna Haldeman Addams, Dec. 26, 1889, JAMC; Ellen Gates Starr to Mary Allen, Thanksgiving, n.d. but probably 1893, EGSP. Ellen viewed the holidays as spiritual occasions calling for church attendance and contemplative prayer. Jane saw them as occasions for an increase in social and artistic events. Ellen Gates Starr to Mary Allen, Christmas Eve 1893, Ellen Gates Starr to Mary Blaisdell, Jan. 2, 1895, EGSP.

17. Ellen Gates Starr to Mary Allen, Thanksgiving, probably 1893, and Ellen Gates Starr to Mary Blaisdell, n.d. but apparently from 1893, EGSP.

18. Ellen Gates Starr to Mary Allen, October n.d., 1890, EGSP.

19. Addams, *Twenty Years*, pp. 147–48.

20. Addams, *Twenty Years*, p. 102. Jane wrote enthusiastic letters to Alice announcing that "new plans are daily becoming clearer to me," that "new things are constantly suggesting themselves" while Ellen confessed her inability to "get the spirit peaceful." When life with Jane at Hull-House brought no peace, Ellen looked forward to her yearly vacation in Deerfield, Massachusetts. JA to Alice Addams Haldeman, Jan. 5, 1890, JAMC; JA to Alice Addams Haldeman, Jan. 8, 1890, SAH; Ellen Gates Starr to Mary Allen, Dec. 30, 1890, EGSP.

21. Ellen Gates Starr to Mary Allen, Dec. 30, 1890, EGSP.

22. Mary Lloyd, "Hull House: A Visit to a Noted Institution," *Philadelphia Public Ledger*, Aug. 5, 1891. Shannon Jackson, *Lines of Activity: Performance, Historiography, Hull-House Domesticity* (Ann Arbor: University of Michigan Press, 2000), discusses the improvisational use of space at Hull-House as a metaphor for the continual creativity in the settlement's program.

23. JA to Alice Addams Haldeman, Oct. 8, 1889, SAH.

24. Rev. Jenkin Lloyd Jones founded All Souls Unitarian Church and was its

energetic minister from 1882 until 1916. He led his congregation into a variety of social gospel activities and guided the editorial work of *Unity* magazine, a Chicago Unitarian publication that often carried articles on Hull-House. Jones's religiosity, like Addams's, centered around the sermon of the deed performed in this life, with the aim of increasing social cooperation and peaceful relations on earth. Richard Harlan Thomas, "Jenkin Lloyd Jones: Lincoln's Soldier of Civic Righteousness," Ph.D. diss., Rutgers University, 1967; Jenkin Lloyd Jones, "What Is Christianity?" published by Unity Mission, n.d., Chicago Historical Society Archives.

25. JA to Jenkin Lloyd Jones, Sept. 2, 1891, Jenkin Lloyd Jones Papers, University of Chicago.

26. JA to Jenkin Lloyd Jones, May 3, 1891, Jenkin Lloyd Jones Papers, University of Chicago.

27. Jenkin Lloyd Jones to JA, May 4, 1891, June 30, 1890, Jenkin Lloyd Jones Papers, Meadville-Lombard Theological Seminary.

28. JA to Jenkin Lloyd Jones, Nov. 3, 1890, Jenkin Lloyd Jones Papers, University of Chicago; Jenkin Lloyd Jones to JA, Feb. 9 and Dec. 21, 1891, Lloyd Jones Papers, Meadville-Lombard Theological Seminary; JA to Jenkin Lloyd Jones, Dec. 26, 1891, Jenkin Lloyd Jones Papers, University of Chicago.

29. Ellen Gates Starr to Mary Allen, October n.d., 1890, and Dec. 7, 1890, EGSP.

30. JA to Lorado Taft, Feb. 3, 1891, Lorado Taft Papers, Chicago Historical Society. "In the Butler Gallery: Venetian Architecture on South Halsted Street: A Juncture of Note that will be formally opened June 10—Arrangement of the Interior—University Extension and Its Purpose—Lectures and Classes at Hull House—with Proposed Summer School at Rockford Seminary—Branches of Study and Training," *Chicago Tribune* May 31, 1891, HHScrapbooks; Richard J. Storr, *Harper's University: The Beginnings* (Chicago: University of Chicago Press, 1966), pp. 61, 197–207. Jane Addams's letter to Taft testifies to her gracious handling of volunteers and to the delicacy of managing the settlement's very crowded schedule. Jane could not fit the esteemed Chicago artist into the Thursday evening college extension lecture series until six weeks from the time of her letter.

31. Addams's attitude toward Rockford improved after it was taken over by Martha Hillard (McLeish) and Sarah Anderson, and after Addams herself joined the board of trustees, but she continued to disparage her own education there. At the end of her first session of summer school, she wrote to Sarah Anderson, "it has been ideal for me to combine Hull-House and Rockford Semry, two places I am so fond of." JA to Sarah Anderson, Aug. 14, 1891, RCA. Rockford Seminary was renamed Rockford College in 1892.

32. JA to Alice Addams Haldeman, February n.d., 1890, SAH; Ellen Gates Starr to Mary Allen, October 1890, EGSP; Helen Culver to cousin Nelly, Jan. 19, 1891, Hull-Culver Papers, UIC; "Pictures for the Poor: Formal Opening Yesterday of Mr. E. B. Butler's Addition to Hull House," *InterOcean*, June 21, 1891; "In the Butler Gallery: Venetian Architecture on South Halsted Street," *Chicago Tribune*, May 31, 1891; "Art for Poor People." Edward Butler was not an art patron; he was a successful businessman and had an interest in educational programs for poor youth. He promised the money for the art gallery building several months before Helen Culver agreed to lease, or donate, the lot next to Hull-House for a permanent new structure. Ellen grew "exasperated" with Culver for being "obdurate," but Jane likely prevailed in the negotiations by acknowledging Culver's legitimate concerns about making such a commitment to a fledgling social experiment.

33. "Art for Poor People."

34. "In the Butler Gallery: Venetian Architecture on South Halsted Street," *Chicago Tribune*, May 31, 1891; "A Local Toynbee Hall: A Valuable Addition Made Today to the Resources of Hull House," *InterOcean*, June 20, 1891; "Chicago's Toynbee Hall: An addition made to the 'Hull House' on Halsted Street," *Chicago Tribune*, June 21, 1891; "Art for Poor People"; "Pictures for the Poor"; "Thrown Open to the Public: Dedication Last Evening of an Important Addition to Hull House," *Chicago Times*, June 22, 1891; "Hull House Opening: Toynbee Hall Duplicated in Chicago—The Edward B. Butler Annex," *Chicago News*, June 22, 1891, HHScrapbooks.

35. During his visit, Barnett gave several talks and one sermon which brought Hull-House even more publicity. "How Toynbee Hall Is Conducted: A Description of the Famous English Institution by Its Founder," *Chicago Tribune*, June 18, 1891; "Lectured on Toynbee Hall: Rev. S. A. Barnett, President of that Institution, in Chicago," *Chicago Globe*, June 22, 1891; "Toynbee Hall's Warden: The Rev. Robert [*sic*] Barnett Tells Something of His Work in London's Slums: An Institution After Which Chicago's New Hull House Is Modeled: God and Law Are Synonymous He Holds," *InterOcean*, June 22, 1891; "Both Preached the Law: The Prophets and Scientific Men Talked on the Same Line," *Chicago Tribune*, June 22, 1891; "Told of Toynbee Hall: Story of Club in East London: In a Sermon at St. James' Rev. F. O. [*sic*] Barnett Praises the Good Work Accomplished by Earnest Young Men in the English Metropolis," *Chicago Herald*, June 21, 1891; "Life Among the Poor: Philanthropic Work Now Being Carried on by Some of London's Young Men: Charity of a Practical Turn Which Does Much to Make Honorable Men of Vicious Youth: Toynbee Hall the Home of the Organization, Whose Members Are Non-Sectarian in Their Manner of Life," *Chicago Times*, June 22, 1891; "Appeal from Whitechapel," *Chicago News*, June 22, 1891, HHScrapbooks.

36. "Art for Poor People."

37. JA to Alice Addams Haldeman, Aug. 12, 1891, SAH; JA to Sarah Anderson, Aug. 14, 1891, RCA; Sarah Blaisdell to Sarah Anderson, Sept. 21, 1891, RCA. Jane's letters claimed Rockford afforded a rest; Blaisdell observed, "Jane was very tired at the beginning of [the summer school], of course not less so as the time went on. She truly gives herself to her work." Blaisdell thought both Jane and Ellen were "doing great work," but thought that Ellen "perhaps better spared herself."

38. JA to Alice Addams Haldeman, June n.d., 1891, SAH.

39. JA to Ellen Gates Starr, Aug. 11, 1879, EGSP.

40. Kellogg, "Hull-House."

41. Frances Hackett, "Hull House—A Souvenir," *Survey* 54 (June 1, 1925): 277. Ellen hinted at her style of supervision in reporting that one male resident "reported some neglect of duty rather ruefully to me one day and I said, 'I'm not going to scold you. My temper has improved.'" Ellen Gates Starr to Mary Blaisdell, n.d., 1893, EGSP. Madeline Wallin, a resident, described Jane as a "really a cosmic individual" who was "far indeed from domineering over anybody" but prevailed because "of her very admirable qualities of mind and disposition. . . . She never drives anyone to work . . . but it is impossible to live here and not feel to some extent the pressure of work to be done." Quoted in Carson, "'Settlement Folk,'" p. 358.

42. Hackett, "Hull House—A Souvenir," pp. 277–78. See, too, Isabel Eaton, "Hull-House and Some of its Distinctive Features," *Smith College Monthly* 1 (April 1894): 7, HHScrapbooks. After a stay at Hull-House, Eaton observed that "the most important

point of difference between Hull-House and other settlements . . . is the spirit in which it is done." She attributed this difference to the "wonderful and inspiring personality" of the head resident, Jane Addams. According to Eaton, the "atmosphere at Hull House is charged with the doctrine embodied by Emerson in the words, 'Trust men and they will be true to you. Treat them greatly and they will show themselves great.' This house," said Eaton, "believes most heartily in the existence of much that is good in the midst of evil, and in the preponderance of good, a doctrine which its head is constantly putting into practice by her goodness."

43. Eliza R. Sunderland, "Hull House, Chicago: Its Work and Workers," *Unitarian* (September 1893): 402, HHScrapbooks.

44. JA to Sarah Anderson, Aug. 14, 1891, RCA. Jane reported to Anderson, at the end of the Hull-House Summer School on the Rockford campus that the Chicago working girls who attended "have gone away quite bewildered with the kindness of the Rockford people." Jane did not "believe it has done them harm to see" people's "goodness and kindness."

45. Hackett, "Hull House—A Souvenir," pp. 277–78; Wallin quoted in Carson, "'Settlement Folk,'" p. 358.

46. Hackett, "Hull House—A Souvenir," pp. 277–78,

47. Addams, "Tolstoy's Theory of Life," *Chautauquan Assembly Herald*, 27 (July 14, 1902): 2. JA to George Haldeman, Dec. 21, 1890, SCHS.

48. The historiography of U.S. immigration history demonstrates that it has taken American historians some time to fully appreciate the multiclass nature of the European immigrant flow between 1870 and 1921 and to flesh out the profile of immigrants by studying homeland conditions. John Bodnar, in *The Transplanted: A History of Immigrants in Urban America* (Bloomington: Indiana University Press, 1985), brings together two decades' worth of scholarship to argue that immigrants were seldom "uprooted" victims but, rather, creative, pragmatic family members who fashioned a "culture of everyday life" out of their traditional cultures and the options, however limited, they faced in the U.S. The literature Bodnar drew upon was vast and has deepened and broadened since he published. For examples of works on immigrant history that are particularly relevant to Jane Addams's experience, see Humbert S. Nelli, *Italians in Chicago, 1880–1930: A Study in Ethnic Mobility* (New York: Oxford University Press, 1970); Dominic Pacyga, *Polish Immigrants in Industrial Chicago: Workers on the South Side, 1880–1920* (Columbus: Ohio State University Press, 1991); James Barrett, *Work and Community in the Jungle: Chicago's Packinghouse Workers, 1894–1922* (Urbana: University of Illinois Press, 1987); Holli and Jones, *Ethnic Chicago*.

49. "A Local Toynbee Hall." On the occasion of the opening of the new reading room in the Butler Art Gallery, where the settlement would henceforth house its station of the Chicago Public Library, this article noted that the Hull-House library carried seventy-five newspapers and periodicals. Many, it said, "come from different sections of the globe and are printed in many different languages so that every visitor, no matter what may be his nationality, may be supplied with interesting reading matter."

50. A long letter from Ellen to her parents, two months after opening Hull-House, expressed such astonishment over the making and eating of pasta with tomato and meat sauce that it is clear neither she nor Jane ate native food while in Italy. The purpose of Ellen's letter was to depict herself and Jane as the neighborhood's true greenhorns and to demonstrate the egalitarian relations that Hull-House fostered

around the dining table, but Ellen's squeamishness about the "gravy" and the hard-as-a-rock meat that their neighbor Mrs. Guido managed to produce under Hull-House's primitive culinary conditions hinted at the patronizing attitude that Ellen disdained in others. Ellen Gates Starr to Caleb and Susan Starr, Nov. 15, 1889, SCPC.

51. Jane Addams, "Outgrowths of Toynbee Hall," Dec. 3, 1890, unpublished manuscript, p. 14, SCPC; "The Objective Value of a Social Settlement," in *Philanthropy and Social Progress: Seven Essays Delivered Before the School of Applied Ethics During the Session of 1892* (New York: Thomas Y. Crowell, 1893), pp. 39–40. In the 1890 speech, Jane distinguished between activities for "foreigners" and the college extension classes, but in "Objective Value," written after at least one more year of experience in the neighborhood, Jane noted that the settlement's classes and lectures attracted "those foreigners who speak English fairly well" and were materially "successful" enough to take advantage of the opportunity to "bring together the old life and the new," p. 37. There is a discrepancy in the records regarding when Jane wrote the "Outgrowths" speech and actually delivered it to the Women's Club. The minutes of the Chicago Women's Club date her delivery as Dec. 3, 1891, and Jane delivered a lecture at Hull-House in December 1891 titled "Outgrowths of Toynbee Hall" according to the *Comprehensive Guide to the Jane Addams Papers*. But correspondence indicates the speech was written and delivered in December 1890 and the *Comprehensive Guide* notes that Jane's cover note for "Outgrowths" dates the speech in December 1890. Given Jane's propensity for recycling speeches, it is possible she delivered versions of the speech twice, a year apart. JA to Anna Haldeman Addams, Dec. 9, 1890, JAMC; Ellen Gates Starr to Mary Allen, Dec. 7, 1890, EGSP.

52. "She Gave up Her Home: Noble Work Being Done Among the People of the West Side: With the Assistance of Lady Friends She Manages a Great Kindergarten and Lecture Course," *Evening Journal,* May 17, 1890, HHScrapbooks. Ellen traced the spontaneous invention of the "creche" to the morning when a neighbor asked to leave her baby, Marcus, at the settlement while she "moved her household effects." Ellen Gates Starr to Caleb and Susan Starr, Nov. 3, 1889, SCPC.

53. Alzina Stevens, "Life in a Social Settlement—Hull House," *Self Culture* 9 (March-August 1899): 43. Stevens herself became a resident at Hull-House in 1893.

54. JA to Katherine Coman, Dec. 7, 1891, Denison House Papers, Radcliffe College/Schlesinger Library; Ellen Skerrett, "The Irish of Chicago's Hull-House Neighborhood," *Chicago History* 30 (Summer 2001): 22–63; Irving Cutler, "The Jews of Chicago," in *Ethnic Chicago*, pp. 131–46.

55. Bright, "Work of Two Women."

56. Jane and her fellow residents found their neighbors to be "dirty, but ready to use our bath-tubs themselves and grateful when we wash their children." Addams, "Outgrowths of Toynbee Hall," Dec. 3, 1890, p. 14, SCPC. In July 1892 the settlement was the site for 980 baths. Addams, "The Objective Value of a Social Settlement," p. 47. For Ellen's characteristically wry commentary on the bathing situation in the neighborhood, see Ellen Gates Starr to Mary Blaisdell, July 25, 1892, EGSP. In 1893, bathing facilities in the neighborhood were increased in two ways. The completion of a new Hull-House gymnasium included twelve showers for those who used the gym. In addition, the residents of Hull-House worked with the Municipal Order League to persuade the Chicago City Council to allocate $12,000 for the construction of public baths in those neighborhoods where they were the most needed. This effort was aided in the Nineteenth Ward because an anonymous local landlord was willing to donate land for

the baths. In November 1893, the city opened the Carter H. Harrison Free Public Bath, with seventeen showers and one tub, just a block away from Hull-House. The bath was named for the Chicago mayor who had been assassinated a month earlier. "Hull House," HHScrapbooks without date or citation; Florence Kelley, "Hull House," *New England Magazine* 18 (July 1898): 554.

57. JA to Alice Addams Haldeman, Jan. 5, 1890, JAMC.

58. Jenny Dow, "The Chicago Toynbee Hall," *Unity*, Mar. 15, 1890, HHScrapbooks.

59. Appleton Morgan, "What Shall We Do with the Dago?" *Popular Science Monthly* 38 (December 1890): 172–79; Ellen Gates Starr to Mary Allen, Dec. 7, 1890, EGSP. As Ellen anticipated, the *Popular Science Monthly* did not print her letter.

60. Addams, "Outgrowths of Toynbee Hall," unpublished manuscript dated December 1890, p. 13, SCPC. The Garibaldi statue was from one of the Italian physicians with whom Jane had established a good working relationship as both a translator and neighborhood liaison to Chicago hospitals. JA to Alice Addams Haldeman, Dec. 18, 1889, JAMC; JA to Mary Addams Linn, Apr. 1, 1889, SCPC.

61. *Chicago Tribune*, headline and date illegible but internal evidence suggests late 1891, HHScrapbooks.

62. Ellen Gates Starr to Mary Blaisdell, Dec. 19, 1890, EGSP; Bright, "Work of Two Women"; Brodlique, "A Toynbee Hall Experiment in Chicago." A very friendly article about Hull-House, written by Rev. J. Frothingham, the father of Jane's seminary pal Nora Frothingham, noted that "care is taken to avoid race antagonism or religious prejudice. What little may have arisen at the first has been allayed by patient, prudent, kindly dealing." Given Rev. Frothingham's relationship with Jane, it is likely that she asked him to make this point as it is not a point that appears in other, more mainstream news treatments. Frothingham was writing for a Chicago Presbyterian publication. Rev J. Frothingham, "The Toynbee Idea," *Interior*, July 7, 1890, HHScrapbooks.

63. Ellen Gates Starr to Caleb and Susan Starr, Nov. 3 and 15, 1889, SCPC. Less than two weeks after Ellen remarked that the Italian women were "embarrassed" by a heterosocial gathering at the settlement, she described an evening of song attended by "lots of Italians," both men and women. It appears that the second gathering was more like a private party for the more middle-class Italians in the neighborhood.

64. Ellen Gates Starr to Caleb and Susan Starr, Nov. 15, 1889, SCPC.

65. Hackett, "Hull House—A Souvenir," p. 277.

66. JA to Anna Haldeman Addams, Dec. 9, 1890, JAMC; Ellen Gates Starr to Mary Allen, Dec. 7, 1890, EGSP.

67. JA to Anna Haldeman Addams, Aug. 11, 1890, JAMC; Jenkin Lloyd Jones to JA, Sept. 23, 1890, Jenkin Lloyd Jones Papers, Meadville-Lombard Theological Seminary; JA to Lorado Taft, Feb. 3, 1891, Lorado Taft Papers, Chicago Historical Society.

68. Addams, *My Friend, Julia Lathrop*. This tribute to Lathrop was the last book Jane Addams wrote; it was published the year Addams died. Robyn Muncy, "Julia Lathrop," in *Women Building Chicago*, pp. 490–92.

69. JA to Alice Addams Haldeman, Dec. 28, 1891 SAH. Lathrop divided her time between Chicago and Rockford for over two years. In June 1893 she made a permanent move to Hull-House. JA to Jenkin Lloyd Jones, Jan. 8, 1893, Jenkin Lloyd Jones Papers, University of Chicago.

70. Addams, *My Friend, Julia Lathrop*, pp. 49, 53.

71. JA to Alice Addams Haldeman, Oct. 8, 1889, SAH.

72. Frothingham, "The Toynbee Idea"; "Hull House: A Visit to a Noted Institution."

73. JA to Alice Addams Haldeman, Oct. 8, 1889, SAH; Hull-House Weekly Programs, January–March 1891, JAMC.

74. Jane Addams, "A Book that Changed My Life," *Christian Century* 44 (Oct. 13, 1927): 1197. In this critical tribute to Tolstoy, Jane captured the evolution in her thinking in the early 1890s.

75. JA to George Haldeman, Nov. 24, 1889, HJFP.

76. JA to Alice Addams Haldeman, Jan. 5, 1890, JAMC.

77. Dorothea Moore, "A Day at Hull House," *American Journal of Sociology* 2 (March 1897): 640. Moore made this claim for the settlement's nonpartisan stance several years after it had actually moved into a more activist, politicized posture.

78. "Art for Poor People"; Porter, "A Home on Halsted Street," *Advance*, July 11, 1889; Kellogg, "Hull-House," *Union Signal*, Jan. 22, 1891. The *Advance* was a Congregational publication; the *Union Signal* was the official organ of the Women's Christian Temperance Union. See, too, "They Help the Poor: Jane Addams' and Ellen Starr's Self-Sacrificing Work Among the Lowly," *Chicago Times*, Mar. 23, 1890; Frothingham, "The Toynbee Idea," HHScrapbooks.

79. JA to Mary Addams Linn, Mar. 13, 1889, SCHS; JA to Ellen Gates Starr, May 3, 1889 and June 4, 1889, EGSP; JA to Henry Demarest Lloyd, Dec. 15, 1891, Henry Demarest Lloyd Papers, Madison, State Historical Society of Wisconsin. In the letter to Lloyd, a former editor at the *Chicago Tribune*, Jane wrote, "We find that Hull-House is to be written up in a series of articles about to appear in *The Century* . . . we are very anxious to write the article ourselves, being more concerned perhaps over the point of view than the correctness of the facts. If you have any 'pull' over Mr. Gilder or any official on the staff we would be very grateful if you would use your influence to this end."

80. Jane thought an article describing her and Ellen as "sweet ladies Bountiful" was "horrid in style, of course," but possessed of "a good deal of truth" in its presentation of the settlement project. JA to Alice Addams Haldeman, Aug. 12, 1890, SAH; Bright, "Work of Two Women." The *Chicago Tribune* was the first paper to publish the story of Jane Addams as a little girl with "decided views of her own on the sort of house she would live in when she grew up." See *Chicago Tribune*, headline and date illegible but internal evidence suggests late 1891, HHScrapbooks. Jane Addams repeated the story, in its final, polished version, in *Twenty Years*, pp. 3–5.

81. Frothingham, "The Toynbee Idea." At the end of this particular article, Frothingham made a veiled appeal for donations of time or money to his Presbyterian readers, noting that "the burden must not be allowed to rest too heavily on the founders, whose strength is already overtaxed." Jane regarded this as a "fairly good article." JA to Jenkin Lloyd Jones, Nov. 3, 1890, Jenkin Lloyd Jones Papers, University of Chicago. For a direct appeal to readers for funds for the promised art gallery, see: "Art for the Masses," *Evening Journal*, May 27, 1890.

82. "Chicago's Toynbee Hall: An Addition Made to the 'Hull House' on Halsted Street," *Chicago Tribune*, June 21, 1891; Brodlique, "A Toynbee Hall Experiment."

83. "Told of Toynbee Hall: Story of Club in East London," *Chicago Herald*, June 21, 1891; "Toynbee Hall's Warden," *InterOcean*, June 22, 1891; "Both Preached the Law: The Prophets and Scientific Men Talked on the Same Line," *Chicago Tribune*, June 22, 1891; "Life Among the Poor: Philanthropic Work Now Being Carried on by Some of London's Young Men."

84. "Told of Toynbee Hall: Story of a Club in East London," *Chicago Herald.*

85. Helen Lefkowitz Horowitz, *Culture and the City: Cultural Philanthropy in Chicago from the 1880s to 1917* (Chicago: University of Chicago Press, 1976). In addition to analyzing the cultural philanthropists' worldview, Horowitz traces Jane Addams's evolution away from a comfortable place at their sumptuous tables. See, too, McCarthy, *Noblesse Oblige.*

86. Frothingham, "The Toynbee Idea"; "Hull House: A Visit to a Noted Institution"; *Chicago Tribune,* headline and date illegible but internal evidence suggests late 1891, HHScrapbooks.

87. "Practical Philanthropy," *Chicago Tribune,* Oct. 16, 1891, HHScrapbooks; "Grace Dodge" biographical entry, *Notable American Women,* vol. 1, pp. 489–92.

88. "Clubs of Working Girls: The Subject of an Interesting Talk by Miss Grace Dodge," *Chicago Tribune,* Oct. 13, 1891, HHScrapbooks.

89. Mary Kenney (O'Sullivan), unpublished autobiographical manuscript, n.d., pp. 62–66, Schlesinger Library, History of Women in America Collection, Radcliffe College. "Mary Kenney O'Sullivan" biographical entry, *Notable American Women,* vol. 2, pp. 655–56; Kathleen Banks Nutter, "Mary Kenney O'Sullivan," in *Women Building Chicago,* pp. 650–53.

90. JA to Henry Demarest Lloyd, Nov. 18, 1891, Henry Demarest Lloyd Papers, Madison, State Historical Society of Wisconsin.

91. JA to Katherine Coman, Dec. 7, 1891, Denison House Papers, Radcliffe College/Schlesinger Library.

92. Ellen Gates Starr to "Family," June 14, 1891, EGSP.

Chapter 14. Unity of Action

1. Kelley's autobiographical treatment, written thirty-six years after the event, claimed that Henry Standing Bear arrived at Hull-House on the same day she arrived. But Ellen Starr said Henry Standing Bear was doing "excellently well" at Hull House six months earlier. Florence Kelley, "I Go to Work," *Survey* (June 1, 1927): 271. Ellen Gates Starr to "Family," June 14, 1891, EGSP.

2. Sklar, *Florence Kelley and the Nation's Work,* is the definitive work on the first half of Kelley's life.

3. Kelley, "I Go to Work," p. 271.

4. Sklar, *Florence Kelley and the Nation's Work,* pp. 177–78.

5. Richard Digby-Junger, *The Journalist as Reformer: Henry Demarest Lloyd and "Wealth Against Commonwealth"* (Westport, Conn.: Greenwood Press, 1996); Chester M. Destler, *Henry Demarest Lloyd and the Empire of Reform* (Philadelphia: University of Pennsylvania Press, 1963).

6. Florence Kelley to Caroline Bartram Kelley, Feb. 24 and May 24, 1892, quoted in Sklar, *Florence Kelley and the Nation's Work,* pp. 178, 182; JA to Sarah Anderson, June 23, 1894, RCA. In February, Kelley told her mother, "It is understood that I am to resume the maiden name, and that the children are to have it. . . . I am better off than I have been since I landed in New York since I am now responsible *myself* for what I do."

7. "Hull House Bureau: Intelligence Office Added to This Worthy Institution," *Chicago Post,* Jan. 23, 1892; "Household Labor," *Union Signal,* Feb. 4, 1892, HHScrapbooks.

8. Linn, *Jane Addams*, pp. 138–39; Sklar, *Florence Kelley and the Nation's Work*, p. 182.

9. Addams quoted this line many times. See "Outgrowths of Toynbee Hall," p. 6, SCPC; "Subjective Necessity for Social Settlements," p. 15; eulogy to Mary Hawes Wilmarth in *The Excellent Becomes Permanent*, pp. 103–4.

10. Sklar, *Florence Kelley and the Nation's Work*.

11. Jane Addams, Address on "How Would You Uplift the Masses?" Report of the Sunset Club, Chicago, Forty-Second Meeting, Feb. 4, 1892, p. 12, Sunset Club Papers, University of Illinois, Chicago.

12. Ellen Gates Starr to Mary Blaisdell, July 25, 1892, EGSP.

13. Kelley, "Hull House," p. 559.

14. Florence Kelley to Caroline Bartram Kelley, Mar. 16, 1892, quoted in Sklar, *Florence Kelley and the Nation's Work*, p. 206.

15. Kelley was hired by the Bureau of Labor Statistics of Illinois in the spring of 1892 and spent a long, hot summer investigating sweatshops in Chicago. In the spring of 1893, she went to work for Carroll D. Wright, head of the U.S. Department of Labor, conducting a door-to-door canvass of Chicago's Nineteenth Ward as part of a larger federal study of urban slums. That research became the basis for *Hull-House Maps and Papers*, a significant contribution to the social survey literature just emerging in the late nineteenth century. See Sklar, *Florence Kelley and the Nation's Work*, chapter 9.

16. "To Wipe Away the Evil: Bricklayers' Hall Speakers Denounce the Sweating System," *Chicago Times*, May 9, 1892. In a subheading of that article, the *Times* quoted Kelley's "startling statement" that the chief officer of the Sanitary Department regarded her complaints about the "sweating dens" as evidence that she was a "crank." "To Stop the System: Mrs. Kelley's Suggestion Regarding the Sweaters," no citation, but internal evidence and scrapbook placement indicate spring 1892; "For Better School Facilities," *Chicago Tribune*, May 9, 1892; "Nineteenth Ward Ill Provided: Women's Alliance Working for an Extension of the School Facilities," *Chicago Herald*, June 9, 1892. The Hull-House Scrapbooks for the period between Feb. 11 and Apr. 4, 1893, contain over a half-dozen articles from various Chicago newspapers reporting on Kelley's sweatshop investigations. The newspaper record for this period indicates that Kelley started out skeptical about government involvement in improving workers' conditions and thought unions were the best agents of regulation over employers. Contact with the sweatshops persuaded Kelley of the difficulty of unionizing within that labor system and of the need for laws to regulate it. For more on the logic of Kelley's transformation, see *Abraham Bisno: Urban Pioneer*, foreword by Joel Seidman (Madison: University of Wisconsin Press, 1967).

17. Addams, *My Friend, Julia Lathrop*, p. 116.

18. "The 'Sweat Shop' Bill," *Chicago Post*, June 14, 1893, HHScrapbooks.

19. "Mill and Shop Hands: Factory Inspectors' Convention," and "To Enforce the Law: International Association of Factory Inspectors: Mrs. Kelley Reads a Carefully Prepared Paper on the Question." No citation but apparently following passage of Illinois factory inspection legislation, HHScrapbooks.

20. "Like Priest and Levite: Men See the Sweaters' Victim and Pass By on the Other Side . . . 3,000 Good Samaritans Who Meet to Protest Against the Evil—Stirring Resolutions Presented by Henry D. Lloyd Unanimously Adopted—Committee Appointed to Do Something in the Matter," *Chicago Times*, Feb. 20, 1893, HHScrapbooks.

21. Addams, *Twenty Years*, p. 201.

22. Addams, "How Would You Uplift the Masses?" p. 12.

23. Florence Kelley's father, William Darrah Kelley, was a founding member of the Republican Party and U.S. Congressman from Philadelphia from 1860 until his death in 1890. Known as "Pig Iron Kelley," the congressman's pro-labor stance was expressed in strong support for a high tariff as an appropriate governmental measure for protecting U.S. prosperity and the working class. For a thorough analysis of Congressman Kelley's views on the role of government in the economy, see Sklar, *Florence Kelley and the Nation's Work*, chapters 1–3. In 1894, Illinois women were permitted to vote in the election for trustees for the University of Illinois. The *Chicago Record* thought to brighten its report of women's participation by noting that "the interest of the feminine contingent" in the Nineteenth Ward "centered around Hull House." "Women Cast Ballots: First Experience at the Polls," *Chicago Record*, Nov. 7, 1894, HHScrapbooks.

24. "Down with Sweaters: Greed of the Merchant Princes," *Chicago Herald*, Feb. 20, 1893, HHScrapbooks. Addams admitted that "the sense that the passage of the child labor law would in many cases work hardship was never absent from my mind." Addams, *Twenty Years*, p. 205.

25. "Ideal and Actual," unidentified San Francisco newspaper, February 1894, HHScrapbooks. Jane Addams was an invited speaker at the Women's Auxiliary of the California Midwinter International Exposition. She attended the meetings with her sister, Alice, and delivered several speeches in Los Angeles and in the Bay Area, including a talk to the "Workingmen of San Francisco," under the auspices of the Socialist Labor Party.

26. "We Must Unite: Laboring People Must Join Hands," no citation but apparently February 1893, HHScrapbooks.

27. JA to Alice Addams Haldeman, Feb. 23, 1893, SAH; JA to Mary Rozet Smith, Dec. 19, 1890, SCPC.

28. JA to Mary Rozet Smith, Feb. 3, 1891, SCPC.

29. Jane Addams, "A Retrospect," Fall 1895. Jane wrote this poem while convalescing from typhoid fever. She may have written it as an accompaniment to a gift of a book by Charles Lamb, the British critic and essayist (1775–1834). In a lengthy section preceding her tribute to Mary, Jane recalled her convalescence from back surgery at Alice and Harry's home in Mitchellville, Iowa. At that time, she had bragged to Ellen about reading Carlyle's *Frederick the Great*, but in this 1895 poem, she fondly recalled reading a great deal of the "gentle Lamb" who wrote of "simple pleasures" and extolled brotherly love. With the gift of the Lamb book, Jane was suggesting that Mary Smith reminded her of Lamb's love of humanity and "simple pleasures . . . amid the holy din of Settlements and public measures." JAPP, reel 45, frame 1596, SCPC. In an undated letter accompanying the gift of a book, Jane told Mary that she wished "there was some book that would express all the gratitude and affection I have for you. I fear that I will have to write one myself to get it all in." JA to Mary Rozet Smith, n.d., SCPC.

30. JA to Mary Rozet Smith, Feb. 3 and 14, 1891, SCPC. Rima Lunin Schultz, "Mary Rozet Smith," in *Women Building Chicago*, pp. 817–19.

31. JA to Ellen Gates Starr, July 1892, EGSP. Jane's mention of "single beds" in this letter means it is quite possible that she and Mary were simply sleeping in the same room, not the same bed.

32. Ellen Gates Starr to Mary Allen, Sept. 5, 1893, EGSP.

33. Ellen Gates Starr to Mary Allen, Sept. 15, 1889, and Aug. 13, 1892, EGSP.

34. Linn, *Jane Addams*, p. 149. Mary Rozet Smith to JA, Sept. 3, 1933, SCPC; Margaret Dreier Robins to JA, Mar. 1, 1934, SCPC. When Mary was ill in 1894, Dr. Alice Hamilton, a Hull-House resident, told her "that she must get well, that she could live without J.A. but J.A. could not live without her." Indeed, Jane referred to Mary's death as "the day of my downfall," and many friends worried, correctly, that the already ailing Jane would not long survive the loss of Mary. Alice Hamilton to Edith Hamilton, Feb. 23, 1894, in *Alice Hamilton*, ed. Sicherman, p. 347. JA to Lillian Wald, Sept. 30, 1934, Lillian Wald Papers, New York Public Library. See also Grace Abbott to JA, Feb. 22, 1934 regarding her "fear" of the "possible effects" of Mary's death on Jane, SCPC; Mary Lewis Langworthy to JA, Feb. 23, 1934, referring to Jane's "almost unbearable loss," SCPC; Graham Taylor to JA, Feb. 23, 1934, calling Mary's death "the greatest loss you could suffer," and Felix M. Warburg, Feb. 23, 1934, expressing his hope that Jane's health was good enough to withstand the shock of Mary's death "with your usual fortitude," SCPC.

35. Linn, *Jane Addams*, pp. 149–50; *Alice Hamilton*, ed. Sicherman, p. 188.

36. JA to Mary Rozet Smith, July 21, 1892, SCPC.

37. Louise deKoven Bowen, *Open Windows: Stories of People and Places* (Chicago: R. F. Seymour, 1946), p. 227.

38. JA to Alice Addams Haldeman, Oct. 28, 1894, JAMC; JA to Mary Rozet Smith, Jan. 27, 1894, SCPC. On a train trip headed toward a speaking tour of the West Coast, Jane wrote to Mary that Alice "asks me every little while if she is as good a traveling comrade as Miss Smith."

39. JA to Mary Rozet Smith Mar. 3, May 4, Oct. 1, 1894, SCPC. The letter in which Jane wrote that "more things would flash" if Mary were there is undated, but was probably written in May 1893, SCPC.

40. JA to James Weber Linn, Mar. 8, 1935, SCPC. This letter, written a little over two months before Jane's death, was part of her ongoing correspondence with Linn about the biography he was writing of his aunt. Here, Jane reported that she had destroyed one-half to two-thirds of her letters from Mary; the ones she saved and sent to Linn were those that showed the settlement's daily activity. Jane asked that even those be read and then destroyed. Fortunately, Linn did not follow his aunt's instructions. By 1935, Jane Addams would have been thoroughly aware that Freudian theory had put an unsavory caste over all same-sex relations and she likely wished to protect her partnership with Mary from unsympathetic eyes. See note 60, Chapter 11, for a discussion of the literature on women's emotional and sexual relationships in the late nineteenth century. The argument here, in regard to Mary Rozet Smith, is similar to that made in regard to Ellen Gates Starr; both women provided Jane Addams with significant emotional attachments over the course of her adult life. If there was a sexual component to either relationship, it seems much more likely to have existed in the relationship with Mary than with Ellen simply because Jane expressed herself in more devoted, romantic terms with Mary, and the relationship with Mary was a more thoroughly satisfying relationship. It would be illuminating to know if Jane Addams did express herself erotically, but the arguments put forth here about Ellen and Mary do not depend on that knowledge.

41. Isabel Smith to JA, Mar. 12, 1934, SCPC.

42. Loving regards to Mary's parents are included in virtually every letter Jane wrote to Mary after the summer of 1892. See, for example, JA to Mary Rozet Smith, Aug. 26, 1893, when Mary and her father had gone to Europe and Jane reported "a

positive pang of homesickness" as she walked up the steps to Mary's home on Walton Place to visit Mary's mother. See JA to Mary Rozet Smith, Dec. 27, 1893, for reference to the "the dear North Side family," SCPC. See also JA to Alice Addams Haldeman, Dec. 4 and 23, 1894 describing a two-week trip to South Carolina with the Smith family, which the Smiths clearly paid for, JAMC. At the end of that trip, Jane wrote to Mary, "I bless you, dear, every time I think of you which is all the time at present." JA to Mary Rozet Smith, Dec. 23, 1894, SCPC.

43. Sklar, "Who Funded Hull House?" pp. 94–115. Sklar performed an invaluable service to all scholars of Jane Addams, Hull-House, and settlements in general by carefully working through the financial records and making sense of Addams's creative fundraising and bookkeeping.

44. JA to Alice Addams Haldeman, Mar. 15, 1892, SAH; *Hull-House Maps and Papers*, by the Residents of Hull-House (New York: Thomas Y. Crowell, 1895), p. 230; "Hull House in Chicago: A Center of Social Reform," *Springfield Republican*, June 24, 1892; "Noble Charity Work: Hull House and What It Is Doing for the Deserving Poor," *Chicago Post*, Feb. 1, 1893, HHScrapbooks.

45. JA to Nettie Fowler McCormick, Mar. 14 and 20, 1894. Nettie Fowler McCormick Papers, Madison, State Historical Society of Wisconsin; JA to Katherine P. Medill, Mar. 20, 1894, *Chicago Tribune*, Company Archives.

46. JA to Mary Rozet Smith, n.d., 1894, SCPC.

47. JA to Mary Rozet Smith, Dec. 19, 1890, SCPC.

48. Sklar, "Who Funded Hull House?" p. 104.

49. "Additions to Hull House: Plans for a Distinct Enlargement of the Social Settlement," *Chicago Record*, Dec. 5, 1894.

50. JA to Mary Rozet Smith, May 1, 1894, May, n.d., 1893, and July 4, 1892, SCPC.

51. Sklar, "Who Funded Hull House?" p. 97. When Mary offered to pay the school expenses for Florence Kelley's daughter, Margaret, Florence told her mother, "Mary Smith is so rich and so generous, and so fond of Margaret, that I do not feel at all embarrassed about accepting her kindness." Florence Kelley to Caroline B. Kelley, Sept. 15, 1898, quoted in Sklar, *Florence Kelley and the Nation's Work*, p. 287.

52. Linn, *Jane Addams*, p. 148.

53. JA to Mary Rozet Smith, Dec. 25, 1892, and n.d., 1894, SCPC.

54. Jane Addams, undated poem to Mary Rozet Smith, SCPC.

55. *Hull-House Maps and Papers*, appendix: "Outline Sketch Descriptive of Hull-House," pp. 207–30; "The Hull House: University Extension Looked upon as Blessing: How the Institution Started Its Growth," no citation but after summer 1893, HHScrapbooks; Chicago Public School Art Society, EGSP; JA to Dr. Bayard Taylor Holmes, Sept. 15, 1892, Amherst College Library. The Hull-House Scrapbooks contain numerous articles charting the growth of the settlement.

56. Ellen referred to Jane as "the chief" in a letter she wrote to Sarah Anderson on Jane's behalf. Ellen Gates Starr to Sarah Anderson Ainsworth, Feb. 8, 1893, RCA; Kathryn Sklar reports that Florence Kelley also referred to Jane as "Chief" on occasion, Sklar, *Florence Kelley and the Nation's Work*, p. 288; Edward L. Burchard to Ellen Gates Starr, Jan. 16, 1938, EGSP.

57. John Dewey to Alice Chipman Dewey, Oct. 7, 1894, cited in Carson, *Settlement Folk*, p. 89.

58. Hackett, "Hull House—A Souvenir," p. 276.

59. Hackett, "Hull House—A Souvenir," p. 277; Eliza R. Sunderland, "Hull House,

Chicago: Its Work and Workers," *Unitarian* (September 1893): 402; Isabel Eaton, "Hull-House and Some of Its Distinctive Features," p. 7. See, too, Louise W. Knight, "Jane Addams and Hull House: Historical Lessons on Nonprofit Leadership," *Nonprofit Management and Leadership* 2 (Winter 1991): 125–41.

60. Kelley, "Hull House," p. 553. For the later emergence of inner and outer circles of influence at Hull-House, see Robyn Muncy, *Creating a Female Dominion in American Reform, 1890–1935* (New York: Oxford University Press, 1991), pp. 13–15.

61. Alice Schoff to JA, June 25, 1894, University of Chicago Library, Miscellaneous Manuscripts Collection; Emily S. Holmes to JA, Aug. 14 [1894], SCPC; Rev. Theodore Crowl, "Hull House," *Presbyterian Messenger*, n.d., 1894, p. 3; Muncy described the system of resident fellowships in *Creating a Female Dominion*, pp. 17–18.

62. Clifford Barnes, "Hull House, Chicago," *Record of Christian Work* (October 1893): 338, HHScrapbooks.

63. In her most quoted comment on this point, Jane said, "The one thing to be dreaded in the Settlement is that it lose its flexibility, its power of quick adaptation, its readiness to change its methods as the environment may demand. It must be open to conviction and must have a deep and abiding sense of tolerance." Addams, "The Subjective Necessity for Social Settlements," pp. 22–23.

64. Jane Addams, "Hull House as a Type of College Settlement," *Proceedings*, Wisconsin State Conference of Charities and Correction (Madison: The Conference, 1894), p. 112.

65. Barnes, "Hull House, Chicago," p. 338; Eva V. Curlin, "One Day in Altruria: A Visit to Hull House in Chicago: What Miss Jane Addams Has Done," *San Francisco Chronicle*, Feb. 4, 1894; "Children Raise Cheers for Maypole," no citation, early May 1894; "Tots in Gay Frolic," June 9, 1894; "Mr. Kent Does not Own 'Poverty Flats,'" *Inter-Ocean*, Feb. 11, 1893, HHScrapbooks. Having denied ownership, Kent then deeded the property over to Jane. See also Addams, *Twenty Years*, pp. 290–91; Nicholas Kelley, "Early Days at Hull House," p. 427; and *Hull-House Maps and Papers*, p. 224. JA to Mary Rozet Smith, Aug. 26, 1893, Mar. 3 and May 1, 1894, SCPC; JA to Nettie Fowler McCormick, Aug. 1, 1893, Nettie Fowler McCormick Papers, Madison, Wisconsin State Historical Society.

66. Kelley, "Hull House," p. 554; "A Social Settlement," no citation, but apparently summer, 1892; "Another Praiseworthy Gift," *Chicago Post*, Dec. 27, 1892; "Hull House Kitchen: Will Prove a Great Boon to Many," *Chicago Herald*, Aug. 12, 1893; "Hull House Kitchen: West Side Philanthropists Open a New Department," *InterOcean*, Aug. 24, 1893; "Hull House Kitchen Opened," *Chicago Record*, Aug. 24, 1893; "Advocates Public Kitchen: Miss Jane Addams's Lecture Before the Chicago Cooking School—Her Idea," no citation but apparently February 1894; "Hull House—A Social Settlement," *Confectioner and Baker and American Caterer* 9: (July 1894), HHScrapbooks; *Hull-House Maps and Papers*, p. 227. Addams was able to smile over her folly in *Twenty Years*, pp. 130–31. JA to Marion Talbot, Oct. 10, 1892, Marion Talbot Papers, University of Chicago Library; JA to Katherine Medill, Mar. 20, 1894, *Chicago Tribune*, Company Archives; JA to Mary Rozet Smith, Mar. 3 and May 1, 1894, SCPC.

67. The Jane Club opened with one flat and seven tenants, including Mary Kenney and her mother, in May 1892. By the time of its second anniversary dance in the Hull-House Gymnasium in May 1894, the club had five flats and fifty tenants. This collective of stenographers, dressmakers, printers, teachers, and bookkeepers, who were both native born and foreign born, each paid three dollars a week for room and board,

out of which they hired a cook. See: *Hull-House Maps and Papers*, pp. 213–14; "Co-operative Club for Women: Successful Outcome of One of Miss Addams's Projects Signalized by a Reception," *Chicago Herald*, May 5, 1892; "The Jane Club," *InterOcean*, July, n.d., 1892; "Life at the Jane Club," *Chicago News*, Nov. 2, 1892; "Jane Club," *Chicago Herald*, Aug. 13, 1893; "Chicago's Girls' Clubs," *New York Sun*, n.d., summer 1893; "Chicago's Jane Club: The Dainty Cooperative Home Life of Forty Working Girls," *New York Sun* article reprinted in the *Philadelphia Times*, Sept. 10, 1893; "One Day in Altruria," Feb. 4, 1894; "A Woman's Club that Does," *Chicago Herald*, May 13, 1894; "Chicago Jane Club: Cooperation Among Working Women," *Chicago Herald*, n.d., May 1894, "With Modest Grace: Descriptions of a Ball at Hull House," *InterOcean*, n.d., late November 1894, HHScrapbooks.

68. Rachel Unruh, "A Door for Leaving and a Key for Coming Home: Working-women, Hybrid Space and the Jane Club, 1892–1920," unpublished graduate paper, Northwestern University, 1999; Joanne Meyerowitz, *Women Adrift: Independent Wage Earners in Chicago, 1880–1930* (Chicago: University of Chicago Press, 1988), pp. 97–101.

69. "How Would You Uplift the Masses?"; Virginia Lull, "Studies at Hull House," no citation, shortly before Easter 1892; "Noble Charity Work: Hull House and What It Is Doing for the Deserving Poor," *Chicago Post*, Feb. 1, 1893; "Hull House: A Chicago Settlement," *Illustrated Christian World*, November 1892, HHScrapbooks.

70. Ellen Gates Starr to Mary Allen, Aug. 13, 1892, EGSP.

71. Samuel Barnett to JA, Dec. 26, 1892, and June 9, 1893, SCPC.

72. Henry C. Adams, introduction, *Philanthropy and Social Progress* (New York: Crowell, 1893), pp. v–xi. In this published volume of selected talks delivered at the Plymouth conference, Jane Addams was the lone female speaker included among four prominent men.

73. Addams, "Outgrowths of Toynbee Hall," December 1890, SCPC. JA to Alice Addams Haldeman, July 1892, SCPC. Edward Burchard to JA, Dec. 10, 1910, SCPC.

74. Ellen Gates Starr to Mary Blaisdell, July 25, 1892, EGSP.

75. Addams, "The Subjective Necessity for Social Settlements," pp. 6, 10–12.

76. Ibid., pp. 17–18.

77. Carl Van Treeck and Aloysius Croft, *Symbols of the Church* (Milwaukee: Bruce Publishing, 1960), pp. 30–34; Heather Child and Dorothy Colles, *Christian Symbols, Ancient and Modern: A Handbook for Students* (New York: Charles Scribner's Sons, 1971), pp. 10–22. Tolstoy, *My Religion*, pp. 93–105; Addams, *Twenty Years*, pp. 51–53, 84. Addams reported in her autobiography that her lectures on the "early interpretation of Christianity" and its relevance for the poor were accepted by the "open-minded" head of the Deaconess's Training School in Chicago, but that she was later blocked from membership on the school's board of directors by "older members" who faulted Hull-House's failure to evangelize. This story effectively defined Addams among those who took their Christianity in nontraditional servings. I am indebted to Rima Schultz and Ellen Skerrett for bringing the Chi-Rho to my attention.

78. Addams, "Subjective Necessity for Social Settlements," pp. 19–20.

79. Ibid., p. 1.

80. Ibid., pp. 1–7.

81. Addams, "Outgrowths of Toynbee Hall," pp. 1–2.

82. Addams, "How Would You Uplift the Masses?" Report of the Sunset Club, p. 12.

83. Jane Addams, "The Objective Value of a Social Settlement," in *Philanthropy and Social Progress*, p. 33.

84. Addams, "Subjective Necessity for Social Settlements," pp. 2, 12–16.

85. Addams, *Twenty Years*, p. 115.

86. "Cool Reasoning at Plymouth," *Springfield Republican*, July 30, 1892; "How Would You Uplift the Masses," *Advance*, Feb. 18, 1892, HHScrapbooks.

87. Ellen Gates Starr to Mary Allen, Aug. 13, 1892, EGSP.

88. Addams, "Objective Value of a Social Settlement," pp. 27–34.

89. Ibid., pp. 35–46.

90. Ibid., pp. 45–46.

91. Ibid., p. 49.

92. Ibid., pp. 50–51.

93. Ibid., pp. 52–54.

94. "The Objective Value of a Social Settlement" was published under the title "Hull House, Chicago: An Effort Toward Social Democracy," *Forum* 14 (October 1892): 226–41. "The Subjective Necessity for Social Settlements" was published under the title "A New Impulse to An Old Gospel," *Forum* 14 (November 1892): 345–58.

Chapter 15. What We Know Is Right

1. Addams, *Twenty Years*, pp. 185–86.

2. Jane Addams, *Peace and Bread in Time of War* (New York: Macmillan, 1922), p. 140.

3. Mary Downs to JA, May 23, 1880, SCPC.

4. Addams, *Twenty Years*, p. 190.

5. Paul T. Phillips, *A Kingdom on Earth: Anglo-American Social Christianity, 1880–1940* (University Park: Pennsylvania State University Press, 1996); Danbom, "*The World of Hope*"; Robert T. Handy, ed., *The Social Gospel in America, 1870–1920* (New York: Oxford University Press, 1966); Ferenc Szasz, *The Divided Mind of Protestant America, 1880–1930* (Tuscaloosa: University of Alabama Press, 1982); Christopher Hodge Evans, ed., *Perspectives on the Social Gospel* (New York: Edwin Mellen Press, 1999); Paul A. Carter, *The Decline and Revival of the Social Gospel* (Ithaca, N.Y.: Cornell University Press, 1956).

6. "And Not Leave the Other Undone," *Advance*, Oct. 20, 1892; Robert M. Jenkins, "The Mission of the Sunday School," no citation, Spring 1894; "Hull House: A Chicago Social Settlement," *Illustrated Christian World*, November 1892; Barnes, "Hull House, Chicago," p. 338; Sunderland, "Hull House, Chicago: Its Work and Workers," p. 402, HHScrapbooks.

7. "Poor Are Ever Welcome: Growth and Work of Hull House, a Most Noble Charity," *Chicago Times*, Sept. 26, 1892; "And Not Leave the Other Undone," *Advance*, Oct. 20, 1892; Rev. Theodore Crowl, "Hull House," *Presbyterian Messenger*, n.d., 1894, p. 3. The editorial in the *Unitarian* for March 1894 said that Addams and her coworkers were "applying literal Christianity." *Unity* magazine, untitled editorial, n.d. November 1892; "Social Settlements," *Churchman*, Nov. 24, 1892. The *Churchman* editorialized, rather combatively, that "none who heard or read [the speeches Jane Addams gave in

Plymouth, Massachusetts] will want to lightly pass sentence of condemnation upon Social Settlements." Willard Thorp to JA, Nov. 7, 1892, SCPC.

8. "Men and Things," *Unity,* July 27, 1893, reviewed a criticism first published in the Episcopal publication *The Living Church* and then reprinted in the liberal magazine *Independent.* The editors of the *Independent* argued that if settlements are worldly, "give us more worldliness." HHScrapbooks. See also Joseph Cook "Robert Elsmere's Mental Struggles," part 3, *North American Review* 148 (January 1889): 106–9. *Robert Elsmere,* by Mrs. Humphrey Ward, traced an Anglican clergyman's conversion away from Christian dogma and toward the social gospel of the settlement house. According to Cook, "the attempt to eliminate the supernatural from Christianity and yet retain its spiritual power is like an effort to cut down a tree and yet retain its fruit season after season and its daily grateful shade," p. 108.

9. Crowl, "Hull House," p. 3; "What Two Little Women Have Done," *Christian Register,* July 1894. In "A Social Settlement," Mary Josephine Onahan described Hull-House as a "non-Catholic convent" and expressed regret that "the Church whose Madonna occupies the place of honor . . . that that church with all her tremendous leverage for good should remain a thing apart, not known, not understood" by the needy masses, *Citizen,* n.d., end of 1894, HHScrapbooks. Onahan argued that "though they have no religious exercises of any sort—at least none are evident to the casual guest—they are certainly animated by the true religious spirit."

10. "How Would You Uplift the Masses?"; "A Home on Halsted Street"; Swing, "A New Social Movement."

11. Addams, "Subjective Necessity for Social Settlements," pp. 17–19. Jane claimed in her Plymouth speech that young men and women "resent the assumption that Christianity is a set of ideas which belong to the religious consciousness, whatever that may be," p. 19.

12. Carrell, "Reflections in a Mirror," p. 228. The Companions of the Holy Cross was a non-residential, lay monastic order founded by Father James Huntington, the Episcopal priest with whom Ellen and Vida, as well as Jane, shared similar views regarding economic and social justice. Vida Scudder joined the Order, also referred to as "the Society of the Companions of the Holy Cross," in 1889. According to Carrell, Ellen joined around 1895 when "the continuing trend toward secularism at Hull House . . . left [her] feeling anxious and isolated." Theresa Corcoran, *Vida Dutton Scudder* (Boston: Twayne, 1982), pp. 8–9; Eleanor J. Stebner, *The Women of Hull House: A Study in Spirituality, Vocation, and Friendship* (Albany: State University Press of New York, 1997), p. 86.

13. Vida Scudder, "The Socialism of Christ," *Dawn* 3 (December 1890): 3–4. Addams, "The Subjective Necessity for Social Settlements," pp. 10–12, 17–19. Ellen Gates Starr to Mary Allen, n.d. 1891 and Aug. 13, 1892, EGSP; Ellen Gates Starr, "A Bypath to the Great Roadway," *Catholic World* 119 (May 1924): 178.

14. Residents' Minutes, Nov. 25, 1893, JAMC, Hull-House Association Records.

15. Edward L. Burchard to Ellen Gates Starr, Jan. 16, 1938, EGSP. Burchard recalled "when Miss Addams led in evening Bible and prayer with every one on their knees. No perhaps that was before Florence Kelley came."

16. Carrell, "Reflections in a Mirror."

17. Membership survey for Ewing St. Church, JAMC.

18. "Will Meet in Sinai: Congress of Liberal Religions: Universalists, Unitarians,

Jews and Independents of America will Assemble in this City May 22, 23, 24 for Cooperation," no citation, HHScrapbooks.

19. "Tells Ministers of Hull House: Miss Jane Addams Appears Before Congregationalists in Oak Park," no citation, May 22, 1894, HHScrapbooks.

20. Stead, *If Christ Came to Chicago.* While researching the book, Stead had regularly visited Hull-House, turning up late at night "wet and hungry . . . and, while he was drinking hot chocolate before an open fire, would relate in one of his curious monologues . . . his adventures." Addams, *Twenty Years,* p. 160. In the same week she met with the Congregational ministers, Stead wrote to ask "how the rumpus which has been made about my Book has affected you at Hull House." He hoped that his positive comments on Hull House in his otherwise harsh book "will not be remembered against you for evil by my enemies." William T. Stead to JA, May 21, 1894, SCPC.

21. Stead, *If Christ Came to Chicago,* p. 346. In an article written during the summer of the World's Columbian Exposition, Stead ranked Jane highest among Chicago's "civic saviors." William T. Stead, "The Civic Life of Chicago: the Impressions of an Observant Englishman," *Review of Reviews* (August 1893): 182. In his 1894 book, Stead criticized the "richer churches in the city" for being "nothing more nor less than social clubs, which are quite out of touch with the masses of the people," p. 270. Dennis B. Downey, "William Stead and Chicago: A Victorian Jeremiah in the Windy City," *Mid-America: An Historical Review* 68 (October 1987): 153–66, and Joseph O. Baylen, "A Victorian's 'Crusade' in Chicago, 1893–1894," *Journal of American History* 51 (December 1964): 419–34.

22. Jane Addams and Ellen Starr, "Hull-House: A Social Settlement," originally published as a pamphlet in February 1893 and revised as an appendix to *Hull-House Maps and Papers,* p. 214.

23. Gilbert, *Perfect Cities;* Miller, *City of the Century;* David Burg, *Chicago's White City of 1893* (Lexington: University Press of Kentucky, 1976); George Ade et al., *The Chicago Record's History of the World's Fair,* (Chicago: Chicago Daily News, 1893); Rossiter Johnson, *A History of the World's Columbian Exposition* (New York: D. Appleton, 1897); Pierce, *A History of Chicago,* vol. 3.

24. "Chicago Letter," *Critic,* n.d., 1893, p. 155; "Jane Club," *Chicago Herald,* Aug. 13, 1893; in "In the White City," an out-of-town reporter visiting the fair found Hull-House to be "as ideal as Christianity itself," no citation, HHScrapbooks.

25. JA to Emily Greene Balch, May 11, 1893, SCPC.

26. Harry Haldeman to Anna Haldeman Addams, Dec. 26, 1893, SAH. Anna Haldeman Addams to Harry Haldeman, June 12 and Sept. 24, 1893, HJFP. Harry had been commenting on George's silence since the spring of 1891. A year later, Harry told Anna that her "officious interference" was disrupting Harry's treatment plan. He argued that "love is a mistake as well as the opium treatment." Harry Haldeman to Anna Haldeman Addams, Apr. 15, 1891, Apr. 19, 1892, and Aug. 15, 1893, SAH.

27. JA to Alice Addams Haldeman, Feb. 10, 1893, SAH; JA to Mary Rozet Smith, Aug. 26, 1893, SCPC.

28. JA to Alice Addams Haldeman, Aug. 20, 1890, SAH.

29. Ellen Gates Starr to Alice Addams Haldeman, Dec. 2, 1892, SAH.

30. Robert A. Woods to JA, June 20, 1893, SCPC; Harry Haldeman to Anna Haldeman Addams, June 26, 1893, SAH. Alice and Marcet made one trip to the fair in May and returned to share the event with the Linns in June, after visiting Anna and

George in Cedarville. Florence Kelley to Caroline B. Kelley, May 27, 1893; Nicholas Kelley Papers, New York Public Library; Anna Haldeman Addams to Harry Haldeman, June 12, 1893, HJFP.

31. Anna Haldeman Addams to Harry Haldeman, Sept. 24, 1893, HJFP.

32. Julian Ralph, *Our Great West* (New York: Harper & Bros., 1893), excerpted in Bessie L. Pierce, *As Others See Chicago: Impressions of Visitors, 1673–1933* (Chicago: University of Chicago Press, 1933), p. 319.

33. Frank and Jerome, *Annals of the Chicago Woman's Club for the First Forty Years of its Organization, 1876–1916*, pp. 103–16.

34. Gayle Gullett, "'Our Great Opportunity': Organized Women Advance Women's Work at the World's Columbian Exposition of 1893," *Illinois Historical Journal* 87 (Winter 1994): 259–76; Jeanne M. Weimann, *The Fair Women* (Chicago: Academy Chicago, 1981).

35. Rima Lunin Schultz, introduction, *Women Building Chicago*, pp. xxx–xxxi; Weimann, *Fair Women*, p. 523; Gayle Gullett, "The Political Use of Public Space: The Women's Movement and Women's Participation at the Chicago Columbian Exposition, 1893," paper presented at the Berkshire Conference on Women's History, Wellesley College, 1987, pp. 11–12. Charles C. Bonney to JA, Jan. 14, 1893, SCPC. Bonney was the president of the World's Congress Auxiliary. This letter makes clear that it was Jane who made the initial request that the auxiliary assign space and time for a Social Settlement Congress. Bonney left it up to Jane to "select and recommend the names of a few others to constitute under your Chairmanship a Committee to make the necessary arrangements." In 1893, there were approximately two dozen settlements operating in the U.S., and the majority were staffed by women. Carson, *Settlement Folk*; Allen F. Davis, *Spearheads for Reform: The Social Settlements and the Progressive Movement, 1890–1914* (New York: Oxford University Press, 1967); Robert A. Woods and Albert J. Kennedy, eds., *Handbook of Settlements* (New York: Charities Publication Committee, 1911).

36. Robert A. Woods to JA, June 20, 1893. SCPC. Addams, *Twenty Years*, pp. 113–14. Jane told Alice that Woods's 1892 book, *English Social Movements* "is quite the best book on the later movements of which the Settlement is one," JA to Alice Addams Haldeman, Dec. 28, 1892, SAH; Carson, *Settlement Folk*, pp. 56–57.

37. Woods's talk at Plymouth was included in the conference's published volume, *Philanthropy and Social Progress*; Scudder's talk was not.

38. JA to Alice Addams Haldeman, Feb. 23, 1893, SAH. Vida Scudder used the distinction between a "social" settlement and a "college" settlement to emphasize her academic credentials. Addams rejected the distinction because Hull House offered college extension courses. Eleanor H. Woods, *Robert A. Woods: Champion of Democracy* (Freeport, N.Y.: Books for Libraries Press, 1929, 1971), p. 67; Vida Scudder, "College Settlements and College Women," *Outlook* 70 (Apr. 19, 1902): 973; Jane Addams, "Hull House as a Type of College Settlement," *Proceedings*, Wisconsin State Conference of Charities and Correction (Madison: The Conference, 1894), pp. 97–115. In "College Settlements and College Women," Scudder pointed to the fall of 1877 as the moment when a "little group" at Smith College first began to discuss the idea of a settlement house. Given Scudder's questioning of Hull-House's academic credentials and Jane's sense of time wasted at Rockford Seminary, Scudder's remark in this 1902 article could have encouraged Jane to imagine what might have happened had she attended Smith in the

fall of 1877 and to claim, in her 1909 autobiography, a real intention to attend Smith as early as 1877. While Jane Addams's Plymouth talks were prominently published in *Forum* magazine, Scudder and Woods were published in an academic journal: Vida D. Scudder, "The Place of College Settlements," *Andover Review* 18 (October 1892): 339–50; Robert A. Woods, "University Settlements," *Andover Review* 18 (October 1892): 319–39. Vida Dutton Scudder, *On Journey* (New York: E. P. Dutton, 1937), pp. 101, 110–11, 135–36, 150; Carrell, "Reflections in a Mirror," on p. 136.

39. Robert Woods to JA, June 20 and 26, 1893, SCPC. Eleanor Woods said that Jane Addams gave a talk on "practical examples of Social Christianity" at the "Evangelical Conference" at the fair, *Robert A. Woods*, p. 81. According to Addams, the "adherents of the most diverse religious creeds, eastern and western, met in amity and good fellowship" at the fair while the "partisan members" of the "social science" congresses "had their feelings hurt because their cause did not receive 'due recognition.'" Addams, *Twenty Years*, pp. 181–82.

40. Vida Scudder to JA, June 15, 1893, SCPC.

41. Robert Woods to JA, June 26, 1893, SCPC.

42. "The World's Fair Congress of Social Settlements," *Unity*, July 27, 1893, HHScrapbooks.

43. Robert Woods to JA, June 26, 1893, SCPC.

44. JA to Henry Demarest Lloyd, July 29, 1893, Henry Demarest Lloyd Papers, Madison, Wisconsin State Historical Society; Jane Addams, "Domestic Service and the Family Claim," *The World's Congress of Representative Women*, vol. 2, ed. May Wright Sewall (Chicago: Rand, McNally, 1894), pp. 626–31. The text from Jane's speech, "Two Belated Trades," which she delivered at the Labor Congress, has not survived. See, Jane Addams, "A Belated Industry," *American Journal of Sociology* 1 (March 1896): 536–50. Much of the text from "Domestic Service" made its way into this journal article; it seems likely that the article's more pointed discussion of the ways in which both domestic service and housewifery were outdated came from the Labor Congress talk.

45. Jane Addams, "Domestic Service and the Family Claim," pp. 626–31.

46. Ibid.

47. JA to Bertha Honore Palmer, Sept. 30, 1893, Jane Addams File, Chicago Historical Society. Jane could have put Palmer in touch with Alzina Stevens, one of Kelley's factory inspectors and a longtime organizer for the Knights. Ann D. Gordon, "Alzina Stevens," in *Women Building Chicago*, pp. 842–44. Nine months after the Chicago fair, in a speech at the California Midwinter International Exposition in San Francisco, Jane took a swipe at the fair's Congress of Women, and at Bertha Palmer's Board of Lady Managers, by claiming that foreign visitors to the Chicago fair were disappointed that American women for all their "advancement did not seem to be awake to that universal consciousness which embraces humanity." "The Ideal and Actual," no citation, February 1894, HHScrapbooks.

48. "Mill and Shop Hands: Factory Inspectors' Convention," no citation, late summer 1893, HHScrapbooks.

49. JA to Mary Rozet Smith, Aug. 26, 1893; minutes, Hull-House Residents' Meeting, Mar. 10, 1894, JAMC, Hull-House Association Records; Miller, *City of the Century*.

50. JA to Mary Rozet Smith, Aug. 26, 1893, SCPC.

51. JA to Alice Addams Haldeman, Apr. 16, 1894, SAH.

52. JA to Sarah Anderson, June 23, 1894, RCA.

53. JA to Mary Rozet Smith, Aug. 26, 1893, SCPC.

54. Jane Addams, "What Shall We Do for Our Unemployed," Sunset Club *Yearbook*, 1893–1894, pp. 81–82. It is possible to date the speech in early November because William Stead was in attendance, and he left Chicago soon after Nov. 12, 1893. Downey, ""William Stead and Chicago," p. 161.

55. Downey, "William Stead and Chicago," pp. 159–61; Baylen, "A Victorian's 'Crusade' in Chicago," pp. 424–25; Graham Taylor, *Pioneering on Social Frontiers* (Chicago: University of Chicago Press, 1930), pp. 29–34.

56. Downey, "William Stead and Chicago," p. 160; Stead, *If Christ Came to Chicago*, pp. 465–66; Douglas Sutherland, *Fifty Years on the Civic Front* (Chicago: Civic Federation, 1943), pp. 4–7. Jane Addams was one of the ten members of the subcommittee formed to "draft and submit a plan of organization and outline the scope of the work to be undertaken by the Civic Federation." W. Turlington Harvey to JA, Dec. 23, 1893, Civic Federation of Chicago Papers, Chicago Historical Society.

57. Destler, *Henry Demarest Lloyd and the Empire of Reform*, p. 351; Sutherland, *Fifty Years on the Civic Front*, p. 7; Albion W. Small, "The Civic Federation of Chicago: A Study in Social Dynamics," *American Journal of Sociology* 1 (July 1895): 79–103; Donald David Marks, "Polishing the Gem of the Prairie: The Evolution of Civic Consciousness in Chicago, 1874–1900," Ph.D. diss., University of Wisconsin—Madison, 1974. For direct evidence of the desire to counter any "impression that 'Civic Federation' is a piece of scholastic idealism" and to emphasize it as "a business man's plan" with a business man's "practicability," see Prof. Albion Small to JA, Dec. 26, 1893, Civic Federation of Chicago Papers, Chicago Historical Society.

58. Stead, *If Christ Came to Chicago*, pp. 468–69.

59. Ibid., p. 467. *Chicago Daily InterOcean*, no citation, May 1894, announcing the creation of Chicago Civic Federation's Conciliatory Committee and listing Jane Addams among the members, HHScrapbooks; Jane Addams testimony before United States Strike Commission, *Report on the Chicago Strike of June-July, 1894* (Washington, D.C.: Government Printing Office, 1895), p. 645.

60. Stanley Buder, *Pullman: An Experiment in Industrial Order and Community Planning, 1880–1930* (New York: Oxford University Press, 1967); Gilbert, *Perfect Cities*, pp. 131–68; Almont Lindsey, *The Pullman Strike: The Story of a Unique Experiment and of a Great Labor Upheaval* (Chicago: University of Chicago Press, 1942).

61. United States Strike Commission, *Report on the Chicago Strike of June-July, 1894*; Buder, *Pullman*; Lindsey, *The Pullman Strike*.

62. Jane Addams Diaries, May 9, 1894, SCPC.

63. Richard Ely, "Pullman: A Social Study," *Harper's New Monthly Magazine* 70 (February 1885): 452–66.

64. Ely, "Pullman: A Social Study," p. 466; Carl Smith, *Urban Order and the Shape of Belief* (Chicago: University of Chicago Press, 1995), pp. 200–208.

65. "Report of the Commissioners," pp. xxi–liv, and Jane Addams testimony, *Report on the Chicago Strike of June-July, 1894*, p. 646.

66. United States Strike Commission, *Report of the Chicago Strike*, pp. xxxii–liv.

67. Ellen Gates Starr to Mary Blaisdell, July 25, 1892, EGSP. "Fined for Being Late: Why Thirty-Five Girls Struck at the Star Knitting Works," *Chicago Herald*, Apr. 27, 1892; "Judge Tuley as Arbitrator," *Chicago News*, Apr. 29, 1892; "Obliged to Pay Back Fines,"

Chicago Tribune, Apr. 30, 1892, HHScrapbooks. Addams, "Judge Murray F. Tuley," *The Excellent Becomes Permanent*, pp. 73–75.

68. George Pullman testimony, United States Strike Commission, *Report on the Chicago Strike*, pp. 556–67.

69. "He Will Not Act: Pullman Ignores the Efforts of Jane Addams on Behalf of Arbitration: She Makes a Final Appeal," *Chicago Mail*, June 1, 1894; "Pullman Is Stubborn: Flatly Refuses to Arbitrate with Striking Employees," *Chicago Times*, June 2, 1894; "Ready to Arbitrate: American Railway Union's Offer: Willing to Submit Grievances Against the Pullman Company to the Civic Federation," *Chicago Herald*, June 2, 1894, Pullman Company Scrapbooks, Newberry Library, Chicago; Jane Addams testimony, *Report on the Chicago Strike*, p. 646.

70. "Ready to Arbitrate," *Chicago Herald*, June 2, 1894; Jane Addams testimony, *Report on the Chicago Strike*, p. 647.

71. "Minds Bent on Peace: Congress of Conciliation and Arbitration Opens," *Chicago Tribune*, Nov. 14, 1894; "Hear the Big Guns: Congress of Conciliation Attracts Big Crowds: Labor Leaders in Line: Status of the Employer and Employee Discussed: Carroll D. Wright Gives His View of Arbitration: Gompers' Optimistic Address," *Chicago Tribune*, Nov. 15, 1894; Ray S. Baker, "The Civic Federation of Chicago," *Outlook* (July 27, 1895); Addams, *Twenty Years*, pp. 213–14; Waldo R. Browne, *Altgeld of Illinois: A Record of His Life and Work* (New York: B. W. Huebsch, 1924), pp. 194–97; Ralph Easley, *The Civic Federation: What It Has Accomplished* (Chicago: Hollister Brothers, 1899), p. 14.

72. Lindsey, *The Pullman Strike;* United States Strike Commission, *Report on the Chicago Strike*, pp. xxi–liv.

73. "Not Lagging: Western Reserve University Keeps in the Van," *Cleveland Plain Dealer*, June 20, 1894. Jane was invited to Western Reserve by Charles F. Thwing, the university's president and a leading advocate of the social gospel and its place in American education.

74. JA to Alice Addams Haldeman, Mar. n.d. 1894, Mar. 17 and 24, 1894; Apr. 8, 16, and 29, 1894, SAH. In the Apr. 29 letter, Jane commented, "Of course, I've had the same unusual expenses this year of the World's Fair that you have had," and reported that she was so broke she'd had to "borrow $200.00 at Freeport" and could not afford to buy the twenty copies of *Philanthropy and Social Progress* that Alice had requested.

75. John Addams Linn to JA, Dec. 17, 1893, SCPC. John found Ellen to be a bit meddlesome in his love life but was hurt that his Aunt Jane did not take his affair of the heart more seriously. The object of his affection, Wilfreda Brockway, married another Hull-House resident, Frederick Deknatel, and John did become an Episcopal clergyman. Alice Hamilton to Agnes Hamilton, Oct. 13, 1897, and July 3, 1898, in Sicherman, ed., *Alice Hamilton: A Life in Letters*, pp. 116–17, 125.

76. JA to Mary Rozet Smith, Dec. 27, 1893, SCPC.

77. Harry Haldeman to Anna Haldeman Addams, June 26, 1893, SAH; JA to Alice Addams Haldeman, Apr. 29, 1894, SAH.

78. JA to Alice Addams Haldeman, March, n.d., 1894; Mar. 17, Apr. 29, 1894, SAH. After Kellogg had finished with the painting, Jane held on to it for a few weeks while Kellogg made a copy for Mary Rozet Smith.

79. Harry Haldeman to Anna Haldeman Addams, May 20, 1894, HJFP.

80. JA to Alice Addams Haldeman, May 11, 1894, SAH.

81. JA to Alice Addams Haldeman, June 29, 1894, SCPC.

82. John Addams Linn to JA, Dec. 17, 1893, SCPC.

83. Rev. John M. Linn signed a "Renunciation" of rights to administer Mary Addams Linn's estate in July 1894, Cook County Probate Division, State of Illinois. In a December 1895 Administrator's Petition to Sell Real Estate once belonging to Mary Linn, Jane Addams is referred to as the "guardian" of Mary's children, Cook County Probate Court, State of Illinois.

84. JA to Alice Addams Haldeman, Dec. 23, 1894, JAMC.

85. Addams, *Twenty Years*, pp. 216–17.

86. Addams, *Twenty Years*, pp. 217–19; Jane Addams, "A Modern Lear," *Survey* 29 (Nov. 2, 1912): 137. Addams wrote this essay in 1894, but was unable to get it published until 1912. A close comparison of surviving drafts indicates that what she wrote in the mid-1890s was virtually identical to what she published in 1912, SCPC.

87. According to her short preface to the published version of "A Modern Lear," the speech "was written in 1894, just after the Pullman strike and read before the Chicago Woman's Club and the Twentieth Century Club of Boston." The *Annals of the Chicago Woman's Club* do not contain any mention of this speech, but Louise deKoven Bowen recalled hearing Jane give a speech comparing Pullman to Lear at a meeting in Chicago. Louise deKoven Bowen, *Growing Up with a City* (New York: Macmillan, 1926), pp. 81–82. For her appearance at the United Charities Building in New York City in May 1895, see "Pullman Follows Lear: Miss Addams, of Chicago, Traces Their Histories in a Speech," n.p., May 4, 1895; "Likens Him to Lear: Miss Addams's Striking Characterization of Pullman," n.p., May 3, 1895, HHScrapbooks.

88. Addams, "A Modern Lear," pp. 133, 137.

89. JA to Alice Addams Haldeman, Aug. 20, 1890, SAH.

90. Jane Addams Notebook, undated, summer 1882, SCPC, and JAPP, reel 27, frame 0369. Like so many phrases Addams used and reused over the years, this one was undoubtedly copied down, without citation, from a book she was reading. A computer search of likely George Eliot texts did not locate it.

91. Addams, "A Modern Lear," pp. 131–37.

92. Ibid., p. 132.

93. Ibid., p. 133. Louise deKoven Bowen, who later became one of Jane's closest friends and one of Hull House's most important financial supporters, recalled this speech as her first exposure to JA. "I remember," wrote Bowen, "she seemed so fair and so dispassionate in her setting forth the reason of the strike . . . I was much impressed by her sympathy for the working man, and the sense of justice which made her see Mr. Pullman's side." Bowen, *Growing Up with a City*, pp. 81–82.

94. Addams, *Twenty Years*, pp. 31–32. In the paragraph following her discussion of her father's close association with Lincoln, she told of seeking solace, during the Pullman strike, by walking in Lincoln Park. Two years later, in defending her association with a political party that had not seated a black delegation from Mississippi, she referred erroneously to "my Abolitionist father." Jane Addams, "The Progressive Party and the Negro," *Crisis* 5 (November 1912): 30.

95. Addams, "A Modern Lear," p. 134.

96. "Not Lagging: Western Reserve University Keeps in the Van."

97. Addams, "A Modern Lear," pp. 133, 134, 136.

98. Ibid., pp. 132, 133, 135.

99. Ibid., pp. 133, 136, 137.

100. Ibid., p. 131.

101. Ibid., p. 137.

102. Ibid., pp. 136, 137.

103. Addams, *Twenty Years*, pp. 185–86; Brown, "Advocate for Democracy," pp. 145–46.

104. For the Socialists' disdain of Jane's moderating politics during the 1912 election, see: "An Oft-Told Tale," *New York Call*, Apr. 25, 1912, and "The Lamb Tags on the Lion," *New York Call*, Aug. 11, 1912. Regarding the post-1894 tensions between Jane and Ellen over labor politics, see Davis, *American Heroine*, pp. 114–17; Carrell, "Reflections in a Mirror," pp. 348–54.

105. John Dewey to Alice Dewey, Oct. 9 and 10, 1894, John Dewey Papers, Carbondale, Southern Illinois University.

106. John Dewey to Alice Dewey, Oct. 10, 1894, John Dewey Papers, Southern Illinois University. Louis Menand, *The Metaphysical Club* (New York: Farrar, Straus and Giroux, 2001), pp. 312–16.

107. John Dewey to JA, Jan. 19, 1896, SCPC.

108. JA to Henry Demarest Lloyd, Feb. 10, 1896, Henry Demarest Lloyd Papers, Madison, State Historical Society of Wisconsin.

109. Brown, "Advocate for Democracy," pp. 142–44.

110. Addams, *Twenty Years*, p. 187.

111. "Notes by a Woman," *Chicago Herald*, June 28, 1894, HHScrapbooks.

Selected Bibliography

Works by Jane Addams Cited

For a complete listing of Jane Addams's writings, see Mary Lynn McCree Bryan, ed., *The Jane Addams Papers: A Comprehensive Guide.* Bloomington: Indiana University Press, 1996, pp. 129–75.

"A Belated Industry," *American Journal of Sociology* 1 (March 1896): 536–50.

"A Book That Changed My Life," *Christian Century* 44 (Oct. 13, 1927): 1196–98.

"The College Woman and Christianity," *Independent* 53 (Aug. 8, 1901): 1852–55.

"The College Woman and the Family Claim," *Commons* 3 (September 1898): 3–7.

Democracy and Social Ethics. New York: Macmillan, 1902.

The Excellent Becomes Permanent. New York: Macmillan, 1932.

The Long Road of Woman's Memory. New York: Macmillan, 1916.

"A Modern Lear," *Survey* 29 (Nov. 2, 1912): 131–37.

My Friend, Julia Lathrop. New York: Macmillan, 1935.

"The Objective Value of a Social Settlement." In *Philanthropy and Social Progress: Seven Essays Delivered Before the School of Applied Ethics During the Session of 1892.* New York: Thomas Y. Crowell, 1893, pp. 27–56.

"The Subjective Necessity for Social Settlements." In *Philanthropy and Social Progress: Seven Essays Delivered Before the School of Applied Ethics During the Session of 1892.* New York: Thomas Y. Crowell, 1893, pp. 1–26.

"Tolstoy's Theory of Life." *Chautauqua Assembly Herald* 27 (July 14, 1902): 2–3.

Twenty Years at Hull House. New York: Macmillan, 1910.

What Then Must We Do? by Leo Tolstoy. Introduction by Jane Addams. London: Oxford University Press, 1934.

Selected Secondary Works Cited

Abel, Emily K. "Middle-Class Culture for the Urban Poor: The Educational Thought of Samuel Barnett." *Social Service Review* 52 (December 1978): 596–620.

———. "Toynbee Hall, 1884–1914." *Social Service Review* 53 (December 1979): 606–32.

Agnew, Elizabeth N. "Charity, Friendly Visiting, and Social Work: Mary E. Richmond and the Shaping of an American Profession." Ph.D. diss., Indiana University, 1999.

Alaya, Flavia. "Victorian Science and the Genius of Woman." *Journal of the History of Ideas* 38 (April-June 1977): 261–80.

Bannister, Robert C. *Social Darwinism: Science and Myth in Anglo-American Social Thought.* Philadelphia: Temple University Press, 1979.

Barker-Benfield, G. J. "'Mother Emancipator': The Meaning of Jane Addams' Sickness and Cure." *Journal of Family History* 4 (Winter 1979): 395–420.

Barnett, Henrietta. *Canon Barnett: His Life, Work, and Friends by His Wife.* New York: G. P. Putnam's Sons, 1921.

Barnett, Samuel, and Henrietta Barnett. *Practicable Socialism: Essays on Social Reform.* 2nd ed. London: Longmans, Green, 1894.

Benstock, Shari, ed. *The Private Self: Theory and Practice of Women's Autobiographical Writings.* Chapel Hill: University of North Carolina Press, 1988.

Blanchard, Mary Warner. *Oscar Wilde's America: Counterculture in the Gilded Age.* New Haven: Yale University Press, 1998.

Boller, Paul. "The New Science and American Thought." In *Social Ideas of American Educators,* ed. Merle Curti. 2nd ed. Paterson, N.J.: Pageant Books, 1959.

Bowen, Louise deKoven. *Growing Up with a City.* New York: Macmillan, 1926.

———. *Open Windows: Stories of People and Places.* Chicago: R. F. Seymour, 1946.

Briggs, Asa, and Anne Macartney. *Toynbee Hall: The First Hundred Years.* London: Routledge and Kegan Paul, 1984.

Brooks, William K. "The Condition of Woman from a Zoological Point of View." *Popular Science Monthly* 15 (June-July 1879): 145–55, 347–56.

———. "Woman from the Standpoint of a Naturalist." *Forum* 22 (November 1896): 286–96.

Bryan, Mary Lynn McCree, ed. *The Jane Addams Papers: A Comprehensive Guide.* Bloomington: Indiana University Press, 1996.

Bryan, Mary Lynn McCree, and Allen F. Davis, *100 Years at Hull-House.* Bloomington: Indiana University Press, 1990.

Carrell, Elizabeth. "Reflections in a Mirror: The Progressive Woman and the Settlement Experience," Ph.D. diss., University of Texas at Austin, 1981.

Carson, Mina Jane. *Settlement Folk: Social Thought and the American Settlement Movement, 1885–1930.* Chicago: University of Chicago Press, 1990.

Cogan, Frances B. *All-American Girl: The Ideal of Real Womanhood in Mid-Nineteenth-Century America.* Athens: University of Georgia Press, 1989.

Collini, Stefan. *Arnold.* Oxford: Oxford University Press, 1988.

Conway, Jill. "Stereotypes of Femininity in a Theory of Sexual Evolution." In *Suffer and Be Still: Women in the Victorian Age,* Martha Vicinus, ed. Bloomington, Indiana: Indiana University Press, 1972, pp. 140–55.

Cook, Blanche Wiesen. "Female Support Networks and Political Activism: Lillian Wald, Crystal Eastman, Emma Goldman." *Chrysalis* 3 (Autumn 1977): 43–61.

Curtis, Susan. *Consuming Faith: the Social Gospel and Modern Culture.* Baltimore: Johns Hopkins University Press, 1991.

Danbom, David B. *"The World of Hope": Progressives and the Struggle for an Ethical Public Life.* Philadelphia: Temple University Press, 1987.

Davis, Allen F. *American Heroine: The Life and Legend of Jane Addams.* New York: Oxford University Press, 1973.

Diliberto, Gioia. *A Useful Woman: The Early Life of Jane Addams.* New York: Simon and Schuster, 1999.

Duis, Perry R. *Challenging Chicago: Coping with Everyday Life, 1837–1920.* Chicago: University of Illinois Press, 1998.

Elshtain, Jean Bethke. *Jane Addams and the Dream of American Democracy.* New York: Basic Books, 2002.

Ely, Richard. *Social Aspects of Christianity and Other Essays.* New York: Thomas Y. Crowell, 1889.

Faderman, Lillian. "Boston Marriages as a Possible Lesson for Today." In *Boston Marriages: Romantic but Asexual Relationships Among Contemporary Lesbians*, ed. Esther D. Rothblum and Kathleen A. Brehony. Amherst: University of Massachusetts Press, 1993, pp. 29–42.

Farrell, John C. *Beloved Lady: A History of Jane Addams's Ideas on Reform and Peace*. Baltimore: Johns Hopkins University Press, 1967.

Fee, Elizabeth. "The Sexual Politics of Victorian Anthropology." In *Clio's Consciousness Raised: New Perspectives on the History of Women*, ed. Mary S. Hartman and Lois Banner. New York: Harper and Row, 1974, pp. 86–102.

Fellman, Anita Clair, and Michael Fellman. *Making Sense of Self: Medical Advice Literature in Late Nineteenth-Century America*. Philadelphia: University of Pennsylvania Press, 1981.

Flanagan, Maureen. *Seeing with Their Hearts: Chicago Women and the Vision of the Good City, 1871–1933*. Princeton: Princeton University Press, 2002.

Fleishman, Avrom. *Figures of Autobiography: The Language of Self-Writing in Victorian and Modern England*. Berkeley: University of California Press, 1983.

Frank, Henriette Greenebaum, and Amalie Hofer Jerome. *Annals of the Chicago Woman's Club for the First Forty Years of its Organization, 1876–1916*. Chicago: Chicago Woman's Club, 1916.

Frank, Stephen M. *Life with Father: Parenthood and Masculinity in the Nineteenth-Century American North*. Baltimore: Johns Hopkins University Press, 1998.

Freedman, Estelle. "Sexuality in Nineteenth-Century America: Behavior, Ideology, and Politics." *Reviews in American History* (December 1982): 196–215.

French, John C. *History of the University Founded by Johns Hopkins*. Baltimore: Johns Hopkins University Press, 1946.

Gilbert, James. *Perfect Cities: Chicago's Utopias of 1893*. Chicago: University of Chicago Press, 1991.

Gosling, F. G. *Before Freud: Neurasthenia and the American Medical Community*. Urbana: University of Illinois Press, 1987.

Grob, Gerald. *Mental Illness and American Society, 1875–1940*. Princeton: Princeton University Press, 1983.

Haldeman-Julius, Marcet. "Jane Addams as I Knew Her." *Reviewer's Library*. Girard, Kan.: Haldeman-Julius Company, 1936.

Hall, Clayton Colman. *Baltimore: Its History and Its People*. New York: Lewis Historical Publishing, 1912.

Himmelfarb, Gertrude. *Poverty and Compassion: The Moral Imagination of the Late Victorians*. New York: Alfred A. Knopf, 1991.

Hirschfeld, Charles. *Baltimore, 1870–1900: Studies in Social History*. Baltimore: Johns Hopkins University Press, 1941.

Holli, Melvin G., and Peter D'A. Jones, eds. *Ethnic Chicago: A Multi-Cultural Portrait*. 4th ed. Grand Rapids: Eerdmans, 1995.

Horowitz, Helen Lefkowitz. *Culture and the City: Cultural Philanthropy in Chicago from the 1880s to 1917*. Chicago: University of Chicago Press, 1976.

———. "'Nous Autres': Reading, Passion, and the Creation of M. Carey Thomas," *Journal of American History* 79 (1992): 68–95.

Houghton, Walter. *The Victorian Frame of Mind*. New Haven: Yale University Press, 1957.

Howe, Daniel Walker. *The Political Culture of the American Whigs*. Chicago: University of Chicago Press, 1979.

Howe, Daniel Walker, ed. *Victorian America*. Philadelphia: University of Pennsylvania Press, 1976.

Jelinek, Estelle, ed. *Women's Autobiography: Essays in Criticism*. Bloomington: Indiana University Press, 1980.

Johansen, Shawn. *Family Men: Middle-Class Fatherhood in Early Industrializing America*. New York: Routledge, 2001.

Kloppenberg, James T. *Uncertain Victory: Social Democracy and Progressivism in European and American Thought, 1870–1920*. New York: Oxford University Press, 1986.

Knight, Louise W. "Biography's Window on Social Change: Benevolence and Justice in Jane Addams's 'A Modern Lear.'" *Journal of Women's History* 9 (Spring 1997): 111–38.

Landow, George P. *Ruskin*. Oxford: Oxford University Press, 1985.

LeQuesne, A. L. *Carlyle*. Oxford: Oxford University Press, 1982.

Levine, Daniel. *Jane Addams and the Liberal Tradition*. Madison: State Historical Society of Wisconsin, 1971.

Linn, James Weber. *Jane Addams: A Biography*. New York: D. Appleton-Century, 1935.

McCarthy, Kathleen D. *Noblesse Oblige: Charity and Cultural Philanthropy in Chicago, 1849–1929*. Chicago: University of Chicago Press, 1982.

Meacham, Standish. *Toynbee Hall and Social Reform, 1880–1914: The Search for Community*. New Haven: Yale University Press, 1987.

Mearns, Andrew. *The Bitter Cry of Outcast London*, ed. Anthony S. Wohl. New York: Humanities Press, 1970.

Miller, Donald. *City of the Century: The Epic of Chicago and the Making of America*. New York: Simon and Schuster, 1996.

Morgan, H. Wayne, ed. *The Gilded Age*. Rev. ed. Syracuse: Syracuse University Press, 1970.

Muncy, Robyn. *Creating a Female Dominion in American Reform, 1890–1935*. New York: Oxford University Press, 1991.

Nettleship, Lois Ellen Shankman. "The Settlement Rationale: A Comparative Study of Samuel Barnett and Jane Addams, 1870 to 1914." Ph.D. thesis, University of Sussex, England, 1976.

———. "William Fremantle, Samuel Barnett and the Broad Church Origins of Toynbee Hall." *Journal of Ecclesiastical History* 33 (October 1982): 564–79.

Olney, James. *Metaphors of Self: the Meaning of Autobiography*. Princeton: Princeton University Press, 1972.

Ostler, Jeffrey. *Prairie Populism: The Fate of Agrarian Radicalism in Kansas, Nebraska, and Iowa, 1880–1892*. Lawrence: University Press of Kansas, 1993.

Ostrander, Gilman. *American Civilization in the First Machine Age, 1890–1940*. New York: Harper and Row, 1970.

Palmieri, Patricia. "From Republican Motherhood to Race Suicide: Arguments on Higher Education of Women in the United States, 1820–1920." In *Educating Men and Women Together: Coeducation in a Changing World*, ed. Carol Lasser. Chicago: University of Illinois Press, 1987.

———. "Patterns of Achievement of Single Academic Women at Wellesley College, 1880–1920." *Frontiers* 5 (1980): 63–67.

Phillips, J. O. C. "The Education of Jane Addams." *History of Education Quarterly* 14 (Spring 1974): 49–65.

Pierce, Bessie Louise. *A History of Chicago*, vol. 3: *The Rise of a Modern City, 1871–1893.* New York: Alfred A. Knopf, 1957.

Rader, Benjamin. *The Academic Mind and Reform: The Influence of Richard T. Ely in American Life.* Louisville: University of Kentucky Press, 1966.

Residents of Hull-House. *Hull-House Maps and Papers.* New York: Thomas Y. Crowell, 1895.

Rodgers, Daniel T. *The Work Ethic in Industrial America, 1850–1920.* Chicago: University of Chicago Press, 1974.

Rosenberg, Charles S. *No Other Gods: On Science and American Thought.* Baltimore: Johns Hopkins University Press, 1976.

———. *The Trial of the Assassin Guiteau: Psychiatry and the Law in the Gilded Age.* Chicago: University of Chicago Press, 1968.

Rosenberg, Philip. *The Seventh Hero: Thomas Carlyle and the Theory of Radical Activism.* Cambridge: Harvard University Press, 1974.

Ross, Dorothy. "Gendered Social Knowledge: Domestic Discourse, Jane Addams, and the Possibilities of Social Science." In *Gender and American Social Science: The Formative Years*, ed. Helene Silverberg. Princeton: Princeton University Press, 1998, pp. 235–64.

Rupp, Leila. *A Desired Past: A Short History of Same-Sex Love in America.* Chicago: University of Chicago Press, 1999.

Schilling, Bernard. *Human Dignity and the Great Victorians.* New York: Columbia University Press, 1946.

Schultz, Rima Lunin, and Adele Hast, editors. *Women Building Chicago, 1790–1990: A Biographical Dictionary.* Bloomington: Indiana University Press, 2001.

Seidman, Steven. "The Power of Desire and the Danger of Pleasure: Victorian Sexuality Reconsidered." *Journal of Social History* 24 (Fall 1990): 47–67.

Sicherman, Barbara. *Alice Hamilton: A Life in Letters.* Cambridge: Harvard University Press, 1984.

———. "Reading and Ambition: M. Carey Thomas and Female Heroism." *American Quarterly* 45 (March 1993): 73–103.

———. "The Uses of Diagnosis: Doctors, Patients, and Neurasthenia." *Journal of the History of Medicine* 32 (January 1977): 33–54.

Sklar, Kathryn Kish. *Florence Kelley and the Nation's Work: The Rise of Women's Political Culture, 1830–1900.* New Haven: Yale University Press, 1995.

———. "Who Funded Hull House." In *Lady Bountiful Revisited: Women Philanthropy, and Power*, ed. Kathleen D. McCarthy. New Brunswick, N.J.: Rutgers University Press, 1990, pp. 94–115.

Smith, Carl. *Urban Disorder and the Shape of Belief.* Chicago: University of Chicago Press, 1995.

Smith-Rosenberg, Carroll. "The Female World of Love and Ritual." *Signs: A Journal of Women in Culture and Society* 1 (Autumn 1975): 1–29.

Stansky, Peter. *William Morris.* Oxford: Oxford University Press, 1983.

Stead, William T. *If Christ Came to Chicago.* Chicago: Laird and Lee, 1894.

Stedman-Jones, Gareth. *Outcast London: A Study of the Relationship Between Classes in Victorian Society.* London: Oxford University Press, 1971.

Tolstoi, Leo. *My Religion*, vol. 17 in *The Novels and Other Works of Lyof N. Tolstoi.* New York: Charles Scribner's Sons, 1899.

Townsend, Lucy F. *The Best Helpers of One Another: Anna Peck Sill and the Struggle for Women's Education.* Chicago: Educational Studies Press, 1988.

Trecker, Janice Law. "Sex, Science and Education." *American Quarterly* 26 (October 1974): 352–66.

Turner, James. *Without God, Without Creed: The Origins of Unbelief in America.* Baltimore: Johns Hopkins University Press, 1985.

Tyack, David, and Elizabeth Hansot. *Learning Together: A History of Coeducation in American Schools.* New Haven: Yale University Press, 1990.

Vicinus, Martha. "Distance and Desire: English Boarding School Friendships." *Signs: A Journal of Women in Culture and Society* 9 (Summer 1984): 600–622.

Waring, Walter. *Thomas Carlyle.* Boston: G. K. Hall/Twayne, 1978.

Zornow, William F. *Kansas: A History of the Jayhawk State.* Norman: University of Oklahoma Press, 1957.

Index

Italicized page numbers indicate illustrations.

Darwinism, 82, 84–87, 89, 94, 145. *See also*
social Darwinism; Herbert Spencer
Debs, Eugene, 283–284
Democratic Party, 20
and machine politics, 167
and Populist Party, 76
depression of 1893, 270, 275, 279–280
DeQuincey, Thomas, 82, 103
Dewey, John, 4, 87, 285, 292, 296
Dodge, Grace, 245
domestic service
in Addams family, 24, 46, 150, 311 n.21
and black women, 172, 355 n.37
Hull-House Household Labor Bureau,
247–248, 251
JA's speeches about at World's Columbian
Exposition, 278–279
Dow, Jenny, 238, 254
Dred Scott decision, 20
Drummond, Henry, 207

education, nineteenth-century
changing views of knowledge, 86
in Cedarville, 35–36
normal schools, 74
public high schools, 100
Teachers' Institute, 19
Washington Hall Collegiate Institute, 17
See also Beloit College; Illinois College;
Rockford Female Seminary; Smith
College; Upper Iowa University;
Vassar; Woman's Medical College of
Philadelphia; women's education
Eliot, George, 88, 96, 120, 140, 146, 165, 195
Ellers, Annie, 96
Ellwood, Mary, 131, *132*
Ellwood, Puss, 131, *132*, 133
Ely, Laura, *104*. *See also* Laura Ely Curtis
Ely, Richard T., 168, 170, 200, 282, 353 n.7
Emerson, Ralph Waldo, 105–108
Engels, Friedrich, 247
Enoch Pratt Library, 154, 167, 353 n.11
Ethical Culture Society, 274

Factory and Inspection Act of Illinois, 251,
279
factory conditions, 243
family claim, 110, 115, 117. *See also* Jane
Addams, family roles of
Farnsworth, Anna, 241
Farrar, William Frederic, 163
fathers of female reformers, 268, 301 n.4, 306

n.2. *See also* John Addams; William
Darrah Kelley
Federation of Labor, 166
first generation of college-educated women.
See women's education
Fort Sumter, 22
Fourteenth Amendment, 47
Franklin, Fabian, 175, 356 n.59
free trade, 96
Freeport, Illinois, 15, 55
free-soil Republicans, 20, 47
Fremantle, Canon William, 199–203
Frothingham, Nora, *104*, 111. *See also*
Nora Frothingham Haworth
Fry, Mary, 311 n.21
Fugitive Slave Act, 20

Galena and Chicago Union Railroad, 18, 48,
303 n.1
garbage inspection, 4
Garfield, President James, 74, 111
Garibaldi, Giuseppe, 239
German Central Labor Union, 166
Gilded Age, 3, 82
Gilman, Charlotte Perkins, 12, 117
Gilman, Daniel Coit, 168, 203
goddess ideal, 87–88, 106
Godwin, William, 195
Goethe, Johann, 64, 82, 105
Grant, President Ulysses, 194
Green, T. H., 205
Guiteau, Charles, 111, 125–126, 329 n.6, 334 n.100
Guiteau, Flora, 111, 183, 186–187, 191, 367 n.134
Guiteau, Luther, 111, 329 n.6
Gunsaulus, Rev. Frank, 214, 230, 281, 370 n.23,
371 n.25

Hackett, Frances, 235–236, 241
Haldeman, Alice Addams
childbearing of, 152, 160, 169
commissions painting of JA, 285
fears Chicago, 275–276
marriage to Harry Haldeman, 42–43, 153,
158, 222
relationship with JA, 127, 158–161, 222–224
Haldeman, George, *40*, *225*
academic diffculties of, 179
attends Beloit College, 56, 61, 73, 112
attends Johns Hopkins University, 136, 148,
156, 339 n.47
childhood companion to JA, 27, 29–30,
33–36

Acknowledgments

In thousands of conversations during the past seventeen years, my friends, colleagues, students, and relatives continually invented new ways of encouraging me in my work on Jane Addams. This book owes its existence to their patience, interest, and loving faith in the endeavor. While I cannot individually thank all to whom I am grateful, I trust that my colleagues will think back on the times they asked, "How's Jane?" and will know that I appreciated their curiosity.

My work on this project benefited at every level, from the most prosaic to the most sublime, by my association with Tom Dublin and Kitty Sklar. In addition to teaching me most of what I know about research, honest analysis of evidence, and the importance of a good story, they also served as my contemporary examples of the lessons Jane Addams tried to teach about the delights of collectivity and mutuality. Whenever I settled into their lakeside home, a veritable beehive of historical productivity, I witnessed the central lesson of Jane Addams's own life: hard work freely chosen and generously shared is not a sacrifice, it is a source of energy and joy.

That lesson was reinforced during the year I spent as a fellow at the Huntington Library in San Marino, California, where my friend and colleague Karen Lystra cheered me over the finish line of this book. By granting me the honor of serving as the Ray Allen Billington Distinguished Visiting Professor at Occidental College and the Huntington Library in 2000–2001, Roy Ritchie, Lynn Dumenil, and the members of the Occidental history department made possible my completion of the manuscript during the happiest sojourn of my professional career. I owe thanks to Grinnell College, Dean Jim Swartz, and my colleagues in the history department for making it possible for me to take advantage of that and other opportunities over the years, and for their continuing support of this project. In addition I am grateful to Elliott Gorn, Jim Grossman, and the other members of the 1998 NEH summer seminar at the Newberry Library "Social Historians Write Biography" for sharpening my analysis of this unique genre of historical narrative.

It is my great hope that the work here reflects the wise counsel I received from colleagues who read and commented on now discarded drafts. I am particularly grateful to Diane Middlebrook, John Milton Cooper, Elaine Tyler

May, Keith Fitzgerald, Barbara Sicherman, Michael Kazin, and the anonymous readers at the University of Pennsylvania Press, all of whom gifted me with smart, straight talk about the structure, tone, and focus of this story. Peter Agree, my editor at Penn, has brought so much integrity and good sense to the project that his praise has been all the more encouraging. My indexer, Kate Babbitt, and the staff at Penn, including Samantha Foster, Noreen O'Connor, and Gail Kienitz, made the final stages of the endeavor a professional pleasure.

To my students at Grinnell College I feel a particular sense of gratitude, not only for allowing me to try out on them my evolving ideas about the Gilded Age, the Progressive Era, U.S. women's history, and the "art" of biography, but also for providing me with solid research on subjects salient to my work; countless hours of photocopying, fact checking, and endnote polishing; and truly candid, insightful commentary on various chapters. Many of my best memories from work on the book include time spent with Rachel Unruh, Catherine Nisbett, Jon Minkoff, Angie Arnold, and Kate Strangio; the names and faces of dozens of other eager Grinnell students populate those memories as well.

Anyone who works on Jane Addams enjoys the added pleasure of belonging to a community of scholars who generously share their curiosity and knowledge about Hull-House and the women and men who enlivened the settlement scene. That community has grown too large to list here, but my work has been especially enriched by Rima Lunin Schultz, whose zest and imagination kept me alert to new ways of looking at the material, and by Mary Lynn Bryan, whose unflagging dedication to the Jane Addams Papers Project extended beyond making the documents available to scholars. She also carefully cautioned me against excesses of interpretation and errors of fact. I am further indebted to the efforts of numerous archivists and librarians who have aided me in large and small ways, including Mary Ann Bamberger, Julia Hendry, and Pat Bakunas of the Jane Addams Memorial Collection at the University of Illinois at Chicago, Peggy Glowacki at the Jane Addams Hull-House Museum on the UIC campus, John de La Fontaine at Occidental College, Wendy Chmielewski at the Swarthmore College Peace Collection, Kathleen Nutter at the Sophia Smith Collection at Smith College, and Mary Pryor at Rockford College.

In the end, of course, it is our family and friends who support and encourage us through undertakings such as this one. I was particularly blessed when my niece, Marcia Hunt, agreed to read chapter after chapter, again and again, prodding my logic, cleansing my prose. In lieu of ever repaying the long-distance companionship she offered over the years, I offer simple thanks. So, too, my daughter, Elizabeth, has spent over half of her life believing in this project. For many more years than she knew, I was carried along on her buoyant confidence; by seeing myself through her eyes, I could envision completion of this endeavor. Other members of my extended family, especially Carter Smith, Anne Taylor Fleming, Karl Fleming, Phyllis Avery, Jon Levitt, John and Linda Hunt, Wendy Fish, and Ben Bycel have offered essential support along the way. Ben, along with my dear friends Mary Lou Locke and Kathleen Murphy Mallinger, provided valuable editorial advice on an early draft; I hope they can see the good effect of their efforts here.

This book is dedicated to my husband, Jim, for support that extended so far beyond reading every word and punctuating every sentence that it would be foolish even to attempt a catalogue of his contributions. Seventeen years ago, when I had no job, no grants, no professional prospects to speak of, I confessed to him a crazy desire to undertake a new look at Jane Addams. His unforgettably communal reply was "then that's what we'll do." And we did.